Queer Iber

Edited by Michèle Aina Barale,

Jonathan Goldberg, Michael Moon, and

Eve Kosofsky Sedgwick

Queer Iberia

SEXUALITIES, CULTURES, AND

CROSSINGS FROM THE MIDDLE AGES

TO THE RENAISSANCE

Edited by Josiah Blackmore *and*

Gregory S. Hutcheson

Duke University Press Durham & London

1999

© 1999 Duke University Press   All Rights Reserved   Printed in the United States of America on acid-free paper ⊗   Designed by C. H. Westmoreland   Typeset in Monotype Fournier by Tseng Information Systems, Inc.   Library of Congress Cataloging-in-Publication Data appear on the last printed page of this book.

This volume is made possible in part by support from The Program for Cultural Cooperation between Spain's Ministry of Education and Culture and United States' Universities as well as the University of Illinois at Chicago's Office of the Vice Chancellor for Research.

Title page art courtesy of The Hispanic Society of America, New York.

Contents

V The Body and the State

Acknowledgments

In May 1994 a session entitled "Queer Iberia" formed part of the 29th
International Congress on Medieval Studies at Western Michigan University in Kalamazoo, Michigan. That occasion, modest in scope, with only a
few participants, fired the opening salvo in a dialogue that over the past
few years has become the wide-ranging, collective scholarly inquiry we
present in this volume. Throughout our editorial work on *Queer Iberia* we
have benefited from the support of colleagues and institutions, and it is
our felicitous task to acknowledge that support here. We extend our thanks
first off to the Society for the Study of Homosexuality in the Middle Ages
(SSHMA) for sponsoring the original Kalamazoo session and for providing a forum within which to begin exploring issues that were, even at that
late date, still taboo in most circles of medieval scholars. We owe much to
the two anonymous readers for Duke University Press for their discerning
and meticulous readings of the manuscript and for the many suggestions
that substantially improved both individual essays and the volume as a
whole; also to Catherine Brown and Anne J. Cruz for their comments on
earlier drafts of the introduction. Sara Lipton gave generously of her expertise as an art historian, while Linde Brocato assisted in tracking down
illustrative material. Our thanks to George Greenia, editor of *La corónica*,
not only for his great enthusiasm for the project since its inception but
for granting permission to reprint portions of essays by Josiah Blackmore
and Louise O. Vasvári that originally appeared in *La corónica*'s pages. We
also wish to acknowledge the University of Chicago Press, which gave its
permission to reprint a revised version of the first chapter of Mark D. Jordan's *The Invention of Sodomy in Christian Theology* (1997). The University
of Illinois at Chicago's Office of the Vice Chancellor for Research and the
Program for Cultural Cooperation between Spain's Ministry of Education
and Culture and United States' Universities provided support in the form of
generous publishing subsidies, without which we would never have dared
to be so ambitious. Our thanks to both these institutions. And there have
been many, many others whose expertise has contributed in discrete ways
to the production of this volume, none more appreciated, however, than

the editorial staff of Duke University Press. Special thanks to both Ken Wissoker (editor) and Richard Morrison (assistant editor) for their sustaining enthusiasm, to Richard in particular for shepherding the book through the intricacies of production, and for his seemingly inexhaustible patience in accommodating our erratic work schedules. And finally, our sincerest thanks to the contributors themselves, not only for their ideas and their contributions, but for making the experience of producing this anthology a testament to the benefits of collaborative scholarship.

Gregory S. Hutcheson and Josiah Blackmore

Introduction

What though Iberia yield you liberty
To snort in source of Sodom villainy?
— *John Marston*

Ever since the Romans named Iberia's western reaches "Extremadura" —
the extreme territories — it has lain on the margins of Europe's consciousness, always the site of difference, always "queer" Iberia.[1] Here it is that the
Romans located the *nec plus ultra,* beyond which there was nothingness, or
worse, every conceivable monster of the imagination. For the Europe of
the *Chanson de Roland,* Iberia was the land of the Saracens, a lusty, black-
skinned people that brought the darkness of Africa dangerously close; so
too the temptations of the soul's darker side. It was the land of literary
modes that turned men away from their innate masculine virtue; of sciences
that upset the balance of the trivium and quadrivium; of heterodoxies that
struck at the very heart of Christian theology.

Iberia represents throughout the Middle Ages Christian Europe's point
of contact with a cultural other that was immense and frightening, as much
a product of the imagination as the leviathans navigating the margins of
medieval maps. It represents as well the space of unnatural sexualities —
"sodomy" in its broad understanding as both aberrance and excess, that
which goes against and beyond nature and God's divine plan.[2] Roland's
Saracens are implicitly defined by a sexuality that exceeds the bounds of a
Christian normativity, one that subverts the teleology of sex and emblematizes the shadow side of European culture. Indeed, in Christian accounts
of Muslim Iberia, sexual excess seems inevitably to cross with cultural (or
racial) otherness, and at times becomes its unique mode of expression. The
eleventh-century Grimaldus, monk at the great monastery of Silos, would
report with regard for neither empirical evidence nor linguistic specificity
that the Saracens consecrated the sixth day of the week to that "shameless
whore" Venus (hence *viernes*), and that "on this day the whole black Ish-

maelite people, following their accursed and senseless religion and their vile abominable tradition (*et insana religione et nefanda atque abhominabili traditione*), abandons itself to irreligious ease and to its unspeakable religious practices (*irreligioso ocio et execrebili cultura*)" (Colin Smith 96, 97). Six centuries later, Iberia (no longer Saracen, but papist, which was infinitely worse) would remain the archetypal site of otherness, the "source of Sodom" for Englishman John Marston, who in 1598 decried the import of abominable vices to English universities (qtd. in Bray 52).

And yet if we subscribe to the myth of medieval Europe—wholly Christian and militant in its Latinity—as the arbiter of cultural normativity, then Iberia is intrinsically queer, not just by reputation but as a consequence of its own historical process. From the moment the Muslimized Berber tribes of northern Africa conquered all but the northwestern corner of the peninsula in 711, Iberia's ties to Christian Europe were tenuous at best. Hegemony would remain for half a millennium in Muslim hands, as would the cultural establishment.[3] Even efforts at *Reconquista*—the military (and no less ideological) reclaiming of Iberia for Christianity—would have the ironic effect of reorienting Christian Iberia toward the south and east and engaging it in a cultural and intellectual activity that was entirely foreign to Europe. Most representative of this reorientation are the schools of translation of Toledo in the twelfth century (serving to introduce Aristotle—by way of Averroes—to greater Europe) and the encyclopedic projects of Alfonso the Wise, king of Castile and León, in the thirteenth. Arabic, not Latin, was the language of culture for Alfonso's age, and Alfonso himself acted, in the words of Francisco Márquez-Villanueva, as "creative manager of the greatest transference of knowledge from East to West seen in the Middle Ages" (76). The renowned Majorcan theologian Ramon Llull knew Arabic, as did Juan Ruiz, author of the *Libro de buen amor*. Only a visitor from north of the Pyrenees would have been shocked to find that the Christian clergy in fifteenth-century Iberia had little command of Latin in this the western outpost (and at one time the shining jewel) of the Islamic world.[4]

Spanish historian Américo Castro coined the term *convivencia*—a "living-together," a coexistence—to describe the unique sociocultural environment of medieval Iberia. Recent scholarship has brought pressure to bear on Castro's idealistic vision, adducing a far more conflictive relationship among Christians, Muslims, and Jews—a slippery alliance with/defiance of the cultural other.[5] What remains, however, is the notion of the Iberian

Middle Ages as a complex matrix of societies and cultures in an ongoing process of definition and redefinition, one template of historical and social order soon replaced by another. By the thirteenth century the balance of power had shifted definitively in favor of the Christian North, with conquests by Afonso Henriques at Lisbon (1147), Pedro II of Aragon at Las Navas de Tolosa (1212), and Fernando III of Castile and León at Córdoba (1236) and Seville (1248). The tremendous promise of *convivencia* — always *in potentia,* never fully realized — gave way to an inexorable and oftentimes violent march toward cultural and religious orthodoxy, with the anti-Jewish pogroms of the late-fourteenth century; heightened anti-Semitism, mass conversion, and inquisition in the fifteenth; and finally the conquest of the kingdom of Granada — the last Muslim foothold on the peninsula — in 1492, followed shortly after by the expulsion of the Jews from Spain in that same year and from Portugal in 1496.

To the early-modern period we might ascribe the creation of a mythic Spanish identity, one intended to meld Iberian history with that of greater Europe by casting Muslims and Jews as interlopers and tracing authentic Spanish character — stoically resistant to change throughout almost a millennium of *convivencia* — back to the golden age of Roman occupation.[6] Perhaps Castro's greatest contribution to Iberian studies was his challenge to this identity, his toppling of a cultural monolith that had held fast from the late Middle Ages to the twentieth century and stood at the very heart of Francoist ideology.[7] Castro and his school effected in essence a "queering" of Iberian history by exposing the Semitic roots of modern Spanish identity and by "outing" as the descendants of Jews or Muslims such icons as Fernando "el Católico," Teresa of Avila, and Cervantes. His was not a campaign of cultural iconoclasm, as some of his detractors have implied, but rather an embracing of difference that obliterated the need to read Spain always as an appendage to greater Europe. It was Castro who brought Spain out of the closet and forced it to face — ultimately to celebrate — the complexities of its cultural and even its racial identities.

It is in this sense that we might understand queerness, as that which normativity — in this case a cultural normativity — must reject or conceal in order to exist. Its presence is always palpable in the incongruities, excesses, or anxieties of normative discourse, but it is only exceptionally given expression, and this only at the margins. It is not surprising, then, that Marcelino Menéndez y Pelayo's monumental *Historia de los heterodoxos españoles*

[A History of Spanish Heterodoxy] should have served less to variegate Spanish cultural history than it did to ensure orthodoxy's privileged position. Indeed, in the obsessive rehearsal of heterodoxy (the work comprises eight volumes), Menéndez y Pelayo in a sense lays the ideological foundations for Franco's ultraorthodox state.

Just as nationalism has informed (and in many ways continues to inform) Spain's reading of its historical past, so too has the study of Iberian sexuality fallen inescapably in line with what Michael Warner exposes as "heterosexual culture's exclusive ability to interpret itself as society" (xxi). A conference entitled "Cuerpo y sexualidad en el Medioevo: Imágenes y concepto" [The Body and Sexuality in the Middle Ages: Images and Concept] is only the most recent manifestation of a critical tradition that continues to assume heterosexuality as the default — the sole legitimate focus — of the study of sexuality.[8] Other efforts strike in the opposite direction by sensationalizing queer sexualities, although the investment is very much the same — that queerness remain queer, a freaky sideshow to the main act of heterosexuality.[9] Even efforts to write a "gay" history defer more often than not to the prerogative of decidedly normative texts — whether Alfonso X's injunction against same-sex copulation or inquisitorial proceedings against sodomites — to determine the behaviors of queerness and the parameters of identity. Such lines of inquiry, while vital for an understanding of sodomy as a legal, moral, even discursive category, nonetheless contribute to the fixing of queerness within a heteronormative framework and confine our discussion to terms of transgression, marginality, or implied resistance at the very best.[10]

Discrete efforts of the past decade have certainly begun to take aim at (male) heterosexuality's privileged position in the historicizing of Iberian sexuality. Norman Roth has foregrounded the theme of boy-love in his studies of Ibero-Arabic verse, while Daniel Eisenberg has gone so far as to suggest the existence of a homonormative society in eleventh-century Granada.[11] Both María Eugenia Lacarra and Mary Elizabeth Perry have studied sexual and/or gender nonconformity in Spain's late-medieval and early-modern periods, while Mary Gossy and Louise O. Vasvári among others have proposed radically new readings of canonical texts.[12] All told, such studies begin to suggest an Iberian sexuality that was, like its cultural identity, dynamic, fluid, constantly challenged and reconstructed — the site of both an encounter and a resistance, an attraction and a repulsion that were not necessarily mutually exclusive. From this deconstructive space there emerges a shifting historical, literary, even moralistic discourse that exposes not only the instability of heteronormativity but, more strikingly, Iberia's ambivalent relationship to any form of fixedness and determinacy. As Louise Mirrer notes of medieval Spain in particular: "[N]o culture reminds us more of the provisional nature of national, religious, and sexual identity" (*Women, Jews, and Muslims* 14).

Queer Iberia is a response to the need for a more systematic examination of premodern and early-modern expressions of sexuality within the context of the growing collaboration between Iberian studies and modern critical theory. It serves in many ways as a complementary volume to Emilie Bergmann and Paul Julian Smith's *¿Entiendes?: Queer Readings, Hispanic Writings* (1995), a collection of studies on the modern Hispanic world that has been instrumental in expanding the "national and linguistic borderlines" (1) of queer theory and its applications.[13] While *¿Entiendes?* begins its historical sweep in the early-modern age, the essays here contained treat of materials ranging from the tenth century to the early seventeenth, and so address, at least preliminarily, Bergmann and Smith's regret "that there are no historical studies for Spanish-speaking nations comparable to those which exist for Britain and the United States."[14] We hope at the same time to call attention to the unique nature of the texts and contexts we study — to the complex range of contentious and revealing intersections among culture, sexuality, literature, and history that not only confound a tradition of normative readings, but confront the geopolitical and chronological biases by which scholarship continues to relegate medieval and early-modern Iberia to the critical closet.

The three essays of "Queering Iberia" serve to launch the scholarly dialogue of the collection, representing as they do distinct theoretical approaches that nonetheless all reveal the confluence of discourses of cultural and sexual difference. Mark D. Jordan considers early accounts of Pelagius, the Christian youth who was martyred in 925 after rebuffing the sexual advances of the Cordoban caliph ʿAbd ar-Raḥmān III. The moral charge of the tale as told by the Iberian cleric Raguel or the Saxon abbess Hrotswitha relies ultimately on the condemnation of same-sex desire as emblematized in the figure of the Saracen, but it is just as dependent on a displaying of the youth's body as the logical object of that desire. Indeed, even while Pelagius's body is being conscripted as a focal point of Christian adoration, it continues to operate as the site of productions of desire that cannot help but inflect that adoration in dangerous ways.

Benjamin Liu challenges the essentialisms inherent in traditional Spanish historicism by reading the Galician-Portuguese *cantigas d'escarnho e de mal dizer* 'songs of scorn and malediction' as the discursive antithesis to law, that space where ethnicity and sexuality are problematized, melded into a site of porosity, confusion, and ultimately the production of new meanings that pose both explicit and implicit challenges to culturally centered normativities. These burlesque works of the twelfth to fourteenth centuries become in essence an emblem of Iberia's unique *morada vital,* as Castro terms it,[15] a neat example of the queerness—both sexual and cultural—that emerges from the clashing and coalescing of meaning and identity. Liu's is the essay that most aligns itself with Castro, the one that identifies the production of queerness as taking place both in response to and despite ideologies, as part of a vital process of becoming and being. While Jordan reads Iberia's queerness as one projected from without—as crucial to Christendom's (and ultimately Christian Iberia's) process of cultural differentiation—Liu taps into Iberia's intrinsic queerness, into those deconstructive spaces that emerge precisely at the point where cultures come into most intimate contact.

Catherine Brown, for her part, challenges philological essentialisms (most emblematized by the likes of Menéndez y Pelayo) by offering a new reading of Alfonso Martínez de Toledo's baldly misogynistic (and homophobic) *Arcipreste de Talavera* (1438). In this "noisiest book ever written," Martínez's stock vituperation of women yields quickly, Brown argues, to the compulsion to *represent* women, to stage in essence a drag performance in which women are no longer the objects of discourse but rather its noisy subjects. Martínez's narrative voice becomes entangled in contradictory desires—"in saying what cannot, even *must* not be said"—and so enacts a "signifying against nature" that exposes beneath the text's apparent asceticism its own resemblence to the fictive women, hypocrites, and effeminates it represents. By taking into account both the complexities of premodern discursivities and the work's textual specificity, Brown offers a corrective for the reductionisms that continue to haunt our reading of canonical texts.

The remaining essays in the collection serve to inflect even further these complementary notions of queer Iberia, to identify or suggest other points of production of queer sexualities that all respond in some manner to the presence, whether real or implied, of the cultural other. In the first essay of "Iberian Masculinities," Sara Lipton explores the ways in which Pedro II of Aragon, who sides with the "heretical" Languedocian nobility in the Albigensian Crusade, is constructed by his adversaries not only as "foreign" or "Spanish," but as "effeminate," controlled by his love for a married noblewoman from Toulouse. Gender and heresy become flip sides of a politically charged discourse, one that is informed less by a "timeless, ahistorical semiotic pattern" than it is by the notion of women as the mediator of value for "the entire economic, social, religious and political network in which aristocratic men lived and functioned."

Louise Vasvári turns to a key episode of the fourteenth-century *Libro de buen amor,* the disputation between the Greek doctor and the Roman *ribaldo,* which she interprets as a staging of male agonistic ritual. Through this highly innovative rereading, the *ribaldo* becomes the enactor of a symbolic "fucking over" of high culture that calls into question the very *auctoritas* of Juan Ruiz's text. Vasvári brings this same semiotic system to bear on other misunderstood or underinterpreted passages of the *Libro de buen amor,* most strikingly the male narrator's sexual victimization (and ultimate degradation) at the hands of the *serranas,* predatory mountain girls who "appropriate male gender roles and disguises, along with powerful — if prosthetic — penile attributes."

Both Lipton and Vasvári point to the arbitrariness of masculinity, as well as its inevitable convergence with — and problematizing by — constructions of sexual and/or cultural normativity. In this they coincide with the methodological framework laid out by Jeffrey Jerome Cohen and Bonnie Wheeler in the recent *Becoming Male in the Middle Ages:* "[W]e are interested in how masculinity — which has for too long functioned as the universal category of being — can be unpacked and reapproached through the eclectic toolbox which the confluence of medieval studies, feminism, gender theory, and cultural studies provides" (xi).[16] In the third essay of "Iberian Masculinities," Roberto J. González-Casanovas demonstrates the ways in which diverse medieval authors (Alfonso X, Ramon Llull, Juan Manuel) subscribe to the reading of male friendship both as an ideal transcending the institutions of marriage and family, and as a "nonnatural, stylized, and anomalous artifact." While never pushing texts to the point of admitting to same-sex desire, González-Casanovas does scrutinize them in such a way that they begin to reveal those "problematic negotiations and 'interstitial' constructions" that appear inevitably along the edges of cultural frontiers.

Underscoring González-Casanovas's analysis is the paradox, noted by David Halperin, that even as male friendship draws its signification from kinship and conjugality — those institutions most constitutive of society — it begins to displace them, "to reduce them to mere *images* of friendship" (85). The essays of "Sources of Sodom" all deal with similar paradoxes, with normative texts that conspire, oftentimes accidentally, in the construction of spaces where sexuality is plurivalent, flexible, bound by nature and discourse, yet unbound and open to deconstructive readings. This section's title (adapted from Marston's verse) speaks to the configuration of Iberia not as a geographically delimited region of vice and villainy, but as the site where a multiplicity of queer discursive spaces obtain in the realms of poetry, narrative, and history.

Josiah Blackmore returns to the Galician-Portuguese *cantigas d'escarnho e de mal dizer,* in which representations of same-sex sexuality are explicit, but always complex and ambiguous, moving freely between a socially mandated abhorrence on the one hand and a curiously modern indulgence on the other.[17] For Blackmore (as for Liu), the *cantigas* undermine legally imposed normativities by serving as "battle/playgrounds for proscribed sexuality and its representation, a site of tensions between deviant sex and the culture that seeks to control it." But they also function as speech acts that can reconstitute the speaker in curious ways, making him an active participant in the recreation of Sodom, "a poetic world inhabited (and often defined) by same-sex interaction."

Gregory S. Hutcheson also subscribes to the idea of sodomy less as empirical act than as Foucault's "utterly confused category" — a category that explodes with meaning in fifteenth-century Castile but which is nonetheless bound by the historical specificity of civil strife and the ascendency of the *conversos,* Jews recently converted to Christianity. Hutcheson examines the case of Alvaro de Luna, the ambitious favorite to Juan II, whose grasp on political power not only gives rise to intimations of sodomy but guarantees his conversion into scapegoat for a host of ills besetting the Spanish body politic. Luna remains as a contaminating presence in both history and text, a locus of anxiety that continually exposes those points where normativity shows its cracks and queerness begins to break through.

Daniel Eisenberg embarks in his essay on a broad-based survey of the "sexual environment" of Muslim Iberia, a society he characterizes as "tolerant and hedonistic," and in which "[h]omosexual pleasures were not only freely available . . . , but they were believed to be more refined than heterosexual ones." In a daring thesis, he proposes the fourteenth-century *Libro de buen amor* as a reactionary response to Muslim homosexuality, the conscious construction of an absolute (Christian) heteronormativity against the queerness of al-Andalus. For Eisenberg, Juan Ruiz's masterwork embodies the moral imperative of the *Reconquista* as it would be so bizarrely summed up by Spanish historian Claudio Sánchez-Albornoz in the present century: without the *Reconquista*, claimed Sánchez-Albornoz, "[h]abría triunfado la homosexualidad, tan practicada en la España mora" (38) [homosexuality, so widely practiced in Moorish Spain, would have triumphed].

Eisenberg's essay already suggests that queerness was never incidental to late-medieval Iberia, never in excess of historical process, but rather utterly essential (whether in its exhibition or its suppression) to efforts to define the boundaries of identity and mount the foundational myths that give the embryonic Spanish nation a reason to be. The three essays of "Normativity and Nationhood" explore more purposefully the emergence of queerness within texts and contexts which, although strikingly different, collaborate in serving the purposes of a state-sanctioned normativity. Michael Solomon's point of departure is *Lo llibre de les dones,* a hygienic and behavioral treatise by the fourteenth-century Catalan moralist Francesc Eiximenis, in which the practice of sodomy is linked explicitly to the notion of contagious disease. By the sixteenth century, disease is no longer simply a matter of internal physiology, but also (and predominantly) of "menacing and inimical entities lurking outside the body." Rendered in this way, Solomon argues, it enters a discursive realm where hygienic and moral imperatives coalesce (in disturbingly familiar ways) to recommend the identification and control/elimination of the subaltern—whether woman, Jew, Moor, or sodomite—as essential to the control of disease and the aversion of biological (and social) dissolution.

Barbara Weissberger studies sodomy's inevitable intersection with discourses of power and social order during Spain's turbulent passage into the modern age. Sodomy is most graphically rehearsed on the body of Enrique IV, king of Castile from 1454 to 1474, who is branded *puto* ("faggot" in Weissberger's translation) and burned in effigy by rebel bands as early as 1465. The merging of sodomy with allegations of impotency not only transforms the king into an emblem of ineffectual power and social disorder, but justifies a posteriori his half-sister Isabel's seizing of power in 1474. Linde M. Brocato, for her part, considers three literary works (Juan de Mena's *Laberinto de Fortuna*, Fernando de Rojas's *Celestina*, and the anonymous *Carajicomedia*) which, despite their stark generic differences, converge in the mapping of female sexuality onto questions of morality, social control, and ultimately the nation-building project of Spain's early-modern age. Both Weissberger and Brocato uncover ironic readings of Isabel la Católica — her projection less as guarantor of Spain's virility/integrity than as a monstrous perversion of womanhood, a virago, not unlike Vasvári's *serranas*, whose agency in historical process cannot help but emasculate the Spanish body politic and breed corruption at every level of society.[18] Isabel announces in her political body what the female body will become for imperial Spain: the alter ego of the sodomite, the site of a confusion of categories and desires that both represents and incites the dissolution of social order.

In "The Body and the State," focus remains on the female body as one of the most active agents of queerness in imperial Spain, the site of multiple and complex crossings of categories that destabilize time and again the twin imperatives of geographical expansion and cultural control. E. Michael Gerli reads the body of Melibea, daughter of the well-heeled Pleberio in Rojas's *Celestina*, as a highly unstable "domain of signification" — the disputed territory in a clash between ideologically charged discourses of class and privilege; it serves, argues Gerli, as the sign of a plutocracy that has lost mastery over itself, "a master trope for challenging and dissolving the boundaries of social and reproductive authority at the center of blood, class, caste, and legitimacy in late fifteenth-century Castile."

Mary Elizabeth Perry traces the trials and fortunes of the historical Catalina de Erauso (born 1592), the celebrated *Monja-Alférez*, or Nun-Lieutenant, whose transgendered body is potentially as dangerous as Melibea's. While Erauso's assuming of male identity and agency does indeed raise significant questions about the relationships among sex, gender, and the body, curiously for her contemporaries it posed little threat, perhaps, as Perry suggests, because her status as nun guaranteed a gender crossing safely beyond the reach of the body and the capacity to pollute or disorder. He was a "paradox of boundaries violated but hymen intact," a hyphenate brought neatly into the service of empire by being made to symbolize, whether as nun or as lieutenant, Spain's ability to defend the borders both of its normative identity and of its geographic expanse.[19]

Such was not the case of the sexually active Elena de Céspedes (born c. 1545), whose body, at once hermaphroditic and Morisco, threatened virtually every means by which imperial Spain wielded power. Stigmatized initially by her status both as female and enslaved, Elena engaged after the emergence of her penis at the age of seventeen in an inventive and highly successful transformation into soldier, surgeon, husband, and finally "proud transgendered subject." Israel Burshatin reads the collected documentation on Eleno/Elena's case as "an exemplary narrative of a frontier culture whose boundaries were being displaced from the political map to the bodies of those subordinated by Castilian and 'old' Christian rule." More intriguing, however, are the voices, bodies, genders, sexualities, and discourses devised or appropriated by Eleno/Elena as a means of resisting normalization as a subaltern, strategies that convert her life story into a "fable of the malleability of genders, bodies, and desires" and her body into a prolific source of queerness.

Paradoxically, where imperial Spain exerts the most pressure, queerness begins to emerge as a spontaneous entity, a vital response to the exercise of power, or rather, a counterresponse that enters as well into the economy of power as understood by Foucault. In this sense, early-modern Iberia presents itself as one of the most compelling case studies for historians of sexuality, a geographical and ideological space where sex is explicitly bound up in the exercise of power, indeed, is obsessively rehearsed in literature, inquisitorial proceedings, and the mandates of conquest as a means by which the state can both legitimize and display the instruments of its authority.[20] That these were the same instruments by which the Spanish state exerted power over the various "others" of its empire (not only the *conversos* and Moriscos of its own shores, but the indigenous peoples of the New World) only emphasizes the presence of race/culture in the forging of technologies of sexuality, perhaps even the inextricability, as Ann Laura Stoler argues, of discourses of race and sexuality.[21] The explosion of sex in early-modern Iberia has of necessity to be explained as a direct consequence of the imperatives of racial purity and cultural orthodoxy that were institutionalized in *Reconquista* and the Inquisition and would come to define the imperial/colonial project. *Limpieza de sangre* (an unsullied bloodline) and *honra* (the integrity of the female body) — both obsessions of the Spanish

Golden Age—are ultimately manifestations of the same master discourse, the conflation of notions of purity and orthodoxy into a reflexive impulse against the threat of racial, cultural, and sexual queerness (and the desires invoked by each).

The loosely chronological order of essays in this collection not only makes apparent dramatic shifts in the parameters of difference as Iberia moves into its modernity, but also suggests *Reconquista* (both in its historical specificity and in a broadly ideological sense) as an inevitable subtext to the narrative of Iberian sexuality. Throughout the age of conquest and colonization—indeed, well into the twentieth century—an "orthodox" Iberia would continue to rub up against the bodies of racial, cultural, and sexual others while denying its own inherent queerness. María de Zayas's exemplary novel *La inocencia castigada* (1647) is highly suggestive in its choice of punishment for the woman who falls victim to both a Moorish spell and her own adulterous desire: she is walled up, kept barely alive in the most secret recesses of her husband's household. Three centuries later, Federico García Lorca would resort to the horse as a potent symbol of transgressive sexuality: a stud grown to twice its size and filling in the darkness, it occupies the corral outside the "four white walls" of Bernarda Alba's (and Spain's) orthodoxy. It would take a Pedro Almodóvar to explode Zaya's "closet" and topple Lorca's "four white walls" through both the flagrant deployment of heterodoxies and the celebration of transgressive desire, indeed, through the reclaiming of Iberia's queerness.

The celebration of queerness is certainly implicit in our project, both in our choice of title and in the sheer delight we take both individually and collectively in the telling of stories of heterodoxy and transgression. But there is a danger in this, one Burshatin points to in the conclusion to his own essay (and, aptly, to the collection as a whole)—the persistent configuration of queerness within "safely marginal and reductive readings of criminology, 'strange loves,' or just plain tabloid history." He challenges us to move the stories we tell out of the "various secret closets and cabinets of wonder"—to naturalize queerness in a sense, make its presence inevitable rather than exceptional in our reading of historical process, literary creation, the deployment of discourse, and the formation of identities.

Such is the "extra step" Michael Warner proposed in 1993: not only the recovery of queer histories and identities as a means to fostering tolerance, but the active imagining of a "necessarily and desirably queer world" (xvi).

And such is what we ultimately mean by "queer Iberia." Only incidentally is it a space bound by history and geography, the domain of a recoverable past; it exists primarily (perhaps paradoxically) as a space within which to rethink the very idea of boundaries, within which to explode categories, multiply centers, and begin imagining a "desirably queer world." As such it poses an explicit challenge not only to Iberianists for whom queerness is best kept in "secret closets and cabinets of wonder," but to historians of (European) sexuality for whom Africa still begins at the Pyrenees.

Notes

1. Notes Paul Julian Smith: "It seems fair to say that Spain itself, geographically separate from the rest of Europe, has often been considered as marginal, even redundant, certainly less 'central' than France or Italy to a received 'European' culture" (*Writing in the Margin* 20). Stoler notes as well that "Spain and Portugal are sometimes eclipsed while Europe largely refers to England, Germany and France" (14 n20).

2. See Bullough for an overview of medieval categories of sodomy, which included masturbation, bestiality, and heterosexual anal intercourse—ultimately any sexual act performed in excess of that necessary for conception. Jordan and Goldberg (*Sodometries*) both expound on the instability of the term in the pre- and early-modern periods, indeed, its existence well into the modern period as "that utterly confused category" (Foucault 101) whose very instability guarantees its effectiveness as a metonymy for difference.

3. See Glick; O'Callaghan; and Reilly for competent accounts of medieval Iberian history; Fletcher and Harvey for accounts of Islamic Iberia in particular.

4. Lawrance summarizes thus the impressions of a German traveler visiting Castile in 1485:

[He was] struck by the "Moorish vices" of the court of Ferdinand and Isabella. The women went veiled in mantillas "in the Saracen manner", the royal officials were "mostly baptized Jews or unbaptized Saracens whom the king makes no attempt to convert", and he heard courtiers refer to Ferdinand and Isabella as "those offspring of a convert Jewess". The priests spoke no Latin, the bishop of Seville was a Jew, and the Grand Cardinal spent his nights in a "harem". (184–85)

5. As Nirenberg notes in perhaps the most critical rereading of Castro's historicism: "[V]iolence was a central and systematic aspect of the coexistence of

majority and minorities. *Convivencia* was predicated on violence; it was not its peaceful antithesis" (245). See also Fletcher (131–56).

6. Such was the consummate positivist Marcelino Menéndez y Pelayo's reading of Spanish literature, as an unbroken line from the Iberian-born Martial and Seneca down to the modern age. Even more striking in its essentialisms is this account of the pre-Roman Tartessians, penned by historian Luis Pericot García in 1952:

> In spite of the passage of three thousand years (one hundred generations), few differences can be noted between the Tartessians and the modern Andalusians, not merely in physical appearance, which must be practically the same, but in their temperament as well. It is enough to recall that the buoyant personality, the facility for dancing, and the fascination with bulls so characteristic of presentday Andalusians were qualities which already adorned them in Antiquity. What will the Tartessian texts tell us when they can speak, or I should say, when we come to understand them? I do not know, but of this I am sure; they will describe a perfectly Spanish society. (Qtd. in Rodríguez-Puértolas 115)

7. It was Manuel Durán who noted the "ideological relationship between Fascism and traditional Spanish historiography" (Rodríguez-Puértolas 116). See Rodríguez-Puértolas for a good overview of Castro's historical project, a project that in purely conceptual terms falls neatly in line with the aspirations of queer scholarship to "redefine the center," as Goldberg would have it, "[o]r, better, to locate a center without a center" (*Queering the Renaissance* 13–14).

8. The conference was convened in Aguilar del Campoo, Spain, in September of 1995. Other recent collaborations, however, have begun to make accommodations for queer sexualities. See, for example, Eisenberg in López Baralt and Márquez Villanueva's *Erotismo en las letras hispánicas: aspectos, modos y fronteras* [Eroticism in Hispanic Letters: Aspects, Modes, and Frontiers]; Paul Julian Smith in Brownlee and Gumbrecht's *Cultural Authority in Golden Age Spain*.

9. Such studies lead to troublesome equations, such as Eslava Galán's conflation of pederasts, sodomites, adulterers, cuckolds, and whores in his sweeping account of sexuality in Spain from pre-Roman times through the present, called, tellingly, *Historia secreta del sexo en España* [Secret History of Sex in Spain]. As problematic is Arjona Castro's conflation of homosexuality and drug addiction in his study of sexuality in Ibero-Muslim society.

10. On Alfonso X, see Boswell (288–89); on sodomy and the Inquisition, see Benassar; Carrasco; Dias; Pérez Escohotado; and Perry. The temptation is strong to reconstruct from inquisitorial records the nature of the sodomite in early-modern Iberia. As Goldberg notes, however, "[A]ny inquiry into [what sodomy

is and how it may be recognized] will never deliver the sodomite per se, but only . . . sodometries, relational structures precariously available to prevailing discourses" (*Sodometries* 20). Netanyahu and Roth (*Conversos*) argue much the same for *converso* identity, alleging that distortions and misinterpretations arise inevitably from an uncritical reading of testimony that was oftentimes forced, ultimately scripted by the inquisitors themselves.

11. For a list of both Roth's and Eisenberg's contributions to gay and lesbian studies, see Eisenberg's essay in this volume.

12. For relevant works by Lacarra and Gossy, see the Works Cited; for Perry and Vasvári, see their respective essays in this volume.

13. See also Smith's earlier *The Body Hispanic: Gender and Sexuality in Spanish and Spanish American Literature* (1989). Expanding the inquiry even further is the newly appeared *Hispanisms and Homosexualities,* edited by Molloy and Irwin.

14. So too does Trexler lament the "critical absence of serious studies on Iberian sexuality before the late sixteenth century" (38), although he himself produces a survey of representations of and responses to nonnormative sexuality up through the age of New World conquest (38–63), in essence doing for medieval Iberia what Boswell did for medieval Europe at large.

15. In King's translation, a "vital disposition and way of life" (34).

16. Mirrer has moved in much the same direction, but with a heightened focus on gender and cultural difference, in a study first published in Lees's *Medieval Masculinities* and later expanded into *Women, Jews, and Muslims in the Texts of Reconquest Castile.*

17. Most remarkable is the virtual legitimization of lesbian desire in the re-frain "Mari' Mateu, Mari' Mateu, / tan desejosa ch' és de cono com' eu!" [Mary Matthew, Mary Matthew, as desirous of cunt as I!].

18. Here we are surely not far from Goldberg's vision of the woman with the strap-on penis, a fantasy in which the act of sodomy "enables the productive confusion and rigorous questioning of a range of presumptions and conventions governing gender, sexuality and the relations of fantasy and acts" (*Reclaiming Sodom* 3).

19. We adopt here Perry's strategy of alternating masculine and feminine pronouns in order to emphasize the "danger, disorder, and power engendered by a boundary-crossing person."

20. For the parameters of this authority, see Cruz and Perry (although both here and in Brownlee and Gumbrecht, sexuality tends to be subsumed under the category of gender).

21. As Stoler asks in her introduction: "Was the obsessive search for the 'truth about sex' in the eighteenth and nineteenth centuries directly culled from earlier

confessional models, as Foucault claims, or was the 'truth about sex' recast around the invention of other truth claims, specifically those working through the language of race?" (6). In her protracted response to this question, Stoler produces a template by which Foucauldian paradigms are made to transcend their geographical and chronological myopia and can be brought more readily to bear on the colonial experience.

For the centrality of sodomy in the discourse of New World conquest, see Goldberg (*Sodometries* 176–222) and Trexler.

Works Cited

Arjona Castro, Antonio. *La sexualidad en la España musulmana.* 2nd enlarged ed. Córdoba: Universidad de Córdoba, 1990.

Benassar, Bartolomé. "El modelo sexual: la Inquisición de Aragón y la represión de los pecados 'abominables.' " *Inquisición española: poder político y control social.* Ed. Bartolomé Benassar. Barcelona: Grijalbo, 1981. 295–336.

Bergmann, Emilie L., and Paul Julian Smith, eds. *¿Entiendes?: Queer Readings, Hispanic Writings.* Durham, N.C.: Duke UP, 1995.

Boswell, John. *Christianity, Social Tolerance, and Homosexuality: Gay People in Western Europe from the Beginning of the Christian Era to the Fourteenth Century.* Chicago: U of Chicago P, 1980.

Bray, Alan. *Homosexuality in Renaissance England.* London: Gay Men's P, 1982.

Brownlee, Marina S., and Hans Ulrich Gumbrecht, eds. *Cultural Authority in Golden Age Spain.* Baltimore: Johns Hopkins UP, 1995.

Bullough, Vern L. "The Sin against Nature and Homosexuality." *Sexual Practices and the Medieval Church.* Ed. Vern L. Bullough and James Brundage. Buffalo: Prometheus, 1982. 55–71.

Carrasco, Rafael. *Inquisición y represión sexual en Valencia: historia de los sodomitas (1565–1785).* Barcelona: Laertes, 1985.

Castro, Américo. *The Structure of Spanish History.* Trans. Edmund L. King. Princeton: Princeton UP, 1954.

Cohen, Jeffrey Jerome, and Bonnie Wheeler, eds. *Becoming Male in the Middle Ages.* New York: Garland, 1997.

Cruz, Anne, and Mary Elizabeth Perry. *Culture and Control in Counter-Reformation Spain.* Hispanic Issues 7. Minneapolis: U of Minnesota P, 1992.

Dias, João José Alves. "Para uma abordagem do sexo proibido em Portugal, no século XVI." *Comunicações apresentados ao 1.º congresso luso-brasileiro sobre Inquisição realizado em Lisboa, de 17 a 20 de Fevereiro de 1987.* Ed. Maria Helena

Carvalho dos Santos. Vol. 1. Lisboa: Sociedade Portuguesa de Estudos do Século XVIII, 1989. 151–59.

Dynes, Wayne R., ed. *Encyclopedia of Homosexuality.* 2 vols. New York: Garland, 1990.

Eslava Galán, Juan. *Historia secreta del sexo en España.* Madrid: Temas de Hoy, 1991.

Fletcher, Richard. *Moorish Spain.* Berkeley: U of California P, 1992.

Foucault, Michel. *A History of Sexuality.* Vol. 1: *An Introduction.* Trans. Robert Hurley. 1978. New York: Vintage-Random, 1990.

Glick, Thomas F. *Islamic and Christian Spain in the Early Middle Ages.* Princeton: Princeton UP, 1979.

Goldberg, Jonathan, ed. *Queering the Renaissance.* Durham, N.C.: Duke UP, 1994.

———, ed. *Reclaiming Sodom.* New York: Routledge, 1994.

———. *Sodometries: Renaissance Texts, Modern Sexualities.* Stanford: Stanford UP, 1992.

Gossy, Mary S. "Aldonza as Butch: Narrative and the Play of Gender in *Don Quijote.*" Bergmann and Smith 17–28.

———. *The Untold Story: Women and Theory in Golden Age Texts.* Ann Arbor: U of Michigan P, 1989.

Halperin, David M. *One Hundred Years of Homosexuality.* London: Routledge, 1990.

Harvey, L. P. *Islamic Spain: 1250 to 1500.* Chicago: U of Chicago P, 1990.

Jordan, Mark D. *The Invention of Sodomy in Christian Theology.* Chicago: U of Chicago P, 1997.

Lacarra, María Eugenia. "La evolución de la prostitución en la Castilla del s. XV y la mancebía de Salamanca en tiempos de Fernando de Rojas." *Fernando de Rojas and 'Celestina': Approaching the Fifth Centenary.* Ed. Ivy A. Corfis and Joseph T. Snow. Madison: Hispanic Seminary of Medieval Studies, 1993. 33–58.

———. "El fenómeno de la prostitución y sus conexiones con 'La Celestina.'" *Historias y ficciones: coloquio sobre la literatura del siglo XV.* Ed. Rafael Beltrán et al. Valencia: Universitat de València, 1992. 267–78.

———. "Parámetros de la representación de la sexualidad femenina en la literatura medieval castellana." *La mujer en la literatura hispánica de la Edad Media y el Siglo de Oro.* Ed. Rina Walthaus. Foro Hispánico 5. Amsterdam: Rodopi, 1993. 23–43.

Lawrance, Jeremy. "Spain and Portugal." *Cultural Atlas of the Renaissance.* Ed. C. F. Black et al. New York: Prentice Hall, 1993.

Lees, Clare, ed. *Medieval Masculinities*. Minneapolis: U of Minnesota P, 1994.

López-Baralt, Luce, and Francisco Márquez Villanueva, eds. *Erotismo en las letras hispánicas: aspectos, modos y fronteras*. Publicaciones de la Nueva Revista de Filología Hispánica 7. Mexico: El Colegio de México, 1995.

Márquez-Villanueva, Francisco. "The Alfonsine Cultural Concept." *Alfonso X of Castile, the Learned King (1221–1284): An International Symposium, Harvard University, 17 November 1984*. Ed. Francisco Márquez-Villanueva and Carlos Alberto Vega. Harvard Studies in Romance Languages 43. Cambridge, Mass.: Department of Romance Languages and Literatures, Harvard U, 1990. 76–109.

Mirrer, Louise. "Representing 'Other' Men: Muslims, Jews, and Masculine Ideals in Medieval Castilian Epic and Ballad." Lees 169–86.

———. *Women, Jews, and Muslims in the Texts of Reconquest Castile*. Ann Arbor: U of Michigan P, 1996.

Molloy, Sylvia, and Robert Irwin, eds. *Hispanisms and Homosexualities*. Durham, N.C.: Duke UP, 1998.

Netanyahu, B. *The Origins of the Inquisition in Fifteenth Century Spain*. New York: Random House, 1995.

Nirenberg, David. *Communities of Violence: Persecution of Minorities in the Middle Ages*. Princeton: Princeton UP, 1996.

O'Callaghan, Joseph F. *A History of Medieval Spain*. Ithaca: Cornell UP, 1975.

Pérez Escohotado, Javier. *Sexo e inquisición en España*. Historia de la España Sorprendente. Madrid: Temas de Hoy, 1992.

Reilly, Bernard F. *The Medieval Spains*. Cambridge: Cambridge UP, 1993.

Rodríguez-Puértolas, Julio. "A Comprehensive View of Medieval Spain." *Américo Castro and the Meaning of Spanish Civilization*. Ed. José Rubia Barcia. Berkeley: U of California P, 1976. 113–34.

Roth, Norman. *Conversos, Inquisition, and the Expulsion of the Jews from Medieval Spain*. Madison: U of Wisconsin P, 1995.

Sánchez-Albornoz, Claudio. *De la Andalucía islámica a la de hoy*. Madrid: RIALP, 1983.

Smith, Colin. *Christians and Moors in Spain*. Vol. 1. Warminster, England: Aris and Phillips, 1988.

Smith, Paul Julian. *The Body Hispanic: Gender and Sexuality in Spanish and Spanish American Literature*. Oxford: Clarendon P, 1989.

———. "Homographesis in Salicio's Song." Brownlee and Gumbrecht 131–42.

———. *Writing in the Margin: Spanish Literature of the Golden Age*. Oxford: Clarendon P, 1988.

Stoler, Ann Laura. *Race and the Education of Desire: Foucault's* History of Sexuality *and the Colonial Order of Things.* Durham, N.C.: Duke UP, 1995.

Trexler, Richard. *Sex and Conquest: Gendered Violence, Political Order, and the European Conquest of the Americas.* Ithaca: Cornell UP, 1995.

Warner, Michael, ed. *Fear of a Queer Planet: Queer Politics and Social Theory.* Cultural Politics 6. Minneapolis: U of Minnesota P, 1993.

I

QUEERING IBERIA

Mark D. Jordan

Saint Pelagius, Ephebe and Martyr

With time, the martyr Pelagius would become younger, more eloquent, ever more desirable. In 925 or 926, when he was martyred, he was thirteen years old, precociously pious, and a prisoner in Córdoba with other Christians. According to the testimony of his fellow prisoners, his beauty was such that the caliph, ʿAbd ar-Raḥmān III, desired to add him to his household as another sexual attendant. Pelagius refused to succumb to the king's desire, as he refused to renounce Christianity. And so, the witnesses say, he was first tortured and then dismembered.

In reading some medieval variations on this story, I do not mean to be the least bit cynical about whatever was suffered in fact by the boy behind them. Who can be cynical about torture, for whatever reason, or about the savageries of religions? But I do mean to examine what cynicism there is already in medieval tellings of the story of Pelagius. The appalling events, whatever they were, became early on the vehicle for increasingly overbearing lessons, both patriotic and religious. From the first, there is no disentangling the "facts" of Pelagius's suffering from the polemical uses of it. Nor is it possible to disentangle the tellings of the passions of Pelagius from the ambivalent relations of Iberian Christianity to the same-sex love it thought was preached and practiced by Islam.[1]

The dating and the interrelation of the earliest texts about Pelagius are not known, though it seems clear that three different kinds of texts were written within fifty years of his death. The first presents itself as a narrative of his passion based on eyewitness accounts. It was written in Iberia before 967 by an otherwise unknown priest, Raguel.[2] The second text is a metrical life of Pelagius by the Saxon canoness Hrotswitha. It may also belong to the 960s (Dronke 56–57). The third text is a Mozarabic liturgy, an office of Saint Pelagius from León, written perhaps around 967 to mark the arrival of the saint's relics — or perhaps thirty years earlier to memorialize his wonders.[3] I am less interested in the precise dating of the works than in the ways their genres transmute the underlying account and deflect its dangers.

Raguel's Witness

The first genre for the telling of Pelagius's death is a narrative constructed from the testimony of eyewitnesses.[4] The narrative does not pretend to be transcribed testimony. It is a well-crafted story of martyrdom, beginning with an invocation of divine aid and ending with a claim on Pelagius as patron of the local church.[5] In between there are deft quotations of Scripture, moral applications, and classical allusions. The author, Raguel, is identified in one manuscript as the "doctor . . . huius Passionis" [teacher of this passion].[6] Raguel is not without his teacherly pretensions. He begins with self-conscious reflections on textual beginnings. He proceeds often through antitheses, which he uses in series to amplify or punctuate the basic narrative. Questions about the exact extent of Raguel's literary learning will soon become important, but his polished and polemical purposes in telling the story stand forth no matter how one decides them. Raguel is eloquent in order to condemn the religion, the morals, and the savagery of the young saint's Islamic jailers.

Pelagius himself was not captured by them. He was given as a substitute for a clerical relative, the bishop Hermoygius. Hermoygius had been taken prisoner after the rout of Christian forces at Valdejunquera in the summer of 920. He was at risk of death because of the hardships of imprisonment. So he arranged for his ten-year-old cousin to take his place, hoping all the while, our chronicler insists, that other captives would be sent in place of his young surrogate. Once in prison, Pelagius lived an exemplary life under divine guidance. He was able to overcome even those temptations that had troubled him in the world. Principal among his flourishing virtues was chastity. He kept his body whole. He "purified the vessel" to prepare it as a fitting chamber in which to rejoice as the "spouse" (*sponsus*) of Jesus, to delight in the bloody embrace of martyrdom as marriage.

Jesus, teaching him inwardly, began to transform Pelagius outwardly. Raguel cannot find words enough for the description. The boy's appearance gave praise to the teacher within: "Cui sane intus manebat instructor Christus ei qui foris erat illuminator, quo ipsum celebraret magistrum specie tenus qui mentem, haud dubium, dignus regebat alumnus" (47–49). He was "singularly ornamented" by the signs of his destination in paradise (46–47): "species iam paradisigena prerogatiue decoraret." His face had a "uenustiorem . . . pulcritudinem" (63) [lovelier beauty]. Indeed, word of this attractiveness reached the Muslim "king" (*rex*) who is not here named by Raguel. (The name is given only in a colophon.) The king sends for Pelagius to be brought to him at banquet. Pelagius is dressed in royal robes and led into the hall, the attendants whispering that he is fortunate to have his beauty carry him so far. The king offers him much to renounce Christ and affirm Mohammed: wealth, opulent clothing, precious ornaments, life in the court. There is even the offer of the companionship of any of the court's young men, with whom Pelagius can do what he will: "Sumes preterea tibi qualem ex his tironunculis elegeris, qui tuis ad votum moribus famuletur" (82–83). The king further promises to free from jail a number of other Christians, including Pelagius's relatives.

All of this Pelagius refuses with a string of contrasts between the passing of temporal things and the eternity of Christ. Ignoring the refusal, the king reaches out to touch Pelagius "joculariter." The adverb is odd. It could mean something like "playfully," but that meaning hardly fits here. In Ovid, who may well be on Raguel's mind, the verb *joco* is used as a metaphor for copulation (Adams 161–62). So *tangere joculariter* may mean at least "to touch sexually" and perhaps even "to fondle" in the quite sexual sense. How else to explain Pelagius's reaction? He strikes the king and spits out a contemptuous question: "Numquid me similem tuis effeminatum existimas?" [Do you think me like one of yours, an effeminate?].[7]

Raguel's Pelagius may mean "effeminate" in the general sense that connects any form of sexual self-indulgence with womanliness. This would seem to go along with the martyr's choice of Paul as model (39–40). But he may also have in mind the more specific sense that *effeminati* has in one passage of the Vulgate. There, in a condemnation of the reign of Roboam, the effeminate are those who commit "omnes abominationes gentilium quas adtrivit Dominus ante faciem filiorum Israhel" (3 Kings 14.24) [all the abominations of the gentiles, which the Lord destroyed before the face of the sons of Israel]. The reference would seem to be both to the destruction of Sodom and to the sexual abominations condemned in Leviticus. So the "effeminate" would seem to be those who "lie with a man as with a woman." Certainly Pelagius's next response emphasizes the sexual character of the king's touch. The martyr rips off the fine gown in which he has been dressed and he stands forth, naked, a muscled athlete of the Greek schools: "Et ilico uestimenta ibi que indutus erat scidit et fortem in palestra se alletam constituit" (93–94).

The king does not immediately command Pelagius's destruction. He thinks rather that the boy might be changed by the "pimping persuasions" of the court's young men. For Raguel, this persistence helps to prove the king's depravity. If we exchange textual frames for a moment, it will seem instead a display of good manners. After all, the king is acting out a role approved by a number of Arabic authors. Islamic rulers, theologians, and poets are frequently depicted as falling in love with socially subordinate boys who then offer resistance. Not a few of the boys are Christian — indeed, they are often Christian prisoners or slaves.[8] A tale heard only a few decades later in Córdoba itself can stand for many. In the *Ring of the Dove*, Ibn Ḥazm tells of the love of Ibn al-Asfar for ʿAjib, a servant of the vizier.[9] Ibn al-Asfar would haunt the mosque where the boy worshipped. One day, infuriated by the unwanted gazes, the boy struck him. Instead of being outraged, Ibn al-Asfar was delighted. His humiliation placed him in the highest rank of lovers and encouraged him in his gentle approaches.[10] The blow Pelagius strikes against the caliph can be read in both ways. For Raguel, it is evidence of the boy's courageous virtue. In narrative formulas more familiar to the caliph and his courtiers, it would have been a charming invitation to further advances. Indeed, thus far the drama of Pelagius and the caliph could very well be a love story in an Arabic anthology. The "martyrdom" would be the caliph's, since exactly this image is used for the sufferings of those who love haughty or inaccessible boys.[11]

But our text is not a piece in an Arabic anthology. It is a passion for Latin Christians. So when further enticement proves unsuccessful, when the king feels his own desires finally spurned, anger seizes him. He orders Pelagius to be seized with iron tongs and twisted about, until he should either renounce Christ or die. Pelagius does neither. So the king demands at last that the boy be cut to pieces with swords and thrown into the river. Raguel describes the dismemberment graphically. What is more, he likens the frenzy of Pelagius's executioners to the mad rites of the Bacchae: "Tam inmania in eum exerto pugione ludibria debacchati sunt" (Rodríguez Fernández lines 107–08) [they were turned into Bacchae through the mad desires that came from beating him], so much so that one would have thought they were sacrificing the boy rather than executing him.[12] Throughout these torments the voice of Pelagius is heard calling out for God's help. The "athlete's" voice is stilled only after he is called to the martyr's crown by the Lord.

The reference to the Bacchae and the emphasis on the unstilled voice are striking, especially in a passage so rich in the customary images of Christian martyrdom. The verb used, *debacchor,* is rare. Both the allusion it incorporates and the archaic tone it carries put the reader in mind of poetic learning, of expertise in pagan mythography. The association seems to be confirmed by what happens in Raguel's narration to the saint's speaking body. The martyr who would not be silent is to be cut apart and then drowned. So it happens. His limbs come to rest on one shore, his severed head on another. Any reader of Latin poetry will hear in these events echoes of the death of Orpheus. Orpheus too was cut apart by a tribe of Bacchae, who seized tools from terrified farmers in order to kill him. His voice had charmed animals with singing, but fell silent under the metal blades. Yet once thrown into the river, Orpheus somehow still sang, borne down toward the sea. Only this miracle is lacking in Pelagius to make the likeness complete.

Is the dismemberment of Pelagius meant by Raguel to call to mind the death of Orpheus? Certainly parts of the myth had been allegorized for Christian purposes long before Raguel began to write. The allegory is presented in Boethius's *Consolation,* for example, and then appropriated by a number of his readers in both vernacular and Latin forms (3 met. 12, lines 76–78).[13] But the part of the myth that matters to the passion of Pelagius is not the already allegorized loss of Eurydice. It is, rather, Orpheus's dismembering because of his refusal to have sexual relations with women after Eurydice's second death. Indeed, Ovid begins his narration of the dismembering by noting that Orpheus taught Thracian men the love of boys (*Metamorphoses* 11.1–84 and 10.83–84). The connection between Orpheus and same-sex love would be registered by later commentators, as it would pass into the vernacular traditions (Bein 50–52). The *Metamorphoses* was known in Spain at the time that Raguel was writing.[14] It may be that he means to Christianize this other part of the Orpheus myth by inverting it: Pelagius becomes the Christian Orpheus because he is dismembered, not just for his purity but for his explicit rejection of same-sex desire.

One can hear other mythic resonances. The martyrdom of Pelagius also inverts or reclaims the well-known tale of Zeus and Ganymede. If Zeus kidnapped the Phrygian boy to be his cup-bearer, the Muslim king wants to abduct Pelagius from Christianity for service in his hall, the approved role for beautiful and beloved boys.[15] The change of condition from the hillsides near Troy to Olympus is no greater than the change from the dark prison to the resplendent court. But Pelagius is in fact called for service at the table of a higher king. His beauty is the visible sign of his having been chosen for the service of Christ, to whom he will be both *sponsus* and *famulus,* both spouse and household intimate. Christ already intends that he should stand beside the heavenly throne in the chorus of virgins (66–67). He who spurned the "crown" of the Muslim tyrant receives the long-promised crown from the hands of Jesus (120). And his spirit flies upward to heaven — as if carried by eagle's wings: "spiritus migrauit ad Deum; corpus uero proiectum est in fluminis alveum" (121). Of course, and to interrupt the series of echoes, it is always difficult to judge how far these literary associations can be assigned to Raguel.

Much riskier, because more speculative, is the question of how far Raguel might have known Arabic or Hebrew poems describing love for boys. Such poems were certainly being written in Córdoba in the years around the death of Pelagius. Indeed, one of 'Abd ar-Raḥmān's ministers is known as a patron of Hebrew poets.[16] But if Raguel knew any poems of this kind, he is at pains to invert their tropes and deny their beauties with scathing silence. In any case, I am content to find poetic precedents only in the most specific case. Raguel does mean to call up Ovid's Orpheus, though he may not have any clear notion of how he will manage the Ovidian allusions once they are called to mind.

Even if all poetic precedents are denied, there can be no denying that Raguel suggests complications in the story that he cannot quite control. Recall, for example, Pelagius's familiarity with practices of same-sex desire. However the king wished to touch him, no single touch could communicate all that is contained in Pelagius's contemptuous question, "Do you think me one of yours, an effeminate?" Pelagius already knows that there are "effeminates" and that they serve for certain kinds of sexual uses. He not only recognizes the king's gesture as sexual, he recognizes the sexual script from which it comes. How does he know this? From the clichés of anti-Islamic polemic preached in Christian communities? He does call the king "dog" (*canis*), one of many animal epithets familiar from anti-Islamic tracts.[17] Or does Pelagius know the king's sexual customs from prison whispers, from the sight of prisoners taken out overnight? Or from the bragging promises of servants? However he knows, Pelagius comes into the presence of the king forewarned that he is a likely object of sexual desire.

So the martyr's next gesture of rejection becomes all the odder. Pelagius strips off the costly robes with which he has been decorated. He thus repudiates "effeminacy." He also exposes that body which is the object of desire. Instead of concealing what the king wants, he presents it more aggressively. Raguel assimilates this to the tradition of Christian martyrology by likening Pelagius to an athlete, naked in the *palestra* (93–94, 119). In context, the gesture taunts the king. Pelagius the martyr is quite plainly Pelagius the ephebe, the type of young male beauty. He rips off his own clothes, as an eager lover might, just in order to show the king what he cannot have. The sight of that body may be one reason why the king is slow to anger, preferring persuasion instead. Only when persuasion fails does the royal desire, exacerbated by Pelagius's display, turn ferocious. Even then, the king hopes that the pain of the iron "forceps" may bring Pelagius to denounce Christ and so recover his body from pain for pleasure.

Pelagius knows the customs of same-sex desire, and he plays with that desire itself when he strips before the king just in order to spurn him. He spurns as well in what he says. When Pelagius proclaims that he "cherishes Christ," when he chooses to die or to suffer "for Christ," when he invokes no one other than "the Lord Jesus Christ," he is speaking the name of his true love in the face of his rival (89, 95, 105, 113). For the king, the choice facing Pelagius seems to be between pleasure and pain, between his own gracious self and a fictive god. For Pelagius, the choice seems to lie between ephemeral and permanent pleasure, between an earthly and a heavenly king, between an imperfect lover and a perfect one. The story of the martyrdom is, through Pelagius's eyes, the story of a passionate triangle in which all the parties are male. He does not deny same-sex love so much as he redefines it by choosing Christ as his lover.

Pelagius redefines it tacitly. It is remarkable that Raguel nowhere gives a special name to the sin that the king wishes to practice on the body of the young martyr. He does not even describe the king's motives except to note that what he heard of Pelagius "pleased" him: "ei obtime sed non recte placuit" (69–70). The ensuing events are placed under general categories of sin. The Moors want to "formam gurgitibus vitiorum . . . obruere" (66) [cover over his form with the torrents of vices]. Certainly there is no detailed description of the acts the king might have wanted to perform with the boy, much less any sense that the king is peculiar in wanting them. If the vices are meant to disgust Raguel's readers, they are also presumed to be familiar to them.

They are familiar not only or principally as acts, but as a cluster of vices. Extravagance, pride in power, and sexual perversion go together for Raguel as they do in late Roman notions of *luxuria,* in some patristic commentary on the story of Sodom, and in early medieval categorizations of sin. Erotic disorder is caught up in a causal network with opulence, which is itself viewed as feminizing, and with arrogance, which is the root of all spiritual disorder. Raguel knows this from many sources. He also knows that the vice of same-sex copulation has been implicated in darker causalities — that it has been linked to bestial cruelty, to the loss of humanity. In Prudentius, for example, Luxury is characterized more by violent rage than by softness (*Psychomachia* 40–52). Raguel's polemical use of Pelagius's suffering against Islam, his appropriation of Pelagius for the cause of Christian Iberia, is perfectly compatible with a simultaneous use of the story to reinforce the nascent theological project of moral categorization. Within this categorization, sexual sins will come to have a more and more prominent place. Indeed, the sins of same-sex copulation will soon become a favorite synecdoche for sin itself.

But not without introducing various instabilities. Raguel's apparently ingenuous testimony to the sufferings of the young boy is polemical and ideological. It is also unstable, so far as it must presume that same-sex desire is familiar, domestic, imaginable. After all, God shows favor to Pelagius by making him desirable, not repulsive. Pelagius is beautiful, not ugly. The boy's body is the body of the ancient ephebe, and the telling of his triumph necessarily calls to mind a string of earlier tales in which ephebes have been loved by gods — or by onlooking poets. The passion of Pelagius as retold by Raguel passes down a number of difficult problems alongside its obvious lessons.

The explicit lessons are, on Raguel's telling, eminently scriptural. The Passion echoes scriptural language throughout, as it recalls the oldest lives of the Christian martyrs. Beneath these obvious lessons lie others, the lessons of Christian struggles against the Muslim regimes. The final request that Raguel makes of the boy-saint is a request for patronage. The martyr who rejected earthly allurements in favor of Christ's promises should now accept the offerings of the local church — the church that struggles against his murderers. There is now no mention of his beauty, only a reference to his refusal of *deliciae* 'pleasures' (133) and *blanditiae* 'enticements' (134). The details of the caliph's proposal are now subsumed in a crusading spirit, reduced only to an outrage that must be avenged. What is to be retained from the story is a sense of Pelagius's patronage in the coming battle to avenge him. Of the problems posed by Ovid or the customs of the Moors or the descriptions of Pelagius's own desire, the listener is to retain only the motive of pious action.

Hrotswitha's Artifice

The story of Pelagius did not remain confined within Iberia. It traveled quickly and far, by unknown means. If the means are unknown, the genres for recording and disseminating the story had been familiar to Christians since ancient times. The story could spread so quickly because it fit — or was made to fit — into one of the oldest of Christian literary forms. The events of Córdoba were not only news, they were confirmation that the God of the ancient martyrs continued to work miracles down to the present day. The passion of Pelagius comes to be incorporated into the writings of the canoness Hrotswitha of Gandersheim in Saxony with just these motives. Much has been written about Hrotswitha, much of it admiring. Rightly so, since her works show eloquence and erudition. Certainly she stands, as an author, above the level reached by Raguel. But my aim here is not to praise Hrotswitha's authorship. It is to notice what changes she makes in rewriting the passion of the desires that Pelagius provoked.

Hrotswitha writes her verse passion of Pelagius, as she writes her plays, according to elaborate symmetries. Some of these are thematic; others are formal or ornamental.[18] Her versification of the martyrdom of Pelagius stands out within these patterns for its newness. Among all her hagiographical texts, it is the only one to record relatively recent events. The next oldest story dates from the eighth century.[19] Moreover, Hrotswitha's title underscores the story's newness: *Passio Sancti Pelagii pretiosissimi martiris qui nostris temporibus in Corduba martirio est coronatus* [The Passion of St. Pelagius, Most Precious Martyr, Who Was Crowned with Martyrdom in Córdoba in Our Own Day].[20] Pelagius is particularly present to Hrotswitha because he is so recent. Indeed her knowledge of him comes not from antecedent texts, but from hearing stories. One of her tasks is to bring these tales under the control of established textual patterns.

Hrotswitha begins to do so in the very first lines: she deploys a literary formula to call upon the young saint. Raguel had invoked Pelagius at the end of his narrative as patron of local churches. The invocation was public and corporate. Hrotswitha begins her verse legend with a personal and passionate call to the boy-saint, who is pictured as a noble knight in the service of the divine king. He is to look down on her, his handmaid, who attends to him in mind and heart. He is to grant her the ability to write of his marvels and his triumph (130.1–11). What Pelagius grants is a poem in several parts, much more suited for non-Iberian audiences than Raguel's relatively terse recital.[21] The poem's first part sets the stage by describing the long-standing idolatry and luxury of the Muslims in Córdoba, a city "inclita deliciis" (131.16) [inclined to delicacies]. The next section narrates the reign of "Abdrahemen," a man "luxu carnis maculatus" (133.73) [stained by the excess of the flesh] and his successful war against the Christian armies. It ends with the capture of Christian leaders and the Muslim ruler's treacherous dickering over the terms of their release. The poem's third part introduces Pelagius, who is distinguished at once by his bodily beauty. Indeed, Hrotswitha mentions his beauty before going on to talk of his prudence and goodness, and she ends the introductory description by noting that he had attained "aetatis primos flores iuvenilis" (136.148) [the first flowers of the age of adolescence].

Differences from Raguel's account have already appeared and not merely in the richness of the artifices employed. In Hrotswitha's telling, for example, Pelagius volunteers for imprisonment in place of his father, a Christian nobleman. There is a direct speech in which the boy pleads with his father to be sent as a substitute, using the argument that his body can better withstand the sufferings to be inflicted. The reader sees Pelagius's filial piety even as attention is drawn to his physical attributes. What is more, the reader gets to hear the boy's extraordinary eloquence. Both eloquence and beauty bring him to the attention of some courtiers once he has been imprisoned. For Hrotswitha, the courtiers are mostly blameless in their dealings with the boy. They wish to free him from the harshness of the prison. Unfortunately, they decide to appeal to their king's special pleasures. The courtiers know that he has been "[c]orruptum vitiis . . . Sodomitis" (138.205) [corrupted by Sodomitic vices]. He wants "to love" beautiful youths "ardently" and join with them in "particular friendship": "Formosos facie iuvenes ardenter amare / Hos et amicitiae propriae coniungere velle" (138.206–07). Surely the king would want to see the "praenitida forma" [outstanding form] of Pelagius—to enjoy his honeyed speech, to have his "corpus candidulus" [shining body] for service in the great hall (139.213–17).

Where Raguel allowed the motive vice to remain nameless and to hang over the whole court as a general condemnation, Hrotswitha names it with the requisite Christian term and confines it to a single, sinning soul. It is the king, and only the king, who has been corrupted by "Sodomitic vices." If Córdoba as a whole was rather too prone to sins of the flesh, ʿAbd ar-Raḥmān was egregiously corrupt, "deterior patribus, luxu carnis maculatus" (133.72) [worse than his parents, stained with the excess of the flesh]. By appealing to his allegedly exceptional vice, the Cordovan courtiers do succeed in persuading the king. He orders Pelagius bathed, swathed in purple, and adorned with a gem-encrusted necklace. The ornamented youth is brought before him. Overcome by the beauty, the king begins to burn. He puts his arm around Pelagius's neck and tries to kiss him. Pelagius responds bitingly to this "pagan king" who is, Hrotswitha says again, "stained by the excess of the flesh" (139.239). No Christian knight who has been washed by baptism will submit himself to barbarian embraces, much less allow his lips to be touched by the filth of demonic kisses (140.243–46). Pelagius urges the king to turn instead to the "stupid men" who will serve him out of a desire for riches. But as in Raguel's story, the king is not angered by this first rebuff. He tries to persuade the "ephebe" gently. "O lascive puer" (140.252) [O lascivious boy], he begins, and then goes on to make his offer of riches, power, ease. At the end, the king puts his hand firmly against Pelagius's face, lays another arm around his neck, and draws him near again for at least one kiss. Pelagius strikes him hard enough to draw blood, which runs down his beard and onto his robes. The king's sorrow turns to rage, and he orders Pelagius's torture.

We need not guess at metaphors to know in Hrotswitha what ʿAbd ar-Raḥmān did to Pelagius. Hrotswitha does also employ metaphors of the game or the joke to describe the king's actions (e.g., 141.271). But she tells the reader quite explicitly how the king touched Pelagius and what he tried to do to him. What she assumes, along with Raguel, is that Pelagius can immediately interpret that kiss as a sexual overture. The kiss is not fatherly or brotherly; it does not bear compassion or pardon. It is felt immediately by the youth as the beginning of a sexual exchange. Indeed, Pelagius retorts to the king that he ought to save his kisses for his fellows Muslims, with whom he shares the stupidity of idolatry (140.246–49).[22] If Hrotswitha's Pelagius is not so vituperative as Raguel's, he is no less well informed about the sexual customs of the Muslim court. So must Hrotswitha's readers be. The "Sodomitic vices" are here condensed into a single kiss, which must be understood as prelude to all of them. The project of moral codification that is suggested in Raguel seems already accomplished and presupposed in Hrotswitha.

The clarity of the moral code makes it imperative that Hrotswitha be equally clear about her own position as narrator, her own relation to Pelagius. The poem begins as a prayer for the saint's help; it ends with note of his patronage. The prologue may be considered formulaic, and the end is not spoken in Hrotswitha's voice. But it is her voice that describes throughout the beauties of Pelagius's body. How does it keep them at a proper distance? By always juxtaposing them with equally sensual descriptions of his eloquence. Indeed, every character in the poem, except one, subordinates appreciation for Pelagius's beauty to appreciation for his beautiful speech. Physical beauty is thus etherealized into verbal beauty. The only exception is the caliph himself, who burns with passion on first seeing Pelagius's face. The caliph wants to love the boy's form before ever hearing him speak (139.231–32). This is a mark of the caliph's depravity. The danger of a woman speaking about the body of an adolescent boy is deflected by making mere reaction to a body something ignoble. Hrotswitha can praise his body safely because she praises his divine eloquence even more enthusiastically.

The poem ends with a longish section on the dispersion and recovery of Pelagius's body. The narrative is considerably more detailed than in Raguel. The recovery of the body is followed by the beginning of a cult of Pelagius. Many persons "of either sex" were moved to sing hymns and offer prayers. After three days, they prepared a fire in which to offer up the body. The fire was to be a vindication of Pelagius's sanctity. Those standing by ask God to show his power in preserving the youth's severed head. After more than an hour in the flames, the head remains intact — the eyes still lustrous. Finally, the faithful break forth in hymns to God.

At least two things are striking in this section. The first is that God's power is shown here in the miracle of preserving Pelagius's physical beauty. Hrotswitha typically abridges or omits the details of the mutilations of martyrdom. She does so here, with a twist. Where Raguel stresses the mutilation of the boy's body, Hrotswitha exalts its intact beauty. The unburned head of Pelagius is much like a female martyr's hymen. It is the physical evidence of his virginity, his innocence of Sodomitic kisses. At the same time, the Christian faithful show themselves more avid fetishists of the physical body even than the lecherous 'Abd ar-Raḥmān. He did not think to collect the pieces of the body he had so much desired. The Christians do, and they begin to enact a reverence much stronger and more persistent than the king's burning desire. The name for that reverence is cult.

Pelagius's Cult

The cult of Pelagius — the cultivation of Pelagius as a saint — was obviously much more than a dispassionate claim that Pelagius lived a holy life and died a holy death. Saints are made popular because they answer any number of needs — institutional needs, civic needs, kinship needs. Pelagius certainly answered them. His death was powerful evidence in anti-Muslim polemic. It was an incitement to vengeance against the Muslim states. It was, in short, the exercise of patriotism by the Christian kingdoms of northern Iberia. The Christian kings of the north were not slow to realize this.

Medieval traffic with saints is very often traffic in saints: the discovery, veneration, exchange, or theft of relics. So with Pelagius. Raguel has told of the faithful coming to collect the remains of the battered boy's body and to give it an honorable burial (122–23). Hrotswitha describes acts of worship toward his body and a miraculous confirmation of his sanctity. What is more interesting, she stresses that the worshipers were of both sexes (145.377). It was two powerful women who are said to have pushed for the recovery of the saint's body from the very ruler who had martyred him. Sancho I of León was urged by his wife, Teresa, and by his sister, Elvira, to sue for peace with 'Abd ar-Raḥmān and to bring the relics back to León, where they would be installed in a new monastery (Menéndez Pidal 2: 422b.31–42). A delegation was sent in 960. The body was recovered only in 967, after both Sancho and the caliph had died. Pelagius was buried in the monastery with ceremony next to the body of "many other bishops" (Menéndez Pidal 2: 424a.50–b.4; cf. Pérez de Urbal and González Ruiz-Zorrilla 163–64). Thereafter the relics became potent political symbols for the Christian rulers. In 985, under the threat of Almanzor's attacks, they were removed from León to Oviedo along with the bodies of the Christian kings (Menéndez Pidal

2: 445b.47–446b.3). The symbolic power would last long in the Iberian imagination. In the *Poema de Fernán González*, the hero is urged into battle against Almanzor by a double dream-vision of Saints Pelagius and Millán.[23] The symbolic power is not only literary. As late as May of 1483, according to the testimony of witnesses under oath, the bones of Pelagius were heard to rattle in premonition of the conquest of Granada (Vaquero 116).

Of course, the political function of the cult of Pelagius is not the only or even the principal motive behind its continuation. The cult spread quickly during the eleventh century and well beyond Galicia and León.[24] From early on, the saint was taken up by communities of religious women.[25] Hrotswitha provides striking evidence for this, but so does the record of church foundings in northern Iberia. The popularity of Pelagius is often explained by pointing out that he is a child saint who embodied in eminent fashion the virtue of virginity. Pelagius could be adopted as a child to the women's community without damage to their purity. Some confirmation of this is found in the popular religion of León. One modern folk song is reported in which Pelagius is invoked as protector of families. The song is clearly written in the voice of a woman, wife and mother, and its petitions are for domestic blessings.[26]

The folk song brings forward what is hidden in any quick narrative of the spread of devotion to the saint. In it, Pelagius is lauded with images of fresh blossoming: "dew-flower," "flower of laurel," "holy rosebud of spring," "red petal." The images want to transmute his body into something less threatening and less sexual than the body of a young adolescent male. If the images are still, almost too obviously, open for erotic readings, they serve nonetheless to turn some attention away from the actual occasion of Pelagius's martyrdom—his beauty, the caliph's desire. It is essential that attention be diverted. Otherwise the cult of Pelagius as saint will reenact the sinful history of the worship of his ephebic beauty.

The danger has already been addressed, of course, in the narratives of Raguel and Hrotswitha. Each of them had to describe Pelagius's physical beauty to an audience of men and women without placing too much emphasis on the young man's body. Raguel's narrative defuses the physical attraction of Pelagius by making Christ its cause and dismemberment its result. The risk may seem less for Hrotswitha, so far as she speaks in the voice of a woman. But her vows make her another one to whom it is not permitted to extol young men's beauty. So she too must attempt to cancel out any purely physical attraction by subordinating the beauty of Pelagius's body to the beauty of his eloquence.

The danger of reenacting illicit desire is greatest for the liturgy. The situation of a Western, Latin liturgy (including the Mozarabic) places the words of the liturgy normatively in the mouths of men. Canonical hours are of course celebrated within women's communities absent a priest, but this is an often unacknowledged exception so far as the authors of liturgy are concerned. The normative voice of the Latin liturgies is male. In the liturgies for Pelagius, this male voice is asked to recall for worshipful memory the story of a man's desire for a boy. The telling of the narrative will require the male voice to admit, if not admire, the youth's physical beauties. Antiphons or hymns about Pelagius's beauty will place praises of his beauty in the mouths of men. More pointedly, the prayers of any liturgy actualize the retold history by applying it to the present situation of the worshipers. To actualize a relation to Saint Pelagius is to place the male voice of the cleric in the position of soliciting Pelagius even while flattering him. That rhetorical position is just the position of the wicked ʿAbd ar-Raḥmān.[27] How can the liturgies for Saint Pelagius escape this rhetorical trap? How can they metabolize same-sex desire into something else?

The best preserved liturgy for the saint is a Mozarabic text for vespers, matins, and mass.[28] It seems to have been written in the 930s or 940s by a distant disciple of the bishop Hermoygius. Perhaps it was a way of repaying the debt owed to the boy who went as substitute for the bishop. A full reading of the text would have to take account of the context created by all of its parts, including those common to all liturgies for martyrs. Here I will look only at the prayers that are proper to the feast. Some of these are spoken in the saint's own voice. Others refer to his actions. None of them is specific about the homoerotic motive behind the martyrdom. One verse of the vespertinal hymn, for example, says that neither the "seculi blanditiae" [blandishments of this age] nor the sword could force Pelagius to deny God. The next verse adds that he cast off the golden necklace given him by the tyrant in order to flee "pomposasque delicias" (192D) [inflated delights]. A prayer from the mass uses similarly vague language: "non adhaesit seculi blanditiis. . . . Perierat autem appetitus ab eo seculi, cesserat amor mundi" (195D). Slightly more specific hints are contained in that same prayer. While Pelagius's contemporaries were living voluptuously ("cum eius consodales voluptuose viverent"), he kept his body intact (195E). The lesson is applied with the plea that those present might be freed from wicked customs and protected from devilish persuasion. Nothing more than this is said about the circumstances of the martyrdom. References to Pelagius's beauty are equally rare and slight. One antiphon for matins begins, "Aspectus erat candidus, vultus quoque angelicus" (195E) [His appearance was beautiful, his face angelic]. The prayer following on it asks rather for the gift of divine strength.

The vagueness of the prayers might seem to be corrected by the short versions of the martyrdom that appear in the preface (*illatio*) to the mass or in the liturgical collections of martyrs' lives. The version preserved in one Mozarabic mass says that the king desired the beauty of Pelagius and thought that the boy might be open to certain vices (196E). But that is a brief mention indeed. The liturgical texts are clearly turning attention away from the particular cause of his martyrdom. They do so by generalizing Pelagius's example. He becomes only a figure for resistance to worldly desires rather than to a quite specific and troubling form of desire. His beauty, moreover, is equally diffused — into the beauty of a distant and ethereal object.

The clearest form of objectification occurs, of course, in the religious art produced by the cult. Very little of the early art survives; what does is not always revealing. A chest adorned with ivory carvings was given by the royal couple in 1053 to receive the relics of Pelagius alongside those of John the Baptist. The carvings show nothing that is particular to the cult of Pelagius. They are adorned with images of the Lamb of God, the evangelists and apostles, archangels and angels.[29] Again, the drawing of the martyrdom of Pelagius in the Pamplona Bibles is a stereotyped rendering distinguished only by the manner of execution.[30] Pelagius is there represented as a bearded, mature man — the same figure that is used in many of the adjacent depictions of male martyrs.

The most striking early image of Pelagius is a façade sculpture taken from the Colegiata de San Isidoro in León. The piece dates to the end of the eleventh or the first half of the twelfth century.[31] The boy-saint is shown holding a Gospel book as if he were a deacon, his hand covered by a dalmatic or deacon's robe. His head is haloed. He looks away into the distance, his expression serene. What is striking is what he wears under his robe. Around his neck there is something like a necklace — the necklace given him by the caliph, perhaps. On closer inspection, it seems the collar of an

Façade sculpture identified as San Pelayo (Saint Pelagius),
from a former portal of the basilica of the Colegiata de San Isidoro,
León (late-eleventh or early-twelfth century). Used with
permission of the Museo de León.

ornamental breastplate, one very similar to a Roman *thorax*.[32] Pelagius may
be wearing the armor of the soldier of Christ or the armor of an Iberian
Christian knight. The soldier of Christ has become simply a noble knight.
But he seems also to have gotten the gifts that the caliph promised—the
gifts of a jeweled collar and luxurious clothing. Pelagius has become for
the eyes of the faithful a beautiful young man dressed for the service of a
king. In this way, the iconography seeks to make visible what the passion
of Pelagius left invisible—namely, the saint's glorification in heaven. The
iconography does this by replicating, in curious ways, the offers made by
the despised caliph.

Pelagius has been transformed from a naked ephebe into a triumphant
military saint. The transformation might be read as an accident of Iberian
politics. Or it might seem to enact a dialectic by which the cause of a military struggle becomes its patron. Pelagius's execution is a cause for which
to fight; Pelagius is soon depicted as a leader in the fight, as a warrior himself. But the transformation from ephebe to glorious captain is also a curious sublimation of homoerotic desire. It would be too obvious for celibate
men to revere Pelagius as a naked "athlete" or spouse of Christ. It is much
easier for them to revere Pelagius as a recognizable adult hero, a comrade
in arms, a soldier. No hint of effeminacy remains—nor of the attraction of
youthful bodies. Pelagius is still to be desired, but now as a model of military power. His body has been changed from that of a defenseless boy to
that of an armored man. Pelagius is no longer at risk of being raped.[33]

Pelagius and the Sublimation of Desire

The tellings and retellings of the passion of Pelagius, his invocation and
representation, are a kind of emblem of medieval theological relations to
same-sex desire. The story explicitly invites the strongest possible condemnations of that desire. These are forthcoming in Raguel and Hrotswitha.
For them, the desire characterizes the most visible enemies of Christianity,
either as a whole or in their rulers. It is depicted, not as something present
within the Christian world, but as something alien, repulsive, imposed
from without. For Raguel, same-sex desire is what unites those who enjoy
the unbelieving king's favor, the benefits of his opulent power. This fact
is known to all, to the courtiers as much as to Pelagius. For Hrotswitha,

Córdoba is the very city of luxury, its ruler a man stained with the vices of flesh. All Christians, again, should know these things.

The condemnations are clear enough, but so are certain hesitations. Raguel is compelled to elide certain details of his narrative, to push the context of same-sex love into silence. He does not say exactly what the king does to Pelagius. He does not explain how the pure Pelagius knew what the king wanted. If Hrotswitha is more explicit about the caliph's advances, she must begin and end her poem by circumscribing Pelagius's desirable beauty — in the beginning, through prayer; in the end, through purifying fire. Pelagius's physical beauty survives the test of fire, but it is only the beauty of his head. It would be too dangerous to imagine the faithful watching for an hour as the naked body of a beautiful young man withstood the flames. Same-sex desire has to be evoked and then contained, made possible but implausible.

The same is true, more strikingly, in the Iberian cult of Saint Pelagius. The Mozarabic liturgy can barely bring itself to mention the cause of his martyrdom. It much prefers to treat Pelagius as a type of the general rejection of worldly desire. His beauty is sometimes mentioned, but never in such detail as to make it troublesome. He is a pure boy, an idealized patron, remote and incorporeal as the heavens. Still, the fact of same-sex desire reasserts itself around the edges. It cannot but appear in the flattery of his beauty that is sung by male choirs. It appears again in some items of iconography. As it begins to act out its own worship of the boy-saint, the Christian community seems as bothered by his beauty as was the Muslim caliph.[34]

Notes

1. I will not treat general questions about the discourses or (hypothesized) practices of same-sex desire in the Islamic regimes. Much that is written about them seems to me problematic. Some studies by American or European scholars, for example, not only overgeneralize from scattered translations, they also enact a belated "Orientalism," a nostalgia for exotic freedoms. Boswell, for example, allows himself to remark that "[i]n early medieval Spain . . . every variety of homosexual relationship was common, from prostitution to idealized love" (196). In fact, and as becomes apparent in more skeptical studies, the construction of same-sex desire in medieval Islamic societies is easily as paradoxical as in medieval Christendom. In what follows, I will mention a few passages from Arabic, Hebrew, or Persian texts that seem to clarify features of the Latin texts

with which I am principally concerned. I do not pretend to read those passages well in their own, very sophisticated contexts.

2. See the summary of scholarly conjecture by Díaz y Díaz ("La pasión de S. Pelayo" 106–10).

3. See Díaz y Díaz ("La pasión de S. Pelayo" 111–12).

4. For what follows, I use the critical edition by Rodríguez Fernández. The edition will be cited by line numbers. The other most easily accessible editions are in Díaz and Díaz ("La pasión de S. Pelayo" 113–16) and in the *Acta Sanctorum*. The version in the *Acta* seems to have been "corrected" throughout to the standards of neo-Latin.

5. The last point leads some to think that the text was composed for liturgical use. Perhaps so, though it is clearly not part of the ordinary office of the saint, which follows it and may well depend on it (Díaz y Díaz, "La pasión de S. Pelayo" 110).

6. From the second *Pasionario* of Cardeña, now Escorial MS b.I.4, f. 127 (Rodríguez Fernández 17); see also *Acta Sanctorum* (181B) and Díaz y Díaz ("La pasión de S. Pelayo" 106).

7. This is the reading of Rodríguez Fernández and Díaz y Díaz (lines 93 and 92, respectively). The *Acta Sanctorum* reads, more suggestively, "Numquid me similem tuis effeminatis existimas?" (184C) [Do you think me like one of your effeminates?].

8. For examples, see Wafer on Abū Nūwās ("Muhammad" 92); Crompton on Ibn Ḥazm (149, 152); Sprachman (192–96).

9. The story is included in the chapter Ibn Ḥazm dedicates to showing how fierce men are rendered suddenly "compliant" through love of a boy (90–91).

10. For some passages illustrating constructions of erotic love as suffering, see Roth ("Care and Feeding" 108–11) and Wafer ("Vision and Passion" 116, 120–25). For the notion that the suffering may be caused by the intensity of beauty (indeed, its intensity as image of the divine), see Wilson (14–18). On "creeping" and other forms of soft pursuit, see Roth (" 'Deal Gently,' " throughout; "Care and Feeding," especially 96–97).

11. See Roth ("Care and Feeding" 113).

12. Earlier editors read "devacati sunt," as in Flórez (23: 235). In editing the *Acta Sanctorum*, the Bollandists had already decided that this was Spanish dialect for *debacchati*, especially since no alternative presents itself. See *Acta Sanctorum* 181C.

13. For some early examples of allegorizations of this passage, see Chance (211–30).

14. See Díaz y Díaz, *De Isidoro al siglo XI*, 31, 81.

15. See Roth ("Feeding of Gazelles" 100).

16. See Roth on Hasdai Ibn Shaprut (" 'Fawn of My Delights' " 161).

17. See Millet-Gérard 101–03 (sexual epithets), 104–08 (animal epithets). For the epithet *canis impurus*, see 147.

18. On the larger patterns, see Dronke (60–64). On the place of the passion of Pelagius, Petroff 83–84.

19. The legend is that of Gongolf, who lived during the reign of Pippin.

20. Hrotswitha, *Pelagius* titulus, in *Opera*, ed. H. Homeyer (Munich: F. Schöningh, 1970), 130 (not given a line number). Subsequent references will be made to the page and line numbers of this edition. Several other Latin editions are available, including that of de Winterfeld in the Monumenta Germaniae Historica.

21. The structure of the poem is capable of several divisions. No single one must be chosen for the present reading to go through. For some other divisions, see the notes to Homeyer's edition; Kirsch (219–220); Petroff (88).

22. Boswell misreads this passage as authorizing same-sex relations among Muslims (198–200). The suggestion cannot stand. Pelagius means to say that demonic kisses between men are caught up in the larger perdition of demon worship. It should also be noted that Boswell, ignoring Raguel's account, tries to read Hrotswitha's poem as a bit of evidence of social history.

23. See Geary (fol. 32v line 14 to 33r line 14 in the transcription). This figure is, I think, "san Pelayo" and not a resurrection of the monk Pelagius who appears earlier in the poem as a prophet of Christian victory.

24. For the spread of the cult in Spain, see Vives (176); Vives and Fábrega Grau (143); Fábrega Grau (1: 227; 1: 297); Colbert (382; 1: 51, 55, 138, 149, 320; 2: 357). See also the remarks on church names in Rodríguez Fernández (16–17, note 13).

25. See Díaz y Díaz ("Passionaires, légendiers, et compilations hagiographiques" 51, 56). The best study of the cult's role in a single community is Colombás.

26. Some verses of the hymn are quoted by García Abad at 148 and 157.

27. It is also, more remotely, the voice of much Arabic love poetry. If we can ask how much of this poetry was known to Raguel, we can also ask how much it served as threatening counterexample to the authors of Mozarabic liturgy.

28. It is printed in *Acta Sanctorum* 191B–197C, which edition I will cite by page number and marginal letter. Another version can be found in the *Patrologia Latina*, ed. J.-P. Migne.

29. The chest is pictured and described in Lasko (153–54). The cathedral of León also holds an embroidered bag with mixed relics, including some from Saint Pelagius (Gómez-Moreno 1: 169). Two other reliquaries, containing respectively teeth and unnamed body parts, are reported in the possession of the Colegiata de San Isidoro in León (Gómez-Moreno 1: 164).

30. Bucher (vol. 2, plate 505 = Amiens MS Lat. 108, f. 228r). Note that the words

of the king's command inscribed around the illumination are an abridgment of the corresponding text in Raguel's *Passio* (101–02).

31. Preserved in the Museo de León, the figure is published in Gaillard (plate 34). Durliat suggests that the figure might have come from "un portail disparu de Saint-Isidore" (388), and I have found no more exact conjecture. For the dating of other parts of the basilica's façade, see Williams ("San Isidoro") who suggests a date as late as 1142. The identification of the figure is, of course, not certain; it has lost any carved label it might have had. Durliat repeats Gaillard's identification of Pelagius without endorsing or denying it (388–89 and fig. 409). Viñayo González thought that there was a much more prominent representation of Pelagius still on the present façade, namely, the vertical figure to the right of the Agnus Dei portal (figures 25, 27). The identification would be quite interesting, not only because the figure is that of a long-haired and very beautiful young man, but because the portal's tympanum can be understood as anti-Muslim polemic (description of the figure, Viñayo González 97; interpretation of the tympanum, Williams, "*Generationes Abrahae*"). Unfortunately, the long-haired figure in question is better identified as Saint Vincent of Avila (Durliat 382–83 and fig. 403).

32. Durliat sees, not a jeweled breastplate, but a jeweled collar above a tunic (389). But the treatment of the ovals on the figure's chest seem to me rather different than the treatment of the cloth around the shoulders.

33. It is interesting to note that Pelagius was not raped by the caliph. In Raguel, this is required for a successful narrative of virginal purity. But it is also, in reverse textual perspective, a refraction of Arabic narratives of chivalry in boy-love. See, for example, the stories of voluntary celibacy in Ibn Ḥazm's chapter on "Compliance" (92).

34. Yet another iconographic transformation was required by Counter-Reformation sensibilities. In bas-reliefs completed in 1633 for the church of San Pelayo in Cicero, we are shown both the presentation to the caliph and the moment before the beheading (Polo Sánchez and Espejo-Saavedra, figs. 24 and 25). In both, the young saint is shown fully clothed — in a cassock.

Works Cited

Acta Sanctorum quotquot toto urbe coluntur, vel a catholicis scriptoribus celebrantur. Junius vol. 7. "Editio novissima." Paris: V. Palme, 1867.

Adams, J. N. *The Latin Sexual Vocabulary.* Baltimore: Johns Hopkins UP, 1982.

Alfonso X. *Primera crónica general de España.* Ed. Ramón Menéndez Pidal. Madrid: Gredos, 1977.

Bein, Thomas. "Orpheus als Sodomit." *Zeitschrift für deutsche Philologie* 109 (1990): 33–55.

Boswell, John. *Christianity, Social Tolerance, and Homosexuality: Gay People in Western Europe from the Beginning of the Christian Era to the Fourteenth Century.* Chicago: U of Chicago P, 1980.

Bucher, François. *The Pamplona Bibles.* New Haven: Yale UP, 1970.

Chance, Jane. *Medieval Mythography: From Roman North Africa to the School of Chartres, A.D. 433–1177.* Gainesville: UP of Florida, 1994.

Colbert, Edward P. *The Martyrs of Córdoba (850–859): A Study of the Sources.* Washington: Catholic U of America P, 1962.

Colombás, García M. *San Pelayo de León y Santa María de Carbajal: biografía de una comunidad femenina.* León: Monasterio de Santa María de Carbajal, 1982.

Crompton, Louis. "Male Love and Islamic Law in Arab Spain." *Islamic Homosexualities.* Murray and Roscoe 142–57.

Díaz y Díaz, Manuel. *De Isidoro al siglo XI: ocho estudios sobre la vida literaria peninsular.* Barcelona: El Albir, 1976.

———. "La pasión de San Pelayo y su difusión." *Anuario de estudios medievales* 6 (1969): 97–116.

———. "Passionaires, légendiers, et compilations hagiographiques dans le haut Moyen Âge espagnol." *Hagiographie, cultures et sociétés (IVe–XIIe siècles).* Paris: Études Augustiniennes, 1981. 49–59.

Dronke, Peter. *Women Writers of the Middle Ages: A Critical Study of Texts from Perpetua to Marguerite Porete.* Cambridge: Cambridge UP, 1984.

Durliat, Marcel. *La Sculpture romane de la route de Saint-Jacques: de Conques à Compostela.* Mont-de-Marsan: Comité d'Études sur l'Histoire et l'Art de la Gascogne, 1990.

Fábrega Grau, Ángel. *Pasionario hispánico.* Madrid: CSIC, 1952.

Flórez, Enrique, ed. *España Sagrada: theatro geográphico-histórico de la Iglesia de España.* 2nd ed. Vol. 23. Madrid: 1799.

Gaillard, Georges. *La sculpture romane espagnole de saint Isidore de Leon à saint Jacques de Compostela.* Paris: Paul Hartmann, 1946.

García Abad, Albano. *Leyendas leonesas.* Madrid: Everest, 1984.

Geary, John S., ed. *Historia del Conde Fernán González: A Facsimile and Paleographic Edition.* Madison: Hispanic Seminary of Medieval Studies, 1987.

Gómez-Moreno, Manuel. *Catálogo monumental de España: Provincia de León (1906–1908).* Madrid: Ministerio de Instrucción pública y Bellas artes, 1925. Rpt. León: Editorial Nebrija, 1980.

Hrotswitha. *Opera.* Ed. H. Homeyer. Munich: F. Schöningh, 1970.

Ibn Ḥazm. *The Ring of the Dove: A Treatise on the Art and Practice of Arab Love.* Trans. A. J. Arberry. London: Luzac, 1953.

Kirsch, Wolfgang. "Hrotsvit von Gandersheim als Epikerin." *Mittellateinisches Jahrbuch* 24–25 (1989–90): 215–24.

Lasko, Peter. *Ars sacra, 800–1200.* 2nd ed. New Haven: Yale UP, 1994.

Menéndez Pidal, Ramón. See Alfonso X.

Millet-Gérard, Dominique. *Chrétiens moʒarabes et culture islamique dans l'Espagne des VIIIe–IXe siècles.* Paris: Études Augustiniennes, 1984.

Murray, Stephen O., and Will Roscoe, eds. *Islamic Homosexualities: Culture, History, and Literature.* New York: New York UP, 1997.

Pérez de Urbal, Justo, and Atilano González Ruiz-Zorrilla, eds. *Historia Silense.* Madrid: Escuela de Estudios Medievales/CSIC, 1959.

Petroff, Elizabeth Alvilda. *Body and Soul: Essays on Medieval Women and Mysticism.* New York: Oxford UP, 1994.

Polo Sánchez, Julio J., and Rocío Espejo-Saavedra. *El Retablo Mayor de Cicero: historia y restauración.* Santander: Fundación Marcelino Botín, 1996.

Rodríguez Fernández, Celso, ed. *La pasión de S. Pelayo.* By Raguel. Santiago de Compostela: Universidade de Santiago de Compostela/Universidade de Vigo, 1991.

Roth, Norman. "The Care and Feeding of Gazelles: Medieval Arabic and Hebrew Love Poetry." *Poetics of Love in the Middle Ages.* Ed. Moshe Lazar and Norris J. Lacy. Fairfax: George Mason UP, 1989. 95–118.

———. " 'Deal Gently with the Young Man': Love of Boys in Medieval Hebrew Poetry of Spain." *Speculum* 57 (1982): 20–51.

———. " 'Fawn of My Delights': Boy-Love in Hebrew and Arabic Verse." *Sex in the Middle Ages: A Book of Essays.* Ed. Joyce E. Salisbury. New York: Garland, 1991. 157–72.

Sprachman, Paul. "*Le beau garçon sans merci:* The Homoerotic Tale in Arabic and Persian." *Homoeroticism in Classical Arabic Literature.* Ed. J. W. Wright Jr. and Everett K. Rowson. New York: Columbia UP, 1997. 192–209.

Vaquero, Mercedes. "La Devotio Moderna y la poesía del siglo XV: elementos hagiográficos en la *Vida rimada de Fernán Gonʒáleʒ.*" *Saints and Their Authors: Studies in Medieval Hispanic Hagiography in Honor of John K. Walsh.* Ed. Jane E. Connolly, Alan Deyermond, and Brian Dutton. Madison: Hispanic Seminary of Medieval Studies, 1990. 107–19.

Viñayo González, Antonio. *L'Ancien royaume de Leon Roman.* Translated into French by Norbert Vaillant. La Pierre-qui-Vire: Zodiaque, 1972.

Vives, José. "Las 'Vitae sanctorum' del Cerratense." *Analecta sacra tarraconensia* 21 (1948): 157–76.

Vives, José, and Ángel Fábrega Grau. "Calendarios hispánicos anteriores al siglo XII." *Hispania sacra* 2 (1949): 29–146.

Wafer, Jim. "Muhammad and Male Homosexuality." *Islamic Homosexualities*. Murray and Roscoe 87–96.

—. "Vision and Passion: The Symbolism of Male Love in Islamic Mystical Literature." *Islamic Homosexualities*. Murray and Roscoe 107–31.

Williams, John. "*Generationes Abrahae:* Reconquest Iconography in Leon." *Gesta* 16.2 (1977): 3–14.

—. "San Isidoro in León: Evidence for a New History." *Art Bulletin* 55 (1973): 171–84.

Wilson, Peter Lamborn. "Contemplation of the Unbearded: The Rubaiyyat of Awhadoddin Kermani." *Paidika* 3.4 (Winter 1995): 13–22.

Benjamin Liu

"Affined to love the Moor"

Sexual Misalliance and Cultural Mixing in

the *Cantigas d'escarnho e de mal diʒer*

La uniformidad limita, la variedad dilata. — *Gracián*

The complex interplay of sexuality, language, and culture in medieval
Iberia is nowhere more evident than in the conflictive arena of religious
difference. Sexual "misalliances," or illicit sexual relations between members of different faiths, violate both the proprieties of sexual behavior and
the limits of what is considered to be acceptable interfaith association.
For this reason, two kinds of texts typically permit themselves to speak of
such encounters: legal codes that seek to establish the limits of acceptable
social conduct, and transgressive texts, such as the burlesque and satirical
Galician-Portuguese *cantigas d'escarnho e de mal diʒer* (CEM),[1] that seek to
exceed the same limits. The cultural anxiety concerning sexual misalliance
has less to do with mere contact than with the concomitant potential for
mixing, for losing both self-definition and group belonging. This anxiety
asserts itself in the desire to control not only sexuality but language as well.
As early as the ninth century, Paulus Alvarus of Córdoba had complained
that Christians living under Islamic rule (*moʒárabes*) had been seduced by
the eloquence of the Arabic tongue.[2] The recurring preoccupation with
mixing — whether sexual, cultural, or linguistic — is apparent in subsequent
etymologies of the very term *moʒárabe* that stress the notion of mixing between Christians and Arabs. The archbishop of Toledo, Rodrigo Ximénez
de Rada (d. 1247), proposes the derivation of the term from *mixti arabi*,
while Pero López de Ayala (d. 1407) furnishes the following definition:
"Mozárabes quiere decir christianos mezclados con alárabes" [*Moʒárabes*
means Christians mixed with Arabs].[3]

Language and culture, as such anxious etymologies show, are inextricably bound. Certainly, etymology and the history of language can become ways of rewriting and stabilizing determined cultural and political narratives. Conversely, as Thomas F. Glick argues, "[t]o take linguistic change as a model for cultural change in general is wholly appropriate. The contact of two different languages provides a microcosm of the contact of cultures" (277). The sixteenth-century Spanish humanist Juan de Valdés had made a similar argument as early as 1535, that Arabisms in Castilian indicate novel things introduced by Arabs: "hallaréis que para solas aquellas cosas, que avemos tomado de los moros, no tenemos otros vocablos con que nombrarlas sino los arávigos que ellos mesmos con las mesmas cosas nos introduxeron" (30) [you will find that only for those things that we have taken from the Moors have we no other words by which to name them except the Arabic ones that they introduced to us along with the things themselves].

While discussing the history of language in pre-Roman Spain, Valdés remarks in passing that warfare and trade are the principal causes of change in language: "griegos fueron los que más platicaron en España, assí con armas como con contrataciones, y ya sabéis que estas dos cosas son las que hazen alterar y aun mudar las lenguas" (23) [the ones who conversed the most in Spain were the Greeks, with arms as well as with commerce, and you already know that these two things are the ones that alter and even change languages]. A third force, cohabitation, emerges in a later passage that explains the Arabisms that came into the language during the period between the Arab conquest (711) and the Catholic Kings' conquest of Granada (1492) nearly eight centuries later:

En este medio tiempo no pudieron tanto conservar los españoles la pureza de su lengua que no se mezclasse con ella mucho de la aráviga, porque, aunque recobravan los reinos, las cibdades, villas y lugares, como todavía quedavan en ellos muchos moros por moradores, quedávanse con su lengua, y aviendo durado en ella hasta que pocos años ha, el emperador les mandó se tornassen cristianos o se saliessen de Spaña, conversando entre nosotros annos pegado muchos de sus vocablos. (29)

[During this interval the Spaniards were not able to preserve the purity of their language enough to prevent a great deal of Arabic from being mixed in with it. Although (the Christian Spaniards) gradually recovered the kingdoms, cities, towns, and villages, many Moorish inhabitants still remained there and continued to speak their language until a few years ago, when the emperor ordered them to become Christians or to leave Spain. By conversing among us they have passed on to us many of their words.]

Valdés expresses the process of language change from Latin to Castilian with such quasi-organic verbs as *mezclar* 'to mix' and *corromper* 'to corrupt,' as well as the word *embaraço*. This last, meaning "impediment" or "encumbrance," also has the secondary sense of "pregnancy," in keeping with Valdés's naturalizing metaphors for language change. These concepts of organic continuity and mixing stand in opposition to the notions of "la pureza de su lengua" [linguistic purity] and the essential preservation of the original parent language, Latin: "Pero con todos estos embaraços y con todas estas mezclas, todavía la lengua latina es el principal fundamento de la castellana" (30) [Despite all these impediments (*embaraços*) and mixtures, the Latin tongue is still the principal foundation of Castilian].

Valdés's narrative of language change covers over precisely the particular encounters that would make up such a process. The disembodied organicity of language figuratively replaces the live utterances that compose the complex weave of the social fabric. Cultural contacts, exchanges, and mixings, of which language change is a sign, are necessarily polymorphous; they resist accommodation to ideas of purity (*pureza*), whether configured in terms of language (as Valdés's formulation is) or, alternatively, sexual conduct, blood, and lineage. Tzvetan Todorov, writing on cultural *mestizaje*, argues that what we call culture arises out of encounters with others recognized to be different: "Identity arises from (the awareness of) difference; moreover, a culture does not evolve except through contacts: the intercultural is constitutive of the cultural" (22). The normalizing fictions of "pure" culture that shape cultural stereotypes are invented precisely out of resistance to such moments of cross-cultural contact, exchange, or mixing.

These moments are often figured as sexual pairings. Octavio Paz takes the couple of Spanish conquistador Hernán Cortés and his indigenous lover, la Malinche, as a foundational myth for Mexican national identity. This identity asserts itself dynamically between the recognition of its heterogeneous origins and the revolutionary desire for rupture with them. As symbolic parents, the "mixed" couple gives rise to a nation constructed out of the violence of conquest and rape, but also out of the productive hybridism of *mestizaje*. Both of these cultural preoccupations are projected onto the sexual relation between Cortés and la Malinche, and find expression in the highly adaptable verb *chingar* 'to fuck,' as for example in the multivalent exclamation "¡hijos de la chingada!" (Grimes). The sexual vocabulary can encompass both the unequivocal violence of taboo language and the complex polysemy of jokes. This language is part of what Paz describes as "un grupo de palabras . . . a cuya mágica ambigüedad confiamos la expresión de las más brutales o sutiles de nuestras emociones y reacciones" (81) [a group of words into whose magic ambiguity we entrust our most brutal or our most subtle emotions and reactions].

In the manifold permutations of such equivocal language, conquest, sex, and commerce come together as highly ambiguous modes of cultural exchange. A single word, in the ambivalent contexts of Iberian *Reconquista*, can open up a constellation of meanings that pertain to different fields of experience. The word *ganancia* 'gain,' for example, has a double signification as both conquered booty and financial profit: both the spoils of military victory and the interest returned on a capital investment. When the Cid, in his capacity as military hero, uses the word *ganancia*, he refers to prospective gains and risks of epic proportions that are very different from those understood by the moneylenders Rachel and Vidas, who finance his expedition (Menéndez Pidal, *Cantar*, vol. 2, s.v. "Gananҫia"). The Cid's *ganancia* is made up of whatever he and his troops can win by force of arms: cities, gold, silver, livestock, clothing, and other forms of wealth (lines 473–81b). For the two moneylenders, by contrast, *ganancia* means specifically the interest due on a loan: "soltariemos la ganançia, que nos diesse el cabdal" (line 1434) [we would relinquish the interest (*ganançia*) were he to repay the principal], they say to Álvar Fáñez after learning of the deception perpetrated against them by the Cid. Neither of these two senses would seem to have anything to do with sex were it not for a third sense, encountered in the expression *hijo de ganancia*, meaning child born out of wedlock. It may be impossible after all to separate the three senses, since the same word is used equivocally in each case. The "magic ambiguity" of brutal and subtle words can produce such reciprocal representations as, for instance, sexual intimacy as an act of war, or combat as an intimate encounter. Because representations of interfaith sexual misalliances touch on highly taboo zones of both conduct and language, it is not surprising that they often take refuge in equivocal registers, especially those of war and commerce, which are more permissible modes of intercultural association.

All three of these areas of interaction—sex, war, and trade—are drawn together by the operation of the equivocal poetics that characterizes the *cantiga d'escarnho* (Rodríguez). The anonymous fourteenth-century poetic treatise that precedes the *cantigas* in the Cancioneiro da Biblioteca Nacional defines the *cantigas d'escarnho* in the following way:

> Cantigas d'escarneo som aquelas que os trobadores fazen querendo dizer mal d'alguẽ ẽ elas, e dizẽ-lho per palavras cubertas que ajã dous entendymentos pera lhe-lo nõ entenderen . . . [*sic*] ligeyramente. E estas palavras chamã os clerigos hequivocatio. (D'Heur 102–03)

> [*Cantigas d'escarnho* are the ones that the troubadours compose when they mean to speak ill of someone in them, but they say it in concealed words that have two meanings so that they will not be understood . . . (*sic*) easily. The learned call these words *equivocatio*.]

Mal diʒer, by contrast, means simply to speak ill of someone without attenuating the language through double meanings, often in the form of direct obscenities.

The combined label *cantigas d'escarnho e de mal diʒer* indicates that the two styles are not mutually exclusive and are in fact often combined in individual *cantigas*. It also points to the extreme heterogeneity of the texts that make up the collection, which range from playful and highly ingenious witticisms to invectives hurled in the most degrading language. The compilation of the corpus began in the Middle Ages as a general counterpoint to the two genres of Galician-Portuguese love lyric: the courtly *cantiga d'amor* and the popularizing *cantiga d'amigo* (Lanciani and Tavani, s.v. "Cantiga de escarnho e maldizer"). The CEM are thus a catch-all, a category of texts that in some way resist categorization.

Roughly speaking, the texts date from the beginning of the thirteenth to the mid-fourteenth century. Their production and preservation was fostered in the courts of such royal patrons as Alfonso X of Castile, the Learned King (r. 1252–84) and his grandson Denis of Portugal (r. 1279–1325). Both of these figure prominently as authors as well as auditors and patrons, among a diverse company of noblemen, courtiers, and professional entertainers (see Ackerlind).

The period of these texts' production witnessed the large-scale military, political and cultural consolidation of the gains of Christian *Reconquista,* epitomized in the taking of Seville in 1248. Pero da Ponte, who is after Alfonso X the most prolific author in the corpus of CEM, offers a panegyric on this occasion to the victorious king Fernando III of Castile, father of Alfonso X, that begins "O muy bon Rey, que conquis a fronteyra" (109–11) [O great King who has conquered the frontier].[4] In the praise poem, Pero da Ponte exalts the conquest of Seville above all other conquests "en todas tres las leys" [in all three religions], that is, Jewish, Muslim, and Christian. Alfonso X, as successor to Fernando III, inherited the riches of the newly conquered territories, as well as the complex tasks of administering them.[5]

Ironically, the very success of Christian military endeavors introduced a whole new set of political and social problems concerning the relations and boundaries between the three religions under Christian domain. The enemy so recently overcome had become neighbor, a situation that called for a shift in strategy from promoting hostile attitudes to encouraging sociable ones, at least within the limits of a relation defined by dominance. The regulations concerning life in close proximity attend to the numerous particulars of social and religious cohabitation: living areas, whether shared or separate, the material exchange of goods and services, conversion of religion or political allegiance (Burns, "Renegades"), and last but not least the physical intimacy of bodies, whether lawful or prohibited. Illicit sexual relations between members of different religions present a challenge to the policies of controlled cohabitation advanced by a Christian authority that formally proscribes such relations without being entirely able to prevent them.

Legislation expresses this desire to exert control over life through control over language. A significant part of the Alfonsine cultural project concerned the establishment of universal legal codes: the *Fuero real* [Royal Code] and especially the *Siete partidas* [Seven Parts] (Craddock). The law, as a representation of a social ideal, is precisely the type of monologic discourse that pretends to be completely univocal and able to regulate its own signification. The penultimate title of the *Siete partidas* — "Del significamiento de las palabras et de las cosas dubdosas et de las reglas derechas" (7.33.0) [Concerning the significance of words and matters which are doubtful][6] — addresses the problem of ambiguities in language and offers a protocol for resolving conflicting interpretations of the letter of the law:

Significamiento et declaramiento de palabra tanto quiere decir como demostrar et espaladinar claramente el propio nombre de la cosa sobre que es la contienda. . . . Et porque segunt dixeron los sabios antiguos las maneras de las palabras et de los fechos dubdosos son como sin fin, por ende non podrie home poner cierta doctrina sobre cada una de las que podrien acaescer: mas sobre las razones generales que son usadas fablaremos, et segunt la semejanza destas podriense librar las otras que acaescen de nuevo. (7.33.1)

[The significance and interpretation of words are intended to show and set forth clearly the proper name of the thing concerning which a dispute has arisen and because, as the learned men of the ancients declared, words and acts of an ambiguous character are, as it were, endless in number and no man can, for this reason, lay down a positive doctrine for every case which may occur; we shall speak of expressions which are general and common, and by analogy, the meaning of others which occur from time to time, can be determined.]

In a revealing conjunction of temporal and hermeneutic authority, only the king is permitted to interpret the letter of law in cases of doubt: "Espaladinar nin esclarecer non puede ninguno las leyes sinon el rey quando dubda acaesciere sobre las palabras ó el entendimiento dellas" (7.33.4) [No one shall interpret or explain the laws except the king, when any doubt arises concerning words or their meaning]. The law, which attempts to restrict the potentially infinite ambiguities of language, is the discursive antithesis of *escarnho* poetry, which thrives on multiplying rather than restricting equivocations and bifurcating senses. Both discourses, of control and of transgression, offer complementary, but not always symmetrical, views of sexual and cultural misalliance. David Nirenberg has recently provided a comprehensive study of sex and violence between majority and minority communities in fourteenth-century Aragon (127–65) that details the "myriad asymmetries of power" and especially the "miscegenation anxiety" that shape interfaith relations (129).

Only in certain combinations of gender and religion, in fact, were sexual relations between members of different faiths explicitly prohibited under the law, specifically in instances involving Christian women and Muslim or Jewish men. The municipal *fueros* 'legal codes' were particularly intolerant of such unions, specifying that both partners in such cases should be burned to death. Mark D. Meyerson cites the provisions of the thirteenth-century *Furs* of Valencia: "Si juheu o serrahi sera trobat que iaga ab cristiana, sien abduy cremats ell e ella" (88, 92n6) [If a Jew or Saracen is found to lie with a Christian woman, let both him and her be burned]. Identical clauses are found in the *fueros* of Baeza and Soria: "Mugier que con iudío o con moro fuere presa, sean quemados ambos" (Ratcliffe 247) [If a woman be caught with Jew or Moor, let both be burned]. The Alfonsine *Siete partidas* are somewhat less indiscriminate in punishing such cases.[7] They prescribe death by stoning for the Muslim man, unless the Christian woman is a *muger baldonada* 'disgraced woman,' or public prostitute, in which case the first offense is punished by a public whipping and the second by death. No such distinctions are made in the title on Jews, which simply prescribes the death penalty for the Jewish man in such cases. For the Christian woman, the punishment depends on her civil status. A virgin or widow loses, on the first offense, half her assets, which revert to her parents, grandparents, or to the king; on the second, she faces the loss of all her assets and the death penalty. A married woman is punished at the discretion of her husband, who may have her burned, free her from penalty, or otherwise do with her as he likes. Finally, a prostitute faces a public whipping for the first offense, and the death penalty for the second.

But double standards seem to apply along the axes of gender and religion. No such prohibitions are articulated for relations involving Christian men and Jewish or Muslim women. Though these too were prohibited under canon law, the ample tolerance for such civil arrangements as concubinage[8] extended in some degree to Christian men's relations with minority women, as historical, literary, and even pictorial documents testify. Yitzhak Baer reports notices of Jewish *barraganas* 'concubines' in Christian Seville (1: 313n), while Meyerson documents the institutionalized prostitution of Muslim women in Valencia. In works of literature, the infamous dean of Cádiz, satirized by Alfonso X in CEM 23, indiscriminately includes *mouras* 'Moorish women' among the many initiates into his esoteric *arte do foder* 'art of fucking' (Márquez Villanueva, "Las lecturas del deán de Cádiz"). The Arcipreste de Hita pursues an Arabic-speaking *mora* without success, saying that he wants to "marry" her (*casar*), referring not to the sacrament of matrimony but rather to concubinage or simply sexual union, given that intermarriage was generally forbidden without a promise to convert before the consummation of the marriage.[9] The illuminations of the Alfonsine *Libro de los juegos* [Book of Games] present a remarkable depiction of the Learned King himself playing chess in the company of two thinly veiled Moorish women (Márquez Villanueva, *El concepto cultural alfonsí* 272–74).

Whereas these relations enjoy a certain tolerance, the punishments for Christian women and Jewish or Moorish men appear inordinately severe. The law, in prohibiting interfaith sexual misalliances, is concerned with something more than interfaith sexuality alone. It protects the hierarchies of power that maintain the dominance, on one hand, of men over women and, on the other, of Christendom over other religious groups. Both women's sexuality and minority religious affiliations connect in ideologies of the "pure," of confinement and control. The special horror, and consequently the horrible punishments, for sexual misalliance and for renegades from the faith derive less from a fear of difference than from fear of hybridity, mixing, and equivocation. Dwayne E. Carpenter has argued that the *Siete partidas'* title on Moors serves to discourage conversion from Christianity to Islam ("Alfonso X el Sabio y los moros" 230–32), and elsewhere has noted that "[i]llicit relations between Jewish men and Christian women do not merely constitute adultery; they represent the linking of believer with unbeliever" (*Alfonso X and the Jews* 92). The *Siete partidas* allow a divorce if one spouse converts to a religion different from that of the other, whether from or into Christianity.[10] The *Furs* of Valencia specifies the same punishment, death by burning, for both sexual misalliances and conversion away from Christianity (Burns, "Renegades" 345; Meyerson 88, 92n6). Inherent in the interfaith sexual encounter is a principle of convertibility and risk taking. Sleeping with the enemy can involve a lapse in one's own religious identity, a kind of apostasy in the flesh; reciprocally, turning away from one's own religion is considered, in the *Siete partidas*, "spiritual adultery" or "spiritual fornication":

[N]on puede acusar de adulterio á su muger el que se tornase herege, ó moro ó judio, et esto es porque fizo adulterio espiritualmiente. . . . Eso mesmo serie del que feciese fornicio espiritualmiente tornándose herege, ó moro ó judio. (4.9.8, 4.10.2)

[A person who becomes a heretic, a Moor, or a Jew, cannot accuse his wife of adultery, and this is the rule for the reason that he himself committed adultery spiritually. The same rule applies to a person who commits fornication spiritually, by turning heretic, Moor, or Jew.]

The law makes special provision for misalliances involving Christian prostitutes. Unlike the married woman, who is given over to the law of her husband, the prostitute is a public concern whose commerce of sex adds an economic dimension to the convertibility of cash, sex, and intimacy with strangers. In the CEM, the *soldadeira* plays this complex part of mediation and exchange. The very name of her office (also called a *mester de foder* 'trade of fucking' in CEM 37), which has to do with *soldada* 'pay' and *soldo*, a type of coin (Latin *solidus*), clearly establishes the link between sex and money. A poem by Pero d'Ambroa narrates such a transaction of objectified labor in the bluntest possible way: "Pedi eu o cono a ũa molher, / e pediu-m'ela cen soldos enton" (CEM 333) [I asked a woman for her cunt, and she asked me for a hundred *soldos*]. The poet, finding this price too high, then asks that the *soldadeira* charge him by the unit ("[F]azed'ora—e faredes melhor—/ ũa soldada polo meu amor / a de parte" [Now make me a retail deal, for love of me, by the piece]), in a grotesque linguistic retailing of the *soldadeira*'s body parts that would render her a mere commodity, compared by the poet to gold and foodstuffs, rather than a sex worker.

The commercial activity of the *soldadeira* in the CEM can also become mercenary, in the approximation of the *soldadeira* to the *soldado* 'soldier.' One of the recurring narratives in the CEM is that of the *soldadeira* who sets off to "moiros guerreiar" (CEM 49) [fight the Moors]. The burlesque frontier romance plays on the equivocal possibilities of martial and sexual struggle between Muslim warrior and Christian woman. In one *cantiga* by Alfonso X, the royal poet tells of the *baralha* 'mix-up,' 'struggle' that the *soldadeira* Domingas Eanes engages with a Muslim *genete* 'horseman' (CEM 25). The language of blows, lances, and wounds that is proper to the epic battle scene here reveals an erotic subtext that deals with sexual positions, genitalia, and venereal disease. These texts parody the language of *Reconquista* epics or panegyrics that celebrate military victories over the Moors (Nodar Manso).

Similarly, in a fragmentary *cantiga* by Afonso Eanes do Coton, a *soldadeira* named Marinha Sabugal wants to bring along an old woman as her companion-at-arms in her *guerra* 'war' against the Moors. The satire of the *velha* 'old woman' is a commonplace in the CEM that comes up in over a dozen poems (see Richlin). The generic character of these satires is attested by CEM 48, in which Afonso Eanes do Coton mocks Orraca López on account of her age in an indirect way: she begs him not to satirize any *velha* at all, for fear that she might be inadvertently mistaken as the intended target. The poem begins by announcing its genre: "A ũa velha quis ora trobar" [Now I wish to compose (a satire of) an old woman]. In this context, the age of Marinha Sabugal's female companion sharpens the incongruity of the scene by pointing to her unfitness—by virtue of age, sex, and sexual orientation—for a combat against the Moors that is at once military and sexual: "mais a velha non é doita da guerra" (CEM 49) [but the old woman is not fit for war].

   The famous Maria Pérez Balteira likewise presents a target for satire on account of her presumed sexual contacts with Moors, although Pero d'Ambroa makes it clear that she has received such "dishonorable" treatment not only from Moors but also from Castilians, Leonese, and "dos mais que á no reino d'Aragon" (CEM 337) [from most everyone in the kingdom of Aragon].[11] The precise degree of Balteira's relations with Muslims has long been a point of controversy that centers on a *tenço* 'poetic debate' between Vaasco Pérez Pardal and Pedr'Amigo de Sevilha (CEM 428). In this poetic debate, Balteira is said to possess the special and mysterious powers of excommunication (*escomungar*) and absolution (*soltar*), the latter of which she learned from a "fi-d'Escalhola," that is, from a member of the Banū Ašqilūla family of Granada.[12] These apparently spiritual powers are no doubt meant to imply magical powers and, equivocally, specific sexual techniques, both of which "Dona Maria" is elsewhere said to possess in fearful degree (CEM 181). Pedr'Amigo goes further to says that her power to *soltar* 'absolve' comes directly from Mecca: "[B]en de Meca ven / este poder" [This power comes from Mecca], "[A]ch'en Meca seu / poder" [She discovered her power in Mecca]. Balteira is said, moreover, to deny the power that God conceded to the Roman Catholic Church: "[O] [poder] que Deus en Roma deu / diz Balteira que todo non é ren" [Balteira says of the power that God granted in Rome that it is all nothing]. The claim that Balteira has explicitly abjured her faith—a requirement for the *muladí* 'renegade' (from Arabic *muwallad*) for acceptance into Islam [13]—lends credence to the connection mentioned above between the interfaith sexual encounter and apostasy. Whether or not to believe Pedr'Amigo is another matter altogether. Might not Balteira simply be considered a female representative of the opportunistic group of thirteenth-century "renegades, adventurers and sharp businessmen" documented by Robert I. Burns?

   As the *soldadeira*'s equivocal narrative of sexual combat with the Moor begins to blur religious boundaries, it also blurs the boundaries of gender and sexual orientation. Men also participate, sexually and militarily, in these mixed melees. One such is Bernal Fendudo (CEM 188). This "split"

Bernal fights the Moors under the gender-bending identity of a male virago or man-like woman: Joan Baveca calls him a *dona salvage* 'wild woman' whose insatiable appetite will conquer the sexual battlefield as all the enemy euphemistically "die" in his power, spent by the force of his passive aggression: "[E] dando colbes en vós, cansaran, / e averedes pos vós a vencer" [They'll tire from raining blows upon you, and then you will be victorious].[14]

The Moorish horseman, the *genete* who rides his *alfaraz* (both words derived from Arabic), is always represented in the CEM as militarily and sexually potent.[15] The longevity of this ambivalent, eroticized image of the Moor is demonstrated by Shakespeare's *Othello*. Iago, though he serves the Moor of Venice, nevertheless says that he is not "affin'd / To love the Moor" (1.1.39–40). The "lascivious Moor" (1.1.126), as Othello is called, is rendered even more alien and more threatening as a sexual figure, and becomes a foil for the construction of Iago's own sense of self-possession. "Were I the Moor," he muses, "I would not be Iago" (1.1.57). Here the difference of persons is made into a difference of kind, as Iago uses his own proper name but refers to Othello only as a member of a category, "the Moor."

If imagining the Moor as "lascivious" highlights his divergence from the norms of Christian society, to imagine him also as homosexual only redoubles this difference. John Boswell has argued that "the regular association of minority sexual preferences with the most dreaded of Europe's enemies inevitably increased popular antipathy toward the minority as well as the Muslims" (279). As mentioned above, the bounds of orthodoxy and normality are fixed by coordinates that are both religious and sexual, so that crossing either line violates both orders.

Crossing lines of belief and sexuality in the CEM is frequently mapped onto the journey *Ultramar* or *alem-mar* 'overseas' to the Holy Land. Balteira, called by Pero da Ponte "a nossa cruzada" (CEM 358) is one such burlesque crusader or female crossover. Another is Álvar Rodríguez, whom the rubrics describe as "un scudeiro que andou aalen-mar e dizia que fora aló mouro" (CEM 324) [a squire who traveled to the Holy Land and who used to say that there he had been a Moor]. Such conversions of convenience are, naturally, condemned by the *Siete partidas*.[16] Álvar Rodríguez thus presents a favorite target for Estêvan da Guarda, who directs five *cantigas* against him (CEM 100–02, 116–17). In one of them, Álvar Rodríguez says that he wants to "tornar-se" [turn around] to the Holy Land, where his life had been better than in his native country: "Ten que lh'ia melhor alen mar / que lhe vai aqui, u naceu e criou; / e por esto diz que se quer tornar" (CEM 101) [He maintains that things went better for him overseas than they do here, where he was born and raised, and for this reason he says that he wants to return]. *Tornar-se* means to return, but it also means to convert, to become a *tornadiço* 'renegade' or turncoat. Along with this line of attack, Estêvan da Guarda, on the authority of a certain Master Ali, also details Álvar Rodríguez's sexual involvement with a young Moorish boy of his own household (CEM 116, 117). Here, though the accusations of apostasy and sodomy may both arise from a distant journey across the sea, they are made to converge on Iberian soil, in the specific representation of an illicit sexual cohabitation between a Christian and a Moor.

Like Álvar Rodríguez, Fernan Díaz is said to have crossed over in geography and sexual orientation during his trip to Ultramar. Airas Pérez Vuitoron not only describes Fernan Díaz's desire for a same-sex union ("casamento . . . d'ome" [marriage of a man]), but also says that nobody has ever witnessed such desire: "e por este casamento del, de pran, / d'ome atal coita nunca viu cristão" (CEM 80, Mérida) [and for this marriage of his, in short, no Christian has ever seen such longing from anyone (for a man)]. Here "Christian" means simply anybody, as the parallel verses in the other two strophes suggest: "[N]unca vós tan gran coita vistes" [You never saw such great longing], "[A]tal coita nunca foi no mundo" [never in the world was there such longing]. However, the expression "nunca viu cristão" still leaves rhetorically open the possibility of non-Christian eyes and experiences, especially if these are undertaken outside the realm of Christendom. Pero Garcia Burgalês (CEM 377) chronicles Fernan Díaz's trip to Ultramar in search of a master jeweler able to set a particular gemstone (*olho*), which is a secondary meaning of an equivocal word — *olho* 'eye' — that a more directly transgressive *cantiga de mal dizer* further glosses as *olho do cuu* 'asshole' (CEM 131). Fernan Díaz's Bataillesque "history of the *olho*" would not be complete without sacred parody: Pero da Ponte, mockingly praising Fernan Díaz as a good Christian for never having loved a woman, and never having failed to love a man, high- or low-born, says that when he dies the New Testament verses "Beati oculi" will be pronounced (CEM 365). The Latin pun on *oculi* and *culi* only amplifies and reconfigures the latent equivocal sense of *olho* as both eye and asshole played on in other *cantigas*.[17] The abasing conflation of face and ass is rendered even more clearly in CEM 340, in which

Pero d'Armea's *bel cuu* 'beautiful ass,' applied with false eyebrows and cosmetics but missing a nose, is favorably compared to a maiden's face.[18]

"Moors" are not encountered only on exotic journeys off Iberian shores. Closer to home, they also coexist within the frontiers of Christian territory. Joan Fernández, for example, is referred to in the CEM as "o mouro" though he was not a Muslim, but, according to the rubrics, only "semelhava mouro" [appeared Moorish] and likely was a Muslim convert to Christianity (CEM 297). Although the *Siete partidas* define Moors univocally as those who believe in Muḥammad as prophet and messenger of God, and prohibit intolerance against Muslim converts to Christianity, the CEM's poetics of equivocation makes no such provision.[19] "Joan Fernández," says one poet of *escarnho*, "fode-a tal como a fodedes vós" [A Moor is fucking your wife, just as you fuck her]. The meaning is clear: Joan Fernández himself is simultaneously intended as both the adulterous Moor and the newly Christian husband, who has been cuckolded, paradoxically, by none other than his past self (CEM 229). The many allusions to circumcision fuse religious and sexual practice in a constant reminder of his convert status. Joan Fernández, himself counted among the "mal talhados" (CEM 51) [ill-fashioned ones], in one *cantiga* wants to do battle against the Moor, with fire, to exact revenge for an ancient injury: "mais quer queimar, ca lhi foron queimar / en sa natura já ũa vegada" (CEM 408) [but he wants to burn, for they once burned him on the penis]. Another poet repeatedly criticizes the "cut" of his dress, his figure, and, by extension, his penis: "Joan Fernandes, que mal vos talharon"; "vola talharon mal"; "sodes vós mal talhado" (CEM 300) [how badly they tailored you; they tailored it badly for you; you are very badly tailored].

By the same equivocal logic, two *cantigas* accuse Joan Fernández of harboring and hiding an *anaçado* 'fugitive Moor' (CEM 297, 409).[20] To shelter a Moor would violate the edicts against cohabitation of Christians with Jews or Muslims;[21] but the irony here is that Joan Fernández, even alone, contradicts those edicts by being himself both a Christian and a "Moor," in the multiple equivocal meanings of the term.

This term *anaçado* (inf. *anaçar*) has an unclear etymological derivation. Apparently cognate to the Castilian *enaciado*, it has at least three possible Arabic etyma that have been proposed: *an-nāẓiʿ* 'renegade'; *an-nāẓiḥ* 'one who is faraway,' 'émigré'; and *an-naẓāḥa* 'rejoicing,' whence Castilian *añacea*. *Anaçar*, besides meaning to become a renegade, also means "to stir up," "to mix" (as in cooking), a sense attested as early as 1318 in Mestre

Giraldo's treatises on equitation and falconry. In light of this second meaning, an unattested vulgar Latin derivation has held sway in many dictionaries (*adnateare*), and many other speculative hypotheses have been advanced.[22] The uncertainty concerning the word's origins, however, should not obscure the characteristic mix of meanings—a convert, and something stirred or mixed up—that gives the word its peculiar savor.

This distinctive combination of senses comes up again in an unexpected context, the cosmic satire, or moral *sirventès*, a well-represented theme in the CEM from the austerity of Martin Moxa to the pathos of the Unknown Troubadour (Tavani 226–32, Scholberg 119–25). The stirring up of people and their mutability in a *cantiga* by Pero Mafaldo echoes the second Psalm almost to the letter: "Vej'eu as gentes andar revolvendo, / e mudando aginha os corações / do que põen antre si as nações" (CEM 399) [I see the people move around and around, and the nations quickly changing their hearts as to what there is between them].[23] Similarly, the famous passage from the end of Paulus Alvarus's *Indiculus luminosus* (854), mentioned briefly above, arises in a rhetorical context that is less well known than the passage itself. The acculturation of young *moçárabes* is taken as a sign of an overturned world and the coming of the Antichrist. This apocalyptic vision uses the figure of *adynata* to express the image of a world upside-down, which Ernst Robert Curtius explains generally as "age's criticism of youth" (98). But Alvarus's criticism is not only of youth, but also of a newly dominant Muslim culture. That Christians should adopt Arabic speech and customs he takes to be a contradiction in terms, an *adynaton*, and the young, culturally mixed *moçárabe* is considered, as the *anaçado* will be centuries later, a monstrous microcosm of a disordered world that is itself mixed up and turned about.

This analogy is made explicit in a poem by Joan Soárez Coelho that is best known for its references to two datable historical events, the Emperor Frederick II's struggle with the Roman papacy and the irruption of the Mongols into Eastern Europe.[24] Joan Soárez Coelho sees in these events— as in the desire of Joan Fernández, "o mouro," to go on crusade—sure signs of the Antichrist and of the world's imminent end (CEM 230). He imagines such oxymoronic possibilities as *o mouro cruzado* or *o mouro pelegrin* (the Moor as Christian crusader or as pilgrim to Jerusalem) all turning on the play in the verb *tornar-se*, 'to turn,' 'to become,' or 'to convert.' The world is not only stirred up ("o mund' é torvado") but, like the *anaçado* himself, it is messed up or mixed up ("o mund assi como é mizcrado"). *Mizcrar,* meaning "to mix" and "to calumniate," breaks with both senses of *puridade,* "secrecy" as well as "purity." [25]

If "purity," in one of its meanings, consists in being able to keep quiet about a secret, then "mixing" implies going public by speaking out loud. This loudness is one of the distinguishing feature of the CEM, which publicly speak ill of others, either directly or in words that are concealed through equivocation. The connection between *mal dizer* and *mizcrar* is made in a *tenço* in which Joan Soárez Coelho suggests to Joan Pérez d'Avoín that he has been duped by a malicious slanderer about a third party:

> — Joan Pérez, por mal dizer
> vos foi esso dizer alguen,
>
> . . . .
>
> mais ben sei eu que o mizcrou
> alguen convosqu'e lhi buscou
> mal, pois vos esso fez creer. (CEM 221)

[—Someone has told you that, Joan Pérez, to speak ill (of him). But I know well that someone has slandered him to you, seeking to do him harm, since he made you believe that.]

Such speaking evil (*mal dizer*) or public slander (*mizcrar*) is a special kind of transgressive speech and, as such, is specifically prohibited in the *Siete partidas:*

Enfaman et deshonran unos á otros non tan solamente por palabra, mas aun por escriptura faciendo cántigas, ó rimas ó dictados malos de los que han sabor de enfamar. Et esto facen á las vegadas paladinamente et á las vegadas encubiertamente. (7.9.3)

[Some men render others infamous and dishonor them not only in speech but also in writing, by making songs or rhymes, or evil statements of those whom they desire to defame. They do this sometimes openly and sometimes secretly.]

Moreover, slanders composed in writing or in rhymes are singled out as particularly reprehensible, even should the accusations prove true, porque el mal que los homes dicen unos á otros por escripto, ó por rimas, es peor que aquel que dicen dotra guisa por palabra, porque dura la remembranza della para siempre si la escriptura non se pierde: mas lo que es dicho dotra guisa por palabras olvidase mas aina. (7.9.3)

[because the evil which men say of one another either in writing, or in rhyme, is worse than that which is spoken in any other way by words, because if not lost the remembrance thereof endures forever, but whatever is stated in another way in words is soon forgotten.]

The CEM, as slanderous texts in rhyme and writing, transgress against both secrecy and purity in the way they loudly mix language, sexualities, and other forms of impure cultural exchanges.

In a *cantiga* by Joan Baveca (CEM 189), a *soldadeira* named Maior Garcia, in order to clear her debts, carries out sexual and economic transactions (*baratar* 'negotiate') with a Christian squire, a Jew, and a Muslim, all in the same day. This same Maior Garcia is mentioned in several other *cantigas* as the lover of various members of the clergy, including a dean and archdeacon (CEM 190, 323, 335). In one instance, Alfonso X says that he will "repossess" the *cadela* 'female dog,' meaning concubine, from a dean—probably the promiscuous dean of Cádiz in CEM 23—as collateral for a dog of his own that the dean has presumably taken: "Penhoremos o daian / na cadela, polo can" (CEM 29) [Let's repossess the *cadela* from the dean, in exchange for the dog]. The object of this humiliating transaction, the dean's *cadela*, referred to as "a maior" [the eldest] is in all likelihood none other than Maior Garcia (Mettman 317–18). In CEM 189, Maior Garcia is herself a debtor upon whom her creditor, a Christian squire, wishes in like fashion to "tomar penhor" [take his due]. She promises to repay him in turn with what she gains from her business with a Jew and a Moor. The entire poem is full of such sexual and economic double entendre. When the Moor agrees to advance her funds, he will only accept a promissory note, in order to secure the loan, that he is permitted to write over her: "[O] mouro log'a carta notou / sobr'ela" [Then the Moor wrote the note over her]. This is a grammatical construction that has clear sexual connotations here and throughout the CEM.[26] The combined transactions of writing and sex produce a *tralado* 'transcript,' a copy or reproduction both of the financial contract and of its sexual author, the Moor himself: that is, both a receipt and a child (Lapa, CEM 189n27).

What would be the significance of this equivocal child, born of the mixed encounters between a Christian squire, a Jew, a Moor, and a prostitute? The *Siete partidas* offer a hybrid etymology for the word *barragana* 'concubine,' which would derive from the union of the Arabic *barran* 'outside' and the Romance *gana* or *ganancia* 'gain' in the multiple senses of the word:

> [*Barragana*] tomó este nombre de dos palabras, de barra que es de arábiga, que quiere decir tanto como fuera, et gana que es de ladino, que es por ganancia; et estas dos palabras ayuntadas en uno, quieren tanto decir como ganancia que es fecha fuera de mandamiento de eglesia; et por ende los que nascen de tales mugeres son llamados fijos de ganancia. (4.14.1)

> [The name *barragana* is derived from two words; one of them Arabic, which means outside, and the other Castilian, which means to gain, and these two words, when united, mean something earned outside the rules of the church. For this reason those who are born of women of this kind are called children of gain (*fijos de ganancia*).]

The etymology of the word *barragana* is as mixed as the *barragana*'s ambiguous child, whose three possible fathers are of three different faiths. The *fijo de ganancia* stands to inherit only an ambivalent cultural legacy of conquest, surplus value, and illegitimacy. Maior Garcia's equivocal *tralado* is a bastard text that, like the CEM themselves, records the profoundly ambiguous realities of cultural mixing in medieval Iberia.

Notes

1. *Cantigas d'escarnho e de mal diχer dos cancioneiros medievais galego-portugueses* (ed. Lapa). All references are to this edition, henceforth abbreviated CEM, and to Lapa's numbering system.

2. *Patrologia latina* (121: 555); Sage (28–31); Lévi-Provençal (94–95); Menéndez Pidal (*Orígenes,* sec. 87).

3. Glick (193, 343n66); Menéndez Pidal (*Orígenes,* sec. 86n1). *Moχárabe* derives from the Arabic active participle *musta'rib* 'Arabized.' The tenth verbal form frequently combines factitive and reflexive or middle senses: "to be made" or "to make oneself" (Wright sec. 61–65). English translations here and throughout are mine unless otherwise noted.

4. Also included and commented in Alvar and Beltrán (*Antología* 158–60). For an echo of the same event through the eyes of the conquered, see Sāliḥ ar-Rundī's lament of the fall of Seville (Monroe 332–37).

5. For a historical overview of the period, see Jackson (ch. 3, "Thirteenth-Century Conquest and Synthesis") and O'Callaghan.

6. The English translations of the *Siete partidas* cited here and throughout are from Samuel Parsons Scott's 1931 translation. Though in some cases the translations do not render the exact letter of the Real Academia de la Historia's 1807 edition, as followed here, they do convey the spirit of the laws.

7. "Qué pena meresce el judio que yace con cristiana" (7.24.9) [What penalty a Jew deserves who has intercourse with a Christian woman]. "Qué pena merescen el moro y la cristiana que yoguieren de consuno" (7.25.10) [What penalty a Moor and a Christian woman deserve who have intercourse with one another]. See Carpenter *Alfonso X and the Jews*, ch. 14, "Forbidden Unions [7.24.9]").

8. Barraganas defiende santa eglesia que non tenga ningunt cristiano, porque viven con ellas en pecado mortal. Pero los antiguos que fecieron las leyes consintieron que algunos las podiesen haber sin pena temporal. (*Siete partidas* 7.14.0)

[The Holy Church forbids Christians to keep concubines, because they live with them in mortal sin. The wise men of the ancients, however, who made the laws, permitted certain persons to keep them without being liable to a temporal penalty.]

9. Juan Ruiz (stanza 1508–12n). For this sense of *casar* as sexual union, compare the equivocal usage of CEM 340: "[S]odes solteiro, e seredes casado" [You are single, but will be married]. See also Roncaglia and Cano Ballesta. The latter remarks on the Arcipreste de Hita's poetics of playful equivocation — "la ambigüedad, el doble sentido encubierto y la desenvoltura ironizante y apicarada" (9) — that bears a striking resemblance to that of the CEM. In law, however, unlike in poetry, these equivocal usages are not admissible, and *casar* must refer only to matrimony: "[N]ingunt cristiano non debe casar con judia, ni con mora, nin con hereja nin con otra muger que non toviese la ley de los cristianos" (*Siete partidas* 4.2.15) [No Christian should marry a Jewess, Moorish woman, a heretic, or any other woman who does not profess the Christian religion].

10. "Qué pena meresce el cristiano ó la cristiana que son casados, si se tornare alguno dellos judio, ó moro ó herege" (*Siete partidas* 7.25.6) [What penalty a Christian of either sex who becomes a Jew, a Moor, or a heretic, deserves]. "Por qué razones se puede facer el departimiento entre el varon e la muger" (4.10.2)

[For what reasons a separation can be made between man and wife]. "Por qué razones el que se face cristiano ó cristiana se puede departir de la muger ó del marido con quien era ante casado segunt su ley" (4.10.3) [For what reasons a party who becomes a Christian can separate from the wife, or husband, to whom he was formerly married according to the rights of his religion].

11. On this literary and historical figure see Alvar.

12. On the historical Banū Ašqilūla, see Harvey (31–37).

13. This is required of would-be converts from Judaism or Christianity as members of the *ahl al-kitāb* 'people of the book' (*Shorter Encyclopedia of Islam*, s.v. "Murtadd").

14. This Bernal Fendudo is probably the effeminate *segrel* Bernal de Bonaval with the sobriquet "split." Bonaval, along with several other personalities in the CEM, could have his own personal songbook not only as author (eighteen songs and one *tenço*) but also as target of abuse (CEM 17, 76, 87, 194, 357), in a sexual and poetic version of Rabelais's Chiquanous 'catchpoles,' who earn their living by being beaten (64; Bakhtin 196). At one point Airas Pérez Vuitoron tells him: "nunca mais escarnid' ome vi" (CEM 76) [I have never seen a man more mocked]. On Bonaval, see Josiah Blackmore's essay in this volume.

15. For example, CEM 21, 25, 60. *Genete* from Arabic *Zanātī; alfaraz* from Arabic *al-faras*. On the perceptions of the *genetes'* military prowess, see Lourie (72–75).

16. "Qué pena meresce el cristiano que se tornare moro, maguer se repienta despues e se torne á la fe" (*Siete partidas* 7.25.5) [What penalty a Christian deserves who becomes a Moor, even if he subsequently repents and returns to our faith].

17. "[N]unc'amou molher . . . / nen desamou fidalgo nen vilão" [He never loved a woman, nor hated a man of high or low estate]. Part of the joke here lies in the negation of the word *desamar,* meaning to hate or dislike: thus "he never hated" or "he never failed to love." For uses of *desamar* see also CEM 81, 127; and Brea Hernández. "Beati oculi" (Luke 10.23, Matt. 13.16). For the pun on *oculi* and *culi* see Hernández Serna (289); Scholberg (108).

18. A perfect visual parallel to this text may be found among the photographs illustrating Georges Bataille's *Erotism.* Labeled only as a "tattooed man," plate 17 depicts a man whose ass is tattooed with a pair of eyes and arched eyebrows.

19. "Moros son una manera de gentes que creen que Mahomat fue profeta et mandadero de Dios" (*Siete partidas* 7.25.0) [The Moors are a people who believe that Mohammed was the Prophet and Messenger of God]. "Qué pena meresce quien deshonrare de dicho ó de fecho á los moros despues que se tornaren cristianos" (7.25.3) [What punishment those deserve who insult converts].

20. On *enaciado* and other terms for converts between Christianity and Islam, see Castro (151–52).

21. "Cómo ningunt cristiano nin cristiana non debe facer vida en casa de judio" (*Siete partidas* 7.24.8) [No Christian, man or woman, shall live with a Jew]. See Carpenter (*Alfonso X and the Jews*, ch. 13: "Social Relations [7.24.8]"). See also the Ordenamiento de Burgos of 1315 that prohibits cohabitation of Christians with Jews or Muslims, cited in Cejador y Frauca (2: 1508n).

22. See Michaëlis (250–57); Corominas (s.v. "Enaciado"); Machado (s.v. "Anaçar"). Rodrigo Fernández Santaella proposed in 1499 a derivation from Latin *initiatus:* "E de aqui llaman *enaziados* casi iniciados a los que se tornan moros" [Whence they call those who have become Moors *enaziados*, as it were, initiated], cited in Alonso (s.v. "Enaciado"). Leo Spitzer has argued for a derivation from Latin *natio*, which, in the spirit of stirring and mixing up of *anaçar*, may perhaps be paired with the also improbable Arabic *an-nās* 'the people' or *anisa* 'to be sociable,' supported by Alonso.

23. On variant readings of these verses, see Spina (46–47). Cf. the Vulgate Psalm 2: "Quare fremuerunt gentes / et populi meditati sunt inania" (Gall.); "Quare turbabantur gentes / et tribus meditabuntur inania" (Heb.) (*Biblia sacra iuxta vulgatam versionem*). Douay-Rheims version: "Why have the Gentiles raged, and the people devised vain things?"

24. For a panoramic history of this period, see Mayer (228–71). Carolina Michaëlis sets the poem's date of composition around 1241–44 (ctd. by Lapa, CEM 230).

25. Castro has identified these words as possible loan translations from Arabic (174–75). The Castilian equivalents are *poridat* and *mezclar* or *mesturar*, as in the *malos mestureros* 'evil gossipers' (line 276) who drive the Cid into exile.

26. Maior Garcia again, in another *cantiga*, finds herself so poor that "se non fosse o arcediano, / non avia que deitar sobre si; / ar cobrou pois sobr' ela o daian" (CEM 323) [were it not for the archdeacon, she had nothing with which to cover herself; once again she sought shelter under the dean].

Works Cited

Ackerlind, Sheila R. *King Dinis of Portugal and the Alfonsine Heritage.* New York: Peter Lang, 1990.

Alonso, Martín. *Diccionario medieval español: desde las Glosas Emilianenses y Silenses (s. X) hasta el siglo XV.* Salamanca: U Pontificia de Salamanca, 1986.

Alvar, Carlos. "María Pérez, Balteira." *Archivo de Filología Aragonesa* 36–37 (1986): 11–40.

Alvar, Carlos, and Vicente Beltrán. *Antología de la poesía gallego-portuguesa.* Madrid: Alhambra, 1989.

Baer, Yitzhak. *A History of the Jews in Christian Spain.* Trans. Louis Schoffman. 2 vols. Philadelphia: Jewish Publication Soc. of America, 1961.

Bakhtin, Mikhail. *Rabelais and His World.* Trans. Hélène Iswolsky. Bloomington: Indiana UP, 1984.

Bataille, Georges. *Erotism: Death and Sensuality.* Trans. Mary Dalwood. San Francisco: City Lights, 1986.

Biblia sacra iuxta vulgatam versionem. Stuttgart: Deutsche Bibelgesellschaft, 1969.

Boswell, John. *Christianity, Social Tolerance, and Homosexuality: Gay People in Western Europe from the Beginning of the Christian Era to the Fourteenth Century.* Chicago: U of Chicago P, 1980.

Brea Hernández, Ângelo José. " 'Se eu podesse desamar,' de Pero da Ponte: um exemplo de 'mala cansó' na lírica galego-portuguesa?" *O cantar dos trobadores* 351–72.

Burns, Robert I., ed. *Emperor of Culture: Alfonso X the Learned of Castile and His Thirteenth-Century Renaissance.* Philadelphia: U of Pennsylvania P, 1990.

———. "Renegades, Adventurers, and Sharp Businessmen: The Thirteenth-Century Spaniard in the Cause of Islam." *Catholic Historical Review* 58 (1972): 341–66.

Cano Ballesta, Juan. "¿Pretende casarse la serrana de Tablada?" *La corónica* 23.1 (1994): 3–11.

O cantar dos trobadores: Actas do Congreso celebrado en Santiago de Compostela entre os días 26 e 29 de abril de 1993. Santiago de Compostela: Xunta de Galicia, 1993.

Cantigas d'escarnho e de mal dizer dos cancioneiros medievais galego-portugueses. Ed. Manuel Rodrigues Lapa. Rev. ed. [Vigo]: Galaxia, 1970. Rpt. in 3rd ed. Vigo: Ir Indo; Lisboa: João Sá da Costa, 1995.

Carpenter, Dwayne E. *Alfonso X and the Jews: An Edition of and Commentary on Siete Partidas 7.24 "De los judíos."* Berkeley: U of California P, 1986.

———. "Alfonso X el Sabio y los moros: algunas precisiones legales, históricas y textuales con respecto a *Siete partidas* 7.25." *Al-Qantara* 7 (1986): 229–52.

Castro, Américo. *La realidad histórica de España.* 8th ed. Mexico: Porrúa, 1982.

Cejador y Frauca, Julio, ed. *Libro de buen amor.* By Juan Ruiz. 2 vols. Madrid: La Lectura, 1913.

[CEM]. See *Cantigas d'escarnho e de mal dizer.*

Corominas, Joan. *Diccionario crítico y etimológico castellano y hispánico.* 6 vols. Madrid: Gredos, 1980–91.

Craddock, Jerry R. "The Legislative Works of Alfonso el Sabio." Burns, *Emperor* 182–197, 257–260.

Curtius, Ernst Robert. *European Literature and the Latin Middle Ages.* London: Routledge, 1953.

D'Heur, Jean Marie. "L'*Art de trouver* du chansonnier Colocci-Brancuti." *Arquivos do Centro Cultural Português* 9 (1975): 321–98. Rpt. in *Recherches internes sur la lyrique amoureuse des troubadours galiciens-portugais (XIIe–XIVe siècles: Contribution à l'étude du "corpus des troubadours."* N.p.: n.p., 1975. 97–171.

Da Ponte, Pero. *Poesías.* Ed. Saverio Panunzio. Trans. Ramón Mariño Paz. Vigo: Galaxia, 1992.

Glick, Thomas F. *Islamic and Christian Spain in the Early Middle Ages.* Princeton: Princeton UP, 1979.

Grimes, Larry M. *El tabú lingüístico en México: el lenguaje erótico de los mexicanos.* New York: Bilingual, 1978.

Harvey, L. P. *Islamic Spain: 1250 to 1500.* Chicago: U of Chicago P, 1990. 31–37.

Hernández Serna, Joaquín. "Erotismo y religiosidad en el cancionero de burlas galaico-portugués." *La lengua y la literatura en tiempos de Alfonso X: Actas del Congreso Internacional (Murcia, 5–10 de marzo de 1984).* Ed. Fernando Carmona and Francisco J. Flores. Murcia: Dpto. de Literaturas Románicas, U de Murcia, 1985. 263–94.

Jackson, Gabriel. *The Making of Medieval Spain.* London: Thames, 1972. [Spanish trans.: *Introducción a la España medieval.* Madrid: Alianza, 1988.]

Lanciani, Giulia, and Giuseppe Tavani, eds. *Dicionário da literatura galego-portuguesa.* Lisboa: Caminho, 1993.

Lapa, Manuel Rodrigues. See *Cantigas d'escarnho e de mal diʒer.*

Lévi-Provençal, É. *La civiliʒación árabe en España.* 6th ed. Madrid: Espasa-Calpe, 1982.

Lourie, Elena. "Anatomy of Ambivalence: Muslims under the Crown of Aragon in the Late Thirteenth Century." *Crusade and Colonisation: Muslims, Christians and Jews in Medieval Aragon.* Aldershot, England: Variorum, 1990. Ch. 7.

Machado, José Pedro. *Dicionário etimológico da língua portuguesa.* 5 vols. Lisboa: Horizonte, 1977.

Márquez Villanueva, Francisco. *El concepto cultural alfonsí.* Madrid: Mapfre, 1994.

———. "Las lecturas del deán de Cádiz en una *cantiga de mal diʒer.*" *Cuadernos hispanoamericanos* 395 (1983): 331–45. Rpt. in *Studies on the* Cantigas de Santa Maria: *Art, Music, and Poetry: Proceedings of the International Symposium on the* Cantigas de Santa Maria *of Alfonso X, el Sabio [1221–1284] in Commemoration of Its 700th Anniversary Year—1981 (New York, November 19–21).* Ed. Israel J. Katz, John E. Keller, et al. Madison: Hispanic Seminary of Medieval Studies, 1987. 329–54.

Mayer, Hans Eberhard. *The Crusades.* Trans. John Gillingham. Oxford: Oxford UP, 1988.

Menéndez Pidal, Ramón, ed. *Cantar de mio Cid: texto, gramática y vocabulario.* 3 vols. Madrid: Espasa-Calpe, 1977.

————. *Orígenes del español: estado lingüístico de la península ibérica hasta el siglo XI.* 4th ed. Madrid: Espasa-Calpe, 1956.

Mérida, Rafael M. " 'D'ome atal coita nunca viu cristão': amores nefandos en los trovadores gallego-portugueses." *O cantar dos trobadores* 433–37.

Mettman, Walter. "Zu Text und Inhalt der altportugiesischen *Cantigas d'escarnho e de mal dizer.*" *Zeitschrift für Romanische Philologie* 82 (1966): 308–19.

Meyerson, Mark D. "Prostitution of Muslim Women in the Kingdom of Valencia: Religious and Sexual Discrimination in a Medieval Plural Society." *The Medieval Mediterranean: Cross-Cultural Contacts.* Medieval Studies at Minnesota 3. St. Cloud: North Star, 1988. 87–95.

Michaëlis de Vasconcellos, Carolina. "Mestre Giraldo e os seus tratados de Alveitaria e Cetraria." *Revista Lusitana* 13 (1910): 149–432.

Monroe, James T. *Hispano-Arabic Poetry: A Student Anthology.* Berkeley: U of California P, 1974.

Nirenberg, David. *Communities of Violence: Persecution of Minorities in the Middle Ages.* Princeton: Princeton UP, 1996.

Nodar Manso, Francisco. "La parodia de la literatura heroica y hagiográfica en las cantigas de escarnio y mal decir." *Dicenda: Cuadernos de filología hispánica* 9 (1990): 151–61.

O'Callaghan, Joseph F. "Image and Reality: The King Creates His Kingdom." Burns, *Emperor* 14–32, 216–20.

Patrologia latina. Ed. J.-P. Migne. 221 vols. Paris, 1844–64.

Paz, Octavio. "Los hijos de la Malinche." *El laberinto de la soledad.* Mexico: Fondo de Cultura Económica, 1993. 72–97.

Rabelais, François. *Le Quart livre.* Ed. Jean Plattard. Paris: F. Roches, 1929.

Ratcliffe, Marjorie. "Judíos y musulmanes en las *Siete Partidas* de Alfonso X." *Alfonso X el Sabio: vida, obra, y época. Actas del Congreso Internacional.* Ed. Juan Carlos de Miguel Rodríguez, Angela Muñoz Fernández, and Cristina Segura Graíño. Vol. 1. Madrid: Sociedad Española de Estudios Medievales, 1989. 237–49.

Richlin, Amy. "Invective against Women in Roman Satire." *Arethusa* 17 (1984): 67–80.

Rodríguez, José Luís. "La cantiga de escarnio y su estructura histórico-literaria: el equívoco como recurso estilístico nuclear en la cantiga d'escarnho de los cancioneros." *Santiago de Compostela: la ciudad, las instituciones, el hombre.* Estudios Compostelanos. 4. Santiago de Compostela: Colegio Franciscano, 1976. 33–46.

Roncaglia, Aurelio. "Glanures de la critique textuelle dans le domaine de l'ancienne lyrique galego-portugaise: le *pardon* de la Balteira et le *casamento* de la 'tendeira.' " *Critique textuelle portugaise: Actes du Colloque, Paris, 20–24 octobre 1981.* Paris: Calouste Gulbenkian, 1986. 19–27.

Ruiz, Juan. *Libro de buen amor.* Ed. Joan Corominas. Madrid: Gredos, 1973.

Sage, Carleton M. *Paul Albar of Cordoba: Studies on His Life and Writings.* Catholic U of America Studies in Medieval History n.s. 5. Washington: Catholic U of America P, 1943.

Scholberg, Kenneth R. *Sátira e invectiva en la España medieval.* Madrid: Gredos, 1971.

Scott, Samuel Parsons. See *Siete partidas.*

Shakespeare, William. *Othello. The Riverside Shakespeare.* Boston: Houghton Mifflin, 1974.

Shorter Encyclopedia of Islam. Ed. H. A. R. Gibb and J. H. Kramers. Leiden: Brill, 1991.

Las siete partidas del rey don Alfonso el Sabio. 3 vols. Madrid: Real Academia de la Historia, 1807. [English trans.: *Las Siete Partidas.* Trans. Samuel Parsons Scott. Chicago: Commerce Clearing House, 1931.] [Concordance: The Text and Concordance of *Las siete partidas de Alfonso X.* Based on the edition of the Real Academia de la Historia, 1807. Prepared by Jerry R. Craddock, John J. Nitti, and Juan C. Temprano. Spanish ser. 60. Madison: Hispanic Seminary of Medieval Studies, 1990. (microfiche ed.)]

Spina, Segismundo, ed. *As cantigas de Pero Mafaldo.* Rio de Janeiro: Tempo Brasileiro, 1983.

Spitzer, Leo. "Enaziado, anaciado." *Revista de filología hispánica* 7 (1945): 160–62.

Tavani, Giuseppe. *A poesía lírica galego-portuguesa.* Trans. Rosario Álvarez Blanco and Henrique Monteagudo. 3rd ed. Vigo: Galaxia, 1991.

Todorov, Tzvetan. "El cruzamiento entre culturas." *Cruce de culturas y mestizaje cultural.* Ed. Tzvetan Todorov. Trans. Antonio Desmonts. Madrid: Júcar, 1988. 9–31.

Valdés, Juan de. *Diálogo de la lengua.* Ed. José F. Montesinos. Madrid: Espasa-Calpe, 1976.

Wright, W. *A Grammar of the Arabic Language.* 3rd ed. 2 vols. Cambridge: Cambridge UP, 1951.

Catherine Brown

Queer Representation in the

Arçipreste de Talavera, or The *Maldeẓir*

de mugeres Is a Drag

E en tanto e a tanto decaimiento es ya el mundo venido quel moço sin hedat e el viejo fuera de hedat ya aman las mugeres locamente. . . . Oy éstos y éstas entienden en amor, e, lo peor, que lo ponen por obra. . . . Mas agora non es para se deẓir lo que ombre vee, que sería vergonçoso de contar; por ende bien pareçe que la fin del mundo ya se demuestra ser breve.

[The world has fallen into such a state of decay that nowadays the beardless youth and the old man full of years alike love women madly. . . . Everyone knows about love these days and, worse, they practice it . . . what one sees today is too shameful to relate. And so, as I have said, it seems to me that the end of the world is at hand.]

　　　　—*Alfonso Martíneẓ,* Arçipreste de Talavera

The world, it seems, was about to end in 1438, when Alfonso Martínez, Archpriest of Talavera, took up his pen and looked around him. And what did he see? His homeland, Castile, had consolidated its Iberian hegemony, but, to believe contemporary moralists, was otherwise in a sorry state. Some twenty years earlier the fire-breathing Valencian preacher Vicent Ferrer had made a sermon tour through the country, passing through Martínez's hometown of Toledo, preaching conversion to Jews and repentance to Christians, apparently to little lasting effect, at least among the latter audience.[1] Castile was ruled by a king who, to believe a late-fifteenth-century chronicler, took orders from his right-hand man on when to sleep with the queen and who cared more for music, poetry, and hunting than for governance.[2] What our Archpriest saw, he says, was love out of order: the too-old and the too-young talking carnalities and, what is worse, putting them into practice.[3] "E por ende, veyendo tanto mal e daño, propuse de algund tanto desta materia escrevir e fablar," the Archpriest says [and so, seeing so much evil and harm, I have set myself to write and speak a little of this matter]; he writes, he continues, to bring things back to order, in order to teach that "amar sólo Dios es amor verdadero, e lo ál amar todo es burla e viento e escarnio" (64) [only the love of God is true love and the love of all else is vanity, wind, and a mockery (14)].[4] Martínez aims to unteach what he calls "amor desordenado" [disorderly love] by holding up a mirror to it, "poniendo algunas cosas en práticas que oy se usan e pratican" (64) [putting certain things in practice that today are in common use].

In the introduction to the text, the author states that he put down his pen on 15 March 1438, naming his book after himself: "[S]in bautismo sea por nombre llamado *Arçipreste de Talavera* donde quier que fuere llevado" (61) [(W)ithout benefit of baptism let it be called, whithersoever it may be borne, the *Archpriest of Talavera* (9)].[5] The *Arçipreste de Talavera* has been taken many places since Martínez sent it traveling under his own name. A vivid, often vitriolic, screed against the world, the flesh and (mostly) women, it apparently enjoyed wide readership. Many of those readers' responses were angry and censorious, for the *Arçipreste de Talavera*'s enthusiastic misogyny won it enemies right away in the courtly, literary circles of fifteenth-century Spain, as Martínez apparently expected it would.[6]

The *Arçipreste de Talavera* is, then, perhaps the most (in)famous argument for sexual order in the Castilian literary canon. However, it was not inducted into the canon so much for its content, as for its earthy and colloquial style. "Very likely the noisiest book ever written" (Martínez, *Little Sermons* 1), the *Arçipreste de Talavera* carries on in the voices of *marginados* speaking out of order—gossips, viragoes, effeminates, sodomites, heretics, and hypocrites—voices ventriloquized in preacherly drag by a narrator who surrenders to the pleasures of vituperation with a singularly anxious delight. In what follows, I will take the Archpriest's conflicted delight in his often scabrous material and in "the sound of his own voice" (Martínez, *Little Sermons* 1) as an occasion to examine the construction of representability around sexual and gender disorder in mid-fifteenth-century Castile. We will see that the *Arçipreste de Talavera* reveals more about the discursive acts of constructing and representing than it does about the constructed or the represented. It may not be surprising, then, to find that representation, as the Archpriest understands and represents it, is far from neutral or transparent; it is, as we shall see, implicated in gender heterodoxy and disorder in the queerest of ways.[7]

Describing Gender

This concern with discursive representation is evident from the very beginning of the *Arçipreste de Talavera*—in its statement of purpose and organization. Since, as we shall see, the *Arçipreste de Talavera* is a text that insistently foregrounds hybrid discursive structures, it is important to distinguish carefully between the narrator and the writer; I shall refer to the former as "the Archpriest" and the latter as "Martínez." The narrator will be talking about gender here, he says; he will also be talking about talking and writing.

> En la primera [parte] *fablaré* de reprobación de loco amor. En la segunda *diré* de las condiçiones algund tanto de las viçiosas mugeres. E en la tercera proseguiré las complisiones de los ombres (quáles son o qué virtud tienen para amar o ser amados). En la quarta concluiré reprobando la *común manera de fablar* de los fados, venturas, fortunas, signos e planetas. (62; emphasis added)

> [In the first (part) *I shall talk* about the reprobation of mad love. In the second *I shall say* a little about the ways of wicked women. In the third I shall do the same for the various complexions of men: what they are and what virtues men have for loving or being loved. In the fourth I shall conclude by condemning the *common way of talking* about fate, luck, fortune, signs, and planets.]

Though the reason for the argumentative bundling of the last with the first three sections is not immediately apparent, all is orderly here, in good scholastic form. This neat separation of discourse-about-men from discourse-about-women rests upon firm theoretical grounds, as we learn when the Archpriest talks about how to talk about gender. "E por quanto comúnmente los ombres non son comprehendidos como las mugeres so reglas generales—esto por el seso mayor e más juyzio que alcançan—conviene, pues, particularmente fablar de cada uno según su qualidad" (204) [since, because of their greater sense and judgment, men are not usually subsumed, as women are, under general rules, it is appropriate to speak of each one according to his quality]. In this gendered version of the wheel of Virgil, ontological differences between "men" and "women" have epistemological consequences, and the rhetoric of gender is characterized by propriety and fit of discourse to its object. Thus constructed, "men" and "women" are stable categories, bound properly to distinct and particular expository ways of talking (*maneras de fablar*). We shall see that Martínez's own practice makes this descriptive rhetoric of gender seem more than a little like wishful thinking;[8] for the moment, though, I would like to listen to these *maneras de fablar* for what they tell us about representation.

Theoretically, since men are stable in their possession of sense and judgment, they can be known and described (presumably by other men) in their particularity, to which is matched the particularizing discourse of the complexions and humors. To women corresponds the discourse of the general rule, endlessly qualified, endlessly repeated: "La muger ser murmurante e detractadora, regla general es dello" (154); "La muger ser de dos fazes e cuchillo de dos tajos non ay dubda en ello" (171); "La muger ser mucho parlera, regla general es dello" (194) [that woman is a gossip and a backbiter may be taken as a general rule (109); it is not to be doubted that woman has two faces, or is a double-edged knife (128); it is a general rule that all women are chatterboxes (153)]. Were we in a taxonomizing and categorizing mood, we might call this discourse of the general rule "misogyny."[9] Fifteenth-century Castilian names it, perhaps more accurately, the *maldezir de mugeres,* the speaking-ill-of-women. I say more accurately, because in the *Arçipreste de Talavera* — as in the genre as a whole — there is at least as much emphasis on the verb ("speaking") and its subject as upon its object ("women"). The representational activity of the genre has less to do with description of a "reality" than with performance; its most urgent questions bear not on the gender(ing) of the *objects* of the verb as on the gendering of its performing subject. For, in the *maldezir de mugeres,* to describe gender is to perform it, a performance that assumes in the *Arçipreste de Talavera* particularly spectacular forms.[10]

Doing Gender

When I tell Hispanists that I work on the *Arçipreste de Talavera,* their reaction is usually one of sympathetic commiseration. Nasty piece of work,
isn't it? they offer; my students agree. There seems to be nothing at all that
we can say about the *maldezir de mugeres,* beyond describing it or performing it by throwing the scholarly equivalent of a hissy fit.[11] If instead we focus
in good medieval fashion upon our terms, we can in fact start to speak.
The first thing we can say is the name: the *maldezir de mugeres* is a speech
act, a performance, and what is so very valuable and remarkable about
the *Arçipreste de Talavera* is that it teaches us to read the *maldezir* as such.
Martínez plays upon the *maldezir de mugeres* as speech act, at once revealing and reveling in its prepositional ambiguity: he speaks ill *about* women
by representing the ill speech *of* women. He is speaking of speech, about
vices of speech; he is speaking an unspeakable, yet endlessly renewed and
inexhaustible discourse, imitated from other texts, of course, but also, he
insists, taken directly from the truth of the world and experiential evidence.

E por ende, veyendo tanto mal e daño, propuse de algund tanto desta materia escrevir e fablar, poniendo algunas cosas en práticas que oy se usan e
pratican, segund oirés, tomando, como dixe, algunos dichos de aquel dotor
de París . . . esto es, de las malas mugeres, sus menguas, viçios e tachas, qué
son, en algund tanto quáles son, e en parte quántas son. Aquí cesa el auctor,
pues non han número nin cuento, nin escrevir se podrían, como de cada día
el que con las mugeres platicare, verá cosas en ellas incogitadas, nuevas e
nunca escriptas, vistas, nin sabidas. (64)

[And so, seeing so much evil and harm, I have set myself to write and speak
a little of this matter, putting certain things in practice that today are in common use, as you will hear, repeating, as I said, some sayings of that Doctor
of Paris . . . that is, about wicked women, their faults, vices, and blemishes,
what they are and, in some degree, how many they are. At this point the
author ceases, for they are numberless and cannot be described, because he
who deals with wicked women will see in them things undreamed of, never
written, seen, or known. (14; modified)]

"¿Quién te mostró esto?" [Who taught you this?], asks a curious student
of misogyny in *Celestina,* the last great work to deploy the *maldezir de*

mugeres in its medieval form. "¿Quién?," replies the teacher, "Ellas. Que desque se descubren, ansí pierden la vergüença, que todo esto y aún más a los hombres manifiestan" (Rojas 99) [Who? Women themselves. As soon as they uncover themselves, they lose their shame: all this and more they reveal to men]. This is precisely the strategy our good Archpriest adopts: to demonstrate women's vicious talkativeness, he shows us how they talk, in imagined harangues that run for pages. He does not merely describe; he *does*. To paraphrase the terminology of twelfth-century pedagogues, the Archpriest does not teach simply *de genere*, about gender; he teaches *per genus*, through gender.[12]

The Archpriest's women are not just the objects of discourse; they are, explosively, the subjects of it. Their discourse sounds at once so thoroughly their own and so uncannily "real" that it is easy to forget that representation here is something more complicated, and more mediated, than simple transcription of "reality." The most celebrated colloquial explosion in the book is, in fact, a representation of a single dry sentence from the treatise *De amore* [On Love] of Andreas Capellanus (most likely the "doctor of Paris" cited above):

> Est et omnis femina virlingosa, quia nulla est quae suam noverit a maledictis compescere linguam, et quae pro unius ovi amissione die tota velut canis latrando non clamaret et totam pro re modica viciniam non turbaret. (Andreas 316)

> [All women are also free with their tongues, for not one of them can restrain her tongue from reviling people, or from crying out all day like a barking dog over the loss of a single egg, disturbing the whole neighborhood for a trifle. (Andreas 317)].

Martínez expands Andreas's descriptive sentence into an astonishing three-page tirade that is simultaneously a scholarly quotation of an Authority, a howling, thumping, plate-throwing quotation of an imaginary housewife, and a literary performance by a writer with an ear of gold.

> Item, por un huevo dará bozes como loca e fenchirá a todos los de su casa de ponçoña: "¿qué se fizo este huevo? ¿quién lo tomó? ¿quién lo levó? ¿A do le este huevo? Aunque vedes que es blanco, quiçá negro será oy este huevo. Puta, fija de puta, dime: ¿quién tomó este huevo? ¡Quién comió este huevo

comida sea de mala ravia: cámaras de sangre, correncia mala le venga, amén! ¡Ay huevo mío de dos yemas, que para echar vos guardava yo! ¡Que de uno o de dos haría yo una tortilla tan dorada que complía mis verguenzas. E no vos endurava yo comer, e comióvos agora el diablo. . . . ¡Ay huevo mío, de la meajuela redonda, de la cáscara tan gruesa! ¿Quién me vos comió? ¡Ay, puta Marica, rostros de golosa, que tú me has lançado por puertas! Yo te juro que los rostros te queme, doña vil, suzia, golosa! ¡Ay huevo mío! Y ¿qué será de mi? ¡Ay, triste, desconsolada! ¡Ihus, amiga! y ¿cómo non me fino agora? ¡Ay, Virgen María! ¿cómo non rebienta quien vee tal sobrevienta? ¡Non ser en mi casa mesquina señora de un huevo! . . ." Y en esta manera dan bozes e gritos por una nada. (149–50)

[Item: she will scream like mad and poison the ears of her household over the loss of an egg. "What happened to that egg? Who took it? Who stole it? Where is my egg? . . . Whore! Daughter of a whore! Tell me, who took my egg? May whoever ate it be eaten by rabies! Ay! my double-yolked egg, I was saving you for hatching! From one or two of you I would have made such a golden omelet! But I didn't get a chance, and now the devil's eaten you. . . . Ay! my egg of the round tread and shell so thick! Who went and ate you? Marica, you whore, you glutton, you've thrown me out of my own house! I swear I'll blister your cheeks for you, you low, filthy pig! Ay! my egg! What will become of me now, poor forlorn wretch that I am? Jesus! Why don't I just die and get it over with? Ay, Virgin Mary! How can one see such a thing and not explode? Not to be even mistress of a single egg in my own house, poor fool!" . . . And in this way they scream and holler over nothing. (103–04; modified)]

Citing Andreas, the Archpriest pretends to cite a woman's speech; he feminizes his voice in order to supply an irrefutable example of woman's wild volubility. In the resulting hybrid construction, words do not describe a "reality" so much as offer themselves as an exemplary performance of a particular way of talking. As the shrew's voice bursts from the text, treatise becomes harangue, and the borders between discourses — masculine and feminine, order and disorder, truth and gossip — begin to blur.

Indeed, it is hard for the Archpriest to maintain the authoritative voice (the preacher's), or even the authoritative gender (the masculine) for more than a few pages at a time. This slippage is especially apparent when the

Archpriest imitates that part of "femininity" most perversely kin to his own brightly colored text: the flowers of feminine rhetoric—that is, cosmetics. Snipes the Jealous Woman:

> "¡Yuy, yuy, pues yuy, vistes y qué vistes, e si lo vistes, pues avrés que contar! Fízonos Dios; maravillámonos nos. . . . ¡Paresçe un eclipsi; reluze como mi ventura qual el día que yo nasçi! Pues ¿si lieva blanquete? ¡A la fe fasta el ojo! Pues ¿arrebol? ¡Fartura! Las çejas bien peladas, altas, puestas en arco, los ojos alcoholados; la frente toda pelada y aun toda la cara." (161)

> ["Pfui and double pfui! Well, now you've seen her and have got something to talk about. God made us all, I suppose, but one wonders. She's as black as an eclipse! She's as white as my luck was the day I was born! Upon my word, she smears whiting up to her very eyes, and paint, no end! Her eyebrows well plucked, high and arched, her eyes darkened with kohl, her face peeled of hairs long and short." (118; modified)]

With the move from exclamation to description, the text enters the literary territory of the *blason,* and begins to partake as much of the rhetorical *artes poetriae* as of catty gossip. As this happens, it becomes hard to identify the subject of discourse, hard to tell the difference between a "man" talking *about* "women," a "man" talking *like* "women," and a "woman" talking like a "woman" about other "women." Such difficulty becomes especially pronounced when the speaker cross-references a previous point in the tirade with the very textual "como de suso dixe" (162) [as I said above]. The shift from a "speaking" and "female" subject to a "writing" and "male" one is complete when a long description of a particular woman's multiple daily makeovers lapses into a generalization of what all women do, cast not in the first, but in the third person plural. *Così,* our narrator tells us, *fan tutte.* "Estas e otras mill mudas fazen; por nueve días fieden como los diablos con las cosas que ponen" (162) [These and a thousand other kinds of packs women wear for nine days on end, and they stink like the devil with the things they smear on their faces (118)].[13]

One might expect that, when the Archpriest turns his attention away from the *maldezir de mugeres,* and toward a discussion of the conditions and complexions of men, the unstable rhetoric of gender characteristic of his version of the *maldezir de mugeres* might no longer operate; men and women, he has told us, are to be talked about in different ways. Such, however, is not the case. Although he now maintains that he intends to speak only of men, the textual practice of the third part of the book belies him.

The Archpriest certainly does not hesitate to criticize men. However, it is difficult for him to talk about men and their humors without talking about women and their wiles; it is equally difficult for him to speak in the man's voice without slipping into the woman's. Take, for example, his discussion of choleric men. The Archpriest begins the scene in the preacher's voice; he introduces a story, then assumes the voices of his characters, both male and female. Things immediately begin to slip: the story, designed to demonstrate the qualities of the man, becomes instead a demonstration of the woman's cunning. After she has provoked her choleric lover to dash outside and avenge some petty offense to her honor, the woman waits for his return and puts on a show for him when he staggers in.

> E quando entra ferido por casa o ha ferido, ráscase la bendita de la promovedora dello las nalgas—con reverençia fablando—diziendo: "¡Cuitada, mezquina, turbada, corrida! ¡Yuy, y que será de mí! Señor, ¿quién vos firió por la cara?" o "¿Quién me vos mató?" o "¿Quién vos dio tal golpe? ¡Virgen María! ¡A tí lo acomiendo, Ihus mío! ¡Bueno, y non me lastimes! ¡Ay, triste de mí! ¡Daca huevos, daca estopa; daca vino para estopadas! Juanilla, ve al çurujano, dile que venga. ¡Corre aína, puta, fija de puta!" (219)

> [And when he is brought back to her house wounded or having wounded, the blessed promotor of it all scratches her arse (speaking with due reverence) and says: "Unhappy creature that I am, shamed and undone! Yuy, what will become of me now? Who cut your face? Who killed you? Who struck you such a blow? Holy Virgin! Dear Jesus, to Thee I commend him! Don't break my heart! Woe is me! Bring me eggs! Bring me lint! Bring me wine to make a compress! Juanilla, run and get the barber! Run, you whore and daughter of a whore!" (183–84; modified)]

The slippage is nearly complete when the woman's voice, drawn into the text as if by a discursive magnet, completely takes over the tale. The moralist's voice slips into the harridan's; description of "man" becomes performance of "woman."

Another kind of discursive slippage appears in the Archpriest's treatment of a different sort of men, the phlegmatics. After a quick description of them, the Archpriest acts out: it is a cold night; the phlegmatic has an appointment to keep with his lover, but hesitates before he leaves. He pokes his head out the door to test the weather and says:

"Iré; non iré; sí iré. Si vo, verme han, mojarme he, me encontraré con la justicia e tomarme ha la espada; correrme ha por las calles la ronda si me encuentra; e si estropieço por ventura, caeré; ensuziarme he de lodo los çapatos de alta grasa. Non iría sin galochas fuera de casa. ¡Guay, si me muerde algund perro en la pierna, o si me dan por ventura alguna cuchillada, o si me dan en la cabeça alguna pedrada, o si me toman en casa, cortarme han lo mío y lo mejor que hé! ¿E si me toman entre puertas o si me cargan de palos? No sé, pues, si me vaya." (222)

["Shall I go? Shall I stay? Yes, I'll go. But then if I do, I may be seen; I may get wet; I may get muddy; I may meet the watch and he will take away my sword, or he may chase me through the streets. And if I stumble I may fall down and muddy my shiny boots. I won't stir out of the house without my galoshes! And, oh, my goodness, suppose some dog bites me on the leg! Or suppose somebody stabs me! Or hits me on the head with a rock! Or, if they catch me in her house, suppose they cut off that which I hold most precious! Or suppose they catch me on the way and give me a beating! I don't know if I'll go." (188; modified)]

The Archpriest, we might say, talks like a phlegmatic here, but it is hard for an attentive reader of the text to perform these lines without hearing the voice of (a) "woman," for fickleness and indecisiveness are included in the Archpriest's general rule defining women (2.5). The Archpriest's performance of "masculine" speech has thus slipped into the feminine: his phlegmatic talks like a woman. Martínez himself calls our attention to this slippage by having the effeminate phlegmatic's lover herself comment on it:

Desque ella vee que está temblando como azogado e más muerto que bivo, e vee que aunque quedase, que non quedava con ella ombre sinón muger, dize ella: "Pues muger por muger, non he menester aquí otra muger." (224)

[So when she sees that he is trembling as if with the ague and is more dead than alive, and when she sees that even if he did stay she would have no man with her, but a woman, she says: "Well, woman for woman, I don't need any more women around here!" (189; modified)]

The Archpriest cannot seem to keep his categories straight. Writing *de genere* (that is, describing gender) is more or less stable, but the narrator's enchantment with representation *per genus* (performing gender) puts his constructions — of his argument, of his characters, and ultimately of gender itself — on very slippery ground. Discourse about "man" (or represented as "masculine") is repeatedly contaminated by discourse about "woman" (or "in the feminine").[14] Speakers are gendered and regendered in mid-discourse, women are viragoes, and phlegmatic men effeminate; the sermon gives way to gossip, and the treatise to monologue, dialogue, and outright fiction making.

The surest sign of such generic instability is the fact that the narrator feels he must assure us that it's not the case.

> Non es esto corónica nin istoria de cavallería, en las cuales a las vezes ponen c por b; que esto que dicho he, sabe que es verdad. . . . E non pienses que el que lo escrivió te lo dize porque lo oyó solamente, salvo por que por prática dello mucho vido, estudió e leyó. . . . Mucha prática e experiençia de todo es maestra e enseñadora porque fable el que lo fabla sin miedo; que paresçe que lo vee cuando lo escrive. (142–43)

> [This is not a chronicle or romance of chivalry, in which at times they put *c* before *b*. Know that what I say here is the truth . . . and do not think that he who writes this speaks merely from hearsay, for he witnessed much of it, and studied and read about the rest. . . . Practice and experience have taught him who speaks to speak without fear, for he seems to see it all as he writes. (96; modified)]

The Archpriest anxiously says he speaks without fear because he writes, not fiction, but immediate and neutral truth, represented "from life." A poor excuse really, because in a world where "non es para se dezir lo que ombre vee, que sería vergonçoso de contar" (64) [what one sees today is too shameful to relate (14)] such life drawing puts the text in an impossible, or at least very uncomfortable position between two other mutually exclusive categories: the speakable and the unspeakable. In this text, the most unspeakable ways of speaking are in fact the most endlessly and pleasurably spoken: the Archpriest tells another story even when he says he won't, talks about women even when he's said they aren't his theme, tells us how unspeakable are sinners' crimes, then tells us all about them.

This aggressively normative text, then, spins out from a core of transgression: the *Arçipreste de Talavera* repeatedly speaks what it brands as unspeakable, represents what it says is unrepresentable, and speaks in the very gendered discourses that it aims to critique and reprove. This preacherly rhetorician's preferred trope is thus preterition, by which the speaker introduces evidence by pretending to suppress it; a venerable move certainly, but one not untainted by dissimulation.[15] It would seem that the Archpriest's protestations of disgust at his material are at the very least disingenuous; one might wonder what this narrator has to cover up.

Queer Representation

Let us now come to ill tongued Hypocrites, who under the colour of griefe and compassion, to bee the better beleeved, lamentably rehearse the ill haps of other; which vice, though it bee common to manie, yet it is most familiar with certaine women, who meeting with other of their Gossips, after the first greetinges, they foorthwith break into these speeches. Have you not heard the hard hap of my unfortunate neighbour[?]
   —The Civille Conversation of M. Steeven Guazzo *(1581)*

Warning of the wiles of women, the Archpriest reminds us of how hard it is to see through their lies and dissimulations (2.6, 2.10). In book 4, he returns to the subject of deceit and seduction in another register. To show how hard it is to find the interior truth of a human soul beneath all the deceptive outer signs of appearance, gesture, and speech, the Archpriest starts to describe a kind of person. He means to tell us about the Beghards (*begardos*), a religious sect related to the Spiritual Franciscans and to those later known as the *alumbrados* or Illuminati.[16] The Archpriest offers the *begardos* as the very image of human artifice and (dis)simulation. He presents them, that is to say, as figures of the Hypocrite, whom Gregory the Great defined thus: "Hypocrita, qui latina lingua dicitur simulator, iustus esse non appetit, sed uideri" (*Moralia in Iob* 18.7) [The hypocrite, who in Latin is called a *simulator*, does not want to be just, but rather to appear so].[17] We have read enough of the *Arçipreste de Talavera* by now to expect that our narrator will not stop at descriptions. We begin this section, then, expecting a performance. We will not be disappointed.

What follows is one of the oddest passages of this very odd book, and one of the least studied (4.1).[18] In it, the Archpriest presents us with categories of male sinners, illustrating each with vivid images and stories. What is strange and wonderful about this section is that it bundles together a whole set of dangerous and unspeakable transgressors, slipping from category to category with no apparent awareness of the (con)fusion of terms. In the same textual bed with the hypocritical *begardos* are all sorts of agents of gender trouble: men who like women too much, men who hate women too much; men who will not hear talk of women, men who talk like women; men who fuck men like men, and men who like to be fucked as if they were women.[19] This eruption of taxonomies in a single jet of discourse calls to mind Vicent Ferrer's metaphor for preaching: it is like spinning, he said, where one thread is spun into another.[20] What, we might ask, is the principle of order here? What drives the spinning of this very queer thread?

The Archpriest begins by speaking of the Beghards in general, presenting them as something of an epistemological puzzle: "Que algunos ay como vigardos, malos de conoscer, por quanto son de muchas guisas e naturas e opiniones, segund sus flacos ingenios les procuran que se retraigan en aquella desimulada vida de bevir entre las gentes" (258) [There are some, like the Beghards, who are hard to know, for they are of many manners and natures and opinions, as their weak wits inspire them to be in that dissimulated life among the people]. The *begardos* make themselves over again and again in a life of endless, and endlessly deceptive, (mis)representation: "[D]isimulan el mal e infingen el bien con disimulados ábitos e condiçiones" (259) [They dissimulate evil and simulate good with dissimulated clothing and conditions].[21] Products not so much of nature as of human ingenuity and artifice, they are brothers in dissimulation to the signifying monkey of African American folklore (Gates). For if human behaviors are signs, then hypocrisy is the very model of perverse signification, as Aquinas suggested:

> Dicendum quod in simulatione sicut in mendacio duo sunt unum quidem sicut signum et aliud sicut signatum. Mala ergo intentio in hypocrisi consideratur sicut signatum quod non respondet signo; exteriora autem vel verba vel opera vel quaecumque sensibilia considerantur in omni simulatione et mendacio sicut signa. (2A, 2AE.III.3; Blackfriars ed. 41.174–75)

> [In deception as in lying there are two elements: one, the sign; the other, the thing signified. In hypocrisy the bad intention stands as the thing signi-

fied that does not match the sign; in all deception and lying words, deeds or whatever appears outwardly are regarded as signs.]

Martínez represents the hypocrite's signifying for us with a vivid picture of Beghard body talk: eyes on the ground, knees bent, they beat their breasts and weep; they sigh and look around them, they raise their hands to heaven (259).

Another way of representing misrepresentation follows, under the guise of more categories of *begardos:*

> E destos bigardos algunos dellos son en dos maneras: ay unos que se dan al acto varonil, desean compaña de omes por su vil acto, como ombres, con los tales cometer. Ay otros destos que son como mugeres en sus fechos e como fembrezillas en sus desordenados apetitos, e desean a los omes con mayor ardor que las mugeres desean a los ombres. (259)

> [Some of these Beghards are of two types: there are some who are inclined to the virile act and desire the company of men with whom, as men, to commit their vile acts. There are others of these who are like women in their deeds and like little sluts in their disordered appetites, and they desire men with greater ardor than women do.]

The Archpriest was talking about religious hypocrites; now, suddenly, he's talking about two kinds of sodomites as if they were subcategories of Beghard. Here we recognize the commonplace bundling of religious with sexual and gender heterodoxy; to say "heresy" in the Middle Ages is often, of course, to say "sodomy," and there is ample evidence of this very slippage in Iberian texts.[22] One could say simply: the Archpriest has heretofore praised proper, orderly behavior by condemning Woman, agent of impropriety and disorder; he has here simply found another set of others through which to construct a religiously and sexually orthodox Castilian subject.[23] This is at least partly true, but to stop here would be to content oneself with righteous critique of an ecclesiastical discourse constructed as hegemonic and internally consistent, a move which, it seems to me, serves more the needs of the critic to "other" the ecclesiastical than it serves the complexities of premodern discursivity. It would also be to ignore the specificity of the *Arçipreste de Talavera* as a *text,* for the *Arçipreste de Talavera*'s deployment of its others is driven by complex and internally contradictory desires. We need to go further, and to ask: what leads this particular text to construct these particular subjects in this particular way?

The Archpriest is most heated in his anger about the second ("effeminate") subgroup of sodomites, about whom, in spite of his emphatic declarations that their behavior is unspeakable, and his repeated promises not to say anything about it, he has quite a lot to tell us. He charges them with being "de naturaleza falleçientes e contra natura usantes contra natural apetito" (259) [deficient by nature, and practicing against nature against natural appetite], but their antinatural behavior, in the Archpriest's imagination, is cast in terms not so much of sexual as of *semiotic* activity. "They are like women in their deeds and like little sluts in their disordered appetites, and they desire men with greater ardor than women do." They are imitation women who are better women than women; simulated "women," then, who disturb the proper (read "natural") relation between the signs of gender and the signified of sex. As the *Arçipreste de Talavera* attempts to represent (and curtail) that disturbance, trouble breaks out on its own textual surface.

> Los más dellos aborreçen las mugeres y escupen dellas, e algunos non comen cosa alguna que ellas aparejasen, nin vestirían ropa blanca que ellas xabonasen, nin dormirían en cama que ellas fiziesen: si les fablan de mugeres, ¡alça Dios tu ira! ¿Qué se dexan dezir e fazer de ficta onestad? E después andan tras los moçuelos besándolos, falagándolos, dándoles joyuelas, dineros e cosillas que a su hedad convienen. Así se les ríe el ojo mirándolos como si fuesen fembras, e non digo más desta corrupta materia e abominable pecado. (260)

> [Most of them despise women and spit on them, and some will not eat anything that women have prepared, nor wear white clothes that women have washed, nor sleep in a bed that women have made: if anyone should speak to them of women, God forbid! What will they let themselves say in their feigning virtue? And afterward, they run after boys, kissing them, praising them, giving them trinkets, or coins or other things fitting for their age. With laughing eyes they look at the boys as if they were women, and I'll say nothing more about this corrupt material and abominable sin.]

These are imitation women who, *like the Archpriest,* imitate, outdo, then deny their models; their femininity is strictly metaphorical, shunning all metonymic contact with their "originals." The extraordinary vividness of the word-painting here makes it easy to miss the underlying incoherence: these woman-hating men, whose desires for other men are more "feminine" than women's are, chase after boys as if the boys were . . . women . . . and they, in a heteronormative (read "natural") model, were men.[24] The "passive" sodomite pursues his desire in an "active" manner; though characterized as "effeminate," he acts like a man, and feminizes his partner; a woman-hater, he seduces a metaphorical woman. The simulations and simulacra are dizzying; the "original" has been expelled, and we have instead a vertiginous pursuit of representations by representations.

No less problematic is the Archpriest's discussion of the first group of ("masculine") sodomites. Though they are initially characterized in terms of sexual acts ("there are some who are inclined to the virile act and desire the company of men with whom, as men, to commit their vile acts"), the sexual is quickly effaced, then troped into other issues: "[N]on se entremeten en la suziedad deste pecado, *sinón en ficta iproquesía*" (260; emphasis added) [They do not get involved with the filth of this sin (i.e., that of the "effeminate" sodomites), *but rather in feigning hypocrisy*]. Again, incoherence at the articulation point of sexual performance and the performance of gender: after sexualizing these men quite explicitly in terms of their acts, he desexualizes them into figures of *ficta iproquesía* in general. He then refigures their hypocrisy as another, and very particular disordering of gender and of sexuality.[25]

> Fázense simplezillos como mugeres . . . aprenden de broslar e fazer bolsillas, caperuças de aguja, coser e tajar e aderesçar altares . . . todas las cosas infingen de fazer como muger, dexando su usar varonil. Infingen delicados, temorosos e espantadisos, e juradores como mugeres . . . quéxanse como mugeres, amortéçense como fenbras. (262–63)

> [They make themselves out to be airheads like women . . . they learn to embroider, do needlepoint, sew, and decorate altars . . . setting aside their virile habits, they try to do everything like women. They make themselves out to be delicate, skittish, and full of oaths like women, . . . they kvetch like women, they faint like women.]

These men make themselves over "feminine," and in spectacular fashion, but they do so in order better to seduce their models under cover of a very gendered continence.

Dan a entender que son vírgenes e que nunca muger conosçieron nin las querrían ver, salvo para las confesar . . . esto porque se fíen en ellos una vez, e porque puedan usar donde mugeres están con toda ficta onestidad. (262)

[They make people think that they are virgins and that they never knew a woman, nor even want to see one, except in confession; . . . this they do so that the women will trust them, and so that they can do their thing where women are with all feigned virtue.]

This group of Beghards, then, like the others, is a category incoherent on the textual surface: they are introduced as men who do the "virile act" with men like men; then they're made over into woman-imitating and woman-loving effeminates who leave aside "virile habits" in order better to seduce not men, but women. This is, in short, some of the queerest straight behavior that one is likely ever to see. "Donde mugeres fermosas ay, allí los ve buscar; bástase que siempre los verás, los falsos, solos entre mugeres: nunca de otro ome quieren compañía. ¡Dios sabe a osadas como las aman de coraçón a las mugeres!" (263) [Go look for them wherever beautiful women are; you'll see them, the false ones, alone among women; they never want the company of another man. God knows how very heartily they love women!]

   Genital sexuality of categories that we would now recognize plays little role in holding these categories of men together; in fact, if we look at it only in these terms, the text becomes chaotically incoherent. What holds these categories together, and holds them in the thread the Archpriest is here spinning, is their *ficta onestad,* the fictioned propriety of their significations. Whatever else they are, these are certainly queer representers, perverters of orthodox signification. These are, then, (dis)simulators, subjects who missignify, who abuse signs for their own pleasure. Their performances are quite literally made up, like the cosmetic asceticism of the first group of Beghards: "Safúmanse las caras con cominos róstigos e con pedra sufre, e con el baho de la yerva orthigosa cuando la cuezen en la olla, porque parescan amarillos e transidos de las abstinençias e ayunos" (262) [They color their faces with smoke from toasted cumin and sulfur, and with stewed nettle juice, so that they look sallow and faint from abstinence and fasting]. Thus the hypocrites and the perversely gendered are bound together by forces more dynamic than those of some monolithic "otherness." They live lives invented, driven by dissimulation.

Making up in the Mirror of Nature

Todas andan entre nos
con espejo para ver
la cara de Lucifer
y escondiendo la de Dios,
porqu'es su natural ser:
píntanse como retablo,
dóranse como oropel,
y el pintor, qu'es el diablo,
desque ha pintado el papel,
viendo a ellas, veis a él.
— *Gloss to Torellas's "Yerra con poco saber,"*
attributed to Juan de Tapia.

non tamen expositas mensa deprendat amator
pyxidas: ars faciem dissimulata iuuat.
— *Ovid*, Ars amatoria

It is no accident that hypocrisy is figured in the *Arçipreste de Talavera* as a sort of spectacular drag. Isidore of Seville, for example, found the very essence of the word *hypocrite* in gender-bending ancient theater:

> E el nombre de *ypocrita* fue sacado de la semejança de aquellos que andavan en los juegos . . . ca fazien de paño de lino engisado semejanças de caras de hombre e pintávanlas de muchas colores e teñiense las manos e los cuellos de tierra blanca . . . un ora en semejança de varón, otra en semejança de muger . . . e en otra manera por hedat, esto es, en semejança de mançebos o de viejos. La qual manera de argumento es trasmudada o trasladada de aquellos que andan con falsa cara e enfíngense ser aquello que non son. (*Etymologías* 10.119; Isidore 1.383)

> [The word "hypocrite" was coined in resemblance to those who acted in plays, . . . for they made from linen cloth images of human faces and painted them in many colors and dyed their hands and their necks with white earth . . . now in the image of a man, now in the image of a woman, . . . now in the image of youths, now of old men. This way of talking is transferred to those who go about with a false face and simulate being what they are not.]

Our many-voiced, many-faced Archpriest is not, of course, immune from accusations of hypocrisy himself, for he is actor as much as author, *histrio* as much as historian—a performer and a *ficto fablador* 'fictive speaker' (cf. the Beghards, Martínez, 261). In fact, he anticipates the charge and anxiously attempts to refute it: I am a sinner, he says, and I expect to be corrected if I misspeak (143; 202–04). And misspeaking is virtually certain, for discursive disorder is an essential characteristic of the Archpriest's wor(l)d. A man whose word matches his deed, the Archpriest says, is so rare as to be miraculous (203), "que el mundo es oy tan malo que *bien dezir es muerte, maldezir es gloria delectable*" (190; emphasis added) [for the world is so wicked today that *to speak good is death, and to speak ill is pure delight* (148)]. The Archpriest's own gloriously catty *maldezir,* then, is in one sense a luxurious surrender to the way of the world: when such pleasures attend it, how can one help but *do the maldezir?* The narrator tells us repeatedly that he is simply "putting certain things in practice that today are in common use," but the line between textual and worldly practice is exceedingly thin. If to show is also inevitably to do, what, exactly, is the Archpriest teaching us?

Predictably enough, the Archpriest himself draws our attention to the problem. "Seré de algunos reprehendido por non saber ellos mi entinçión—la qual solo Dios sabe en este paso non ser a mala parte—porque algunas cosas pongo en prática dirán que más es avisar en mal que corregir en bien" (190) [I shall be scolded by some for setting down these things, for they will say that I teach wickedness instead of correcting it; but they are ignorant of my purpose, which God knows is not evil in this matter (148)]. He does not expect us to imitate his text's imitations, but rather to be mortified at the verisimilitude of the text's imitations of us—at the knowledge that our secrets are known.

> Diga cada cual su voluntad, que yo non lo digo por que lo así fagan, mas porque *sepan* que por mucho que ellos nin ellas encobierto lo fagan e fazen, que *se sabe.* . . . E las que *saben* que ge lo entienden, que de algo dello se dexarán. . . . Esto sea quanto a mi escusaçión, por quanto *sé* bien que si dixe, de mí ha de ser dicho. (190; emphasis added)

> [Let them say what they please, for I do not talk about evil so that they will go out and do it, but to let men and women *know* that however secretly they do or may do evil, that it is *known.* . . . And those women who *know* that these

things are *known* may reduce their evil-doing to some degree. . . . Let this be my justification, for I know that as I have spoken, so I shall be spoken of.]

The question, then, is how much the *Arçipreste de Talavera* is not just the mirror, but also the very spit and image of its sinners. Like his women, the Archpriest is prolix, fond of the word and fond of its sound. "El callar le es muerte muy áspera" [To keep silent would be death itself], he says, speaking of Woman; "non podriá una sola hora estar que non profaçase de buenos e malos" (154) ["not for a single hour could she refrain from taking everyone to pieces, good and bad alike" (109)]. He chatters, he gossips, he backstabs, he tells secrets; he slips into the mode he characterizes (and rejects) as feminine, even as he describes it.

The narrator is aware of this slippage from discourse *de genere* to discourse *per genus*—from talking *about* to talking *like*—but the explanation he offers ultimately creates more problems than it solves. Since any attempt at translation of this difficult passage is necessarily an interpretation, I will begin with the Castilian original, cited in paleographic transcription from the manuscript.[26]

E po^r q<uan>to q<ual>- / quier sabio les manj[fie]sto poco mas / o menos la muger q<ue> es q<ui>e<n> es po^r / ellas e<n> el mu<n>do vjno destruyçio<n> / e oy dura no<n> es honesto dellas / mas fablar. no<n> diga<n> q<ue> no<n> fue / muge^r el que co<n>puso este co<n>pe<n>dio / sy no<n> çesara mal fablar por ho- / nestitat. pero los vjçiosos de / las criminasas bueno es rredar- / guy^r (f. 13v, lines 33–44; Martínez, *Text and Concordances* 32)[27]

Lesley Byrd Simpson renders it thus: "And now, since it is manifest to any wise man whatever what women are, more or less, and how it was through them that destruction came into the world and still endures, it is not fitting longer to speak of them. Let it not be said that he who composed this book was a woman, for if he had been, from honesty he would cease this evil speaking. But it is well to attack the vices of wicked women" (*Little Sermons* 47). Simpson's translation implies that feminine speech is governed by *hones(ti)dad* (honesty, virtue, propriety), something the Archpriest repeatedly declares to be false. It seems to me that the sense of the penultimate sentence is more something like this: "Because, for honesty's sake, the composer of this work might not have avoided speaking evil, let it not be said that he was behaving like a woman." Although the Archpriest says it is not honest to speak of Woman, he speaks of her in order to correct her. His *maldeʒir* thus justified by its honest intent the Archpriest is protected from accusations of backstabbing, cattiness, and femininity.

However, the force of the double negative — "*non* digan que *non* fue muger" [let it *not* be said that (the composer of this work) was *not* a woman] — for a moment creates the unspeakable illusion that the subject here is, in fact, female, or at least discursively feminine. If virtuous, "masculine" discourse cannot speak of dishonesty, cannot speak in detail about the vices, then to speak of Woman, even with the intention of speaking ill of her, is to speak like her. According to the Archpriest's logic, then, the *maldeʒir de mugeres* is a *feminine* and femininizing discourse.

His own text's *honestidad,* then, is as *ficta* as that of the queer dissimulators he so enthusiastically represents. Like them, his text mimes women spectacularly; outdoes women, in fact, in femininity (an honest woman myself, I have never heard a female as "feminine" as the Archpriest's), yet loathes and rejects them with a passion as highly interested as that of his second group of sodomites.[28]

We could say of the narrator what he says of women: "[S]u deseo . . . non es otro sinón secretos poder saber, descobrir e entender" (173) [What she desires . . . is nothing less than to know, discover, and understand secrets]. The Archpriest talks about people who have secrets and people who tell secrets; he talks about secrets in a textual world of the purest paranoia. "Pero esta es la verdad: la mejor e la más peor tanto pierde dándose al loco amor quel morir le será vida, *ora se sepa ora non se sepa. Sé* empero cierto, que de *non saberse* sería imposible" (70; emphasis added) [But this is the truth: the best woman and the worst, both, lose so much by surrendering to mad love that death would be life to her, *whether the affair be known, or whether it be unknown. I know* one thing for sure: it would be impossible for it *not to be known*]. He talks about secrets, and then simultaneously cloaks and reveals them with preterition, that most dissimulating and titillating of tropes: "Por ende," he concludes, "lo que contesçe desta materia escrevir non se podría" (70) [thus, what comes of this material cannot be be written].

The *Arçipreste de Talavera*, then, is a text with its own unwriteable secret. It is not a single, simple biographical secret of the *Weekly World News* variety ("ALFONSO MARTÍNEZ IMPRISONED FOR SODOMY!" "ARCHPRIEST'S LOVE NEST WITH HOUSEKEEPER!"). It is more complicated than that. The *Arçipreste de Talavera* is a text dedicated to saying what must be said, and which finds itself ever more tightly entangled in saying what cannot, even *must* not be said. Entangled, that is, in desire and (and desire for) representation.

We began this essay by imagining the view from Alfonso Martínez's window. What did he see when he looked around him? What the Archpriest sees he shows and tells us, in lively and vivid detail—unspeakable things, shameful to recount.

> Dentro en Tortosa yo vi fazer justiçia de una muger que consintió que su amigo matase a su fijo porque los non descubriese. Yo la vi quemar porque dixo el fijo: "Yo lo diré a mi padre, en buena fe, que dormistes con Irazón el pintor." (117)

> [In Tortosa I saw a woman executed who had got her lover to murder her son to prevent her exposure. I saw her burned with my own eyes! All this because her son had said to her: "I'm going to tell my father that you have slept with Irazón the painter." (68)]

What he sees in this story stands well for what he sees and shows us throughout his book: a multiply covered, multiply disclosed secret. A secret revealed to the adulteress's son, covered up by her murderous lover, revealed in court, and, finally, published by our good Archpriest. Martínez's story is driven by the forces of disorder: woman and desire, with some help from a painter—like the Archpriest himself, a representer of the visual world. "Destos enxiemplos mill millares se podrían escrevir," he says later, "pero de cada día contesçen tantas destas porfías, quel escrevir es por demás" (179) [Thousands on thousands of stories like these could be written, but so many things like this happen every day that to write about them would be gilding the lily]. Writing, that is, is superfluous, so vivid is the natural occurrence.

If the *Arçipreste de Talavera* has a secret, then—something unsayable that keeps begging to be said—it is the text's nature as second nature—as the touched-up image in the devil's mirror, the made-up painting, the simulacrum. As Quintilian, that most sober of rhetoricians, stoutly declares, style should be "natural and unaffected" (8.18), not calling attention to itself with "meretricious finery" (8.26) or "the effeminate use of depilatories and cosmetics" (8.20). Now, to many modern critics, the style of the

Arçipreste de Talavera has felt like the most natural thing in the world.[29] "In its good parts," says Menéndez y Pelayo, "there is no trace of literary imitation, but rather the direct impression of Castilian reality" (Menéndez y Pelayo, *Orígenes* 1: 181).

Martínez's words feel so "natural" that they make even readers as erudite as Menéndez y Pelayo forget their artifice, forget that they are dressed-up, made-up representations. In book 4, the Archpriest cautions his readers not to take representations at their word, nor ways of talking to the letter: "Así que non diga ninguno: 'Yo vi la muerte en figura de muger, en figura de cuerpo de ome, e que favlava con los reyes, etc., como pintada está en León', que aquello es *ficçión natural contra natura*" (271–72; emphasis added) [So let no one say: "I saw death in the figure of a woman, in the figure of the body of a man; it was talking with kings, etc., just as it is painted in León," *for that is a natural fiction against nature*]. The fictive representation produced in the fresco and in the text that represents it is profoundly paradoxical: simultaneously natural and unnatural, simulation and dissimulation at once, it sneakily leads us to mistake *signans* for *signatum* — to signify against nature. If the *Arçipreste de Talavera* itself has a secret, it is how much, under its narrator's preacherly discursive asceticism and Archpriestly continence, which he himself calls "capa para cobrir otros muchos pecados" (96) [a cloak to cover many sins (47)], the text in fact resembles its made-up hypocrites, effeminates, and women.

Notes

1. For more on Vicent Ferrer's Castilian sermon tour of 1411–12, which included Toledo, where Alfonso Martínez was born in 1398, see Cátedra.

2. I have in mind here the portrait of King Juan II (r. 1406–54) in Fernán Pérez de Guzmán's *Generaçiones y semblanças* (c. 1458). For more on Pérez de Guzmán's reading of Juan II, see Hutcheson's contribution to this collection; on the "gender trouble" that characterizes the discourses of aristocratic fifteenth-century Castile, see the essays by Brocato and Weissberger also in this volume.

3. For useful overviews of the courtly vogue and reactions to it in this period, see Gerli ("La 'religión de amor' "); Boase; Whitbourn.

4. The Spanish text is drawn from the edition of E. Michael Gerli, and the English translations of books 1–3 from the version by Lesley Byrd Simpson. Trans-

lations from book 4 are mine, as are all other uncredited translations. I will make more general references to the *Arçipreste de Talavera* by giving book and chapter number, separated by a period (e.g., "2.5" for "book 2, chapter 5").

5. The name of Martínez's book has proven ungainly; contemporary readers quickly renamed it *Corbacho,* a title in a sense illegitimate, since the *Arçipreste de Talavera* in fact draws little from Boccaccio's archmisogynist *Corbaccio.* The other title often given it, *Reprobación del amor mundano* [Reprobation of Mundane Love], is more germane, but, as we shall see, does not name the textual activity of the book in a really satisfactory manner. Its English translator responded to this nominational problem by inventing a name of his own: since "the original title has no meaning for the English reader" (Martínez, *Little Sermons* 7) he baptised it *Little Sermons on Sin.*

6. The *Arçipreste de Talavera* is preserved in one manuscript, Escorial h.III.10, copied in 1466; it formerly belonged to the library of Queen Isabel of Castile. Five printed editions survive from 1498 to 1547; the printed editions differ from the MS text in significant ways: starting with Seville 1498, for example, the book is rechristened *Corvacho* (in the explicit) and expanded with a savagely comic palinode.

7. A note on terminology: this essay will use the word "queer" with its contemporary political overtones intact, to indicate, not practicing "homosexuals" or "homosexual" practice, but subjects which evade, escape, or confuse (hetero)-normative codes of behavior, most often, but not always, gender binarism. Both the aesthetic and the semiotic fields of "representation" are active in my uses of the term.

8. In fact, this rhetorical separation of men and women is explicitly contradicted four pages later: "Lo que te digo en este caso en los ombres entiende de las mugeres: ombre sanguino, ombre colórico, ombre flemático, ombre malencónico" (209) [[W]hat I have told you about men applies equally to women: sanguine, choleric, phlegmatic, and melancholic (173; modified)]. To begin to make sense of this apparent contradiction in Martínez's scriptural practice, we might remember Bloch's observation that "the reduction of Woman to a category implies in our culture . . . an appropriation that is not present when identical genderizing statements are applied to man or men" (5). It would be fruitful to supplement Ciceri's study of the dialectic of generalization and particularization characteristic of Martínez's own style ("Gli *exempla*") from this gendered and gendering point of view.

9. See the definition of "misogyny" proposed by Bloch: "a speech act in which woman is the subject of the sentence and the predicate a more general term" (4). It follows, then, that "any essentialist definition of woman . . . is the fun-

damental definition of misogyny" (6). This grammatical reading of discourse-about-"woman" could fruitfully be undertaken in the mirror twin of the *maldezir de mugeres*, the so-called profeminist genre so popular in the later Middle Ages. Overviews of the *maldezir de mugeres* may be found in Ornstein; Cantarino; Lacarra; Muriel Tapia.

10. Following upon Bloch's suggestion that medieval misogyny is a speech act, we might add that in Austin's terms it may well be regarded as a *performative*, a discourse that, according to Austin, "is a part of the doing of an action, which . . . would not normally be described as, or as 'just,' saying something" (Austin 5). As we shall see, in spite of its vociferous claims to the contrary, the *maldezir de mugeres*, like an Austinian performative, "do[es] not 'describe' or 'report' or 'constate' anything at all, [is] not 'true' or 'false' " (Austin 5). For gender as performance and the term "doing gender," see Butler.

11. A reviewer of a recent anthology of medieval texts about the "woman question," for example, begins by sighing, "How difficult it is to review this book! . . . After some two hundred pages of misogynist writings, scrupulously catalogued, simply to write a review, rather than sit down and howl or demonstrate on street corners, seems too small a response" (Smith).

12. Twelfth-century theoreticians of the trivium, drawing on Cicero (*De Inventione* 1.6.8), make much of a distinction between acting *de arte*, about an art, and *per artem*, through an art. That is, for example, writing about poetry as opposed to writing poetically. See also Hugh of St. Victor (*Didascalicon* 3.5).

13. It is amusing to note that when the speaking voice slips back into the feminine, it is to imagine "herself" a man, and imagine the possibility of lovemaking with such a painted lady: "Si yo hombre fuera, antes me degollara que a tal mi cuerpo diera. ¡O, Señor Dios, por qué non me feziste ombre, que mal gozo vean de mi si por tal como ella penara una noche nin de mi casa saliera!" (162) [If I were a man, I'd cut my throat before I'd lie with such! Oh Lord God, why didst Thou not make me a man, for I'd be damned if I'd suffer a single night for such a woman, or even leave my house for her! (119; modified)].

14. This contagious quality of the "feminine" — the difficulty of speaking *about* Woman without speaking *like* her — is perhaps the most fascinating characteristic of misogyny as a discourse. Thus to deconstruct misogyny — that is, to recognize the absolute dependence of the discourse upon its suppressed other, to recognize the ways in which the discourse *performs* as well as censures the construct Woman — is to my mind the most intellectually and politically fruitful response. Only thus can we begin to step outside the tight circle of complicity spun by these texts.

15. Quintilian allies *praeteritio* to irony and dissimulation (*Institutio Oratoria*

9.2.44–48); see also Lausberg (§884–85, s.v. *praeteritio*). Dissimulation and preterition are, of course, tropes in Western cultural discourses of homosexuality (Chiffoleau) and in the rhetoric of the closet (Sedgwick 203).

16. Beghards, Beguines, and Spiritual Franciscans were especially active in Aragon and Catalonia in the fourteenth century; they were still a presence when Alfonso Martínez lived there in the 1420s. For more on the Beghards in Iberia, see Lea (214–20); Menéndez y Pelayo (*Historia de los heterodoxos* 2: 581–83); Fernández Conde (160–74); Pou i Martí.

17. For a history of "hypocrisy" in medieval ecclesiastical usage, see Amory.

18. The only substantive treatment of this section that I have been able to find is in Penna's edition (*Arcipreste* xli–xlii); we shall return to his comments below. Ciceri gives a brief semiotic reading of the hypocrite's "mystifying behavior"; she mentions the interweaving here of women and sodomites, but she does not address issues of gender and sexuality ("*Arcipreste de Talavera:* il linguaggio del corpo" 202–04). In what follows I discuss the Archpriest's groups of *begardos* one by one; the text, however, jumps back and forth from one to the other, an argumentative structure which further blurs the borders between them.

19. The Archpriest is concerned only with male transgressors here, and women, when they appear, play decidedly secondary roles: erotic partners seduced and rejected; erotic models imitated and rejected. Given the overwhelming association of "Woman" in the *Arçipreste de Talavera* with deception, Martínez's insistence on the male sex of his protagonists here is surely worthy of note.

20. "La preycació és comparada al filat, que hun fil es ligat ab altre" (Vicent Ferrer, qtd. in Gerli, "*Ars praedicandi*" 438) [Preaching is compared to spinning, for one thread is attached to another].

21. Though the terms "simulation" and "dissimulation" both appear in the discourse on hypocrisy, the difference between them is important. Alfonso de Cartagena, in his *Doctrinal de caballeros* [Handbook for Knights] (1487), defines them thus: "El sim<u>lar es fazer acto fingido . . . disim<u>lar es no<n> fingir lo q<ue> no<n> fizo / mas no<n> demostrar ni<n> de- / zir lo q<ue> fizo" (f. 27v) [To simulate is to feign an act falsely, to dissimulate is not to feign what one did not do, but rather not to reveal or speak what one did]. Simulation, as its association in Castilian with the verb *(in)fingir* implies, makes fiction from whole cloth, while dissimulation rather covers (or closets) another story.

22. The physician Villalobos, in the first attested Castilian use of the word *alumbrado* to designate a member of a social subgroup (1498), takes them quite simply to be sodomites, and offers remedies by which their illness might be cured (an instance of the mutual and pernicious attraction between sex/gender heterodoxy and disease) (*Sumario de Medeçina* f. 16v). Amusingly, just as Villalobos subsumes a religious category under a pathological one, so Lea, following

Menéndez y Pelayo, alludes to this passage in a religious context without mentioning the sexual (*Historia de los heterodoxos* 219). The best-known cases of such bundling of heresy with sodomy are the Templars and the Albigensians. Bibliography on this bundling of heterodoxies is ample; for starters, see Chiffoleau; Moore; Boswell (283–86); Goodich (7–10).

23. Heterodoxy is forever the trait of the other, of course; so it is not surprising to find classic Spanish historiographers like Menéndez y Pelayo intent on fixing the foreign origin of heresies. What is more surprising is to see the forms this gesture takes among contemporary scholars: Penna, for example, sees in Martínez's representation of the sodomites in book 4 "crude Castilian masculinity reacting against the semitic element in the environment" (Martínez, *Arcipreste* xlii), even though there is absolutely no textual indication of anything "semitic" about the sodomites. To this catalog of unacceptable, unnaturalizable others — queer, heretic, Jew — literary scholarship of the fifties and sixties added another: misogyny itself, which critics seem eager to fix on anyone but the Castilian man in the street. Ornstein's classic study of the *maldezir de mugeres* brands the discourse ascetic and monkish, and stresses the Catalan antecedents of many of the Castilian texts; in the case of the acerbic misogyny of Fernando de Rojas and Luis de Lucena we are reminded that "we are not in the presence of Spaniards nor of Castilians, but rather of Jews" (231). Cantarino, for his part, tries to exonerate Catholicism of misogyny, and fixes its origin on the Arabs and the Greeks.

24. It bears noting here that the Castilian, like my translation, is ambiguous here about exactly who — the pursuers or the pursued — is behaving "like women": our queer subjects look at boys "como si fuesen fembras" [as if they were women], leaving ambiguous whether the subject of the verb "to be" is the woman-hating men or the boys they pursue. It is as if the Archpriest's writing *itself* queered these subjects, then, for both woman-haters and their love interests are gendered at once and in sequence both masculine and feminine.

25. In his edition, Penna suggests that the "feminine" submission of the Beghard to the will of God drives the Archpriest's transition to speak of sodomites, and then to the "ambiguous virility" of those Beghards who consort too much with women (xli). For him, what holds the arguments together here is the "characterization of hypocrisy on a sensual plane" (lxi); it seems to me, however, that there is more of the erotic and (perversely) semiotic here than of sensuality.

26. One great Martínez scholar shrugs, "The meaning of this passage is unclear" (Richthofen 496n4). The textual transmission of the *Arçipreste de Talavera* attests to the "illegibility" of this difficult passage, which appears only in the manuscript. In her edition, Ciceri suggests that it was a marginal annotation introduced by a scribe (not the scribe of the Escorial manuscript, however — Naylor reproduces it as body text in his paleographic edition), which then fell

from the printed texts by *homeoteleuton* (Martínez, *Arcipreste*, ed. Ciceri 2.139). No other modern editor of the text comments on this point, though each represents it in slightly differing ways.

27. Resolutions of scribal abbreviations are in angle brackets, and editorial emendations in square brackets; superscripts are as they appear in the manuscript, and line breaks are indicated by a slash.

28. It is interesting to note in this context that the Archpriest seems to regard good women as truly (as opposed to preteritionally) unrepresentable, at least in his text. He consigns them to the extratext, where they themselves become neutral representers: "[E]s dicho que las buenas non han par nin que dezir mal dellas; antes como espejo son puestas a los que miran" (109) [[O]f good women it is said that they have no equal, nor should they be ill-spoken of; rather, they should be placed like a mirror for men to look at (61)]. Woman, it seems, is always already representation, whether she is the devil's mirror or man's.

29. The *Arçipreste de Talavera* was inducted into the canon of Castilian literature for this stylistic "naturalism"; however, the discomfort and disingenuousness of many scholars with regard to the text's misogyny makes one wonder if the "naturalness" of misogyny is not an issue as well.

Works Cited

Alfonso de Cartagena. *Doctrinal de caballeros.* Burgos: Fadrique de Basilea, 1487. Transcription by Catherine Soriano, correction by James Ray Green. Available in electronic form in *ADMTYE* (Madrid: Micronet, 1992).

Amory, Frederic. "Whited Sepulcres: The Semantic History of Hypocrisy in the High Middle Ages." *Recherches de théologie ancienne et médiévale* 53 (1986): 5–39.

Andreas Capellanus. *Andreas Capellanus on Love.* Ed. and trans. P. G. Walsh. London: Duckworth, 1982.

Aquinas, Thomas. *Summa theologiae.* Latin text and English trans. Blackfriars ed. 64 vols. New York: McGraw-Hill, 1964–1972.

Austin, J. L. *How to Do Things with Words.* Ed. J. O. Urmson and Marina Sbisà. 2nd ed. Cambridge, Mass.: Harvard UP, 1962.

Bloch, R. Howard. *Medieval Misogyny and the Invention of Western Romantic Love.* Chicago: U of Chicago P, 1991.

Boase, Roger. *The Troubadour Revival: A Study of Social Change and Tradition in Late Medieval Spain.* London: Routledge and Kegan Paul, 1978.

Boswell, John. *Christianity, Social Tolerance, and Homosexuality: Gay People in*

Western Europe from the Beginning of the Christian Era to the Fourteenth Century. Chicago: U of Chicago P, 1980.

Brown, Catherine. "The Archpriest's Magic Word: Representational Desire and Discursive Ascesis in the *Arçipreste de Talavera*." *Revista de estudios hispánicos* 31 (1997): 377–401.

Butler, Judith. *Gender Trouble: Feminism and the Subversion of Identity*. New York: Routledge, 1990.

Cantarino, Vicente. "El antifeminismo y sus formas en la literatura medieval castellana." *Homenaje a don Agapito Rey*. Ed. J. Roca-Pons. Bloomington: University of Indiana, Department of Spanish and Portuguese, 1980. 93–116.

Cátedra, Pedro M. *Sermón, sociedad y literatura en la Edad Media: San Vicente Ferrer en Castilla (1411–1412). Estudio bibliográfico, literario, y edición de los textos inéditos*. [Valladolid]: Junta de Castilla y León, Consejería de Cultura y Turismo, 1994.

Chiffoleau, Jacques. "Dire l'indicible: remarques sur la catégorie de *nefandum* du XIIᵉ au XVᵉ siècle." *Annales* 45.2 (1990): 289–324.

Ciceri, Marcella. "*Arcipreste de Talavera:* il linguaggio del corpo." *Marginalia hispanica*. Rome: Bulzoni, 1991. 179–206.

———. "Gli *exempla* dell *Arcipreste de Talavera*." *Marginalia hispanica*. Rome: Bulzoni, 1991. 161–78.

Fernández Conde, Javier, ed. *La iglesia en los siglos VIII–XIV*. Vol. 2, pt. 2, of *Historia de la iglesia en España*. Biblioteca de Autores Cristianos. Madrid: Católica, 1984.

Gates, Henry Louis. *The Signifying Monkey: A Theory of Afro-American Literary Criticism*. New York: Oxford UP, 1988.

Gerli, E. Michael. "*Ars praedicandi* and the Structure of the *Arçipreste de Talavera*, Part I." *Hispania* 58 (1975): 430–41.

———. "La 'religión de amor' y el antifeminismo en las letras castellanas del siglo XV." *Hispanic Review* 49 (1981): 65–86.

Goodich, Michael. *The Unmentionable Vice: Homosexuality in the Later Medieval Period*. N.p.: Dorset Press, 1979.

Gregory the Great. *Moralia in Job*. Ed. Marc Adriaen. Corpus Christianorum 143, 143A, 143B. Turnholt: Brepols, 1985.

Isidore of Seville. *Las Etimologías de San Isidoro romanceadas*. Ed. Joaquín González Cuenca. Acta Salamanticensia, Filosofía y Letras 139. 2 vols. Salamanca: CSIC, 1983.

Lacarra, María Jesús. "Algunos datos para la historia de la misoginia en la edad media." *Studia in honorem profesor Martín de Riquer*. Ed. Carlos Alvar et al. Barcelona: Quaderns Crema, 1986–87. 1: 339–61.

Lausberg, Heinrich. *Manual de retórica literaria.* 3 vols. Madrid: Gredos, 1966.

Lea, Henry Charles. *Chapters from the Religious History of Spain.* 1890. New York: Burt Franklin, 1967.

Martínez de Toledo, Alfonso. *Arcipreste de Talavera.* Ed. Marcella Ciceri. Studi, testi e manuale 3. 2 vols. Modena: STEM.-Mucchi, 1975.

————. *Arcipreste de Talavera.* Ed. Mario Penna. Turin: Rosenberg and Sellier, [1955].

————. *Arçipreste de Talavera o el Corbacho.* Ed. E. Michael Gerli. Madrid: Cátedra, 1981.

————. *[Arcipreste de Talavera] Little Sermons on Sin.* Trans. Lesley Byrd Simpson. Berkeley: U of California P, 1959.

————. *The Text and Concordances of the Escorial Manuscript H.III.10 of the "Arcipreste de Talavera" by Alfonso Martínez de Toledo.* Microfilm. Ed. Eric Naylor. Madison: HSMS, 1983.

Menéndez y Pelayo, Marcelino. *Historia de los heterodoxos españoles.* Biblioteca de Autores Cristianos. 2 vols. Madrid: Católica, 1956.

————. *Orígenes de la novela.* Ed. Enrique Sánchez Reyes. Obras completas 13.1.[1905]. Madrid: CSIC, 1961.

Moore, R. I. *The Formation of a Persecuting Society: Power and Deviance in Western Europe, 950–1250.* Oxford: Blackwell, 1987.

Muriel Tapia, María Cruz. *Antifeminismo y subestimación de la mujer en la literatura medieval castellana.* Caceres: Guadiloba, 1991.

Ornstein, Jacob. "La misoginia y el profeminismo en la literatura castellana." *Revista de filología hispánica* 3 (1941): 219–32.

Pou i Martí, José María. *Visionarios, beguinos, y fraticelos catalanes (siglos XIII–XV).* Ed. A. Abad, J. Martí Mayor and J. M. Arcellus. Madrid: Colegio Cardenal Cisneros, 1991.

Quintilian. *Institutio Oratoria.* 4 vols. Trans. H. E. Butler. Loeb Classical Library 124–27. Cambridge, Mass.: Harvard UP, 1976.

Richthofen, Erich von. "Alfonso Martínez de Toledo und sein *Arcipreste de Talavera*, ein kastilisches Prosawerk des 15. Jarhunderts." *Zeitschrift für romanische Philologie* 61 (1941): 417–537.

Rojas, Fernando de. *La Celestina.* Ed. Dorothy Sherman Severin. Madrid: Cátedra, 1987.

Sedgwick, Eve Kosofsky. *Epistemology of the Closet.* Berkeley: U of California P, 1990.

Smith, Lesley. Review of Blamires et al., *Woman Defamed and Woman Defended. Bryn Mawr Medieval Review,* 9 May 1995. Available at listserv@brynmawr.edu.

Villalobos, Fransisco López de. *Sumario de la medecina.* Salamanca: Impresor de

Nebrija para Antonio de Barreda, 1498. Transcription by Michael T. Ward and María Teresa Pajares Giménez; correction by María Jesús García Toledano. Available in electronic form in *ADMYTE* (Madrid: Micronet, 1992).

Whitbourn, Christine. *The "Arçipreste de Talavera" and the Literature of Love.* Occasional Papers in Modern Languages 7. Hull, England: University of Hull, 1970.

II

IBERIAN MASCULINITIES

Sara Lipton

"Tanquam effeminatum"

Pedro II of Aragon and the Gendering of Heresy

in the Albigensian Crusade

In grateful and affectionate memory of John E. Boswell

In the year 1208, Pope Innocent III authorized the launching of a military campaign—generally called a crusade—against the Albigensian Cathars (dualist heretics in Languedoc) or, more accurately, against the Languedocian Catholic lords accused of tolerating and protecting them. The crusading forces were largely made up of clerics and members of the minor nobility from northern France, and they were opposed by almost all the residents of Languedoc—Catholic and Cathar, noble, burgher, and peasant—with the exception of a handful of clerics loyal to the pope. Although the military campaigns and the long-term political effects of this crusade have been exhaustively studied, its intellectual and ideological underpinnings, and, more importantly, its social aspects, have received far less scholarly attention.[1] One area that particularly merits greater notice than it has yet been accorded is that of sex and gender, for in the polemics of the Albigensian Crusade, gendered terms are placed squarely at the center of this religious, territorial, and military struggle.

Such notice is worthwhile and long overdue. First, because careful reading of this gendered terminology, which draws upon a host of classical and medieval antifeminist tropes, can help illuminate the social matrix underlying the Albigensian Crusade; and, second, because the failure of historians to deal with this terminology has, I believe, resulted in a distorted understanding of the Albigensian heresy, the crusade, and its participants.

In this essay I focus on one specific context in which sexual and gendered rhetoric was conspicuously employed: the discourse surrounding the participation of Pedro II of Aragon in the Albigensian Crusade. The letters, chronicles, and poems generated by this crusade regularly discuss Pedro's entry into the hostilities in sexual and gendered terms. I will suggest that in this discourse "woman" becomes the mediating term by means of which "value" (negative or positive) is ascribed to the protagonists of the crusade and the religious and political projects they represent. The resulting rhetorical centrality of female agency corresponds to a striking degree to the position occupied by women in the economic and political life of the aristocracy.

Pedro II stands at the center of the questions of identity raised by the Albigensian Crusade both because of who Pedro was and what the crusade purported to be. Heir to the kingdom of Aragon, the county of Barcelona, and many other territories on either side of the Pyrenees, Pedro earned the sobriquet *el Católico* through a series of measures that proved his devotion to the Catholic cause and the papacy. A persecutor of heretics in his own realm, a stalwart fighter of Muslims, a symbolic vassal of the pope, Pedro was widely proclaimed a genuine Christian hero in 1212 for his role in a stunning and pivotal victory over Muslim forces at Las Navas de Tolosa.[2] And yet, when Pedro entered the Albigensian Crusade, it was in order to fight against the papal forces who claimed to have come to Languedoc to repress heresy.

The outbreak of the Albigensian Crusade was highly problematic for Pedro. As feudal overlord to many of the Languedocian nobles under attack, and, moreover, as a king with considerable political interests in and ambitions concerning Languedocian lands, Pedro could not look with equanimity at the arrival of an army consisting mostly of land-hungry northern French lords. At the same time, as a loyal Catholic and a king who had sworn fealty to the pope, he could hardly openly oppose the repression of heresy. His approach in the first years of the crusade, then (to somewhat simplify and telescope a series of complicated maneuvers), was to stay out of the fighting and try to protect his vassals' (and his own) interests through diplomacy—largely in the form of letters and messages directed toward the papal court. The thrust of this diplomacy was to assert that the war had gone seriously astray—to undermine the articulated motivations of the invaders and challenge the sincerity and authority of the clerics promoting the crusade. Finally, in early 1213, Pedro put the case for his vassals to the pope's legates in Languedoc.[3] In the correspondence generated by two councils held by these legates—at Lavaur and at Orange—a contest over the valuation of Pedro and his allies as heretics is indirectly engaged through questions of the feminine, effeminacy, and sexuality.

The exchange is inaugurated in a letter addressed by Pedro to the Council of Lavaur in February 1213. In this letter Pedro denies that his vassals are heretics and requests that the lands taken from them be returned. The letter begins with the following words:

> Quoniam sacrosancta mater ecclesia non solum verbera, sed ubera quoque docetur habere, devotus ecclesiae filius Petrus, deo miserante, Rex Aragonensis, pro comite Tolosano, ad sinum eiusdem matris ecclesiae cupiente redire . . . petit humiliter . . . quod . . . restituatur . . . ad possessiones.[4]

> [Since the Sacrosanct Mother Church is taught to have not just *verbera* but also *ubera*, Pedro by the mercy of God King of Aragon humbly seeks in behalf of the Count of Toulouse that she restore his rightful possessions to the Count, who desires to return to the bosom of Mother Church.]

The word *verbera* can be translated as "whips" or "scourges," but I think the contrast being exploited by Pedro is most clearly conveyed in the translation: "We are taught that Sacrosanct Mother Church has not just *rods* but *breasts*." In this highly skillful opening gambit, Pedro (or his secretary) uses the venerable topos of a nurturing Mother Church to undermine the aggressive (masculine) policies of the crusade leaders. At the same time, Pedro underscores his allies' Catholicism and masculine, active natures, insisting that each of his vassals in turn "nec fuit unquam haereticus nec eorum susceptor, sed potius impugnator" (Vaux-de-Sarnay 2: 70; *RHGF* 19: 72) [never was a receiver of heretics, but rather was an attacker of heretics]. This homological pair of receiver and attacker echoes the distinctions between passive and active (that is, female and male) sexuality that the letter earlier invoked; it may also resonate with medieval conceptions of homosexuality.

The prelates at the council responded to Pedro's challenge by directing a letter in February or March 1213 to Pope Innocent III, emphatically accusing Pedro's vassals of supporting heresy and warning of dire consequences should the crusade not proceed. This letter inverts Pedro's gendered homological pairings and represents the political and religious menace—figured in this instance by the city of Toulouse—as a sexual one. The prelates tell the pope that "timendum est et cavendum ne venenum hydrae,

hoc est, dolosissimae civitatis Tolosae, si non tanquam membrum putri-
dissimum succidatur . . . inficiat iterum et corrumpat"[5] [we must fear and
beware lest the venom of the Hydra—that is, the most treacherous city of
Toulouse—should once again corrupt and infect, if it is not cut off like a
most putrid member]. The letter goes on to exhort the pope that the city of
Toulouse, "fermentatissima civitas illa cum sceleratis omnibus spurciteis et
sordibus, quae se infra tumidum ventrem viperae receperunt, cum in sua
malitia non sit inferior Sodoma et Gomorrha, debito exterminio radicitus
explantetur"(*RHGF* 19: 570–71) [that most vexatious city, together with
all the wicked smut and filth, vipers which found refuge within her swollen
womb, must be uprooted, since in her malice she is not inferior to Sodom
and Gomorrah].

The "hydra" is the classical many-headed serpent, which, growing back
two heads for each one cut off, was finally slain by Hercules; it was used to
signify heresy from the earliest Christian period.[6] Reminiscent of that other
threatening serpent-like female, Medusa, the sign is a dizzyingly complex
subject, one that has been studied extensively by Freud and post-Lacanian
critics, who have focused on the fetish character of such figurations.[7] What
is important, here, are its effects. The identification of Toulouse as a "hydra" possessing a penetrated womb serves to gender heresy as a menacing
and sexually active form of femininity, whose ambiguity the prelates of
Lavaur simultaneously affirm and seek to repress by (paradoxically) calling
for its castration. The comparison of Toulouse to Sodom and Gomorrah
similarly underscores the figure's sexual iniquity and ambiguity, as these
cities were generally held by medieval exegetes to have been destroyed on
account of "unnatural carnal perversions"—particularly sodomy.[8]

The papal legates won this diplomatic round. Pope Innocent directed a
stern letter to Pedro in which he castigated the king for deceiving him,
adopting the very words of the prelates of Lavaur in comparing the excommunicated city of Toulouse to "a putrid member" that had to be cut
off.[9] Nevertheless, the pope ordered that the crusade be suspended pend-
ing a thorough investigation of the situation. But Pedro was no longer in
the mood to wait. He decided to put an end to the war before reinforcements for the crusaders could arrive from northern France and, assembling
an army, joined the count of Toulouse in his principal city. Their destination was a stronghold called Muret, held by a small band of crusaders a
short march away. Although they vastly outnumbered both the defenders

and the crusaders who rushed to support them, Pedro's forces were routed and he himself was killed in the battle (12 September 1213). The Battle of Muret was probably the crucial military encounter of this stage of the war; it also stands at the center of the valuations and countervaluations of Pedro's political and military character in terms of sexual identity. For Pedro's decision to go to war challenged the religious classifications carefully constructed by the promoters and propagandists of the crusade. Their response was to echo the correspondence generated by the Council of Lavaur in invoking polarities perceived to be less ambiguous—that is, by invoking categories of gender difference.

An oft cited (but little analyzed) example of this technique appears in a chronicle of the Albigensian Crusade written by the cleric Guillaume de Puylaurens around the year 1250.[10] In his account of the events leading up to the Battle of Muret, Guillaume relates that as the crusaders were on their way to help defend the stronghold of Muret from the forces of King Pedro II, they stopped at the Abbey of Boulbonne. There Simon de Montfort, leader of the crusaders, met a monk named Amaury. Guillaume continues:

Nam, ut ego audivi post plures annos dominum Maurinum abbatem Apamiae, virum fide dignum et per omniua laudibilem referentem, qui prius sacrista Apamiae castri habebat custodiam, ipse apud Bolbonam exivit obviam eidem Comiti venienti, et, audito eo quod veniret succursurus obsessis, et etiam si eum exspectarent in campo, cum obsessoribus commisurus, ait ei sacrista, "Vos habetis paucos socios respectu adversariorum, in quibus est Rex Aragonum, vir in bellis experientissimus et probatus, habens secum Comites et exercitum magnum valde, et non est par cum tam paucis contra Regem et tantum multitudinem experiri." Quid ad hanc vocem protulit literas de sua almoneria, dicens, "Legite istas literas." Quas cum legisset, invenit in eis quod Rex Aragonum quandam nobilem uxorem cujusdam nobilis Tolosanae diocesis salutabat, persuadens quod ob amorem ejus ad expellendos de terra Gallicos veniebat, et alias blanditias continebant. Quibus lectis, respondit ei sacrista, "Quid vultis dicere propter istud?" Qui ait, "Quid volo dicere? Sic Deus me adjuvet, quod ego Regem non vereor, qui pro una venerit contra Dei negotium meretrice." (Duvernoy 78–80; *RHGF* 19: 208)

[Now, as I heard many years later from Lord Amaury, abbot of Pamiers, . . . this same Amaury went out to meet the count, and having heard from him that he would go to relieve the besieged garrison, and also that he would meet the besiegers if they waited for him in the field, remarked to Simon that "you have few comrades compared to your adversaries, among whom is the king of Aragon, an experienced and proven warrior, having with him counts and a great army, and it is not an equal match to test against a king and such a multitude with so few." In response, Simon took letters out of his wallet and said, "Read these." When (Amaury) had read them, he found that in them the king of Aragon saluted a certain noble woman, wife of a noble man of the diocese of Toulouse, protesting that it was for love of her that he had come to chase away the French (*Gallicos*) from the land, and they contained other flatteries. After he read the letters, Amaury asked Simon, "What is your point?" "What do I want to say?" replied Simon, "That, accordingly, God may come to my aid, for I do not fear a king who will have come against the business of God for the sake of one whore!"]

Guillaume then adds his own comment, suggesting that Simon had obtained a copy of the letters from a servant or secretary of the noble woman, "quas secum Comes ferebat in testimonium coram Domino contra illum, qui tamquam effeminatum sibi posse resistere pro Dei confidentia non timebat" (Duvernoy 78–80; *RHGF* 19: 208) [which letters the count carried in testimony before God against (Pedro), for, confident in God, (Simon) did not fear that one who was like an effeminate could resist him].

The passage has attracted considerable attention, if not inspired a great deal of serious thought, on the part of historians. At least two scholars have speculated on the identity of the woman in question;[11] one has pondered whether the letter was written in prose or in verse (Duvernoy 81n2); and another, rushing to Pedro's defense, questioned the existence of the letter, of the conversation between Simon and Amaury, of the amorous relationship, and of the woman herself.[12] A typically vague and uncritical comment on the episode is that of Jonathan Sumption, who, in order to demonstrate that Simon was well informed about Pedro's movements, mentioned that one of Pedro's messengers, carrying a "suggestive" letter to a lady of Toulouse, had been intercepted by Simon's men (164). Sumption does not elaborate on what the letter suggested either to Simon or to himself. Neither Sumption nor any other scholar has yet commented on what any social historian who takes seriously the question of gender must consider of particular interest—the way in which the chronicler repositions Pedro's deviation from his "assigned" military, political, and religious role as a deviation from sexual and gender roles represented as normative.

Of course, aligning heresy with either excessive or ambiguous sexuality (especially sodomy) was by no means novel in medieval Catholic texts—it was, in fact, a venerable topos by the thirteenth century.[13] Yet, in spite of considerable scholarship on the subject, the ideological impetus for this alignment, and, more importantly, its effects—how the sexualized rhetoric resonates within any given context—remain largely unexamined. The case of Pedro, as yet unnoticed as an example of this polemical strategy, is an instructive one, since (unlike in the case of the vast majority of accused heretics) we know a great deal about Pedro's sexual life and proclivities; this knowledge renders the polemical aspects of the epithets attached to him unusually transparent.

Perhaps the most noteworthy aspect of Guillaume's narrative is that, as in the letters of the Council of Lavaur, the "female," the "feminine," and sexuality assume (against all likelihood, given that the subject is, after all, a medieval military encounter) center stage. Pedro is marked as "effeminate" because he allows himself to be motivated by love for a woman, who is also explicitly identified as a noblewoman of Toulouse, as a wife, and as a whore. Since in this context a native of Toulouse is necessarily regarded as a heretic, this (literary) figure of the woman operates to merge the question of orthodoxy with that of sexuality. Moreover, as a wife who has resorted to "harlotry" the Toulousaine is a woman who has escaped the control of a male, and who through her sexuality in turn controls a male. The entire phenomenon of heresy is thus incarnated in a single woman, whose inversion of power relationships turns Pedro into something resembling herself (an inversion of gender) by motivating his political decisions.[14]

The strategy is strikingly similar to that seen in the letter of the papal legates: an ambiguous religious and social identity is subsumed within another realm—that of sex and gender. One extreme end of the newly defined continuum is consequently represented by this woman, who signifies the identification of heresy with femaleness, sexuality with immorality. And because the figure of the woman functions as a synecdoche—a part which stands for the whole—these traits are also, by extension, projected onto the woman's native city, Toulouse, and onto Languedocian society. Simon, the embodiment of maleness and Catholicism (and Frenchness), is located at the other extreme; and Pedro, the ambiguous and boundary-blurring figure, stands in the middle. Once a Christian warrior like Simon, he is now transformed into the "opposite" (as constructed in the narrative) — an effeminate, and consequently a heretic — by the fact that he allowed his lust (or his courtly affectations? — I'll come back to this point later) to master him.

The realignment of political and religious value with effeminacy in Guillaume's work, and in the letters of Pedro and the papal legates, is of course neither unprecedented nor arbitrary. Like most works of medieval rhetoric, it self-consciously relies upon an index of venerable literary models in which sexuality, especially female sexuality, is invested with negative worth.[15] However, two models in particular are especially relevant for an analysis of the range of possible meanings conveyed by the term *effeminatus* in Guillaume's chronicle: the Vulgate and Roman historiography.

The term *effeminatus* appears in nine places in the Vulgate version of the Hebrew Scriptures, in each case in a similar context: condemnations of the contamination of sacred precincts with idolatrous practices.[16] For example, in Hosea 4.13–14, God rebukes the Israelites for idolatry and debauchery with the following words:

> Ideo fornicabuntur filiae vestrae,
> Et sponsae vestrae adulterae erunt,
> Non visitabo super filias vestras cum fuerint fornicatae,
> Et super sponsas vestras cum adulteraverint,
> Quoniam ipsi cum meretricibus conversabantur,
> Et cum effeminatis sacrificabant;
> Et populus non intelligens vapulabit.[17]

[For although your daughters will fornicate and your wives commit adultery, I will not punish your daughters when they shall have committed fornication, nor your wives when they shall have committed adultery: because (the Israelite men) themselves have trafficked with prostitutes, and offered sacrifice with effeminates, and a people without understanding is doomed].

In this context, the word *effeminatis* refers to male temple prostitutes, who formed a part of pagan worship. As in Guillaume's narrative, *effeminatis* is used in a metaphorical sense: temple prostitution is made to stand for the whole of pagan worship, and, ultimately, for all transgressions against

God's law. The actual practice of sodomy (if, indeed, that was the nature of temple prostitution) is secondary in heinousness to the resulting inversion of spiritual and gender norms, which, like a disease, is infectious, tainting not only those Israelite men directly involved but the Israelite women as well.[18] Read in the light of such Bible texts, to be "like an effeminate" is to sin against God and to pose a threat to the spiritual purity of God's people. Guillaume's characterization of Pedro as "effeminate," then, identifies him with biblical transgressors against God and God's chosen people, and Pedro's opponents — Simon and the crusaders — with the true Israel.[19]

Effeminacy was also a central indicator of value in Roman historiography, most instructively (for this analysis) in Plutarch's *Life of Antony*. A principal strategy of this work is to construct a comparison between Octavian (Caesar), who represents all things Roman, dutiful, masculine, and warlike; and Antony, who, in succumbing to the allures of Cleopatra, represents all things Oriental, degenerate, and effeminate. For example, Plutarch relates that when Antony was spending time with his wife Octavia, Cleopatra sent friends to lure him away. According to Plutarch, "they so softened and effeminized him" [molliuerunt et effoeminarunt] that he forsook his lawful Roman wife and returned to Cleopatra in Alexandria.[20]

Like Plutarch's Antony, Guillaume's Pedro is treated apotropaically — as the representative figure of an ambiguous and menacing alterity, which must be relocated within secure boundaries. Plutarch's Antony is a Roman who resides in and sides with the East; Guillaume's Pedro is a Catholic who opposes the Catholic cause. Both are men who are supposed to lead but instead follow women; they are consequently equated with "effeminates."

Also informing Guillaume's characterization of Pedro was the Aragonese king's well-publicized sexual and marital adventures, which Guillaume made a point of incorporating into his chronicle. The very first mention of Pedro in Guillaume's chronicle deals, in fact, with his marital history. In a chapter that significantly interrupts the historical recitation, Guillaume tells us that Pedro married and twice abandoned the daughter of a woman whom he had also once abandoned, and that he did not remain faithful to either (Duvernoy 56–57). Guillaume is correct in saying that Pedro tried to divorce his wife, but errs grossly in saying that he had earlier abandoned her mother. The modern editor of Guillaume's *Chronica* is at a loss to explain the error, and speculates that perhaps a phrase was left out by the scribe. This is possible, of course, but it is interesting that the effect of such an omission is to significantly magnify Pedro's lack of control over his sexual and marital life.

Guillaume's "feminization" of Pedro is by no means an isolated case. A remarkably similar approach is apparent in another contemporary explanation for Pedro's defeat in the Battle of Muret. According to the autobiography of Pedro's own son, Jaime I, "The night of the day that the battle [of Muret] was fought the King [Pedro] had spent in debauchery [havia jugat ab una dona (had played with a woman)], so that as I afterwards heard his own seneschal . . . say, the King was so exhausted by the preceding debauch, that he could not stand up [at mass], when it came to the reading of the Gospel, but kept his seat all the while it was read." Again, Pedro is portrayed as having been weakened by a woman, and his spiritual and military deficiencies are related to his lack of sexual control: "Thus, through bad order, through our sins, and through the Murelians fighting desperately since they found no mercy at my father's hands, the battle was lost." [21]

Jaime I also echoes Guillaume de Puylaurens in attributing Pedro's decision to enter the war to his vulnerability to feminine allures (although he lays the bulk of the blame for Pedro's lapses on duplicitous Languedocian lords). According to Jaime, Pedro broke with Simon de Montfort because he took pity on the Languedocian lords, who in their fear of the northern invaders offered their lands to the Aragonese king if he would come to their aid. When his father was about to take possession of the land, the Languedocian lords said,

> Com gitarets nostres mullers de nostres cases, mes nos e eles ne seren vostres, en faren vostra volentat. E per aquesta manera noli atenyan co que li prometien, e mostraven li llurs mullers, e llurs filles, e llurs parentes les plus belles que podien trobar. E can sabien que ell era hom de fembres tolien li son bon proposit, e feyan lo mudar en co que ells volien.[22] (Forster 12–15)

> ["How can you turn our wives out of our houses? We and they will be yours; we will do your will." But in this way they did not do what they promised him: they showed him their wives and daughters, and their kinswomen, the fairest they could find. And when they knew that he was a woman's man, they took away his good purpose, and (made him do) what they wished.]

By contrast, the chronicles highlight Simon de Montfort's marital harmony and proper control over his wife, most notably in a passage that simultaneously serves (yet again) to effeminize Pedro. A history of the Albigensian Crusade written by a northern monk named Pierre des Vaux-de-Sarnay, who was a nephew of a leader of the crusade, relates the following story: On the night before the Battle of Muret (which Pierre calls the fourth day before the Ides of September), Simon's wife, the countess of Montfort, had a terrifying dream. She dreamt that blood flowed out of Simon's arms in great abundance. The next morning she told Simon about her dream and said that she was very disturbed. The count replied, "This is womanish speech [locuta de mulieribus]; do you think that I follow dreams or auguries in the Spanish manner? Indeed, even if I had dreamed that I'd been killed in battle, I would go freely and confidently, that I might oppose the stupidities of Spaniards and of men of this land, who pay attention to dreams and auguries." The count then sent his wife to Carcassonne to round up reinforcements, and she obediently complied (*RHGF* 19: 84).

The similarities in technique to Guillaume's anecdote are striking. The recourse to well-known Roman historiography (Plutarch, again, tells us that Caesar's wife, Calpurnia, urged him not to go to the Forum on the day of his assassination—the Ides of March—because she'd had a bad dream the night before); the alignment of femininity with cowardice; the association of cowardice with infidelity, since belief in the significance of dreams and augurs was by this time labeled heretical by Catholic theologians (Kruger 11–13) (and since the "men of this land" mentioned by Simon can only mean Albigensian heretics); and, of course, the seemingly gratuitous imposition of these negative qualities onto Pedro, since clearly "Spanish manners and stupidities" must recall the Iberian king whom Simon is marching to combat. The phrase also serves, again, to align cultural with gender and religious characteristics, underscoring the orthodoxy and rationality of the "French" cause by emphasizing the heterodox and irrational (female) nature of Languedocian and Spanish culture.

However, the role of gender in crusade polemics is not limited to the stigmatization of Pedro as effeminate. Rather, "femininity" is a shifting concept by means of which either positive or negative value emerges in relation to a political position. For a Languedocian troubadour lyric accepts the northerners' alignment of Pedro with women and with southern culture, although it inverts their estimation of his consequent worth, presenting him as a defender of ladies, "courteoisie," and southern culture against "French" interlopers. The Toulousain troubadour Raimon de Miravel composed a song for Countess Leonora, wife of Raymond of Toulouse and sister of Pedro II, which called on Pedro to repel the crusaders with the following words: "King [Pedro] has promised me that I will recover [my castle] shortly and that my Audiart [Raymond of Toulouse] will recover Beaucaire. Then ladies and lovers will be able to return to the joy that they have lost."[23]

Moreover, although the chronicles that are supportive of the Aragonese king utterly reject this casting of Pedro in the role of courtly and romantic hero, they also place "women" at the heart of the issue. The *Chanson de la croisade albigeoise* [Song of the Albigensian Crusade], a verse chronicle in Languedocian highly hostile to the crusaders and sympathetic to Pedro, asserts that Pedro's primary motives for going to war were to protect the interests of his sisters, who were married, respectively, to the count of Toulouse and to his son.[24] The anonymous *Gesta veterum comitum barcinonensium* [Deeds of the Former Counts of Barcelona] and the *Chronicle of San Juan de la Peña,* the official chronicle of the Crown of Aragon, make this same claim more emphatically, not once, but twice: "The king went to the lands of Toulouse only for the purpose of giving aid to his sisters, as was stated above, and not to help any infidels or enemies of the orthodox faith, of which he was a member and in which he persisted faithfully and without blemish all his life."[25]

Of course, the Albigensian Crusade is far from the only context in which the male/female homology serves to identify the superiority or inferiority of a given political constituency. Wayne Rebhorn has called attention to accusations of effeminacy and homosexuality among professional rhetors in Quattrocento Italy; Neil Hertz discusses in a fascinating essay the gendering of the 1848 political convulsions in France; and Laura Levine offers a recent examination of fears of effeminization associated with Elizabethan drama. It is clear that the dynamics of male-female sexual relations present themselves as relevant metaphors in a wide variety of contexts concerned with issues related to power, dominance, and hierarchy.

I am not citing these examples in order to argue that the gendering of heresy should be considered merely one more manifestation of a timeless, ahistorical semiotic pattern. On the contrary, this phenomenon *must* be historicized because it lies at the heart of what has to date been presented as the normative history of these events. Indeed, the irony is that precisely by not contending with the gendered homologies of the Albigensian chronicles, modern historians have uncritically perpetuated them.

I will briefly comment on two instances of this perpetuation because they serve to illuminate my conclusions.

In the specific case of Pedro, modern comment on Guillaume's anecdote has not only failed to examine but has generally reinforced his gendered invective. Austin P. Evans, a leading twentieth-century historian of the Albigensian Crusade, cited the anecdote as evidence that Simon fought with confidence because Pedro had come to the support of the count of Toulouse for what he perceived to be "frivolous" reasons (Evans 301). This remark implicitly ratifies Guillaume's charges, since the homology serious/frivolous is conventionally gendered male/female. The only historian who has given the passage more than glancing consideration is Michel Roquebert. Roquebert believes that the letter was probably genuine, pointing out that it was rather standard procedure for those versed in courtly love to dedicate combat to a woman. Of course (Roquebert points out), the lady of Toulouse would not have believed a word of Pedro's protestation, nor would he have expected her to, but both would have taken pleasure in the fiction nonetheless. According to Roquebert, Simon's failure to recognize the subtleties of courtly love conventions testifies to his rusticity, since he was ignorant not only of the courtly customs of Languedoc, but even of the refined manners already popularized in his own northern region by writers such as Chrétien de Troyes (Roquebert 4: 180). Like Evans, Roquebert accepts Guillaume's representation of Simon and Pedro as diametric opposites (although reversing their value in his estimation) and perpetuates an implied linkage of gender and culture in adopting the pairing refined/rustic in association with the warring figures.[26]

In a more general sense, the gendering of heresy has been perpetuated in modern historiography in that almost every modern writer on the subject of the Albigensian heresy—most notably Walter Wakefield, Arno Borst, and Gottfried Koch—repeats emphatically and without substantiation the assertion that women were disproportionately numerous and influential among the Albigensian heretics.[27] This belief continues in spite of the fact that an empirical study of the question published in 1979 strongly indicated otherwise (Abels and Harrison).[28] I am not asserting that women were *not* important participants in Catharism, but I do urge that the texts on which such claims are based should be carefully reexamined. Since the writings of the Cathars themselves were almost entirely destroyed, the only basis for this assumption are the writings of Catholic polemicists—whose assertions concerning gender among the Albigensians must, as I hope I have demonstrated, be read as ideological constructions.

What, then, is signified by the fact that heresy is addressed in gendered and sexual terms in these sources? I mentioned the second fallacy — the unsubstantiated assumption that women were disproportionately influential among heretics — because it nevertheless points indirectly to what I believe to be a certain truth about the role of women in the Albigensian Crusade.

One inescapable observation is that all the women "heretics" or "seductresses" highlighted in the chronicles, from Pedro's alleged paramour and the troubadour's beloved to Pedro's sisters and the kinswomen of the duplicitous lords of Languedoc, are members of the aristocracy. These aristocratic women are not, however, presented as important in themselves; their importance lies in the fact that through interaction with them the quality of their male connections is revealed: men (Simon and Pedro in this case) are assessed according to the extent to which they dominate or are dominated by their women. In occupying such a pivotal, yet effaced role, the aristocratic women function in a way reminiscent of and analogous to the "general equivalent" — that Aristotelian concept of currency, which in and of itself has no value, and therefore can be used to affix value to other commodities. This likeness is neither coincidental nor irrelevant. For although the central position attributed to heretical women clearly differentiates (and probably was intended to differentiate) the heretical religion from Catholicism, which granted no such status to women, it echoes — or perhaps parodies — the role played by women in the aristocratic society that conducted the Albigensian Crusade.

For exactly in this period, the French aristocracy was experiencing certain economic and political developments in which women played a role analogous to the pivotal, if effaced, role played by the feminine in the diplomatic and ideological exchanges I have just presented. According to Georges Duby, between about 1180 and 1230 nonprincely aristocrats endured a significant loss of power, authority, and financial dominance; they responded by "closing ranks," that is, creating a self-conscious aristocratic ethos, culture, and identity (178–85).

The encroachment on the power and solvency of the aristocracy came from various directions, but, above all, from two sources: the Crown and the bourgeoisie. And in each case, "woman" was the mediator in the exchange of wealth or power. First, the great territorial princes were vigorously working to expand the scope and force of their power and prerogatives—inevitably at the expense of lesser lords. One aspect of this policy consisted of augmenting their domains through dynastic alliances with leading heiresses;[29] another consisted of cultivating dynastic ideology that emphasized royal lineage. This was an especially central strategy in France, where the Capetians buttressed their claims to Carolingian blood via marriage to princesses descended directly from Charlemagne.[30]

Secondly, the rapidly expanding monetary economy for the first time provided the aristocracy with serious economic competition—the bourgeoisie. The aristocracy reacted to the rise of a prosperous bourgeoisie by elevating the aspects of a "noble" lifestyle—aristocrats' banquets, castles, and especially their wives' clothing became ever more luxurious in an attempt to visually and culturally distinguish themselves from their middle-class competitors. Yet such ostentation simply exacerbated their financial difficulties: as land prices and profitability stagnated, the aristocracy became ever more indebted to the bourgeoisie that controlled liquid capital.

Thirdly, as part of the move to "close ranks" and preserve distance from and superiority to prosperous and influential but base-born *arrivés,* aristocratic ideology placed ever greater stress on birth and lineage (Bisson, "Medieval Lordship" 754). If kings and great princes benefited most from this development, nonprincely aristocrats by no means repudiated it. The symbolic value if not political influence of women naturally increased as family replaced military service as the primary source and indicator of nobility.

Finally, these hard-pressed lords constructed a uniquely aristocratic literary culture. In this culture, courtly love rituals and rhetoric that provided an outlet for knightly activity and enterprise while encouraging reverence for the lord's wife (now accorded an elevated but largely passive role) featured prominently. Here, too, aristocratic women took center stage but nevertheless remained objects of male regard rather than subjects.

As the medium by which inherited lands were exchanged and political control transferred or augmented, as the signifiers of their husbands' wealth and status, as the focal points for the elaborate courtly rituals that came to define knightly culture, then, aristocratic women were at the center of the changes affecting French nobles.

These same changes were intimately intertwined with the Albigensian Crusade. Simon de Montfort and the northern French lords who responded most enthusiastically to the call for the crusade were just the kind of middle-level aristocrats most vulnerable to the transformations described above.[31] The two kings involved — Philip Augustus of France and Pedro II of Aragon — were among the most ambitious and successful princes of their day.

Now, many historians have already pointed out the secular and territorial aspects of the northern (and for that matter southern) nobles' interest in the crusade. However, no one has yet asked how these economic interests may have affected the ideology and rhetoric of the crusade; nor has anyone yet made the attempt to link the gendered terms by which the crusade was represented to the mechanisms of exchange at the heart of the structural changes of the early thirteenth century. The anxiety or ambivalence felt by the economically pressed nobles of France about the encroachment on their lands and authority by the French and Aragonese Crowns, the increasingly ritualistic nature of their military roles, and the growing significance of their domestic households in defining their status may well be associated with the establishment of the figure of the woman as the mediator of value at the center of the discourse surrounding this event. In assessing a man's worth in relation to his control over women, the texts are using women as figures for the entire economic, social, religious, and political network in which aristocratic men lived and functioned.

Let me emphasize that I am *not* suggesting that the chroniclers used gendered or courtly rhetoric to mask the "real" economic or geopolitical nature of the Albigensian Crusade. Rather, the war was inevitably seen and described by contemporaries in relation to the encompassing symbolic economy of their society.[32] And what is striking is the extent to which this symbolic economy — and its basic assumptions about the significance of courtly rhetoric and the role of women — is shared by northern and southern writers. The northern texts reject courtly values not because they are "foreign" but because in this particular project the northern lords were seeking to expand through conquest — to infiltrate the southern aristocracy and take advantage of just those situations that caused their own economic distress. Similarly, I have noted how vehemently the Catalan and Aragonese royal sources — those promoting a figure seeking to capitalize on aristocratic vulnerability — also reject "courtly" values. The Languedocian texts embrace courtly values because they epitomize the hegemony Languedocian lords were fighting to preserve. In this reading, I find myself in agreement with Howard Bloch, who saw in secular courtly love literature and misogynistic clerical literature opposite sides of the same coin.

If I can only hesitantly offer some observations about the conditions that may have been associated with the gendering of heresy, I can point with greater confidence to some concrete effects. The success of the crusade inaugurated intensive regulation in Languedoc of various areas of life seemingly peripheral to the question of heresy but in which women were intimately involved, including marriage, inheritance laws, and prostitution.[33] Although this activity has been studied in some depth, it remains unexplained; it seems likely that such legislation is connected to the prominence accorded women in the ideology of the crusade. It is also notable that the overwhelming targeting of women during the witchcraft prosecutions of the later Middle Ages and the early-modern period directly echoes the forms of discourse established in this period—I mention this not to posit a direct causal connection but to suggest investigation into similarities in the economic and social contexts.

As a postscript, I would like to note that the French barons who overpowered Languedoc in the Albigensian Crusade did not get to keep it. Simon de Montfort was killed by a catapult (allegedly operated by women!) while besieging the city of Toulouse in 1218. Unable to control the conquered territories, the son of Simon de Montfort handed them over to the king of France. The rest of Languedoc was eventually incorporated into the domain of the French Crown through a dynastic alliance: by the treaty that closed the war, the daughter and heiress of the count of Toulouse was married to the brother of the king of France. Because the marriage was childless, the county of Toulouse reverted to the French Crown, and the unification of France as we know it was achieved as a result of the Albigensian Crusade and through the mediation of a woman.

Notes

1. The bibliography on the Albigensian Crusade is extensive; for the primary English-language studies and recent and/or noteworthy works in French see the Works Cited.

2. There is, as yet, no modern biography of Pedro II of Aragon. Most works on

medieval Catalan and Spanish history discuss his participation in the Albigensian Crusade in the context of the expansion of the kingdom of Aragon. For comprehensive bibliographies, see O'Callaghan; and Bisson (*The Medieval Crown*).

3. On Pedro's involvement in the Albigensian Crusade, see O'Callaghan (249–51); Bisson (*The Medieval Crown* 38–39); and especially Roquebert (4: 43–229).

4. A copy of this letter is included in Vaux-de-Sarnay (2: 69–72). See also *Historia albigensium* in *Receuil des Historiens des Gaules et de la France* (henceforth *RHGF*); Peter's letter is on 19: 72. The letter also appears in *Patrologia latina* (henceforth *PL*) 216: 839–40, but here "verbera" is rendered "verba," a misreading that considerably blunts the force (not to say the sense) of the contrast. All translations are my own unless otherwise specified.

5. This may be found among the letters of Pope Innocent III in *RHGF* 19: 570–71; it also appears in *PL* 216: 836, but is mistakenly dated to March 1212. I adopt the dating of *RHGF* because of the mention (in the penultimate line of the letter) of the cleric Thedisius, who was one of the delegates sent by the Council of Lavaur to Pope Innocent (see *RHGF* 19: 76).

6. See, for example, Ambrose (20; bk. 1, ch. 6, line 46); Cassian (237; bk. 1, ch. 1, lines 1–24). Bernard of Clairvaux made frequent use of the imagery, as in the *Sermo de conversione ad clericos* (94). For a summary of the bestiary tradition, see Malaxecheverria.

7. Freud held that a multiplication of phallic symbols signals castration; this is, of course, explicitly called for in the prelates' letter. See especially Hertz ("Medusa's Head").

8. See, for example, the Glossa on Genesis 19 in *Biblia latina cum glossa ordinaria* 1: 55.

9. Vaux-de-Sarnay (99); *RHGF* (19: 76); and *PL* (216: 849–52). Again, Migne's reading is defective: the phrase in question is omitted.

10. The best edition of Guillaume de Puylaurens's chronicle is *Chronica magistri Guillelmi de Podio Laurentii*, ed. Jean Duvernoy (with French translation; henceforth Duvernoy). See also *RHGF* (19: 193–225). Although Guillaume's chronicle was not completed until about 1270, according to Duvernoy the sections narrating the Battle of Muret were written by 1250.

11. Vaissette and de Vic (6: 422) and Étienne Baluze, in his continuation of the *Marca hispanica* of Petrus de Marca, bk. 4, col. 522.

12. Auguste Molinier, in Vaissette 6: 422n2.

13. On the frequent accusation that heretics engaged in homosexual behavior and/or sodomy, see Moore; Goodich; and Boswell (283–86; bibliography in accompanying notes). See also Camille (90–92 and n. 36).

14. The strategy of embodying heresy within a female figure has many paral-

lels in the Albigensian chronicles. I am presently preparing an article on these passages.

15. See esp. Bloch ("Medieval Misogyny" 87–117).

16. 3 Kings 14.24, 15.12, 22.47; 4 Kings 23.7; Job 36.14; Prov. 18.8; Isaiah 3.4; and Hos. 3.13–14.

17. The translation is my own rendering of the Vulgate text.

18. On sodomy as infectious disease, see Solomon in this volume.

19. An interesting parallel from twentieth-century Palestine is cited in Kupferschmidt: "We have begun to see some youngsters who do not care anymore about religion. . . . [T]hey are becoming effeminate, and play up their charms like women" (250). I am indebted to Daniel Monk of the State University of New York at Stony Brook for this reference.

20. Plutarch (5: 193–94). Note also that Plutarch has Octavia, Antony's dutiful Roman wife, dissuade her brother from attacking Antony on her behalf with the remark, "[I]t would be intolerable to have it said of the two greatest commanders in the world that they had involved the Roman people in a civil war, the one out of passion for, the other out of resentment about, a woman" (194). I am indebted to Kate Cooper of Manchester University for directing my attention to this work.

21. *The Chronicle of James I of Aragon* (17–18). At the time of the Battle of Muret, Jaime was in the custody of Simon de Montfort (to whose daughter he had been betrothed); although Jaime allegedly heard the account of Pedro's activities the night before the battle from companions of his father—eyewitnesses to the proceedings—the construction that Jaime put on this event and on his father's reasons for entering the conflict may well reflect attitudes prevalent in Simon's camp. Modern comment on this passage again has not only failed to note but has even extended the polemical dimensions of this charge. O'Callaghan (251) repeats the assertions of the chronicle of Jaime I without comment (thereby, presumably, ratifying it): "Pedro II, who, according to the Chronicle of his son, Jaime I, had spent the preceding evening in amorous pursuits and was too tired to stand for the reading of the gospel in the morning's mass, fell on the field of battle." Chaytor (80) not only accepts that Pedro lost the battle because he spent the night with a woman, but seems to imply that the entire Aragonese army was similarly exhausted by a night of debauchery!

22. I have slightly modified Forster's translation of this passage; I would like to thank David Nirenberg of Rice University for his help with this.

23. The text of the canso appears in Switten (161–62); the politics of the poem are discussed in Siberry (160). It is just possible that a poem like this lies at the bottom of Guillaume's "letters"—although the putative existence of some actual

text in no way detracts from the polemical nature of Guillaume's incorporation of the passage into his chronicle.

24. "And since [Raymond of Toulouse] is my brother-in-law, who's married my sister, and since I've married my other sister to his son, I will go to help him against these miserable people who want to disinherit them" (*Chanson de la croisade albigeoise* vv. 2765–68).

25. *RHGF* (19: 23) and *The Chronicle of San Juan de la Peña* (60). Note that this explanation was embraced by Vaissette and Baluze (see note 11 above).

26. Roquebert did not address the fact that, whatever the depths of Simon's ignorance (and I find it far from credible), Guillaume de Puylaurens and his readers would certainly have been familiar with the conventions of courtly love literature. Guillaume's portrayal of Simon and his own added comment therefore constitute a knowing and explicit rejection of the courtly love ethos, and fall squarely within the tradition of antifeminist rhetoric.

27. For a review of this position, see Abels and Harrison (215–17).

28. Abels and Harrison do not address the question of how the misconception came to dominate historiography; I suggest that it may well be traced to the rhetorical strategies examined in this essay and the one I am preparing.

29. See Bisson ("The Problem of Feudal Monarchy," esp. 463 and 472); Shneidman (1: 3).

30. See Spiegel; Lewis.

31. On possible economic motives for Simon's involvement in the crusade, see Varagnan. I am not particularly convinced by Varagnan's thesis (that Simon was seeking to control a crucial trade route), but the description of the changing economic conditions faced by lords of Simon's type is solid. It is interesting to note that Bisson described the earlier crusades as designed in part to provide a lordly reputation ("Medieval Lordship" 749).

32. These considerations may help account for the centrality of courtly love rhetoric in the "letters" mentioned by Guillaume de Puylaurens. Roquebert was, I believe, absolutely right to point out its prominence in these texts. However, for reasons explained below, I cannot endorse Roquebert's dichotomy, pitting "courtly" southerners against "rustic" northerners.

33. See Statutes 39 and 45 of the Council of Pamiers (Mansi 22: 855–63), for example, and Carbasse (107).

Works Cited

Abels, Richard, and Ellen Harrison. "The Participation of Women in Languedocian Catharism." *Medieval Studies* 41 (1979): 215–51.

Ambrose. *De fide. Opera.* Pt. 8. Ed. Otto Faller. Corpus Scriptorum Ecclesiasticorum Latinorum 78. Vienna: Hoelder-Pichler-Tempsky, 1962.

Belperron, Pierre. *La Croisade contre les albigeois et l'union du Languedoc à la France (1209–1249).* Paris: Plon, 1945.

Bernard of Clairvaux. *Selected Works.* Trans. G. R. Evans. New York: Paulist P, 1987.

Biblia latina cum glossa ordinaria: Facsimile Reprint of the Editio Princeps Adolph Rusch of Strassburg 1480/81. 4 vols. Turnhout [Belgium]: Brepols, 1992.

Bisson, Thomas N. *The Medieval Crown of Aragon: A Short History.* Oxford: Clarendon P, 1986.

———. "Medieval Lordship." *Speculum* 70 (1995): 743–59.

———. "The Problem of Feudal Monarchy: Aragon, Catalonia, and France." *Speculum* 53 (1978): 460–78.

Bloch, R. Howard. "Medieval Misogyny." *Continuity and Change: Political Institutions and Literary Monuments in the Middle Ages: A Symposium.* Ed. Elizabeth Vestergaard. Odense [Denmark]: Odense UP, 1986.

———. *Medieval Misogyny and the Invention of Western Romantic Love.* Chicago: U of Chicago P, 1991.

Borst, Arno. *Die Katharer. Schriften der Monumenta Germaniae Historica* 12. Stuttgart: Hiersemann, 1953.

Boswell, John. *Christianity, Social Tolerance, and Homosexuality: Gay People in Europe from the Beginning of the Christian Era to the Fourteenth Century.* Chicago: U of Chicago P, 1980.

Camille, Michael. *The Gothic Idol: Ideology and Image-Making in Medieval Art.* Cambridge: Cambridge UP, 1989.

Carbasse, Jean-Marie. "La Condition de la femme mariée en Languedoc (XIIIe–XIVe siècles)." *Cahiers de Fanjeaux* 23 (1988): 99–112.

Cassian, John. *De incarnatione domini contra Nestorium. Opera.* Pt. 1. Ed. Michael Petschenig. Corpus Scriptorum Ecclesiasticorum Latinorum 17. Vienna: F. Tempsky, 1888.

Chanson de la croisade albigeoise. Ed. Eugène Martin-Chabot. 3 vols. Paris: Belles-Lettres, 1931–61.

Chaytor, H. J. *A History of Aragon and Catalonia.* New York: AMS P, 1933.

The Chronicle of James I King of Aragon. Trans. John Forster. London: Gregg International, 1968.

Chronicle of San Juan de la Peña. Trans. Lynn H. Nelson. Philadelphia: U Pennsylvania P, 1991.

Corpus scriptorum ecclesiasticorum latinorum. Vienna, 1866–.

Duby, Georges. *The Chivalrous Society.* Trans. Cynthia Postan. Berkeley: U of California P, 1977.

Duvernoy. See Puylaurens.

Evans, Austin P. "The Albigensian Crusade." *A History of the Crusades.* Ed. K. M. Setton. Vol. 2. Philadelphia: U of Pennsylvania P, 1962.

Forster. See *Chronicle of James I.*

Goodich, Michael. *The Unmentionable Vice: Homosexuality in the Later Medieval Period.* Santa Barbara, Calif.: Clio Books, 1979.

Griffe, Elie. *Le Languedoc cathare au temps de la croisade (1209–1229).* Paris: Letouzey et Ané, 1973.

Hamilton, B. *The Albigensian Crusade.* London: Historical Association, 1974.

Hertz, Neil. *The End of the Line: Essays on Psychoanalysis and the Sublime.* New York: Columbia UP, 1985.

Innocent III. *Letters.* In *Patrologia latina.* Vols. 214–17. Ed. J.-P. Migne. Paris: n.p., 1844–64.

Koch, Gottfried. *Frauenfrage und Ketzertum im Mittelalter.* Berlin: Akademie Verlag, 1962.

Kruger, Stephen F. *Dreaming in the Middle Ages.* Cambridge: Cambridge UP, 1992.

Kupferschmidt, Uri M. *The Supreme Muslim Council: Islam under the British Mandate for Palestine.* Leiden: E. J. Brill, 1987.

Levine, Laura. *Men in Women's Clothing: Anti-Theatricality and Effeminization, 1579–1642.* Cambridge: Cambridge UP, 1994.

Lewis, Andrew L. *Royal Succession in Capetian France: Studies on Familial Order and the State.* Cambridge: Cambridge UP, 1981.

Malaxecheverria, I. "L'Hydre et le crocodile médiévaux." *Romance Notes* 21.3 (1981): 376–80.

Mansi, Giovanni Domenico. *Sacrorum conciliorum nova et amplissima collectio.* Vol. 22. Graz: Akademische Druck, 1961.

Marca, Petrus de. *Marca hispanica sive limes hispanicus.* Ed. Étienne Baluze. Paris, 1688.

Moore, R. I. *The Formation of a Persecuting Society: Power and Deviance in Western Europe, 950–1250.* Oxford: Basil Blackwell, 1987.

O'Callaghan, Joseph. *A History of Medieval Spain.* Ithaca: Cornell UP, 1975.

Paladilhe, Dominique. *Simon de Montfort et le drame cathare.* Paris: Librairie académique Perrin, 1988.

Patrologia latina. Ed. J.-P. Migne. Paris: n.p., 1844–64.

Plutarch. *Vitarum parallelarum plutarchi.* Vol. 5. Leipzig: Impensis Golth. Theoph. Georgi., 1776.

Puylaurens, Guillaume de. *Chronica magistri Guillelmi de Podio Laurentii.* Ed. Jean Duvernoy. Paris: Éditions du CNRS, 1976.

Rebhorn, Wayne A. *The Emperor of Men's Minds: Literature and the Renaissance Discourse of Rhetoric.* Ithaca: Cornell UP, 1995.

Recueil des historiens des Gaules et de la France. Vol. 19. Ed. M. Bouquet and L. Delisle. Paris: Académie des inscriptions et belles lettres, 1880.

Roquebert, Michel. *L'Épopée cathare.* 4 vols. Toulouse: Privat, 1970–89.

Shneidman, J. Lee. *The Rise of the Aragonese-Catalan Empire 1200–1350.* New York: New York UP, 1970.

Siberry, Elizabeth. *Criticism of Crusading, 1095–1274.* Oxford: Clarendon P, 1985.

Spiegel, Gabrielle M. "The *Reditus Regni ad Stirpem Karoli Magni:* A New Look." *French Historical Studies* 7 (1971): 145–74.

Strayer, Joseph R. *The Albigensian Crusades.* New York: Dial P, 1971.

Sumption, Jonathan. *The Albigensian Crusade.* London: Faber and Faber, 1978.

Switten, Margaret Louise. *The Cansos of Raimon de Miravel: A Study of Poems and Melodies.* Cambridge, Mass.: Medieval Academy of America, 1985.

Vaissette, Joseph, and Claude de Vic. *Histoire générale de Languedoc.* 16 vols. Toulouse: Privat, 1872–92.

Varagnan, André. "Croisade et marchandise: pourquoi Simon de Montfort a assisté au croisade albigeois." *Annales: ESC* 1 (1946): 209–18.

Vaux-de-Sarnay, Pierre de. *Hystoria albigensis.* Ed. P. Guébin and E. Lyon. 3 vols. Paris: Champion, 1926–39.

Wakefield, Walter L. *Heresy, Crusade and Inquisition in Southern France, 1100–1250.* London: Allen and Unwin, 1974.

Louise O. Vasvári

The Semiotics of Phallic Aggression and Anal Penetration as Male Agonistic Ritual in the *Libro de buen amor*

The semiotics of phallic aggression and anal penetration refers to sex not as a hetero- or homosexual act but as a game of dominance and submission, reinterpreted as insertive and receptive sexual roles, where the male organ becomes a kind of weapon and where the passive position is equated with dishonor, weakness, and feminization. It includes actual physical phallic orosexual aggression, such as rape, as well as its linguistic and paralinguistic displacements, such as insults, verbal dueling, and aggressive humor, all of which have an equal iconic function to humiliate an adversary physically, morally, and psychologically. The real-world use of phallic aggression as a weapon of war has recently been tragically demonstrated in the former Yugoslavia, where an international team investigating the atrocities found that rape was systematically being used against both women and men, with the conscious intention of demoralizing and terrorizing communities (*New York Times,* 9 Jan. 1993). Illustrative of the "humorous" reappropriation by popular culture of this phallic semiotic system are the visual jokes that circulated in photocopy lore during the Gulf War about Sadam Hussein as a sissified Iraq being anally penetrated by the Iwo Jima flag (Dundes, "Interview").[1]

The marginalized language of popular or carnivalesque insults and obscene humor obsessively plays with the language of phallic aggression, a conscious understanding of which can help clarify much medieval humor, as I shall attempt to illustrate here through a discussion of several key episodes in the *Libro de buen amor* [Book of Good Love].[2] It will first be necessary to go into some detail about the semiotic rules of orosexual aggression in order to prepare for the discussion of the specific examples from the *Libro de buen amor,* where I hope to illustrate that taking into account phallic discourse will help to recuperate these and other long misunderstood and underinterpreted passages in the work.[3]

After my introductory theoretical discussion, I shall continue with the the key episode of the agonistic encounter between the Greek scholar and the Roman streetwise trickster, which is a mime of anal rape. Next, I will treat in some detail the episode of the baker girl Cruz as a "screwing" of the protagonist, sacrilegiously represented as a "planked" Christ figure. I will follow with briefer mention of three other episodes, that of the painter Pitas Pajas, who is cuckolded by his virile young apprentice, the anal rape of *Don Carnal* 'Sir Flesh' in the textualized ritual carnival battle of Flesh and Lent, and, finally, of the total humiliation of the protagonist, when he falls prey to predatory virilized wild mountain girls who attack him with the aid of their powerful prosthetic penile attributes.

The Grotesque Grammar of OroSexual Aggression

Ong, in his *Fighting for Life: Contest, Sexuality, and Consciousness,* argues that both aggression and sexuality are affected by *agon* or contest, demonstrating the importance of dominance among the higher species in biological evolution, and that the struggle for dominance is more critical for males in helping them to manage their insecurity and establish their sexual identity.

Historically, among the earliest surviving attestations in material culture of the equation of violence and phallic display are Bronze Age petroglyphs. These endow the generative organ with the power of the spear, the sword, and the ax in their depiction of erections in sexual and aggressive scenes, as well as with other physical activities, such as plowing and sailing, which can be regarded as examples of male power in a wider sense (Vanggaard 102 ff., figs. 9, 10, ll).

Phallic aggression signaled by phallic display is likely to be biologically inherent in human nature and related to the semiotic significance among many mammals of dominance mounting, where the defeated adversary, regardless of sex, is forced to assume the coital position of the female as an indicator of submission.

Support for the biological relatedness of phallic display and aggression comes from clinical observations made of the hypothalamus of apes to determine the neurological basis of penile erection. Results of these experiments, although they are as yet controversial, claim to show the close association in the brain mechanisms linking combative, sexual, and oral behavior, which one researcher has aptly dubbed the "oro-sexual mechanism in aggression" (Neuman [18]; see also LeVay; Vasvári, "Festive Phallic" 105n9). However, because tendencies toward overt aggressive genital activity are even more taboo in our present civilization than erotic activities, we have tended to repress the dominance-submission symbol function of phallic signaling, even as we continue to utilize many displaced rituals of phallic discourse, such as pantomimes of anal rape, including "goosing" someone, "giving him the finger" (or the whole forearm), or, conversely, self-debasement through baring the head, kneeling, or hand kissing.

A cursory review of sexual terms across languages makes it evident that to connote activity-power-dominance, the single most persistent semantic constant is the description of the male organ as a piercing, stabbing, wounding, stinging, pricking instrument with which the active male agent demonstrates his dominance over a subordinate partner through violent sexual penetration, as, in the English nouns *prick, tool, pecker, plunger, shaft, pistol;* Spanish *carajo* (etymologically "a little pointed stake"); and verbs like *to screw, nail, drill, plank, bang, knock (up), ream, hump;* Spanish *clavar;* French *enfiler, enfoncer, clouer, foutre, filer dedans, taper, toquer, chiquer, estamper;* Italian *chiavare;* and so on. All these terms are generally understood as something a male does to a female, although they are equally applicable between an "insertive" and a "receptive" male.

There is semantic evidence that in such sexualized acts of violence what is primary is not sexuality per se but the display of aggressive power. For example, when passivized, verbs of violence, while maintaining their sexual meaning, are, at the same time, subject to relexicalization to connote that the passive subject has been rendered powerless by the active agent through trickery, as in English *to get screwed/shafted/reamed/fucked (over),* that is, to be the subject of any act of aggression, regardless of the sex of the victim or of the aggressor. Italian is particularly rich in such expressions, for example, *essere fottuto/ fregato, averlo in culo, essere inculato/buggerato/infinocchiato* (and cf. the slightly less obvious English *to get a raw deal*), all of which have the double connotation of anal copulation/deceit (Guiraud; Vasvári, "Semiología"; Zlotchew, "Rhetoric,"

"Metáforas"; Grimes). The process of relexicalization is maintained when these verbs are nominalized to denote an active male agent, so that, for example, someone engaged either in sexual activity or prone to cheat or compete unfairly can be referred to as a *shaftsman* or *shaft-artist* who *gives someone the shaft*, or who *slips it to him*.

The same phallic display of dominance can be achieved through gestures, by, for example, the "phallic" hand, where the stiff middle finger (Lat. *digitus virile/impudicus/infamis*) is extended to represent the penis. It can be held up with the bent fingers on either side curled below to represent the testicles, and also with the whole hand and arm rising with a reaming, undulating motion, while the other hand repeatedly strikes on the upper arm muscle (as, for example, in the Sp. gesture known as the *[corte de] manga* or *manganeta*, Port. *manguito*, Braz. *fazer a banana*). Other variants of the gesture include grimaces and accompanying finger gestures, such as biting the thumb (as in the famous scene of adolescent aggressive sexual bravado in *Romeo and Juliet* 1.1), or the eyelid pull (Sp. *ojo*), thumping one's nose derisively while extending the fingers (known as the "Shanghai gesture" or *cocking a snook*) (Wagner; Gilmore and Cuhl; Allen; Driessen).

The male agonistic drive may also seek outlet in rituals as diverse as sexual jokes, insults, graffiti, football, cockfighting, and chess. For example, Silva Tellez (96–97) describes the smearing of walls with graffiti as an aggressive exhibitionist discourse privileged by its anonymity and marginality, as in the free-floating aggression implied in the following graffito: "[Q]uerido estudiante, alégrese que lo que tiene en la mano no tiene en el culo" [Dear student, be glad that what you hold in your hand isn't in (i.e., being shoved up) your ass]. Legman (728–29) describes adolescent insult contests ("playing the dozens") in a black community, in which insulting the wrong person is referred to as "*mounting on* the wrong guys." In a classic article Dundes describes ritual insult exchanges between adolescent Turkish boys, in which the aim is to force one's opponent into a passive role, which may be done indirectly by defining the opponent's mother or sister as wanton sexual receptacles, or directly by casting him as a submissive anus that is forced to take the brunt of the verbal duelist's attacking phallus. In other articles, Dundes, citing evidence of folk speech, shows how American football also represents a form of ritual combat in which males prove their masculinity at the expense of other males by feminizing them ("Into the Endzone," "American Game"). Similarly, for Spanish, Suárez-Orozco cites Argentinean football cheers such as "Hoy a los peruanos les rompemos el culo" [Today we'll rip open the Peruvians' ass], while Goldenberg analyzes games involving stick and balls as phallic dramas serving as an elaborate channeling of male desire. Cockfighting is an even more evident case of male agonistic ritual (Garry; Dundes, "Gallus as Phallus"; Vasvári, "Fowl Play").

Given the potentially neurological orosexual basis of aggression, the equivalence of the semantic fields of sex and violence might well be a semantic universal, as is the additional superposition of the field of alimentary activity, which also involves the penetration of the body by external elements. The mouth and the anus used, respectively, for ingestion and excretion of food, can, at the same time, also serve for sexual "ingestion," their ambiguity and potential interchangeability becoming particularly emphasized (as in, for example, *sausage/weenie* as food, penis, or excrement).

In displays of violence, actual or threatened, oral and anal penetration serve equally well to humiliate an adversary, as in Catullus's "[P]edicabo ego vos et irrumabo" [I'll fuck you in the ass and in your mouth], with which he threatens to ravish two men, who had ostensively accused him of being effeminate because of the delicacy of his verse (Richlin).[4]

In the Middle Ages, in twelfth-century Scandinavian society references to effeminacy in Old Norse eddas were used as a literary motif and cultural symbol. For example, in the *Saga of Gisli*, a wooden effigy of two men engaged in a homosexual act is carved as an insult to the partner depicted in the pathic position (Johnston). Verbal ritual insults included one man saying of another that he had been used by another man, given birth to his children, or that he turns into a woman every ninth night; or he might be called a mare, bitch, or any other kind of female animal. All these insults connoted unmanliness in general, such as cowardice, flight from battlefield, or treachery to kinsmen, derived from the basic sexual meaning that a man who subjects himself to another in sexual affairs will do the same in other respects (Martínez-Pizarro; Sorensen; Gade; Swenson; Clover). The Scandinavian sagas clarify why in medieval Spanish, as well, the most serious insults against males included charges of being *gafo* 'leper'/'sexual pervert,' *sodomita, fudidoencul[o]* 'fucked in the ass,' *traidor* 'traitor,' *puta* 'whore,' *rocina* 'female horse' (Walsh; Madero). Similar verbal assaults today include English *shove/stick it up your ass,* and Spanish *mandarlo tomar por el culo* 'have him get it up the ass' (Legman 141–42; Brandes, *Metaphors* 95–96, "Male" 116).

In a 1931 essay (later suppressed from his "complete works") Borges discussed this active/passive dichotomy, denouncing what he dubbed the *dialéctica fecal* 'fecal dialectic' of the Buenos Aires underworld, where there exists "una especie de veneración para el agente activo — porque lo embromó al compañero" (qtd. in Balderston 29) [a kind of veneration for the active partner — because he put something over on his companion]. The same sexual bravado is eloquently described for Mexican Spanish by Octavio Paz, who says that there are only two possibilities in the ego identity of the Mexican *macho,* who must either inflict actions implied by *chingar* or suffer them himself: "El chingón es el macho, el que abre. La chingada, la hembra, la pasividad pura, inerme ante el exterior" (68–70) [The fucker is the male who opens up (the other). The one fucked (over) is the female, pure passivity, powerless against attack].[5] Compare also the depiction of the ultimate phallic aggression, even beyond rape, in Carlos Fuentes's *La muerte de Artemio Cruz,* where Palomino Molero is killed with his testicles hung down to his thigh and a pole rammed up him from behind. Significantly, the passage is eliminated in the English translation. Compare also American prison subculture, where predatory males (*wolves*) become dependent for self-esteem on their assertion of sexual dominance and on the degradation of their weaker victims (*punks*), whom they taunt with phrases such as "We're gonna take your manhood," "We're gonna make a girl out of you" (Weiss and Friar 238).

The same popular equation of male sex identity and power is depicted with black humor in Tony Kushner's hit play *Angels in America.* In one scene Roy Cohn threatens to destroy his doctor's career, when the latter dares to imply Cohn has AIDS. Cohn explains: "Homosexuals are not men who sleep with other men. Homosexuals are men who in fifteen years of trying cannot get a pissant antidiscrimination bill through City Council. Homosexuals are men who know nobody and who nobody knows. Who have no clout. Does this sound like me, Henry? . . . Roy Cohn is not a homosexual. Roy Cohn is a heterosexual man, Henry, who fucks around with guys" (133).

Male Agonistic Ritual in the *Libro de buen amor*

An understanding of the "grotesque grammar" I have described is particularly necessary for the understanding of what is arguably the key episode of the *Libro,* the dispute conducted in sign language between the Roman country bumpkin and the learned Greek (stanzas 46–63). Considerable scholarly attention has been given to this *exemplum,* because by its strategic placement as the "threshold" story after the introductory material and before the main body of the work and by its theme—what is proper interpretation?—it is meant to provide directions about how to read the whole work.

Various scholars have suggested that the episode is a parody of monastic sign language, that its humor resides in the misunderstanding between the Greek's theological understanding of the signs and the *ribaldo* or "rogue's" streetwise interpretation and reply, or that both the Greek and the Roman are "right" in their interpretations (Fleischmann; De Lope, "Signe"; Seidenspinner-Núñez; Vasvári, "Festive Phallic"). The episode is not likely to be simply a parody of monastic customs, where use of sign language was based on humility and not aggression (Umiker-Sebeok and Sebeok). Notwithstanding Quintilian's belief that gestural language was universally understood (a view of which Juan Ruiz, the author of the *Libro,* was likely also incidentally making fun as much or more than of monastic sign language), in all periods sign language has been systematically used for both high—abstract legal and ecclesiastical—meaning and, in folk culture, for low meaning. The structure of the tale also shows it to be a parodic textualization of the many agonistic dialectical and rhetorical practices of the universities, verbal exchanges conducted orally, containing a heavy residue of primary orality, diffused with academic orality (Ong, *Fighting* 24–27, "Orality"). During *disputationes* 'public examinations' students would joust verbally with fellow students or a master, their aim being to come out "on top."

In the context of the horizon of expectations of the text's original reception, it is hard to conclude that the Roman rogue didn't come out "on top" in the agonistic dispute. The *ribaldo* as a folk character represents all that is considered "low," aggressively sexual and scatological, and he is a mocker of reason, authority, and abstract language. The very name *ribaldo* 'scoundrel'/'cad'/'charlatan,' as well as its synonyms, such as *arlote,* have associations not only with trickery and blasphemy, but also with sex and prostitution (Frago García 262–64; Webber). The rogue is the power of the corporeal at its most grotesque, which seeks to debase all higher principles. It is his folkloric role to ridicule his antagonist by the more aggressive

power of his more debased oral-anal bodily cycle of alimentation, defeca-
tion, and sexual ingestion. Usually depicted as short, dark, and hairy but
with a bald pate, the rogue, like his predecessor the Latin *mimus calvus* 'bald
mime,' becomes a kind of personified talking phallus, with his bald head
as the *glans penis* (Bakhtin 20; Camporesi 128). The technique of rogues,
whether Marcolf, Till Eulenspiegel, Aesop, or Panurge, consists of playing with words and with gestures, in emptying them of their content and
lowering everything to the sexual or scatological level, replying to established wisdom with sardonic practical truths, mocking and outwitting with
secular blasphemy, and in the process not only besting the adversary but
also of enjoying the other's realization that he has been "shafted."

In the episode it is described in detail how, when in the supposedly theological debate the learned Greek lifts one finger to signify that there is one
God, he is understood by the *ribaldo* as threatening to poke out the latter's
eye. The *ribaldo* therefore feels compelled to reply with a three-fingered
threatening gesture, with extended middle finger and contracted fingers on
either side, a stock gesture to represent the penis and two testicles. With
this and with the following gesture, where the rogue menaces with his
closed fist ("mostró puño cerrado"), he is not *only* threatening to smash up
the learned Greek's face but is *also* flashing his adversary two paralinguistic
threats of anal rape, which, as I discussed in the context of twelfth-century
Scandinavian literature, was semantically equivalent to one of the most
serious medieval ritual insults, taunting someone as being *fodido (en culo)*
'fucked (in the ass).'

There is also ample documentation from the fourteenth and fifteenth centuries of, for example, the use of the *digitus virilis* (cf. Ger. *elfte/steife Finger* 'the eleventh/stiff finger') with this meaning in carnivalesque genres
(Aigremont 328; Catholy 247). Compare the visual pun in *The Rutland
Psalter* (c. 1260), apparently the manuscript illustrator's suggestion as to
what the learned Latin scribe can do with his pen, where on one page the
letter *p* of Latin *conspectu* 'penetrate visually' is elongated into the margin so that the tail of the letter ends up in the anus of a prostrate fish-man
by joining up with the arrow shot by an exotic archer (Camille 21, ill. 6).
Compare also, in contemporary American culture, where "giving someone the finger" is still an obscene gesture, roughly equivalent to "shove it
up your ass," as is the related gesture of the clenched fist. Although the
latter is today often interpreted as a positive political gesture ("up with

the people"), in their origin *all* expletives with the particle "up" are a sign of threatened rape, as becomes evident in other expressions syntactically equivalent to "up with the people," such as "up the establishment" and "up your ass," the former accompanied by a raised fist and the latter by raising the middle finger ([Rancoeur]-Laferrière 57–58; Morris 160). Compare the Russian gesture of the arm thrust out with fist, roughly translatable as "up yours," and also the raised thumb that, while in Western Europe and the Americas a signal of approval, is used in Greece as a vulgar taunt (*katsa pano* "sit on this"). Compare also the signs for the Greek fist-phallus and finger-phallus, the latter known as *kolodakhtylo* 'the finger for the ass,' with which one can accuse another male of being *poustis* 'pathic' (Petropoulou; Collett; Bremmer and Roodenburg; Driessen; Gundersheimer).

Nor is it surprising that the rogue would understand the Greek's threat to stick his finger in his eye as a stock sexual insult to which he must respond in kind, given that in agonistic folk genres, such as riddles, the eye regularly stands for either the vulva or the anal orifice, based on fanciful analogies of shape, mucosity, and pilosity (cf. standard Sp. *ojo del culo* 'asshole,' Eng. *brown eye* 'anus' [in reference to anal copulation]). Further, blinding (as in the case of Oedipus's self-mutilation) is a recognizable symbol of castration. Thus, to stick the index finger brusquely toward another man's eye is to threaten him with rape, a gesture rediscovered by surrealism in the famous scene of the raped eye in Buñuel's *Le chien andalou*.

The *ribaldo*, in the first part of the story at least, talks only with signs, which allows him even more extreme linguistic play because gestures as a second-order semiotic system are even *more* subject to ambiguity than is language. Gestures also allow the rogue—and the *juglar* 'jongleur,' who we must remember is the performer of the joke—to make ample use of ostentatious kinetic and paralinguistic features, which cannot be successfully translated into the format required by the orthographic exigencies of the written page but must be heard and seen, and are, hence, now forever lost to us, although partially retrievable from the context. For example, the raised finger might have been accompanied by a subtle—or not so subtle— rotation of the forearm and a slight upward thrust (*la manga*), and maybe a smirk and an arched eyebrow.

The *ribaldo* uses his whole body as *penis cum glandis* to act out the insult to his adversary. None of his gestures are spontaneous but are standard signs learned like a vocabulary and executed as part of a ritualized competitive interaction—they articulate the dominant notion of masculinity, which is by definition competitive. The real fool is the Greek doctor who doesn't understand the polysemic nature of sign systems and hence of the whole debate as scholarly theological discussion versus a ritual insult exchange, which depends on the player's skill in selecting appropriate retorts to provocative insults, with the goal to force his opponent into the female position. In such ritual exchanges failure to respond constitutes a form of surrender, so that if one cannot retort to a phallic insult, he essentially admits that he is reduced to the female receptive role. That is, the learned Greek doctor, and by extension all of high culture, was fucked over, and he didn't even know it!

In contrast to the *ribaldo* episode, the tale of the protagonist's misadventures with the baker girl Cruz and the roguish go-between Ferrán García, is one which virtually all scholars have had to admit to being obscene, even if they didn't "get" some of it (well, no, there *was* one who claimed it was all a serious religious allegory). The episode (stanzas 112–21) relates how the protagonist "Juan Ruiz" tries to arrange a tryst with an inappropriately lower-class baker girl, but his friend, whom he had unwisely used as the go-between, ends up stealing the girl. As the author puts it: "The conycatcher got to eat the meat and the sweet roll and left me chewing my own cud." "Eating" *carne* 'meat'/'flesh' and *pan dulce* 'sweet roll' both connote the female organ, with *pan* also sacrilegiously alluding to the ingestion of the communion wafer, while *rumiar* 'chew'/'ruminate' and here clearly also "masturbate" continues the sacrilegious reference to the ingestion of the host at the same that that it plays on the medieval clerical practice of *ruminatio,* the psychic integration of memorized sacred texts by constant repetition (Morlaàs; Riché 136). At the end of the Cruz story the protagonist gets his revenge, by getting the last word "in" with the displaced tool of his *logos* to recount in an obscene rhyme the story of his humiliating *cruciar* 'planking' caused by the girl with the suspiciously phallic name of Cruz.[6]

The Cruz episode, with its sexualization of the semantic field of bread making, eating, and ingestion, and of cony hunting and eating, represents the complete melding of violence and oro-sexuality. To give a good "flavor" of how the *pan dulce* joke would have been received by Juan Ruiz's audience, we can compare still surviving nonverbal jokes about stereotypically lascivious *panaderos* in contemporary folk culture, as in the New Mexican Spanish riddle: "¡Adivina cómo [el panadero] hace los 'donus'!"

[Guess how the baker makes doughnuts?], with the punchline, expected
to be delivered with the same appropriate kinetic arm movement that the
juglar might have used to mime the rogue's body language (González).

Some years ago ("Semiología"), I tried to show that the whole Cruz episode is a multileveled sacrilegious sacred parody, centered on the polyse-
mous syntagm *súpome el clavo echar* 'he knew how to drive in the nail'/'he
really screwed me good.' On the parodied allegorical level the episode is
a mock *Imitatio Christi*, where the protagonist's cuckolding by his *compañero* 'buddy'/'companion' and his sexual suffering is equated to Christ's
mocking and martyrdom on the cross. The crucifixion was an easy target
for sexual double entendres in medieval culture, given that the feminized
sexual representation of Christ's suffering was a common verbal and visual
motif in both high and low culture, playing on the fact that the sexual component of the Crucifixion is subsumed under the term "passion," which can
connote both suffering and sexuality. Bakhtin (320) argued that in popular
culture the traditional Corpus Christi procession had a clearly expressed
carnivalesque character with a prevailing bodily note and that the popular marketplace aspect of the feast was a parody of the church ritual of
the Corpus Christi. During the same period, however, devout worshipers
would in all seriousness mutilate themselves out of religious fervor, driving nails into their bodies or whipping and hanging themselves in imitation
of the crucifixion, believing that the blood that flowed from their bodies
mingled with the blood of Christ's wounds (Bynum 162). Similarly, the
sacred language of mysticism also emphasized the depiction of the passive, humiliated flesh of the crucified or "planked" Christ on the cross,
where he is both verbally mocked and physically perforated by nails, his
side is opened by a spear, and his head crowned with sharp thorns. It is
no coincidence that the term *planking*, a standard form of execution that
much antedates Christianity, also connotes violent sexual penetration. In
mystical language Christ was also described in feminized terms as having
gestated and given birth on the "hard marriage bed of the Cross" to the
Church through his bleeding uterine-like wound, whose heart blood was
equated with the life-giving force of menstruation (Boullet 966; Guldan
ill. 27; Bynum ill. 4; Wirth ills. 51, 52; Debroise et al.).

It would have been inevitable that less well-intentioned audiences would
have been sensitive to the extreme sexual suggestiveness of such language.[7]
A similar debased representation of Christ's crucified body becomes the

crux of the joke in several French *fabliaux* on the cuckolded husband theme, as in *Le Prestre crucifié*, where a husband, by profession a carver of crucifixes, goes off to market to sell an enormous crucifix, which he carries on his back, that is, he "carries his cross/sign of his cuckoldry" while his wife is at home sporting with her lover (Montaiglon 194–97).[8]

While the "cross" Juan Ruiz has to bear–losing a girl of low class and lower morals to a pimp—is clearly akin to that of the cuckolded crucifix carver, the play on words is even more overdetermined because the girl herself is called *Cruz* 'Cross,' in folk religions the emblem of male reproductive power, which Christianity, after trying vainly to prohibit, later coopted by adapting as a sign of salvation (Gamble 318–34; Michalski 436; De Lope, "Signe"). It, therefore, becomes evident that the Cruz episode can only be fully understood on the debased corporeal meaning of the term, *clavo* 'nail'/'penis' and *echar el clavo* 'to drive in the nail'/'to copulate'/'to trick.'[9] In spite of the overwhelming documentation attesting to the sexual suggestiveness of the key term *echar el clavo*, Joset has called me to task for having had the temerity to claim that *echar el clavo* in the context of the Cruz episode could mean anything more than simply "deceive" when "it is exactly the opposite that happens to the unfortunate protagonist, who was not able to 'drive in his nail' and, unless he is accused of being a homosexual, he would not have much appreciated 'the nail' of the messenger" (*Nuevas* 70–71; translation mine). Joset fails to grasp that the point is precisely that the wily Ferrán García as go-between achieved a kind of double-shafting, where by "screwing" the baker girl, he simultaneously also managed to "screw" or "shaft" the protagonist. As we saw in the *ribaldo* episode, this is precisely the traditional duty of rogues (see further my "Don Hurón"). Also, as Conlon pointed out in relation to Don Juan, the *burlador* is always linked in a basic way with all the men he victimizes through his sexual conquest of his victim's women. That the woman remains merely as object in the between-mate culture is clearly all the more suggestive in the *Crux* episode, where the seducer is repeatedly characterized as the dupe's close *compañero [de la cucaña]*, a term which it would be appropriate to translate colloquially as "asshole buddy," given that *compañeros/compañones* also denote the testicles (seen as "inseparable companions of the *ego*"), and given the phallic connotations of *cucaña* '(may)pole.' In addition, *compañero* is made even more suggestive by the fact that it has embedded within it the the term *pan*, and all its sexual allusiveness (De Lope, "Signe" 80–81).[10]

The impact on the *Libro*'s audience of the religious-erotic connotative symmetries between sexual nailing and Christ's crucifixion in the Cruz episode can perhaps be better appreciated by the comparison with the impact on modern Hispanic audiences of the rewriting of the Crucifixion as homosexual gang rape by René Marqués in his *La mirada* [The Gaze]. The first unexpurgated edition of this work was published in 1976, two years after Spanish censors had refused to publish it with the inclusion of the objectionable passage, where Marqués details the precise symmetries between the "sexual nailing" of the willing first-person protagonist and Christ's Crucifixion in the eleventh station of the *Via Crucis*.[11]

The *fabliau* of the cuckolded painter Pitas Pajas (stanzas 474–85) inevitably plays on the same polysemy of copulation and deception that we have seen in the Cruz episode, but it is even more inventive because, like the story of the *ribaldo*, it manages to do so in more than one semiological register. Pitas Pajas, the unfortunate merchant and "pintor de Bretaña" [painter from Brittany] paints a lamb under his wife's bellybutton to keep her virtue intact while he goes off on a business trip. The lamb gets erased by consistent heavy rubbing by Pitas's virile young apprentice, who, when he hears Pitas Pajas is about to return, quickly substitutes a picture of a full-horned ram, an obvious symbol of his duped master's cuckoldry. Had the painter's younger rival found his way into the *ribaldo* story, he could have contented himself with flashing the appropriate finger gesture to let the older man know of his dishonor. But since this tale is more complex, with the "traces of the other man" motif grafted on to the basic cuckolded merchant story line, the trickster must, in addition, leave material signs of his agency and of his dupe's dishonor. The umbilical fresco painted by Pitas's rival functions as an aggressive exhibitionist discourse, with the apprentice functioning as a kind of graffiti artist, who, like the anonymous Kilroy, leaves his mark everywhere. Because the younger more virile man is also a painter, hence also the dupe's professional rival, he is offered the narrative opportunity to "screw" poor Pitas Pajas with his appropriate "tool," the more effective (brush)strokes he is able to administer to Pitas's willing wife.[12] Poor Pitas Pajas's cuckoldry is *also* signaled onomastically through his acoustically and semantically transparent name, which connotes "fool"/"impotent"/"masturbator," as in expressions like *soplapijas* 'cocksucker,' *pitoflojo* 'limpcock,' both connoting lack of adequate virility.

Nor does Pitas Pajas's other profession as *mercader* 'businessman' allow him any other folkloric role but that of the impotent, weakling husband, as we can see in a Sephardic wedding song collected in Tetuán, where a young wife complains that her mother married her to a "mercader flamengo . . . que tiene las patas largas" [Flemish merchant who has enormous feet] and only wants to sleep on their wedding night, where the groom's overlarge feet stand for his lack of sexual "standing" power (Cohen and Anahory-Librowitz).

The verses that end the Pitas Pajas story, couched in the erotic cony hunt terminology of the Cruz story, are equally applicable as a moral to both tales, claiming, in effect, that the cuckolding of both protagonists was their own doing because they were not "up" to finishing the job for themselves.

In a previous study, I discussed the first part of the mock epic alimentary battle of Flesh and Lent in the *Libro* (stanzas 1067–1314), fought with both live animals and prepared meats and ludicrous if appropriate weapons like pots and platters. Central to the carnivalesque verbal games of the episode is the creation of an antilanguage, whose basic form is the relexicalization or semantic reinterpretation of central metaphors of the three major symbolic levels of carnival: food, sex, and violence, which I dubbed the "gastro-genital" level (Vasvári, "Gastro-genital"). As we have already seen in the Cruz episode, these semantic fields can exist simultaneously, superimposed, alternating, or intermingled with one another. For example, edible soldiers of the two armies of Flesh and Lent, such as the *gruesso tocino* 'fatty bacon,' *pixota* 'hake,' *puerco* 'piggy,' *ostra* 'oyster,' *liebre* 'hare,' *conejo* 'cony,' and others, function simultaneously in three semantic fields: violence, gastronomy, and sexuality, as respectively combatants or cadavers (depending on the stage of the battle), prepared foods and/or live animals, and sex organs of one or the other sex. In this episode of "carnival as rape" the violent sexual relexicalization revolves around the key terms *luchar/lidiar* 'do battle'/'copulate,' and *matar* 'kill'/'copulate'/'rape.' Male sharks "kill" female partridges and castrate capons, while the acoustically phallic *pixota* 'hake' (recalling *pija* 'penis') threatens the *puerco* 'piggy'/'vulva' with rape (on *puerco* as "vulva," see Vasvári, "Múltiple transparencia"). Victory in Carnival consists in the act of "stuffing" the enemy like a carnival sausage, preferably anally.[13] The most important of Don Carnal's vassals in the *Libro* is the personified *Don Jueves Lardero* 'Fat Thursday,' but whose name also suggests "Ritual Carnival Buggerer," as in the French carnival terms *larder* 'to stuff strips of fatback into a piece of meat with a wide needle'/'to copulate,' and, hence, *lardeur* 'active homosexual.'[14]

Calendar rites make it obligatory for *Don Carnal* 'Sir Flesh' to be vanquished in the first round of the battle with Lent. For his further derision, he is placed in singular combat with a series of phallic fish and vegetables because anal rape, seen as the worst possible form of humiliation, was therefore, naturally a popular carnival topic. In the first round of battle Carnal is anally attacked by a series of fishy and leguminous troops, all in the service of *Doña Cuaresma* 'Lady Lent' (whose role in carnival is, however, always played by a man in drag). As is to be expected, the Lenten troops are subject to the same rules for relexicalization that served to eroticize Carnal's army. The eel figures prominently in the episode, along with lobsters, octopus, and crabs, all of which, because of the multiplicity of their members are reinterpreted as polyphallic (Bowen). In addition, both the eel and the crab were associated with sodomy because they hide in the mud ("anal excrement") and because they can function both in water and on land.[15] The eel was further characterized by its ability to slip out of the fingers of the person who grasps it and, alternately, to slip easily into any opening it wants.

Poor Carnal is also anally attacked by a leek, a plant commonly cultivated as an aphrodisiac in medieval Europe for its supposed ability to produce semen. This was a belief based on phallic aspect of the leek, with its elongated shape and white "head" and green, that is, lusty, "tail," and hard texture when fresh, which, however, quickly goes limp when heated. The agonistic phallic symbolism of leeks becomes even more obvious in the cult of the giant leek, where cultivating leeks is accompanied by intense passion and male rivalry among the almost exclusively male competitors, with growers sitting up all night to protect their leeks from marauders, and washing, polishing, grooming, shampooing, and plaiting the hairs of their leeks for display (Kirkup).[16]

Carnal's ritual punishment spectacularizes his whole body, so as to degrade it within the spatialized social categories of high/low-male/female, to the site of shame for both sexes, the space of the feminine. His pathic humiliation is considered the just reward for his phallic bravado before the beginning of the battle. When in her declaration of war Cuaresma had complained that Carnal had raped her lands, "vertiendo mucha sangre" [shedding much blood], the greasy Jueves Lardero was the first of

Carnal's vassals to counterchallenge to rape her once again. The *liebre*, another of Carnal's phallic vassals, tops Lardero's boast, by threatening to infect Cuaresma with venereal disease. Carnal, in his own parodic letter of counterchallenge to Cuaresma, signed in blood, dubs her "flaca, vil e sarnosa" [scrawny, ugly, and mangy (as a result of venereal disease)], and he vows to give her a "bloodletting" and to have her "cuero maduro" [old hide], an insult to her old, wrinkled, and diseased *pudendum*.

Carnal's utter humiliation in the first round of battle through anal "force-feeding" of Lenten foods is turned right side up, as it were, when during his subsequent imprisonment, a friar, in a parody of the discourse of penitentials, imposes an appropriate ascetic discipline on him of semistarvation on a Lenten diet. The discipline is meant for him to atone for his fleshy sins by mortifying the "flesh" in a very practical way. The connection is made very clear when he is forced also to abstain from "probar la lucha" (stanza 1164) [engaging in copulation]. By virtue of his calendar function, Carnal is able to regain his fleshy strength in spite of his meager Lenten diet, and he soon flees his imprisonment. The bloody imagery continues in his stay with a Jewish ritual slaughterer.[17] Later, in his triumphant return after Lent as *roi de fête*, accompanied by his alter ego, Don Amor, Carnal himself will be described as a butcher/slaughterer/rapist covered with skins and hides, with a bloody rag around his waist, all suggestive of bloody tokens of past sexual conquests. He is now ready to *desollar* 'flay'/'skin'/'fleece' any animal in sight, where *desollar* has the same sexual connotation as English *skin the live rabbit* or as Calisto's vulgar remark to Melibea in *Celestina* about having to pluck a chicken before one eats it.

There remains one form of humiliation *still* more debasing to Juan Ruiz and to any male than violation by another male, and that is to be violated by a woman. Since sexual violence, particularly rape is normally assumed to be an offense perpetrated by males on females, its male victims are seen as doubly humiliated in that by being physically penetrated they are also reduced to the level of "female" passivity and receptivity. Thus, the final level of humiliation is for the male to be raped by a female, and this is precisely what awaits the protagonist as pilgrim in the *sierra*, where he falls prey to predatory virilized females who appropriate male gender roles and disguises, along with powerful—if prosthetic—penile attributes (stanzas 950–1042).

The *Libro* is in large part a hilarious recounting of the protagonist's and his various alter egos' sexual failures with all classes of women, from the baker girl Cruz that we have examined to nuns, a Moorish girl, and even an ugly old woman.[18] But the protagonist has even worse luck with the burly *serranas* 'mountain girls' who pursue him, where it is precisely the virilization of these women and the carnivalesque topsy-turvy sexual power relationship that this implies that are at the core of the hilarity of these episodes. Variants of the protagonist's misadventures repeat themselves with three *serranas*, of which I can only briefly mention a few salient details.[19] The protagonist-pilgrim's many moments of sexual humiliation in the mountains include being accosted by an enormous bestial *serrana*, Alda, whose virility is signaled by her black beard, wide, black, hairy neck, and her pinky, which is bigger than the pilgrim's own middle finger. Given that in medieval physiognomies as well as in popular tradition extreme hairiness, the girth of the neck, and the size of fingers were commonly thought to be reliable indications of penis size (recall the discussion above about the middle finger as *digitus virilis*), Alda did not even have to engage in an actual sexual encounter with the protagonist for her to prove that she was the better endowed.[20]

While there is no actual sexual contact between Alda and the protagonist, he does find himself forced to do the sexual bidding of two other transgendered (i.e., manly but apparently heterosexual) dominatrix *serranas*, *La Chata* 'Snub-nose'/'Pussy' and *Gadea*, where both names are also variants of Saint Agatha, in turn, a christianization of the popular *Lou Gat* 'Cat Saint' (and the female as fearful *vagina dentata*), whose feast day of 5 February is still an occasion for carnivalesque rites or reversal where women rule and men obey. Juan Ruiz is drubbed behind the ear by Gadea with her enormous phallic staff, a kind of parodic reverse Incarnation, which according to some theological interpretations occurred through the ear canal. La Chata likewise beats the unfortunate pilgrim with her enormous phallic staff and carries him off on her back as if he were an empty *çurrón* 'leather shepherd's pouch.' The empty pouch (like the bagpipes in another semantic register), because it is made of hide and easily inflated or deflated, is a standard carnivalesque sign for the scrotum. At the same time in medical discourse the empty pouch is a reference to orchidectomy, a form of castration of domestic animals but also of diseased human male organs through the surgical excision of the testicles from the scrotum, which is not itself removed but remains as a little empty bag (Spink and Lewis ch. 69).

We have seen that in the *Libro de buen amor* the Greek scholar is fucked by the fickle finger of fate, Juan Ruiz as protagonist is planked by a pimp, Pitas Pajas's picture is painted by a pricklier paintbrush, Don Carnal is stuffed by a leek with a frisky green tail, and the protagonist as pilgrim in the *sierra* encounters great difficulties in scaling that most fearful mountain, the *mons Veneris*. In phallic discourse — whether serious or festive — adult male victims placed in a pathic role are much more humiliated than females would be in an equivalent role, as they have become the object of sexual role inversion. In the folk concept of *machismo*, which place high value on "manliness" defined as a hypermasculine masquerade, the essence of virility resides in the testicles, as illustrated, for example, by the Spanish expressions *tener cojones / ser cojonudo / un hombre de cojones* (Pitt-Rivers; Ingham; C. Nelson; Brandes, *Metaphors;* Carrier, *De los otros;* Gilmore and Cuhl). A "real man" is constantly required to prove his masculine identity and to protect himself from potential feminization by obsessively performing agonistic games of power by subjecting someone else to sissificaton. Macho posturing is accompanied by a generally professed disgust of homosexuality, with the term applied only to those who play the anal recepetive sex role in a homosexual encounter, while the active partner does not undergo identity transformation (Murray; Almaguer; Lancester; Piedra). For example, a man might stealthily go up behind a regular drinking companion at the bar and grab his testicles from behind, or he may approach a group on a street corner or in a bar and grab the buttocks or even penis of someone in the group to suggest that he wants to "make" him, in both cases to the general amusement of all present. The *macho* performer might also displace the scoring to the verbal level by, for example, greeting a friend named Martín with: "Hola, Martín Cholano," where the "straight" spelling hides the onomastic joke, which is orally "opened up," where it is pronounced as "hincho el ano" [I swell up/stuff your ass].[21]

Any man who doesn't know how to play the aggression game is judged lacking in masculinity and therefore to be effeminate (or *manso* 'timid'/ 'weak'/'henpecked'/'impotent'), regardless of his actual sexual orientation. We have seen that this is the case of the Juan Ruiz persona, who is symbolically castrated by his *compañero,* a term synonymous with being *cojonudo,* and by the time a *serrana* gets through with him, he ends up symbolically reduced to a limp empty scrotum that she can throw over her shoulder.

Notes

I want to thank George Greenia, editor of *La corónica*, for permission to reprint sections of an earlier article (Vasvári, "Phallic"), which appeared in vol. 22.2 (1994), where it was awarded the John K. Walsh Prize for Best Article for 1994.

1. Cf. Piedra on the equivalence of "war and bed games" of colonization.

2. For the best English translation, see Willis; the most accessible Spanish editions are Joset and Blecua.

3. For similar rereadings in modern popular cultural texts, cf. Gabbard on jazz and Paul on Chaplin comedies (where Charlie is literally made "the butt" in sight gags).

4. Cf. also Parker; and for Greek, Keuls; and Bremmer.

5. Cf. the most recent studies on Mexican hypermachismo and homosexuality by Carrier; also Balderston and Guy (118–32).

6. Cf. Laferrière, "Writing Perversion."

7. For an unequivocally intentionally debasing misreadings of the supposed strictly allegorical understanding of such mystical terminology, see the graphic example in the Fitzpayn Book of Hours (c. 1300), where the planked Christ in an illustrated capital is juxtaposed in the margin by a cartoon of a little squirrel connoting the male organ, burrowing a hole in the vellum page, a perverse and obscene parody parallel to his adjacent wound (Camille 38–41 and ill. 17). Cf. Vasvári, "Tale of Taillying," on small furry animals as sexual organs.

8. And the same theme in *Le Prestre teint* and *Connebert* (Livingston 255–69; 29–32).

9. In addition to my earlier documentation in "Semiología," compare also contemporary Cuban slang *clavar*, male penetration of the female, and the American-Spanish dialect Pachuco *steal, rip off, screw, fuck, lay;* Ger. */an/nageln, Nagel;* as well as the exact parallel of *echar el clavo* in Fr. *river son clou* 'rivet' / 'clinch' / 'nail' / 'screw,' where *rivette* is also 'prostitute' / 'pathic homosexual' (Huguet; Polkinshorn; Spalding).

10. Joset, who not only seems unable to deal with any potential homoerotic implications of the Cruz episode but even with suggestion of its sexual playfulness, further criticized me for insufficiently rigorous and serious documentation of connotative language, claiming that it is necessary to stay only with the meaning "deceive" for *echar el clavo,* because it is "well attested." This is a specious argument, one regularly utilized to avoid having to accept heterodox rereadings of canonized authors who have become the object of uncritical obeisance. The "attestation" on which Joset would insist is impossible, given the suppression, in the name of morality or of good taste, of obscene and suggestive language

in dictionaries, and the falsification and bowdlerization, both conscious and un-conscious, and outright destruction of offensive texts in almost all periods. What Whinnom said of one genre applies to many: "[T]he history of courtly love, as well as that of love poetry of the *cancionero* songbooks, has been the history of fal-sification and suppression of inconvenient data" (28; translation mine). Because of the systematic expurgation of the history of sexuality, documentation must often be sought in other languages, in noncanonized oral and dialectal forms, and in later attestations. In the case of *clavo/echar, clavo*, documentation from all these sources is so rich, and the context in which it occurs in the *Libro* is so sug-gestive, that if Joset wants to claim the validity of his willfully castrated reading, it is he who has the responsibility of disproving the weight of evidence against it.

11. The thieves on the right and left sides of the crucified Christ become, in Marqués's story, hippie guitarists whose penises are nails that the protagonist is forced to grasp so that his arms are extended in the form of a cross. The protago-nist is figuratively nailed to the cross by being anally penetrated by his friend Julito, who will later boast "te clavé en la carcel" [I screwed you in jail]. To com-plete the crucifixion scene, another young man frenetically nails his small pointed "lance" between the crucified victim's nipple and right side, while masturbating prison guards with their pants around their ankles play the voyeuristic role of the Roman soldiers. The protagonist's "passion" ends "between pleasure and pain" in the dying anguish of sexual climax: "bautizado con el líquido sagrado, como un llanto también trágico y final, definitivo" [baptized with the sacred liquid, as with tears, also tragic and final, definitive]. In a later hallucinatory scene of castration the protagonist is kidnapped for ransom and his severed testicles are sent to his mother and later carried around by his homosexual lover in a black bag or *bolso* (*bolsa* is Spanish slang for testicles [Hortas; Cruz-Malavé 143–44]). The combination of travesty, profanation, sacrilege, and sexual degradation that can be achieved by the linguistic games in texts as temporally distant from one another as the *Libro de buen amor* and *La mirada* is nevertheless a common one. Compare the same combination of sexual degradation and religion in Bernard Malamud's *Pictures of Fidelman*, where Arthur, a Jew formerly sexually enslaved by the Catholic *dominatrix* Annamaria Oliovino, manages to extract his revenge on her only when he returns disguised as a priest, where by another reenactment of the Crucifixion, "pumping slowly, he nailed her to the cross."

12. Recall that the Lat. slang term *penicillus* 'little penis,' also the etymology of Eng. *pencil*, also meant "paintbrush"; and compare the related sexual connota-tion of writing as "penetrating stone or skin," as in Eng. *to score*, either "to make a permanent mark on a clean surface" or "succeed in copulating with someone."

13. Cf. the same concept in the English curse "stuff it up your . . . ," and in French *se la farcir* 'to stuff her,' i.e., "to copulate with a woman."

14. Cf. the fifteenth-century Fr. carnivalesque *sottie des lardeurs* in Ida Nelson.

15. Compare the Eng. expression AC/DC, albeit in a different semantic field.

16. Note the similarity with male grooming of cocks for cockfight competitions (Dundes "Gallus").

17. On the folk fantasy of the *shochet* 'ritual slaughterer' as rapist, see Gilman 346n35.

18. On which see Vasvári, "Chica cosa."

19. See further Vasvári, "Peregrinaciones"; the aggressive female sexuality in carnival in Bettelheim.

20. Cf. the similar features of the *Quijote*'s Aldonza Lorenzo, recently outed as butch by Gossy.

21. Cf. Eng. sexual onomastic jokes like *Eileen Back*, *Dick Hertz*, *Seymour Hare* (Rennick).

Works Cited

Aigremont [Siegmar Baron von Schultze-Gallera]. "Beiträge zur Hand- und Finger-symbolik und Erotik." *Anthropophyteia* 10 (1913): 314–29.

Allen, Keith. "Some English Terms of Insult Invoking Sex Organs: Evidence of a Pragmatic Driver for Semantics." *Meaning and Prototypes: Studies in Linguistic Categorization*. Ed. Savas L. Tsohatzidis. London: Routledge, 1990. 159–94.

Almaguer, Tomás. "Chicano Men: A Cartography of Homosexual Identity and Behavior." *The Lesbian and Gay Studies Reader*. Ed. Henry Abelove et al. New York: Routledge, 1993. 255–74.

Bakhtin, Mikhail. *Rabelais and His World*. Trans. Hélène Iswolsky. Cambridge, Mass.: MIT P, 1968.

Balderston, Daniel. "The 'Fecal Dialectic': Homosexual Panic and the Origin of Writing in Borges." Bergmann and Smith 29–45.

Balderston, Daniel, and Donna J. Guy. *Sex and Sexuality in Latin America*. New York: New York UP, 1997.

Bergmann, Emilie L., and Paul Julian Smith, eds. *¿Entiendes?: Queer Readings, Hispanic Writings*. Durham, N.C.: Duke UP, 1995.

Bettelheim, Judith. "Ethnicity, Gender, and Power: Carnival in Santiago de Cuba." *Negotiating Performance*. Ed. Diana Taylor and Juan Villegas. Durham, N.C.: Duke UP, 1994. 176–212.

Blecua, Alberto, ed. *Libro de buen amor*. By Juan Ruiz. Madrid: Cátedra, 1992.

Boullet, Jean. *Symbolisme sexuel dans les traditions populaires*. Paris: Jean-Jacques Pauvert, 1961.

Bowen, Barbara. "Lenten Eels and Carnival Sausages." *L'Esprit créateur* 21.1 (1981): 12–25.

Brandes, Stanley. "Male Sexual Ideology in an Andalusian Town." *Sexual Meanings: The Cultural Construction of Gender and Sexuality.* Ed. Sherry B. Ortner and Harriet Whitehead. Cambridge, Mass.: Harvard UP, 1981. 216–39.

———. *Metaphors of Masculinity: Sex and Status in Andalusian Folklore.* Philadelphia: U of Pennsylvania P, 1980.

Bremmer, Jan. "Greek Pederasty and Modern Homosexuality." *From Sappho to De Sade: Moments in the History of Sexuality.* Ed. Jan Bremmer. London: Routledge, 1989. 1–14.

Bremmer, Jan, and Herman Roodenburg, eds. *A Cultural History of Gesture.* New York: Columbia UP, 1991.

Bynum, Caroline Walker. "The Female Body and Religious Practice in the Late Middle Ages." *Fragments for a History of the Human Body.* Ed. Michel Feher. New York: Urzone; Cambridge, Mass.: Harvard UP, 1989. 160–219.

Camille, Michael. *Image on the Edge: The Margins of Medieval Art.* Cambridge, Mass.: Harvard UP, 1992.

Camporesi, Piero. *Rustici e buffoni: cultura popolare e cultura d'élite fra Medioevo ed età moderna.* Torino: Einaudi, 1991.

Carrier, Joseph M. *De los otros: Intimacy and Homosexuality among Mexican Men.* New York: Columbia UP, 1995.

———. "Mexican Male Bisexuality." *Journal of Homosexuality* 11.1–2 (1986): 75–85.

Catholy, Eckehard. *Das Fastnachtspiel des Spätmittelalters: Gestalt und Funktion.* Tübingen: Max Niemeyer, 1961.

Clover, Carol J. "Regardless of Sex: Men, Women and Power in Early Northern Europe." *Speculum* 68 (1993): 363–87.

Cohen, Judith R., and Oro Anahory-Librowitz. "Modalidades expresivas de los cantos de boda judeo-españoles." *Revista de tradiciones populares* 41 (1986): 189–209.

Collett, Peter. "Meetings and Misunderstandings." *Cultures in Cross-Cultural Interaction.* Ed. Stephen Bochner. Oxford: Pergamon P, 1982. 81–98.

Conlon, Raymond. "The *Burlador* and the *Burlados:* A Sinister Connection." *Bulletin of the Comediantes* 42.1 (1990): 5–22.

Cruz-Malavé, Arnaldo. "Toward an Art of Transvestism: Colonialism and Homosexuality in Puerto Rican Literature." Bergmann and Smith 137–67.

Debroise, Olivier, Elisabeth Sussman, and Marthe W. Teitelbaum, curators. *El Corazón Sangrante/The Bleeding Heart.* Boston: Institute of Contemporary Art, 1991.

De Lope, Monique. "Le Signe et la croix." *Mélanges offerts à Maurice Molho.* Vol. 1. Spec. issue of *Ibérica* (1988): 69–81.

Driessen, Henk. "Gestured Masculinity: Body and Sociability in Rural Andalucia." Bremmer and Roodenburg 237–57.

Dundes, Alan. "The American Game of 'Smear the Queer' and the Homosexual Component of Male Competitive Sport and Warfare." *Parsing through Customs.* Ed. Alan Dundes. U of Wisconsin P, 1987. 178–84.

———. "Gallus as Phallus: A Psychoanalytic Cross-Cultural Consideration of the Cockfight as Fowl Play." *The Cockfight: A Casebook.* Ed. Alan Dundes. Madison: U of Wisconsin P, 1994. 241–84.

———. "Interview." *California Monthly* Sept. 1993: 31–33.

———. "Into the Endzone for a Touchdown: A Psychoanalytical Consideration of American Football." *Western Folklore* 37 (1978): 75–88.

Fleischmann, Suzanne. "Signs and Co-Signs in the *Libro de buen amor.*" *Le Gai Savoir: Essays in Linguistics, Philology, and Criticism.* Ed. Mechthild Cranston. Potomac: Studia Humanistica, 1984. 157–67.

Frago García, Juan A. "Sobre el léxico de prostitución en España durante el siglo XV." *Archivo de filología aragonesa* 24–25 (1979): 257–73.

Fuentes, Carlos. *La muerte de Artemio Cruz.* Mexico City: Fondo de Cultura Económica, 1977.

Gabbard, Krin. "Signifyin(g) the Phallus: *Mo' Better Blues* and Representations of the Jazz Trumpet." *Cinema Journal* 32.1 (1992): 43–62. Rpt. *Jammin' at the Margins: Jazz and the American Cinema.* Ed. Krin Gabbard. Chicago: U of Chicago P, 1996. 138–59.

Gade, Kari Ellen. "Homosexuality and Rape of Males in Old Norse Law and Literature." *Scandinavian Studies* 58 (1986): 124–41.

Gamble, Eliza Burt. *The God-Idea of the Ancients, or Sex in Religion.* 1897. Rpt. in *The Story of Phallicism.* Ed. Lee A. Stone. 1927. New York: Ams Press, 1976.

Garry, Marvin. "The Cockfight in Andalusia, Spain: Images of the Truly Male." *Anthropological Quarterly* 57 (1984): 60–70.

Geary, John S., et al. *Florilegium Hispanicum: Medieval and Golden Age Studies Presented to Dorothy Clotelle Clarke.* Madison: Hispanic Seminary of Medieval Studies, 1983.

Gilman, Sander. *Sexuality: An Illustrated History.* New York: Wiley, 1989.

Gilmore, David D., and Sarah Cuhl. "Further Notes on Andalusian Machismo." *Journal of Psychoanalytic Anthropology* 10.4 (1987): 341–60.

Gilmore, M., and D. D. Gilmore. "Machismo: A Psychodynamic Approach to Spain." *Journal of Psychological Anthropology* 2 (1979): 281–300.

Goldenberg, Naomi R. "On Hockey Sticks and Hopscotch Patsies." *Returning*

Words to the Flesh: Feminism, Psychoanalysis and the Resurrection of the Body. Ed. Naomi R. Goldenberg. Boston: Beacon P, 1990. 42–57.

González, Alicia María. " 'Guess How Doughnuts Are Made': Verbal and Non-verbal Aspects of the *panadero* and His Stereotype." *"And Other Neighborly Names": Social Process and Cultural Image.* Ed. Richard Bauman and Roger D. Abraham. Austin: U of Texas P, 1981. 104–22.

Gossy, Mary S. "Aldonza as Butch: Narrative and the Play of Gender in *Don Quijote.*" Bergmann and Smith 17–28.

Grimes, Larry M. "The Linguistic Taboo: Examples from Modern Mexican Spanish." *Bilingual Review* 4 (1977): 69–80.

Guiraud, Michel. "Le Champ morpho-sémantique du mot *tromper.*" *Bulletin de la Société de Linguistique de Paris* 63 (1968): 96–109.

Guldan, Ernst. *Eva und Maria: Eine Antithese als Bildmotiv.* Graz-Köln: Verlag Hermann Böhl, 1966.

Gundersheimer, Werner. "Clarity and Ambiguity in Renaissance Gesture: The Case of Borso d'Este." *Journal of Medieval and Renaissance Studies* 23.1 (1993): 1–17.

Hortas, Carlos. "René Marqués's *La mirada:* A Closer Look." *Latin American Literary Review* 8.16 (1980): 201–04.

Huguet, Edmond. *Dictionnaire de la langue française du seizième siècle.* Paris: Didier, 1965.

Ingham, J. "Culture and Personality in a Mexican Village." Diss. U of California-Berkeley, 1968.

Johnston, George, trans. *The Saga of Gisli.* Toronto: U of Toronto P, 1963.

Joset, Jacques, ed. *Libro de buen amor.* Madrid: Taurus, 1990.

———. *Nuevas investigaciones sobre el "Libro de buen amor."* Madrid: Cátedra, 1988.

Keuls, Eva C. *The Reign of the Phallus: Sexual Politics in Ancient Athens.* New York: Harper and Row, 1985.

Kirkup, James. "Phallic Worship: Some Personal Meditations on a Sacred Theme." *The Sexual Dimension in Literature.* Ed. Alan Bold. Totowa: Vision and Barnes and Noble, 1982. 145–62.

Kushner, Tony. *Angels in America: A Gay Fantasia on National Themes.* New York: Theatre Communications Group, 1993.

Laferrière, Daniel. "The Writing Perversion." *Semiotica* 18 (1976): 217–33.

———. [Rancoeur-Laferrière, Daniel]. "Some Semiotic Aspects of the Human Penis." *Quaderni di studi semiotici* 24 (1979): 37–82.

Lancester, Roger N. "Subject Honor, Object Shame." *Life Is Hard: Machismo, Danger, and the Intimacy of Power in Nicaragua.* Berkeley: U of California P, 1992.

Legman, Gershon. *Rationale of the Dirty Joke: An Analysis of Sexual Humor.* 2nd ser. New York: Breaking Point, 1975.

LeVay, Simon. *The Sexual Brain.* Cambridge, Mass.: MIT P, 1993.

Livingston, Charles H. *Le Jongleur Gautier Le Leu: étude sur les fabliaux.* Cambridge, Mass.: Harvard UP, 1951.

Madero, Marta. "L'Injure et le corps en Castille aux XIIIe et XIVe siècles." *Atalaya* 5 (1994): 231–48.

Malamud, Bernard. *Pictures of Fidelman.* New York: Farrar, Straus, Giroux, [1969].

Marqués, René. *La mirada.* Río Piedras, P.R.: El Antillana, 1975.

Martínez-Pizarro, Joaquín. "On Níd against Bishops." *Mediaeval Scandinavia* 11 (1978–79): 149–53.

Michalski, André S. "Juan Ruiz's *troba caʒurra:* Cruz cruzada panadera." *Romance Notes* 11 (1969): 434–38.

Montaiglon, Anatole, and Gaston Reynaud. *Receuil générale et complet des fabliaux.* Vol. 1. Paris: Librairie des Bibliophiles, 1878.

Morlaàs, J. "Manducation alimentaire—manducation de la parole." *Annales médico-psychologiques* 136.2 (1978): 233–55.

Morris, Desmond. *Gestures, Their Origin and Distribution.* New York: Stein and Day, 1979.

Murray, Stephen O., ed. *Male Homosexuality in Central and South America.* Gai Saber Monographs. San Francisco: Instituto Obregon, 1987.

Nelson, Cynthia. *The Waiting Village: Social Change in Rural Mexico.* Boston: Little, Brown, 1971.

Nelson, Ida. *La Sottie sans souci: essai d'interpretation homosexuelle.* Paris: Éditions Honoré Champion, 1977.

Neuman, Gerard G. "Past and Present Thinking on Aggression: An Introductory Overview." *Origins of Human Aggression: Dynamics and Etiology.* Ed. Gerard G. Neuman. New York: Human Sciences P, 1987. 17–28.

Ong, Walter J. *Fighting for Life: Contest, Sexuality, and Consciousness.* 1989. Amherst: U of Massachusetts, 1989.

———. "Orality, Literacy, and Medieval Textualization." *New Literary History* 16 (1984–85): 1–11.

Parker, W. H. *Priapea: Poems for a Phallic God.* London: Croom Helm, 1988.

Paul, William. "Chaplin and the Annals of Anality." *Comedy-Cinema-Theory.* Ed. Andrew Horton. Berkeley: U California P, 1991. 109–30.

Paz, Octavio. *El laberinto de la soledad.* 2nd ed. México: Fondo de Cultura Económica, 1969.

Petropoulous, Elias. "Fist-Phallus." *Maledicta* 3 (1979): 103–07.

Piedra, José. "Nationalizing Sissies." Bergmann and Smith 370–409.

Pitt-Rivers, Julian. *The People of the Sierra.* Chicago: U of Chicago P, 1954.

Polkinhorn, Harry, et al. *El libro de caló: Pachuco Slang Dictionary.* San Diego: Atticus P, 1983.

Rennick, Robert M. "Obscene Names and Naming in Folk Tradition." *Names* 16 (1960): 207–09.

Riché, Pierre. "Le Rôle de la mémoire dans l'enseignement médiévale." *Jeux de mémoire: aspects de la mnémotechnie médiévale.* Ed. Bruno Roy and Paul Zumthor. Montreal: Les Presses de l'Université de Montréal, 1985. 133–48.

Richlin Amy. "The Meaning of *Irrumare* in Catullus and Martial." *Classical Philology* 76.1 (1981): 40–46.

Ruiz, Juan. See Blecua.

Seidenspinner-Núñez, Dayle. "On 'Dios y el Mundo': Author and Reader Response in Juan Ruiz and Juan Manuel." *Romance Philology* (1988–89): 251–66.

Silva Tellez, Armando. *Una ciudad imaginada.* Bogotá: Universidad Nacional de Colombia, 1986.

Sorensen, Preben Neulengracht. *The Unmanly Man: Concepts of Sexual Defamation in Early Northern Society.* Trans. Joan Turville-Petre. Odense: Odense UP, 1983.

Spalding, Keith. *An Historical Dictionary of German Figurative Usage.* Oxford: Basil Blackwell, 1984.

Spink, M. S., and G. L. Lewis, eds. and trans. *Albucasis on Surgery and Instruments.* Berkeley: U of California P, 1973.

Suárez-Orozco, Marcelo M. "A Psychoanalytic Study of Argentine Soccer." *Essays in Honor of Alan Dundes.* Ed. L. Bryce Boyer et al. Hillsdale, N.J.: Analytic P, 1993. 211–34.

Swenson, Karen. *Performing Definitions: Two Genres of Insult in Old Norse Literature.* Studies in Scandinavian Literature and Culture 3. Columbia, S.C.: Camden House, 1991.

Umiker-Sebeok, Jean, and Thomas A. Sebeok. *Monastic Sign Language.* Amsterdam: Mouton, 1987.

Vanggaard, Thorkil. *Phallos: A Symbol of Its History in the Male World.* New York: International Universities P, 1972.

Vasvári, Louise O. "*Chica cosa es dos nueẓes:* Lost Sexual Humor in the *Libro del Arcipreste.*" *Revista de estudios hispánicos* 24.1 (1990): 1–22.

———. "Don Hurón *Trickster:* un arquetipo psico-folklórico." *Actas del tercer congreso de la Asociación Hispánica de Literatura Medieval.* Ed. María Toro Pascua. Salamanca: Biblioteca Española del Siglo XV, 1995. 1121–26.

———. "Festive Phallic Discourse in the *Libro del Arcipreste.*" *La corónica* 22.2 (1994): 89–117.

———. "Fowl Play in My Lady's Chamber: Textual Harassment of a Middle English Pornithological Riddle and Visual Pun." *Medieval Obscenity: Social*

Control and Artistic Creation in the European Middle Ages. Ed. Jan Ziolkowski. Leiden: Brill, 1998. 110–35.

———. "Gastro-genital Rites of Reversal: The Battle of Flesh and Lent in the 'Libro del Arcipreste.' " *La corónica* 20.1 (1991): 1–15.

———. "Múltiple transparencia semántica de los nombres de la alcahueta en el 'Libro del Arcipreste.' " *Medioevo y literatura: actas del quinto congreso de la Asociación Hispánica de Literatura Medieval*. Ed. Juan Paredes. Granada: U de Granada, 1995. 453–63.

———. "Peregrinaciones por topografías pornográficas en el *Libro de buen amor*." *Actas del sexto congreso de la Asociación Hispánica de Literatura Medieval*. Ed. José Manuel Lucía Megías. Alcalá: Universidad de Alcalá, 1997. 1567–72.

———. "Pitas Pajas: Carnivalesque Phonosymbolism." *Revista de estudios hispánicos* 26 (1992): 135–62.

———. "La semiología de la connotación: lectura polisémica de 'Cruz cruzada panadera.' " *Nueva revista de filología hispánica* 33 (1983) [1985]: 300–24.

———. "A Tale of 'Taillying': Aesop Topsy-Turvy in the *Libro de buen amor*." *Journal of Interdisciplinary Hispanic Studies/Cuadernos interdisciplinarios de estudios literarios* 2 (1990): 13–41.

Wagner, Max Leopold. "Phallus, Horn und Fisch: Lebendige und verschüttete Vorstellungen und Symbole, vormehrlich im Bereiche des Mittelmeerbeckens." *Romania Helvetica* 4 (1937): 79–130.

Walsh, John K. "The Names of the Bawd in the *LBA*." Geary et al. 151–64.

Webber, Edwin J. "The *ribaldo* as Literary Symbol." Geary et al. 131–38.

Weiss, Carl, and David James Friar. *Terror in the Prisons: Homosexual Rape and Why Society Condones It*. New York: Bobbs-Merrill, 1974.

Whinnom, Keith. *La poesía amatoria de la época de los Reyes Católicos*. Durham, England: U of Durham, 1981.

Willis, Raymond S., ed. and trans. *Libro de buen amor*. Princeton: Princeton UP.

Wirth, Jean. *L'Image médiévale: naissance et développements (VIe–XVe siècles)*. Paris: Méridiens Klincksieck, 1989.

Zlotchew, Clark M. "Metáforas agresivo-sexuales en inglés y en español." *Foro literario* 7.12 (1984): 46–49.

———. "The Rhetoric of Hispanic Machismo: A Historical Perspective." *Maledicta* 3 (1979): 110–22.

Roberto J. González-Casanovas

Male Bonding as Cultural Construction in Alfonso X, Ramon Llull, and Juan Manuel

Homosocial Friendship in Medieval Iberia

Cultural Interpretations of Friendship

Praise of male friendship abounds in official and popular texts from every culture and in every period. Like love, it appears to be a human ideal based on universal experience that anyone can appreciate. Also like love, it offers a broad term that encompasses many types and levels of social phenomena, while it refers to value systems open to multiple interpretations and contradictory manipulations. Traditionally *philia*, or intimate friendship, is shown to be ethically superior to *eros,* or sexual love: "Friendship is to be distinguished from other forms of love in that its partners are chosen according to moral criteria and behave in a moral way. Friendship is the ethical form of *eros*" (Alberoni 31; translation mine). As a complement to familial and conjugal ties, male friendship is often depicted as transition and counterweight to collective allegiances; it can also serve as a channel for same-sex affections that are seen as both essential to proper gender development and vulnerable to homoerotic attachments. Despite its ambiguities, it seems to be a central category of human relations and virtues in the imaginative matrix, ideological code, and textual canon of Western European cultures in the Greco-Roman and Judeo-Christian traditions: poets like Homer immortalized heroic companions (Achilles and Patroclus), philosophers like Plato and Aristotle devoted treatises to *philia,* orators like Cicero expounded on true *amicitia,* Hebrew chroniclers memorialized personal bonds among heroes (David and Jonathan) and with God, while Christian preachers exemplified fellowship among believers as well as intimacy with

God-made-man. In medieval culture, close same-sex friendships emerged as a basic component of chivalry and courtesy: both male bonding among knights-in-arms and affectionate relations among male courtiers seemed to reach new heights of cultural refinement, esthetic expression, and ethical exemplarity.

The problems inherent in the typical descriptions and conventional evaluations of friendship should become manifest, however, to those who are engaged in the study of cultural poetics along the revisionist lines developed over the last twenty years by Michel Foucault and many others. A comparative reading of critical studies from C. S. Lewis and Francesco Alberoni to Foucault and David Halperin would indicate that friendship is continuously being redefined within and across cultures; in addition, its hybrid nature constantly evolves in relation to the symbiotic phenomena of love and sexuality and to the parallel institutions of family and marriage. When friendship is analyzed from anthropological, societal, historicist, "archeological," and mythological points of view—as a cultural field of shifting relations and polarities, as well as a cultural artifact of constructed meanings and values—then its fundamental historicity and textuality need to be established. For "new medievalists" (those whose interest in cultural interpretation as such is informed by theories of historical reception, sociopolitical rhetoric, and mythopoetic hermeneutics),[1] the study of male friendship in medieval Iberian texts can offer important critical insights: what appears to be a basic category of human experience turns out to be an elaborate construction that develops in complex ways along historical, social, and textual frontiers of cultures. In the case of male bonding, or heroic friendship between male aristocrats, as represented in Castilian and Catalan texts from 1256 to 1335, the cultural frontiers include those between paganism and Christianity, as well as those between Islam and Christendom; those between clerical authority and chivalric utopia, as well as those between aristocratic power and courtly ethics; and those between affection and sexuality, as well as those between same-sex relations and like-gendered affinities.

In general terms, such cultural frontiers lead to the emergence of syncretist models of social relations in medieval Iberia: they are centered on the hierarchy and symmetry of aristocratic male friendship; predicated on the good counsels that derive from mutual interest, loyalty, and service; based on classical, biblical, Christian, and Muslim sapiential traditions; and manifested in various forms of ethical and utopian discourse. These models culminate in the many translations and compilations (fables, miracles, laws, chronicles) edited at the court of Alfonso X the Learned, King of Castile (r. 1252–84). They also come to fruition in unique works of didactic, reformist, and mystical exemplarity written in Catalan by Ramon Llull (1232–1316) and chivalric treatises and popular stories written in Castilian by Juan Manuel (1282–1348).

This is an era that can be characterized by the parallel encouragement of *convivencia* (ethnic and cultural symbiosis) and *mudejariζación* (Arabized styles of life and art), as well as the promotion of secular authority (according to Oriental wisdom and Roman law placed in the service of a royal-aristocratic rather than a papal-clerical agenda) and vernacular expression (for official and popular writing centered at the court but disseminated beyond its confines).[2] The particular construction of heroic-male bonding, within the more general syncretist network of social relations and chivalric ideals, would seem to fit directly into the heart of characteristically late-medieval Iberian *mentalités* and institutions of courtly life, which are themselves the result of the dynamically interacting and evolving cultural frontiers of the Reconquest in the crucial period of the mid-thirteenth to mid-fourteenth centuries (when Christian domination of the peninsula is definitively established and the kingdoms of Aragon, Castile, and Portugal emerge as nation-states).

These centuries witness the renaissance and reformation of all the Christian kingdoms of Reconquest Iberia, which give rise to the Ibero-Romance languages (Castilian, Galician-Portuguese, and Catalan) as the dominant oral and written media for court, chancery, scholarship, and literature. Considered the "founder of Castilian prose," Alfonso X seeks to extend the military conquests and juridical institutions of his father Fernando III (conqueror of Córdoba in 1236 and of Seville in 1248) with cultural and intellectual conquests of his own; by means of systematic projects of translation, edition, revision, and synthesis, he seeks to colonize for Castile all fields of knowledge represented in medieval Iberia, whether national and universal history, law, science, pious verse, or didactic prose.[3] Ramon Llull is revered as the "father of Catalan literature"; born in Majorca only three years after its conquest from the Moors by Jaume I in 1229, he forsakes his aristocratic life at the royal court as a result of a religious "conversion" experience and strives to renew both Iberian and European Christendom with an extraordinary series of missionary *summas* in Latin and Catalan and exemplary utopias in Catalan, with which he aims at the conversion to Christianity of the whole world. According to this vision, all new or renewed Christians, from lowly individuals to mighty nations, as well as from nominal Christians to former infidels, are to form an evangelical community under papal authority.[4] Juan Manuel, nephew of Alfonso X and co-regent for Alfonso XI, is admired as the "first Castilian prose stylist"; he follows the Learned King's example in promoting vernacular writing based on the cultural synthesis of Ibero-Mediterranean traditions, but with the difference that, in the midst of his agitated life as magnate and statesman, he dedicates himself, rather than groups of scholars and scribes, to the task of authoring important works for the court, such as histories, sociopolitical treatises, genealogies, and didactic tales and counsels. All are designed to uphold his own conservative brand of aristocratic ethos and chivalric ethics in the midst of what he perceives to be a period of national crisis and moral decadence.[5] Given the late-Reconquest phenomena of crossing frontiers to colonize cultural discourse as well as ethnic territory, what cultural significance, then, does heroic male bonding enjoy along the textual frontiers and in the ideological colonies?

On closer scrutiny, from what emerges as the culturally "exemplary" yet ideologically "ex-centric" point of view of heroic male bonding, it can be shown that the crosscultural interactions that characterize this period not only promote a novel syncretism but also reveal anew familiar tensions. These tensions lend themselves to the critical and nuanced analysis of contemporary theories about the cultural discourses of sexuality and gender. In effect, when such theories are applied to the three representative writers chosen, noble male friendships are seen to involve problematic negotiations and "interstitial" constructions that develop along the horizontal margins and vertical edges of the various cultural frontiers. In the law code of *Siete partidas* from 1256 to 163, Alfonso X's scholars endorse the clerically defined centrality of matrimony, while they praise a classical model of male friendship as the superior form of human bonding; in the process, appeals to nature and reason prove contradictory, as do the insistence on male control of social relations and exhortation to training in concord based on "homophilia." Llull presents his *Llibre d'Amic e d'Amat* [Book of the Friend and Beloved] (composed in 1276 but included in 1283–85 in the novel *Blanquerna,* or *Libre de Evast e Blanquerna*) as a series of mystical confessions and parables on the Christian's devotion to the human-divine Christ: to optimize his reception (by clergy, nobles, bourgeois), he sees the need to imitate what he considers the Sufis' affective style and to drama-tize what he most admires in the "homophilic" code of chivalry; he comes to allegorize the soul's encounter with Christ in the "erotic" (albeit styl-ized and sublimated) discourse of a male friend-as-lover's intimacy with his male friend-as-beloved. Juan Manuel includes in his 1335 collection of tales *El conde Lucanor* two exempla on Saladin (25 and 50) that raise issues, respectively, of surpassing family and religious ties by same-sex chival-rous friendships and of reconstructing different-sex love as male-gendered noble friendship; for him the representation of an ethical *philia*, within "homosocial" and "homotextual" networks, culminates in sapiential tran-scendence of both heteroerotic and "homophilic" conventions. Before ex-amining constructions of aristocratic male bonding in detail, it is necessary to pause to define terms and establish models for analysis.

Critical Models:
Constructions and Ambiguities of Male Friendship

Crucial to any discussion of male bonding in medieval texts on friend-ship is the problem of defining the exact parameters of the relationships (as cultural ideals and textual phenomena rather than actual practices). For the purposes of this study, it is important to distinguish the follow-ing terms: *homosociality, homophilia, homoeroticism,* and *homosexuality,* as well as *gendered role. Homosociality* refers to the preference in professional and recreational relations for members of the same sex; it is reflected in the model of all-male camaraderie that still predominates in traditional Medi-terranean societies. *Homophilia* here signifies a predilection for same-sex friendships based on close intimacy, which can extend over the full range of emotional attractions and sentimental expressions that lie outside genital interaction; it is illustrated in notions of blood brothers and boon compan-ions that often characterize heroic male couples in literature from Homer to Hemingway. *Homoeroticism* develops homophilia further by stressing "romantic love" within the same sex, which can include passionate expres-sions and courtship rituals that lead to physical intimacy with or without genital behavior; according to Boswell (*Christianity, Social Tolerance, and*

Homosexuality), it is present (at times encoded) in medieval love lyrics and letters among certain male clerics and poets; it is also documented in medieval Arabic and Hebrew poetry on male love for adolescent boys.[6] As for "homosexuality," it is a term that should be excluded from cultural studies of classical and medieval texts so as to avoid anachronistic confusions with contemporary notions of gay sexuality (*pace* Boswell): in modern theory it points to the explicit and self-conscious concept of a personality type based on (often exclusive) same-sex attractions, whether or not they are expressed in emotional, physical, or social ways; however, in premodern codes of penitential and legal documents, its approximate term, sodomy, only denotes genital *acts* between persons of the same (male) sex that are categorically condemned as unnatural (Thomas Aquinas, *Summa theologiae*, question 54, art. 1–2), and therefore sinful and criminal, but it does not characterize a particular sexual *type* (a nineteenth-century development). Finally, *gendered role* means the cultural fashioning in all communities of psychosexual identities (as opposed to biosexual behavior), so that men (or women) are encouraged to be more or less masculine or feminine in their self-representation and social interaction. Central to this study are issues of homosociality, which underlies aristocratic utopia, and of homophilia, which contributes to heroic virtue, as well as of gender roles, which acquire a "masculine conscience" in chivalric male bonding and a "feminine sensibility" in mystical male union.

Here it would be useful to turn back to the question of cultural interpretations of friendship. In Lewis one finds: "To the ancients, friendship seemed the happiest and most fully human of all loves; the crown of life and the school of virtue" (55). As ideal, male friendship often refers to a process of humanization that goes beyond the natural life of the human animal and the social life of the citizen, so that the fullest affects and best effects in life can result from its cultivation: "Friendship is . . . the least *natural* of loves; the least instinctive, organic, biological, gregarious and necessary. . . . This . . . 'non-natural' quality in friendship goes far to explain why it was exalted in ancient and medieval times" (56). But given primarily same-sex manifestations in male-dominated societies (57–59, 68), along with modern categorizations and condemnations of homosexual orientation (as well as the older anathema toward homosexual acts), Lewis needs to emphasize nonsexual (nonerotic and nongenital) aspects of virtuous male bonding: "It has actually become necessary in our time to rebut the theory that every firm and serious friendship is really homosexual" (59). This forms part of Lewis's task of "rehabilitating" *philia* (57) from both neglect and distrust in the face of the dominant *eros*. His defense of friendship gives equal weight to ethical and esthetic values that lie beyond sex and sentiment: "Friendship . . . [has] not so much survival value, as what we may call 'civilization value' . . . something . . . which helps the community not to live but to live well. . . . Friendship is unnecessary, like philosophy, like art. . . . It has no survival value; rather it is one of those things which give value to survival" (65, 67). For Lewis, *philia,* unlike *storge* (familial affection), *eros* (sexual passion), or *agape* (selfless charity), constitutes the most gratuitously self-fulfilling of the four loves.

Ironically, an interest in the critical rehabilitation and cultural sublimation of same-sex *philia* also characterizes Foucault's analysis of the construction of Greek pederasty. This finds its textual correlative in the "ascetic Socrates": "Xenophon presents a Socrates who draws a strict dividing line between love of the soul and love of the body, disqualifies the love of body in his own person, makes love of the soul the true love, and seeks in friendship (*philia*) the principle that gives value to every relation (*synousia*)" (233). Foucault shows that rituals of homoerotic courtship evolve into ethical discourses of homophilia. For him, it is this particular development in the valorization of intimate male friendships that gives rise to the cultural ascetics and poetics of self-mastery and self-fashioning in ancient Greece: "[T]he Greeks developed arts of living, of conducting themselves, and of 'using pleasures' according to austere and demanding principles. . . . [T]he requirement of austerity that was implied by this self-disciplined subject was not presented in the form of a universal law . . . but as a principle of stylization of conduct for those who wished to give their existence the most graceful and accomplished form possible" (249–50). In contrast to Lewis's apologetic reaction to modern society's fear of contamination of homophilia by homoeroticism, Foucault stresses the cultural and critical debate that historically accompanies conceptualizations of love and friendship. For him, the "discourse of erotics" is seen to be bound up with the continuous reformations of esthetics and ethics across cultures and eras.

The critical interpretation of homophilia can also be seen to present other types of difficulties than those of Lewis's "sexual contamination" or Foucault's "ascetic sublimation." As Halperin explains, the cultural representation of friendship, particularly homophilic relations, is fundamentally different from other constructions sanctioned by traditional authority and social institutions. Significantly, he begins his essay on "Heroes and Their Pals" with a reference to E. M. Forster's early novel, *The Longest Journey* (1907): "Forster has accurately understood what he calls 'the irony of friendship' — its paradoxical combination of social importance and social marginality, its indeterminate status among the various forms of social relations. Friendship is the *anomalous* relation: it exists outside the more thoroughly codified social networks formed by kinship and sexual ties; it is 'interstitial in the social structure' of most Western cultures" (75). What Halperin brings out (also noted by Lewis 56) is the very marginalization of friendship: its pursuit as a human perfection and its representation as a heroic ideal occur outside the regular networks and official status accorded to family and spouses (as well as to citizens and coreligionists, one might add). Hence, as Halperin further notes (83–85), there is a double irony in the cultural construction of male bonding: its very ambiguity derives from its hybrid borrowings from kinship and sexuality; and its contingency makes it seek a transcendence of what are perceived to be the established natural and societal ties: "Friendship is parasitic in its conceptualization on kinship relations and on sexual relations. That is, it must borrow terminology and imagery from these other spheres of human relations in order to identify and define itself" (84). Constructions of male bonding can therefore be seen to thrive along the textual, societal, and ideological frontiers of human culture and of historical cultures.

Alfonso X's *Siete partidas*

A selection of Iberian texts from the thirteenth century should serve to highlight key contexts for the construction of late-medieval notions of friendship as *philia* and *homophilia*. This is a critical period that marks the last stages of a certain phase of centuries-old (yet intermittent) cultural experiments in tolerance for same-sex affections (studied by Boswell; cf. Gauvard 92 and Le Goff 189), as well as in recognition of marginal-gender values (such as "feminine" virtues in courtesy and in piety, studied respectively by Solé and by Vauchez 157–68), before official domination, orthodoxy, and intolerance are firmly consolidated. It is a century that includes the founding of the Inquisition (1231), codification of penitentials and canon law by Ramon Penyafort (1229–34), and systematization of doctrine in Thomas Aquinas's *Summa theologiae* (1269–72). It also witnesses renewals of clerical and lay devotion based on the humanity of Christ and the feminization of spirituality by male and female religious writers (studied respectively by Cousins and by Bynum). It is framed by the Fourth Lateran Council of 1215, which reaffirms clerical celibacy and matrimonial integrity, and the trial of the Templars in 1307, which combines accusations of heresy and sodomy (Barber 178–82, 190–91). As the century progresses, clerical authority imposes a uniform, dogmatic vision of the Christian church and society based on domination by celibate males and control of "natural" heterosexual desire in the sacrament of marriage (reflected in Alfonso X's *Siete partidas*, parts 1 and 4). At the same time, aristocratic idealizations of same-sex friendship and companionship find expression in chivalric epics, romances, and treatises, as well as in vernacular reworkings of classical ethics (found in *Siete partidas*, parts 2 and 4).[7]

In Alfonso X's *Siete partidas*, which constitutes a utopian law code (as López Estrada has shown), court scholars balance social dangers and communitarian ideals with respect to various human conditions. This is the case for the regulation of conjugal relations between the two sexes:

> Matrimonio . . . es uno de los más nobles e más honrados de los siete Sacramentos de la Sancta Eglesia. . . . [E]s mantenimiento del mundo, e que faze a los omes beuir vida ordenada naturalmente, e sin pecado, e sin el qual los otros seys Sacramentos non podrían ser mantenidos, nin guardados. E por esso lo pusimos en medio de las siete partidas deste libro; assí como el coraçón es puesto en medio del cuerpo. (4 gen. prol., 2: 453)[8]

> [Matrimony is one of the noblest and most honorable of the seven Sacraments of Holy Church. (I)t maintains the world and causes men to live a regular life according to nature and free from sin; without it the other six sacraments cannot be maintained or observed. Hence we placed it in the middle of the seven parts of this book, just as the heart is placed in the middle of the body. (877)]

But this clerically defined conjugal ideal is shown to have negative underpinnings. It is accompanied by a misogynist view of sexual and social disorder among men caused by women when there is no proper male domination and regulation: "Contiendas, e homezillos, e soberuias, e fuerças, e otras cosas muy tortizeras . . . nascerían por razón de las mugeres, si casamiento non fuesse" (4.12 prol., 2: 465) [(Q)uarrels, homicides, insolence, violence, and many other very wrongful acts would take place on account of women if marriage did not exist (886)]. A more positive aspect of utopian harmony underlies the projection onto society of what, in the cultural contexts of classical philosophy and medieval chivalry, can be seen to be male-like bonds of friendship:

> Amistad, segund dize Aristóteles, es vna virtud que es buena en sí, e prouechosa a la vida de los omes. . . . E concordia es vna virtud que es semejante a la amistad. E desta se trabajaron los Sabios, e los grandes Señores, que fizieron los libros de las leyes, porque los omes biuiessen acordadamente. (4.27.1, 2: 629–30)

> [(F)riendship, according to Aristotle, is a virtue which is intrinsically good in itself and profitable to human life. Concord is a virtue similar to friendship; the sages and great lords who made books of law favored bringing it about so that men might live together in unity." (1003)]

As for sexual interaction between men, it is defined as the sin of sodomy and classified as a sacrosanct taboo, the violation of which often brings fatal consequences:

> Porque de tal pecado como este nascen muchos males a la tierra do se face, et es cosa que pesa mucho a Dios con ella, et sale ende mala fama non tal solamente a los facedores, mas aun a la tierra do es consentido. (7.21 prol.)

> [(M)any evils arise from an offense of this kind in the country where it is committed, and it is something which causes great grief to God, and a bad reputation results therefrom, not only to those guilty of it but also to the land where it is permitted. (1427)] [9]

Such pronouncements reveal an Alfonsine preoccupation (based on clerical regulation) with the official control of sexuality, in promoting matrimony and prohibiting sodomy, as well as with the ethical commendation of interpersonal friendship (essentially male) as the basis for collective harmony (embracing all); while in one case the "natural appetites" of sexuality are checked by procreative institutions, in the other case "natural bonds" of affinity are developed as voluntary forms of social obligation. In each case, however, there is a chain of responsibility that connects individual and group, believer and church, subject and nation, so that whatever works for the good or evil of one party also affects the others. But such reciprocity is still asymmetrical: the cultural context and reception of the *Siete partidas* make it clear that it is a gendered hierarchy (masculine aristocracy and clergy) that is to interpret and apply the predominantly homosocial discourse of human order. At the same time, a sort of ethical ripple effect is intended: by cultivating moral excellence among noble males, some degree of minimal virtue will spread (by interaction and imitation) among commoners and even women. Aristocratic male *philia* thus fosters the "common good."

As for the clerically defined proscription of sodomy in *Siete partidas* 7.21, it is worth noting that, only one generation before the fatal trial in 1307 of the Templars for heresy and sodomy, with subsequent dissolution of the order and execution of its leaders, Alfonso X himself is quite capable of manipulating the law to suit political circumstances. It is likely that charges of sodomy and treason were combined to justify the executions in 1277 of his own brother Fadrique by hanging and the noble Simón Ruiz de los Cameros by burning. This is the view of O'Callaghan, who also observes, referring to the passage quoted above (7.21.1), "Because homosexual acts were thought to bring disaster upon the kingdom that permitted them, the penalties were extremely harsh" (*The Learned King* 241); he adds a pertinent allusion found in the Alfonsine *Cantigas de Santa Maria* [Songs of Santa Maria]: "E ben com' ard' estadal / Ardeu a carne daqueles que non querian moller" (no. 235, lines 73–75) [Just as the candle burns, so also burned the flesh of those who did not want woman]. That national disasters follow the prevalence or tolerance of sodomy among the aristocracy was a significant argument against the Templars, whose disastrous loss in 1291 of Acre, the last crusader stronghold in the Holy Land, was attributed to divine chastisement for alleged sodomy (Barber 190–91). As marginal and anomalous phenomena, close male friendships, especially among prominent members of the aristocracy, could be seen to be susceptible to the sexual "contaminations" of homoeroticism and sodomy, as well as vulnerable to the political "corruptions" of conflicting loyalties and even treason.

It is significant that, in part 4.27 of the *Siete partidas*, essentially homophilic constructions of friendship inherited from classical antiquity (Aristotle and Plato via the Church Fathers and Arab scholars [the latter connection studied by Walzer 240–42]) come to serve as models for all, even nonhomophilic, situations in contemporary medieval society. A fundamental tension, even contradiction, underlies the new broad contexts being imposed on such Aristotelian homophilic ethical constructions as "Amistad es cosa que ayunta mucho la voluntad de los omes, para amarse mucho. Ca segund dixeron los Sabios antiguos, el verdadero amor passa todos los debdos" (4.27 prol., 2: 629) [Friendship is something which induces persons to love one another greatly, for, as the ancient wise men declared, true love is the most important of all obligations (1003)]. It is one thing to follow Aristotle's discussion of friendship in personal relations:

> Aristóteles . . . dixo que eran tres maneras de amistad. La primera es de natura. La segunda es la que ome ha a su amigo, por uso de luengo tiempo, por bondad que aya en él. La tercera es la que ome ha con otro, por algund pro o por algund plazer que ha dél, o espera auer." (4.27.4, 2: 631)

> [Aristotle said there are three kinds of friendship: first, that of nature; second, that a man has for his friend, from intercourse of long duration by the affection which he has for him; third, that a man has for another for some advantage or pleasure which he obtains or expects to obtain from him. (1004–05)]

But it is quite a different matter to extrapolate communal harmony from the cultivation of generalized, generic friendship: "E concordia es vna virtud que es semejante a la amistad. E desta se trabajaron los Sabios, e los grandes Señores, que fizieron los libros de las leyes, porque los omes biuiessen acordadamente" (4.27.1, 2: 630) [Concord is a virtue similar to friendship; the sages and great lords who made books of the law favored bringing it about so that men might live together in unity (1003)]. For there to be a good and just social order, are all subjects, all aristocrats, or all Christians, meant to become the truest and best of friends like heroic male companions? Perhaps, as Halperin suggests, such a vision derives from classical utopia itself, in which one finds the ethical exaltation and mythical transcendence of homophilic discourse: "[I]n Plato's *Republic* . . . the utopian effort to unite all the citizens of the just city in the bonds of fraternal love effectively does away with the social significance of real brothers and sisters, of both kinship and conjugality, altogether. Having begun by borrowing its social significance and representational elements from kinship and conjugality, in other words, male *philia* ends up (in Plato's fantasy, at least) displacing them entirely" (86).

It is also significant that Alfonso X's utopia draws upon classical constructions of essentially male friendship, rather than upon evangelical challenges of the more radical forms of Christian utopia based on charity toward all one's neighbors (and enemies). Is Christian charity somehow to be inferred by Alfonso's contemporaries from the advocacy of homophilic ethics and civic concord modeled on Greek philosophy? Such an attempt would be problematic: as Lewis points out, ordinary association, intimate friendship, and Christian charity are all disparate concepts with distinct origins and divergent aims; it is not simply a question of degree of affinity but of kind of relationship (61–62, 120–21). Paradoxically, in the Alfonsine social utopia, what originally were homophilic paradigms of noble friendship are appropriated as communitarian standards: somehow they are meant to guide those who are not essentially "like" (in gender or class) and who have only the slightest "affinity" (in attraction or obligation).

In recapitulating classical and clerical formulas of order, Alfonso X takes an ideological leap of faith (Aristotelian and Thomist) from aristocratic homophilia to social utopia:

Dixo Aristóteles que si los omes ouiessen entre sí verdadera amistad, non aurían menester Justicia nin Alcaldes que los judgassen: porque aquella amistad les faríe complir, e guardar aquello mismo, que quiere e manda la Justicia. (4.27.1, 2: 629–30)

[Aristotle stated that if true friendship existed among men, they would have no need of courts or magistrates to judge them, because friendship would cause them to do and observe what justice orders and directs. (1003)]

In effect, this type of utopian syncretism confuses two types of *philia* that are clearly distinguished in classical ethics. As Price explains, there are two socially significant processes contemplated in Aristotelian *philia*. One is contractual obligation by transpersonal political or economic association: "[T]here must in effect be an actual partnership. So we have an instance of *philia* whenever a pair or group of human beings is interacting in a way intended to benefit one another through beneficence or co-operation according to some shared conception of benefit" (159–60).

The other is transcendent formation by interpersonal moral interaction: "Aristotle envisages the emergence of that reciprocal concern and respect which constitute the best kind of friendship, linking individuals not merely as satisfiers of one another's incidental needs, but as partners in a life of personal self-realization" (238). It is the latter which, in formulations of classical ethics and medieval chivalry, is often exemplified in idealized and sublimated forms of homophilia, so that it can then be said that "the moral end of love is to transcend itself in friendship" (249). But in *Siete partidas*, it is assumed that what can be achieved individually among élites (loyal male companionship, if not quite heroic male bonding) can be extended to flourish among all sexes, estates, and conditions. True, in Alfonsine utopia, aristocratic male friendship is not the foundation of Christian society (as marriage is, both as sacrament and as civil status), but it does serve as its best cement.

Ramon Llull's *Llibre d'Amic e d'Amat*

Llull's *Llibre d'Amic e d'Amat* [Book of the Friend and Beloved], along with the novel *Blanquerna* in which it is included as a semiautonomous section (bk. 5, chs. 99 and 100), presents certain difficulties as a hybrid text: it is based on mixed religious and literary cultures and it is designed for mixed reception by clergy and laity (aspects of *Blanquerna* studied by González-Casanovas, *The Apostolic Hero*). It also purports to offer the protagonist's mystical confessions, based on personal experience and examples of "Sufi preachers," as a guide to contemplation within the apostolic utopia of a reform of contemporary Christendom. In the process, Llull represents chivalric and courtly concepts of love and friendship in such a way as to exemplify the archetypal Christian man who falls in love with Christ, as well as becomes his boon companion:

> Dementre que Blanquerna plorava e adorava, e en la sobirana stremitat de ses forces havia pujada Déus sa ànima, qui.l contemplava, Blanquerna se sentí exit de manera, per la gran frevor e devoció en què era, e cogità que força d'amor no segueix manera com l'amich ama molt fortment son amat. On, per açò Blanquerna fo en volentat que fées *Libre d'Amic e Amat*, lo qual amich fos feel e devot crestià, e.l amat fos Déu." (bk. 5, ch. 99; 3: 10)

[While Blanquerna wept in adoration, God raised his soul to the limit of its power to contemplate Him, so that he fell into a rapture out of great fervor and devotion; he pondered that the force of love follows no order when the Friend greatly loves his Beloved. That is why Blanquerna wished to write the *Llibre d'Amic e d'Amat,* in which the Friend is a faithful and devout Christian, and the Beloved is God].[10]

Thus, the narrative framework in the novel proper (the prelude contained in bk. 5, ch. 99) serves to prepare the reader for the orthodox pious reception and spiritual allegorization with which to decode the parables of love that follow (the 366 prose "verses" and "moral metaphors" that make up ch. 100).

Nonetheless, upon entering the sequence of parables, the reader finds not only exemplary confessions of spiritual autobiography (the struggle to serve Christ in preaching to fellow Christians and missions to infidels, as in nos. 287 and 337) and symbolic personifications of theological doctrines (such as the Augustinian spiritual trinity of the memory, understanding, and will, as in nos. 18 and 298), but also lyrical passages that, in their effort to embody and inspire devotion, are striking for their use of homophilic expression (not at all homogenital but at times truly homoerotic). On the one hand, one finds the textual representation of emotional intimacy between the two male lovers: "L'amat enamora l'amich, e no.l plany de son languiment, per ço que pus fortment sia amat e en lo major languiment atrop l'amich plaer e reveniment" (no. 31, 3: 17) [The Beloved shows his love to the Friend, who does not complain of languishing, so that he may be loved more strongly, and in so much languishing the Friend finds pleasure and renewal]. This constitutes the transposition of courtly love — as well as other conventions of courtly literature, such as dawn songs, love letters, and prisons of love (as in nos. 26–27, 130, 168) — into a spiritualized form of homoeroticism. On the other hand, one finds the symbolic idealization of virtuous affinity between the two male friends:

Les condicions d'amor són que.l amich sia sufirent, pacient, humil, temorós, diligent, confiant, e que s'aventur a grans perills a honrar son amat. E les condicions del amat són que sia vertader, liberal, piadós, just, a son amich. (no. 33, 3: 18)

[The conditions of love are that the Friend be long-suffering, patient, humble, fearful, diligent, trusting, and that he risk great dangers so as to honor his Beloved. And the conditions of the Beloved are that he be true, generous, merciful, and just towards his Friend.]

Here a Christianized form of homophilia is exalted: it is expressed in culturally fixed terms not only of courtly sentimentality but also of chivalric formation; and it serves to construct exemplary relations of perfect human love between the Friend and the Beloved. The Friend is at various times represented as the Fool of Love:

> Anava l'amich per una ciutat com a foll, cantant de son amat; e demanaren-li les gents si avia perdut son seny. Respòs que son amat havia pres son voler, e que ell li avia donat son entendiment; per açò era-li romàs tan solament lo remembrament, ab què remembrava son amat." (no. 54, 3: 22)

[The Friend went through a city like a fool, singing of his Beloved; the crowds asked him if he had lost his mind. He answered that his Beloved had captured his will, and that he had given him his understanding, so that all he had left was his memory, with which he remembered his Beloved.]

This image, which recalls Pauline and Franciscan pious conceits of the Christian as God's fool among the worldly wise, reflects the autobiographical figure of Ramon the Fool in *Blanquerna*, who forsakes vain courtliness for itinerant preaching with popular parables (bk. 4, chs. 79–83 and 87). But in the *Llibre d'Amic e d'Amat* the Fool of Love also corresponds to a form of homophilic exaltation as a symbol for true devotion, which is not satisfied with the common affections of conventional society or nominal Christians: "Escarnien e reprenien les gents l'amich per ço cor anava com a foll per amor. E.l amich menyspreava lurs scarns, e reprenia les gents per ço cor no amaven son amat" (no. 148, 3: 43) [The crowds mocked and scolded the Friend for going about like a fool of love. The Friend scorned their mockery and scolded the crowds for not loving his Beloved]. The Beloved is identified as Christ, God-made-man, who appears as a figure of radical human love, whose friendship is expressed in extravagant homophilic terms: "Entresenya's l'amat a son amich de vermells e novells vestiments; e estén sos braços per ço que l'abraç, e enclina son cap per ço que li dó un besar, e està en alt per ço que.l puscha atrobar" (no. 91, 3: 31) [The Beloved shows himself to his Friend in new red clothes; he extends his arms to embrace him, inclines his head to kiss him, and stays raised above him so that

he might find him]. This is a striking symbol of what is after all the crucified Christ; nevertheless, it is textually constructed as an ever intimate and
totally generous male friend-lover. In its cultural context, it is clear that for
Llull and his readers, rather than a poetic license that borders on sacrilege
and heresy, this homophilic image represents an idealization as well as an
exaggeration of male bonding as humanized love.

Evidently, the homophilia and homoeroticism explicit in some (not all
or even most) of the prose verses, as well as implicit in the overall narrative framework that allegorizes what is undeniably a male "love affair," are
also meant to be interpreted within the textuality of pastiche (vernacular
popularizations of what are commonly understood to be Sufi and Christian
expressions of mystical love) and parable (symbolic challenges to devotion
based on evangelical models of fully human responses to Christ's empa-
thy and compassion). Given the textual artifice and spiritual artifact of a
dramatized yet sublimated homophilia, as well as the conventional and
transposed cultural dimensions of its discourse and narrative, it is impossible to determine Llull's own ethical view of male bonding as such. (We
know that he was a Majorcan of noble estate close to the Aragonese crown,
who at age thirty abandoned his love poetry and paramours at the court, as
well as a wife and two children, in response to a conversion experience; it
was this that led him to dedicate the rest of his long, solitary life and auto-
didactic, eccentric career to theological writing, missionary teaching, and
reform propaganda along the margins of the Dominican and papal centers
of power.) His influential *Llibre de l'orde de cavaleria* [Book of the Order
of Chivalry] (written around 1275, soon translated into several languages,
and printed in English in 1484 by William Caxton) only makes the usual
reference to knights honoring their peers (86).

There are two models of homophilic and even homoerotic medieval textualities with which Llull, as noble courtier and missionary to Islam, would
have been quite familiar. One is the example of the Sufis, which he and his
protagonist cite as literary (rather than theological) point of departure for
writing the *Llibre d'Amic e d'Amat*:

> Blanquerna . . . remembrà . . . que los serrayns an alcuns hòmens religio-
> sos . . . qui són més preats enfre ells . . . , qui han nom 'sufies,' e aquells
> han paraules d'amor e exemplis abreuyats e qui donen a home gran devoció.
> (Bk. 5, ch. 99; 3: 10)

[Blanquerna remembered that the Saracens have some religious men who are highly regarded by them, who are called 'Sufis'; they use words of love and short examples to effect great devotion.]

For Llull this is a characteristic effort to appropriate the form and spirit of Muslim devotions for Christian renewal: in another work, *Cent noms de Déu* [Hundred Names of God], he offers a pious counteroffensive to Islamic veneration of the ninety-nine divine attributes; and elsewhere in *Blanquerna* (bk. 4, ch. 80) he holds up to Christian crusaders and missionaries the example of Saracen assassins as devotees willing to suffer martyrdom for their faith. In the case of the Sufis, it is interesting to note that for Llull they represent not so much mystical visionaries and poets as popular preachers and pious minstrels:

Molts galiadors e arlots . . . preycaven als sserrahins l'*Alcorà* e les benanances de parays; e tan devotes paraules preycaven, que quaix tots aquells qui los scoltaven se ploraven. . . . Los sserrayns preycaven de devoció e de consideracions en la glòria de paraís e en les penes infernals, e per açò avien devoció als sermons e ploraven per devoció. (Bk. 4, ch. 93; 2: 241)

[Many goliards and minstrels would preach to the Saracens on the Koran and the blessings of paradise; they preached with such devoted words that almost all who heard them would weep. Saracens preached devotion and represented the glory of paradise and pains of hell, and so felt devotion in their sermons and devoutly wept.]

This simplification of Sufi mysticism as a model of affective devotion excludes references to the autobiographical and symbolic examples of homoerotic friendship for which they are equally famous.[11] In one point Llull may have been influenced by a general, popularized knowledge of Sufi expressions of piety as sublimated forms of homophilic union. It is summarized by Burckhardt:

Full, integral love . . . gives a sort of subjective infallibility [that applies] to all that forms part of the 'personal' relationship of the adorer to his Lord. It is in the object, Beauty, that love virtually coincides with knowledge. . . . [T]he most lofty station of the soul is not a psychological correlative of knowledge . . . but is integral love, the complete absorption of the human will by the Divine attraction. It is the state of being 'lost in love' of which Abraham is the human prototype. (31, 33, 34)

This idealization and sublimation of homophilia, which leads to spiritual transcendence and divine communion, found its most sublime expression in Plato and his followers, whose influence continued into the Christian and Muslim Middle Ages and beyond. As Price notes,

> According to the *Symposium*, love is the desire to beget in beauty. . . . A goal of Plato's preferred lovers is mental union in a shared life. . . . Platonic love that is not satisfied by physical procreation is indeed fundamentally, and essentially, homoerotic. . . . Thus if mental union is conceived on the model of mental pregnancy, it does indeed point to pederasty. . . . If peder-astic desire is particularly susceptible to sublimation, then it is natural that those particularly capable of sublimation should incline towards pederasty; by contrast, those content with physical pleasure should be relatively indif-ferent about what form it takes. (228)

Such a paradigm (as much Platonic and Augustinian as it is Sufi), that of falling in love with divine truth and beauty in a personal relationship of transcendent intimacy, would have been widely diffused along the reli-gious and intellectual frontiers of Reconquest Iberia and the Mediterranean known by Llull.

Sufi models do not account, however, for the culturally specific refer-ences to expressions of courtly sentimentality and chivalric companionship found in the *Llibre d'Amic e d'Amat*. More important than general parallels with Sufi devotion, then, is the need to recognize to what extent homo-erotic poetics and homophilic ethics fundamentally characterize certain constructions of medieval chivalry found in codes, rituals, and texts. As Gauvard observes of medieval knights,

> Among men profound sentiments were developed, when it concerned those of the same class and age, or youths who were initiated by the same sponsor. Their bonds began with a simple camaraderie and finally attained friendship, which often . . . was mixed up with love. This friendship was sealed by ges-tures that were not in the least ambiguous: they would drink from the same cup and share the same mattress until the day they died, when the friends'

dearest wish was to be buried next to each other, so as to rise together from their grave on the day of Judgment. (92; translation mine)

A famous medieval literary example of aristocratic homophilia is provided by *Ami et Amil* (c. 1200). Its erotic dimensions and critical issues are noted by Gauvard (cf. Boswell 1980: 239–40, Rosenberg 12–13):

[It] narrated the exemplary friendship of two young noblemen, who when they met "fell into each other's embrace with such force, and hugged one another with such tenderness, that they almost stifled themselves. . . ." After they tumbled off their horses and fell to the ground, they covered each other's faces with kisses from nose to chin in a public display of great eroticism. These, then, were the forms of love taken by friendship between two [medieval noble] men. Can it also have been homosexuality? This issue remains open, but the terms with which to define it are not always exact, since they are anachronistic. (92; translation mine)

With this type of homophilic textuality conspicuously present in Llull's day, it is not surprising that the chivalric and courtly mirror of intimate male friendship should serve as a central feature of his effort to show the most sublime and passionate form of human love for the human figure of Christ.

To confirm the appeal of this model for Llull, one has only to turn to a later work in which he develops it with greater textual and narrative complexity (but less mystical and lyrical exaltation): in 1298–99 he writes *Arbre de filosofia d'amor* [The Tree of Philosophy of Love], which includes a section on "Fulls d'amor" [Leaves of Love]. This consists of an allegorical narrative about the chivalrous male Friend, whose passion for the Beloved (Christ) leads him to confessions and languishments in the prison of love; his zeal leads him to escape and go on a love pilgrimage to the Holy Land; at the Holy Sepulcher he expires out of ecstatic compassion and desire for union with his Beloved; later at his funeral there are solemn and affective displays by a procession of "Noble Young Men of Love" (*donzels d'Amor*):

Sobre'l vas e la péra d'amor escriviren los donzels d'amor aquest títol: "Aysí jau l'amic, mort per son amat e per amor; amic qui à amat son amat ab bona, gran e durable amor." . . . Can lo títol agren escrit los donzels d'amor e agren [daurades] les letres ab desirers, suspirs e plors d'amor . . . tot ensems acompanyaren la dona d'amor tro a la casa on l'amic morí per amor. (Bk. 5, ch. 83, 130–31)

[On the tomb and burial stone of love the Noble Youths of Love wrote this inscription: "Here lies the Friend, who died for his Beloved and his love; the Friend who loved his Beloved with a good, great, and lasting love." When the Noble Youths of Love had written and gilded the letters with their desires, sighs, and tears of love, all went together to accompany the Lady of Love to the house where the Friend died for love.]

It seems that Llull's construction of mystical parables with chivalric and courtly forms of homophilia not only persisted but grew even more elaborate in his later works. Clearly such expressions appealed to him and he thought they would also appeal to his readers.

What the modern reader finds in Llull's *Llibre d'Amic e d'Amat* are new twists to the esthetics of sublimated love. Both "civilized" and pious self-constructions of explicitly male subjects and objects of desire become the sustained theme of those 366 verses and moral metaphors: "Anava l'amich desirant son amat, e encontrà's ab -II- amichs qui ab amor e ab plors se saludaren, e s'abraçaren e.s besaren. Smortí's l'amich: tant fortment li remembraren los -II- amichs son amat" (no. 59, 3: 24) [The Friend went about desiring his Beloved and found two friends who greeted each other with love and tears, embraced, and kissed. The Friend fainted, for the two friends reminded him so much of his Beloved]. Both "ascetic" and mystical transformations of conspicuously male bodies and minds, as loci of divine grace, serve as the climax to a five-part work of religious exemplarity in the world:

Encontraren-se l'amich e.l amat, e foren testimonis de lur encontrament saluts, abraçaments, e besars, e làgremes e plors. E demanà l'amat al amich de son estament; e l'amich fo enbarbesclat en presència de son amat. (no. 117, 3: 37)

[The Friend and the Beloved met. Witnesses to their meeting were greetings, embraces, kisses, tears, and weeping. The Beloved asked the Friend about his condition; the Friend was perplexed in the presence of his Beloved.]

To these aspects should be added the elaboration of a gendered complementarity within the homophilic narrative. The Friend is feminized as the subject of companionship: he is characterized as receiving loving advances, languishing in dependence, suffering bodily passion, expressing wordless gestures, and indulging in unrestrained emotions that turn him into the helpless Fool of Love. The Beloved, in turn, is masculinized as the object of attraction: he is represented as initiator of stages in relations, heroic champion, wise and gentle teacher, and militant for virtue, who becomes the active Martyr of Love.

It is noteworthy, then, that Llull does not hesitate to embrace homophilic discourse as a symbolic medium for no less than spiritual self-transcendence within the orthodox piety of the human imitation of Christ. There is no denying that in attempting to describe and exemplify the most intimate, passionate, and sublime friendship of the devout Christian for the incarnated Christ, Llull has recourse to representations of male bonding in homophilic terms: "Encontraren-se l'amich e.ll amat, e dix l'amich: 'No cal que.m parles; mas fe'm senyal ab tos hulls, qui són paraules a mon cor, con te dó ço que.m demanes'" (no. 29, 3: 17) [The Friend and Beloved met, and the Friend said: "You do not need to speak to me, but give me signs with your eyes, which are words to my heart, so that I might give you what you ask of me"]. Given the wide availability (indeed dominance) of heteroerotic models in sacred and profane literature of his day (cf. Solé and Vauchez 186), it is clear that Llull's privileging of homophilic relations represents a deliberately positive valuation of intimate male friendship within the homosocial, masculine-gendered ideals of high chivalric culture. It is equally clear that he felt confident that his audience of clerical, aristocratic, and bourgeois (literate and pious) élites would receive his parables of male bonding as constructive challenges to their devotion and reformation. For, in highlighting virtuous forms of homophilia as images of the truest and best love, Llull believed himself to be definitely within the bounds of his readers' chivalric culture: he was still speaking their own ritual language, referring to their liminal experiences, and appealing to their communal values.

Juan Manuel's *El conde Lucanor*

In Juan Manuel's *El conde Lucanor*, the utopian discourse of male bonding in Christian chivalry comes to be expressed, not in the erudite disquisitions of Alfonsine jurisprudence or in the affective parables of Lullian devotion, but in the more dispersed narrative framework of popular anecdotes, dialogues, and moralities exchanged by the eponymous aristocrat and his trusted counselor Patronio. In this process, the construction of male friendship comes to be contextualized in the cultural frontiers of Iberian *reconquista* and *convivencia* (the crusade for reconquest of Iberia from the Moors, along with the cultural symbiosis of Christians, Muslims, and Jews), just as it is also integrated into traditions of Mediterranean sapience and folklore. Among the fifty tales included in the collection, there are two ex-empla (nos. 25 and 50) on Saladin, the historical and legendary figure of the crusading East. These are outstanding for their cultural background, ethical exemplarity, psychological development, and narrative skill (see González-Casanovas, "Didáctica y *Bildung*"). They also serve to illustrate the cultural paradigm and narrative discourse of heroic male bonding that is most characteristic of aristocratic eras and frontier societies, and of the epic-chivalric textualities that arise from them. The model is summarized by Halperin (in the contexts of a discussion of *Gilgamesh*, the *Iliad*, and the Books of Samuel):

[H]eroic friendship [is] better captured by terms like comrades-in-arms, boon companions . . . something that only males can have . . . only in couples. . . . The male couple constitutes a world apart from society at large, yet it does not merely embody a "private" relation. . . . [It] helps to structure — and possibly to privatize — the social space; it takes shape in the world that lies beyond the horizon of the domestic sphere, and it requires for its expression a military or political staging-ground. . . . [I]t depends for its meaning on the meaningfulness of social action. . . . Those repre-sentations . . . all seem to exhibit a similar paradox: although their textual strategies make kinship and conjugality into privileged loci of signification for representing friendship, they also make friendship into a paradigm case of human sociality. They invoke kinship and conjugality . . . only to displace them, to reduce them to mere *images* of friendship. (77, 85)

Such critical distinctions can provide useful references to help modern readers understand Juan Manuel's image of Saladin's heroism.

Example 25 shows that the sultan's relation to the count of Provence is that of valiant comrade, intimate friend, and trusted counselor, who helps decide the other's family matters. These involve issues of noble power and inheritance: whoever marries the count's daughter will govern the county and beget an heir, as well as rule during the count's captivity overseas. It is thus striking that Saladin's counsel, to have the daughter marry a "real man" in every sense of the word, is predicated on a radical heroic-masculine ethics, which is intuitively grasped in male bonding:

> Saladín respondió assí . . . : "Mas el mío consejo es éste: que casedes vuestra fija con omne." El conde gelo tovo en merçed, et entendió muy bien lo que aquello quería dezir. . . . [E]l soldán . . . tovo que más de preçiar era el omne por las sus obras que non por su riqueza, nin por nobleza de su linage. (145–46)

> [Saladin answered thus: "My counsel is this: that you marry your daughter to a man." The count thanked him for it, and understood quite well what it meant. The sultan thought that a man was more to be prized for his acts than for his wealth or noble lineage.] [12]

Example 50 presents Saladin as all-powerful potentate, whose exploits are already accomplished, so that he currently lacks a heroic agenda to challenge him as well as a heroic companion to bring out his fullest nobility; instead, in his courtly leisure and solitude he encounters a married woman with whom he falls in love and runs the risk of compromising his virtue (as well as hers). It is thus remarkable that he should find in her his ultimate challenge, a quest for knowledge of the greatest virtue (*vergüença* or a sense of shame), which leads him to find self-knowledge, confront his conscience, and struggle to conquer his own desire with his own virtue:

> Quando la buena dueña esto oyó, dexósse caer en tierra ante los sus pies, et díxol assí, llorando muy fieramente: "Señor, vós avedes aquí dicho muy grandes dos verdades: la una, que sodes vós el mejor omne del mundo; la otra, que la vergüença es la mejor cosa que le omne puede aver en sí. Et señor, pues vós esto conosçedes, et sodes el mejor omne del mundo, pídovos por merçed que querades en vós la mejor cosa del mundo." (251–52)

> [When the good lady heard this, she fell on the ground at his feet, and, weeping very violently, said to him: "My lord, you have said two great truths: one, you are the best man in the world; the other, shame is the best thing that a man can have in himself. Since you recognize this and are indeed the best man in the world, my lord, I beg you for pity's sake to seek for yourself the best thing in the world."]

Foucault's ascetic self-mastery and Halperin's socialized self-transcendence thus find textual correlatives in Saladin. He is led to reconstruct within himself the complete male hero thanks to a woman, whose poised speech, valiant defiance, and prudent counsel in effect represent a textual substitute for the noble male companion that is so conspicuously absent in example 50. In this narrative process, the woman's emergent textuality displaces the feminine object of bodily desire with a masculine subject of prudent restraint; rather than submit to seduction or rape, she asserts a male-like chivalric appeal to moral reason and self-control. Instead of male bonding as such, we find a challenge to aristocratic masculinity: it is now Saladin's turn to seek, in himself, what is a real man, true noble, and best friend. In this ethical process, his sexual desire for the woman as woman is sublimated into a masculine relation of *philia:* "Et commoquier que la él amava ante de otro amor, amóla muy más dallí adellante de amor leal et verdadero" (ex. 50, 252) [Although he had loved her before with another type of love, he loved her much more henceforth with a true and loyal love]. This textual transformation in Juan Manuel recalls Solé's observation about the cultural transposition of masculine chivalric values onto courtly relations between noble men and women: "In its complete formulation, [medieval] European love would thus represent the extension to intersexual relations of values at first belonging to masculine friendship" (100; translation mine).

In Juan Manuel's two exempla on Saladin, several levels of irony are at work. The mirror of chivalry for Christian readers is not a fellow Christian, eminent for his religious zeal or noble credentials, but a Saracen enemy who commends himself for his integrity and prudence: "Et todo este bien vino al conde por el buen consejo que el soldán le dio que casesse su fija con omne" (ex. 25, 150) [And all these good things befell the count as a result of the good counsel which the sultan gave him that he marry his daughter to a (real) man]. The exemplar of heroic male bonding finds his truest friends not among Muslim male peers but in a Christian noble captive and in a Muslim subject woman, who remind the sultan of the need to balance power with ethics:

Señor, commo quier que yo só assaz muger de pequeña guisa, pero vien sé que el amor non es en poder del omne, ante es el omne en poder del amor. . . . [A]ssí sé otra cosa: que quando los omnes, et señaladamente los señores vos pagades de alguna muger, dades a entender que faredes quanto ella quisiere, et desque ella finca mal andante et escarnida, preçiádesla poco [et], commo es derecho, finca del todo mal. (Ex. 50, 246–47)

[My lord, although I am only a weak woman, still I know that love is not in the power of men, but rather man is in the power of love. Another thing I know: when you men, especially lords, satisfy your desires with a woman, you pretend to do whatever she wants, but as soon as she finds herself ill used and mocked, you prize her little, and according to your right, she comes out badly.]

The proofs of loyalty and nobility take the forms, not of heroic companionship in military or political action, but of trustworthy service by means of good counsels in noble domestic affairs and matters of conscience: "Quando Saladín esto oyó, gradesçió mucho a Dios, et plógol más porque açertó en l' su conseio, que sil oviera acaesçido otra pro o otra onra por grande que fuesse" (ex. 25, 149) [When Saladin heard this, he gave many thanks to God, and he was happier for finding the right counsel, than if any benefit or honor had befallen him]. Finally, the textual construction of aristocratic virtue is expressed, not in relation to transcendent systems of society or religion, but in reference to more contingent frames of interpersonal relations and intrapersonal values: "Loaron mucho el entendimiento et el esfuerço et la lealdad del yerno del conde. Otrossí, loaron mucho las vondades de Saladín et del conde, et gradesçieron mucho a Dios porque quiso guisar de lo traer a tan buen acabamiento" (ex. 25, 150) [They praised greatly the count's son-in-law's understanding, efforts, and loyalty. They also praised Saladin's and the count's virtues, and gave many thanks to God for having him come to such a good end]. In contrast to the Alfonsine vision for an extended masculine harmony and to the Lullian quest for an intensified masculine compassion, Juan Manuel's exempla constitute modest and internalized expressions of affinity, while at the same time they offer paradoxical and cross-cultural constructions of male chivalric mimesis.

Where examples 25 and 50 stand out is in developing certain key emphases within homosocial order and homophilic expression. First, they elaborate upon the mirror image of friendship that allows true friends to function as two halves of the same whole:

Et commo quier que estava preso, sabiendo Saladín la grand vondat del conde, fazíale mucho bien et mucha onra, et todos los grandes fechos que avía de fazer todos los fazía por su conseio. Et tan bien le conseiava el conde et tanto fiava dél el soldán que, commo quier que estava preso, que tan grand logar et tand grand poder avía, et tanto fazían por él en toda la tierra de Saladín commo farían en la suya misma." (Ex. 25, 144)

[Although the count was being held captive, Saladin knew his great virtue; he favored and honored him greatly so that all the great deeds to be done by him would be done according to his counsel. The count counseled him so well and the sultan trusted him so much, in spite of his captivity, that he came to hold a great place and great power, and they would do for him as much in all of Saladin's lands as would be done in his own country.]

Second, they stress gendered identification, even between different sexes, with respect to the masculine-defined virtues of just rule, self-controlled power, and words of honor: "Quando Saladín todas estas buenas razones oyó et entendió cómmo aquella buena dueña, con la su vondat y con el su buen entendimiento, sopiera aguisar que fuesse él guardado de tan grand yerro, gradesçiólo mucho a Dios" (ex. 50, 252) [When Saladin heard all these good statements and understood how this good lady by her virtue and understanding had managed to keep him from such a great wrong, he gave many thanks to God]. Third, they promote a paradigm of ongoing formation and perfection in chivalric ethics:

Et ya por la dueña non fiziera tanto; mas, porque él era tan buen omne, tenía quel era mengua si dexasse de saber aquello que avía començado; ca, sin dubda, el grant omne grant mengua faze si dexa lo que una vez comiença, solamente que el fecho non sea malo o pecado; mas, si por miedo o trabajo lo dexa, non se podrá de mengua escusa. (Ex. 50, 248)

[He would no longer do as much for the lady; but since he was such a good man, he considered that it would be to his discredit to abandon the search to know what he set out to learn; for undoubtedly the great man discredits himself greatly if he abandons what he began, as long as it is not evil or sinful; but, if out of fear or difficulty he abandons it, his discredit cannot be excused.]

Fourth, they illustrate the need to correspond fully to the highest expectations that friends and others have of one's virtues:

> Aquel fijo de aquel rico omne . . . tovo que, pues Saladín lo escogiera por omne, et le fiziera allegar a tand grand onra, que non sería él omne si non fiziesse en este fecho lo que pertenesçía . . . : que él fiava por Dios que él le endereçaría porque entendiessen las gentes que fazía fecho de omne. (Ex. 25, 146–47)

> [That son of a great noble thought that since Saladin had chosen him for a man, and had raised him to such a great honor, that he would not be a man if he were not to do in this event what corresponded to him: for he trusted in God to guide him in such a way that the crowds might understand that he was performing a man's deed.]

Fifth, they project a model of homotextual formation that reinforces the didactic and narrative frames. On the one hand, within the exempla one finds the mutual recognition of friends by their shared ways of thinking and speaking:

> Quando el cavallero ançiano oyó esta razón, entendióla muy bien; et otrossí, conosçió en la palabra que aquél era Saladín; ca él visquiera muy grand tiempo con él en su casa et reçibiera dél mucho bien et mucha merçed. (Ex. 50, 249)

> [When the old knight heard this statement, he understood it quite well; likewise, he recognized in that speech that it was Saladin; for he had lived for a very long time with him in his household and had received from him much good and favor.]

On the other hand, one encounters confirmation of years of friendship at court and in council recapitulated toward the end of Patronio's lengthy and generous dialogues with Lucanor:

> Agora, señor conde Lucanor, demás de los enxiemplos et proverbios que son en este libro, vos he dicho assaz a mi cuydar para poder guardar el alma et aun el cuerpo et la onra et la fazienda et el estado, et, loado a Dios, segund el mio flaco entendimiento, tengo que vos he complido et acabado todo lo que vos dixe. (Pt. 5, 304)

[Now, my lord Count Lucanor, in addition to the exempla and proverbs to be found in this book, I have told you as much as I can about safeguarding soul, body, honor, wealth, and estate, and, praise be to God, by my weak understanding, I consider that I have fulfilled and completed all that I told you that I would do.]

Through Patronio's good counsels and Lucanor's good reception their own male bonding has been constructed.

Juan Manuel relates Saladin's prudent heroism to Patronio's sage counsels. He thus underscores the textual elaboration of friendship via speech acts: these articulate and exemplify chivalry in ritual dialogues about heroic initiation, profession, recognition, acclamation, and rededication; they are paralleled in the narrative frame of each story, with the sequential recitation of Lucanor's aristocratic obligations, Patronio's appeal to moral reason, illustration of the dilemma by exempla drawn from their common field of experience, Patronio's wise and courtly counsel, and Lucanor's noble valuation and appropriation of it for himself, his court, and his book. Saladin and Patronio both come to affirm an essentially homotextual relationship: it is expressed in words of communal self-correction and self-evaluation by the élite, based on verbal rehearsal and application of chivalric codes, realized as esthetic and ethical discourses that perfect a practical art of eloquence, performed by experienced interpreters for noble initiates and intimates, received by true peers with sympathetic hearts and like minds, and interpreted as a mutual challenge to virtue. Such homotextual discourse in effect represents a sublimation of homophilia in courtly narrative and aristocratic dialogue.

Conclusions: Cultural Ethics of Male Friendship

In medieval cultures, male bonding often consists of the heroic representation of same-sex companionship, as well as the aristocratic exemplification of like-gendered affinities, both of which are seen to emerge in patterns of virtuous formation. For chivalric culture, such a model can develop in a variety of forms and on multiple levels. But most involve a shared quest for personal fulfillment through ethical interaction, which transcends the natural limits and societal boundaries of sex, marriage, and family. In part, this reflects the post-Augustinian duality of body and spirit, so that what is most human (and God-like) is what rises above (but not against) nature; male "true friends" achieve a supranatural formation in virtue that goes beyond natural gratification of procreative appetites by "good spouses" (or antinatural perversion in "evil acts" of sodomy). In part, this also responds to an asymmetry in medieval society between men and women, so that not only power but also virtue is seen to reside in greater measure in male élites; male "best friends" thus extend domination by a male aristocracy to the exaltation of masculine chivalry. As a special case one finds the spiritualization of chivalry and courtesy represented by Llull's *Llibre d'Amic e d'Amat*. Here there are two types of asceticism, which correspond to religious convention and to ethical constructionism: in one, family, world, and body are disowned to pursue contemplation in a hermitage (in Llull's novel, the former pope Blanquerna, as hermit, writes the *Llibre*), while in the other, perfection of self and others (aristocratic and bourgeois readers) is promoted through companionship with Christ in culturally determined terms of the highest human/male friendship then advocated. Despite the appropriations of homophilia found in clerical and aristocratic authority, and in spiritualizations of chivalry, there remain the problematic nature and paradoxical example of male bonding as a "marginal" phenomenon and "superfluous" discourse: beyond the stability of family and marriage in the cultural construction of official institutions lies the contingency of friendship as the cultural stylization of interpersonal interaction. Male friends, especially true, noble, and virtuous ones, can complete each other's lives but are not essential to them.

In late-medieval Iberian texts, male bonding is constructed within shifting cultural frontiers. These not only reflect contemporary religious cultures that coexist in the peninsula during the Reconquest but also relate to historically dominant cultures that overlap in the medieval "authorities." As a cultural-frontier phenomenon, male friendship is a nonnatural, stylized, and anomalous artifact (to combine terminology from Lewis 56; Foucault 2: 249–50; and Halperin 75). Its fundamental "difference" emerges in didactic textuality drawn from the traditional wisdom and natural philosophy that flourish in the Iberian *convivencia:*[13] while everyone (Jew, Christian, and Muslim) supposedly knows what constitutes a good ruler, subject, soldier, husband, father, or son, it is rather more difficult to define the true, good, and best male friend as such; for the friend is to be recognized by personal traits of character and subjective attributes of virtue, rather than by natural ties of blood and sex or by official categories of law and doctrine. This point is made by Juan Manuel in *El conde Lucanor:* "Los buenos amigos son la mejor cosa del mundo, et . . . quando biene grand mester et la grand quexa, que falla omne muy menos de quantos cuyda" (ex. 48, 235) [Good friends are the best thing in the world; but when great need and trouble arise, one finds far fewer than he expects]; to which he adds, as a major stumbling block to friendship: "Non a cosa en l' mundo en que omne tanto nin tan de ligero se engañe commo en cognoscer los omnes quáles son en sí et quál entendimiento an" (ex. 50, 244) [There is nothing in the world in which one can so easily be deceived as in knowing what men are truly like and what are their intentions]. Male friendship's peculiar difficulty also emerges in cultural (rather than ideological) tension between pagan reason and Christian doctrine, which is exacerbated in systematic appropriations of Aristotelian philosophy by Thomist theology, and accentuated in competing systems of canon law and Roman jurisprudence (as in *Siete partidas*): among many types and degrees of "natural obligations" can be found varieties of friendship that range from profitable association to highest human love; but only matrimony, as sacrament and civil status, receives recognition from church and state. Discussion about the good friend and companion involves multiple, and at times contradictory, layers of reference to heroic archetypes, biblical exemplars, ethical prototypes, social contracts, political networks, and ecclesiastical prescriptions. Ultimately, such constructions of male bonding must deal with the fundamental cultural frontier that operates in late-medieval and Renaissance Europe: a secular humanism privileges *philia* as an "ascetic" formation (critical, esthetic, ethical) for good subjects or knights in this world (as in Juan Manuel's *El conde Lucanor*); but a spiritual humanitarianism converts *philia* into a "mimetic" approximation (conscientious, conformational, and compassionate) to Christ by Christians as pilgrims to the next world (as in Llull's *Blanquerna*). The classical quest for self-fulfilling virtuous excellence (*arete*) and the evangelical counsels of selfless spiritual perfection (*caritas*) come to lay divergent claims on constructions of heroic, aristocratic male friendship within chivalric culture.

Taken together, the selected texts by Alfonso X, Ramon Llull, and Juan Manuel serve to show the poetic transformation and ethical reformation that arise in representations of chivalric homophilia within utopian, devotional, and didactic contexts. As a constitutive and idealized, yet also hybrid and marginalized, discourse on the excellence and virtue of all true friendship, noble male bonding transcends not only sex-based marriage and interest-defined society, but also same-sex relations and like-gendered affinities. The way it accomplishes cultural transcendence leads, beyond the common necessity to struggle for survival (or salvation) of the individual and group, to what (to paraphrase Lewis and Foucault) is constructed as an aristocratic "art of civilized living" with the truest and best companions.

Notes

1. For new-medievalist critical theory and practice, see the collections of studies edited by Brownlee et al.; Nichols; Paden; and Zumthor.

2. On the cultural history of Reconquest Iberia, see the surveys of Hillgarth (*The Spanish Kingdoms*) and O'Callaghan (*A History*), as well as the major exposition of *convivencia* in Castro.

3. For background on Alfonso X's reign and renaissance, see the useful general survey by Procter; the well-balanced and up-to-date biography by O'Callaghan (*The Learned King*), with extensive bibliography; the cultural synthesis and revision in Márquez-Villanueva; and the critical essays edited by Burns. On contemporary critical approaches to Alfonsine texts and contexts, see González-Casanovas ("Text and Context").

4. Good introductions to Ramon Llull's life, works, and thought, are found in Badia and Bonner; Bonner; Hillgarth (*Ramon Llull*); and Riquer. On the importance of *Blanquerna* as a late-medieval religious utopia, see González-Casanovas (*The Apostolic Hero*).

5. On Juan Manuel as didactic author and aristocratic propagandist, see the studies by Biglieri; Diz; and Ruiz; as well as the critical essays edited by Macpherson. For a basic introduction to his life, times, and works, see Sturcken.

6. In a series of key articles published between 1982 and 1991, Norman Roth has studied medieval Arabic and Hebrew poetry—both in general and in Iberia—that deals with boy-love as the romantic and lyrical construction of *ephebophilia* (homophilic relationships based on the pursuit by adult males of adolescent objects of desire). While Roth distinguishes conventional metaphors from genuine affections, he also points to the close relationship between cultural realities and literary idealizations: Jewish and Muslim men wrote about their own experiences of falling in love with beautiful youths in highly refined yet personal works.

Such verse flourished in periods of relative tolerance for ephebophilic love affairs, which in these cultures often did not extend to other forms of homophilic relations.

7. *Siete partidas*, pt. 4, has been studied by González-Casanovas ("Gender Models") in terms of the cultural ideology of gender in "nature" and "society," and by Stone in terms of the models of social and moral relations presented in the law code.

8. Numbers refer to part.title.law, followed by volume: page. The translation is Scott's.

9. In Scott's notes to the 1931 English translation of the *Siete partidas*, which betray his own era's official condemnation of homosexuality, he quotes a passage from an earlier Castilian law code, the *Fuero juzgo* (3: 5): "Los que yacen con los barones, o los que lo sufren, deuen seer penados por esta ley en tal manera, que después que el iues este mal supiere, que los castre luego a ambos, e los dé al obispo de la tierra en cuya tierra ficieran el mal" (Scott 1428n1) [Those men who lie with men or who submit to it should be punished by this law so that, once the judge has ascertained this evil, he will castrate both men and hand them over to the bishop in whose land they committed the evil act (translation mine)].

10. All translations of passages from Llull are my own.

11. Meddeb and Menocal have pursued various literary parallels between Llull and the Sufis, but they have dealt with them in terms of the cross-cultural poetics of lyrical love rather than in terms of the gender and sexual constructions of lyrical personae.

12. All translations of passages from Juan Manuel are my own.

13. Such traditional wisdom and natural philosophy represent for Márquez-Villanueva parts of the bases of *mudéjar* or Arabized culture in thirteenth-century Castile.

Works Cited

Alberoni, Francesco. *L'amitié*. Trans. N. Drusi. Paris: Pocket, 1995. [Originally published in Italian in Milan: Garzanti, 1984.]

Alfonso X. *Cantigas de Santa Maria*. 3 vols. Ed. W. Mettmann. Madrid: Clásicos Castalia, 1986–89.

———. *Siete partidas*. 4 vols. Ed. Gregorio López [Latin glosses of 1555 ed.]. Madrid: Benito Cano, 1789. English translation ed. and trans. S. P. Scott. Chicago: American Bar Association, 1931.

Aquinas, Thomas. *Summa Theologiae*. Latin text and English trans. Blackfriars ed. 64 vols. New York: McGraw-Hill, 1964–72.

Badia, Lola, and Anthony Bonner. *Ramon Llull: vida, pensamiento y obra literaria*. Barcelona: Quaderns Crema, 1993.

Barber, Malcom. *The Trial of the Templars*. Cambridge: Cambridge UP, 1978.

Biglieri, Aníbal A. *Hacia una poética del relato didáctico: Ocho estudios sobre "El conde Lucanor."* North Carolina Studies in Romance Languages and Literatures. Department of Romance Languages. University of North Carolina, 1989.

Bonner, Anthony. "Introduction." *Selected Works*, by R. Llull. Princeton UP, 1985. 1: 3–89.

Boswell, John. *Christianity, Social Tolerance, and Homosexuality: Gay People in Europe from the Beginning of the Christian Era to the Fourteenth Century*. Chicago: U of Chicago P, 1980.

————. *Same-Sex Unions in Premodern Europe*. New York: Vuillard, 1994.

Brownlee, Kevin, Marina S. Brownlee, and Stephen G. Nichols, eds. *The New Medievalism*. Baltimore: Johns Hopkins UP, 1991.

Burckhardt, Titus. *Introduction to Sufism*. London: Thorsons, 1995.

Burns, Robert I., ed. *Emperor of Culture: Alfonso X the Learned of Castile and His Thirteenth-Century Renaissance*. Philadelphia: U of Pennsylvania P, 1990.

————, ed. *The Worlds of Alfonso the Learned and James the Conqueror: Intellect and Force in the Middle Ages*. Princeton: Princeton UP, 1985.

Bynum, Caroline W. *Jesus as Mother: Studies in the Spirituality of the High Middle Ages*. Berkeley: U of California P, 1982.

Castro, Américo. *España en su historia: cristianos, moros y judíos*. 3rd ed. Barcelona: Crítica, 1984.

Cousins, Ewert. "The Humanity and Passion of Christ." *High Middle Ages and Reformation*. Vol. 2 of *Christian Spirituality*. Ed. J. Raitt. New York: Crossroad, 1987. 375–91.

Diz, Marta Ana. *Patronio y Lucanor: la lectura inteligente "en el tiempo que es turbio."* Potomac: Scripta Humanistica, 1984.

Foucault, Michel. *The Use of Pleasure*. Vol. 2 of *The History of Sexuality*. Trans. R. Hurley. New York: Random House, 1985.

Gauvard, Claude. "Hótan hoi hippótes philiontoúsan sto stóma" [When Knights Kissed in the Mouth]. *Historía eikonographeméne* [*History Illustrated* (Athens)] 27, 323 (1995): 91–93.

González-Casanovas, Roberto J. *The Apostolic Hero and Community in Ramon Llull's "Blanquerna": A Literary Study of a Medieval Utopia*. New York: Peter Lang, 1995.

————. "Didáctica y *Bildung* en el *Conde Lucanor*: del consejo a la educación de Saladino." *Anuario medieval* 2 (1990): 78–90.

————. "Gender Models in Alfonso X's *Siete partidas*: Sexual Politics of 'Nature' and 'Society.' " *Sex and Sexuality in the Middle Ages and Renaissance.* Ed. Jacqueline Murray and Konrad Eichenbichler. Toronto: U of Toronto P, 1996. 42–60.

———. "Text and Context in Alfonsine Studies: Is the 'New Medievalism' for Alfonsistas?" *Exemplaria hispanica* 1 (1991–92): vii–xxxiv.

Halperin, David M. *One Hundred Years of Homosexuality.* London: Routledge, 1990.

Hillgarth, J. N. *Ramon Llull and Lullism in Fourteenth-Century France.* Oxford: Clarendon, 1971.

———. *The Spanish Kingdoms, 1250–1516.* 2 vols. Oxford: Clarendon, 1976.

Juan Manuel. *El conde Lucanor.* Ed. J. M. Blecua. Madrid: Clásicos Castalia, 1969.

Le Goff, Jacques. "Le Refus du plaisir." *Amour et sexualité en Occident.* Ed. G. Duby. Paris: Seuil, 1991. 177–92.

Lewis, C. S. *The Four Loves.* 1960. London: Harper Collins, 1977.

López Estrada, Francisco. "El sentido utópico de las *Partidas.*" *Las utopías.* Ed. J.-P. Étienvré. Madrid: Casa Velázquez, U Complutense, 1990. 205–14.

Llull, Ramon. *Arbre de filosofia d'amor.* Ed. G. Schib. Barcelona: Barcino, Els Nostres Clàssics, 1980.

———. *Cent noms de Déu* [selections]. In *Poesies.* Ed. R. d'Alòs-Moner. Barcelona: Barcino, Els Nostres Clàssics, 1928: 34–41.

———. *Libre d'Amic e Amat.* In *Libre de Evast e Blanquerna,* bk. 5, chs. 99–100, 3: 9–96.

———. *Libre de Evast e Blanquerna.* 4 vols. Ed. S. Galmés et al. Barcelona: Barcino, Els Nostres Clàssics, 1954.

———. *Llibre de l'orde de cavaleria.* Ed. M. Gustà. Barcelona: Edicions 62, 1980.

Macpherson, Ian, ed. *Juan Manuel Studies.* London: Tamesis, 1977.

Márquez-Villanueva, Francisco. "The Alfonsine Cultural Concept." *Alfonso X of Castile, the Learned King (1221–1284): An International Symposium, Harvard University, 17 November 1984.* Ed. Francisco Márquez-Villanueva and Carlos Alberto Vega. Harvard Studies in Romance Languages 43. Cambridge, Mass.: Department of Romance Languages and Literatures, Harvard U, 1990. 76–109.

———. *El concepto cultural alfonsí.* Madrid: Mapfre, 1994.

Meddeb, Abdelwahab. "Religión del otro: Ibn ʿArabí/Llull." *Cruce de culturas y mestizaje cultural.* Ed. T. Todorov. Madrid: Júcar, 1988. 131–44.

Menocal, María Rosa. "Love and Mercy at the Edge of Madness: Ramon Llull's *Book of the Lover and Beloved* and Ibn ʿArabî's 'O doves of the arâk and the bân trees.' " *Catalan Review* 4.1–2 (1990): 155–77.

Nichols, Stephen, ed. *The New Philology.* Spec. issue of *Speculum* 65 (1990): 1–108.

O'Callaghan, Joseph. *A History of Medieval Spain*. Ithaca: Cornell UP, 1975.

———. *The Learned King: The Reign of Alfonso X of Castile*. Philadelphia: U of Pennsylvania P, 1993.

Paden, William D., ed. *The Future of the Middle Ages: Medieval Literature in the 1990s*. Gainesville: U of Florida P, 1994.

Price, A. W. *Love and Friendship in Plato and Aristotle*. Oxford: Clarendon, 1989.

Procter, Evelyn S. *Alfonso X of Castile, Patron of Literature and Learning*. Oxford: Clarendon, 1951.

Riquer, Martí de. "Ramon Llull." *Història de la literatura catalana*. Barcelona: Ariel, 1964. Vol. 1. 197–352. 11 vols.

Roth, Norman. "The Care and Feeding of Gazelles: Medieval Arabic and Hebrew Love Poetry." *Poetics of Love in the Middle Ages*. Ed. M. Lazar and N. Lacy. Fairfax: George Mason UP, 1989. 95–118.

———. " 'Deal Gently with the Young Man': Love of Boys in Medieval Hebrew Poetry of Spain." *Speculum* 57 (1982): 20–51.

———. " 'Fawn of My Delights': Boy-Love in Hebrew and Arabic Verse." *Sex in the Middle Ages: A Book of Essays*. Ed. Joyce E. Salisbury. New York: Garland, 1991. 157–92.

———. " 'My Beloved Is Like a Gazelle': Imagery of the Beloved Boy in Religious Hebrew Poetry." *Hebrew Annual Review* 8 (1984): 143–65.

Ruiz, María Cecilia. *Literatura y política: el "Libro de los estados" y el "Libro de las armas" de don Juan Manuel*. Potomac: Scripta Humanistica, 1989.

Scott, S. P. See Alfonso X, *Siete partidas*.

Solé, Jacques. "Les troubadours et l'amour-passion." *Amour et sexualité en Occident*. Ed. G. Duby. Paris: Seuil, 1991. 95–103.

Stone, Marilyn. *Marriage and Friendship in Medieval Spain: Social Relations According to the Fourth Partida*. New York: Peter Lang, 1990.

Sturcken, H. Tracy. *Don Juan Manuel*. New York: Twayne, 1974.

Vauchez, André. *La spiritualité du Moyen Âge occidental, VIIIe–XIIIe siècles*. Rev. ed. Paris: Seuil, 1994.

Walzer, Richard. "Platonism in Islamic Philosophy." *Greek into Arabic: Essays on Islamic Philosophy*. Oxford: Bruno Cassirer, 1962. 239–43.

Zumthor, Paul. *Speaking of the Middle Ages*. Trans. Sarah White. Lincoln: U Nebraska P, 1986.

III

SOURCES OF

SODOM

Josiah Blackmore

The Poets of Sodom

The literary activity of medieval Iberia known as Galician-Portuguese lyric flourished between the late twelfth century and the first quarter of the fourteenth. It includes a substantial number of love lyrics known as the *cantigas de amigo* 'friend's songs' and the *cantigas de amor* 'love songs,' as well as the satiric and often scurrilous *cantigas d'escarnho e mal dizer* 'songs of scorn and malediction,' hereafter CEM.[1] This poetic corpus depicts early Iberian culture in a carnival of mischievous, licentious, and lively detail. In a celebration of the scandalous and the transgressive, the CEM offer a rich field of study to the scholar who endeavors to understand the kinds of parameters — religious, linguistic, political, and sexual — that defined life in Portugal and Spain in the Middle Ages. Most of the CEM poets were also practitioners of the sober love lyric, but it is in the composition of the satiric verses that these writers are at their imaginative and inventive best. The CEM form a repository of poetic virtuosity.

It should come as no surprise, then, that in this arena of uninhibited *poesis* the poets engage sexuality in flagrant terms, and in so doing cast sex decisively as a category of cultural discourse. Within the numerous sex-themed poems we find thirty-six that manifest same-sex imagery and language in varying degrees of elaboration, from off-hand allusion and innuendo to unambiguous declaration and accusation.[2] These poems cover a wide range of topics, persons, and events; yet despite their heterogeneity, there is a common preoccupation among the "poets of Sodom" with the power dynamics involved in (poetically) speaking about sodomy.[3] These power dynamics constitute the focus of my analysis here.

It has been something of a critical commonplace to assume that the treatment of sodomy in this poetry is necessarily condemnatory.[4] The unmentionable vice and its wholesale condemnation by medieval canon and civic law would seem to offer a transparent and unquestionable premise for poets intent on seeking targets for public ridicule and derision. But such an assumption erases the complex and ambiguous nature of many of these texts.

Ultimately, within the satiric space of the CEM, we witness a willed recreation of Sodom, a poetic world inhabited (and often defined) by same-sex interaction. While the poets can invoke sodomy in a spirit of aggression and condemnation, this is not unequivocally the case: as a whole, these poems are at once indictful and playfully tolerant, double voiced, moving freely between the poles of abhorrence and indulgence. Here, then, is a space of fluid sexuality and attitudes toward it, where incursions into the "unnatural" realm of the sodomite border provocatively on the edge of an alternate norm. These texts are telling battle/playgrounds for proscribed sexuality and its representation, a site of tensions between deviant sex and the culture that seeks to control it. The poets of Sodom both impose social or cultural orthodoxies and complicate them, delineating the boundaries of sex and poetry and then reveling in their crossing.

The Rule of Sodomy

The understanding of the thirteenth century in Western Europe — the core period of production for these *cantigas* — as one of particular intolerance toward sodomy in large part derives from the widespread drafting and revising of legal codes. In Iberia, even in the midst of a thriving sociocultural climate that was anything but normative when it came to sexuality, we find harsh legislation against sodomy, perhaps most influentially in the *Fuero real* and *Siete partidas* of Alfonso X.[5] Alfonso's sodomy legislation revisits and updates the Visigothic laws of the seventh century (known as the *Forum judicum* [c. 650], translated into Castilian as the *Fuero juzgo*) that contain sections on both male concubines and sodomites.[6] What the actual enforcement practices of Alfonso's laws were is unknown (Boswell 289), and it might well have been that the strict laws ironically sponsored a kind of tolerance from lack of enforcement (Foucault 101). But the letter of the law attests to the construction of an unequivocal ideal of sexual transgression.

The role of sodomy in the *cantigas* relates in part to the strictures of the law as it is substantiated through discourse. If we look at the corpus of local municipal laws (Port. *foros,* Sp. *fueros;* many predate the Alfonsine legislation), we find a wealth of information about regional social habits and customs, including sexual ones. These texts forge a direct alliance between sodomy, speaking, and the law in the form of stipulations against insults (Port. *denostos,* Sp. *denuestos*).[7] As the formulations are largely standardized due to copying practices between municipalities (Walsh 157), I cite as representative the following:

De denostos

Qvi dixer a outro: "cornudo" ou: "fududi[n]cul" ou: "gafo" ou "iudeo" ou: "traydor", o a moller: "puta" ou: "ceguladera" ou: "gafa", peyte .V. mor. (Cintra 56)[8]

[On insults

He who would say to another (man): "cuckold" or "fucked-in-the-ass" or "leper" or "Jew" or "traitor," or would say to a woman "whore" or "adulteress" or "leper" is to be fined 5 *morabatins*.]

We may ask: what, precisely, do these laws prohibit? We first might suppose that certain words are the object of this legislation, but in fact what is being regulated here is also — we could even say primarily — the speaker as a self-authorized interpellator. He who uses these insults is situating someone else within a legally constituted category of marginality; there is a presumed authoritative claim to the existence of a transgression. To say to another man *cornudo* is to act as the intruding, adulterous third party in a matrimonial bond — the act of saying *cornudo* constitutes the one thus addressed *as* a cuckold. Similarly, to say *fududincul* is the same as constituting someone as a sodomite.[9] It is significant that the law formulates the offense in terms of the verb *diƶer a* 'to say to' and not *chamar* 'to call,' since *chamar* would shift the emphasis from the speaker of the word to the word itself. He who constitutes *himself* as subject (self-) constructs an authority to act as the police through language. "De denostos," it could be said, rather than regulating the use of certain words, regulates the self-constitution of a speaker as a lawful interpellator.[10]

Two of the poets of Sodom map out these power dynamics of law, language, and sodomy in CEM 71 and 104. Let us consider first, CEM 71, by Airas Nunes:

O meu senhor, o bispo, na Redondela, un dia,
 de noite, con gran medo de desonra, fogia;
 eu, indo mi aguisando por ir con ele mia via,

achei ũa companha assaz brava e crua,
que me deceron logo de cima da mia mua:
azêmela e cama levavan-na por sua.

E des que eu nacera nunca entrara en lide,
pero que já fora [a] cabo Valedolide
escontra donas muitas fazer, e en Molide.
E ali me lançaron a min a falcacrua;
a[i], maos escudeiros trage o Churruchão [e assua];
el á taes sergentes, ca non gente befua!

Ali me desbulharon do tabardo e dos panos
e non ouveron vergonha dos meus cabelos canos,
nen me deron por ende grãas nen adianos;
leixaron-me qual fui nado no meio de la rua;
e un rapaz tinhoso — que o Deus peon [d]estrua! —
chamava-mi "mia nona, velha fududancua!"

[One day, my lord the bishop, with great fear of dishonor,
was fleeing by night in the Redondela;
I, getting ready to meet him on the way,
found a very savage and cruel group
who threw me off my mule right away:
they took my beast and belongings as their own.

And since I was born I never entered a fight,
although I've been to Valladolid
and Molide because of many women.
And there they put handcuffs on me;
oh, what wicked squires Churruchão assembles and brings with him.
His officials are of this quality — not people of low condition!

There they stripped me of my tabard and other clothes
and showed no respect for my white hair.
They gave me no covering or anything in return;
they left me as I was born in the middle of the street,
and a tumor-ridden boy — may God destroy him in this manner! —
called me, "My lady, my old fucked-in-the-ass!"]

Nunes narrates a scenario violent in idiom and imagery that accelerates in clues suggesting a sodomitic theme, one encapsulated by the stinging punchline of the poem (the insult issued by a tumor-ridden youth). The nocturnal encounter that begins the poem is a common setting for homosexual meetings in the CEM. The attack on the pacific, self-declared heterosexual pedestrian (lines 7–9) develops throughout the poem as a gradual process of disempowerment and passivization: the speaker is pulled from his mount, robbed, disrobed, and handcuffed. The placing of handcuffs in such a brutal fashion and the fact that the boy with tumors issues the insult "Mia nona, velha fududancua!" conspire to imply that the victim is raped by the officers of Churruchão, or at least by the diseased youth.[11]

The forced passivity and the sexual repositioning of the poet into "unnatural" space dramatizes the process of interpellation discussed above in relation to the insult laws. CEM 71 relates a scenario in which the issuer of an insult creates the conditions of his own interpellative pronouncement; it is significant that the insult closes the text, as if to suggest that the movement of the *cantiga* is to construct a moment where an already marginalized figure—the tumorous youth, marginalized by virtue of his diseased body and apparent sodomitic activities, and therefore representing a conflation of the *foros*'s *leproso* and *fududincul*—constitutes himself as an interpellator. The ignominy of the insult here derives from its application by the aggressor (someone who in effect "creates" a sodomite by rape, then indicts his victim for being "fucked in the ass"), and by the fact that the *rapaz tinhoso*, whose own marginal or transgressive character preexists the utterance of the insult, boasts an authority to speak peremptorily.[12] Reading CEM 71 against the insult laws in general and the specification of speaking as sodomy in particular raises the possibility that Nunes is poetically tackling the logic that governs the laws—that is, whatever action may or may not have been visited on the elderly protagonist, the fact that a claim to truth is made (participation in sodomy) by a *rapaz tinhoso* justifies his outburst of derisive, poetic laughter.

The regendering of the narrator completes the offensive movement of CEM 71. We know the speaker is a man in line 16 (*nado* 'born' is masculine), yet the insult *velha fududancua* is grammatically feminine. All occurrences of *fududincul* in the CEM are in the feminine, yet this feminine form is not attested in the *foros* as a possible insult spoken to a woman. *Fududancua* (variant of *fududincula* [fem. form of *fududincul*]) is a term of derision for prostitutes (Díaz 410). Nunes's use of the feminine applied to a male speaker not only complicates our understanding of the word in the CEM as having a necessarily feminine referent (*fududancua* may be a kind of in-joke among the poets of Sodom and their targets), but adds another level to the insult in CEM 71 by feminizing the victim with language generally reserved for prostitutes.[13]

Comparable to CEM 71's aggressive language is the bullying exchange of CEM 104:

> Esta foi feita a un cavaleiro, que lhe apoínham que era puto.
>
> Un cavaleiro me diss' en baldon
> que me queria põer eiceiçon,
> mui agravada, como ome cruu.
> E dixi-lh' enton como vos direi:
> —Se mi a poserdes, tal vo-la porrei,
>   que a sençades ben atá o cuu.
>
> E diss' er-m' el: —Eiceiçon tenh' eu já
> tal que vos ponha, que vos custará
> mais que quanto val aqueste meu muu.
> E dixi-lh' eu: —Poi-lo non tenh' en al,
> se mi a poserdes, porrei-vo-la tal,
>   que a sençades ben atá o cuu.
>
> —Tal eiceiçon vos tenh' eu de põer—
> diss' el a min—per que do voss' aver
> vos fique tanto que fiquedes nuu.
> E dixi-lh' eu: —Coraçon de judeu,
> se mi a poserdes, tal vos porrei eu,
>   que a sençades ben atá o cuu.

[This poem was composed against a gentleman whom they said was a bugger.[14] A gentleman arrogantly said to me
    that he wanted to bring a particularly nasty
    lawsuit against me—so crude a man is he.
    And I'll tell you what I said to him:

"If you put it to me, so will I put it to you
   that you'll feel it all the way down to your ass."

And he further said to me: "I already have a lawsuit
to bring against you that will cost you
more than that mule of mine is worth."
And I said to him, "Since you leave me no choice,
if you put it to me, I will put it to you so
   that you'll feel it all the way down to your ass."

"Such a lawsuit will I bring against you,"
he said to me, "that of your belongings
you'll have as much left so as to be nude."
And I said to him, "By the heart of a Jew,
if you put it to me, so will I put it to you
   that you'll feel it all the way down to your ass."]

Here the poet addresses an unnamed interlocutor who has threatened a lawsuit, and the *cantiga* records the verbal sparring match between the two speakers. The humor of CEM 104 certainly depends on our surmising a cause of the legal action and reckoning it against the language of threat and counterthreat. The mention of the gentleman's reputation as a *puto* in the rubric, together with the poem's tacit acknowledgment that this individual feels he has the law on his side enough to warrant a legal threat, suggests that an infraction of the stipulations against insults is the implicit premise of this poem. CEM 104 invites us to speculate on an altercation already in progress: had Estêvan da Guarda called the *cavaleiro* "fududincul," and is he outraged that such a *puto* would dare respond in such a fashion? Da Guarda tellingly situates the image of the *cuu* 'ass' centrally in his poem via its reiterative presence in line-final position of the refrain; consequently, *cuu* is linked phonetically and semantically with *muu* and *nuu*. Gonçalves (40, 42) argues for *muu* as symbolic of a male same-sex partner. So the ass in this poem is a sodomitic one, and the dominant verb *põer* 'to put' vacillates between meaning "to put legal action to" and "to put it to" in a sexual sense. What the interlocutors in CEM 104 are fighting over is control of the subject position of *põer*: each struggles to make the other the object, or the passive recipient, of the verbal action. When the *cavaleiro* threatens "to put legal action to" the poet, the poet responds with vehement indignation and turns the phrase back on its issuer, mockingly referring to the ass as both that which gave the gentleman his bad name and as a clue to the text's joke. The poet predicates his victory in this power struggle on his ability "to put it to" the *cavaleiro,* to "fuck him over" once and for all. There may be a threat of (sodomitic) violence here. The fight for subject position, this tug-of-war between the speakers to inhabit *põer* actively lies at the bottom, so to speak, of Estêvan da Guarda's poetic conflation of law, recrimination, and sodomy.

The Nefarious Muse

The intersection between speaking and sodomy evidenced in the *foros* forms part of the "force relations" (Foucault 93) or power over discursive culture outlined in the tracts of Alfonso X.[15] In other words, Alfonso (in such works as the *Siete partidas*) provides rules for how speaking is to be juridically employed and regulated, how discourse is to enact and, reciprocally, be shaped by power in the service of cultural-political hegemony. That the act of speaking can carry ideological (political, sexual, religious, cultural) weight is a necessary presupposition to keep in mind when reading laws that delimit the parameters of "transgressive" language or uses of language. Consider CEM 17, Alfonso's famous reproach to the Galician master-poet Pero da Ponte:

> Pero da Ponte, pare-vos en mal
> per ante o Demo do fogo infernal,
> por que con Deus, o padre spirital,
> minguar quisestes, mal per descreestes.
> > E ben vej' ora que trobar vos fal,
> > pois vós tan louca razon cometestes.
>
> E pois razon [a]tan descomunal
> fostes filhar e que tan pouco val,
> pesar-mi-á en, se vos pois a ben sal
> ante o Diaboo, a que obedecestes.
> > E ben vej' ora que trobar vos fal,
> > pois vós tan louca razon cometestes.

Vós non trobades come proençal,
mais come Bernaldo de Bonaval;
por ende non é trobar natural,
pois que o del e do Dem' aprendestes.
      E ben vej' ora que trobar vos fal,
        pois vós tan louca razon cometestes.

E poren, Don Pedr', en Vila Real,
en mao ponto vós tanto bevestes.

[Pero da Ponte, may things go badly for you[16]
because, in front of the devil from the fire of hell,
you decided to fail in your duty toward God,
the spiritual father, and you committed a grave irreverence.
      And I see now that your art has failed you,
        since you could write about so foolish a theme.

And since you have chosen such an unusual topic,
and one which is worth so little,
it will grieve me if you succeed now
in your pact with the devil.
      And I see now that your art has failed you,
        since you could write about so foolish a theme.

You do not compose like a Provençal,
but like Bernaldo de Bonaval;
and therefore your poetry-making is not natural,
for you learned it from him and from the devil.
      And I see now that your art has failed you,
        since you could write about so foolish a theme.

And therefore, Don Pedro, in Vila Real
you drank too much, and that is your misfortune.]

The possible reasons for Alfonso's reproach to the Galician poet have elicited a fair amount of critical speculation.[17] Some believe that CEM 17 is nothing more than one blow in a good-natured poetic sparring match between the monarch and the poet, while others read Alfonso's declaration that Pero da Ponte's poetry making is "not natural" as an indictment of a series of poems containing "ideas scarcely orthodox in terms of religious subject matter" (Lapa 30). This last hypothesis (so far the most widely accepted) holds that Pero da Ponte, following the example of Bernal de Bonaval, wrote a series of poems that contravened the increased orthodoxy in both style and content espoused in Provençal lyric after the Albigensian Crusade. The admitted disadvantage to this thesis is that no such poems by either da Ponte or Bonaval survive, making necessary the presumption of a lost group of texts.[18] In this line of thought, then, "non é trobar natural" refers to an "unnaturalness" characteristic of religious heterodoxy.[19]

But Pero da Ponte's candid treatment of sodomy as poetic subject matter in his oeuvre persuasively argues for a reading of CEM 17 in which "non é trobar natural" may refer to transgression of a sexual nature as well, and allows us to read Alfonso's text against texts of da Ponte that do survive.[20] Alfonso regards da Ponte as one who has acted *contra naturam* in his choice of sodomy as poetic topos,[21] as having opposed a dominant poetic ideology that mandates the alliance between desire and poetry as a hetero-erotic orthodoxy; poetic and sexual ideologies hence coalesce. CEM 17 is a legislation of the parameters of (poetic) transgression, and even in the *cantigas*, Alfonso warns, it is possible to transgress too much. The infractions Alfonso identifies target sexual, not solely spiritual, deviance: failing in his duty to God and the denial committed (line 4), the foolish theme that proves Pero da Ponte obeys the devil in his art (lines 7–10). These infractions, with their severely moralistic tone, fall within the scope of Alfonso's definition of *escándalo* 'scandal' in the *Siete partidas:* "['escándalo'] tanto quier dezir cuemo fecho o dicho o muestra por que los omnes se mueuen a fazer pecado mortal" (Van Scoy 42) ['scandal' refers to a deed or word or gesture by which men are moved to commit mortal sin]. And one cannot overlook the reference to Bernaldo de Bonaval, who was a reputed sodomite (Lopes 320); this may be the tacit point of comparison in line 14.[22]

The difference of critical opinion surrounding CEM 17 demonstrates an ambiguity that Alfonso could very well have intended. *Both* sexual and spiritual orthodoxy may be found here in an indictment where the "judge" strategically refrains from mentioning the poetic crime committed.[23] Alfonso's (studied?) ambiguity opens up CEM 17 as a theoretical text and brings sexual orthodoxy to the fore as one of the boundary posts of poetic ideology.

Pero da Ponte's CEM 342 may have been one of those texts that incited

Alfonso to compose CEM 17, a *cantiga* that itself aligns sexual deviance and poetry:

> Eu digo mal, com' ome fodimalho,
> quanto mais posso daquestes fodidos
> e trob' a eles e a seus maridos;
> e un deles mi pôs mui grand' espanto:
> topou comigu'e sobraçou o manto
> e quis en mi achantar o caralho.

> Ando-lhes fazendo cobras e sões
> quanto mais poss' e and' escarnecendo
> daquestes putos que s'andan fodendo;
> e ũu deles de noit' asseitou-me
> e quis-me dar do caralh' e errou-me
> e [er] lançou depós min os colhões.

> [I curse, like a studly man,[24]
> as much as I can those guys who get fucked,
> and I write poetry about them and their husbands;
> one of them gave me a huge fright:
> he bumped into me and lifted up my cloak
> and tried to stick his cock in me.

> I go around composing verses and music about them
> as much as I can, and I scorn
> those buggers who go around fucking one another;
> and one of them attacked me at night
> and tried to shove his cock in me, but missed:
> (standing) behind me, he only ended up thrusting his balls.]

CEM 342's singularly explicit imagery has predictably caused critical unease. Lapa and Lopes read the poem as essentially anecdotal, as a "strange 'confession'" (Lopes 153) of a homosexual adventure, "truly surprising" (Lopes 154) in that Pero da Ponte would so casually and publicly claim such an experience as his own. Scholberg categorically declares that "the gross tone of the poem does not hide the poet's repugnance toward these perverts and 'their husbands,' and it makes manifest that what is being dealt with here is no mere insulting topic or humorous fiction, but a real and living vice" (108–09). Lopes posits (153–54) that CEM 342 is a *cantiga de maldizer aposto*, a type of composition in which the poet speaks in the voice of another, thereby exonerating Pero da Ponte from the uncomfortable responsibility of claiming firsthand experience with (attempted) sodomy.

Far from being merely a "surprising confession" to actual personal experience with *putos* 'buggers,' da Ponte uses sodomitic imagery here in a scandalous, metaphoric game to address the broader issue of poetry itself. CEM 342 is first and foremost about scornful *trobar*, and constitutes one of the many instances in the CEM (and in the Galician-Portuguese lyric in general) where the practice of poetry is foregrounded. It is a text about poetry and power, one configured as a power shuffle between poet and sodomite.[25] The *rapprochement* between poetry and sex presents itself at the outset, when Pero da Ponte explicitly mobilizes the satiric genre ("Eu digo mal"), immediately likening his capacity for *mal dizer* to sexual potency ("com' ome fodimalho"). The equation between poetry and sex is further elaborated in the rhyme pairs "and'escarnecendo"/"s'andan fodendo" and "sões"/"colhões." What's more, the poet tells us that he taxes his skill to the extreme ("Eu digo mal . . . quanto mais posso") when writing about "daquestes fodidos," and so sodomy emerges as a theme *par excellence* in his work, one that challenges his poetic skill to the fullest. But most significant is the fact that this *cantiga* is a response to a real or imagined encounter where the unnamed assailant attempts to penetrate the poet (that is, feminize by making passive); had the attacker succeeded, the poet would have joined the ranks of the *fodidos*.

The attempted penetration not only impugns the poet's self-declared reputation as an "ome fodimalho" (and therefore the active partner in sex), but in the symbolic idiom of the *cantigas* passive sodomy can represent bad poetic skill. Da Ponte guards his status as active partner in sex (and therefore talented *trobador*) by poetic cursing. He establishes *mal dizer* as a supreme test of poetic skill, a skill that is best foregrounded by a brush with (and victory over) sexual deviance. In this way the poet maintains the upper hand in the power struggle: while his actual sexual capacity remains *in potentia*, he mobilizes it figuratively in the form of poetry, and dominates his sodomitic antagonist discursively, ultimately "sodomizing" him in return. Poetic cursing thus emerges as a form of active sexuality.

Fernan Díaz, *Meirinho*

As we have seen to this point in the discussion, sodomy in the CEM can play a key role in an interrogation of satiric, poetic speaking. Sodomy is a productive notion; it might not speak its name, but it certainly generates texts. We now turn our attention to a figure in the CEM that gives sodomy flesh and bones, and by association, a name: Alfonso X's *meirinho* 'bailiff,' Fernan Díaz, touted as a paragon of homosexual promiscuity desirous of bedding every man "from Estorga to San Fagundo" (CEM 80).[26] Díaz is the subject of nine *cantigas* in which his homosexuality underwrites a game of *equivocatio* based on sexual and political positioning. Díaz's fame is more literary than historical, and like that other great challenger of sexual mores, the *soldadeira* Maria Balteira, Fernan Díaz's unfettered and unorthodox sexuality makes him the object of poetic fascination. The nine *cantigas* about him constitute a minicycle of texts based on homosexual desire and conjointly present the *meirinho* as one of the more famous citizens of queer Iberia.

The Díaz poems typify the attitude of (bemused) tolerance toward queer sexuality I mentioned at the outset of this essay. These are not acerbic texts, meant to excoriate Fernan Díaz in the public eye; rather, the CEM poets shake a smiling finger at the *meirinho,* whose real offense is not so much his taste for men as it is his exploitation of political position to gain sexual favors. Promotion to an important administrative post, for instance, serves as both metaphor and motive for Fernan Díaz's move from passive to active sodomy—that is, a move *into* power is a move into active sexuality— formulated in the prepositional *ir atrás/ir adeante* (to go behind)/(to go ahead) in CEM 81:

> [e] pois vos Deus ora tanto ben fez,
>   punhade d'ir adeant' ũa vez,
> ca, atra aqui, fostes sempr' a derredo.

> [Since God has done so well for you this time,
>   make an effort and go ahead once and for all,
> since, until now, you've always been behind.]

This jockeying between passive and active sodomy underlies as well the joke in Pero Garcia Burgalês's CEM 381, where the expression *fazer justiça* means both "to administer justice" and "to perform (active) sex":

Que muito mi de Fernan Díaz praz,
  que fez el-Rei Don Afonso meirinho,
    e non cata parente nen vezinho
  con sabor de tee-la terra en paz.
  Se o pode por mal feitor saber,
  vai sobr' el; e, se o pode colher
    na mão, logo d' el justiça faz.

E porque á Don Fernando gran prez
  das gentes todas de mui justiceiro,
    o fez el-Rei meirinho, dês Viveiro
  atá Carron, ond' outro nunca fez;
  e se ouve de mal feitor falar,
  vai sobr' el, e non lhi pod' escapar,
    e faz-lhi mal jogo por ũa vez.

E cuidará d' el queno vir aqui,
  que o vir andar assi calado,
    ca non sabe parte nen mandado
  de tal justiça fazer qua[l] lh' eu vi:
  leixou a gente adormecer enton
  e trasnoitou sobr' un om' a Leon,
    e fez sobr' el gran justiça logui' i.

[I'm glad that King Alfonso thought
  to make Fernando Díaz sheriff,
for he spares neither friend nor relative
  but always keeps the land quite calm:
  if a wrongdoer comes to his notice,
  he lays down the law, and getting hold
    of the man, he really lays it on.

Because Fernando is considered
  by all around to be very fair,
  he was made sheriff from Viveiro
to Carrion, where no one ever served,
  and if he hears a wrongdoer's near,
  he lays down the law, going in search
of the man, to deal him his just deserts. (*sic*)

Let every visiting man take heed
to keep out of sight, avoiding misdeeds,
for with Fernando you've no idea
of the brutal justice I have seen:
he waited till all were asleep and then
spent the whole night on a man in León,
laying on a justice you wouldn't believe!][27]

CEM 127, below, is a particularly interesting text in that it elaborates on the leitmotific game of Díaz's positionality by removing the *meirinho*'s sexual tactics from the scene of poetic speaking. Estêvan Faian's poem plays on the prepositions *su* 'under' (line 14), *deante* 'in front of' (line 20), and *de trás* 'behind' (line 21), imbricating Díaz's exercise of vocation with the seeking out of sexual alliances with other men. Ostensibly, the poet is telling the *meirinho* that he would find no man willing to work under him, no "vassals" should he marry a certain woman and move to her region of the country. The joke, of course, is that the poet knows that Díaz is considering marrying the woman as a way to gain access to men in this other *terra* 'land,'[28] and he knows that no man there would allow himself to be "dominated" (sexually) by Díaz:

Fernan Díaz, fazen-vos entender
que casaríades desta dona ben;
e nós teemos que vos é mal sen,
per quant' est' o que vos quero dizer:
por que a dona é de terra tal,
Don Fernando, que, per ben nen per mal,
non poderedes i un om' aver.

Ante, faredes i vosso prazer
en quererdes con tal dona casar,
Fernan Díaz? —ca é de [tal] logar
que non podedes, per nen un poder,
aver nulh' ome, ca as gentes son
de tal natura, se Deus mi pardon,
que non querran i su vós guarecer.

E sei, Don Fernando, per quant' aprendi,
non poderedes esta dona aver,

ca seus vassalos, com' ouço dizer,
non queren om' estranho sobre si:
ca dizen que sabedes lousinhar
ome deant' e sabedes buscar
gran mal de trás a muitos, com' oí.

[Fernán Díaz, they would have you understand
that you would do well in marrying this woman:
and we think this would be bad for you,
in view of what I want to tell you:
because this woman is from such a land,
Don Fernando, for good or for bad,
you won't be able to have a man there.

Before anything else, would it really please you
in wanting to marry such a woman,
Fernán Díaz? Because she's from such a place
that you would not by any means be able
to have any man, because the people
are of such a nature — God forgive me —
that they will not want to live under you.

And I know, Don Fernando, from my experience,
that you will not be able to have this woman,
because her vassals, as I hear,
do not want a strange man over them:
for they say you know how to flatter
a man to his face (lit., "before a man") and that you know how to find
great evil behind many, as I have heard.]

Unlike the other Fernan Díaz texts, here there is a closer, more ambiguous relationship between Díaz's form of desire and the voice of the poet. The declaration "We think this would be bad for you" (line 3) suggests that the advice offered in the poem is not entirely hostile, although it is not clear precisely who the "we" is, for whom the poet is acting as spokesperson. Is it a community defined by political interests? By a common form of desire? There is an implied familiarity here because the poet is quite knowledgeable about Díaz's tactics for finding sexual partners. The claim to knowledge of Díaz's stratagems through hearsay (lines 17, 21) may well be part of the poetic joke, for if the speaker is familiar with Díaz he surely knows in much greater detail the specifics of Díaz's plans.

The comic tension in this poem derives in large part from a basic distinction drawn between a "here" (the space from which the poet speaks and in which Díaz resides) and a "there" (the place where the *dona* is, with the company of potentially uncooperative vassals). "There" is where the inhabitants would not readily accept an "om' estranho sobre si" [strange man over them] because they are of a different "nature." Fernan Díaz would be a stranger in a strange land, a target of a kind of xenophobia. Faian's poem taunts us with the possibilities of a strangeness that is abhorred or rejected "there," but which is tolerated or even embraced "here." We are left wondering about the basis of the alienation much as we are about the basis of community in line 3. The implied contrast between the "natures" of the people residing in the unnamed "there" and "here" spaces of the poem teasingly suggests that the place from which the poet speaks is a place where heterodox desire can exist in relative peace. In the face of such rejection, Faian enjoins the *meirinho* to stay where he is, to remain in his own queer space.[29]

Women on the Verge

Female homosexuality is rare in the CEM corpus, perhaps because the subversive potential of sodomy in Iberian culture depends primarily on an assumed patriarchal, heteronormative order. The *foros*, for instance, are silent on lesbianism, and this silence implicitly constructs agency of deviant sexuality in phallocentric terms.[30] References to women are found briefly in CEM 49, where the *soldadeira* (or military-camp prostitute) Marinha Sabugal, is accompanied by an old woman "a que quer ben, e ela lhi quer mal" (line 3) [whom she loves, but who doesn't love her]; in CEM 213, another *soldadeira*, Dona Ourana, is advised to engage in sex only with men as opposed to women (line 24); or in CEM 244, yet another *soldadeira* by the name of Maria Leve appears to want to live only where young women can be found. Nonetheless, these few occasions do inscribe women into the demography of the sodomitic CEM and require us to consider this poetic world as one not exclusively inhabited by men.

I want to conclude this essay with a *cantiga* by Afonso Eanes do Coton

(CEM 41), one of the most exuberantly teasing compositions of all the poets of Sodom:

> Mari' Mateu, ir-me quer' eu daquen,
> por que non poss' un cono baratar;
> alguen que mi o daria nõno ten,
> e algũ[a] que o ten non mi o quer dar.
> Mari' Mateu, Mari' Mateu,
> tan desejosa ch' és de cono com' eu!
>
> E foi Deus já de conos avondar
> aqui outros, que o non an mester,
> e ar feze-os muito desejar
> a min e ti, pero que ch' és molher.
> Mari' Mateu, Mari' Mateu,
> tan desejosa ch' és de cono com' eu!

> [Mary Matthew, I want to leave here
> because I can't get any cunt;
> there are people who would give it to me although they don't have one
> and those who have one won't give it to me.
> Mary Matthew, Mary Matthew,
> as desirous of cunt as I!
>
> And it was God who made cunts in abundance here,
> for there is no lack,
> and Who also made both you and I want them
> even though you're a woman.
> Mary Matthew, Mary Matthew,
> as desirous of cunt as I!]

Pimenta reads this as a "bitter reflection" of a "society incapable of satisfying [the poet] sexually," manifesting a "fear-hatred toward the carriers of perversion" (123). Yet I would argue that the poet's "complaint" is not bitter in tone but highly playful; he is not vilifying Maria Mateu but engaging in a ludic competition based on a solidarity of desire. Coton and Maria Mateu both desire women with the same zeal. Coton, far from denouncing Maria Mateu as a pervert, openly addresses her in good-natured complicity. Those who would "give it to him" are not possessed of a *cono*, and those who are have no interest in him whatsoever. Coton's competitor is onomastically both female and male, a crosser of neat gender categories and orthodox sexuality who is quite capable of getting her woman. And, most remarkably, Coton characterizes the direction of one's sexual desire as an innate quality, part of an individualized blueprint. In this sense both Maria Mateu and Fernan Díaz anticipate what will come to be thought of in our century as lesbian and gay identity.

Notes

1. All CEM references are to Lapa 1995. For biographical information on individual poets, see Jensen (lxiii–cxiii) and Tavani (275–330). Unless otherwise noted, all translations of both primary and secondary texts are my own.

2. The numbers of the poems, following Lopes (376), are: on male homosexuality: 56, 62, 73, 75, 80, 81, 83, 104, 116, 117, 127, 131, 132, 168, 188, 194, 232, 340, 342, 348, 365, 372, 377, 378, 380, 381, 404, 424 (I add CEM 17 to this list — see discussion in "The Nefarious Muse," below; Gonçalves convincingly adds 90, 91, and 92 to the sodomitic canon); on female homosexuality: 41, 49, 213, 244.

3. I use "sodomy" and "homosexuality" interchangeably in this essay. I understand "homosexuality" following Boswell's definition of the term as referring to "all sexual phenomena between persons of the same gender" (44), although I am aware, of course, that the term is anachronistic. "Sodomy" is overall the preferable term since it parallels the medieval *sodomia*, but it must be kept in mind that this word covered a wide range of sexual activity, including same-sex contact. And while the texts under discussion here foreground sexuality, they do not do so in a manner that could be considered erotic — hence I avoid "homoerotic(ism)."

4. The first significant treatment of these poems is the series of annotations on individual texts made by Lapa in his editions of the CEM. Scholberg provides brief comments (106–09) on the "real and living vice [of homosexuality]" (109), although these comments are essentially recapitulations of Lapa. Both Lapa and Scholberg employ an indiscriminate critical terminology, equating "pederast" with "sodomite" and "homosexual." Martins refuses to consider the poems at all, dismissing them in the following terms: "Active or passive homosexuality, it matters little. . . . Homosexuality with venereal diseases, the homosexuality of the *segrel* Bernaldo de Bonaval, with his wet clothing clinging to his body, homosexuality with Moors, the brutal verses of Pero da Ponte . . . all of this has little value. There are matters to know and pass over and matters on which we should linger. Here one should just take note and move on. Such satires don't even in-

spire one to laugh—and this, literarily, disqualifies them" (110–11). In recent years, these poems have begun to claim more systematic attention (see Pimenta; Gonçalves; Madero, *Manos* [passim]; Mérida; Arias Freixedo; and Lopes). For a study of homosexuality in Italian poetry roughly contemporaneous with the CEM, see Dall'Orto.

5. Of particular interest is the formulation in the *Fuero real:* "Although we are reluctant to speak of something which is reckless to consider and reckless to perform . . . it happens that one man desires to sin against nature with another. We therefore command . . . [that] both be castrated . . . and on the third day after be hung by the legs until dead" (Boswell 288). Boswell observes: "This law is remarkable not only for its severity but also for its reference to 'nature': no European civil law prior to the thirteenth century had either prescribed death for homosexual acts or related their gravity to 'nature' " (288).

6. The *Forum judicum* (Latin text in *Fuero juzgo* [Latin] 46 and *Leges et consuetudines* 1: 42) was known in both Spanish and Portuguese territories. For the Castilian translation of the concubine/sodomite laws, see the *Fuero juzgo* (Castilian 62–63); Bailey (92–94); Boswell (174–76); Goodich (73); and Trexler (43–45) comment briefly on these passages. Trexler points out (44–45, 202n29) that the *Forum judicum* as well as Alfonso's *Fuero real* and his *Siete partidas* recognize the active/passive distinction in same-sex intercourse. For a slightly later Visigothic law against sodomy, see the Latin and Castilian texts of Toledan Council XVI in *Concilios visigóticos e hispano-romanos* (500–01).

7. Madero (*Manos*) provides an interesting and well-documented treatment of various kinds of injury (including verbal injury) in medieval Castile and León especially as they relate to notions of the body and honor (also see Pimenta). Of particular interest to the present essay are the sections on homosexuality (68–70, 124–27). Madero is certainly right when she observes that "the poems of scorn that refer to homosexuality do so in terms of gesture (*una gestualidad*)" (68), but these "gestures" must be understood as elements of a broader interrogation of the boundaries between sodomy and discourse.

8. This citation represents the wording in the *foros* of Castelo Rodrigo, Alfaiates, and Castelo-Bom (this last one redacted in Latin); the *foro* of Castelo-Melhor is virtually identical (see *Leges et consuetudines* 2: 911). For corresponding sections from several Spanish *fueros,* see Walsh (157–58). Madero comments on the individual words listed as *denuestos* in *Manos* (49, 62–70, 108–13, 117) and "L'Injure" (234–36).

9. The *foros* identify *fududinculo* as the spoken term of insult. For further clarification of this distinction, consider the following passage from the *Fuero de Cuenca* (see Madero, *Manos* 62, 108, for brief comment):

Del que fuere fallado en pecado sodomitico
Qual quier que fuere fallado en pecado sodomitico, quemenlo; [e] qual quier
que a otro dixere "yo te fodi por el culo", si pudiere ser prouado aquel pecado
que es verdad, quemenlos amos; si non, quemen a aquel que tal pecado dixo.
(353)

[Concerning him who is found guilty of the sodomitic sin
Whoever is found guilty of the sodomitic sin is to be burned; and whoever says
to another (man) "I fucked you in the ass," if that sin can be proved to be true,
both shall be burned; if not, he who said such a sin will be burned.]

Del que dixere a otro sodomitico
El que dixere a otro que faze pecado sodomitico, por el dicho peche, çinquenta
mr. (839)

[Concerning him who says to another (man) "sodomitic"
He who says that another commits the sodomitic sin, for said sin (is to be fined)
50 *morabatins*.]

Scrutiny of the second passage reveals that *sodomitico* is not a term of insult; the
use of *sodomitico* does not necessarily identify the word as a *denuesto*, but as part
of an elliptical expression that is best understood as "Concerning him who says
to another [man] *that he is* sodomitic." The first passage is remarkable in its equation of speaking as a form of sodomy. The fact of saying "Yo te fodi por el culo"
claims a referential truth value that the law recognizes and seeks to regulate. It
is the claim to truth that the law targets, and not the act itself.

10. Here is a document that serves as an interesting complement to Butler's
discussions of interpellation, which focus more on the dynamic between interpellator and interpellated than on the authority of the interpellator to speak in
the first place. In contrast to what could be termed Butler's "transitive" model of
interpellation, this text evidences a reflexive one where the very power to perform interpellation is at issue. See *Bodies That Matter* (ch. 4) and *Excitable Speech*
(1–41).

11. The tumor as a sign of sexual deviance is the point of Pero Viviaez's CEM
404, in which the poet responds to an inquiry as to how to recognize a "Pero
Tinhoso" (Peter Tumorous). The refrain in the three-stanza *cantiga* informs that
"aquel é Pero Tinhoso que traz o toutiço nũu / e traz o câncer no pisso e o
alvaraz no cuu" [Pero Tinhoso is the one whose head is naked / and who has
a cancer on his dick and a tumor on his ass]. Here the tumors represent the infected location of sodomitic activity (Lapa 256): on the penis (active), and on

the ass (passive). Pero Tinhoso's bald head sponsors a reading of sexual deviance through his body; for instance, Trexler (44) notes that lay persons found guilty of (active) sodomy, according to the Toledan Council laws of 693, were to be shaved bald and excommunicated. The bald head may also refer to a circumcised penis, thus implicating Jews as agents of diseased sexuality (my thanks to one of the anonymous readers for Duke University Press for this latter interpretation). Heterodox or diseased sexuality is thus graphically depicted on/through Pero Tinhoso, a male body troped as both active and passive and therefore as the grotesque site of cancerous growth.

12. His words preclude the possibility of response since they close the text and therefore finalize the poetic scenario.

13. An alternate translation of "mia nona, velha fududancua!" that posits ironic (self-) recognition would be "you old queen!" Madero (*Manos* 186) observes that in the *Fuero juzgo*, *tinnoso* is another term of insult, the use of which is punishable by fifty lashes.

14. I have translated *puto* as "bugger"; in the medieval idiom, *puto* generally denotes passive partner in male-male intercourse (Lapa 83), and its use is derogatory.

15. Parts of the discussion in this section originally appeared in Blackmore, "Locating."

16. The English translation cited here is basically that of Jensen (57), although in a few instances I have modified it. I translate the first line following Lapa's 1970 emendation of the original (see Lapa 30); Jensen (435) opts for the reading of the first edition (1965), translating this first line as "Pero da Ponte, things took a bad turn for you." Additionally, Jensen translates "trobar" in line 5 as "inspiration" and in line 13 as "write." Finally, Jensen translates "non é trobar natural" (line 15) as "your writing is not according to the rules."

17. See Snow (43 ff.) for studies on this poem through 1977.

18. "It seems to us that his [i.e., Alfonso X's] irony is targeting some texts of Pero da Ponte and Bernal de Bonaval that were unfortunately lost" (Lapa 29); equally, Michaëlis de Vasconcelos (2: 458), Alvar and Beltrán (182). The heterodoxy of Pero da Ponte's lost poetry would have had to have been fierce indeed, since religious topics were targeted by other CEM poets but were spared public reprimand.

19. For discussions of possible meanings of *trobar natural* as it relates to Provençal lyric, see Gruber and Van Vleck (139–46).

20. See CEM 342, 348, 365, and 372.

21. This reading of the poem is briefly suggested by Lopes (320n1).

22. CEM 188 by Joan Baveca identifies a Bernal Fendudo [Bernal Split] as the target of satire, thought by Lapa (130) to refer to Bernal de Bonaval. The adjec-

tive *fendudo* 'split,' with its possible implication of meaning "rent" by penetration is one reason for positing Bonaval's homosexuality (for further comment, see Benjamin Liu's essay in this volume). In CEM 194, Baveca again takes aim at "Don Bernaldo" on account of his wet clothes; Freixedo reads the wetness as meaning covered in semen (53). Of note too is the reference in line 16 of this poem to "vosse ome" [your man].

23. A good part of the ambiguity resides in the use of *demo/diabo* 'devil' in lines 2, 10, and 16. *Demo* can mean the devil, but also the penis (Tavani 197). For a well-known example of this latter meaning see CEM 23.

24. *Fodimalho* is a problematic word that has no easy equivalent in English (for remarks on its possible etymology, see Lapa 221; and Panunzio's edition of Pero da Ponte [154–55]), but according to Lapa and Panunzio it means "sexually capable," "given to intercourse." I have used "studly" to indicate this quality of sexual potency; Friedrich's translation is "breeder."

25. CEM 342 can be read as an example of what Louise O. Vasvári calls the "semiotics of phallic aggression" (see her essay in this volume for elaboration). Vasvári explains that sexual passivity is part of a game of dominance and submission, where such passivity equals dishonor, weakness, and feminization.

26. The poems about Fernan Díaz are 80, 81, 83, 127, 365, 377, 380, 381, and 424.

27. The translation is that of Richard Zenith (183).

28. *Terra* can be roughly translated as "land," but it commonly refers to a region *within* a country.

29. In contrast to the perceived safety of "here" in CEM 127, we read of another unspecified "there" in line 8 of CEM 188, the location of Bernal Fenudo's "battles" with the Moors that earn him the title of *dona salvage* 'savage woman' (see Benjamin Liu's essay in this volume for a discussion of the figure of the Moor in the CEM).

30. For a survey of lesbian sexuality/female sodomy in medieval and early modern Europe, see Brown. Alfonso's *Siete partidas* were glossed in the sixteenth century by Gregorio López to extend punishment for sodomy to women (Brown 72). An interesting instance of the possibility of women as phallic perpetrators of sodomy is found in an anecdote related by Francesc Eiximenis (d. 1409) in his *Terç del crestià:*

Jo fuý una vegada en una ciutat de Spanya e yo aquí present; fou aquí penjada matex una fembra qui aytants anys havia tengut aquí offici de savi en àbit d'om mascle, e havia haüdes duas mullers, e presas en la faç de la sgleya dues fembres per títol de mullers, e la segona que havia presa viuda, acusà-la que no era hom, ans era fembra; e axí estech trobat. E com fos conclús aquí que aquella qui havia axí preses les mullers, de fet era stada sodomita, havent a fer ab aquelles fem-

bres que·s deÿen ésser stades ses mullers aytants anys. Empero de benignitat de
la senyoria, e per tal cant havia leyalment e piadosa servida la cosa pública en
offici de sag per gran temps, no fou cremada mas fou penjada ab aquell artifici
al coll ab lo qual havia jagut carnalment ab les dues fembres. (ch. 609)

[I was once in a city in Spain and was present when a woman was hanged who
had for some years held a judicial office while clothed in masculine attire, and
had taken two wives. And she had taken the two women as wives before the
church; and the second of them was a widow who accused her of not being a
man but a woman and indeed that was the case. The conclusion was reached
on the spot that the one who had taken the women in this way had actually
been a sodomite, having taken up with those women who must have been her
women for a number of years. Given the clemency of the authorities, and because she had loyally and piously served the republic as a judicial officer for a
long time, she was not burnt but was hanged with that artifice around her neck
with which she had carnally lain with the two women].
(My thanks to Jill R. Webster for this text and for its translation.)

Clearly what's at issue here is the condemned woman's coopting of male/phal-
lic power by cross-dressing and by acting as the active partner in sex with the
help of an artificial penis (Brown 495n3 references a sixteenth-century case of
nuns being hanged for "using material instruments"). The form of her punishment mirrors that prescribed for men in documents like Alfonso X's *Fuero real*
and *Siete partidas:* death together with castration (achieved symbolically here
with the artificial penis hung around her neck). Trexler (57) notes the practice of
hanging a convicted sodomite's testicles around his neck.

Works Cited

Alfonso X, el Sabio. *Foro real*. [Portuguese translation of *Fuero real*.] Ed. José de
    Azevedo Ferreira. 2 vols. Lisboa: Instituto Nacional de Investigação Cientí-
    fica, 1987.
————. *Fuero real*. Colección Filológica 3. Ed. Azucena Palacios Alcaine.
    Barcelona: Promociones y Publicaciones Universitarias, 1991.
Alvar, Carlos, and Vicente Beltrán. *Antología de la poesía gallego-portuguesa*.
    Madrid: Alhambra, 1985.
Arias Freixedo, Xosé Bieito, ed. *Antoloxía de poesía obscena dos trobadores galego-
    portugueses*. Colección Plural 5. Santiago de Compostela: Edicións Positivas,
    1993.

Bailey, Derrick Sherwin. *Homosexuality and the Western Christian Tradition*. 1955. Hamden: Archon Books–Shoe String P, 1975.

Bernal de Bonaval. *Poesie*. Ed. Maria Luisa Indini. Biblioteca di Filologia Romanza 32. Bari: Adriatica, 1978.

Blackmore, Josiah. "Locating the Obscene: Approaching a Poetic Canon." *La corónica* 26.2 (1998): 9–16.

Boswell, John. *Christianity, Social Tolerance, and Homosexuality: Gay People in Western Europe from the Beginning of the Christian Era to the Fourteenth Century*. Chicago: U of Chicago P, 1980.

Brown, Judith C. "Lesbian Sexuality in Medieval and Early Modern Europe." *Hidden from History: Reclaiming the Gay and Lesbian Past*. Ed. Martin Duberman, Martha Vicinus, and George Chauncey Jr. New York: Penguin, 1990. 67–75, 495–500.

Butler, Judith. *Bodies That Matter: On the Discursive Limits of "Sex."* New York: Routledge, 1993.

———. *Excitable Speech: A Politics of the Performative*. New York: Routledge, 1997.

[CEM]. See Lapa.

Cintra, Luis F. Lindley. *A linguagem dos foros de Castelo Rodrigo: seu confronto com a dos foros de Alfaiates, Castelo Bom, Castelo Melhor, Coria, Cáceres e Usagre. Contribuição para o estudo do leonês e do galego-português do século XIII*. 1959. Lisboa: Imprensa Nacional-Casa da Moeda, 1984.

Concilios visigóticos e hispano-romanos. Ed. José Vives, Tomás Marín Martínez, and Gonzalo Martínez Díez. Barcelona: Consejo Superior de Investigaciones Científicas, 1963.

Dall'Orto, Giovanni. "L'omosessualità nella poesia volgare italiana fino al tempo di Dante: appunti." *Sodoma: rivista omosessuale di cultura* 3 (1986): 13–37.

Díaz, Esther Corral. "A figura da *velha* nos cancioneiros profanos galego-portugueses." *O cantar dos trobadores* 403–14.

Eiximenis, Francesc. *Terç del crestià*. Barcelona: Biblioteca de Catalunya, Ms. 458.

Foucault, Michel. *The History of Sexuality*. Vol. 1: *An Introduction*. Trans. Robert Hurley. 1978. New York: Vintage-Random, 1990.

Friedrich, Ellen L. " 'No olho do cuu': A Look at Homoerotic Expression in Some Galician-Portuguese *Cantigas*." Queer Iberia session. 29th International Congress on Medieval Studies, Kalamazoo, Michigan. May 1994.

Fuero de Cuenca (Formas primitiva y sistemática: texto latino, texto castellano y adaptación del Fuero de Iznatoraf). Ed. Rafael de Ureña y Smenjaud. Madrid: Academia de la Historia, 1935.

Fuero juzgo en latín y castellano, cotejado con los mas antiguos y preciosos códices por la Real Academia Española. Madrid: Ibarra, 1815. (The Latin and Castilian texts are paginated independently.)

Gonçalves, Elsa. "A mula de Joan Bolo." *Poesia de rei: três notas dionisinas.* Lisboa: Cosmos, 1991. 35–62.

Goodich, Michael. *The Unmentionable Vice: Homosexuality in the Later Medieval Period.* Santa Barbara, Calif.: ABC-Clio, 1979.

Gruber, Jörn. *"Porque trobar é cousa en que jaz entendimento:* Zur Bedeutung von *trobar natural* bei Marcabru und Alfons dem Weisen." *Homenagem a Joseph M. Piel por ocasião do seu 85.° aniversário.* Ed. Dieter Kremer. Tübingen: Niemeyer, 1988. 569–79.

Jensen, Frede, ed. and trans. *Medieval Galician-Portuguese Poetry: An Anthology.* Garland Library of Medieval Literature A/87. New York: Garland, 1992.

Lapa, M. Rodrigues, ed. *Cantigas d'escarnho e de mal dizer dos cancioneiros medievais galego-portugueses.* 3rd ed. Lisboa: João Sá da Costa, 1995. (1st ed. 1965, 2nd ed. 1970.)

Leges et consuetudines. Vol. 2 [pts. 1 and 2] of *Portugaliae monumenta historica.* 1856–1917. 6 vols. Nendeln, Lichtenstein: Kraus Reprint, 1967 (only vols. 1–5 reprinted).

Lopes, Graça Videira. *A sátira nos cancioneiros medievais galego-portugueses.* Imprensa universitária 102. Lisboa: Estampa, 1994.

Madero, Marta. "L'Injure et le corps en Castille aux XIIIe et XIVe siècles." *Atalaya: revue française d'études médiévales hispaniques* 5 (1994): 231–48.

―――. *Manos violentas, palabras vedadas: la injuria en Castilla y León (siglos XIII–XV).* Humanidades/Historia 341. Madrid: Taurus, 1992.

Martins, Mário. *A sátira na literatura medieval portuguesa (séculos XIII e XIV).* Biblioteca Breve 8. Lisboa: Instituto de Cultura e Língua Portuguesa, 1986.

Mérida, Rafael M. *"D'ome atal coita nunca viu cristão:* Amores *nefandos* en los trovadores gallego-portugueses." *O cantar dos trobadores* 433–37.

Michaëlis de Vasconcellos, Carolina, ed. *Cancioneiro da Ajuda.* 2 vols. Halle: Max Niemeyer, 1904.

O cantar dos trobadores: actas do Congreso celebrado en Santiago de Compostela entre os días 26 e 29 de abril de 1993. Santiago de Compostela: Xunta de Galicia, 1993.

Pero da Ponte. *Poesie.* Ed. Saverio Panunzio. Biblioteca di Filologia Romanza 10. Bari: Adriatica, 1967.

Pimenta, Berta Martinha C., Leonardo Parnes, and Luis Filipe Llach Krus. "Dois aspectos da sátira nos cancioneiros galaico-portugueses: 'sodomíticos' e 'cornudos.'" *Revista da Faculdade de Letras (Univ. de Lisboa)*, 4th ser., 2 (1978): 113–28.

Ramos, Maria Ana. "La Satire dans les *cantigas d'escarnho e de mal dizer:* les péchés de la langue." *Atalaya: revue française d'études médiévales hispaniques* 5 (1994): 67–84.

Scholberg, Kenneth R. *Sátira e invectiva en la España medieval*. Madrid: Gredos, 1971.

Snow, Joseph. *The Poetry of Alfonso X, el Sabio: A Critical Bibliography*. Research Bibliographies and Checklists 19. London: Grant and Cutler, 1977.

Tavani, Giuseppe. *A poesia lírica galego-portuguesa*. Trans. Isabel Tomé and Emídio Ferreira. Colecção Estudos de Cultura Portuguesa 1. Lisboa: Comunicação, 1988.

Trexler, Richard C. *Sex and Conquest: Gendered Violence, Political Order, and the European Conquest of the Americas*. Ithaca: Cornell UP, 1995.

Van Scoy, Herbert Allen. *A Dictionary of Old Spanish Terms Defined in the Works of Alfonso X*. Ed. Ivy A. Corfis. Madison: Hispanic Seminary of Medieval Studies, 1986.

Van Vleck, Amelia E. *Memory and Re-Creation in Troubadour Lyric*. Berkeley: U of California P, 1991.

Walsh, John K. "The Names of the Bawd in the *Libro de buen amor*." *Florilegium Hispanicum: Medieval and Golden Age Studies presented to Dorothy Clotelle Clarke*. Ed. John S. Geary. Madison: Hispanic Seminary of Medieval Studies, 1983. 151–64.

Zenith, Richard, trans. *113 Galician-Portuguese Troubadour Poems*. Manchester, Eng.: Carcanet, 1995.

Gregory S. Hutcheson

Desperately Seeking Sodom

Queerness in the Chronicles of Alvaro de Luna

The *Encyclopedia of Homosexuality* wastes precious little time in outing Juan II, king of Castile from 1405 to 1454, and what's more, exposing him as the junior partner in Spain's preeminent gay coupling: "The most famous homophile relationship in Spanish history is that between Juan II and his older lover Álvaro de Luna (ca. 1390–1453), who shared a bedroom for years" (640). What ensues is a tale so heavy in intrigue, romance, and victimization of the gay underdog that it cannot help but beg comparison with *Edward II* (more Jarman's than Marlowe's):

> The relationship began when the king was three, with the appointment of Álvaro as his page (*doncel*). The bond which quickly emerged between them was so strong that those hostile said the king was victim of an *hechizo* or enchantment. . . . When the young king was seven, his mother exiled Álvaro and kept the king virtually a prisoner, a period that ended only with her death six years later. . . . Save for a later period when the king was again prisoner and Álvaro exiled, which was intended to end their relationship, Juan and Álvaro remained together for thirty-five eventful years. They struggled together against a hostile aristocracy, sometimes fleeing together from superior force. The end came with Juan's remarriage after his first wife's death; his new wife, mother of the prudish Isabella the Catholic, was able to force the dismissal and then the execution of Álvaro. The king died a year later. (641)

While the tale is factual in the details of the telling, what gives pause is its baldly anachronistic interpretation of events through the lens of sexual, even romantic love. Suffice it to say that social opportunism and political expediency are far more plausible determinants in the course of Juan II and Luna's "relationship" than are the trials and fortunes of starcrossed lovers.

And while some sources do indeed corroborate that the two "shared a bed-room for years," Bray reminds us that such sleeping arrangements were not uncommon practice throughout the early-modern period, and by no means fall outside the bounds of acceptable convention for friendship in its broader understanding as social and political contract.[1]

And yet there is queerness to be had here, a queerness derived less from bedchamber politics than from the figure of Alvaro de Luna. Called by his contemporaries both "the greatest man uncrowned" and "perverse tyrant," "virtuous and blessed *Maestre*" and "noxious beast," Luna became the ob-sessive focus of a debate over the nature of power and the privileges of caste that could not help but slip into discourses of the unnatural. Not a few sources refer suggestively to his "peculiar habits" or to Juan II's "exces-sive love" for his favorite; still others make explicit reference to a vice they dare not name. That political power is the primary concern here rather than sexuality is clear enough to those of us steeped in a healthy Foucauldian skepticism; less clear is the extent to which sodomy emerges solely as a by-product of the debate, a convenient catchword for the violation of social, political, or racial boundaries that crisscrossed the body politic of fifteenth-century Spain. Indeed, the most scrupulous efforts to tie together the loose ends of Luna's public escapades only serve to unravel even further the mat-ter of his private life, exposing always at the core the perplexing question of his extraordinary influence over the king.[2]

I deploy "queerness" here as an unstable term, one that pushes simulta-neously in the directions of heterodoxy and the sodomitic act without ever fully arriving at either. It is precisely the instability of the term that makes it so readily applicable to Luna, himself a locus of anxiety in an age that was fast becoming obsessed with absolutes. The old Christian guard cer-tainly played a major role in defining the parameters of Luna's queerness, indeed, had need of it as a means of feeding its own compulsion toward orthodoxy. But Luna was not so much queered by texts and contexts as he was himself the source of queerness, the destabilizer even of those works intent on reinscribing him as the locus of normativity. It is in the queer spaces of these texts—in their anxieties, inconsistencies, and excesses— that Luna most spontaneously and most provocatively resides. And it is here that sodomy might be had, if it is to be had at all.

De tu resplandor, ¡o Luna!

In most accounts of the reign of Juan II, the king and his favorite constitute two sides of a single protagonist; Luna reads as the strong arm to the king's political body, the pragmatic side to the ideal of kingship, a Macchiavellian prince *avant-la-lettre*. He is a politician to the core, a victim ultimately of the political intrigue of his age or, in later, more literary turns of the tale, of the fickleness of Fortune, perhaps because it seemed impossible to account otherwise for his extraordinary rise and fall.[3]

His beginnings could not have been less auspicious. Alvaro de Luna was born not in Castile but Aragon, the bastard son of a nobleman of the same name. In essence dispossessed by his father, who died when he was a boy, he found his way eventually to the Castilian court, where the favor he enjoyed with the infant king quickly became a *cause célèbre*. By Juan II's majority (1419), Luna had already assumed the *privanza* — the highly coveted post as the king's intimate advisor and constant companion. From this point on, even dispassionate accounts make note of the fact that Luna was the one "que mas tenía en la voluntad del Rey" (*Crónica de don Juan II* 380–81) [who was most favored by the king].

As king, Juan II was notoriously incompetent — far more taken with courtly pomp than matters of state — a circumstance that made all the more excusable, even desirable, the displacement of power into his *privado*.[4] Luna, for his part, expended the bulk of his energies in defense of the Crown, or rather, in defense of the Crown as he sought to invent it. He envisioned a centralized and self-sufficient government, a well-oiled administrative machine that in the ideal gave impetus to the rise of the modern Spanish state, but which on a more immediate plane served to guarantee Luna's own indispensibility.[5] His staying power was indeed remarkable, due in great part, no doubt, to the king's devotion, but no less so to his ability to forge alliances, defuse opposition (at times unscrupulously), and play factions off one another to his own advantage. All told, Luna dictated the course of Castilian politics for almost four decades, garnering in that time the most prestigious posts in the land (*condestable* [constable] of Castile in 1422 and *maestre* [grand master] of the military order of Santiago in 1445). He accrued such a vast amount of wealth that a contemporary would say of him: "[O]pinion fue de él solo tener más tesoro que todos los grandes onbres e perlados d'España" (Pérez de Guzmán 46) [Rumor had it that he alone possessed more treasure than all the grandees and prelates in Spain].

Opposition to Luna was certainly not wanting; voiced as early as 1425 by the Crown of Aragon, it gained force over the next three decades, culminating finally in the call for Luna's execution in 1453. Especially vitriolic was the widely circulated "Memorial de agravios" [Record of Grievances] addressed to Juan II by the highest-ranking members of Iberian nobility in 1440.[6] Charges here revolve in the main around Luna's "vanagloria e soberuia e desordenada cobdiçia" (324) [vainglory and pride and unbridled avarice], in the service of which he engages in corrupt practices of every imaginable sort, from usurpation of royal finances to nepotism, from extortion to wanton acts of violence. Most offensive, however, is Luna's calculated alienation of the Spanish nobility, the *naturales* 'native-born', in deference to *estrangeros* 'foreigners, outsiders':

[S]ienpre se á travajado por yndinar a vuestra señoría contra vuestros naturales . . . con yntención de mejor seguir su estado. . . . E así apartados los vuestros naturales, metió e puso en vuestra casa, en guarda de vuestra rreal persona, muchos estrangeros, en gran difamaçión e ynjuria déllos. (330)

[He has always endeavored to turn your lordship against your *naturales* so as to better carry out his own designs. And once your *naturales* were out of the way, he introduced many *estrangeros* into your house, in watch over your royal person, much to the dishonor and shame of (those same *naturales*).]

Estrangero is an ambiguous term in this context, one that sets itself in both horizontal opposition to those who are native-born and vertical opposition to those who could claim a birthright to status and rank.[7] And yet it cannot help but implode as well, assuming a third, more furtive meaning intended to provoke a knee-jerk reaction within an increasingly anxious *status quo*. Widespread anti-Jewish violence at the end of the fourteenth century had occasioned the mass conversion of Jews to Christianity and the creation of a *converso* class—converted Jews who suddenly found themselves in a position to lay claim to both the identity and the privilege of the old Christian caste. Embraced initially by the body of Spanish Christendom, *conversos* soon fell victim to the resentment and mistrust of the rank and file. By the mid-fifteenth century they had become less equals in the faith than the sign of ambiguous identity, of a slippage between cultural systems—a new, even more insidious threat posed by the *estrangero*, only now from within.[8]

Limpieza de sangre, an uncontaminated bloodline, was of the essence in the matter of Christian identity, or so the agitator Pero Sarmiento would proclaim in the revolt of Toledo in 1449; and the *sangre limpia* that coursed through the veins of old Christians had of necessity to course through the veins of the Spanish body politic.[9] Luna worked in flagrant opposition to this mandate through the introduction of *estrangeros* into the bureaucratic machine. His appointees were at times family members, at times commoners, but more often than not they were descendents of the Jews who had been the driving force in Castilian affairs of state and finance for the previous two centuries. Jews and *conversos* remained the most capable administrators in the kingdom, and as such were key to Luna's invigoration of the Crown's finances and authority.[10] But what for Luna was a common-sense maneuver, for old Christians represented an act of aggression against their birthright as *naturales* of the kingdom. Far from being the redeemer of a kingdom in crisis, Luna was the conduit for a willed contamination of the Spanish body politic.

The slide from here to sodomy is inevitable, already implied in the term *natural*, which is contrasted not only with *estrangero*, but just as explicitly with "unnatural," *contra naturam:* "Hay dos maneras de prinçipar e señorear sobre la gente," the "Memorial" stipulates in its opening lines, "la vna natural, derecha e vuena, la otra tiránica e contraria" (320) [There are two ways to rule over people, the one natural, good and true, the other tyrannical and contrary]. Luna belongs definitively to the latter camp, and his hold on power is "desordenado," "perverso," "no . . . natural ni derechamente avido, mas por otras maneras muy contrarias a toda natural rrazón" (329) [disordered; perverse; not acquired through natural or principled means, but rather through other means contrary to all natural reason].

What is only implied in such highly suggestive formulations is made explicit later in the text in what constitutes the first charge in public record of Luna's practice of sodomy:

Otrosy, . . . ha traydo a vuestra muy notable e linpia corte la más suzia e aborreçible cosa a Dios e a natura que se fabla entre todos los viçios, lo qual fué sienpre más denostado en España, en especial en la generaçión de estos vuestros rreynos . . . , a que por fealdad non se puede onestamente nonbrar nin declarar por la presente. (331)

[Furthermore, he has brought to your most distinguished and blameless court the filthiest of all vices, that thing most detestable to both God and nature, which has always been condemned most in Spain, especially among the people of your own realms, and whose repulsiveness is such that we cannot bring ourselves to name it.][11]

That Juan II is the passive recipient of Luna's practice of the "unmentionable vice" is implied in the accusation of sorcery that immediately follows:

[E]s nos forçado . . . afirmar lo que por todos se dize, que el dicho condestable tiene ligadas e atadas todas vuestras potencias corporales e animales por mágicas e deavólicas encantaciones. (332)

[We are forced to acknowledge that which everyone is saying, that the aforementioned *condestable* has bound up all of your bodily and spiritual faculties through the use of diabolical magic spells.][12]

The king is simultaneously bewitched and buggered, compelled (in language that almost begs to be read sexually) to yield, to give "tan gran logar e posada a tan enormes fechos e tan contrarios a toda onestidad e rrazón que tolerables non devían ser" [utter license to acts so egregious and so contrary to all decency and reason that they should never have been tolerated].

Sodomy runs as a subtext throughout the "Memorial," oscillating wildly between literal and figurative meanings and producing in Luna an agent of corruption and contamination who engages wantonly in the simultaneous "screwing over" of each of the king's two bodies. He introduces not only *estrangeros* but sodomy itself into the "most distinguished and blameless court," entirely undermining its role in the formation of the aristocratic class and converting it instead into a site of perversion.[13] In an act of lèse-majesté, he dominates, renders passive, and finally eliminates the king's authoritative presence, using "entera e largamente de todo vuestro rreal poder, así avsoluto como ordinario" (320) [freely and completely all of your royal power, both absolute and ordinary]. Luna becomes the *nefandum* (that which cannot be spoken) in its most dangerous sense, the perpetrator of abominable acts veiled in a silence that masquerades as majesty. It is this

"silence trompeur," Chiffoleau argues, that emerges as the point of intersection between the *nefandum* and the *crimen majestatis,* necessitating efforts
"to make the accused speak the unspeakable precisely in order to protect
the zone of silence and mystery that surrounds legitimate power" (302).[14]

Luna was never made to speak the unspeakable, it would seem, nor did
Juan II respond formally to the letter of 1440.[15] Nonetheless, by 1453 he
seems to have extricated himself entirely from Luna's influence, so much
so that in June of that year the *condestable* was beheaded by royal decree
in the city of Valladolid and his head kept on public display for well over a
week. No source gives a satisfactory explanation as to why the king turned
so quickly and decisively against his *privado* after almost four decades of
virtually absolute dependency. His second wife, Isabel of Portugal — whom
he had married, ironically enough, at Luna's instance — surely had a hand in
it, although perhaps not as heavy a hand as is implied in the *Encyclopedia of
Homosexuality.* Greater pressure was undoubtedly exerted by Juan Pacheco,
the ambitious counselor and confidant to Crown Prince Enrique, as well as
by members of the nobility who had been displaced by Luna's political program.[16] And Netanyahu suggests that it was the *conversos* themselves who
were ultimately to blame, resentful as they were of radical shifts in policy
made by Luna as a consequence of the Toledo rebellion in 1449 (681 ff.).

Neither does the public apology composed by Juan II shortly after Luna's
execution clear up matters any.[17] In the main it parrots many of the charges
(and much of the rhetoric) of the "Memorial de agravios," leaving open
the question of how active a part the king actually had in its composition.
Given its wide distribution, there remains little doubt that its immediate
purpose was the bolstering of public support a posteriori for Luna's execution and the defusing of threats of reprisal on the part of pro-Luna factions.
Indeed, specific mention is made at letter's end of these factions and of acts
of aggression that had already been perpetrated against the king.

While sodomy is never named, it is certainly referenced obliquely in
the charges of lèse-majesté that comprise the majority of the document.
More striking is the recourse to a decidedly apocalyptic discourse, one that
concentrates in Luna all of the evil besetting the common good. Luna is
no longer simply the "perverse tyrant," but Lucifer himself, "queriéndose
igualar comigo" (684) [desiring to make himself my equal] and carrying out
his evil designs "con elacion é luciferna sobervia" (688) [with delight and
Lucifer-like pride].[18] The marquis of Santillana, scion of the powerful Men-

doza family, gives much the same reading to Luna in his poetic "De tu resplandor, ¡o Luna!" [Of your radiance, o Luna!], a piece composed shortly after Luna's execution. Here the double entendre (Luna-Moon) expands into the triple meaning of Luna-Moon-Lightbearer (i.e., Lucifer).[19] In his treachery, in his ambition, but primarily in his "desiring to make himself my equal" (which is both the sin of Lucifer and the vain desire of the *converso*), Luna enters inevitably into a metonymic relationship with the Jews, and the punishment visited on his body becomes a presage of the punishment that would be visited on the body of Spanish Jewry forty years later.

Luna represents time and again the site of contamination, whether of the court, of the Spanish body politic, or of Christendom itself. He possesses, whether through force or enchantment, the king's will and ultimately his crown. He is the low-born, the outsider, the Jew. In sum, he is a "sodomite" in virtually every social and political inflection of the term, enough so that the chronicler Alonso de Palencia would begin his contemptuous account of the reign of Enrique IV with the figure of Luna, "en cuyo tiempo tuvieron origen en Castilla los infames tratos obscenos que tan vergonzoso incremento tomaron después" (2: 30) [in whose time Castile witnessed the beginnings of those vile and obscene relations that would proliferate so shamelessly afterward].[20] So flagrant are the contiguous charges, so watertight the "sodomitic" case made against Luna that the sexual act is quite literally beside the point. Indeed, it would seem to corroborate Jonathan Goldberg's conviction that any inquiry into sodomy "will never deliver the sodomite per se, but only . . . sodometries, relational structures precariously available to prevailing discourses" (20). We are left, then, still desperately seeking Sodom.

Aquel exçesivo e maravilloso amor

Serving as something of a check to the feeding frenzy enjoyed by anti-Luna factions at Luna's expense is the *Generaciones y semblanças* [Genealogies and Portraits], a collection of thumbnail sketches composed by the aristocrat and littérateur Fernán Pérez de Guzmán toward the end of Juan II's reign. Pérez de Guzmán's subjects are the leading political figures of his day: kings and queens, blue-bloods and prelates, or the untitled but no less powerful bureaucrats who managed to put their own stamp on the course of Spanish history. To these portraits (composed in the main before 1450) are appended heftier accounts of Luna and Juan II shortly after the death of the latter in 1454.

Pérez de Guzmán eschews traditional historiography and its sycophancies in favor of an objectivity whose parameters he lays out in his introduction. The historiographer, he feels, should not only be eyewitness to the events of his age but delay publishing his account of these events "biviendo el rey o prínçipe en cuyo tienpo o señorío se hordena, por quel estoriador sea libre para escrivir la verdad sin temor" (3) [while the king or prince whose reign it recounts is still alive, this so that the writer of the history is free to speak the truth without fear]. Although Pérez de Guzmán subscribes to a strict code of ethics bound up inevitably in the binarisms of a persecuting society, this code he applies as rigorously to the powerful as he does to the weak, to friend as well as foe. Few if any figures in his *Generaciones y semblanças* are entirely virtuous, and in fact most are beset by a series of vices that can only be seen as inherent in the human species. Ultimately, lines are blurred between aristocracy and bureaucracy, between church and state, between old Christian and new. Indeed, while the portrait of Don Pedro de Frías, cardinal of Spain, is far from complimentary—"non fue muy devoto nin onesto, nin tan linpio de su presona como a su dignidad convenía" (36) [he was not very devout or principled, nor as clean in his person as the dignity (of his office) might have dictated]—the portrait of the *converso* Pablo de Santa María, "ebreo de grant linaje de aquella naçión" (28) [noble scion of the Hebrew nation], is not only deferential, but constitutes one of the earliest and most eloquent defenses of the *converso* caste against the alarmism of the old Christian guard.[21]

What we might expect given the equalizing agenda of the *Generaciones y semblanças* is a demythification of Luna and a probing of the polemical discourse that casts him so spontaneously as Jew, as tyrant, even as sodomite. This expectation does indeed seem to bear itself out, most obviously in the occasional bursts of apologetic language—"[a]yudó a muchos" (45) [He helped many]; "perdonó a muchos" [he forgave many]; "estorvó algunas muertes" (47) [he prevented the death of some]—but more significantly in the generalization of specific charges to implicate the broad range of Spanish society. Luna remains the monster of excess in his avarice and ambition, but the nobility is not far behind:

[Q]uanto quier que la prinçipal e la original cabsa de los daños de España fuese . . . la cobdiçia e ambiçión exçesiva del condestable, pero en este casso non es de perdonar la cobdiçia de los grandes cavalleros que por creçer e avançar sus estados e rentas . . . dieron lugar a ello. (47)

[Although the cause of Spain's ills was first and foremost the *condestable*'s excessive avarice and ambition, as blameworthy in this case was the avarice of those grandees who indulged the *condestable*'s excesses in hopes of increasing their own estates.]

So too is desire to control the king's will made endemic to the nobility at large:

[L]a verdad es ésta . . . : que quanto quier que los señores prínçipes e los grandes onbres que los siguían dixiesen que lo fazían por fazer libre la voluntad del rey . . . , e por amor de la república e por amor e utilidad e provecho comunal, pero . . . que la entençión final era poser e aver aquel lugar del condestable, e veyendo que el rey era más para ser rigido que rigidor, creían que qualquier que dél se apoderase le governaría a él e por consiguiente al reino, e podrían acresçentar sus estados e casas. (50)

[The truth is this: that although the princes and their noble entourage claimed that they (plotted against Luna) in order to ransom the king's will — out of love for the republic and for the benefit of the common good — their ultimate goal was to gain possession of the *condestable*'s post, for, seeing that the king was more apt to be ruled than to rule, they believed that whoever gained power over him could govern both him and his kingdom, and so they might hope to increase their own estates.]

What is remarkable here is the frank interrogation into the nature of "truth"; Pérez de Guzmán quite literally deconstructs anti-Luna polemic by exposing its underside, breaking down its binarisms, and reducing its altruistic discourse to pure rhetorical ploy. Even sorcery, that charge immediately contiguous to sodomy, is revealed to be no more than smoke and mirrors behind which the aristocracy conceals its own desires to "possess" the king.[22]

The general thrust of Pérez de Guzmán's account would seem to be a neutralization (although certainly not a vindication) of the *privado* together with a censuring of the nobility at large. The two camps are merged into a collective antagonist whose ambitions and factiousness are responsible for the sorry state of Spain: "de todos estos males fueron cabsa los pecados de los españoles" (53) [the sins of the Spaniards were the cause of all these ills]. Luna, far from being the unique site of perversion, is merely the *primus inter pares*. The text assures a porosity between the two camps that makes the charge of "sodomy" undesirable, even dangerous. Even if launched solely against Luna, it would spread through the entire of the Spanish body politic, converting the text itself into the site of contamination and Pérez de Guzmán into the author of his own buggering.

Needless to say, sodomy is never mentioned by name. And yet Pérez de Guzmán crafts subtle distinctions between Luna and the aristocracy that end up being equally provocative. Although he devotes substantial passages to the slights committed by aristocratic factions against the Crown, he falls just short of accusing these factions of lèse-majesté: "[Y]o bien los escusaría de deslealtad o tiranía çerca [de] la presona del rey e de su corona" (51) [I would readily excuse them of any disloyalty or tyranny with regard to the person of the king or his crown]. He also falls short of neutralizing entirely the queerness that surrounds Luna's rise to power and control over the king. Luna remains for Pérez de Guzmán a "cavallero sin parientes" (41) [knight without family], a "fijo bastardo" (44) [bastard son] who, in his presumption, forgets the "homill e baxa parte de su madre" (45) [base and humble origins of his mother]. By depriving Luna of normative social alliances, Pérez de Guzmán blocks any natural access he might claim to the playing fields of Spanish politics.[23] Rather his rise is intrusive, unnatural, defined almost exclusively by an enigmatic *potençia* whose reach is "tan grande e tan exçesiva" (40) [so great and so excessive] that no member of the body politic is left untouched:

> Ca non solamente los ofiçios e estados e merçedes de que el rey podía prover, mas las dignidades e benefiçios eclesiásticos, non era en el reino quien ossase suplicar al papa nin aun açebtar su provisión . . . sin consentimiento del condestable. Así lo tenporal e spiritual todo era en su mano. Toda la abtoridad del rey era firmar las cartas, mas la hordenança e esecuçión dellas en el condestable era. (40)

> [(This was true) not only (of) the offices, estates, and favors the king was empowered to grant, but also (of) ecclesiastic dignities and benefices; there

was no one in the kingdom who dared make a request of the pope or even abide by his pronouncements without the *condestable*'s approval. So it was that all matters, whether temporal or spiritual, were in his hands. All of the king's authority was reduced to signing decrees, while it was the *condestable* who ordered them and carried them out.]

Just as the king is rendered utterly passive in his political body, so too is he immobilized in his physical body, and the instrument of his sexual *potençia* held just as firmly in Luna's grasp:

[A]un en los actos naturales se dió assí a la ordenança del condestable, que seyendo él moço e bien conplisionado e teniendo a la reina su muger moça e fermosa si el condestable ge lo contradixiese, non iría a dormir a su cámara della, nin curava de otras mugeres, aunque naturalmente asaz era inclinado a ellas. (40–41)

[Even in acts of nature he gave himself over to the *condestable*'s charge; although he was a young man and well disposed, and the queen his wife was young and beautiful, he would not go to sleep in her chamber if the *condestable* objected, nor would he pay heed to other women, even though he was by nature quite inclined to do so.][24]

It is here, in perhaps the most voyeuristic moment of the *Generaciones y semblanzas*, that Luna is made to work most explicitly *contra naturam;* in his compromising of the king's "natural inclination" (i.e., heterosexual desire), what appears to be a simple act of lèse-majesté skirts dangerously close to something left unnamed.

The suspicion of sodomy is not entirely contained in the figure of Luna, however; in a radical departure from the "Memorial de agravios," Juan II is rendered as less the passive victim to unnatural desire than the propagator of his own forms of queerness. His integrity is already severely compromised earlier in the text through mention of his "strange condition," a passion for language and learning to the virtual exclusion of matters of governance:

E porque la condición suya fue estraña e maravillosa, es nesçesario de alargar la relación della. . . . Plazíale oir los onbres avisados e graçiosos e notava mucho lo que dellos oía, sabía fablar e entender latín, leía muy bien, plazíanle mucho libros y estorias, oía muy de grado los dizires rimados e conoçía los viçios dellos. . . . Pero como quier que de todas estas graçias oviese razonable parte, de aquellas que verdaderamente son virtudes e que a todo omne, e prinçipalmente a los reyes, son nesçesarias, fue muy defetuoso. Ca la prinçipal virtud del rey, después de la fee, es ser industrioso e diligente en la governaçión . . . de su reyno. (38–39)

[And because this condition of his was so marvelous and strange, it behooves us to give an extensive account of it. He enjoyed listening to learned and witty men and he took note of what he heard them say, he spoke and understood Latin, he read very well, he greatly enjoyed books and histories, he listened with great relish to poetic works and was himself familiar with their pleasures. And yet, although he was reasonably adept in all of these areas, he was defective in those that truly count as virtues and that are necessary for every man, most of all for kings. For the primary virtue of the king, faith aside, is industry and diligence in the governing of his kingdom.]

Pérez de Guzmán stresses the essential nature of Juan II's "defectiveness" when he makes the claim that no one can hope to explain it except "Aquél que fizo la condiçión del rey tan estraña" (41) [the One who made the king's condition so strange (to begin with)]; indeed, neither his marriage to his first wife, the daughter of the consummate warrior-king Fernando of Aragon, nor his succession to the throne of Castile, nor even Luna's numerous exiles and eventual execution served to divorce him from his "natural condition," that is, "aquella remisión e nigligençia cassi monstruosa" (42) [that almost monstrous carelessness and negligence] with which he had brought the ship of state to rack and ruin.[25]

Of note here is the slippage of "natural" from a heteronormative meaning to a denaturalizing one: Juan II represents both a "natural inclination" toward heterosexual desire and a "natural condition" that reverses the direction of that desire, implying open complicity in the sodomizing at the very least of his political body. His body becomes the site of confused categories, a spawning ground for discourses of unnatural desire. Indeed, he seems to enter into a sadomasochistic contract with Luna: "Tanta e tan singular fue la fiança que el rey fizo del condestable e tan grande e tan exçesiva su potençia" (40) [So great and extraordinary was the trust the king placed in his *condestable* and so great and excessive the *condestable*'s power]; "[L]a inclinaçión natural pudo en él aver tanto vigor e fuerça que de todo punto sin algunt medio se sometiese a la hordenança e consejo del condestable"

(41) [So strong a hold did his natural inclination have on him that he gave himself over entirely and without reserve to the charge and counsel of the *condestable*]; "[L]e ovo aquel exçesivo e maravilloso amor" (45) [He felt (for Luna) an excessive and extraordinary love]. Throughout the account, the site of perversion shifts from the king to Luna and back again—from the utter passivity (*nigligençia*) of the one to the absolute control (*potençia*) of the other—and ultimately it never anchors itself, nor does Pérez de Guzmán seem to want it to: "[Y]o non sé quál destas dos cosas es de mayor admiraçión, o la condiçión del rey o el poder del condestable" (41) [I don't know which of these two things is more extraordinary, the condition of the king or the power of the *condestable*]. It is precisely in this in-between space—a space of tension and irresolution—that Juan II and Luna's relationship is at its most provocative, and sodomy, though unnamed, is most graphically enacted.

Guardando en ellos secreto tanto

Never does Pérez de Guzmán voice openly the charge of sodomy as the "Memorial de agravios" had done or as subsequent historiographers would do throughout the early-modern age. And yet the sodomitic script is unmistakable. Indeed, what lends it greater force is how it emerges almost accidentally from the slippages of text. Equally provocative is the absence—and inevitable presence—of sodomy in the *Crónica de don Álvaro de Luna,* a full-length biography composed by one of Luna's more stalwart partisans shortly after the *condestable*'s execution.[26] Unabashedly apologetic, it constitutes a conscious rescripting of Luna in terms that counter point by point the charges launched against him throughout his tenure at court. Every episode of Luna's life is read as conclusive evidence of his gallantry, his generosity of spirit, and his absolute loyalty to the king. So too are his last days recounted in terms that make heavy-handed use of allusions to the Passion of Christ[27] and finally consign this "virtuoso e bienadventurado Maestre" (434) [virtuous and blessed *Maestre*] to the company of the saints. It becomes quickly evident that this is not history, but hagiography, where Christology mixes with romance in the invention of a Luna who is both heroic and holy. And yet it is not a matter of degree, as would be the case of romance, but rather of negation, reconfiguration, and denial. The *Crónica* is ultimately an extended defensive reflex in which extremes respond to extremes and hyperbole becomes the language of default. Its defenses are most heightened (and its silences most resounding) at precisely those points where the danger of slippage is greatest.

One such point is the question of Luna's humble origins, which for the anti-Luna camp continued to justify his being branded as an interloper. That Luna's biographer is keenly aware of the polemic is evidenced in his obsession with the nature of nobility in the opening lines of his text:

> Quistión fué muy antigua . . . en qual . . . de los ombres resplandescía más la
> nobleza e fidalguía: en aquellos que nascían de claros linajes . . . , e por su des-
> merescer e escuros fechos . . . manzillaban la limpia sangre de sus linajes, o
> en aquellos que de humildes e baxos linajes, por los grados de la virtud e de la
> noble carrera de la vida, sabían subir e acumbrar en la silla de la nobleza? (7)

> [A question of old was this: in which men was nobility more resplendent, in
> those born of illustrious lineage who, through their lack of merit and ignoble
> deeds, sullied the pure blood of their ancestors, or in those who, through
> virtuous deeds and the noble course of their lives, managed to rise up from
> their base and humble origins and mount the throne of nobility?]

All agree, the biographer concludes, that this second group is more noble, and so to this second group, it would seem, Luna belongs. And yet what seems in essence a very deliberate response to Pérez de Guzmán—ultimately a subtle attack on the privileges of birth—curiously falls away as the biographer assigns his protagonist to a third caste, to those who "no sólo merescen rescebir gloria para sí mesmos, mas acrescientan la de los sus pasados" (8) [not only deserve to obtain glory for themselves, but who augment the glory of their ancestors]. The biographer, evidently uncomfortable with a purely constructionist view of nobility, launches into a protracted encomium of Luna's paternal line in the folds of which his mother is entirely obscured:

> Clara e sabida cosa es que entre las casas prinçipales . . . del reyno de Ara-
> gón fué e es vna dellas la casa de Luna, así por nobleza de linaje como por
> mucha antigüedad e grandeza de patrimonio, e avn porque salieron siempre
> de aquella notables e escogidos hombres. (8)

[It is well known that among the principal houses of the kingdom of Aragon, one such house was and is that of Luna, renowned as much for the nobility of its lineage as it is for its great antiquity and the grandness of its legacy, and also because it has always produced notable and distinguished men.]

Within the hyperbole, however, the initial question lingers, and so the suggestion of "base and humble origins"; although the author strives to re-insert Luna into normative alliances through frank denial of his maternal line, the specter of Luna's mother remains to haunt us as much with her sudden absence as she does elsewhere with her undesirable presence.

This is only one of many instances in which the text doubles back on itself, bringing to the surface precisely that which it seeks to hide. Such ambiguities of textual intention cannot help but inflect in curious ways the *Crónica*'s reading of that most slippery of areas by far, Luna's relationship with the king. Curiously, little effort is made to obscure the king's obses-sion with his *privado,* and indeed, it is fleshed out as nowhere else, not only in the public sphere but initially (and primarily) in far more intimate spaces:

[E]l Rey de noche nin de día non . . . quería estar sin don Áluaro de Luna, e lo aventajaba sobre todos los otros, e no quería que otro alguno lo vistiese ni tratase. (19–20)

[The king could not be without Don Alvaro de Luna whether by day or by night; he favored him above all others, and did not want anyone else to dress him or tend to his needs.]

[S]i el Rey salía a dançar, no quería que otro caballero ninguno . . . dançase con él, saluo don Áluaro, ni quería con otro cantar, . . . ni se apartaba con otro a aver sus consejos e fablas secretas tanto como con él. (27)

[If the king got up to dance, he did not want any other knight to dance with him except Don Alvaro, nor did he want to sing with any other; neither did he seclude himself with any other to speak of secret matters as much as he did with him.]

While such obsession can be attributed within this specific context to the king's tender age (both passages correspond to his preadolescence), the biographer makes little point of the fact. Indeed, he implies instead a sophisticated political sense on the part of the king in his account of Luna's departure for Aragon (occasioned, we are told, by a courtly conspiracy against him):

El Rey quando vido que todavía era dispuesto don Áluaro de Luna de se partir, non pudo sufrir que las lágrimas no le viniesen a los ojos; e como quiera que el Rey era niño, que aun non avía más de diez años, bien entendió que aquello se hazía por apartar dél a don Áluaro de Luna, e abraçándolo muy amigablemente díxole que si todavía quería su seruicio se viniese luego para él. En esta manera se partió don Áluaro de Luna de la corte por aquella vez, e non solamente quedó el Rey triste por su partida, mas todas las doncellas e dueñas de la casa de la Reyna, maldiziendo en sus coraçones a los que avían tenido manera con la Reyna que don Áluaro partiese de la corte. (21–22)

[When the king saw that Don Alvaro de Luna was still intent on leaving, he could not help the tears coming to his eyes; and even though the king was a boy—he was no more than ten at the time—he understood well that this was being done to separate him from Don Alvaro de Luna. Embracing him very affectionately, he told him that if he still desired his service he need only come to him. So it was that Don Alvaro de Luna departed from the court on that occasion; not only the king was saddened by his departure, so too were all the damsels and ladies of the queen's household, who cursed in their hearts those who had persuaded the queen that Don Alvaro should leave the court.]

Sharp lines are drawn here and throughout the first dozen or so chapters of the *Crónica* between the men of the court (those who contrive Luna's absence) and the women (those who desire his presence), between the breakdown of homosocial alliances and the consummation of romantic ones. Of note is the king's constant association with the second camp, his very deliberate insertion into the realm of female desire. Indeed, through recourse to all the *topoi* of romance—secret trysts, displays of grief, the collusion of the ladies of the court, and a foreshadowing of Luna's eventual return and vindication—both *privado* and king are cast as lover and beloved in a tale of romance that becomes so essential a part of the text that it resurfaces time and again, most poignantly 120 chapters (almost forty years) later in the aftermath of Luna's execution:

Mandólo matar su muy amado e muy obedesçido señor el Rey, el qual, en lo mandando matar, se puede con verdad dezir se mató a sí mismo; ca non duró después de su muerte si non sólo un año e çincuenta días, los quales todos . . . le fueron días de dolor e de trabajo. Ca muchas vezes . . . lo vieron los suyos llorar con mucha amargura por la muerte del su leal Maestre. (434)

[It was his lord the king, whom he had always loved and obeyed, who ordered Luna's death, and in so doing, it might truthfully be said that the king killed himself; for he did not last after Don Alvaro's death more than a year and fifty days, all of which were for him days of toil and suffering. For quite often his servants saw him crying bitterly over the death of his loyal *Maestre*.][28]

So it is that within the realm of desire there is as much a doubling of authorial intent as elsewhere, as much an effort to magnify desire as there is to defuse it, reconfigure it, generalize it, or push it behind closed doors. And ironically, here as elsewhere, it is the very act of closing doors that opens up "secret" spaces in the texts, spaces that confound strictly homo-social readings, spaces where queerness resides. What draws our attention are not the public displays of affection between Juan II and Luna, but rather the "speaking of secret matters," allusions to an intimacy that exists out-side the public forum, outside the scope of the text itself, in a realm that is unspoken, unmentioned, perhaps unmentionable. Secrets proliferate, pre-dominantly in matters of love. The author confesses that while Luna "[f]ué muy enamorado en todo tienpo; guardó gran secreto a sus amores" (207) [was forever deeply in love, he kept his loves a great secret]. And elsewhere:

E si otras veces razonaban algunos alabando a sus amigas, e contando sus casos de amores, don Álvaro los sabía assí graciosamente dezir, que todos avían muy grand voluntad de le oír fablar, e el Rey sobre todos. E don Álvaro se ouo tan discretamente sus amores, guardando en ellos lealtad e secreto tanto, que por aquello era mucho más amado e preciado de todas las dueñas e donzellas. (28)

[And if at other times his companions discoursed in praise of their lady-loves and told tales of their passions, Don Alvaro gave such delightful accounts that everyone was extremely eager to hear him speak, especially the king. And Don Alvaro was so discreet in matters of love and kept them such a secret that for this reason he was even more greatly loved and appreciated by all the ladies and damsels.]

More intriguing is the reference to a conspiracy of silence in which the author himself participates:

> E yo no niego que algunas grandes señores se pudiesen aquí nombrar en esta Historia, las quales verdaderamente fueron presas del su amor, e se ofresçieron a mayores peligros que los flacos coraçones de las mugeres deben ser obligados por cabsa dél; mas no sería honesta cosa que . . . la fama e vida de algunas de aquéllas el su historiador, recontando sus fechos, en alguna manera manzillase. (28)

> [And I do not deny that several great ladies could be named in this history who were truly held captive by his love, and subjected themselves to greater peril than the weak hearts of women should have to sustain for reason of it; but it would not be prudent for the author of (Don Alvaro's) history to taint in some way the reputation of these women for the sake of recounting his deeds.]

The biographer teases us relentlessly by alluding to a secret and never revealing it, by maintaining a silence that is at once resolute and highly suggestive. This is silence as Sedgwick has theorized it, one that "accrues particularity by fits and starts, in relation to the discourse that surrounds and differentially constitutes it" (3). What claims to be discretion in the *Crónica de don Alvaro de Luna* cannot help but enter into an intense dialogue with "secret matters," with the king's "excessive and extraordinary love," with "the filthiest of all the vices, that thing most detestable to both God and nature," and so constitute not only the performance of "closetedness" but ultimately the construction of sodomy.

Silence is only one — and by no means the least significant — of what Foucault refers to as a "polyvalence of discourses," that series of discontinuous segments whose distribution "we must reconstruct, with the things said and those concealed, the enunciations required and those forbidden" (100). Sodomy, as that "utterly confused category," is perhaps most resistant to this sort of reconstruction. As we have seen, it is in its paradoxical nature to be most present when it is concealed, most elusive when it is explicitly named. Indeed, the blatant accusations of the "Memorial de agravios" are rooted far more, perhaps even exclusively, in the ideologies of a persecuting society—in an understanding of the king's body in a metaphorical sense as the Spanish body politic and of Luna as the agent of perversion and contamination. Luna represents the point where "unnatural" assumes the double meaning of "not natural" and "not-of-us," the point where sexual and cultural otherness fall into a lockstep, provoking as much an impulse toward heteronormativity as they do toward orthodoxy.

Sodomy slips into the cracks, however, precisely when it no longer carries a distinct sociocultural charge, and yet it is at this point that it begins to assume its most tangible form. Behind the hyperbole, astride the language of romance, within the closets of the *Crónica de don Alvaro de Luna* lurks the specter of sodomy, ever present (like Luna's mother) in its conspicuous absence. Indeed, the *Crónica* conspires almost inevitably with Pérez de Guzmán and the "Memorial de agravios" in the production of a sodomitic script that both emerges from and is constitutive of the biographies of Luna and Juan II, that engages in a queering of history through the very act of narration. In the final analysis, sodomy need not be discovered, invented, or inserted into the tale of Luna's rise and fall—it is already of the essence.

Notes

1. The *Crónica de don Alvaro de Luna* notes that when Juan II selected Luna as his sleeping companion, "el escándalo fué grande" (33) [there arose a great outcry], not due to any impropriety, but rather because "el adelantado Pero Manrrique e otros grandes omes avían procurado mucho acostarse a los pies del Rey, mas non les avía seído dado lugar" [the *adelantado* Pero Manrique and other grandees had greatly desired to sleep at the king's feet, but the privilege had never been granted to them]. Unless otherwise indicated, all translations of primary sources are my own.

2. Scholarship nonetheless continues to engage in a bowdlerization of source materials: Jaen's narrative account of the life of Luna omits any intimations of homosexuality, while Round's superb analysis of Luna's final years makes only a passing reference (*The Greatest Man Uncrowned* 8). And Netanyahu goes no further than alluding suggestively to the king's "addiction" to Luna's company (219). Only Brocato, in an unpublished paper, points to sex as one of the central axes of contemporary sources, although she is reluctant to read into these sources the "unequivocal assertion that [Juan II and Luna] were lovers."

3. Both Golden Age theater and the ballad tradition would capitalize on the

theme (see MacCurdy; Pérez Gómez). Even as far afield as England Luna is invoked as exemplar of the favorite's fall from grace, most notably in *Several Tracts against Popery: Together with the Life of Don Alvaro de Luna*, composed by the eighteenth-century polemicist Michael Geddes.

4. This displacement of power constitutes the core of polemic over Luna throughout his tenure in Juan II's government. The anonymous first author of the *Crónica de don Juan II* (the official account of the reign of Juan II) makes no mention of him until 1419, when he is appointed *privado* and first begins to flex his political muscle. It is only in 1426, when authorship of the *Crónica* passes to the *converso* Alvar García de Santa María, that Luna comes to occupy center stage — acknowledgment, no doubt, of the *privado*'s favorable policies toward the *converso* class (Netanyahu 242). The unofficial *Crónica del halconero de Juan II*, authored by the king's head huntsman, Pedro Carrillo de Huete, is steadfastly neutral (see Carriazo's introduction, xii), although it remains a goldmine for documentation of anti-Luna polemic. As for the *Crónica de don Álvaro de Luna*, it is unapologetically biased in favor of Luna, and as such can only be trusted in the bare bones of its historical narrative. Serving as counterbalance are the highly critical portraits of Juan II and Luna composed by Fernán Pérez de Guzmán shortly after the death of both. Both the *Crónica de don Álvaro de Luna* and Pérez de Guzmán's *Generaciones y semblanzas* will be taken up later in this essay. For comprehensive modern assessments of Luna's governance, see Suárez Fernández and Netanyahu.

5. Notes Round: "What the Catholic Monarchs were able to do with Castilian government was done with the government which Alvaro de Luna made and staffed" (*The Greatest Man Uncrowned* 21).

6. Among whom the *infantes* of Aragon (Juan, by then king of Navarra, and his brother, Enrique), Grand Admiral Fadrique, and other grandees of the Castilian court. The "Memorial de agravios" (so named by its twentieth-century editor Juan de Mata Carriazo) is included almost in its entirety in the *Crónica del halconero*, at least partially in the *Crónica de don Juan II*, and was taken up again in later chronicles, including the revision, or *Refundición*, of the *Crónica del halconero*, composed by the cardinal Lope Barrientos sometime after 1454. Given its wide circulation, the "Memorial" undoubtedly formed the basis for much of what later historiographers had to say about Luna, this despite (or perhaps because of) its overtly libelous intent. For a consideration of the "Memorial," see Carriazo's preliminary study in his edition of Barriento's *Refundición* (cviii–cxii). All citations in the present study are to the *Crónica del halconero*.

7. That Luna himself embodies the *estrangero* — he is both foreign born and the bastard son of a plebeian mother — did not go unnoticed: he is ultimately an out-

sider, or so the letter implies, a *poseur* who achieved rank and status only by concealing his true station, "olvidando quien él hera" (324) [forgetting who he was].

8. The work of Spanish historian Américo Castro continues to provide valuable insight into this period, in particular into the rise of a self-aware *converso* class that figured prominently in Spanish society and culture throughout the early modern period. In English, see his *The Structure of Spanish History* and *The Spaniards: An Introduction to Their History*. Rodríguez-Puértolas offers an uncritical overview of Castro's contributions to Spanish historicism, while Smith lays bare his essentializing tendencies. Most recent work on *conversos* engages actively in the debate over the sincerity of conversion and the question of essential *converso* identity. See especially Freund and Ruiz, Roth, and, of course, Netanyahu, who, at complete variance with Baer, argues that *converso* backsliding was less a reality than a pretext for inquisition and the Spanish move toward absolutism.

9. Among the more salient points of Sarmiento's manifesto was his exclusion of *conversos* from administrative posts:

[D]eclaramos que . . . los conversos del linage de los judios, por ser sospechosos en la fé de nuestro Señor e Salvador Jesuchristo, en la qual frecuentemente bomitan de ligero judaizando, no pueden haber oficios ni beneficios públicos ni privados por donde puedan facer injurias, agravios e malos tratamientos a los christianos viejos lindos. (Ruano 193)

[we declare that *conversos* of Jewish lineage, inasmuch as they are suspect in the faith of our Lord and Savior Jesus Christ, which they frequently mock and defile by adhering to their Jewish practices, may hold neither offices nor benifices, whether public or private, through which they might bring insult, injury, or harm to the old Christian caste.]

10. Netanyahu is only the most recent scholar to comment on Luna's pro-Jewish and pro-*converso* policies (see 236 ff.). Roth goes so far as to claim that Luna was himself of *converso* stock (89), although he provides no documentation.

11. Alfonso V of Aragon had already alluded in 1425 to Luna's "maneras exquisitas" [peculiar habits] with which he "había procurado gran familiaridad del Rey" [had achieved great intimacy with the king] (qtd. in Paz y Melia's introduction to Palencia's *Crónica de Enrique IV,* livni). But the "Memorial" constitutes the first actualization of a discourse of sodomy with reference to Luna. Interestingly, what remains unnamed here is named for the first time only in the following century by the Aragonese historian Jerónimo de Zurita, who, in one of his annotations to the *Abreviación* (a later, abridged version of the *Crónica del halconero*), "llama a la cosa por su nombre y advierte que este pasaje había sido

suprimido en la versión impresa" [calls the thing by name and notes that this passage had been suppressed in the printed version] (from Carriazo's introduction to his edition of Barrientos's *Refundición*, cxi).

12. The charge of sorcery comes as no surprise, given the associations of sodomy with sorcery or, more generally, with heresy since the late eleventh and early twelfth centuries: see Boswell (283–86); Brundage (473); Goodich (7–10). The "Memorial" discourses elsewhere on the tyrant's (and by extension Luna's) heretical disposition: "Lo primero, que en lugar de amar a Dios e guardar su ley ama más e codicia las obras peruersas e malas" (322) [Firstly, rather than loving God and keeping his commandments he loves all the more and desires only perverse and evil works].

13. Fear of recruitment is not only implied but made explicit in the charge of sodomy: "[L]os grandes honbres e otros de vuestros rreynos e señorios han muy grande temor de enviar criar e dominiar a vuestra rreal corte e palaçio los fijos ny las fijas" (331) [The grandees and others of your kingdoms and domains are much afraid to send either their sons or their daughters to your royal court and palace to be brought up]. Notable here is the inclusion of both male *and* female as likely victims of Luna's perverse influence.

14. The translation is my own. These efforts, Chiffoleau maintains, are an earmark of the rise of absolutist power in late medieval France. There is nonetheless ample evidence in Spain's historical record as well of the conflation of sodomy and lèse-majesté. The Medina del Campo ordinance, for example, passed by the Catholic Monarchs in 1497, deemed proof of sodomy sufficient "if it matched that necessary to convict someone of *lèse-majesté* or heresy" (Trexler 46).

15. Notes the *Crónica del halconero*: "A estas cosas el señor Rey no respondió" (333) [To these charges the king gave no reply].

16. See O'Callaghan (564–66); Suárez Fernández (176–79). Round provides without a doubt the most extensive and best-documented account of Luna's final days. However, although he does much to tease out the complex political intrigue of the period, he too seems at a loss to provide definitive answers.

17. The text of the apology is to be found in the *Crónica de don Juan II* (684–91).

18. This reading of Luna is reinforced throughout the letter through reference to specific assaults on the body of Christianity: deliberate disregard for the church's authority (or rather, for the king's authority in the appointment to ecclesiastic posts) (685–66); the seizure of monies intended for the *Reconquista* (686); the surrender of Christian territories (and their inhabitants) to the Muslims through reckless administration (687); and alliances with the Moors and with the devil himself (689). Juan II, for his part, is cast not as the innocent victim of Luna's treachery but as the compassionate Christ. Luna's misdeeds

fueron por mí toleradas por largos tiempos en mucha paciencia, siguiendo la manera que Nuestro Señor tiene con los pecadores, la muerte é perdicion de los quales no quiere, mas que se conviertan é vivan. (685)

[were tolerated by me with great patience for a long time, this in keeping with our Lord's treatment of sinners, whose death and perdition he does not desire, but rather that they might convert and live.]

19.   O luna mas luminossa
         que la lus meridiana . . .
         vn ser atan prosperado
         no vio onbre terrenal. (lines 3–4, 9–10)

[Oh moon more luminous than the light of midday, no earthly man ever saw such a prosperous being.]

The best known of Santillana's anti-Luna works, however, is the "Doctrinal de privados," an ironic handbook for *privados* composed in Luna's own voice that capitalizes on the charges of ambition and avarice.

20. See Weissberger in this same collection for a full-length study of Palencia's discursive effeminizing/sodomizing of Enrique IV, Juan II's son by his first wife, María, sister of Alfonso V of Aragon.

21. For an appraisal of this *semblança* in particular, see Netanyahu (606–09).

22. "E ansí algunos se movieron contra el condestable diziendo quél tenía al rey engañado e aun malifiçiado . . . , pero la final entençión suya era aver e poser su lugar" (47) [So it is that some charged the *condestable* with beguiling the king and even bewitching him, but their real intention in doing so was to gain possession of his post].

23. Ultimately the point of Pérez de Guzmán's *Generaciones y semblanzas* is not merely descriptive, but normative in the mapping out of social alliances — *generaciones* — upon which economic processes and political structures could rely. Virtually all accounts express the same degree of wonderment at Luna's utter lack of alliances. See, for example, the *Crónica de don Juan II* (691); Santillana's "De tu resplandor, ¡o Luna!" (lines 19–22).

24. Also, "nin le dexava estar nin usar quando quería con la segunda reyna su muger" (43) [nor did he allow him to be with the second queen his wife or enjoy her when he so desired]. Brocato makes a point of Pérez de Guzmán's obsession with sexual habits, noting that "[h]ardly a figure isn't somehow marked sexually as either honorable, illegitimate, or loose," an obsession that underscores the discursive relationship between deployment of alliance and deployment of sexuality. Cf. Santillana's suggestive accusation in his "De tu resplandor ¡o Luna!":

> Los dones que la natura
> otorga a todo animal
> en que toda criatura
> reçibe goso espeçial
> solaz de muger y fijos
> le fesyste aborreçer
> por sobrado engrandeçer
> y faser condes tus fijos. (lines 99–106)

[The gifts that nature affords to every animal and from which every creature derives a singular joy—the company of wife and children—you caused him to abhor so that you might raise up your own sons beyond their due and make them counts.]

25. Even after Luna's death, "el rey se quedó en aquella misma remisión e nigligençia que primero, nin fizo abto alguno de uirtud nin de fortaleza *en que se mostrase ser más onbre que primero*" (44, emphasis added) [the king persisted in the same carelessness and negligence as before; neither did he perform any act of virtue or strength *in which he showed himself to be any more of a man than before*]. The anti-intellectualism evident throughout this account is pervasive in fifteenth-century courtly society (see Round, "Renaissance Culture," and Russell), due in great part, the Castro school would maintain, to the overwhelming *converso* presence among the intelligentsia.

26. In the introduction to his edition of the *Crónica de don Álvaro de Luna*, Carriazo gives strong reasons for identifying the author as one Gonzalo Chacón, a retainer in the company of Luna during the last few years of the latter's life (xxv). Since the evidence is not conclusive, however, I prefer to leave the work anonymous. Carriazo further speculates that the text was begun before the death of the *condestable* and completed sometime after 1478.

27. Notes Round: "Don Alvaro appears as victim, Christlike in his majestic innocence, betrayed and immolated at the liturgical climax of the Christian year" (*The Greatest Man Uncrowned* 67). Pérez de Guzmán had already resorted to the same analogy, although ironically: "[E]l día que debiera ser de resureçión fue pasión del dicho condestable" (43) [what should have been the day of Resurrection was the *condestable*'s passion].

28. Even the eighteenth-century historian Juan de Mariana could not avoid a romantic reading of the sources:

[N]ecesario es confesar hobo alguna causa secreta que de tal suerte trabó entre sí al rey de Castilla y á don Alvaro de Luna, así aficionó sus corazones y ató sus voluntades, que apenas se podian apartar. . . . Ningun dia amaneció alegre para el Rey . . . despues que le quitaron á Don Alvaro. Dél hablaba entre dia, y dél pensaba de noche, y ordinariamente . . . se le representaba la imágen del que ausente tenia. (2: 85)

[It must be acknowledged that there existed some secret accord between the king of Castile and Don Alvaro de Luna that captured their hearts and took such hold of their will that they could scarcely be separated. Not a happy day dawned for the king after Don Alvaro was exiled from his side. He spoke about him during the day, thought about him at night, and was constantly besieged by the image of him who was absent.]

Equally suggestive is Mariana's attribution of the king's affection to astral influences: "Sin duda tienen algun poder las estrellas, y es de algun momento el nacimiento de cada uno; de allí resultan muchas veces las aficiones de los príncipes y sus aversiones" (2: 85–86) [Doubtless the stars play a role, and an individual's birth is of consequence; from these oftentimes the affections and aversions of princes derive]. In his account of both the causes and the effects of Juan II's affection, Mariana resorts unapologetically to the commonplaces of medieval theories of love.

Works Cited

Baer, Yitzhak. *A History of the Jews in Christian Spain.* 1961. Philadelphia: Jewish Publication Society of America, 1978.

Barrientos, Lope de. *Refundición de la Crónica del halconero.* Ed. Juan de Mata Carriazo. Madrid: Espasa-Calpe, 1946.

Boswell, John. *Christianity, Social Tolerance, and Homosexuality: Gay People in Western Europe from the Beginning of the Christian Era to the Fourteenth Century.* Chicago: U of Chicago P, 1980.

Bray, Alan. "Homosexuality and the Signs of Male Friendship in Elizabethan England." *Queering the Renaissance.* Ed. Jonathan Goldberg. Durham, N.C.: Duke UP, 1994. 40–61.

Brocato, Linde. "*Amor tan espeçial, fiança tan exçesiva, tan singular poder:* Alvaro de Luna, Juan II, and the Order of Saturn." Don Alvaro de Luna: Interrogating the Bad Boy of Fifteenth-Century Castile. 30th International Congress on Medieval Studies. Western Michigan University, Kalamazoo, Mich. 6 May 1995.

Brundage, James A. *Law, Sex, and Christian Society in Medieval Europe.* Chicago: U of Chicago P, 1987.

Carrillo de Huete, Pedro. *Crónica del halconero de Juan II.* Ed. Juan de Mata Carriazo. Madrid: Espasa-Calpe, 1946.

Castro, Américo. *The Spaniards: An Introduction to Their History.* Trans. Willard F. King and Selma Margaretten. Berkeley: U of California P, 1971.

———. *The Structure of Spanish History.* Trans. E. L. King. Princeton: Princeton UP, 1954.

Chiffoleau, Jacques. "Dire l'indicible: Remarques sur la catégorie du *nefandum* du XIIe au XVe siècle." *Annales ESC* 45.2 (March–April 1990): 289–324.

Crónica de don Álvaro de Luna. Ed. Juan de Mata Carriazo. Madrid: Espasa-Calpe, 1940.

Crónica de don Juan II. In *Crónicas de los reyes de Castilla.* Vol. 2. Ed. Don Cayetano Rosell. Madrid: Biblioteca de Autores Españoles, 1953.

Foucault, Michel. *The History of Sexuality.* Vol. 1: *An Introduction.* Trans. Robert Hurley. 1978. New York: Vintage-Random, 1990.

Freund, Scarlett, and Teófilo F. Ruiz. "Jews, Conversos, and the Inquisition in Spain, 1301–1492: The Ambiguities of History." *Jewish-Christian Encounters over the Centuries.* Ed. Marvin Perry and Frederick Schweitzer. New York: Peter Lang, 1994. 169–95.

Geddes, Michael. *Several Tracts against Popery: Together with the Life of Don Alvaro de Luna.* London, 1715.

Goldberg, Jonathan. *Sodometries: Renaissance Texts, Modern Sexualities.* Stanford: Stanford UP, 1992.

Goodich, Michael. *The Unmentionable Vice: Homosexuality in the Later Medieval Period.* Santa Barbara, Calif.: ABC-Clio, 1979.

Jaen, Didier T. *John II of Castile and the Grand Master Alvaro de Luna.* Madrid, 1978.

"Juan II of Castile (1405–1454)." *Encyclopedia of Homosexuality.* 2 vols. Ed. Wayne R. Dynes. New York: Garland, 1990.

Mariana, Padre Juan de. *Historia de España. Obras del Padre Juan de Mariana.* Biblioteca de Autores Españoles. Vols. 30–31. Madrid: Ediciones Atlas, 1950.

MacCurdy, Raymond R.: *The Tragic Fall: Don Alvaro de Luna and Other Favorites in Spanish Golden Age Drama.* North Carolina Studies in Romance Languages and Literatures. Chapel Hill: Department of Romance Languages, University of North Carolina, 1978.

Netanyahu, B. *The Origins of the Inquisition in Fifteenth Century Spain.* New York: Random House, 1995.

O'Callaghan, Joseph. *A History of Medieval Spain.* Ithaca: Cornell UP, 1975.

Palencia, Alonso de. *Crónica de Enrique IV.* Ed. A. Paz y Melia. Biblioteca de Autores Españoles 257. Madrid: Ediciones Atlas, 1973.

Pérez de Guzmán, Fernán. *Generaciones y semblanzas.* Ed. R. B. Tate. London: Tamesis Books, 1965.

Pérez Gómez, Antonio, ed. *Romancero de don Alvaro de Luna.* Valencia, 1953.

Rodríguez-Puértolas, Julio. "A Comprehensive View of Medieval Spain." *Américo Castro and the Meaning of Spanish Civilization.* Ed. José Rubia Barcia. Berkeley: U of California P, 1976. 113–34.

Roth, Norman. *Conversos, Inquisition, and the Expulsion of the Jews from Spain.* Madison: U of Wisconsin P, 1995.

Round, Nicholas G. *The Greatest Man Uncrowned: A Study of the Fall of Don Alvaro de Luna.* London: Tamesis Books Unlimited, 1986.

———. "Renaissance Culture and Its Opponents in Fifteenth-Century Castile." *Modern Language Review* 57 (1962): 204–15.

Ruano, Eloy Benito. *Toledo en el siglo XV: vida política.* Madrid: Consejo Superior de Investigaciones Científicas, 1961.

Russell, Peter. "Arms versus Letters: Towards a Definition of Spanish Fifteenth-Century Humanism." *Aspects of the Renaissance: A Symposium.* Ed. Archibald R. Lewis. Austin: U of Texas P, 1964. 47–58.

Santillana, Marqués de. "De tu resplandor, ¡o Luna!" *Poesías completas.* 2 vols. Ed. Manuel Durán. Madrid: Castalia, 1987. 2: 177–89.

———. "Doctrinal de privados." *Poesías completas.* 2: 157–77.

———. "Hércules contra Fortuna." *Poesías completas.* 2: 154–57.

Sedgwick, Eve Kosofsky. *Epistemology of the Closet.* Berkeley: U of California P, 1990.

Smith, Paul Julian. "*La Celestina*, Castro, and the *Conversos*." *Representing the Other: 'Race', Text and Gender in Spanish and Spanish American Narrative.* Oxford: Oxford UP, 1988.

Suárez Fernández, L. *Nobleza y monarquía: puntos de vista sobre la historia política castellana del siglo XV.* Valladolid: Universidad de Valladolid, 1975.

Trexler, Richard C. *Sex and Conquest: Gendered Violence, Political Order, and the European Conquest of the Americas.* Ithaca: Cornell UP, 1995.

Daniel Eisenberg

Juan Ruiz's Heterosexual "Good Love"

Provar omne las cosas non es por end peor,
e saber bien e mal, e usar lo mejor.
—*Juan Ruiz*, Libro de buen amor

[To try things out is not so bad;
Knowing good and evil, one can choose the best.]

The topic of this essay is the meaning of the most canonical work from the rich Spanish corpus of erotic and sexological literature, the work that is customarily dished out, in small doses, to students of Spanish literature. The topic of the *Libro de buen amor* [Book of Good Love] is sex. Although the word used is "love," at the time it was a synonym for sex, a term that did not exist in the sense in which it is most often used today. Love and sex were not clearly distinguished. The *Libro de buen amor* teaches men how to seduce women, how to gain access to their beds, and how to identify the most desirable candidates. It also describes seductions of women, seductions by women, and the consequences of inattention to women's great sexual desire (see Braidotti).

As often happens with erotic literature, the *Libro de buen amor* has been censored. It is the oldest example of censorship in Hispanic literature of which I am aware. The pages containing the consummation of the protagonist's pursuit of Doña Endrina were torn out many years ago, and from more than one manuscript. Also, and it is again a unique case in Hispanic literature, there are entire episodes missing: love songs, satirical songs (*cazurros*), and sexual songs (*de burlas*) alluded to in the surviving text but missing from all the manuscripts (see Walsh). It is possible that censorship was also a factor in their disappearance.

The first publication of the work, in the eighteenth century, was controversial (Buchanan 173). The editor, the scholar Tomás Antonio Sánchez, mutilated it because he found it morally offensive.[1] He at least marked his

deletions with ellipses, and therefore his edition is a handy guide to the
sexual passages of the work.

Yet we should not congratulate ourselves for our alleged superiority over
these censors of previous centuries. The work is still censored in the books
in which the largest number of readers meet it: in undergraduate antholo-
gies. That the "small woman" provides *solaz* 'comfort' in bed (strophe 1609)
is not found in *Five Centuries of Spanish Literature* of Barrett, nor in *Representative Spanish Authors* of Pattison and Bleznick, nor in the *Antología general de la literatura española* of Ángel and Amalia del Río. In the *Introducción
a la literatura española* of Peñuelas and Wilson this strophe is suppressed,
and in addition another (1616), which calls the small woman "terrenal
paraíso" [earthly paradise] and notes that she is "mejor . . . en la prueva
que en la salutaçión" [better in the proof than in the salutation]. They are
also missing in *España en su literatura* of Adams and Keller, in its newly revised edition of 1991. Some college professors and students, at least in the
United States, are not up to reading about women who are good in bed.

Although the *Libro de buen amor* deals with sex, the interpretation of the
work is problematical, subject to the most divergent opinions. What is Juan
Ruiz's perspective on the sexual acts he portrays? Why is he providing sex
education? How is this instruction to be reconciled with his attitude toward
the Virgin Mary, whom he calls "comienço e raíz . . . de todo bien" (19a)
[beginning and root of all good]? In short, what, for him, *is buen amor*?

The *Libro de buen amor* loudly proclaims that it is a didactic work. The author calls it a *libro de testo* 'textbook' (1631). Nevertheless, it is also a book
that insists on its correct interpretation. It is an instrument, and its lesson
depends on how it is played (70ab). At the same time, its lessons are hidden (68a); one has to understand them and arrive at the sense of the work
(68c), says Juan Ruiz. The reader has the responsibility of discovering the
work's meaning, which according to the author is hidden.

Juan Ruiz's hidden meaning has yet to be completely discovered. Considering his overt references to the work's meaning and lessons, our current
chaos about its interpretation, the critics' confusion, is surprising. Responses have taken two paths. First, some propose that Juan Ruiz sought
ambiguity, that he did not have a clear message.[2] In its more extreme form
it is alleged that he did not know what he wanted to say, or that he intended to confuse the reader, such confusion being supposedly healthy
and modern. But, as with Cervantes's alleged ambiguity, we must keep the

cultural context of these authors in mind. Ambiguity was no virtue in the fourteenth century, nor in the seventeenth. No treatise taught ambiguity, nor was it praised or even discussed. (According to Corominas, the term is first documented in Spanish in the sixteenth century.) The wise author had something to say to his readers. He might say it poorly, but not from a desire to deceive or mislead. Yet sometimes, with the passage of years and then centuries, the context is lost and the message becomes obscure.

The second answer to the problem of Juan Ruiz's sexual message turns to the debate over clerical celibacy. According to Zahareas, "the very composition of the poem is related to the socio-religious situation of celibacy and concubinage" (79). A small digression: why is clerical celibacy still treated as an ideal? That Spanish priests, in the Middle Ages or later, enjoyed female sexual partners and opposed clerical celibacy with all their strength seems to me much to their credit.[3] If there was "laxity" among the Spanish clergy, all the better, and no thanks to Cardinal Cisneros for suppressing it (one of several big mistakes from a great cultural criminal, as I have discussed elsewhere ["Cisneros"]). Of course Queen Isabel did not put up the slightest resistance to her confessor Cisneros's innovations.

Returning to our topic, to take the *Libro de buen amor* as an attack on clerical celibacy is unacceptable. The work is not directed to Juan Ruiz's superiors in the Catholic Church. It is less a defense of women than a defense of pleasure. It gives instruction on seduction and deals especially with the love of nuns. Nuns, the archpriest informs us, "tienen a sus amigos viciosos" (1333b) [keep their boyfriends in vices]. I know of no other even potential combination of an attack on clerical celibacy with advice for that typically Spanish figure, the *galán de monjas* 'suitor of nuns.'

Juan Ruiz is indeed opposed to celibacy, of both nuns and priests. He fears its evil consequences. I believe that scholars, such as Dagenais, are correct when they search outside the text for the keys to its interpretation. I did the same with *Don Quijote* (*Interpretación*).

As my title implies, I wish to propose a new meaning for Juan Ruiz's enigmatic *buen amor*. My source is not new instances of medieval Spanish texts in which these words appear; many of these have already been gathered without producing a solution.[4] What I have to offer is a new interpretation of the present texts. In short, my thesis is that Juan Ruiz's *loco amor* 'mad love' is not love of women, opposed to "good love" for God, since this explanation leaves the text full of mysteries and contradictions. The situation is more complex. I wish to suggest that the love that is really mad, for Juan Ruiz, is the love of young men. In medieval Spain, love among males was frequently associated with a lack of Christian patriotism, even a secret sympathy for Islam, a disposition for treason.

Between the two extremes — the loves of God and of young men — in the central, ambiguous position, is woman. In the precise and often repeated term of Juan Ruiz, it is the *dueña*, the woman who is not a virgin. The *dueña* is the correct woman, the available woman: neither virgin nor married.

If Juan Ruiz gives sex education, which he describes as a "saber sin pecado" (15c) [science without sin], it is to avoid a great sin. "Entiende bien mi libro e avrás dueña garrida" (64d) [understand well my book, and you'll get a pretty *dueña*].

My evidence for this thesis is drawn from the sexual environment in which an archpriest of Hita would have lived. Among other things I wish to show that the history of sexual behavior, which seemingly still causes discomfort in some quarters, can help us to understand a Spanish classic.

That there was much homosexual activity in medieval Iberia is beyond any doubt, although it is seldom discussed. There is no general study of the topic.[5] In the Christian kingdoms of the north, for which little evidence of homosexual love is known before the fifteenth century, such homosexual activity as there was must have been furtive. In Muslim Spain, called al-Andalus, the situation was quite the reverse. Although homosexual acts were prohibited, the prohibitions were never enforced nor was there even a pretense of doing so. The culture was so tolerant and hedonistic that I would not be surprised to see it resurrected as a potential model for us today. Nowhere in the Islamic world have there been, to my knowledge, more sensual and tolerant periods (see Norman Daniel, esp. 141, 321). Its acceptance of pederastic love, and hashish as well, has yet to be imitated (see Valdés Fernández; Arié [326]; Rosenthal).

Not only has the topic been little studied, the loss of source materials has been enormous. The period most relevant to Juan Ruiz — the Nasrid kingdom of fourteenth- and fifteenth-century Granada — is particularly obscure, thanks to the systematic destruction of its manuscripts by Cardinal Cisneros (Eisenberg, "Cisneros"). I am obliged to use information from earlier and subsequent periods.

During the caliphate and *taifas* periods and, to the best of our knowledge, in Nasrid Granada, homosexuality was practiced by monarchs.[6] It was courtly love—from this, perhaps, the resistance to the theory of Islamic origin of the concept. We know that ʿAbd ar-Raḥmān III, the wise bibliophile al-Ḥakam II, and ʿAbd Allāh de Granada preferred boys.[7] The kings al-Muʾtamid of Seville and Yūsuf III of Granada wrote pederastic poetry.[8] Muḥammad VI, king of Granada, was also given to pederasty (Arié 327). The woman who wanted to seduce him had to dress as a boy.[9]

In all countries and periods, subjects imitate the practices of their rulers. Bouhdiba says in *Sexuality in Islam,* referring specifically to Córdoba, Baghdad, and Kairwan:

> The cities had in their suburbs or in the surrounding countryside highly frequented pleasure gardens, with open-air cabarets and cafés set up on the farms attached to Byzantine, Roman, or Persian castles, or even Christian monasteries. In the best viticultural traditions, the monks provided plenty of wine and pretty girls for the "joyous companions of sincerity," the *fityāna sidqin* of which Abu Nawas [*sic*] speaks. These taverns were places where many kinds of pleasure were served up without shame and without exclusion. Singers, dancers, gamblers, but also pleasure-seeking young fellows, homosexuals of both sexes, taught the art of pleasure, without let or hindrance, to a youth whom Islam had freed from any sense of shame or guilt. (131)[10]

Many love poems addressed to youths have come down to us.[11] The *Poemas arabigoandaluces* compiled by Emilio García Gómez were scandalous at the time of their publication, first in the *Revista de occidente* and then as a book, just before the libertarian Second Republic.[12] Poems are dedicated to the cupbearer, the carpenter, and so on: love that crossed class lines.[13] The verses of Ibn Quzmān, also made available by García Gómez, describe an openly bisexual lifestyle. There exists a third collection, *The Banners of the Champions* (Ibn Saʿīd), also first translated by García Gómez.[14] Ibn Ḥazm of Córdoba's famous treatise on love, with the typically picturesque Arabic title *The Ring of the Dove*, contains many anecdotes about homosexual lovers.[15]

The following unpublished and untranslated Arabic manuscripts exist in the former royal library in the Escorial monastery: *Modesty Abandoned, and the First Fuzz on the Cheek; An Apology for the Love of the First Fuzz of the Cheek,* and *The Scholar's Garden and the Delight of the Wise Man;* together with others that can or must be heterosexual, such as *The Passion of He Who Moans, and the Tear of He Who Cries; The [Female] Slave Market; A Description of the Burning Lover; The Inlaid Girdle, on the Benefits of Sexual Intercourse.*[16] Again I must point out the richness of Hispanic erotology, even if we do not know the provenance of these texts: in no other library, Western or Islamic, are similar texts found. Their publication and translation would be worthy topics for theses.

Finally, we have abundant evidence from sixteenth-century North Africa or Maghreb (today's Morocco, Algeria, and Tunisia). This region had strong ideological and demographic links with al-Andalus. In the final periods of Muslim presence in Spain there was large-scale emigration to North Africa. In earlier centuries there had been much immigration from North Africa to al-Andalus, with family ties between the two regions extending over generations.

By far the best-documented North African city in this period is Algiers. Christian prisoners reported to their home countries that male homosexuality was common there to an extent inconceivable in Europe. The *Topografía e historia general de Argel* [Topography and General History of Algiers], originally published by Diego de Haedo,[17] states that sodomy is publicly esteemed in Algiers (1: 177). Algerian *morabutos* [holy men] "are usually enormous sodomites, and proud of it, and they practice the bestial sin publicly in the middle of the market, or on the main street, in front of everybody, and the Moors and Turks are so blind that they praise this behavior, and consider it good" (Haedo 1: 111). A different lifestyle, to be sure, from that of Christian Spain. I do not know even today where in the world sodomy may be freely practiced in public, much less that it receive general applause. But who knows what future behavior will be? Who would have believed, fifty years ago, that pornographic movies would be sold openly today?

If this were not enough, among Sephardic Jews, while they lived in Muslim Andalusia, pederasty was not just tolerated but the norm among the upper classes. In contrast with Iberoarabic homosexuality, that of Sephardic Jews has been amply studied, in English and in Hebrew (although not in Spanish). A good beginning is the classic article published in the Spanish journal *Sefarad*, in 1955, during the Franco period, but in English: "The Ephebe in Medieval Hebrew Poetry." It would never have appeared if it had been in Spanish. Roth and others have published subsequent studies.[18]

According to an article in *Aspects of Jewish Culture in the Middle Ages,*

in Spain there was a "courtly aristocratic culture involving romantic indi-
vidualism [in which there was] intense exploration of all forms of liberating
sexuality, heterosexuality, bisexuality, homosexuality. Ask your average
suburban rabbi his views on homosexuality and he will tell you there is
nothing more un-Jewish than this, oy-veh. But not if you study Spanish
Jewish culture. Homosexuality is central to it" (Cantor 184–85).

During the Spanish Middle Ages, Judaism reached heights of culture and
political and military power unknown between biblical times and the modern state of Israel. There existed a Jewish kingdom in medieval Spain, the
eleventh-century Zirid kingdom of Granada, whose Muslim ruler was a
powerless figurehead. There exists no full treatment of it. In Zirid Granada
Jews were not *dhimmi* 'second-class citizens,' as they were elsewhere in
Muslim Spain, but the governors and generals. There is plentiful source material on the period, among it much pederastic poetry, and by good fortune
the memoirs of the last Zirid monarch have survived.[19] The Alhambra was
built, according to a well-documented theory of Bargebuhr, as a new Jewish Temple, one thousand years after the destruction of the Second Temple
of Jerusalem. What remains of it, besides some foundations, is the famous
Fountain of the Lions. The twelve lions represent the twelve Jewish tribes
of the Old Testament. This theory has received little attention in Spain;
that the Alhambra may have had a Jewish origin was unacceptable to the
dominant Spanish authority on al-Andalus, García Gómez (Bargebuhr 9–
10, 195–96).

In the Zirid kingdom of Granada, pederasty was even more widespread
than in other parts of al-Andalus. It was seen as authorized by the Bible,
as part of the Jewish nationality: the sacred homosexuality of the biblical
books of *Kings,* and the homosexuality of the great poet-king David. (This
line of discussion is taboo in modern Judaism.) The Hebrew language permitted direct and unfiltered access to these holy texts, and to pederastic
poetry. As Jews soon had to incorporate themselves into Christian Spain,
as the Muslim territory shrank, the language itself became associated with
the occult, magic, and mysticism (see Eisenberg, "Judaism").

Homosexual pleasures were not only freely available in Jewish and Muslim Spain, but they were believed to be more refined than heterosexual ones.
A priceless scrap of information reveals that male prostitutes in twelfth-
century Seville charged more than the female ones, and had a higher-class
clientele. The female prostitutes were for the farmers.[20] In a Jewish poem

of the period, the womb is spoken of as *Sheol* 'hell.'[21] In a later report, Muslims looked down on the Christians for rejecting boys as sexual partners; they believed that "the Gauls and those living in northern countries are insensible of pleasure; that it is only themselves who have the true smack of voluptuousness."[22] In sixteenth-century Algiers, again according to Haedo, "[s]odomy is honorable, because he who supports more boys (*garçones*) has higher status (*es más honrado*). Their patrons take better care of them than of their own wives and daughters. Many of the Turks and renegades, who are great and old men, not only want no other wives than these boys, but boast of never having known a female, rather they despise them and don't want to set eyes on them" (1: 176–77).

The hedonism and sexual tolerance of al-Andalus were destined to disappear. It is important to note, however, that in conflict with what the early historians tell us, the beginning of their destruction and a great step toward it arrived not from the north but from the south, with the puritan Almohads. It was they who destroyed the libraries of Córdoba, and split a more or less united caliphate into the small *taifas* kingdoms, unable to defend themselves from the Christians. We should remember that the Christians who lived under Islam in al-Andalus, called Mozarabs, were just as hedonistic as the Muslims, if not more so. I quote from an Iberoarabic legal treatise of the period: "Muslim women should be forbidden to enter the abominable churches of the Christians, because their priests are libertines, fornicators, and sodomites. Also Christian women should be prohibited from entering churches at times other than prayers and feast days, because in the churches they eat, drink, and fornicate with the priests, and there is no priest that does not have at least two of these women to sleep with."[23] So much for the Mozarabic priests, according to this source: libertines, fornicators, and sodomites. A different sort of Christianity from the one that the Christian kingdoms sought to impose on southern Iberia.

It is also true that Andalusian hedonism, and especially homosexual practices, alarmed northern Europe. One needs to recall the strong pressure from the French on the small Christian kingdoms of the north of the Iberian peninsula.[24] Without this pressure, perhaps they would not have fought for centuries against their neighbors to the south. It is questionable, for example, whether Alfonso VI would have conquered Toledo without the influence of Constance, one of his French wives.[25]

Medieval Christians exaggerated Andalusian homosexuality, making the topic even more sensitive than it already was. Mohammed was for them the great libertine, champion of all forms of sexuality.[26] Homosexuality was, for the Christians, a contagious malady, superficially very attractive. There was no need for a *Book of Evil Love* to depict its attractions. Christian emigration to Granada has yet to be studied, but we know that it existed,[27] and it seems likely that sexual freedom was one of its attractions. Sánchez-Albornoz, clearly alarmed at the prospect, even said that "[w]ithout the Reconquest, homosexuality, so widely practiced in Moorish Spain, would have triumphed" (38). This is a picturesque worry: triumphant homosexuality seems an oxymoron. It would mean the extinction of the human race. Yet even a near-contemporary of ours saw homosexuality as a real and powerful threat.

What disturbed the Christians was not a chaste love between men — what we would today call "platonic."[28] The problem was the expression of this love in genital acts. To indulge in these was both sacrilege and treason. Not only was this pleasure viewed as contagious, it was also incurable. He who indulged was lost forever. He would never give it up. The danger could only be controlled with the bonfire and the gallows, and these measures were employed.[29]

The existence of homosexual pleasures in Europe was perceived as a threat to the family and to the security of women. Homosexuality in the Christian kingdoms also made them militarily vulnerable, or so it was thought. Although by the fourteenth century Granada was little threat to Castile, there was a great fear, even an exaggerated fear, of invasions from the south.

According to the Christians, homosexuality made men weak. It made them poor soldiers, less able to defend their country. The evidence was the Christians' progress: the victories of the champions of heterosexuality over the depraved, sodomitical Muslims. Although we lack a study of the concept of chastity in medieval Spain, Christians unanimously attributed the so-called loss of Spain to the Muslims to the sexual license of the eighth-century King Rodrigo. They also believed that Christian chastity or continence, compared with the sexual indulgence of Iberian Muslims of all periods, made possible the beginning and progress of the "Reconquest."[30]

History was written to reflect this interpretation. According to late-medieval Castilian historians, the birth of the idea of "reconquering" Spain was attributed to Alfonso II of León, called "The Chaste," lord of the fictitious but also chaste vassal Bernardo del Carpio, called the "archetype of the Hispanic hero." (The Cid would not achieve this status until the end of the nineteenth century.)[31] Baths facilitated sex as well as cleanliness; so the Catholic Isabel closed those of Granada after conquering it. Three centuries earlier, Alfonso VI had destroyed the baths in Christian Spain, and began the central phase of the "Reconquest" by conquering Toledo.

Finally, to some extent Iberoarabic sexuality depended on the capture and importation of Christian slaves by raiding parties. We do not know the extent, and the topic also has yet to be studied in depth, but it seems safe to say that although the dependence was not complete, it was still significant. We know that Iberian "Arabs," like the renegades and other inhabitants of Algiers in the sixteenth century, preferred, as sexual partners, Christian slaves, both male and female. Native women and boys, and black Africans, were less valued.[32] Like the existence of eunuchs — "manufactured" in al-Andalus by Jewish physicians — this sexual use of slaves was a serious problem for the Muslim world in general, provoking the enmity of the Christian kingdoms whose children were stolen and neutered. The boy Saint Pelagius was martyred for opposing the sexual desires of ʿAbd ar-Rahmān III. After his sanctification he was celebrated in a poem of the Saxon nun Hroswitha.[33]

So the fight against Andalusian homosexuality was fundamental for the Christians. It is an important part of the context of the Reconquest, and of the expulsion of the Jews. It also seems to be related to the delayed imposition of clerical celibacy in Castile. *Barraganía* (the priests' keeping of "housekeepers") was a defensive measure. Until Islam was conquered and its libertinism abolished, one could not deprive the priests of their female friends.

I have spoken at length about sexual behavior, but not about Juan Ruiz. One cannot but conclude that Juan Ruiz knew something, and perhaps a great deal, about what I have just presented. His familiarity with Iberoarabic civilization would not only be logical in a man from Hita, in the kingdom of Toledo; it is found in the text itself. "Después fiz muchas cánticas . . . para judías e moras" (1513ab) [I wrote many songs for Jewish and Moorish girls], he tells us. He uses Arabic words.[34] Various commentators have pointed out the Arabic background of his concepts of female beauty[35] and of literature.[36] Besides the songs for Jewish girls, Juan Ruiz displays in several places his knowledge of Jewish culture: that the Jews had their own butchers, governed by religious laws, for example. There were two synagogues and a midrash (a rabbinical school) in Hita.[37]

It seems, then, unavoidable to conclude that Juan Ruiz was well informed about homosexual behavior among Iberian Muslims and Jews. Given the Christian position on the subject, it follows that the sexual teachings of his *Libro de buen amor* offer an alternative and are intended as a weapon against what he understood to be bad love. According to the Archpriest, female sexual partners are abundant. In the mountains they practically rape the men. Sexuality and Catholicism are compatible, he suggests in the parody of the canonical hours. Marriage, although a protection against lust (1593), is not indispensable. "No ha muger en el mundo, nin grande nin moçuela, que trabajo e serviçio no la traya al espuela" (612bc) [There is no woman in the world, neither old nor young, that work and persistence cannot bring to heel]. Love is beneficial: it makes the stupid man *sutil* 'wise,' the coward daring, the lazy quick (156). It makes the old man cast off his age and keeps the young man young (157ab).

Success can be had by following some easy principles. "Vençerse la dueña non es cosa tan maña" (621d) [To win a *dueña* is not so hard a task]. "Mugeres e varones por palabras se conosçen" (677cd) [Women and men meet each other through words]. "Dil' juguetes fermosos, palabras afeitadas con gestos amorosos; con palabras muy dulçes, con dezires sabrosos, creçen mucho amores e son más desosos" (625) [Tell her charming tales, polished language with loving gestures; with very sweet words, with tasty speech, love grows and with it desire]. Above all, avoid excess in wine (528b).

Women want a happy man as lover (626b); happiness makes men beautiful (627a). According to Doña Endrina, the woman kissed and embraced has been conquered (685). "Por mejor tiene la dueña de ser un poco forçada que dezir: 'Faz tu talente,' como desvergonçada" (631ab) [The *dueña* prefers to be pressured rather than to shamelessly say "Have at it"]. Do not tire of pursuing her (623b), and if there are difficulties, one can turn to those effective servants, the professional go-betweens.

In short, "sey sotil e acuçioso e avrás tu amiga" (648b) [be shrewd and diligent and you'll have your sweetheart]. There is a woman for you. If Juan Ruiz tells of the advantages of love of women, if he teaches the techniques to achieve a happy heterosexual life, if he assures us that we are surrounded

by seducible, lusty women (if they don't seem so in the street, they will
be in bed), if he teaches that Christianity need not be identified with celibacy, if he paints the strength of the attraction to women, an attraction that
one need not resist because its consequences are healthy, according to the
poem (155–57). . . . If Juan Ruiz does all this, then the logical implication is
that he is opposed to homosexuality, and fighting against it.

Two other points: Juan Ruiz's esteem for Ovid (429)[38] also reflects his
heterosexualism. Ovid was seen in the western Middle Ages as the classical author who defended the love for women as superior to that for young
men,[39] the author who taught (according to *Libro de buen amor*, 612) that
there is no woman, of any age, who cannot be seduced. Ovid's homosexual
counterpart, as seen in the medieval West, was Virgil; Juan Ruiz only cites
him as an example of lust (265).[40]

Also, Juan Ruiz cites Aristotle as authority:

> Como dize Aristótiles, cosa es verdadera,
> el mundo por dos cosas trabaja: la primera,
> por aver mantenençia; la otra cosa era
> por aver juntamiento con fenbra plazentera. (71)

> [Wise Aristotle says, and what he says of course is true,
> That all men struggle most for two things: first, what he must do
> To feed himself and keep alive, and second, in this view,
> To have sex with a pleasing woman who is compliant, too.]

Aristotle never said this, we now know.[41] The world is run by many other
things than these two: for example, by the desire for fame, or to create or
enjoy beauty, or simply to reproduce oneself and thus survive, in this way,
death. But it fits perfectly with the medieval image of Aristotle. It would
never have been attributed to the Middle Ages' wise homosexual, Plato.

Where is homosexuality, or boy-love, treated openly in his *Libro*? Nowhere. Juan Ruiz never mentions it. He created a poetic world from which
pleasurable homosexual practice is absent.[42] Cervantes didn't mention the
eroticism of Don Quixote's favorite author Feliciano de Silva, not even to
attack it, fearing—I conclude—that even criticism would be counterpro-
ductive. Juan Ruiz the same.[43] He does not mention the love of young men,
not even to attack it.

For Juan Ruiz the sensuality of the south of the Iberian peninsula has been converted into gastronomy. The "carnal" man loves "carne" (meat), not sex. The "pleasures of the flesh" are the pleasures of eating lambs, sheep, goats, cows, and bulls (1214–15).[44]

In the *Libro de buen amor* there is neither pregnancy nor children. There are hardly any male figures at all, and the author makes extensive use of animal fables. According to the author, "solo, sin conpaña, era penada vida" (1317d) [life without companionship, alone, was only pain] but it does not seem that male companionship would have had much to offer him. His only "conpañero" (113c) [companion] in the work, a Ferrand García who appears briefly as a messenger, betrays him. In the mountains there are no men, only women. What men exist are minor and sexually unattractive characters. The absent lover Pitas Payas is only present in a story. There is a mayor of Bugía, in África, who meaningfully is a monkey (323), and don Cabrón his vassal (327).[45] Love is not represented by the usual young Cupid, but by the burly Don Amor, married to Lady Venus; that Juan Ruiz's Love is not a child is often noted. Also present is the fat Don Carnal. None of them is an attractive object for anyone's amorous thoughts.

Juan Ruiz even battles lexically against the love of boys. The term used in the Castilian Middle Ages for homosexuality was *garçonía,* and the ephebe was a *garçón:* a Gallicism with the nasty (and of course untrue) suggestion that boy-love was a French import. Juan Ruiz gives the word a new meaning: his *garçón* wants to marry three women (189).

I will close by looking at two of the concluding passages of the work. After another review of sins, the arms the Christian can use against them, the need to be vigilant against our enemy the devil, we find two adjacent episodes. These — the praise of the small *dueña,* followed by the defects of Don Hurón — have traditionally been treated as unrelated.

In fact the episode of Don Hurón, "moço del Arçipreste" (1618) [the Archpriest's boy] and the only young man found in the work, has hardly been examined. It is a bit surprising that despite the abundance of research on the *Libro de buen amor,* no one, to my knowledge, has considered whether the typical archpriest would have an "apostado donçel" (1619c) [handsome young man], and if so, what his duties would have been.

What the text does suggest is that no one would ever want to have such a lad as servant, nor allow him in one's house. Boys are liars, thieves, drunkards, dirty, stupid, lazy, and incompetent. But instead of the boy, one has a better option: the *"dueña chica"* [little dueña]. She is, both physically and morally, the lesser of two evils (1617cd). The famous episode of the little woman is introduced with Christ's words, "Bendichos, a mi venid!" (1605d) [Blessed ones, come to me!].

And so I close. Juan Ruiz says, in conclusion, "fizvos pequeño libro de testo, mas la glosa . . . es bien grand prosa" (1631ab) [I made you a small textbook, but the gloss is a long piece of prose]. "Entiende bien mi libro" (64d) [Understand my book well], he asks. "La manera del libro entiéndela sotil" (65b) [be subtle in your interpretation]. Such has been my goal in this study.

Notes

I would like to express my appreciation to Francisco Márquez Villanueva, Steven Kirby, John Dagenais, and José Antonio Cerezo for their comments on drafts of this essay, and the readers and editors of this volume for suggestions. An earlier version was delivered in Spanish at the Primer coloquio de erótica hispana, Montilla, Spain, 1993, and prior to that at the Kentucky Foreign Language Conference, 28 April 1989. It appeared in Spanish as "El buen amor heterosexual de Juan Ruiz."

The epigraph is from *Libro de buen amor*, 76. The text used in the present study is that of Joset, noting his "Correcciones de urgencia" (*Nuevas investigaciones* 148–50). There is controversy concerning the text of the *Libro de buen amor;* I have excluded from my discussion those sections whose authenticity has been called into question by modern scholars, particularly the prologue and the framing verses. Translations from the Spanish are my own, although I have had at hand and recommend the translation of Daly, and have taken from it the translation of the stanza on Aristotle.

1. Castro (395); in *Cambio 16* (25 January 1993), 84, we find that it was Sánchez himself who tore the pages from the manuscripts of the work.

2. "The Archpriest does not offer a moral *dictum* or *sentençia* to his reader because such reductiveness would not be effective, authentic, or apposite for his purpose and world view. What he chooses to do instead is to dramatize—both in style and theme—the problematic complexity of human experience and of reality" (Seidenspinner-Núñez 259).

3. For an introduction to the topic, see Eslava Galan (105–08), who observes: "[T]he Spanish cleric was more of a skirt-chaser (*mujeriego*) than his European

colleagues" (106). The same position is found in Linehan, *Spanish Church* (29–30, 52). I would like to express my appreciation to Francisco Márquez Villanueva for calling my attention to this book.

4. For the bibliography on these collections, along with other new examples, see Joset (129–47); also Álvarez; and Márquez Villanueva.

5. "Sodomy was common in Muslim Spain" (Arié 327). Some information can be found in Arjona. See also Continente Ferrer; Eisenberg ("Granada," "Homosexuality," "Slavery," and "Spain"). On medieval Islamic homosexuality in general, see Pellat ("Djins" [Sex] and "Liwāt" [Homosexuality]). The unsigned article on "Homosexuality," attributed previously to John Boswell (Dynes), is attributed to Pellat and pointedly annotated by Schmitt in his reprint.

6. "The Andalusian chronicles have pointed out the tendency to pederasty (*hubb al-walad*) of the caliph al-Hakam II; according to them, the libertinism had spread after the disappearance of al-Mansūr b. Abī ʿĀmir and in the period of the last Umayyads. At the beginning of the 11th century . . . Córdoba was full of libertines boasting of their vile deeds; sodomy was openly practiced. The *taifas* kings have often been criticized for having permitted such a spirit of disobedience and libertinism to develop on Andalusian soil. Possibly the division of Spain into small principalities and the weakness of authority worsened the moral corruption. However, one must note that the accusations of immorality against the Andalusian rulers come from later historians, paid by the Almoravids or the Almohads, who boasted, at the beginning, of their sober customs and moral purity. In reality, the *taifas* kings were just as given to pleasure as their predecessors or the Almoravid and Almohad governors that came after them" (Arié 326).

7. On ʿAbd ar-Rahmān III, see discussion of the martyrdom of the boy Saint Pelagius discussed below. On Al-Hakam II, see note 6. On ʿAbd Allāh, see his *Tibyān* (191–92, and page 25 of the introduction by Tibi). Tibi's translation, although based on the same unique manuscript, differs substantially from the less annotated translation of ʿAbd Allāh by Lévi-Provençal and García Gómez (*El siglo XI en 1ª persona* 330–31). Tibi proposes and annotates many different readings, and the differences between the translations are impressive. The sentence that in Lévi-Provençal and García Gómez reads (from the Spanish): "The king of Granada only wanted to amass riches, love beautiful women and invite ephebes" (330), in Tibi reads: "The prince of Granada coveted money and was fond of good-looking boys and of their company as boon companions" (191). The sentence that in Lévi-Provençal and García Gómez reads: "Regarding my invitations to ephebes to attend my parties, since a moderate use of wine was necessary—something for which God must have forgiven me—, why do you have to concern yourself with my drinks and my guests?" (331), in Tibi says: "As for taking boys as boon companions, they were not employed for wine-bibbing

and caresses as this would have entailed the use of some wine from which God has turned me away" (192).

8. On al-Mu'tamid, see Nykl (137). The poetry of Yūsuf III is mostly without translation into any European language. One example is found in Monroe (372). An introduction to Yūsuf is provided by Moral Medina.

9. "The second caliph of Córdoba, al-Ḥakam [II], had a well-stocked harem and, nevertheless, reached the age of forty-six without having had children; perhaps men interested him more than women. A Basque Christian slave succeeded in making him a father: she was very young, smart, and pretty, and she adopted a Baghdad custom: abandoning female garments, she dressed as a lad. The caliph from then on called her by the male name she had adopted: Chafar" (Dufourcq 134–35).

10. Bouhdiba cites Abu Nuwas, but the more customary transcription of this name is Abū Nuwās. He also points out that "[h]omosexual relations were relatively encouraged by the Arabo-Muslim societies, to the detriment of intersexual relations" (200).

11. There is a small anthology in the chapter "Perversión" (123–28) of the homophobic book of Sánchez-Albornoz. On this topic, see Continente (esp. 16–18).

12. Some information on the context and influence of this collection may be found in Anderson (18–19). There are three independent partial translations of this collection, by Lane; Franzen; and Middleton and Garza-Falcón.

13. "Boy-love in the Arab Empire was a powerful force of reconciliation between races, religion and social classes" (Marc Daniel 65). The author cites on the same page some surprising examples of interreligious love, all by Hispanic authors.

14. The first English translation, sanitized, was by Arberry. The new translation of Bellamy and Steiner is far superior.

15. My thanks to Nicholas Heer, who has confirmed this from the Arabic text (personal communication, 1 June 1995). There is a translation to the Spanish by García Gómez, to the English by Arberry.

16. Ctd. by Márquez Villanueva (*Orígenes* 38n70). The titles as given by Márquez Villanueva, which I have translated into English, are *El abandono del pudor y el primer boẓo de la mejilla; Excusas sobre el amor del primer boẓo en la mejilla; El jardín del letrado y las delicias del hombre inteligente; Ardor del que gime y lágrima del que llora; El mercado de esclavas; Descripción del enamorado ardiente;* and *El cinturón incrustado, sobre las ventajas de las relaciones sexuales.* For other unpublished Islamic erotological works, see Bouhdiba (142–46). The treatise *Mufākharat al-jawārī wal ghilmān* [Boasting Match over Maids and Youths], which he cites as untranslated at that time, has been published in English in al-Jahiz. The

only other example known to me of an Islamic erotological work with homosexual content, and available in a Western language, is *Les délices des coeurs* of Aḥmad al-Tīfāshī. The homosexual portion has been translated from the French by Edward A. Lacey.

17. As set forth in my "Cervantes, autor," I believe the author was Cervantes, the only significant writer among those imprisoned in Algiers.

18. The *Sefarad* article is by Schirmann. For those by Roth, see the Works Cited in the present essay. See also Eisenberg ("Judaism"). A historical study, although it attributes homosexuality exclusively to Arabic influence, is that of Assis. According to Leneman, the book of Zemach and Rosen-Moked deals with the erotic poetry of Samuel ha-Naguid.

19. ʿAbd Allāh; see note 7.

20. "Female prostitution existed principally in the cities; the clientele was the urban lower class (*plebe*) and, above all, the farmers who came to town for its market" (Arié 327).

21. Carmi (316). The author of the poem is Ibn Gabirol.

22. Chorier (284). On the bibliographical problems of this book, see Foxon (38–43).

23. The text is taken from Sánchez-Albornoz (129). A slightly different translation is found in Levi-Provençal and García Gómez (150).

24. "The Gauls, of all people, have the greatest abhorrence for this strange Venus" (Chorier 284).

25. On the wives of Alfonso VI, see Palencia. On their influence and the perception of the Toledan monarch as "effete," see also Martínez, and Cantarino (165).

26. See Norman Daniel (101–02, 144, and 160). Again the sixteenth-century sources, prima facie applicable to late Islamic Spain, are much more abundant: "Most of the acts of the practitioners [of Islam] were identified . . . with lust (*lujuria*)" (Bunes Ibarra 218). "They practice a large number of sexual aberrations" (224). "There is no variety of this sin [lust] that they do not use, and they locate their happiness both in this world and in that to come" (235). "Mohammed was one of the most sensual (*carnal*) men that has ever existed. . . . As he knew that he was a fraud, to win the support of the idolaters he permits and legalizes their vile passions" (235). "Celibacy is almost a sin. . . . They believe that the Muslims serve their Prophet better, the more immodest (*deshonesto*) acts they commit, and they do not respect their step-daughters, sisters-in-law, and female relatives" (236). "The enjoyment of pleasure is, according to the opinion of the Spaniards, the goal of Muslims" (239).

27. We know the name of one emigrant: "Almançor of León, scribe and secretary of the King of Granada, my Lord, for Castilian" (*Relaciones* 89 and 136).

28. The identification of chaste love as "Platonic" is an error, apparently cre-

ated by the mad Don Quixote. There is no example earlier than Cervantes. See my *Interpretación* (132n60); in the earlier *Study,* 124n58.

29. "[Sodomy] is against the public good, since it prevents the multiplication of the human species. . . . The people . . . considered sodomy (*el pecado nefando*) as a 'contagious' (*pegajoso*) vice, from which, once contracted, those infected could free themselves only with difficulty. . . . Fire was the only appropriate treatment, since once a man took up this vice, no one nor anything, other than fire, could move him to forsake it" (Herrera 262–63). Examples of executions of homosexuals by hanging are found in Münzer (82, 264), by burning in Ayala (157–58).

30. The concept of the Reconquest, that is, the recovery of territory illegally conquered and occupied by Muslim invaders, is the predominant theme of traditional Castilian historiography of the Middle Ages. However, it is rejected by revisionist historians and by the present writer. See Linehan (*History* 1–21, 95–127).

31. On Alfonso II and Bernardo del Carpio, see ch. 2 of my *Interpretación*.

32. Márquez Villanueva (*Orígenes y sociología* 172). Although the term "Arabs" is widely used and the culture was self-identified as Arabic, I put it in quotation marks because the proportion of ethnic Arabs was small.

33. See Aguilera Camacho; and Flórez (105–31). In the present volume, Jordan reviews the literature on Pelagius; this article reached me only after mine was completed.

34. See Martínez; Márquez Villanueva ("Nuevos arabismos").

35. Notes López-Baralt: "The 'problems' which plague Juan Ruiz's pretty girl disappear when seen in an Arabic literary context" ("Bella" 83). See also her "Juan Ruiz y el Šeyj Nefzawī."

36. For example, "behind Juan Ruiz resounds the echo of a long tradition of Hispano-Islamic literary pride" (Castro 412); "his art consisted in harmonizing in a Castilian and Christian fashion the two fundamental tendencies in Arabic literature of the preceding centuries, sensuality and moral exemplarity" (442). Note that the various versions of Castro's book differ significantly in their treatment of the *Libro de buen amor.* On these revisions, see Joset (*Nuevas investigaciones* 59–60).

37. See Cantera Burgos; and Lacave. Criado de Val points out that "[t]he Jewish community of Hita, as it appeared at the time of its liquidation, was very different from those of the rest of the peninsula. It was not isolated in special quarters or 'ghettos,' nor was it outside the town walls, but spread throughout all the streets of the town, with its houses adjacent to those of the Castilian nobles" (144).

38. See the note of Joset to the passage. Juan Ruiz's alleged use of Ovid has been strongly attacked by Márquez Villanueva (*Orígenes y sociología* 95n216).

39. Ovid "preferred girls to boys, because in these sorts of amusements he liked a reciprocal and not a selfish enjoyment. He said that he delighted in love

'which dissolves on both sides.' Hence it was that 'boy's love affected him less' "
(Chorier 281).

40. A then famous passage in the *Georgics* refers to pastoral homosexuality;
Virgil was also seen as a magician. See Chorier 281 ("Maro" is Virgil); and Spargo.

41. See the note of Gybbon-Monypenny in his edition (123), and also Rico.

42. Vasvári, in this volume, unveils allusions to penetrative sodomy (only) as a
punishing or aggressive, but not pleasurable act.

43. Silva is mentioned in the first chapter of *Don Quixote*. I pointed out the
need for a study of his eroticism in "Research Topics" (86).

44. On the eroticism of the episode of Don Carnal and Doña Cuaresma, see
Márquez Villanueva ("Carnaval" 182–83 and the bibliography cited there).

45. *Cabrón* 'he-goat' in Spanish is strongly associated with lust, and is a dirty
word.

Works Cited

'Abd Allāh ibn Buluggin. *El siglo XI en 1ª persona: las* Memorias de *'Abd Allāh,
último rey z̄īrī de Granada, destronado por los Almorávides (1090)*. Trans. E.
Lévi-Provençal and Emilio García Gómez. 4th ed. Madrid: Alianza, 1982.

———. *The Tibyān: Memoirs of 'Abd Allāh B. Buluggin last Zīrid Amīr of Granada*. Emended, trans., and ann. Amin T. Tibi. Leiden: Brill, 1986.

Adams, Nicholson B., and John E. Keller, with the assistance of Rafael A.
Aguirre. *España en su literatura*. 3rd ed. New York: W. W. Norton, 1991.

Aguilera Camacho, Daniel. "El drama de San Pelagio: poema de la monja sajona
Roswitha." *Boletín de la Real Academia de Córdoba de Ciencias, Bellas Letras
y Nobles Artes* 20 (1949): 29–44.

Al-Jahiz. "Boasting Match over Maids and Youths." *Nine Essays of al-Jahiz*.
Trans. William M. Hutchins. New York: Peter Lang, 1989. 139–66.

Álvarez, Nicolás E., " 'Loco amor,' 'goliardismo,' 'amor cortés' y buen amor: el
desenlace amoroso del episodio de doña Garoça en el *Libro de buen amor*."
Journal of Hispanic Philology 7 (1983): 107–19.

Anderson, Andrew. *Lorca's Late Poetry: A Critical Study*. Liverpool: Francis
Cairns, 1990.

Arié, Rachel. *España musulmana (siglos VIII–XV)*. Vol. 3 of *Historia de España*,
ed. Manuel Tuñón de Lara. Barcelona: Labor, 1984.

Arjona Castro, Antonio. *La sexualidad en la España musulmana*. 2nd enlarged
ed. Córdoba: U de Córdoba, 1990.

Assis, Yom Tov. "Sexual Behaviour in Mediaeval Hispano-Jewish Society." *Jew-*

ish History. Essays in Honour of Chimen Abramsky. Ed. Ada Rapoport-Alpert and Steven J. Zipperstein. London: Peter Halban, 1988. 25–59.

Ayala, Francisco. *La imagen de España.* Madrid: Alianza, 1986.

Bargebuhr, Frederick P. *The Alhambra: A Cycle of Studies on the Eleventh Century in Moorish Spain.* Berlin: de Gruyter, 1968.

Barrett, Linton Lomas. *Five Centuries of Spanish Literature, from The Cid through the Golden Age.* New York: Dodd, Mead, 1962.

Bouhdiba, Abdelwahab. *Sexuality in Islam.* London: Routledge and Kegan Paul, 1985.

Braidotti, Erminio. "El erotismo en el *Libro de buen amor.*" *Kentucky Romance Quarterly* 30 (1983): 133–40.

Buchanan, Milton A. "Notes on the Life and Works of Bartolomé José Gallardo." *Revue hispanique* 57 (1923): 160–201.

Bunes Ibarra, Miguel de. *La imagen de los musulmanes y del norte de África en la España de los siglos XVI y XVII: los caracteres de una hostilidad.* Madrid: CSIC, 1989.

Cantarino, Vicente. *Entre monjes y musulmanes: el conflicto que fue España.* Madrid: Alhambra, 1978.

Cantera Burgos, Francisco. "La judería de Hita en el cuadro de los núcleos judíos de Guadalajara." *El Arcipreste de Hita: el libro, el autor, la tierra, la época. Actas del I Congreso Internacional sobre el Arcipreste de Hita.* Madrid: SERESA, 1973. 439–46.

Cantor, Norman. "Disputatio." *Aspects of Jewish Culture in the Middle Ages.* Albany: SUNY P, 1979. 181–86.

Carmi, T., ed. *Penguin Book of Hebrew Verse.* Harmondsworth, U.K.: Penguin, 1981.

Castro, Américo. *The Structure of Spanish History.* Trans. Edmund L. King. Princeton: Princeton UP, 1954.

Chorier, Nicolas. *The Dialogues of Luisa Sigea.* Trans. not specified. North Hollywood, Calif.: Brandon House, 1965.

Continente Ferrer, J. M. "Aproximación al estudio del tema de amor en la poesía hispano-árabe de los siglos XII y XIII." *Awrāq* 1 (1978): 12–28.

Corominas, Joan. *Diccionario crítico etimológico de la lengua castellana.* 4 vols. Bern: Francke, 1954.

Criado de Val, Manuel. "La aljama de Hita según el inventario de sus bienes antes de la expulsión." *Historia de Hita y su Arcipreste: vida y muerte de una villa mozárabe.* Madrid: Nacional, 1976. 144–48.

Dagenais, John. *The Ethics of Reading in Manuscript Culture: Glossing the* Libro de buen amor. Princeton: Princeton UP, 1994.

Daniel, Marc. "Arab Civilization and Male Love." Trans. Winston Leyland. *Gay Sunshine* 32 (1977); rpt. in *Gay Roots: Twenty Years of Gay Sunshine*. Ed. Winston Leyland. San Francisco: Gay Sunshine P, 1991. 32–75.

Daniel, Norman. *Islam and the West: The Making of an Image*. Edinburgh: Edinburgh UP, 1960.

Del Río, Ángel, and Amalia A. de Del Río. *Antología general de la literatura española*. 2nd corrected and enlarged ed. New York: Holt, Rinehart and Winston, 1960.

Dufourcq, Charles-Emmanuel. *La Vie quotidienne dans l'Europe médiévale sous domination arabe*. Paris: Hachette, 1978.

Dynes, Wayne R., ed. *Encyclopedia of Homosexuality*. 2 vols. New York: Garland, 1990.

Eisenberg, Daniel. "El buen amor heterosexual de Juan Ruiz." *Los territorios literarios de la historia del placer: I Coloquio de Erótica Hispana*. Ed. José Antonio Cerezo, Daniel Eisenberg, and Víctor Infantes. Madrid: Libertarias, 1996. 49–69.

———. "Cervantes, autor de la *Topografía e historia general de Argel* publicada por Diego de Haedo." *Cervantes* 16.1 (1996): 32–53.

———. "Cisneros y la quema de los manuscritos granadinos." *Journal of Hispanic Philology* 16 (1992 [1993]): 107–24.

———. "Granada." Dynes, *Encyclopedia*.

———. "Homosexuality." *Encyclopedia of Medieval Iberia*. Ed. Michael Gerli. New York: Garland, in press.

———. *La interpretación cervantina del* Quijote. Trans. Isabel Verdaguer. Madrid: Compañía Literaria, 1995. Rev. trans. of the English original: *A Study of Don Quijote*. Newark, Del.: Juan de la Cuesta, 1987.

———. "Judaism, Sephardic." Dynes, *Encyclopedia*.

———. "¿Por qué volvió Cervantes de Argel?" *Essays in Golden Age Literature Presented to Geoffrey Stagg on His Eightieth Birthday*. Ed. Ellen Anderson and Amy Williamsen. Newark, Del.: Juan de la Cuesta, in press.

———. "Research Topics." *Journal of Hispanic Philology* 13 (1988): 85–87.

———. "Slavery." *Encyclopedia of Medieval Iberia*. Ed. Michael Gerli. New York: Garland, in press.

———. "Spain." Dynes, *Encyclopedia*.

Eslava Galán, Juan. *Historia secreta del sexo en España*. Madrid: Temas de Hoy, 1991.

Flórez, Enrique, ed. *España sagrada*. Vol. 23. Madrid, 1767.

Foxon, David. *Libertine Literature in England, 1660–1745*. New Hyde Park, N.Y.: University Books, 1965.

García Gómez, Emilio, comp. and trans. [Arabic to Spanish]. *Andalusian Poems.*

Trans. [Spanish to English] Christopher Middleton and Leticia Garza-Falcón. Boston: D. R. Godine, 1993.

————, comp. and trans. [Arabic to Spanish]. *In Praise of Boys: Moorish Poems from al-Andalus.* Trans. [Spanish to English] Erskine Lane. San Francisco: Gay Sunshine P, 1975.

————, comp. and trans. "Poemas arabigoandaluces." *Revista de occidente* 62 (1928): 177–203.

————, comp. and trans. *Poemas arabigoandaluces.* 1930. Madrid: Espasa-Calpe, 1940.

————, comp. and trans. [Arabic to Spanish]. *Poems of Arab Andalusia.* Trans. [Spanish to English] Cola Franzen. San Francisco: City Lights, 1989.

Haedo, Diego de. *Topografía e historia general de Argel.* Ed. Ignacio Bauer y Landauer. 3 vols. Madrid: Sociedad de Bibliófilos Españoles, 1927–29.

Herrera Puga, Pedro. *Sociedad y delincuencia en el Siglo de Oro.* Madrid: Católica, 1974.

Ibn Ḥazm, ʿAlī ibn Aḥmad. *El collar de la paloma: tratado sobre el amor y los amantes.* Trans. Emilio García Gómez. Madrid: Sociedad de Estudios y Publicaciones, 1952.

————. *The Ring of the Dove: A Treatise on the Art and Practice of Arab Love.* Trans. A. J. Arberry. London: Luzac, 1953.

Joset, Jacques. *Nuevas investigaciones sobre el* Libro de buen amor. Madrid: Cátedra, 1988.

Ibn Quzmān. *Todo Ben Quzmán.* Ed. and trans. Emilio García Gómez. 3 vols. Madrid: Gredos, 1972.

Ibn Saʿīd al-Maghribī. *The Banners of the Champions.* Trans. James Bellamy and Patricia Steiner. Madison: Hispanic Seminary of Medieval Studies, 1989.

————. *El libro de las banderas de los campeones.* Trans. Emilio García Gómez. 2nd ed. Barcelona: Seix Barral, 1978.

————. *Moorish Poetry: The Pennants.* Trans. [bowdlerized] A. J. Arberry. Cambridge: Cambridge UP, 1953.

Lacave, José Luis. "El rabí Açelyn y su posible identificación." *El Arcipreste de Hita: el libro, el autor, la tierra, la época. Actas del I Congreso Internacional sobre el Arcipreste de Hita.* Madrid: SERESA, 1973. 479–82.

Lázaro Carreter, Fernando. Review of Márquez Villanueva, *Orígenes. ABC Literario* 30 April 1993. 7.

Leneman, Helen. "Reclaiming Jewish History: Homo-erotic Poetry of the Middle Ages." *Changing Men* 18 (Summer/Fall 1987): 22–23.

Levi-Provençal E., and Emilio García Gómez. *Sevilla a comienzos del siglo XII: el tratado de Ibn ʿAbdūn.* 2nd ed. Seville: Servicio Municipal de Publicaciones, 1981.

Linehan, Peter. *History and the Historians of Medieval Spain*. Oxford: Clarendon P, 1993.

———. *The Spanish Church and the Papacy in the Thirteenth Century*. Cambridge: Cambridge UP, 1971.

López-Baralt, Luce. "La bella de Juan Ruiz tenía los ojos de hurí." *Nueva revista de filología hispánica* 40 (1992): 73–93.

———. "Juan Ruiz y el Šeyj Nefzawī elogian a la dueña chica." *La torre* nueva época 1 (1987): 461–72.

Márquez Villanueva, Francisco. "El buen amor." *Relecciones de literatura medieval*. Seville: U Hispalense, 1977. 45–73.

———. "El carnaval de Juan Ruiz." *Arcadia: estudios y textos dedicados a Francisco López Estrada*. 2 vols. *Dicenda* 6–7 (1987–88). 1: 177–88.

———. "Nuevos arabismos en un pasaje del *Libro de buen amor* (941 ab)." *El Arcipreste de Hita: el libro, el autor, la tierra, la época. Actas del I Congreso Internacional sobre el Arcipreste de Hita*. Madrid: SERESA, 1973. 202–07.

———. *Orígenes y sociología del tema celestinesco*. Barcelona: Anthropos, 1993.

Martínez, H. Salvador. "Alfonso VI, Hero in Search of a Poet." *La corónica* 15 (1986): 1–16.

Martínez Ruiz, Juan. "La tradición hispano-árabe en el *Libro de buen amor*." *El Arcipreste de Hita: el libro, el autor, la tierra, la época. Actas del I Congreso Internacional sobre el Arcipreste de Hita*. Madrid: SERESA, 1973. 187–201.

Monroe, James T. *Hispano-Arabic Poetry: A Student Anthology*. Berkeley: U of California P, 1974.

Moral Medina, Celia del. "El *Dīwān* de Yūsuf III y el sitio de Gibraltar." *Homenaje al prof. Darío Cabanelas Rodríguez, O.F.M.* 2 vols. Granada: U de Granada, Departamento de Estudios Semíticos, 1987. 2: 79–96.

Münzer, Hieronymus. *Viaje por España y Portugal en los años 1494 y 1495*. Ed. Julio Puyol. Madrid, 1924. [Also issued in the *Boletín de la Real Academia de la Historia*, 1924.]

Nykl, A. R. *Hispano-Arabic Poetry and Its Relations with the Old Provençal Troubadours*. Baltimore: n.p., 1946.

Palencia, Clemente. "Historia y leyenda de las mujeres de Alfonso VI." *Estudios sobre Alfonso VI y la reconquista de Toledo. Actas del II Congreso Internacional de Estudios Mozárabes (Toledo 20–26 Mayo 1985)*. Toledo: Instituto de Estudios Visigótico-Mozárabes, 1988. 281–90.

Pattison, Walter Thomas, and Donald W. Bleznick. *Representative Spanish Authors*. 3rd ed. New York: Oxford UP, 1971.

Pellat, Charles. "Djins" [Sex]. *Encyclopaedia of Islam*. New ed. Leiden: Brill, 1960–.

[Pellat, Charles]. "Liwāt" [Homosexuality]. *Encyclopaedia of Islam*. New ed. Leiden: Brill, 1960–. Rpt. with annotations by Arno Schmitt. *Sexuality and Eroticism among Males in Moslem Societies*. Ed. Arno Schmitt and Jehoeda Sofer. New York: Harrington Park, 1992. 151–67.

Peñuelas, Marcelino C., and William E. Wilson. *Introducción a la literatura española*. New York: McGraw-Hill, 1969.

Relaciones de algunos sucesos de los últimos tiempos del reino de Granada. Ed. E. L[afuente] y A[lcántara]. Madrid: Sociedad de Bibliófilos Españoles, 1868.

Rico, Francisco. " 'Por aver mantenencia': el aristotelismo heterodoxo en el *Libro de buen amor*." *Homenaje a José Antonio Maravall*. 3 vols. Madrid: Centro de Investigaciones Sociológicas, 1985. 3: 271–97.

Rosenthal, Franz. *The Herb: Hashish versus Medieval Muslim Society*. Leiden: Brill, 1971.

Roth, Norman. "The Care and Feeding of Gazelles: Medieval Arabic and Hebrew Love Poetry." *Poetics of Love in the Middle Ages*. Ed. Moshe Lazar and Norris J. Lacy. Fairfax, Va.: George Mason UP, 1989. 95–118.

———. " 'Deal Gently with the Young Man': Love of Boys in Medieval Hebrew Poetry of Spain." *Speculum* 57 (1982): 20–51. Rpt. in *Homosexual Themes in Literary Studies*. Ed. Wayne R. Dynes and Stephen Donaldson. New York: Garland, 1992. 268–99.

———. " 'Fawn of My Delights': Boy-Love in Hebrew and Arabic Verse." *Sex in the Middle Ages: A Book of Essays*. Ed. Joyce E. Salisbury. New York: Garland, 1991. 157–72.

———. "Loving the 'Other': Boys and Women among Jews, Muslims and Christians." Unpublished.

———. " 'My Beloved Is Like a Gazelle': Imagery of the Beloved Boy in Religious Hebrew Poetry." *Hebrew Annual Review* 8 (1984): 143–65.

———. "Satire and Debate in Two Famous Medieval Poems from al-Andalus: Love of Boys vs. Girls, The Pen and Other Themes." *Maghreb Review* 4 (1979): 105–13.

Ruiz, Juan. *Book of Good Love*. Trans. Saralyn Daly. University Park: Pennsylvania State UP, 1978.

———. *Libro de buen amor*. Ed. G. B. Gybbon-Monypenny. Madrid: Castalia, 1988.

———. *Libro de buen amor*. Ed. Jacques Joset. 2 vols. Clásicos castellanos 14 and 17. Madrid: Espasa-Calpe, 1974.

Sánchez, Tomás Antonio. *Colección de poesías castellanas anteriores al siglo XV*. Madrid: A. de Sancha, 1779–90.

Sánchez-Albornoz, Claudio. *De la Andalucía islámica a la hoy*. Madrid: RIALP, 1983.

Schirmann, Jefim. "The Ephebe in Medieval Hebrew Poetry." *Sefarad* 15 (1955): 55–68.

Seidenspinner-Núñez, Dayle. "On 'Dios y el mundo': Author and Reader Response in Juan Ruiz and Juan Manuel." *Romance Philology* 42 (1989): 251–66.

Spargo, John. *Virgil the Necromancer: Studies in Virgilian Legends.* Cambridge, Mass.: Harvard UP, 1934.

al-Tīfāshī, Aḥmad. *Les délices des coeurs.* Trans. René R. Khawam. Paris: Phébus, 1981.

———. *The Delight of Hearts, or, What You Will Not Find in Any Book.* Trans. (abridged) Edward A. Lacey. San Francisco: Gay Sunshine P, 1988.

Walsh, John K. "Juan Ruiz and the *Mester de clere_ía:* Lost Context and Lost Parody in the *Libro de buen amor.*" *Romance Philology* 33 (1979): 62–86.

Zahareas, Anthony. "Celibacy in History and Fiction: The Case of *El libro de buen amor* [*sic*]." *Ideologies and Literature* 1 (1977): 77–82.

Zemach, Eddy, and Tova Rosen. *A Sophisticated Work* [Hebrew]. Jerusalem: Keter 1983.

IV

NORMATIVITY

AND

NATIONHOOD

Michael Solomon

Fictions of Infection

Diseasing the Sexual Other in Francesc

Eiximenis's *Lo llibre de les dones*

[W]hen there is a lack of preaching, epidemics of disease rage unchecked.
— Humbert of Romans, *De eruditione praedicatorum*

Although we seldom consider Francesc Eiximenis (1340–1410) a medical theorist, to think that one of the most prolific writers of the later Middle Ages avoided speaking out on the nature and cause of human illness would be foolhardy. Like most moralists of his age, Eiximenis claimed that disease was tightly linked to sin. Like most clergymen and preachers, he believed that humans who committed sexual sins were particularly susceptible to the pains and sufferings associated with disease.

In chapter 14 of his *Lo llibre de les dones* [The Book of Women], Eiximenis identifies five forms of lechery: fornication, adultery, incest, sacrilege, and sodomy (339). Although he routinely describes and harshly condemns each sin, the Franciscan adds an extra dimension to his description of sodomy. He tells us that when "men with men or women with women" act against the ways of nature, the temperament of these sinners becomes corrupt. Thus corrupted, the air around them becomes contaminated resulting in terrible plague-like conditions. Implied in his discussion is the idea that sodomy not only condemns the sinner, but that it leads to pestilence and disease. Although Eiximenis's denunciation of sodomy is far from original, the prolific distribution of *Lo llibre de les dones* in the sixteenth century offered a powerful model of contagion that would later coalesce in the popular imagination with burgeoning theories of communicable diseases. His treatment of the "sin against nature" participated in the late-medieval and early-Renaissance process of diseasing the sexual other, a process of

long-standing social and political consequence that aided in forging identities based on biological and popular images of disease.

During the late-fifteenth and early-sixteenth centuries a profound shift
occurred in the way humans imagined the cause of illness. From antiquity
and throughout most of the Middle Ages, medical theorists frequently envisioned disease physiologically, as an imbalance in the bodily temperament or as a corruption of vital bodily fluids. With the repeated epidemic
outbreaks beginning with the Black Death in 1348 and the coming of new
contagious diseases such as syphilis, the popular and scientific gaze began
to focus increasing on disease as a discrete entity. Medical theorists began
to write extensively on the presence of little seedlets (*seminaria*) that could
"creep" (*inserpere*) into a healthy body, adhering and propagating in the
humors, eventually leading to putrefaction and dissolution.[1]

It is true that Hippocrates and his followers had discussed the transmissibility of certain diseases in the Hippocratic corpus, and that ancient and
medieval thinkers identified various communicable diseases such as leprosy, scabies, smallpox, and measles (Nutton, "The Seeds of Disease" 34).
But during the later Middle Ages, the idea that disease could travel from
afar and attack a healthy body gained greater acceptance, capturing the
popular and scientific imagination. The image of the martyred Saint Sebastian on the cover of many plague treatises not only reminded the public of
the saint's status as patron of the plague, but also powerfully illustrated the
mechanics of contagion. In the image of the saint's bound and arrow-ridden
body, one could clearly see the way hundreds of foreign entities could travel
through the air, piercing and infecting an individual at multiple points.

Increasingly, humans imagined disease as a real entity that like a wild
beast could move secretly and attack unexpectedly. To keep well required
more than merely balancing the humors, controlling one's intake of food,
or regularly eliminating excessive fluids from the body. To be healthy required that humans identify, avoid, and control those menacing and inimical entities lurking outside the body. This required a general etiological
shift that would force humans to rethink the very nature of the world at
large and the potential pathologies that lurked therein.

The biomedical concept of ontological disease was translated popularly
in the later Middle Ages as diseased otherness. For the public, disease became located in an ambiguous place beyond; it was something that dwelled
"over there," in other countries, in other cities, within the bodies of other

Image of Saint Sebastian riddled with arrows, from the title

page of *Regimiento contra la peste* by Fernando Alvarez (Seville

c. 1500). Used with permission of the Biblioteca Nacional.

people. It was something that soldiers and travelers could bring with them from foreign places. For the first time in history we have epidemics extensively identified along national boundaries. Syphilis, for example was variously called during the sixteenth century "French scabies" (*gallica scabies*), the "Spanish sickness," the "Castilian disease," the "Italian malady," and the "Portuguese sickness" (Quétel 22). Attempts to describe the etiology of disease also focused on distant origins. Diaz de Isla, in his early treatise on syphilis (1538), was the first to suggest that this sickness was born in the New World, specifically in the island of Hispaniola.

Perhaps the most troubling aspect of ontological disease, the one with the

most profound social consequences, was the idea of an agent or an inter-
mediary that could transmit the seeds of disease from one place, or from
one person, to another. Since the so-called *seminaria* or *fomes* of which
medical theorists spoke were undetectable to the popular eye, the agents to
which the seeds adhered quickly became imagined as the disease itself. In
the popular imagination, disease moved from place to place in the bodies
and belongings of the infected other. From a hygienic and therapeutic
standpoint, it became imperative to identify these agents to avoid them, to
control them, and when necessary, to eliminate them. Increasingly during
the later Middle Ages and Renaissance, people thought that the ability to
control disease and preserve the general well-being was linked to the ability
to identify the agents who could transmit their afflictions to the healthy.

The hygienic imperative to recognize the agents of disease served as a
compelling instrument of social control. Disease, we should keep in mind,
is a social construct that is often indifferent or in opposition to the corporeal status of the individual's body.[2] Throughout the centuries any belief
or practice thought to undermine or disrupt the social order could be regarded as a manifestation of a diseased individual.[3] Ideologically bound,
the construction of disease has traditionally played itself out on the body of
the subaltern, specifically on the bodies of those whose gender, ethnicity,
nationality, and sexual practices were deemed threatening or undesirable.

In most cultures, the right to read the signs of the body and to determine
who is healthy and who is diseased is held by a small group. In the later
Middle Ages clergymen, including preachers and moralists, shared with the
learned physician the responsibility of "diseasing" the undesirable other. I
use the verb "to disease" here not in the common sense of making someone else sick, but in a more restricted sense of convincing the public that
certain individuals are unhealthy and therefore are in need of being subjected to all the limitations imposed on the sick. To disease a human being
requires the discursive process of infecting that person. Etymologically
speaking, to infect (*inficio*) meant to mark, color, stain, or dye an object.[4]
It is the combination of the etymological sense of marking and the later
pathological connotations that constitutes the act of diseasing. Embedded
in the hygienic imperatives of sixteenth-century public health is the idea
that to be free from illness, one must heed the warnings of clergymen and
physicians when they suggested that women, Jews, Moors, and sodomites
could spread the contagious elements of disease contained in their bodies.

Traditionally, medical historians have granted little space to the role of preachers and moralists in the dissemination of medical knowledge. Popular medical historiography has often characterized the Middle Ages as a period in which religious men frustrated the efforts of "rational" and "scientific" thinkers. This view is deceptive. It not only fails to recognize that many learned clergymen understood and accepted the basic principles of humoral medicine; it also obscures the clergyman's role in helping the sick imagine, and by that understand and accept, the biomedical nature of their illnesses.[5]

Nothing drives human beings to consider the workings of their own body more than the onset of sickness. When illness strikes, humans immediately sense that the world is out of order, that they are moving toward dissolution and even death. As Michael Taussig points out, illness interrupts daily routines, causing the patient to question the previously uncritical acceptance of cultural life. Illness turns people into "metaphysicians and philosophers" who seek meaning for their pain and answers for questions such as "why me?" (4). It is in these moments of pain and disorientation that the words of religious men powerfully resurface and stick to the sick person's mind.

Although preachers and moralists seldom interjected lengthy scientific discussion of biological disorder into their treatises and sermons, they were fond of producing images of disease and bodily afflictions. Often this served as a strategy to modify a sinner's behavior. For example, it was common for priests to dissuade the penitent from frequenting prostitutes by describing the horrible symptoms of leprosy, a disease thought to be transmitted through illicit sexual relations (Payer 131; Jacquart and Thomasset 183–88). Curiously, medical writers often used the rhetorical skills of preachers to help in the conceptualization of disease. Medical historians have noted that medieval "medical nomenclature developed slowly and so long as medical knowledge was restricted, a narrative, descriptive style was used to evoke a picture of disease, where nowadays one word, a simple disease name, would suffice" (Veith 221). Therefore, the Middle Ages was a time when "anatomical or physiological explanation was a melting-pot in which scientific knowledge was amalgamated with the *exempla*" (Jacquart and Thomasset 5). We should not be surprised, therefore, to find inscribed within a preacher's homilies, sermons, anecdotes, and fables information about the workings of the human body, the nature and cause of illness, and the hygienic and therapeutic steps to be taken for prevention and cure. It is in this sense that Francesc Eiximenis's *Lo llibre de les dones* functioned during the later Middle Ages, as a powerful instrument for helping people imagine disease.

Lo llibre de les dones emerged from the tradition in the kingdom of Aragon of writing hygienic and behavioral treatises of moral and medical contents for the nobility. Eiximenis dedicated the work to dona Sancxa Xemèmneç d'Arenós, countess of Prades, designing it, as explicitly stated in the prologue, to help her to keep her health and live a life of virtue (8). Contrary to the title, the work is not exclusively about women. The early Castilian translator, Alfonso de Salvatierra argued that the largest part of the work spoke to men rather than women (Wittlin xxxvi). Encyclopedic in scope, the work rambles through remedies for common vices (anger, laziness, lust), discussion on the nature of marriage, instructions on how to offer a proper Ave Maria or Paternoster, definitions of sins, advice for widows, descriptions of life in hell, and speculations on such topics as whether women are converted into men in heaven.

Although Eiximenis wrote *Lo llibre de les dones* in the final decade of the fourteenth century, it was probably better known during the first part of the sixteenth century. In 1495 an estimated two hundred copies were printed in Barcelona. A Castilian translation appeared in 1452 (Wittlin xxxv). Like other medieval guides to moral and hygienic behavior, such as Jaime Roig's *Spill* and Alfonso Martínez's *Arcipreste de Talavera*, Eiximenis's *Lo llibre de les dones* held great appeal for sixteenth-century readers who lived at the time when the threat of syphilitic *bubas* created the need for greater speculation on the nature of epidemic disease.

In *Lo llibre de les dones,* Eiximenis suggests that those who commit acts of sodomy bring corruption upon themselves and scourges on others. Sodomy, he argues, is a sin so terrible that its practitioners deserve to be burned. Appropriating references and images of corrupted nature, putrefaction, and pestilence, he forcefully links the practice of sodomy with contagious disease. This diseasing of sexual otherness, generated at the end of the fourteenth century, coalesced enthusiastically a hundred years later with new medical notions of contagion, helping to develop fears and myths about the infectious nature of sexual otherness.

Eiximenis begins his diseasing of the sexual other by insinuating that acts of sodomy cause or lead to sickness. By describing same-sex practices within the context of sin — "aquest peccat" (339) — Eiximenis already links these acts to disease. The idea that sin is at the root of all illness was a commonplace in ecclesiastic and medical writings (Delaunay 10). Iberian physicians supported wholeheartedly the papal order that required a confessor to visit the severely sick to address the root of their affliction.[6] Alfonso Chirino, court physician for Juan II, proclaimed outright that certain diseases could only be healed by confession (437). Arnau de Vilanova instructed physicians, saying that "when you come to a house, inquire before you go to the sick whether he has confessed, and if he has not, he should do so immediately or promise you that he will do so immediately, and this must not be neglected because many illnesses originate on account of sin and are cured by the Supreme Physician after having been purified from squalor by the tears of contrition" (141).

Disease was also thought to be a punishment for sin.[7] The punitive miracles that circulated in the later Middle Ages clearly illustrated how moral transgression quickly resulted in a physical ailment. Sexual sins were especially conducive to divine punishment. The fifteenth-century *Espéculo de los legos,* a source book of *exempla* and other materials for preachers, includes a story about a man who wanted to have sex with his wife on All Saints' Day. While the rest of the Christians went to mass, he took his wife to bed. During the act of making love they were both injured, and the following morning they were found stone dead, wrapped in each other's embrace. "Be assured," the commentator warns us, "that just as their bodies were then wrapped together, their souls are now wrapped in hell" (186).

The relation between sexuality and disease permeates the dominant medieval models of illness. Church fathers promoted the idea that when Adam and Eve introduced sex and the evil of lust by partaking of the fruit of the tree of knowledge, they also brought disease into the world. Saint Bonaventure articulated the general suspicion of many healers by explaining that "the sexual act itself is diseased, for it cannot be performed without disorder" (Brundage 424). Sex was identified as the means by which horrible afflictions were thought to be passed from human being to human being. Leprosy, perhaps the most dreaded, the most symbolically saturated, and certainly the most socially stigmatized disease of the Middle Ages, was linked to hypersexuality in the patient who was thought to transmit venereally the horrors of autoamputations, nasal destruction, facial coarsening, and vocal changes.

In *Lo llibre de les dones,* Eiximenis draws on a long-standing tradition in which sexual acts are privileged as a major cause of disease. In the initial chapters he reminds the reader that it was Adam's love of carnal pleasure that led to the Fall and the resulting pain, suffering, and sickness (17). Later he warns that any sexual activity brings with it endless physical and spiritual maladies including shortening of the sinner's life and a weakening of the heart. Insinuated in his presentation of sodomy is that this particular sex act, like all sexual acts, is etiologically linked to disease.

The next step in diseasing sexual otherness is to suggest that acts of sodomy not only bring illness to the sinner, but that those who engage in such acts become agents of disease. Eiximenis claims that sodomy brings with it the corruption of human nature: "porta ab si corrupció de natura humana" (339). Although the term *natura humana* has various meanings throughout Eiximenis's extensive works, there is no denying its biological underpinnings and its pathological connotations. One fundamental notion of ancient and medieval disease is that illness occurs when the body's nature or natural constitution becomes corrupted. This corruption was thought to develop when individuals experienced the effects of the so-called *contra-naturals:* fevers, abscesses, accidents, and usually, any pathological condition. Therefore an act *contra natura,* as preachers like Eiximenis traditionally described sodomy, is inextricably linked to biological corruption.

In medieval and early-Renaissance epidemiology, corruption was thought to be a prerequisite for contagion. According to sixteenth-century medical theorists such as Girolamo Fracastoro, contagion took place when "a similar corruption of the substance of a particular combination" passes from one thing to another (Nutton, "The Reception" 200). By claiming that those who commit sodomy corrupt their nature, Eiximenis creates a conceptional foothold for ontological hygienics. He forcefully implies that this corruption is not only the result of an individual suffering from disease, but rather that this corruption can threaten healthy individuals. By identifying those who participate in sodomy as diseased individuals, Eiximenis sets the stage for claiming that these people can spread their corruption and effectively act as agents of infection.

The image of transmissibility insinuated in Eiximenis's description of corrupt nature becomes more explicit when he claims that the air around those who commit sodomy also becomes corrupt: "Car dien los sants que corromp l'ayre (386)." [8] Medieval hygienic treatises stated frequently that the primary rule for preserving one's health was to breathe good air. Arnau de Vilanova, for example, initiates his *Regiment de Sanitat* with a lengthy discussion on the necessity of carefully identifying the type of air in which one works and sleeps, warning that the air changes according to the season and geographical location (103–10).

When Eiximenis claims that sodomy corrupts the air, he not only draws the reader's attention to this general hygienic imperative, but also alludes to one of the oldest notions of communicative disease. From antiquity natural philosophers spoke of the "seeds" of disease that traveled through the air. Varro (116–27 BCE) spoke of little animals, too small to be seen, "which by mouth and nose through the air enter the body and cause severe diseases" (Temkin, "Health and Disease" 426). Lucretius argued that plague-bearing seeds "were carried into the air and borne upwards to be transported by wind or clouds to the farthest parts of the earth," where they "were taken in with the air which we breathe and were thus absorbed into the body" (Nutton, "The Seeds of Disease" 20). Late-medieval plague treatises contain extensive discussion of the relation between air and pestilence. Typical is the explanation in the first chapter of Velasco de Taranta's Castilian version of his *Tratado de la peste* [Treatise on the Plague]:

> La pestilencia es dolencia contagiosa e assi peude infecionar a los otros de qualquiere complexion que sean, como proceden de ellos malos fumos e poçoñosos que corrompen el aire e los humores; y el aire que espiran es ya corrupto e corrompe el aire que esta cabe ellos e, por consiguiente, a los otros que resollando toman aquel aire. Desto se sigue manifestamente que los que estan cabe el ferido de peste e los assistentes deuen bobuer les el rostro e poner lo haza al fuego o haza la ventana o puerta, para que no attraya a si el aire por el doliente resollado, que es ya corrupto. (23)

> [Pestilence is a contagious suffering and as such can infect others despite their complexion; since it proceeds from bad and poisonous vapors that corrupt the air and the humors; and since the air that they breathe is already corrupt, it corrupts the air that is next to them, and consequently, it corrupts those who take in this air. From this we can clearly deduce the attendants who are near one injured by the plague should turn their heads toward fire, or toward the window or door so as not to inhale the sufferer's breath that is already corrupt.] [9]

By insisting that those who participate in same-sex relations corrupt the air, Eiximenis identifies these people as plague-afflicted intermediaries who could inflict their sickness on the healthy.

The final step in Eiximenis's diseasing of sexual otherness is his description of the miasmic conditions that he claims prevail in the area where the cities of Sodom and Gomorrah had once stood. After explaining how God destroyed these cities with "terrible tribulations" (*terribles tribulacions*) and fire from the sky (*foch del cel*), he insinuates that the counternatural acts of individuals can lead to disintegration and putrefaction. According to Eiximenis, who draws from traditional geographical legends, the entire area where the cities once stood is now a lake of dead water in which no fish can live and over which no flying bird can survive: "tota aquella terra és estany d'aygua morta en qué no viu peys, ne aucell no.n passa dessús qui vischa puys" (338).

Closely connected to the idea of bad air is the notion of miasmas, those polluted and putrid locations — swamps, battlefields laden with dead bodies, garbage dumps — from which harmful vapors arise. Eiximenis clearly communicates the image of miasmas in his description of the region of Sodom and Gomorrah. In medieval epidemiology, miasma, with its conditions of fetidness, rotting, and decay, was thought to constitute the final state of those who suffer from pestilence and the origin of contagious diseases. Miasma theory contends that the sick individual and the objects in the world around that person also are pestiferous. Increasingly the putrid state of the diseased other was thought to excrete its deadly vapors into the objects of the world, contaminating clothing, tableware, and furniture, leaving these things in a state of contagious decay.

By linking the act of sodomy with images of sin, bodily corruption, unhealthy air, and putrefaction, Eiximenis effectively lodges sexual otherness firmly within the category of infectious diseases. More troubling is that in his attempt to denounce acts of sodomy, Eiximenis also "identifies" those who engage in same-sex practices as agents of disease.

The presence of sexual identities in the Middle Ages is a difficult and highly disputed topic among many medievalists. One aspect that has yet to be fully investigated is the way the shift toward ontological disease forced humans into categories that eventually were adopted as forms of identity. To participate in a sexual sin made one a sinner, but in the later Middle Ages to commit the sin of sodomy differentiated this specific type of sinner as a diseased and infectious human being. Unlike other sinners, those who practiced sodomy increasingly found themselves on the wrong side of the division between the healthy and the diseased. This crossing, as Sander Gilman has argued, becomes salient to one's definition of self. And "whenever an image of difference projected onto a group within a society has sufficient salience for an individual in the stereotyped group as to be completely internalized, the individual acts as if the image is a pattern for self definition whatever the validity or implications of the charge of difference or the image imposed" (5).

Ontological notions of disease offered people in the sixteenth century a sense of control over their illnesses, providing them with a tangible entity upon which they could act. Perpetuated in the writings of moralists such as Eiximenis was the idea that humans could best deal with the rampage of disease and its ensuing biological dissolution by locating it in the bodies of the sexual other. In this way humans thought to gain a sense of comfort knowing that the cause of disease can be controlled, contained, and if need be, eliminated. A frightening pattern, often left undocumented in the history of modern epidemiology (germ theory, bacteriology virology), is the way the fight against disease with all its bellicose metaphors and combative strategies, has repeatedly been a fight against the ethnicity, gender, and sexual practices of others.

Notes

1. On premodern theories of contagion, see Nutton.

2. See Eisenberg; Young (264); Kleinman and Sung (8); Kleinman, *The Illness Narratives* (3–8); Engelhardt ("Ideology and Etiology" 257).

3. Any type of behavioral aberration, complaint, criticism, or discontentment can be somatized and pathologized. For specific examples see Fisher; Showalter; Engelhardt ("The Disease of Masturbation"); and Hare.

4. Temkin points to a chapter in Theodorus Priscianus's medical textbook (written during the sixth century CE) which bears the title *De infectionibus capillorum* [On the Dyeing of Hair]. He suggests that the modern-day notion of infection evolved from the connotation of poisonous substances used in dyes, noting that the English word "stain" still maintains the double meaning of dyeing and of polluting, tainting, and spoiling. Temkin also points to the "analogy with a tincture where a small drop of dye-stuff suffices to color a large amount of fluid,"

arguing that it "played an important role in medieval alchemy and medicine. It helped to explain how the whole body could become sick from mere contact or inhaled breath" ("An Historical Analysis of the Concept of Infection" 457, 461).

5. See Temkin (*Hippocrates in a World of Pagans and Christians*); Amundsen and Ferngren ("Medicine and Religion: Early Christianity through the Middle Ages").

6. Pope Innocent III prohibited physicians from visiting a sick person more than twice without the patient being visited by a priest (Lateran IV, canon 22). Similar edicts were pronounced in the Second Council of Ravinna (1311), the Council of Paris (1429), and the Council of Tortosa of 1429 (Delaunay 3). See Amundsen ("The Medieval Catholic Tradition" 88–89); Amundsen and Ferngren ("Medicine and Religion: Early Christianity Through the Middle Ages" 125). The Valencian *Furs* of 1328 echoed these prohibitions, requiring all physicians to inform seriously ill patients of the need to confess their sins to an ecclesiastical authority. In 1329 King Alfons IV of Aragon obliged physicians and surgeons to swear each year before the *justiciar* that they would not treat anyone seriously ill or wounded who had not first made confession. See García-Ballester et al. (59–61).

7. See Ell, "Concepts of Disease"; Amundsen and Ferngren ("Medicine and Religion").

8. Eiximenis reiterates his claim that sodomy pollutes the air in his chapter "Qui tracta del tocar" [Which treats the sins of touch]: "[E] qui, segons que ells dien, escura e corremp l'ayre on se fa, e per lo qual se n'entrà en abís tota la terra" (386) [The air becomes dark and corrupt where it (sodomy) is committed and for this reason the whole world enters into an abyss].

9. Translations of primary sources are mine.

Works Cited

Amundsen, Darrel W. "The Medieval Catholic Tradition." *Caring and Curing: Health and Medicine in the Western Religious Traditions*. Ed. Ronald L. Numbers and Darrel W. Amundsen. New York: Macmillan, 1986. 65–107.

Amundsen, Darrel W., and Gary B. Ferngren. "The Early Christian Tradition." *Caring and Curing: Health and Medicine in the Western Religious Traditions*. Ed. Ronald L. Numbers and Darrel W. Amundsen. New York: Macmillan, 1986. 40–64.

———. "Medicine and Religion: Early Christianity through the Middle Ages." *Health/Medicine and the Faith Traditions*. Ed. Martin E. Marty and Kenneth L. Vauz. Philadelphia: Fortress P, 1982. 93–131.

Arnau de Vilanova. *Regiment de sanitat* [early-fourteenth-century translation of *Liber de regimine sanitatis,* trans. from Latin into Catalan by Berenguer Sariera]. Ed. Miquel Batllori. *Arnau de Vilanova: Obres Catalanes.* Vol. 2. Barcelona: Editorial Barcino, 1947.

Brundage, James A. *Law, Sex, and Christian Society in Medieval Europe.* Chicago: U of Chicago P, 1987.

Chirino, Alfonso. *Espejo de medicina.* Ed. Angel González Palencia and Luis Contreras Poza. Madrid: J. Cosano, 1944.

Delaunay, Paul. *La Médecine et l'église.* Paris: Editions Hippocrate, 1948.

Diaz de Isla, Rodrigo. *Tractado contra el mal serpentino: que vulgarmente en España es llamado bubas que fue ordenado que el ospital de todos los santos d'Lisbona . . .* Seville, 1539.

Eisenberg, Leon. "Disease and Illness: Distinctions between Professional and Popular Ideas of Sickness." *Culture, Medicine and Psychiatry* 1 (1977): 9–23.

Eiximenis, Francesc. *Lo llibre de les dones.* Ed. Frank Naccarato. Barcelona: Curial Edicions Catalanes, 1981.

Ell, Stephan R. "Concepts of Disease and the Physician in the Early Middle Ages." *Janus* 65 (1978): 153–67.

Engelhardt, H. Tristram, Jr. "The Disease of Masturbation: Values and the Concept of Disease." *Concepts of Health and Disease.* Ed. Arthur L. Caplan et al. Reading: Addison-Wesley, 1981. 267–80.

———. "Ideology and Etiology." *Journal of Medicine and Philosophy* 1 (1976): 256–68.

Espéculo de los legos. Ed. José María Mohedano Hernández. Madrid: Consejo Superior de Investigaciones Científicas, 1951.

Fisher, Sue. *In the Patient's Best Interest: Women and the Politics of Medical Decisions.* New Brunswick: Rutgers UP, 1986.

García-Ballester, Luis, Michael McVaugh, and Agustín Rubio Vela. *Medical Licensing and Learning in Fourteenth-Century Valencia.* Philadelphia: American Philosophical Society, 1989.

Hare, E. H. "Masturbatory Insanity: The History of an Idea." *Journal of Mental Science* 108 (1962): 2–3.

Humbert of Romans. *On the Formation of Preachers* [*De eruditione praedicatorum*]. Trans. Simon Tugwell. *Early Dominicans: Selected Writings.* New York: Paulist P, 1982. 183–370.

Jacquart, Danielle, and Claude Thomasset. *Sexuality and Medicine in the Middle Ages.* Princeton: Princeton UP, 1988.

Kleinman, Arthur. *The Illness Narratives: Suffering, Healing, and the Human Condition.* New York: Basic Books, 1988.

Kleinman, Arthur, and Lilias H. Sung. "Why Do Indigenous Practitioners Successfully Heal?" *Social Science and Medicine* 13B (1979): 7–26.

Nutton, Vivian. "The Reception of Fracastoro's Theory of Contagion: The Seed That Fell among Thorns?" *Osiris* 6 (1990): 196–234.

———. "The Seeds of Disease: An Explanation of Contagion and Infection from the Greeks to the Renaissance." *Medical History* 27 (1983): 1–34.

Payer, Pierre J. "Sex and Confession in the Thirteenth Century." *Sex in the Middle Ages: A Book of Essays.* Ed. Joyce E. Salisbury. New York: Garland, 1991. 126–44.

Quétel, Claude. *History of Syphilis.* Baltimore: Johns Hopkins UP, 1990.

Showalter, Elaine. *The Female Malady: Women, Madness, and Culture in England, 1830–1980.* New York: Pantheon Books, 1985.

Taussig, Michael. "Reification and the Consciousness of the Patient." *Social Science and Medicine* 14B (1980): 3–13.

Temkin, Owsei. "Health and Disease." *The Double Face of Janus and Other Essays in the History of Medicine.* Baltimore: Johns Hopkins UP, 1977. 419–39.

———. *Hippocrates in a World of Pagans and Christians.* Baltimore: Johns Hopkins UP, 1991.

———. "An Historical Analysis of the Concept of Infection." *The Double Face of Janus and Other Essays in the History of Medicine.* Baltimore: Johns Hopkins UP, 1977. 456–71.

Veith, Ilza. "Historical Reflections on the Changing Concepts of Disease." *Concepts of Health and Disease.* Ed. Arthur L. Caplan et al. Reading: Addison-Wesley, 1981. 221–30.

Velasco de Taranta. *Tratado de la peste.* Ed. María Nieves Sánchez. Madrid: Arco, 1993. 15–76.

Wittlin, Curt. "Introducció." Eiximenis, *Lo llibre de les dones.* xi–xxxvii.

Young, Allan. "The Anthropologies of Illness and Sickness." *Annual Review of Anthropology* 11 (1982): 257–85.

Barbara Weissberger

"¡A tierra, puto!"

Alfonso de Palencia's Discourse of Effeminacy

The sexualized discourse of the pro-Isabelline chronicles of late-fifteenth-century Castile vividly illustrates what Gregory Bredbeck identifies as "the simple but central principle that the articulation of order demands means of accounting for disorder, and these means frequently involve issues of sex, sexuality, and eroticism" (47). The present essay analyzes the intersection of transgressive sexuality and the sociopolitical order in Spanish historiography written at a critical juncture in the construction of Europe's first modern nation-state and world empire: the struggle for the throne of Castile waged by Isabel I and her supporters against the legitimate heir, Princess Juana, daughter of Isabel's half-brother, King Enrique IV (r. 1454–74).[1]

My particular focus is the representation of the putative homosexuality of Enrique IV as a figure for political and social disorder in the *Crónica de Enrique IV,* written after 1477 by Alfonso de Palencia in his capacity as royal chronicler to Queen Isabel of Castile.[2] I first identify and analyze a "discourse of effeminacy" fashioned by Palencia and several of his contemporaries — Fernando del Pulgar, Diego de Valera, and Juan de Flores, among others — and employed to denigrate Enrique as a man and discredit him as monarch. I then situate this rhetorical weapon ideologically as a propagandistic strategy in the Trastamaran/Isabelline program of political legitimation, centralization, and expanded royal power.[3] My ultimate goal, however, is to uncover the double-edged nature of that powerful rhetorical weapon, showing that the homophobic construction of an impotent, sodomitical, and therefore effeminate Enrique is inseparable from the simultaneous misogynistic construction of a masculinized Isabel, whose gender-inappropriate power and authority produces, I argue, an unacknowledged political and sexual anxiety in the humanist authors of her official story. Finally, I go beyond the regiocentric analysis to discuss some of the broader implications of these male sexual and gender anxieties for the rise of humanism in Spain as in the rest of Europe. The *crónicas,* I suggest, are significant texts for understanding the deeply patriarchal values embedded in the humanist project of the *letrados.*[4]

My ideological analysis of the *crónicas* as cultural products that seek to disclose and contain threats to early modern cultural masculinity is necessarily indebted to the work of the New Historicists. Scholars such as Stephen Greenblatt, Maureen Quilligan, and Louis Adrian Montrose, have greatly altered the way we read the texts created by the subjects of that other Isabel, Elizabeth I of England.[5] Montrose's work in particular shows how the unmarried woman at society's symbolic center embodied a challenge to the homology between hierarchies of rule and of gender: "A range of strategies was generated by means of which this ideological dissonance, this contradiction in the cultural logic, could be variously articulated and obfuscated, contained and exploited" (309).[6] In Spain, one very effective strategy of this sort is the Palencian "discourse of effeminacy" that is the subject of this essay.[7]

Any discussion of the embedding of sexual and political power relations must also acknowledge the work of Michel Foucault, especially the first volume of his *History of Sexuality.* I have also found useful for my theoretical framework the more recent work of queer theorists — Gregory Bredbeck, Alan Bray, Jonathan Goldberg, and Eve Kosofsky Sedgwick — all of whom in turn are indebted to Foucault. Particularly important has been Sedgwick's more strictly feminist formulation of queer theory. She is careful both to treat homosexuality as a point in the continuum of male homosocial desire that is constitutive of patriarchy and to make plain the misogyny that always underlies homophobia. As she states, "[H]omophobia directed by men against men is misogynistic and perhaps transhistorically so. By 'misogynistic' I mean not only that it is oppressive of the so-called feminine in men, but that is oppressive of women" (20). This concept has helped me to clarify the subtle and complex ways in which homophobia and misogyny interact in the chroniclers' stigmatization of a feminized Enrique IV and to recognize that the anxieties produced by the behavior of Enrique and Isabel arise from a perceived instability of gender roles and identity. For as we shall see, the wild accusations against Enrique and the more cautious ones against Isabel have as much to do with gender role violations — on the one hand, Enrique's passivity and a failure to control others, especially his adulterous queen, and on the other, Isabel's will to power and an unseemly domination of her husband—as with any real or imagined sexual transgressions.

At the same time, it is important to keep in mind that to identify an individual as a "homosexual" in the Renaissance is anachronistic.[8] As Foucault was the first to affirm, before the late-nineteenth century there simply was no consciousness of homosexuality as a definable identity or subjectivity. Rather, in the early-modern period I am dealing with, the homosexual was defined as a sodomite. This juridical category designated any person, man or woman, who participated in any sexual act not having as its goal procreation within marriage, that is, any act that threatened the structures of alliance and consequently the power hierarchy and social stability maintained by those structures (37–38).[9] Sodomy was thus viewed as a temptation to which anyone, and especially unformed adolescents who did not as yet have their appetites under control, might succumb.[10]

Expanding upon Foucault's insights, Alan Bray's fundamental *Homosexuality in Renaissance England* affirms that in the early-modern period sexual acts stigmatized as sodomitical in fact only became visible when those who performed those acts, or were accused of performing them, were persons who threatened the established social order: heretics, traitors, spies, and so on (25). This "utterly confused" (Foucault 101) and "slippery" (Bredbeck 21) character of sodomy before the advent of modernity thus makes it virtually impossible to untangle the threads of race, class, gender, ethnicity, and sexuality that are tightly knotted in many Renaissance texts, including many works shaped by and shaping the profoundly exclusionary ideology of Isabelline Spain.[11]

The awareness that the sodomitical belongs to an undifferentiated catalogue of otherness informs Bredbeck's analysis of the ideological uses of the "poetics of sodomy" in Renaissance satire, in which homoeroticism becomes embedded within a mythology of the unnatural, the alien, and the demonic (5). Precisely because it is fundamentally synecdochic, sodomitical discourse provides "a way to encompass and demonize a multitude of sins—everything from foreign languages to monstrous men—with a minimum of signs" (13–14). The use of sodomy to attack undifferentiated vice helps to explain the diffuseness that we shall find in Palencia's stigmatization of Enrique, as well as its constant slippage into attacks on Jews, Moors, Portuguese, *conversos, parvenus,* and women, including the virago Isabel.[12] In its aggressive intent to demonize elements that threaten the integrity of orthodox social structures, discursive sodomy in fifteenth-century Castilian texts thus serves a deeply conservative purpose that perfectly suited the exclusionary nature of Isabel's political program. The establishment of the Inquisition under the aegis of the Crown (1478) and the expulsion of the Jews (1492) are only the two most famous accomplishments of her reign that can be adduced to prove this point.[13]

The recent investigations of Inquisition attacks on the *pecados abominables* 'abominable sins' by historians Bartolomé Benassar and Rafael Carrasco are helpful in understanding the politics and poetics of sodomy in early-modern Spain. Carrasco, for example, rigorously documents the confusion of the category of sodomy for a slightly later period, noting that "behind the sodomite, bearer of pestilence, is the outline of the converso. They are joined in the worst popular insult that could be hurled: 'faggot Jew!.'"[14] In a similar vein, Arturo Firpo suggests that the marked sexualization of much political writing of the fifteenth century, for example, the obscene "Coplas del Provincial" [The Provincial's Verses], in which the anonymous satirist hurls accusations of sodomy and Judaizing against contemporary aristocrats and clergymen, is due to two interrelated factors. First, the new racist preoccupation with *limpieza de sangre* 'purity of blood,' with its inevitable links to sexual control and heightened conjugal normativity, and second, the growing confusion in the noble lineages since the reign of Alfonso X (1252–84). In addition to the large numbers of bastard aristocratic offspring, there was the added disorder produced by the many *parvenus* receiving advancement at court (148).

The slippery poetics of sodomy pervades Palencia's physical and psychological portrait of Isabel's predecessor in the *Crónica de Enrique IV*. The following comments on Enrique's appearance, character, behavior, and tastes are culled from the "Primera década" [First decade], which recounts events occurring from 1440 until 1468, when the death of Isabel's brother, Prince Alfonso, made the succession of a woman to the throne of Castile a real possibility. In his physical description of the king, Palencia notes his "gran semejanza con el mono" (1: 11) [great similarity to a monkey], and observes that he "respiraba con delicia la fetidez de la corrupción, y el hedor de los cascos cortados de los caballos, y el del cuero quemado . . . que por este sentido del olfato podía juzgarse de los demás" (1: 12) [sniffed with delight the stench of putrefaction, and the stink of the shaved hooves of horses, and of burned leather so that by the sense of smell one could judge the others]. He strongly disapproves of Enrique's apparent solitary nature, noting that he "huía del trato de las gentes" (1: 39) [ran away from social relations] and that "enamorado de lo tenebroso de las selvas, sólo en las más espesas buscó el descanso" (1: 11) [enamored of the darkness of the forests, only in the deepest ones did he find rest].

In the chronicler's view, these traits damaged Enrique's marital relations with Juana (although as we shall see, Palencia and his fellow chroniclers are distinctly ambivalent about assigning culpability for the sexual failure of the marriage). Palencia describes the king as "enteramente ajeno al conyugal afecto" [totally devoid of conjugal affection] and reproves "las repentinas ausencias, la conversación a cada paso interrumpida, su adusto ceño y su afán por las excursiones a sitios retirados" (1: 11) [the sudden absences, the constantly interrupted conversation, his severe scowl, and his delight in excursions to secluded places].

The monarch's sartorial tastes are also censured: "su indigno traje y más descuidado calzado" [his unworthy dress and more careless footwear]; "su traje de lúgubre aspecto, sin collar ni otro distintivo real o militar que le adornase" (1: 11) [his lugubrious-looking clothes, without the adornment of a chain or other royal or military insignia].[15] The reproach targets something rather more serious than an unprincely lack of ostentation, since the primary role of the king in the medieval period was that of warrior. Enrique's credibility in this role is further compromised by his fascination with Islamic culture.[16] Thus, for example, Palencia reproves the king for going to a siege of Granada "más a contemplar la ciudad que a combatirla" (1: 71) [more to contemplate the city than to fight against it], and he objects that Enrique "prefirió, a usanza de la caballería árabe, la gineta, propia para algaradas, incursiones y escaramuzas, a la más noble brida, usada por nosotros . . . imponente y fuerte en las expediciones y ejercicios militares" (1: 11) [preferred the short stirrups used by Arab cavalry, suitable for marauding, incursions, and skirmishes, to our more noble bridle, imposing and strong in expeditions and military exercises]. The king's maurophilia not only has an adverse effect on his personal habits, it also casts a shadow over his religious orthodoxy, for "hasta en el andar, en la comida y en la manera de recostarse para comer, y en otros secretos y más torpes excesos, había preferido las costumbres todas de los moros a las de la religión cristiana" (1: 74) [even in his walk, in his food, and in his manner of reclining when eating, and in other secret and more indecent excesses, he had preferred the customs of the Moors to those of the Christian religion].

Enrique displays a similarly deplored indifference to class and race hierarchy, demonstrated by his choice of advisers. Palencia condemns his "agregar a su séquito a otros muchos secuaces . . . cuyos nombres y apellidos no recordaban ciertamente el lustre de antiguas familias, antes bien la más abyecta condición" (1: 74) [adding to his retinue many other followers whose names certainly did not bring to mind the lustre of the ancient families, rather the most abject condition]. He also blames him for constructing "un vasto y magnífico edificio donde se encerraba a solas con los rufianes . . . de los cuales los más queridos eran un enano y un etiope tan horrible como estúpido" (1: 230) [a vast and magnificent building where he shut himself up with ruffians of which the most favored were a dwarf and an Ethiopian as horrible as he was stupid].

It is difficult to find a common denominator for such a variegated series of personality traits and affinities, among them introversion, sensuality, exoticism, misanthropy, cowardice, a love of nature and the hunt, passivity, and generosity. But that is precisely the point: Palencia creates a synecdochical chain that ties the king's multifarious stigmatized traits to his "nefandas iniquidades" (1: 73) [abominable iniquities]; "toda suerte de liviandades" (1: 52) [all manner of licentiousness]; "vicios infames" [disgusting vices]; and "innumerable abusos . . . cuya enumeración me sonroja y me apena" (1: 83) [innumerable abuses whose enumeration makes me blush and pains me]. Broadly speaking, Palencia's reticence reminds us that sex between men had been famous throughout the Judeo-Christian tradition precisely for having no name, for being "unspeakable" and "unmentionable," its very namelessness and enforced secrecy a form of social control (Sedgwick 94). On a rhetorical level, it is the very lack of specificity, the undefined and indefinable nature of the sodomitical, that gives Palencia's discourse its persuasive force. It makes the Henrician "abominable vice" infinitely expansive and highly contaminating. It easily reaches apocalyptic levels: "el germen de la ruina universal que a toda prisa se venía encima" (1: 73) [the seed of the universal ruin that was fast approaching], the "corrupción de la humanidad entera" [corruption of all humanity];[17] and a "general trastorno" (1: 83) [general upheaval], and the sodomites with whom the king surrounds himself become nothing less than demonic: "amigos de las tinieblas . . . poseídos de cierta rabia para exterminar el bien y acarrear las catástrofes" (1: 83) [friends of darkness possessed of a certain rage to exterminate goodness and to cause catastrophes].

Simple but powerful evidence of the effectiveness of the "discourse of effeminacy" fashioned by Palencia is the uncritical transmission of the epithet *el Impotente* for Enrique throughout more than five hundred years of Spanish historiography. William Phillips's judicious treatment of the monarch and his reign summarizes the vast and long-lasting influence that Palencia has had on Spanish historiography. He provides a partial list of the historians from the fifteenth through the twentieth centuries who have accepted more or less at face value Palencia's homophobic interpretation of politics and society in the last half of the fifteenth century. It includes, to name only the most prominent, Fernando del Pulgar, Diego de Valera, Andrés Bernáldez, Lorenzo Galíndez de Carvajal, Gonzalo Chacón, William H. Prescott, J. H. Mariéjol, R. B. Merriman, and Gregorio Marañón.[18] This enumeration of Palencian historians could easily be extended into the present. The Columbus Quincentenary recently contributed new hagiographic portrayals of Isabel as the virile restorer of order and light to a nation weakened by the dark chaos of Enrique's effeminacy. One example among the many that could be cited is the 1992 biography of Isabel by the distinguished historian Luis Suárez Fernández, who describes Enrique as "inconstant, cyclothymic, cowardly, abundantly endowed with the goodness of the weak who hand over everything" (21).

According to Orestes Ferrara, author of the first important revisionist treatment of Enrique's reign, the imputation to Enrique of "abominable iniquities" was widely disseminated only after his death in 1474. It functioned largely to bolster the prior accusation of impotence, which had begun circulating ten years earlier, two years after the birth of Enrique's heir, Juana of Castile, whose legitimacy was thereby challenged by the nobles opposed to her father. The rumor, promoted as fact in Isabelline propaganda, and popularly crystallized in the long-lasting sobriquet *la Beltraneja*, a pejorative reference to Juana's presumed fathering by Enrique's favorite, Beltrán de la Cueva, has never been convincingly proven. But it was absolutely required to justify "the triumph of the collateral branch over the direct branch, [which] was determined by arms, not law" (Ferrara 340).

Historical evidence of the king's impotence ranges from the documentary to the fanciful, but absolutely none of it is conclusive (Azcona 20–22;

O'Callaghan 573). A complete catalog of the "proof" of the sovereign's impotence marshaled by his contemporaries cannot be attempted here, but a few examples may serve to illustrate its questionable nature. There is the failure of Enrique's first wife Blanca de Navarra to produce an heir after three and a half years of marriage, leading to the king's petitioning the pope for a divorce; the related claims that Blanca had bewitched the king, causing his temporary impotence; the 1464 declaration in defense of Juana's legitimacy by the king's physician, Fernández de Soria, that at the age of twelve, Enrique "had lost his potency," but had later recovered it. Also adduced are Enrique's own supposed allusions to the illegitimacy of his daughter in 1464, when he declared his half-brother Alfonso heir to the throne: "Be it known that I, in order to avoid any manner of scandal that may occur after our death regarding the succession to my kingdom . . ." (qtd. in Paz y Melia lvii), and again in 1468, after Alfonso's death, in the pact he was coerced into signing at Toros de Guisando in order to avert a civil war, in which he named Isabel legitimate successor to the Castilian throne "in order that the kingdom not remain without legitimate successors of the lineage of said King and said Princess" (qtd. in Paz y Melia lvi) and agreed to a divorce from Juana because "it is public knowledge and manifest that the Queen Doña Juana, for a year now has not been chaste in her person as befits the service of said King" (qtd. in Paz y Melia lviii).

In addition, numerous anecdotes pertaining to this highly charged issue have survived, among them the king's deathbed refusal, despite the urging of his confessor, to clarify the questions surrounding his rightful heir; the testimony of a number of Segovian prostitutes, expert witnesses called upon during the divorce proceedings to testify as to the proper functioning of the royal member: "[H]e had a virile member that was firm and paid its debt in potent seed just like any other male" (qtd. in Sitges 47); the joke about Enrique's penis told by one Gonzalo de Guzmán on the occasion of the king's wedding to Juana and recorded by Palencia: "[D]ecía . . . que había tres cosas que no se bajaría a coger si las viese arrojadas en la calle, a saber: la virilidad de don Enrique, la pronunciación del Marqués y la gravedad del arzobispo de Sevilla" (1: 76) [He said that there were three things that he would not bend down to pick up if he saw them thrown in the street, namely, Don Enrique's sex, the marquis's speech (a reference to Juan Pacheco's stutter), and the archbishop of Sevilla's dignity]; the rumors that princess Juana's nose had been broken at birth to compensate for the fact that she bore no physical resemblance to Enrique, and that an attempt had been made, also at her birth, to exchange her for a male child born on the same day in the same town (Paz-y Melia lviii–lix); and the German doctor Hieronymus Münzer's diagnosis of the king's problem, based on conversations with members of Isabel's court twenty years after Enrique's death: "[H]is member was thin and weak at the base but large at the head, so that he could not have an erection," and "his semen was thin and watery" (qtd. in Liss 47).

The blatantly propagandistic nature of most of the historiography of Enrique's reign and the fact that it was closely overseen by Isabel is indubitable. There is ample evidence, presented by the historian Jaime Vicens Vives and others, that the queen ordered the revision of chronicles and falsification of documents in order to legitimate *a posteriori* her assumption of the throne.[19] But as Brian Tate states in the indispensable *Ensayos sobre la historiografía peninsular del siglo XV,* the chroniclers' severe moral condemnation of Enrique's reign, as well as their identification of the year 1464 (when the aristocrats, rallying around Prince Alfonso, presented their seditious "Carta-protesta" to Enrique) as the nadir of the Castilian monarchy, must be considered in conjunction with the belief held by those same writers that the succession of Isabel was the result of providential intervention.

The messianic tone of fifteenth-century historiography in Castile has been amply discussed in light of the *converso* origins of many of the chroniclers, Palencia included.[20] It has not, however, been situated in the context of the period's sex/gender system and its interrelationship with the operations of power, that is to say, in terms of the sexual politics of the early-modern period. This gendered perspective is, however, detectable in Tate's discussion of the "recuperative modeling" of the fifteenth-century chronicles from Rodrigo Sánchez de Arévalo on:

[T]he native historian seems to have awakened to a new sense of the integrity of his country and the uniqueness of its historical experience. . . . The Romans were presented as undermining the rough virtues of the primitive Iberians with their introduction of effeminate and sophisticated pleasures such as hot baths and wine-drinking. The Visigoths, although they were equally colonizers, were seen as spiritual brothers of the Iberians, being praised for their virility and their great vigor, the ultimate cause of the collapse of decadent Rome. (*Ensayos* 293–94)

The chroniclers' insistence that the virile Castilian temperament was inherited from the Iberians and the Visigoths is bolstered by proof, often invented, of an uninterrupted line of descent from the primitive tribes to the Castilian sovereigns.[21] In this foundational myth Isabel embodies the fulfilment of the Castilian God-given mission—"Hispaniam restaurare et recuperare"—to restore what the last Visigothic king, Rodrigo, had destroyed: the integrity of the Castilian political body.[22]

Since the thirteenth century, historians had blamed the destruction of Spain on Rodrigo's rape of the daughter of his political enemy, Count Julian, which was said to have provoked the latter to a calamitous act of vengeance, an invitation to his North African allies to invade the peninsula.[23] For my purposes, what is most significant about the reiterated historiographical motif of *reintegratio Hispaniae* is its conceptual linking of sociopolitical integrity and virility, that is, of the political body and the (masculine) physical body. Interestingly, although tradition most frequently assigns blame to the male half of the Edenic couple of Rodrigo and "la Cava," the latter is not represented as entirely innocent (her name is derived from the Arabic for whore [Colin Smith 52]). In similar fashion, Palencia and Pulgar hold both Enrique and his queen to blame for the chaos of the pre-Isabelline period.[24]

In the *crónicas* the identification of the destructive temptresses "la Cava" and Eve becomes a foundational pre-text for the association of a restorative Isabel and the Virgin. Palencia repeatedly figures the Catholic Queen as a redeeming Ave to Castile's originally sinful Eva. At one point in his narrative, speaking of the havoc wreaked in Castile by Enrique's adulterous wife Juana, Palencia underscores the connection between the Virgin and Isabel as follows: "Al cabo, frágil mujer y antiguo principal instrumento de la desgracia de la humanidad, para cuya reparación fue escogida una Virgen y madre singularísima, a fin de que por la extraordinaria e insigne virtud de una mujer se remediase el pecado original que la corrupción de otra introdujo en el mundo desde sus comienzos" (1: 132) [Finally, she was a fragile woman and ancient chief instrument of the disgrace of humankind, for whose reparation was chosen a Virgin and exceptional mother, so that through the extraordinary and renowned virtue of one woman the corruption that another introduced into the world from its beginnings might be remedied].

Cultural materialists have extensively analyzed the use of the human body as a fundamental symbolic site of social systems.[25] In the early-modern period this mode of representation can be observed, for example, in the concept of the king as the head of state or in the theory of the monarch's two bodies—the one physical and temporal, the other divine and eternal—which attempts to account for the immortal but human nature of sovereignty.[26] In his account of the so-called Farce of Avila (1465), the crucial moment of the struggle for power between Enrique and the high nobility (the future Isabelline faction), Fernando del Pulgar describes the bishop of Calahorra's attempt to impede the dethroning of Enrique's effigy in precisely such terms: "Notorio es, Señores, que todo el Reyno es habido por un cuerpo, del qual tenemos el Rey ser la cabeza; la qual si por alguna inhabilidad es enferma, parecería mejor consejo poner las melecinas que la razón quiere, que quitar la cabeza que la natura defiende . . . porque si los Reyes son ungidos por Dios en las tierras, no se debe creer que sean subjetos al juicio humano" (*Crónica* 230) [It is well-known, my lords, that the entire kingdom is considered to be a body, of which we take the king to be the head; which if ill due to some weakness it would seem best to administer those medicines that reason prescribes, rather than to cut off the head that nature defends, because if kings are annointed by God on earth, we should not consider them subject to human judgment]. This conciliatory mood did not, however, prevail, and the rebel band of Juan Pacheco, Pedro Girón, and Archbishop Carrillo carried out the dramatic act of ripping away the effigy's phallic symbols of power, the scepter and the sword, and then throwing the violated sovereign body to the ground with the cry, "¡A tierra, puto!" [Eat dirt, faggot!].[27]

The graphic corporeal symbolism with which the chroniclers depict the ritual dethronement of Enrique, subtly analyzed by Angus MacKay, leaves no doubt that the task of "restoring" Castile that begins with this act of treason and is brought to fruition by Isabel and Fernando is conceived of in violent sexual terms. It represents a restoration of a native virility corrupted not only by the repeated invasions of foreign, effeminate peoples, first the Romans and later, more catastrophically, the Muslims, but also by the equally effeminate internal enemy who represents a similar threat to the health of the masculine body politic.

It is important to remember that Enrique is not the first of these degenerate enemies from within. In his *Compendiosa Historia Hispanica* (c. 1470) Rodrigo Sánchez de Arévalo records the legend of the buffoon who, addressing Pedro I as he lies dying in the tent of Bernard du Guesclin, suggests that the king has had an unnatural friendship with him.[28] The accusation of sodomy against Pedro I, legitimate king of Castile murdered in 1369 by his brother, Enrique II, founder of the Trastamaran dynasty has an important function in Arévalo's chronicle. It is a discursive displacement of a double anxiety concerning the legitimacy of the Trastamaran line founded by Enrique II: double because he was both bastard and usurper. The slur reveals the sexualization of political relationships in the generation of historians writing immediately before Palencia. Sánchez de Arévalo's chronicle leaves little doubt about the fundamental role that the discourse of effeminacy, that is, of transgressive sexuality and gender instability, played in the foundational myths of the Trastámara dynasty, myths crafted to a large extent by the fifteenth-century *cronistas*.

Palencia, in building on this precedent, goes much further, to create a kind of genealogy of sodomy and illegitimacy.[29] He claims that Juan II, great-grandson of Enrique II and father of Enrique IV and Isabel, himself had homosexual propensities, "como quiera que . . . ya desde su más tierna edad se había entregado en manos de Don Alvaro de Luna, no sin sospecha de algún trato indecoroso y de lascivas complacencias por parte del Privado en su familiaridad con el Rey" (1: 9) [since from his most tender youth he had put himself in the hands of Don Alvaro de Luna, not without the suspicion of indecorous behavior and lascivious pleasures on the part of the favorite in his relationship with the king].[30] This suggestion in turn casts doubt upon Enrique IV's legitimacy, just as the latter's familial abnormality — "encenegado desde su más tierna niñez en vicios infames" (1: 74) [wallowing in disgusting vices since his most tender youth] — promotes the ultimate goal of fostering suspicion about his daughter Juana's legitimacy.

Returning to the reign of Enrique, we can now posit that the effeminacy obsessively associated with him in Palencia's *Crónica de Enrique IV* responds to an anxiety of legitimacy on the part of Isabel and her apologists that is very similar to that of Enrique II, since although not illegitimate of birth like her great-great-grandfather, she is equally a usurper. But the significance of the sodomitical genealogy invented for Enrique IV by Palencia and eagerly adopted by most other Isabelline chroniclers extends beyond the immediate context of the fierce struggle for the Castilian throne. It constitutes an important strategy in the ambitious political program of the new queen: nothing less than to impose on her heterogeneous and fractious subjects the patriarchal values of unity, homogeneity, and centralism that she considered essential to building a strong nation-state and imposing her absolute authority over it.

Isabel and Fernando clearly appreciated the effective and enduring role that the chronicles could play in the propagation of these patriarchal values. To cite Ferrara once again: "They moved from a victory of arms to a triumph of paper. Isabel, with her natural vigor, oversaw the account of the chroniclers in order to ensure a verdict favorable to posterity" (340). Ironically, this contemporary historian's naturalization of Isabel's vigor is in itself evidence of the propaganda program's success, since the enduring perception of the queen's vigor largely results from a concerted effort to construct her public persona as masculine,[31] a construction that is coterminous with that of her half-brother as "an execrable monster because he was not at all a man" (1: 74).

The rhetorical masculinization of Queen Isabel is a topic too extensive for me to treat adequately in the space allowed.[32] A single example from the chronicles must suffice. It is contained in the fascinating and little-studied *Crónica incompleta* (written after 1477) whose author has only recently been identified as Juan de Flores, official chronicler to the Catholic Monarchs as well as author of three extremely popular late-fifteenth-century sentimental romances.[33] Flores repeatedly extols Isabel's manliness in handling difficult affairs of state and military matters. In recounting her delicate negotiations with the politically fickle archbishop of Toledo, for example, he notes that "no como muger, mas como esforçado varon toma bien en el alma el peso de tan grand cuydado" (208) [not like a woman, but like a brave man she takes to heart the weight of such a great responsibility]. He also praises the bellicosity of the queen: "mas avn en cosas de la guerra ningund varon tanta soliçitud y diligençia podiera poner" (310) [but even in matters of war no man could be so diligent and solicitous]. And on the occasion of the retreat of the Castilian troops from the siege of Toro, the chronicler puts in Isabel's mouth "palabras de varón muy esforçado más que de muger temerosa" (238) [words more appropriate to a brave man than to a fearful woman]. In this extraordinary harangue the enraged but self-controlled sovereign skillfully manipulates gender stereotypes in order to castigate the cowardice of the Castilian forces, led by none other than Fernando:

"Yo en mis palaçios, con coraçon ayrado y con dientes çerrados y puños apretados, como si en la mesma vengança estouiera conmigo mesma peleando, estaua, y si tal ansia a uosotros, caualleros, tomara, el mayor peligro de vuestros enemigos fuera menor que el de vosotros mesmos. De mi saña, seyendo muger, y de vuestra paçiençia, seyendo varones, me marauillo." (241–42)

["There I was in my palace with an angry heart, gritted teeth, and clenched fists, as if I were fighting with myself out of revenge, and if such anguish had taken hold of you, sirs, the greatest danger presented by your enemies would have been less than your own to yourselves. Being a woman, I am amazed at my anger, as I am at your patience, being men."]

Fernando's response to his wife's scolding can only be described as whining:

"Yo me creya que veniendo desbaratados, oviera en vuestra lengua palabras de consuelo y esfuerço; y veniendo sanos y honrrados ¿os quexays? ¡Grand trabajo ternemos con vos de aquí adelante! Mas siempre las mugeres, avnque los hombres sean dispuestos, esforçados hazedores y graçiosos, son de mal contentamiento, espeçialmente vos, señora, que por nasçer está quien contentar os pueda." (245)

["I thought that if we arrive wounded you would have on your tongue words of consolation and encouragement; but seeing us arrive safe and with our honor intact, you berate us? What trouble we shall have with you from now on! But even when men are well disposed, brave, capable, and elegant, women are difficult to please, especially you, madam, because the man who can please you is yet to be born."] [34]

The inversion of gender roles and power relations in Flores's portrayal of the royal couple reveals the radical contradiction at the heart of the reciprocal gender construction of Enrique and Isabel. In the context of the gender ideology of the early modern period, the virile woman that Flores and others praise is as abnormal, as threatening as the effeminate man they repudiate so violently. The woman who rules is nothing short of monstrous, due to her inversion of the power hierarchy on which the patriarchal social institutions of the family, the church, and the state rest. Resistance to that inversion in the late-medieval and Renaissance periods has been well-documented, most extensively for Elizabethan England.[35] Clear evidence of the same attitude in Spain can be seen in a letter of 1486 written by Francisco de Rojas, an agent of the Catholic Monarchs sent to Rome to petition the pope that Isabel be granted perpetual administration of the Spanish military orders, a position accruing enormous power and wealth. He reports back to Fernando:

> "Certifico a vuestra magestad que conceder el Papa que fuese para la reina sola fue la más dificultosa cosa de acabar de quantas en Roma despaché. Porque el Papa y todos los cardenales y letrados habían por cosa contra todo derecho y por cosa monstruosa que mujer pudiera tener administración de órdenes." (qtd. in Azcona 728)

> [I certify to your majesty that the most difficult of the many tasks I had to achieve in Rome was having the pope grant that (the administration) be exclusively the queen's right. Because the pope and all the cardinals and the jurists considered it to be completely illegal and a monstrous thing that a woman should be allowed the administration of orders.]

With this attitude in mind we can more readily understand why Palencia's discourse of effeminacy soon slips into a misogynistic discourse. It becomes evident that for him it is the category Woman, and in particular the unsubmissive, willful woman-on-top, who functions as the most basic alterity and greatest threat to masculine identity and power. In a recent article Tate has pointed out the surprisingly overt criticism of Isabel that begins to accumulate in the pages of the *Crónica*, particularly in the second and third "Decades." He suggests that it is part of the chronicler's general stern disapprobation of what he considers a typically feminine "urge to dominate," a will to power that has no less disastrous consequences for the public sphere than male homosexuality.

Tate marks as the beginning of Palencia's censure of Isabel his description of her precipitous self-proclamation as queen upon the death of her half-brother ("Políticas" 170). It appears to have been entirely Isabel's idea to have her chief steward, Gutierre de Cárdenas, lead her procession through the streets of Segovia holding aloft an unsheathed sword. The appropriation of this phallic symbol of royal authority by a female sovereign did not go unremarked by the populace: "No faltaron algunos sujetos bien intencionados que murmurasen de lo insólito del hecho, pareciéndoles necio alarde en la mujer aquella ostentación de los atributos del marido" (2: 155) [There were some well-intentioned subjects who muttered about its unprecedented nature, for it seemed to them that it was foolishly ostentatious for a wife to display the attributes of the husband]. Palencia here levels his criticism not only at the gender inappropriateness of the new sovereign's ceremonial symbolism, but also, and more importantly, at her refusal to adopt, even for the sake of appearances, the role of queen consort. Furthermore, he invests this initial uxorial usurpation with dark portent, judging that "[d]e aquí surgió el germen de graves contiendas a gusto de los Grandes, fomentadores de nuevas alteraciones, como más a las claras se verá luego" (2: 155) [this created the seed of grave disputes amenable to the grandees, fomenters of new disturbances, as shall be seen later].

In fact, a common technique employed by Palencia to strengthen his criticism of Isabel is to ventriloquize it into Fernando. Concerning the same ostentation of the sword, for example, he has the king say: " 'Quisiera que . . . tú, Palencia, que leíste tantas historias, me dijéseis si hay en la antigüedad algún antecedente de una Reina que se haya hecho preceder de ese símbolo, amenaza de castigo para sus vasallos. Todos sabemos que se concedió a los Reyes; pero nunca supe de Reina que hubiese usurpado este varonil atributo' " (2: 162) [I would like you, Palencia, who have read so many histories, to tell me if there is in antiquity any precedent of a queen who had herself preceded by that symbol, a threat of punishment to her vassals. We all know that it was granted to kings, but I have never known of a queen who had usurped this masculine attribute].

As Tate shows, the stronger and more dominating the picture that Palencia paints of Isabel, the weaker and more submissive his portrayal of Fernando; her gender role transgressions have the effect of feminizing him, making him dangerously uxorious (168). I would take this a step further, to suggest that the process ends up associating Fernando with Enrique, who "[e]mbrazó la adarga con más gusto que empuñó el cetro" (1: 11) [embraced the shield more eagerly than he grasped the scepter] and whose weakly grasped scepter was in the chroniclers' view properly snatched away by Isabel's future supporters at the Farce of Avila.[36]

Palencia's gradual self-distancing from Isabel comes to a dramatic cli-

max during the preparations for the famous Cortes of 1480[37] when queen
and royal chronicler openly clashed, ostensibly over the future of the monarchs' heir, Prince Juan. The underlying issue, however, seems to have been
precisely the problem of conjugal relations of power. The struggle of wills
between sovereign and servant had a predictable outcome: the marginalization of Palencia and the promotion of his colleague Fernando del Pulgar
(1420?–1490?), who was a more submissive servant, that is, less resistant to
royal censorship of his work (Tate, "Décadas" 226). In his ungrateful treatment by his patron, "taimada maestra del disimulo y del engaño" (López
de Toro 167) [a sly master of pretense and deception], Palencia, consciously
or unconsciously, aligns himself with Fernando as a victim of Isabelline
emasculation. In this way, paradoxically, he both enhances his status as
confidant to the king and assimilates them both to the royal genealogy of
effeminacy that he had originally created to defame Enrique IV.

What then are we to make of the contradictory attitude of Palencia to
the virile queen he has been in good measure responsible for fashioning?
I suggest that the discourse of effeminacy that Palencia aims at Enrique
for the purpose of promoting Isabel's political legitimacy and authority
also plays a more personal role in his work. It expresses and contains the
sexual and political anxiety that her anomalous power arouses in the ambitious intellectual, and, we may assume, in the equally ambitious nobles
and courtiers that would have formed his readership. However, whereas
Tate sees a change occurring in Palencia's attitude to his sovereign, I maintain that the negative view of her masculinity is present all along, inherent
in the rhetorical slippage — from sexuality to gender, from homophobia to
misogyny — characteristic of the poetics of sodomy.

The following are but two examples of Palencia's profound misogyny,
reiterated throughout the *Chronicle:* "un sexo tan débil y tan propenso a
los placeres" (1: 82) [a sex so weak and so inclined to pleasures]; "esa pasión propia del sexo que las hace precipitarse de su grado a los impulsos
del deseo, y ansiar que todo se pierda con tal que su anhelo se cumpla"
(1: 18) [that passion characteristic of the sex that makes them willingly
plunge into the promptings of desire, and to wish for the destruction of
everything provided that their desire be fulfilled]. It is significant that such
outbursts almost always occur at crucial political junctures, as can be seen
in the invective he hurls at the powerful Leonor de Pimentel after his ac-

count of the Portuguese invasion of Castile in 1476 (Tate, "Políticas" 169). According to the chronicler, the countess of Plasencia was accused at the time of unspecified "horrendos crímenes, y recordando la caída de nuestro primer padre, funesta para todo el género humano, decían que del mismo modo, por la maldad de aquella mujer, todo caminaría a completa ruina" (2: 194) [horrendous crimes, and remembering the fall of our first father, fatal for the entire human race, people said that in the same way, because of that woman's evil, everything would go to complete ruin].[38] But by far the woman most frequently compared to Eve in the *Crónica* is the wife of Enrique, the supposedly adulterous Juana de Portugal.[39]

In Palencia's narration of the matter of Juana's adultery there is a curious equivocation. On the one hand, he claims that the liaison between the queen and the king's favorite, Beltrán de la Cueva, putative father of Juana of Castile, was forced on Juana by the king: "[T]erminado el vano simulacro de sus bodas, empezó a descubrir sus propósitos para con la Reina, sometiéndola a una constante seducción. Así creyó lograría precipitarla a que buscase el placer en ilegítimas relaciones" (1: 82) [The false simulacrum of his wedding over, he began to disclose his goal to the queen, subjecting her to a constant seduction. In that manner he thought he would manage to rush her into seeking pleasure in illicit relations]. At the same time, he is vitriolic in censuring the queen's licentiousness, as in the famous description of her arrival in Castile to marry Enrique, accompanied by her equally loose ladies-in-waiting:

> Ninguna ocupación honesta las recomendaba. . . . Las continuas carcajadas en la conversación, el ir y venir constante de los medianeros, portadores de groseros billetes, y la ansiosa voracidad que día y noche las aquejaba, eran más frecuentes entre ellas que en los mismos burdeles . . . consumían la mayor parte en cubrirse el cuerpo con afeites y perfumes, y esto sin hacer de ello el menor secreto, antes descubrían el seno hasta más allá del estómago. (1: 75)

[They had no honest occupations to recommend them. Their continuous laughter, the constant comings and goings of the go-betweens, carriers of vulgar missives, and the anxious voraciousness that afflicted them day and night were more frequent among them than in the very brothels; they consumed most of the time in covering their bodies with cosmetics and perfumes, and they did this without the least secrecy, but rather they uncovered their breasts to below their bellies.]

Palencia's discursive construction of Juana's body is remarkably similar to the representation of queenship in many medieval French romances where "reproductive sexuality, through which the queen is empowered, is displaced by a transgressive sexuality, through which she loses status and influence at court" (McCracken 40).

Juana also functions as a springboard for Palencia's generalized misogyny: "los males que ordinariamente acarrean las pasiones de las mujeres, las cuales por lo común adoptan o sugieren los peores consejos" (1: 21) [the evils commonly caused by the passions of women, who generally adopt or suggest the worst advice]. For example, he charges that Juana "fomentó después la perfidia de los Grandes, para el cabo, como originaria de Portugal, propagar por este reino las llamas que habían de destruirle" (2: 194) [later fomented the perfidy of the grandees so as to finally, as a native of Portugal, spread throughout this kingdom the flames that were to destroy it], and then seamlessly conflates the sins of this specific woman with those of her entire gender: "mujeres habían sido siempre causa de la perdición de España" (2: 194) [women had always been the cause of Spain's ruin]. By blaming Juana for the Portuguese invasion of Castile, Palencia associates her in his readers' minds with that other ambiguously stigmatized woman, the daughter of Count Julian, who was also held responsible for a foreign, feminizing invasion. Both cataclysms are thereby represented as earthly repetitions of the expulsion from Paradise, and both women, as descendants of Eve. This genealogy of powerful sinful women, I would argue, ultimately serves to recuperate the geneaology of weak transgressive men (Pedro I–Juan II–Enrique IV) discussed above.

In view of Palencia's profound misogyny and his ambivalence toward his royal patron's power, it is not entirely surprising that his genealogy of sinful women should incorporate Isabel herself. When Palencia refers to her attempts to marginalize Fernando he complains that the queen, "al fin mujer" [a woman after all], is full of "arrogancia y prepotencia" (2: 165) [arrogance and haughtiness]; he castigates "la vanidad de la Reina . . . persuadida de que la postergación del marido redundaría en su propia gloria y poderío" (2: 168) [the vanity of the queen, persuaded that the subordination of her husband would redound in her own glory and might]; and he bitterly laments that she is in no way disposed to accept "las condiciones del gobierno que desde los más remotos siglos favorecían al varón" (2: 165) [the conditions of government that from the remotest centuries favored the male].

A brief comparison of Isabel's situation with that of her English namesake is useful at this point. Unlike Elizabeth I, who symbolically manipulated the fact of her virginity in order to maintain absolute authority by impressing upon her subjects the inviolability of her two bodies, the natural and the political, Isabel I of Castile did not have the option of remaining unmarried. To restore the integrity of Spain, damaged by the invasions of foreigners and by the sexual sins of its monarchs, she had to produce a legitimate heir, preferably male. Her great triumph in this regard must therefore be considered her successful evasion of what her modern biographer, Tarsicio de Azcona, calls "the traffic in blue blood" (106), that is, Enrique's repeated attempts to forge political alliances with foreign princes by offering them his sister's hand in marriage. There is no doubt that Isabel herself chose Fernando as consort, by means of a process that remains largely unexplained.[40] It is equally true that she considered him precisely that, a consort, instead of adopting the properly subordinate uxorial role on which her most intimate advisers like Fray Martín de Córdoba insisted.[41] In his *Jardín de nobles doncellas* [Garden of Noble Maidens], an advice treatise addressed to Princess Isabel shortly after Prince Alfonso's death in 1468, the cleric counsels the following: "Pues como dezimos que el rey es padre, por esta misma razón dezimos que la reina es madre" (88) [Since we say that the king is a father, for this same reason we say that the queen is a mother]. The maternal role of the queen consists of acting as *abogada* 'lawyer' and *escudo* 'shield'; her proper function, like the Virgin's, is to intercede on behalf of her subjects with the real power on the throne, the fearsome *juez* 'judge' and *espada* 'sword,' that is, the king (87–88).[42]

What we witness in Palencia's growing discomfort with the virile queen whose image he helped to create is his gradual, dismayed realization that it is in reality Isabel and not Fernando who rules supreme in Castile.[43] The gender role inversion that he, like Flores, observes in the royal couple becomes every bit as threatening as Enrique's sexual inversion. It represents the political instability that did not of course end with the ascension of Isabel to the throne, but continued to threaten the stability of the state and the career of its ambitious official historian.

This brings me to the broader cultural implications of Palencia's discourse of effeminacy, that is, the role of gender ideology in the rise of humanism in early modern Castile. Almost fifty years ago, José Maravall noted the important political and cultural role of the *letrados*. These men of letters with advanced degrees in canon or civil law began, in the reign of Isabel's father Juan II (r. 1406–54), to dominate the royal courts and advisory councils and to populate the growing bureaucracies of the court and the church, and later the Inquisition.[44] The growing class consciousness and pride that attended their social and political ascendancy was based not on lineage, but rather on their position as royal subjects with exclusive access to the civil, secular *ciencia* that the monarchs increasingly relied on for the administration of affairs of state (346–47). The *letrados'* assiduous cultivation of this working relationship can be seen in their frequent and hardly disinterested warning that the good monarch surrounds himself with and seeks counsel from *hombres de saber* 'learned men' while the tyrant distances and mistreats them (354). And for the many *conversos* among the *letrados*, starting with the extremely influential Alonso de Cartagena (1384–1456),[45] dependency on the monarchy held special significance since "within a Castilian society that was becoming increasingly anti-*converso*, [s]upporting the Castilian monarchy . . . usually meant supporting the only ally in power the *conversos* possessed" (Kaplan 56).

Jeremy Lawrance has more recently reaffirmed the role of the *letrados* as conduits for the introduction of Italian humanist attitudes, methods, and texts to Spain. Lawrance stresses the overtly political motive behind much of the humanist project in Castile that results from the close relationship between sovereign and humanists. The placement of their learning at the service of the regalist and centralist cause of the Trastámara dynasty produced in the *letrados* a narrow chauvinism, a decided anti-Italian bias, and a consistent subordination of humanistic philological concerns to nationalistic ones (253–54). The monarchy in turn encouraged the humanists' allegiance to the establishment by swelling the ranks of the *letrados* and increasing their financial support: the percentage of *letrados* doubled under Juan II and Enrique IV and tripled under the Catholic Monarchs (Tate, "Historiografía" 18).[46]

None of these excellent studies deals with the gender issues I have raised above in regard to Palencia, a *letrado* whose broad humanist interests produced not only the *Crónica de Enrique IV,* but also geographical and

antiquarian studies of Spain, Lucianic satires and allegories in Spanish
and Latin, vernacular translations of Plutarch and Josephus, and a Latin-
Spanish dictionary dedicated to Isabel (Lawrance 230). In order to find
such a treatment, we must turn to recent feminist scholarship on northern European humanist writers of a somewhat later period, in particular,
Barbara Correll's analysis of Erasmus's *Colloquia* (1496–1529) and *De civili-
tate morum pueriliem* (1530). Correll examines the Erasmian colloquies on
marriage and the education of boys for their role in the discursive structuring of feminine and masculine identity in the Renaissance. She identifies in
both texts

> a kind of psycho-political crisis of masculine identity and authority among
> members of a rising intellectual bourgeoisie who sought to negotiate posi-
> tions of authority in a power structure still largely determined by the heredi-
> tary nobility and the institution of the Church. . . . The conflict between the
> two groups' claims to power reveals sexual anxiety in that shifting notions
> of subordination and superiority call attention to women as designated sub-
> ordinates who — because of the ascribed and increasingly codified roles they
> reflect — *might* threaten the uneasy dynamics of power. (241) [47]

In Erasmus's treatises, the discursively constructed Woman functions as
an essential negative that can be overcome by civilizing labors and education (246). Thus, for example, Correll links Erasmus's advice to married
women to accommodate to the demands of the elementary sociopolitical
unit that is marriage by cultivating subordination (that is, getting their husbands to stop abusing them by using behavior modification techniques) to
his own personal situation as a humanist seeking to placate church authorities critical of his teachings. The implication is that when used by the male
administrative underling or the court intellectual, the strategy of cultivating subordination that Erasmus advocates for the married woman will be
rewarded with social mobility and professional patronage. But, as Correll
notes, the scheme of tutoring and nurturing one's superiors "retains connections to notions of feminine decorum and duty, and discloses the uneasy
presence of the socially constructed feminine, threatening to erupt from its
place within the new cultural manhood" (257).

Also applicable to the construction of gender in humanism is Patricia
Parker's work on the anxieties of effeminacy which attended any man
whose province was the art of words. Loquacity, she recalls, was gender-

coded as a feminine excess in the Renaissance and as such was a central concern of the abundant conduct literature addressed to women. In her analysis of Erasmus's *Lingua, sive de linguae usu ac abusu* (1525), Parker finds that the author decries the spread of the feminine "disease of the tongue" to men, a contamination of the *brevitas* associated with the manly style by the *copia* of feminine speech. The anxious recognition of the infection of male rhetoric by female excess, that is, the fear of effeminacy, shadows the whole enterprise of the humanists, men who deal professionally in words, not weapons. In Erasmus's *Lingua,* furthermore, the gender coding of language and literary endeavor is extended to national types, leading to the "opposition of effeminizing East and more virile Rome" ("On the Tongue" 448), an opposition that we have seen is central to the historiographic texts of Castile.

A sexual anxiety was elicited by the shifting relations of power between the aristocracy and the humanists, and by the latter's "cross-gendered" dependence on the art of words for their new curial status: this phenomenom is clearly applicable to Palencia and his fellow chroniclers.[48] In the Castilian case, the sexual anxiety of the humanists is further complicated by issues of class and ethnicity, as suggested in the following description by Fernando del Pulgar, a *converso* like his rival Palencia: "Vemos por experiencia algunos omnes destos que iudgamos de baxa sangre forçarles su natural inclinación a dexar los oficios baxos de los padres, e aprender ciencia e ser grandes letrados" (*Letras* 71) [We know by experience that some men whom we judge to be of low birth are forced by natural inclination to abandon the lowly occupations of their fathers and learn sciences and become eminent men of letters].

Whether they project the threat of effeminacy as Enrique, discursively constructed as "Woman" in his homosexuality, effeminacy, weakness, lack of control, and passivity, or as Isabel, constructed as "Man" in her usurpation of male power and display of unwomanly traits, the Isabelline chroniclers urgently concern themselves with the fashioning of secular masculine identity, a process in which "woman has an essential function, projected as the horror of effeminacy which must be contained" (Correll 258). The chronicles of Palencia, Pulgar, Valera, and Flores, to cite only the ones I have dealt with herein, deserve further study as important documents of the gender ideology that informed Isabel's construction of Spanish nationhood. The abiding influence of that ideology can be seen in the tellingly redundant epithets in the title of Luis Suárez Fernández's 1992 biography:

Isabel, mujer y reina [Isabel, woman and queen]. Five hundred years after the sovereign of Europe's first modern nation-state sent Columbus on his way, her gender still troubles.[49]

Notes

1. The struggle can be said to have lasted from 1462, the year of Juana's birth, to 1479, when Isabel and her husband Fernando II, recently crowned king of Aragon, united the kingdoms of Castile and Aragon to form a single powerful political entity.

2. *Crónica de Enrique IV* is the title Antonio Paz y Melia gave to his 1904–07 translation of the original Latin, *Gestarum Hispaniensium decades* [Decades of the Deeds of Hispania], commonly known as *Décadas* for its Livy-inspired temporal organization. Although Palencia's chronicle centers on the reign of Enrique IV, it treats events occurring between 1440 and 1477, in many of which the author personally intervened. Subsequent references to the *Crónica* are to the more accessible 1973–75 three-volume edition in Biblioteca de Autores Españoles and appear parenthetically in the text as volume and page number; references to the Spanish translation of the fourth "Decade" by José López de Toro are indicated by page number. All English translations of this and other works quoted in this essay are my own. The original *Décadas* has never been published in its entirety; José López de Toro edited the fourth *Decade* alone in 1970. Jeremy Lawrance and R. Brian Tate are currently working on a much-needed edition of the complete Latin work. On Palencia's life, see Paz y Melia (*Cronista*) and Tate ("Biography").

3. The Trastamaran dynasty, an illegitimate branch of the Burgundian house that ruled Castile since the twelfth century, held the Castilian throne from 1369, when Enrique II came to power by murdering his brother Pedro, through 1504, the year of Isabel of Castile's death. The term "Isabelline" refers to the thirty years (1474–1504) that Isabel reigned as sovereign, first of Castile alone (1474–79) and subsequently of Castile and Aragon jointly, with Fernando II.

4. The term *letrado* is used by Hispanists to refer in particular to humanist scholars and writers of the latter part of the fifteenth century in Castile, most of them holding advanced degrees in canon or civil law. They increasingly displaced the *caballeros* or noblemen as members of royal courts and advisory councils, partly because of the perception that their loyalty would not be divided between king and kin. In calling the *letrados* humanists, I am conscious of the elements that set Iberia's "Renaissance" and "humanism" apart from the traditional conceptualization of these terms, closely linked to the particular political situation of

northern Italian city-states in the fifteenth century. As Nader states, "Agrarian, monarchical, rural Castile *did* produce a Renaissance. . . . Renaissance historians have ignored this" (16).

5. See in particular the studies of Greenblatt, Montrose, and Quilligan, which analyze the unsettling force that Elizabeth I had, as monarch and as woman, on male subjects like Sydney, Spenser, and Shakespeare; the various ways that she consciously exploited the anxiety she provoked; and the dramatization and containment of such anxiety in works such as *Faerie Queene* and *A Midsummer Night's Dream.*

6. I deal with the important difference between the married Isabel and the virgin Elizabeth below.

7. I have adapted the phrase "discourse of effeminacy" from the similar "anxieties of effeminacy" that Parker ("Gender Ideology") has found to pervade male-authored works in sixteenth-century France.

8. See Boswell for a general overview of the attitude toward and treatment of homosexuals in medieval Europe.

9. It is noteworthy that there were significant differences in the ways that sodomites were prosecuted by the Inquisition and the civil authorities, even in the same city, as Perry discusses.

10. In his *Crónica de los Reyes Católicos,* roughly contemporaneous with Palencia's chronicle, Fernando del Pulgar blames Enrique's homosexuality on his being introduced at the age of fourteen to "unseemly pleasures" that he was unable to resist because of his inexperience and which became a habit of depravity (235). In the biographical collection, *Claros varones de Castilla* [Illustrious Men of Castile] (*terminus post quem* 1483), he reiterates the point, writing that in his youth "he gave himself over to certain pleasures that adolescence normally demands and that propriety should refuse" (5).

11. See, for example, the analyses of Fernando de Rojas's *Celestina* (first published in 1499) by Paul Julian Smith and Gossy.

12. Unfortunately, most modern Spanish scholarship on the reign of Enrique still embraces this kind of sodomitical slippage, especially toward xenophobia. In Menéndez y Pelayo's classic study *Antología de poetas líricos castellanos,* for example, the eminent scholar laments "the royal nuptial bed, stained with scandalous lewdness . . . and custom infected with the secret and enervating contagion of Oriental vices" (6: 2–3). Cf. the totalizing statement of Palencia's modern editor, Paz y Melia: "These despicable habits, which are everpresent, have periods of recrudescence, like the fifteenth century, owing to relations with the Moors, which required the Edict of the Catholic Queen establishing the terrible punishment of burning at the stake; the seventeenth century, due to Italian influences; and our own time, because of cynical and foreign doctrines" (lviii–liv).

13. Of course, as Paul Julian Smith reminds us, following Américo Castro, the exclusionary ideology that supports the Catholic Monarchs' project of nation-building, a project in which such texts as Palencia's participate, is deeply vexed since "Spanish faith in *casticismo* is counterbalanced by an awareness of a lack of clear divisions between the three communities [Christian, Moorish, Jewish] even as late as 1500, and of their history as one of relational development" (47).

14. The English translation of "puto judío" cannot fully convey the pejorative sense of this masculinization of "puta," which figures the Jewish male subject both as a whore and as the passive partner in the homosexual act.

15. It should be noted that wearing Moorish garb was considered fashionable as far back as the thirteenth century. See Bernis for the practice in Palencia's time.

16. References to Enrique's preference for Arab military tactics recur throughout the *Crónica*. I am grateful to Jeremy Lawrance for reminding me of their deeply pejorative nature.

17. See Solomon in this same anthology for a discussion of the discursive linking of sodomy to contagion.

18. Marañón's 1934 analysis of Enrique's reputed impotence and homosexuality is noteworthy for its purported scientific framework. While ostensibly criticizing Palencia, Marañón relies on his text and a variety of homophobic "facts" to diagnose Enrique's problem as a case of "displasic eunochoid acromegaly" (78) that rendered him "incompletely impotent" (60). See Eisenberg for a critique of Marañón's unreflective acceptance of Palencia's homophobic representation of the king.

19. An example of the former, according to Julio Puyol, is Pulgar's *Crónica de los Reyes Católicos*, commissioned by Isabel in 1482 specifically to justify her assumption of the throne. A similar case is Enríquez del Castillo's *Crónica del rey don Enrique el Cuarto*, which he rewrote to be more flattering to the Catholic Monarchs after the original manuscript was destroyed following his arrest by her supporters. See also Avenoza's study of a recently discovered manuscript in the library of the University of Santiago de Compostela containing, among other texts, another version of Castillo's chronicle in which the description of Enrique is much more degrading than in the more widely known version. For examples of the falsification of documents under Isabel (including the famous Pact of Toros de Guisando), see Vicens Vives (209–43, 282–87).

20. For example, as he begins his record of the reign of the Catholic Monarchs, Palencia uses the light imagery that is a common stylistic feature of Isabelline messianism: "For this reason I commence the narration of admirable events with the gladness of one who, after sharp pains, achieves a deserved well-being; like he who . . . trembling with joy sees once again the light that, lost to darkness, re-

mained for a long time in gloom" (2: 159). On fifteenth-century messianism and the *conversos,* see Castro (*Aspectos*) and Cepeda Adán.

21. Archbishop Rodrigo Jiménez de Rada in his thirteenth-century *De rebus Hispaniae* traced the ancestry even further back, claiming that the Iberians were themselves descended from Tubal, grandson of Noah. The lineage was often re-iterated by later historians (Castro, *Realidad* 3–4).

22. The restoration was deemed realized by Nebrija ("Hispania tota sibi resti-tuta est") with the fall of Granada, the last Muslim kingdom in Spain (qtd. in Tate, *Ensayos* 296).

23. In reality, as O'Callaghan notes: "The circumstances that led to the Muslim invasion of the peninsula . . . are involved in extraordinary confusion. In later accounts of the conquest it is not always possible to separate truth from legend" (51–52).

24. In one of the most famous ballads of the cycle about Rodrigo, "En Ceuta está don Julián," the poet laments "que por sola una doncella / la cual Cava se llamaba / causen estos dos traidores / que España sea domeñada / y perdido el rey señor" (Colin Smith 52) [because of a single maiden who was called la Cava these two traitors (the other being Bishop Oppas) cause Spain to be conquered and the king our lord lost].

25. For English uses of such corporeal symbolism, see Stallybrass and White and the essays in Burt and Archer.

26. Kantorowicz and Axton discuss this medieval political theory.

27. This violent curse, borrowed for the title of my essay, is recorded in Diego de Valera's chronicle, *Memorial de diversas haʒañas* (33). I am indebted to David Weissberger for the English translation.

28. It most likely belongs to the oral tradition; Tate notes that the anecdote is not found in any other written source (*Ensayos* 89). Leonardo Funes has kindly pointed out to me the ambiguity of Tate's wording in his discussion of this sod-omitical couple: the "him" in question may be either the French ally of Enrique de Trastámara or the buffoon himself. I have been unable to consult Arévalo's chronicle in order to clarify the target of the slander.

29. Palencia's sodomitical genealogy forms part of a generalized "cult of geneal-ogy" that permeates fourteenth- and fifteenth-century Castilian culture. Tate notes that the cult's "insistence on the Visigothic inheritance is nothing more than a facet of the political struggle between the monarchy and the nobility" (*Ensayos* 121).

30. On the discourse of sodomy as deployed by other chroniclers of the reign of Juan II, see Hutcheson in this volume.

31. Jonathan Goldberg reminds us that in textual representations of Elizabeth I

of England, there is frequent slippage from *vir* to *virago* to *virtus* (*Sodometries* 40 n14).

32. It is, for example, a common feature of courtly lyric, as in the poem by Cartagena, where the queen as courtly goddess inspires both love and fear, i.e., is represented as simultaneously maternal and paternal (qtd. in Jones 57).

33. See Gwara and Parrilla for the able detective work.

34. This complaint could easily have been uttered by another of Flores's characters, Grimalte, the long-suffering courtly lover of the similarly ungrateful and overbearing Gradissa in his sentimental romance *Grimalte y Gradissa*. The connection between hapless courtly lover and humiliated royal consort is not fortuitous; the romance, written toward 1495, most certainly circulated at court.

35. Marcus and Jordan are useful starting points.

36. It should be noted that the cause-and-effect relationship of the gender hierarchy inversion that Palencia reproves is never totally clear. See Mirrer on the same blurring in the contemporary ballads, which, in their frequent portrayal of strong women, suggest that female power and its destabilizing consequences are due to men's inability to control them.

37. It was at this time that the Royal Council, the mainspring of Fernando and Isabel's government, was reorganized to subordinate the magnates in favor of the petty nobility and the *letrados*, who could be expected to support royal authority more fully.

38. Surtz discusses in detail the political accomplishments of this strong aristocratic woman and an interesting containment strategy adopted by her confessor.

39. See McCracken for a discussion of the way that the medieval king's political authority at court was shown in romance to be compromised by "his (un)knowing complicity in the adulterous relationship between his wife and her lover" (43). In the case of Enrique the complicity is represented as not only knowing but instrumental.

40. See Azcona (106–07) for a lucid discussion of Isabel's evasions of the European exchange of royal women.

41. At their wedding in 1469, Fernando took an oath to obey the laws and customs of Castile. Her 1474 self-proclamation as queen marginalized Fernando, clearly assigning him the role of royal consort, a treatment that Fernando strongly resented (Azcona 213). Palencia narrates these power struggles in great detail and has the king protest the insult to his masculinity and the rumors of the people who "atribuía a bajeza aquel abandono de su cualidad de varón con la que borraba . . . hasta la ley de naturaleza y renunciaba a un derecho tan divino como humano" (1: 167) [attributed to baseness that disregard for his manliness which erased even natural law and renounced a right no less divine than human]. There was in fact a

considerable segment of the Castilian population that had always defended male succession over female and therefore thought of Fernando as their true monarch.

42. We recall the symbolic sword that Córdoba's addressee was to flaunt at her coronation a few years later. In my "*Jardín*" I discuss in some detail the gender ideology of Fray Martín's treatise.

43. Gómez Manrique's poem "Regimiento de príncipes" betrays a similar preoccupation with the Catholic Monarch's gender role inversion when he warns Fernando against the danger of kings listening to the advice of women, citing the example of Sardanapalus, "effeminate prince" (171).

44. Tate notes Palencia's awareness of his status as a servant of the Crown: "Palencia writes from the chancery as a *letrado* and with the consciousness of a *letrado*, insisting repeatedly on the need for a readjustment of seignorial relations with the crown" ("Preceptos" 47–48).

45. See Di Camillo for an excellent study of Cartagena, whom he calls "the first Spanish humanist" (16).

46. In her 1979 study of the noble Mendoza family, whose members included many of the most important writers of the late-fifteenth and early-sixteenth centuries in Spain, Nader goes so far as to contend that the *letrados*, with their theory of monarchy placing the king at the apex of a divinely ordained and immutable hierarchy of institutions administered by anonymous bureaucrats, actually "rejected the most basic religious and historiographical assumptions of the humanists" (132). I am indebted to the anonymous reader of my manuscript for drawing my attention to this.

47. See Kelly's classic formulation of women's loss of power during the Renaissance (19–50).

48. Juan de Lucena, a member of Isabel's court and author of *Epístola exhortatoria a las letras* [Epistle Exhorting to Letters] and several other humanist works, pointed to an "afán de discusión" [argumentative zeal] as one of the distinguishing traits of his circle of scholars (qtd. in Maravall 358).

49. I am grateful to Ron Surtz, most incisive and gentle of critics, for his comments on an earlier draft of this essay. Any remaining shortcomings are entirely my own.

Works Cited

Avenoza, Gemma. "Un nuevo manuscrito de las *Generaciones y semblanzas:* la *Crónica de Enrique IV* y la propaganda isabelina." *Anuario medieval* 3 (1991): 7–22.

Axton, Marie. *The Queen's Two Bodies: Drama and the Elizabethan Succession.* London: Royal Historical Society, 1977.

Azcona, Tarsicio de. *Isabel la Católica: estudio crítico de su vida y su reinado.* Madrid: Biblioteca de Autores Cristianos, 1964.

Benassar, Bartolomé. "El modelo sexual: la Inquisición de Aragón y la represión de los pecados 'abominables.'" *Inquisición española: poder político y control social.* Ed. Bartolomé Benassar. Barcelona: Grijalbo, 1981.

Bernis, Carmen. "Modas moriscas en la sociedad critiana española del siglo XV y principios del siglo XVI." *Boletín de la Real Academia de la Historia* 144 (1959): 198–210.

Boswell, John. *Christianity, Social Tolerance, and Homosexuality: Gay People in Western Europe from the Beginning of the Christian Era to the Fourteenth Century.* Chicago: U of Chicago P, 1980.

Bray, Alan. *Homosexuality in Renaissance England.* London: Gay Men's P, 1982.

Bredbeck, Gregory. *Sodomy and Interpretation: Marlowe to Milton.* Ithaca: Cornell UP, 1980.

Burt, Richard, and John Michael Archer, eds. *Enclosure Acts: Sexuality, Property, and Culture in Early Modern England.* Ithaca: Cornell UP, 1994.

Carrasco, Rafael. *Inquisición y represión sexual en Valencia: historia de los sodomitas (1565–1785).* Barcelona: Laertes, 1985.

Castro, Américo. *Aspectos del vivir hispánico.* Madrid: Alianza, 1970.

———. *La realidad histórica de España.* Rev. ed. Mexico: Porrúa, 1966.

Cepeda Adán, José. "El providencialismo en los cronistas de los Reyes Católicos." *Arbor* 17 (1950): 177–90.

Córdoba, Martín de. *Jardín de nobles donzellas.* Ed. Harriet Goldberg. North Carolina Studies in the Romance Languages and Literatures 137. Chapel Hill: U of North Carolina P, 1974.

Correll, Barbara. "Malleable Material, Models of Power: Woman in Erasmus's 'Marriage Group' and *Civility in Boys.*" *English Literary History* 57 (1990): 241–62.

Di Camillo, Ottavio. *El humanismo castellano del siglo XV.* Valencia: Fernando Torres, 1976.

Eisenberg, Daniel. "Enrique IV and Gregorio Marañón." *Renaissance Quarterly* 29 (1976): 21–29.

Ferrara, Orestes. *Un pleito sucesorio: Enrique IV, Ysabel de Castilla y la Beltraneja.* Madrid: "La Nave," 1945.

Firpo, Arturo. "Los reyes sexuales: ensayo sobre el discurso sexual durante el reinado de Enrique de Trastámara (1454–1474)." *Mélanges de la Casa de Velázquez* 20 (1984): 212–27; 21 (1985): 145–58.

Flores, Juan de. *Crónica incompleta de los Reyes Católicos.* Ed. Julio Puyol. Madrid: Academia de la historia, 1934.

Foucault, Michel. *The History of Sexuality.* Vol. 1: *An Introduction.* Trans. Robert Hurley. 1978. New York: Vintage, 1990.

Goldberg, Jonathan, ed. *Queering the Renaissance.* Durham, N.C.: Duke UP, 1994.

————. *Sodometries: Renaissance Texts, Modern Sexualities.* Stanford: Stanford UP, 1992.

Gossy, Mary S. *The Untold Story: Women and Theory in Golden Age Texts.* Ann Arbor: U of Michigan P, 1989.

Greenblatt, Stephen. *The Power of Forms in the English Renaissance.* Norman, Okla.: Pilgrim Books, 1982.

————. *Renaissance Self-Fashioning from More to Shakespeare.* Chicago: U of Chicago P, 1980.

Gwara, Joseph. "The Identity of Juan de Flores: The Evidence of the *Crónica incompleta de los Reyes Católicos.*" *Journal of Hispanic Philology* 11.2 (1987): 103–29; 11.3 (1987): 205–22.

Jones, Roy. "Isabel la Católica y el amor cortés." *Revista de literatura* 21 (1962): 55–64.

Jordan, Constance. *Renaissance Feminism: Literary Texts and Political Models.* Ithaca: Cornell UP, 1990.

————. "Women's Rule in 16th-Century British Political Thought." *Renaissance Quarterly* 40 (1987): 421–25.

Kantorowicz, Ernst. *The King's Two Bodies: A Study in Medieval Theology.* Princeton: Princeton UP, 1957.

Kaplan, Gregory B. "Toward the Establishment of a Christian Identity: The *Conversos* and Early Castilian Humanism." *La corónica* 25.1 (1996): 53–68.

Kelly, Joan. *Women, History, and Theory.* Chicago: U of Chicago P, 1984.

Lawrance, Jeremy N. H. "Humanism in the Iberian Peninsula." *The Impact of Humanism on Western Europe.* Ed. Anthony Goodman and Angus MacKay. London: Longman, 1990. 220–58.

Liss, Peggy. *Isabel the Queen: Life and Times.* New York: Oxford UP, 1992.

López de Toro, José. See Palencia.

MacKay, Angus. "Ritual and Propaganda in Fifteenth-Century Castile." *Past and Present* 107 (1985): 3–45.

McCracken, Peggy. "The Body Politic and the Queen's Adulterous Body in French Romance." *Feminist Approaches to the Body in Medieval Literature.* Ed. Linda Lomperis and Sarah Stanbury. Philadelphia: U of Pennsylvania P, 1994. 38–64.

Manrique, Gómez. *Cancionero de Gómez Manrique.* Ed. Antonio Paz y Melia. 2 vols. Madrid: Imprenta A. Pérez Dubrill, 1885.

Marañón, Gregorio. *Ensayo biológico sobre Enrique IV de Castilla y su tiempo.* 10th ed. Madrid: Espasa-Calpe, 1964.

Maravall, José. "Los 'hombres de saber' o letrados y la formación de su conciencia estamental." *Estudios de historia del pensamiento español.* 3rd ed. Vol. 1. Madrid: Ediciones Cultura Hispánica, 1983. 333–62.

Marcus, Leah. *Puzzling Shakespeare: Local Reading and Its Discontents.* Berkeley: U of California P, 1988.

Menéndez y Pelayo, Marcelino. *Antología de poetas líricos castellanos.* 10 vols. Madrid: Consejo Superior de Investigaciones Científicas, 1944–45.

Mirrer, Louise. *Women, Jews, and Muslims in the Texts of Reconquest Spain.* Ann Arbor: U of Michigan P, 1996.

Montrose, Louis Adrian. "Celebration and Insinuation: Sir Philip Sidney and the Motives of Elizabethan Courtship." *Renaissance Drama.* New Series 8 (1977): 3–35.

———. "The Elizabethan Subject and the Spenserian Text." *Literary Theory / Renaissance Texts.* Ed. Patricia Parker and David Quint. Baltimore: Johns Hopkins UP, 1986. 303–40.

———. " 'Shaping Fantasies': Figurations of Gender and Power in Elizabethan Culture." *Representations* 1 (1983): 61–94.

Nader, Helen. *The Mendoza Family in the Spanish Renaissance: 1350–1550.* New Brunswick: Rutgers UP, 1979.

O'Callaghan, Joseph F. *A History of Medieval Spain.* Ithaca: Cornell UP, 1975.

Palencia, Alfonso de. *Crónica de Enrique IV.* Trans. A. Paz y Melia. 3 vols. Biblioteca de Autores Españoles 257, 258, 267. Madrid: Atlas, 1973–75.

———. *Cuarta Década de Alonso de Palencia.* Ed. and trans. José López de Toro. 2 vols. Archivo Documental Español 24, 25. Madrid: Real Academia de la Historia, 1970–74.

Parker, Patricia. "Gender Ideology, Gender Change: The Case of Marie Germain." *Critical Inquiry* 19 (1993): 337–64.

———. "On the Tongue: Cross Gendering, Effeminacy, and the Art of Words." *Style* 23 (1989): 445–65.

Parrilla, Carmen. "Un cronista olvidado: Juan de Flores, autor de la *Crónica incompleta de los Reyes Católicos.*" *The Age of the Catholic Monarchs: 1474–1516. Literary Studies in Memory of Keith Whinnom.* Ed. Alan Deyermond and Ian Macpherson. Special Issue of *Bulletin of Hispanic Studies.* Liverpool: Liverpool UP, 1989. 123–33.

Paz y Melia, Antonio. *El cronista Alonso de Palencia: su vida y sus obras.* Madrid: Hispanic Society of America, 1914.

Perry, Mary Elizabeth. *Gender and Disorder in Early Modern Seville*. Princeton: Princeton UP, 1990.

Phillips, William D. *Enrique IV and the Crisis of Fifteenth-Century Castile (1425–1480)*. Cambridge, Mass.: Medieval Academy of America, 1978.

Pulgar, Fernando del. *Claros varones de Castilla*. Ed. Robert Brian Tate. Oxford: Clarendon, 1971.

———. *Crónica de los Reyes Católicos*. *Crónica de los reyes de Castilla*. Ed. Cayetano Rosell. Vol. 1. Biblioteca de Autores Españoles 70. Madrid: Atlas, 1953. 223–511.

———. *Letras, Glosa a las "Coplas de Mingo Revulgo"*. Ed. J. Domínguez Bordona. Clásicos Castellanos. Madrid: Espasa-Calpe, 1949.

Puyol Alonso, Julio. "Los cronistas de Enrique IV." *Boletín de la Real Academia de la Historia* 78 (1921): 399–415; 79 (1921): 11–28, 118–44.

Quilligan, Maureen. *Milton's Spenser: The Politics of Reading*. Ithaca: Cornell UP, 1983.

Sedgwick, Eve Kosofsky. *Between Men: English Literature and Male Homosexual Desire*. New York: Columbia UP, 1985.

Sitges, J. B. *Enrique IV y la excelente señora llamada vulgarmente Doña Juana la Beltraneja*. Madrid: n.p., 1912.

Smith, Colin. *Spanish Ballads*. Oxford: Pergamon P, 1964.

Smith, Paul Julian. *Representing the Other: 'Race,' Text, and Gender in Spanish and Spanish-American Narrative*. Oxford: Clarendon, 1992.

Stallybrass, Peter, and Allon White. *The Politics and Poetics of Transgression*. Ithaca: Cornell UP, 1986.

Suárez Fernández, Luis. *Isabel, mujer y reina*. Madrid: Ediciones Rialp, 1992.

Surtz, Ronald E. "Fray Juan López en travestí: sus *Historias que comprenden toda la vida de Nuestra Señora*." V Jornadas Internacionales de Literatura Española Medieval. Universidad Católica de Argentina, Buenos Aires. 23 Aug. 1996.

Tate, Robert Brian. "Alfonso de Palencia: An Interim Biography." *Letters and Society in 15th-Century Spain: Studies Presented to P. E. Russell on his Eightieth Birthday*. Llangrannog, Wales: Dolphin Book Co., 1993. 175–91.

———. "Alfonso de Palencia y los preceptos de la historiografía." *Nebrija y la introducción del renacimiento en España*. Actas de la III Academia Literaria Renacentista. Ed. Victor García de la Concha. Salamanca: Ediciones Universidad de Salamanca, 1981. 37–51.

———. "Las Décadas de Alfonso de Palencia: un análisis historiográfico." *Estudios dedicados a James Leslie Brooks*. Ed. J. M. Ruiz Veintemille. Barcelona: Puvill, 1984. 223–41.

———. *Ensayos sobre la historiografía peninsular del siglo XV*. Trans. Jesús Díaz. Madrid: Gredos, 1970.

————. "La historiografía del reinado de los Reyes Católicos." *Antonio de Nebrija: Edad Media y Renacimiento.* Ed. Carmen Codoñer and Juan Antonio González Iglesias. Salamanca: Ediciones Universidad de Salamanca, 1994. 17–28.

————. "Políticas sexuales: de Enrique el Impotente a Isabel, maestra de engaños (magistra dissimulationum)." *Actas del primer congreso anglo-hispano.* Vol. 3 *Historia.* Ed. R. Hitchcock and Ralph Penny. Madrid: Castalia, 1994. 165–75.

Valera, Diego de. *Memorial de diversas hazañas.* Ed. Cayetano Rosell. Biblioteca de Autores Españoles 70. Madrid: Atlas, 1953.

Vicens Vives, Jaime. *Historia crítica de Fernando II de Aragón.* Zaragoza: Diputación Provincial, 1962.

Weissberger, Barbara. "*Jardín de nobles donzellas* y la formación de Isabel I." V Jornadas Internacionales de Literatura Medieval Española. Universidad Católica de Argentina. 23 Aug. 1996.

Linde M. Brocato

"Tened por espejo su fin"

Mapping Gender and Sex in Fifteenth-

and Sixteenth-Century Spain

The panorama of fifteenth-century Spain is as complicated as that of the late-fourteenth century, when Don Enrique de Trastámara won a civil war to depose the legitimate heir, his half-brother Pedro I, known as "el Cruel," and so became Enrique II of Castile (r. 1369–79). Indeed, just as the fourteenth century closes with rabidly anti-Semitic preaching and the outbreak in 1391 of pogroms that swept from Sevilla to Valencia in a matter of months, so too does the fifteenth with inquisition and the expulsion of those Jews who had resisted conversion throughout the century's difficulties. The Trastámara epoch, ruled by Enrique II's successors, is the crucial period of the construction of an orthodox Spanish and Catholic identity purified of its others — ethnic (Jews and Moors), religious (heretics, *conversos,* and non-Christians), and sexual (those who deviate from an orthodox late-medieval Catholic sexual morality) — categories often conflated in the discourses of the period, as several of the essays in this volume show.

Although the beginnings of this identity construction are clear in the policies of Juan I, successor to Enrique II, the imposition of orthodoxy by the Catholic Monarchs, Isabel and Fernando, is better known, since it culminated in the institutionalized control of dissent via the Inquisition (established in 1478), the expulsion of Jews (1492), and the forced conversion of Muslims to Christianity (1502). Nonetheless, questions of national identity preoccupy the fifteenth century, taking form in lengthy reflections on gender and identity and even lengthier reflections on social order. These themes are often intertwined, in fact, and embody and textualize debates about the relationship of gender and sex to social order that surface throughout the period, whether in the pro- and antifeminist stands on "the woman question"; in the moralizing looks at history and biography; or in the political satire that circulated in collections of poetry (*cancioneros*).[1] That is, these pervasive debates use bodies to work out a vision of the past, present, and future that maps gender and sex onto social and often geographical space as a means of locating lines of force, whether for order or for chaos.

Not surprisingly, both in and outside of Spain these discussions often took a biographical form that made use of galleries of positive and negative examples. Classical authors such as Titus Livius, Plutarch, and Valerius Maximus furnished the model for Giovanni Boccaccio, who wrote his *De casibus virorum illustrium* [The Fates of Illustrious Men] between 1350 and 1360, and for the Castilian Fernán Pérez de Guzmán, who finished his *Generaciones y semblanzas* [Families and Portraits] sometime after 1454. Boccaccio also uses the form for the debate on women and love in his *De claris mulieribus* [Concerning Famous Women] (1361); so too Alvaro de Luna in his *De las claras y virtuosas mugeres* [Concerning Famous and Virtuous Women] almost a century later.[2] This tendency to the particular makes social and political conflict concrete through the bodies of both monarchs and subjects, which become metaphors in the effort to think collectively through social issues. Thus, to speak of the body politic accurately reflects this kind of concrete thinking about issues that are both abstract in their workings and quite material in their consequences, for the metaphorical bodies in question also become the very real bodies of individuals as social vision is realized. Since the political *body* is inscribed in the cultural production of the late-fifteenth century as the basis of morality as both public and private, the discussion requires broadening to more fully include the body as gendered and sexual, an analytical move that sheds light on a crucial moment in Castilian letters and culture, and perhaps on our own time.

Fifteenth-century writers tend to see a strong correlation between *eros* and the *polis*, and it is their view of the fifteenth century that has predominated. For example, Pérez de Guzmán's gallery of historical figures is in part organized around details of gender and sexual behavior. Our lay view of the fifteenth century basically follows the pattern he establishes: a morally bankrupt society, in which a sexually chaotic and self-interested nobility is in conflict with weak and sexually problematic monarchs (Juan II [r. 1406–54] and Enrique IV [r. 1454–74]), is finally controlled via the imposition of religious orthodoxy, an orthodox Catholic moral code, and a strong central government in the hands of the perfect couple, Fernando and Isabel, the Catholic Monarchs (r. 1474–1506).[3]

Another side of the social critique in fifteenth-century literature is embodied in the obscenely satirical poetry of protest savaging nobles and clergy alike for their decadence, a poetry rife with patent disgust for political elites that is often expressed through sexual and ethnic slurs.[4] Juan II's alleged incapacity as king and his abdication of government almost entirely into the hands of his favorite, Alvaro de Luna, whom he named Constable of Castile, prompted not only outrage on the part of some of the noble houses, but also rumors that the source of Luna's power over the king lay either in witchcraft or in a relationship of a homosexual nature.[5] Such authors as Fernán Pérez de Guzmán (1378?-1460?) and Iñigo López de Mendoza, the marquis of Santillana (1398–1458), both members of the powerful Mendoza family opposed to the upstart bastard Luna, wrote bitter denunciations of the greed, rapacity, and sexual immorality of their contemporaries, especially attacking Luna.[6]

This elaboration of moral and social vision and cultural identity around sex is, I would argue, the central problematic in three generically very different yet tightly related works of the period. Juan de Mena's *Laberinto de Fortuna* (1444) is thoroughly foundational in its parsing of sociopolitical reality (although it is not usually read in quite this way) and serves as a model for Fernando de Rojas's *Celestina* (1499 onward), which attempts to work out the same problematic.[7] Yet the imposition of morality is, much as in our own time, a political and not simply a moral endeavor. Although explicit dissent largely disappears during the "moral" reign of the Catholic Monarchs (cf. Varo 88n86, citing Rodríguez Puértolas), it remains spectacularly and resolutely present in the political satire of the anti- as well as noncanonical *Carajicomedia*, published anonymously in 1519.[8]

All three works textualize the debate in similar ways, for which reason they can be seen to be not only complicitous in their reflections on the sorry state of affairs in Castile, but coherent in locating the problem along the coordinates of gender and sex. Neither do they differ much in their suggested cure for the chaos that ensues from uncontrolled desire and unsettled masculinity: the authoritarian imposition of masculine dominance (of various kinds) to produce order. *Carajicomedia* in its misogyny may well agree with *Laberinto* and *Celestina* on women and sex as a problem; but because of this, it works to deflate any righteous solution imposed from above in the context of Isabelline Spain. This contrasts with *Laberinto* and *Celestina*, which see the imposition of moral virtue as the basis of social order.

Indeed, as we read these texts sequentially through their articulations of gender, sex, and social order, we will find not only more and more explicit representations of a wide variety of sexual possibilities, but also a progressively more virulent parsing of the deleterious effects of undisciplined sex (women) on masculinity. Yet part of what makes these representations so graphic is not only the mapping of certain kinds of sex/uality[9] (corrupt, destructive, and chaotic) onto certain kinds of bodies (female, ethnic, non-Christian), but the textual violence that is turned on those bodies — a violence that resonates clearly with the physical and political violence turned on real bodies in Spain and elsewhere, then and now.

Mena's Moral Labyrinth

Juan de Mena (1411–56) is among the best known and most influential of the fifteenth-century poets, as can be seen in the frequent reprinting of his most famous work, *Laberinto de Fortuna* [Labyrinth of Fortune].[10] Mena trained at Córdoba and Salamanca, served the pontifical court in Florence, and was Latin secretary to Juan II (Cummins 13); he never openly opposed the monarch or the royal favorite, and so remained a much admired court poet (as opposed to Pérez de Guzmán, who ended up in virtual exile). His *Laberinto de Fortuna*, finished in 1444 and presented to the king (at the time under house arrest by his royal cousins, the Infantes of Aragon), is an allegorical poem that takes stock of the political and moral state of Castile. Mena does this via an ekphrastic reading of the House of Fortune, rescuing Spain's heroic past from oblivion, pointing toward epic, and aiming at reform by inspiring the monarch to the aggressive imposition of moral order. For Mena, the violent correction of Castile's moral state is but preparatory to the task of expelling her most powerful other, the Moors; indeed, he implies that Castile has become unable to undertake the *Reconquista* because of moral decay.

Laberinto consists of a framework in which Mena's voice is complexly positioned, but with the different positions conflated.[11] In addition to being the court poet who authors the work, his voice/persona is at once situated outside the work — as the *vates* of both the invocation that opens the allegorical vision of Fortune's *laberinto* and the exhortation that closes it — as well as within the vision itself as reader and (e)narrator of its representations.[12]

The invocation declares Mena's desire to understand the instability of Fortune, and he demands to be shown her house; in response, he is snatched away by Belona (the goddess of war) to Fortune's abode. Once in her specular realm (16–17), however, he is unable to see clearly, and so Providence descends to lead him within to behold the representations of the moral and historical world that it contains. The narrator is charged by Providence to enarrate truthfully what he sees, a task he protests as impossible, given the power of those whose vices he should reveal.[13]

Fortune's edifice is adorned with a *mappa mundi* around its ceiling, and each of the seven concentric circles representing the Ptolemaic universe contains three wheels — Past, Present, and Future (62). Each wheel has images (*simulacra*) (59b) of exemplary figures, which Mena enarrates like a *grammaticus*, explicating the difficulties of the text for his reader(s). In each order, Mena does what he promised in his invocation: "virtudes y vicios narrar de potentes" (6d) [to narrate the virtues and vices of the powerful] as a corrective vision.

The circles or orders organize the virtues and vices according to the influence of the planets/gods that dominate them: Diana, Mercury, Venus, Phoebus, Mars, Jupiter, Saturn. In each, the wheel of the Past is still and the figures represented therein are clearly labeled, serving to prompt the poet's memory to enarrate and evaluate their significance to the present. The wheel of the Present turns, but Mena is cautious in naming its negative examples while exhorting the king to correct their vices. The wheel of the Future is both still and shrouded, forbidden to mortal vision since only God may know what is to come.

As we have already seen, *Laberinto* as object is literally presented to the king, as well as being addressed to him throughout. Each circle ends with an exhortation to the king to make real the moral order that Mena's understanding reveals via its examples (see table 1). As can be seen from the poem's basic structure diagrammed in the first three columns of the table, only the circles of Diana and Venus explicitly attend to sexual matters. However, a closer reading of the text, articulated in the fourth column of the table, shows that in fact issues of sexual otherness coded generally as

TABLE I: The Orders of Mena's *Laberinto*

Order	Those Included	Contemporary Figures	Virtue/Vice Addressed to King
1 Moon/Diana	The chaste/hunters	(+) Juan II, his wife, María of Aragon; his sister, María of Castile, wife of Alfonso V; [María de Coronel]	Chastity as *Temperance*/"vile couplings" plus any vice in general
2 Mercury	Orators/merchants	(-) Castilian clergy in general, who sell their offices	[Integrity in office and duties]/*Avarice*
3 Venus	Good lovers; evil lovers	(-) Macías	"clean, virtuous Catholic love"/ "libidinous fire of Venus"
4 Sun/Phoebus	Those who seek knowledge: contemplatives, poets, philosophers, musicians; magicians and witches	(+) Enrique de Villena; (-) "nuevas Medeas y nuevas Publiçias"	*Prudence*/"damned arts"
5 Mars	Warriors	(ambivalent): Juan II, his forebears, and a whole series of figures from the recent past	*Fortitude*/[violence for profit]
6 Jupiter	Kings; tyrants	(+) Juan II	*Justice*/[tyranny]

TABLE 1: Continued

Order	Those Included	Contemporary Figures	Virtue/Vice Addressed to King
7 Saturn	Rulers (nobles?)	(+) Alvaro de Luna; (-) nobles who consult the *Maga* of Valladolid	———

vice are not only a constant theme but a dominant organizing principle throughout. As we follow Mena through the house of Fortune, it becomes clear that the return to epic glory proposed for Castile requires the violent discipline or eradication of such others, the stabilization of masculinity (traditionally defined as the locus of virtue) and violent domination of women's sex/uality.

In the very beginning of the poem's allegory, the order of Diana, Juan II along with his wife and his sister are represented as paragons of chaste marital fidelity.[14] Mena suggests further that Juan II's wife, María of Aragon, is more apt at inspiring or imposing virtue than anyone, although a woman. "Más mesurada que toda mesura" (72) [more measured than all measure],

> si fuesse trocada su umanidat, . . .
> a muchos faría, segund que yo creo,
> domar los su vicios con su justedat. (76egh)

That is, if she were a man ("if only her 'humanity' [sex] were switched"), she "would make many tame their vices with her justness."

A nameless but epic female figure of chastity is also adduced. "Digna corona de los Coroneles" (79c) [worthy crown of the Coronel family], Mena encodes her violent act of self-discipline in antonomasia:

> la muy casta dueña de las manos crueles
> . . . .
> que quiso con fuego vencer sus fogueras. (79bd)

[the very chaste lady of the cruel hands who chose with fire to conquer her burning.]

In El Brocense's gloss we learn her story:

[E]stando el marido ausente vínole tan grande tentación de la carne que determinó de morir por guardar la lealtad matrimonial, y metióse un tizón ardiendo por su natura, de que vino a morir. (259)

[While her husband was absent, such great temptation of the flesh came to her that she decided to die in order to guard marital loyalty, and so she inserted a burning brand into her sex, from which she subsequently died.]

This is not only a heroically ascetic gesture as Mena would have it, but mimetic self-punishment as suicidal masturbation—a concrete antonomasia in which masturbation takes on a different inflection. Indeed, in this story Mena's art condenses his themes into one narration of exemplary violence: the husband at war with the ethnic other; the wife at war with the inner sexual other of lust. Nor can we fail to note that this supposedly exemplary moment would have been and should be the origin of all those texts largely reserved to men and war—glory and fame, which are oral texts; prose and verse, which are written ones—and a temple dedicated to the "casta dueña," although Mena ironically leaves her individual name unspoken even as he memorializes her.[15]

María de Coronel is ostensibly a heroic example of chastity (or threat) for libidinous women, in one concise and elliptical stanza; at the same time, her action is an ascetic gesture that cannot be named but is invoked by allusion. Even more nameless are the "baxas presonas" [common people] uncommemorated by Fame, but who "han de los vicios menor pensamiento" [have less thought of vice] and who "roban las claras e santas coronas" [steal illustrious and holy crowns] of virtue (80). Juan II's role, according to the final exhortation of this circle, is to "zelar" [zealously guard] political life by making laws that also apply to the powerful, that is, legislating morality "por que pudicicia se pueda guardar" (231) [so that sexual shame/modesty can be maintained], and so that, by equal punishment, the nobles learn chastity and flee "viles deleites" (233) [vile delights].[16]

Next Mena reads the circle of Mercury, in which avarice and the improper use of office invert the proper order, and in which the moralizing representations target the Castilian clergy, again unnamed. Significantly, he protests here, as in the invocation, his fear of pointing out particulars; he further underscores the cost of this fear in the workings of language itself, since fear can make words mean their opposite, for example, "buenos nos faze llamar los viciosos" (93f) [(fear) makes us call the viceful good] (92–94; see also

Pérez de Guzmán's prologue). The venality of the clergy also reverses the proper order of exemplarity, further distorting the mirror of society. Under the sophistical guise of clerecy, evil clerics "dissipan . . . los justos sudores / de simples e pobres e de labradores" (95bc) [dissipate the just sweat of the simple and poor and of laborers], and thus fail as examples, "cegando la santa católica vía" (95d) [closing off the holy Catholic way]. Thus, if divine and exemplary violence like the earthquake of Caesarea were to occur, it would be the townspeople, not the local church and its clergy, that would be spared (96–97). In this mapping of virtue and vice, we again see that those of "baxa sangre" (80) [low blood]—just how low in the social order is not clear—are not only more virtuous than the clergy and therefore more exemplary, but also exploited by their supposed leaders. Mena thus maps social disorder onto the different social and individual bodies as well as language, a chaotic decadence that invites a violent cure from above.

As he proceeds to view the order of Venus, Mena makes brief mention of that manifestation of Venus concerned with turning lust into virtue by means of marriage.[17] This circle is primarily dedicated to a catalogue of sexual sinners, including homosexuals, "los maculados de crimen nefando, / de justa razón e de toda contrarios" (101gh) [those stained with unspeakable sin, contrary to all and right reason], although most of the exemplars are guilty of incest, adultery, and bestiality, since the sin of sodomy itself is unspeakable.[18] Again invoking phallic violence, Mena exhorts Juan II to use "el regio cetro de [su] potencia / fiera" (114bc) [the regal scepter of (his) royal potency] to destroy the "viles actos del libidinoso / fuego de Venus" (114ef) [vile acts of the libidinous fire of Venus] and to make "los humanos sobre todo caten / el limpio cathólico amor virtuoso" (114gh) [all humans observe clean and virtuous Catholic love].

It is a male figure—Macías, paragon of courtly lovers and virtual emblem of Iberian courtly love poetry—whose voice is lifted in ventriloquized warning against love, although he himself can't give it up. The warning is clearly directed to men rather than to women, although the parade of depravity that fills this section of the text is equally attributed to both. Macías's autoelegy is a condemnation of the religion of love that is the provocation of courtly poetry (of which Mena himself was a practitioner) and was the cause of Macías's violent death (he was run through by a jealous husband) (Vanderford).

Mena enarrates the next order (the Sun or Phoebus Apollo) as implicitly concerned with illicit love and bad women as well, since the "dañadas artes (129b) [damned arts] condemned in it are those of "nuevas Medeas e nuevas Publiçias" (135g) [new Medeas and new Licinias] who have lost *pudici-cia* (131ef) from being wounded by Venus's arrow and don't know how to "darse reparos amando" (130f–h) [give (themselves) relief because loving]. Mena suggests that Castile is afflicted with a plague of mysterious deaths due to poisoning by these wanton women, inner others whose internal and external violence destroy the social fabric of the state (135). Of note here is that, in direct contrast to the problem of witchy women, Mena makes Don Enrique de Villena the positive example of learning by erasing his common reputation as both womanizer and necromancer and protesting the burning of his books ordered by Juan II upon his death (125–28; compare Pérez de Guzmán 32–33). Indeed, according to Mena in this order, it is the monarch's duty to encourage licit knowledge (presumably among men like Villena and Mena himself), and to "fazer destroir los falsos saberes" (134b) [destroy false knowledge] (violence countering violence) among women rather than maintain permissive laws that allow such death-dealing (female) monsters to disrupt society by killing men and destroying marriage.

The *simulacra* of the circle of Mars are concerned with matters of war and *Reconquista,* and this fifth circle is the appropriate location of Mena's most prominent ekphrasis, that of Juan II's *silla* 'throne.' While this epic order has little that is explicitly related to matters of sex/uality, in it Mena calls for a return to the *Reconquista* as "virtüosa, magnífica guerra" (152a) [virtu-ous, magnificent war], the solution for the civil strife afflicting Castile. The final exhortation that Mena addresses to the king is a call to *Fortaleza* 'For-titude,' which is not simply force, but implies constancy as well as virtue. Afraid only of "las cosas que son desonestas" (213c) [those things that are dishonest],[19] it "huye, desdeña, depártese çedo / de las que diformes por vicio se fazen" (213ef) [flees, disdains, departs immediately those who make themselves deformed through vice].

Finally, in the circle of Jupiter, the last order with a moral exhortation at the end, Mena declares Juan II a "novel Augusto" [new Augustus] who should "[sanar] . . . los reinos" [heal (his) kingdom] of the excessive zeal and "fambre tirana" [tyrannical hunger] for gain of some of his (unnamed) servants (230abd). However, justice heals not only abuse of power and office, but other vices as well; in Mena's scheme, it is the primary means of healing Castile's ills, not only scepter and garment of the soul ("Justicia es un çeptro que el cielo crió, / . . . / ábito rico del ánimo puro," 231ac), but also an incorruptible "açote que pugne los viçios" (231g) [whip that punishes vice]. Like Augustus, Juan II should combine political and legislative power in order to combat decadence.

There is in addition an excursus in this sixth circle directed to the common folk to exhort them not to envy the powerful (223) since "las [sus] riquezas son más naturales" (223h) [(their) riches are more natural]. In a significant articulation of natural virtue onto socialized bodies, Mena declares that the wealthy and powerful envy the gifts of nature given common people: beauty, beautiful bodies, naturalness (*desenvoltura*), prudence and moderation, strength, courage, health (225d–f). Mena closes this mapping of virtue (with its implied opposite mapped onto elites) with an image of the powerful to contemplate: "[P]ues vet ser en ellos non tanta virtud, / nin toda en riquezas la buena ventura" (225gh) [So see in them there is not as much virtue, nor is all blessing (*ventura*) in riches]. Here the common subjects naturally and corporeally possess all of the virtues Mena is trying to inspire in the king.

From the order of Saturn, which has no final definition and exhortation, Mena enarrates only one directly offered example: that of Alvaro de Luna, favorite of Juan II and Constable of Castile, paragon of virtue and prudence. Yet the layout of the circle is the usual opposition of positive and then negative examples:

> las grandes personas en sus monarchías,
> e los que rigen las sus señorías
> con moderada justicia temidos
> . . . los que non punidos
> sufren que passen males e viçios
> e los que pigros en los sus ofiçios
> dexan los crímenes mal corregidos. (232b–d, e–h)

[great persons in their monarchies, lords who, being feared, rule their realms with moderated justice, those who allow that evils and vices go unpunished, and those who, negligent in their duties, leave crimes poorly punished.]

In this circle, however, there is one last woman besides the two primary female figures of the poem. Of the first two, Fortune is here tamed like an unruly mount by the Constable (235); the other, Providence, is completely enamored of Luna (234). Mena presents the third, the *maga* 'sorceress' of Valladolid, via an extended deployment of the conjuring scene from Lucan's *Pharsalia*. She is employed by some nobles who wish to know the outcome of the civil wars (245) and undertakes an incantation to know the future from the body of a man so evil that he was denied burial—he died in unjust battle, a significant fact given Mena's moral purpose, especially visible in the circle of Mars.

The prophecy from this foul and undead flesh is procured through the *maga*'s domination of the man's body by magic and gender-bending phallic violence: "con viva culebra lo fiere y açota" (249c) [she wounds and beats it with a living serpent], and, as it begins to tremble, nears it "con besos impíos" (252e) [with obscene kisses] to ask her clients' question. The latter take the cadaver's prophecy that Luna will be "desfecho" (256e) [undone] as grounds for changing alliances, ignoring that the majority of the cadaver's reply is an exhortation to turn against the Moors rather than each other (253–57).[20] Here, the *maga* wields a clearly phallic instrument in an aggressively sexual violation of all propriety, transgressing as well the express prohibition of knowledge of the future, and Mena condemns both practitioner and clients.

To summarize, then, Mena's poem denounces vice and calls Spain to (epic) virtue in reconquering both the Spanish body (politic) and Spanish lands lost to the Moors. These two activities are seen as integral to one another; his call to (kingly) virtue is a call to salutary violence against the vitiation of inner and outer others. Finally, throughout *Laberinto*, Mena clearly maps vice and virtue onto bodies, essentially based in gender and sexual behaviors, via a series of readings of examples that are an overtly graphic series of ekphrastic and memorial representations.

In this ethical scenario of the punishment of vice, it is most often women who are punished rather than men—witness the contrast between Villena and the women of the order of Apollo. Though the male member is an equal instrument of sexual license, it is instrument and not recipient of punishment in the *Laberinto*, even in the hands of the *maga* of Valladolid. Yet the horrifying sexes (*naturas* or *umanidates*) of women, like that of María de Coronel, must be disciplined by phallic instruments. In this odd juxtaposing of symbolic instruments of torture with "real" bodies and their parts, the order of virtue is a violent economy of phallic power with its predilect modality—the penetration and punishment of women.

In projecting virtue onto bodies, *Laberinto* tells us again and again that women are the irredeemably other locus and source of vice unless tamed and contained or punished and eradicated. Though the queen is the very paragon of virtue, she would have to be male to have perfect virtue and to impose it by whatever force necessary, and María de Coronel's self-destruction is horrifyingly exemplary. Lustful women go crazy and lose all restraint, like Medea and Licinia who scheme to murder their husbands and secretly destroy the entire social order from within. The *maga* of Valladolid, with her improper assumption of a phallic instrument of power (the snake), provides fodder for insurrection against Luna, himself a paragon of all virtues in his masculine perfection. Further, Mena's moral gaze maps the proper lines of gender and of sex, and calls for their (violent) imposition as integral to and preparatory for the epic (re-)imposition of Christian rule over the peninsula.

Mena's contribution to the debate on order, then, is that, on the one side, the monarch must display and enforce his proper royal and phallic power ("the royal scepter of [his] fierce potency") to heal the social and political chaos of the realm. From the other side, though, he also suggests that this monarch (and therefore Castile) suffers from a lack of proper masculinity, and that vice (and therefore civil strife) is due in part to this insufficiency, which is gendered feminine in opposition to the masculinity ascribed to *vir*tue. Although the poem addresses Juan II, he is framed between paragons of virtue—his wife and his sister (masculine in their virtue) and Luna—examples offered for his edification that also imply his lack.

Inner others, if not controlled, lead to vice, emasculation/feminization, and dissension. Further, violence is necessary to manage them, whether punishment by legal fiat (inflicted by regal sword, scepter, or whip), self-punishment, or simply by channeling the violence into all-out war against a common other: the Moor.[21] The infliction of this social and moral discipline is a restoration of the proper masculinity necessary in a *vir*tuous, that is, *man*ly, monarch and his realm.

Fortune's labyrinth is the world, a fallen maze of vice because its inhabitants give themselves over to feminizing appetites and passions, whether lust, avarice, or fear. Seen from Mena's Providential perspective, (sexual) vice is interwoven throughout its chaotic fabric. For Mena, Castile, while under the domination of moral decadence, is a moral labyrinth of inextricable error (Doob, ch. 6, esp. 157–58), and moral choices must be made not for the well-being of one's own soul (not an explicit concern of *Laberinto*) or one's own fame, but rather for the well-being of the *polis*, for which moral and sexual otherness (women and lust) are equally destructive. So it will remain, unless the "libidinous fires of illicit love" are transformed into virtue by "clean, virtuous Catholic love" — a heteronormative moral order imposed from above to stabilize identity and appetite, gender and desire.

Rojas's Urban Labyrinth of Love

Although Fernando de Rojas's *Celestina* does not obviously resemble *Laberinto*, Mena's labyrinthine world reappears in it as the moral site of *Celestina*'s city, and the text often directly echoes *Laberinto* and articulates the former's epic and allegorical vision in the mode of a particular case. This is clear in the final *auto* as Pleberio, bereft patrician father, laments the death of his child, echoing Mena as he addresses Fortune, life, and the world:

> Yo pensaba en mi más tierna edad que eras y eran tus hechos regidos por alguna orden; agora, visto el pro y la contra de tus bienandanzas me pareces *un laberinto de errores*, un desierto espantable, una morada de fieras, juego de hombres que andan en corro. . . . (396–97; emphasis mine)[22]

> [I thought in my more tender years, that both thou and thy actions were governed by order, and ruled by reason: but now I see thou art pro and con; there is no certainty in thy calms. Thou seemest now unto me to be a *labyrinth of errors;* a fearful wilderness; an habitation of wild beasts; a dance full of changes.]

As he stands in the ruins of his life and at the end of his daughter's story, Pleberio begins his lament — key in understanding the text as a whole — with words that resonate with *Laberinto:*

> O fortuna variable, ministra y mayordoma de los temporales bienes, ¿Por qué no executaste tu cruel ira, tus *mudables ondas*, en aquello que a ti es sujeto? . . . [D]iérasme, *fortuna flutuosa*, triste la mocedad con vegez alegre. (396–97; emphasis mine)

> [Oh variable fortune, and full of change, thou ministress and high stewardess of all temporal happiness, why didst thou not execute thy cruel anger upon

me? Why didst thou not overwhelm him with thy mutable waves, who professes himself to be thy subject? . . . Thou mightest, O fortune (fluctuant and fluent as thou art), have given me a sorrowful youth and a mirthful age.][23]

Further, Fernando de Rojas explicitly alludes to Mena in the prefatory letter that appears in editions of the work from 1500 onward (6–7). His allusion also points to the beginning of *Celestina*'s textual life as the *Comedia de Calisto y Melibea* [Comedy of Calisto and Melibea], a sixteen-*auto* novel in dialogue, largely written by Rojas, a student of law at Salamanca (Mena's *alma mater*), who claims to have found the unsigned first *auto*, perhaps attributable to Mena or Rodrigo Cota.[24] This "found text" begins the story of the love affair between Melibea, Pleberio's daughter, and Calisto, a young local nobleman whose servingman Sempronio solicits the aid of the city's procuress to make Melibea accessible to his master, with fatal results.

However, the *Comedia* soon becomes the *Tragicomedia de Calisto y Melibea* (1500 or 1502), with Rojas's addition of a prologue recounting public response to the work and five more *autos* prolonging the love affair, as his readers begged.[25] In his prefatory letter, Rojas, like Mena, explicitly offers his text as a literary gift with reforming intentions, in this case a service to his hometown, filled with young men held captive by love. Rojas, then, situates *Celestina* precisely in the same social mode as *Laberinto*, and part of its service is "avisos y consejos contra lisongeros y malos sirvientes y falsas *mugeres* hechizeras" (6–7; emphasis mine) [advice and counsel against flattering and evil servants and false witches], emphasizing equally conflicts of class and gender.[26] In this reading, Rojas's adaptation of Mena offers a more concrete view of what happens when love is rampant in the *polis*. The city's maze of streets with its houses—Celestina's, Calisto's, Pleberio's—is presented as an edifying mirror, a map of vice, and a set of defensive arms for a place and its community, and its characters must be read in a similar mode as Mena's *simulacra*.[27]

Mena's possible paternity as well as the influence of his work on *Celestina* have been noted, and the paratext of Dorothy Severin's recent critical edition is littered with allusions to the *Laberinto* (cf. Castro Guisasola; Lida de Malkiel, *La originalidad artística*). Mena's importance to *Celestina* goes beyond mere citation, and, as a formative intertext, is both integral and crucial to *Celestina*'s basic vision.[28] For our purposes, the most important effect of this is that both grapple with the issue of what is wrong with Spain and what can be done to remedy it, *Laberinto* mapping the disorder in epic and satire and from a cosmic viewpoint (Weiss, "Juan de Mena's *Coronación*" 123); *Celestina* mapping it in a prose text in dialogue with a sublunar perspective.

In spite of their generic differences, though, both attribute their work to a social and political need for a cure from the ills of love, and both employ a basically violent set of metaphors: that of weapons. As we have seen, however, *Laberinto* offers a set of offensive weapons against the otherness of vice, whether internal or externalized in women and Moors; its map of gender and sex/uality is a battle plan. *Celestina*, in contrast, is a set of "defensivas armas" (6–7) [defensive arms], a metaphorically ekphrastic suit of armor necessary to defend the young compatriots of Rojas and his unnamed dedicatee from the vitiation of love; its map makes visible the dangers inherent in the territory in order to flee them like Mena's Fortitude. In the face of the public acclaim of *Celestina*'s plot, Rojas closes the text of the *Tragicomedia* with protestations of the (negative) exemplarity beneath the lascivious surface of the text:

> No dudes ni ayas vergüença, letor,
> narrar lo lascivo, que aquí se te muestra
> que siendo discreto verás que es la muestra
> por donde se vende la honesta lavor. (404–05)

[Do not doubt nor be ashamed, reader, to read out the lascivious matter which is shown you here, for being discreet you will see that it is the sample from which honest work is sold.]

Although working the same moral problematic, *Celestina* leaves dream vision and, via fiction, enters the spinning material world of the present described and critiqued by Mena from afar. If Mena runs the gamut in enumerating the sexual world outlined in the circle of Venus, *Celestina* runs the same gamut from fornication to homosex/uality, but also includes an aura of violence as well as a mercenary atmosphere of sexual interchange. In joining the pervasive debate taken up by Mena, *Celestina* textualizes the implications for gender and incarnates them, makes *Laberinto*'s philosophical argument take on (punished) flesh, and remaps its social analysis.

In the fifteen *autos* of the *Comedia* and then the twenty-one of the *Tragicomedia*, men and women are bound up in relationships of both desire and conflict, within and across the lines of rank. The social mapping here is dual, as the love interest of the young nobles is paralleled by the sexual liaisons of the commoners who serve them. Sempronio is the lover of Elicia, a prostitute managed by Celestina; Pármeno is persuaded to join their cause when Elicia's cousin Areúsa is procured for him by Celestina. For Celestina herself sex/uality is now mostly a spectator sport, but she's no less active for that.

Equally on display in the text are conflictive structures of gender and sex/uality, in an array not unlike Mena's, and in more particular detail. In addition to the apparently "normal" courtly heterosex/uality of Melibea and Calisto that is the ostensible focus of this *Comedia* or *Tragicomedia*, aspects of the violent and mercenary underworld of sex/uality in this unnamed city also characterize Calisto himself and his relationship to Melibea.

Sempronio is the first character presented to us as an active lover, although his beloved is a local prostitute (who is free if not *gratis* with her sexual favors). As an expert on sex, in the first *auto* he employs in succession two conflicting defensive weapons offered by fifteenth-century medicine as therapy for *amor hereos:* misogyny's punishing rejection of women and sex, and humoral theory's emphasis on therapeutic sex for relief of superfluidity (Solomon). But Sempronio also wants, as Celestina puts it, "más estar al sabor, que al olor deste negocio" (146–47) [to rather have taste than scent this business].

Here, too, Sempronio invokes sodomy as integral to the blasphemous religious structure Calisto (in courtly tradition) has invoked. Tellingly enough, this occurs in the same curative misogynist discourse, when Calisto contests Sempronio's right to offer a condemnation of women as inferior to men by declaring Melibea divine: "¿Mujer? ¡O grosero! ¡Dios, dios!" (34–35) [A woman? O thou blockhead, she's (God)!]. Sempronio takes literally and ridicules the courtly metaphor that casts the beloved as divine (masculine "Dios" in Spanish); punning on the signifier's grammatical gender (masculine), he makes it "peor invención de pecado que en Sodoma" (34–35) [a worse invention of sin than in Sodom], explaining his laughter with "porque aquéllos procuraron abominable uso con los ángeles no conocidos y tú con el que confiesas ser Dios" (34–35) [for they did but go about to procure abominable use with angels whom they knew not, and thou with her whom thou confessest to be a god].

Calisto laughs along with this joke; his lust, it seems, is straight if still illicit. Nonetheless, he is perversely exhibitionist throughout the text, welcoming the servants' presence at his tryst. "Bien me huelgo que estén semejantes testigos de mi gloria" (314–15) [I should be proud to have such witnesses as she of my glory], he says, while Melibea refuses such witnesses of her error.[29] His refusal to temper his rough advances on Melibea are, he says, *necessary* to any man "que hombre sea" (314–315) [any man that is a man]; this particular sexual conquest, that is, penetrating Melibea's body, is therefore testimony to his masculinity, to his sex/uality in general (cf. Weiss, "Alvaro de Luna" 248–49). That is, Calisto wishes to make a spectacle of his own masculinity and potency, proving it with his sex. Not just a parody of the courtly lover in his foolish misapplication of love theory, Calisto is also a negative example in his feminized and self-centered passivity, disloyalty, and hedonism, meant to reveal the perversion and social disruption proceeding from courtly love, and so teach a lesson about the moral cost of vitiated masculinity.

In the end Pármeno is no more moral, although he resists Celestina's advances with all the arguments a Mena would offer against both lust and avarice. As a loyal servant, he even offers the ungrateful Calisto suggestions for licitly pursuing Melibea, many of which also echo *Laberinto* (Castro Guisasola 158–67). Abandoned by Calisto as (non)exemplary master, Pármeno too is seduced by his own lust into fornication and hypocrisy with a local prostitute through Celestina's mediation.

As in *Laberinto*, the clergy, though again nameless and present only within Celestina's nostalgic stories of her prime, are lovers in abundance in her world. Perhaps most troubling to Sempronio is this portrait of the world of Celestina's golden youth (perhaps virtually contemporary with Mena's, to mix *fictitia* with *realia*), a world in which she was sought after and rewarded by almost every cleric in town. Not only did she manage their affairs, but she got a share of the firstfruits of the entire diocese — wine, fine food, staples — the "just sweat" of the common folk as Mena would say (Severin/Mabbe 213 ff.; *Laberinto* 95bc). In her reminiscing, then, Celestina incarnates Mena's condemnation of the sins of the clergy in the order of Mercury (*Laberinto* 95 ff.).

Using Celestina as the prototype of all women, Rojas takes on female sex/uality in much more concrete detail than Mena. We have seen that she is clearly polymorphously perverse in *auto* 7 where she panders Areúsa to Pármeno, as well as her reminiscing in *auto* 9 about the good old days of her youthful career as a prostitute and madame. The latter monologue makes her out not only to be a "puta vieja alcoholada" (50–51) [old bawd . . . be-daub'd with painting], but also quite *alcohólica*, and still actively lustful, provoked in this instance by the sexual roughhousing at her table. Celes-tina is voyeuristic; if Calisto wants to show, Celestina wants to see, a point made in both *autos*.

Further, in *auto* 7 Celestina reveals her own interest in Areúsa's body, as well as desire to watch her coupling with Pármeno (whom Celestina had apparently tried to fondle as a child; cf. 66–67). In addition to the penetra-tion of her gaze as she begins her persuasion of Areúsa, Celestina also lays hands on the young woman, whose words seem to indicate that Celestina is feeling her up, a possibility reinforced by the latter's reported pleasure in repairing hymens.[30] Celestina's excursus to Areúsa on one as the worst number, especially in terms of numbers of sexual clients, reveals her as both mercenary and insatiable, and she mediates the illicit circulation of sexes (some repaired), running the gamut of sexual perversions and possibili-ties, from hetero- to homosex/uality, from voyeurism to child molesting to pandering. This range of perverse sex/uality is mapped concretely onto her body, violently inscribed with its scars and frenetically punished by Sempronio and Pármeno's sword, rather than onto the mythological and historical figures of Mena's allegorical *enarratio*.[31]

Even Melibea, "doncella brava" (140–41) [gallant lady (more at "untamed maiden")] to be tamed by Celestina via the phallic power in Calisto's name, becomes more celestinesque as her appetites dominate her. Melibea's appe-tites are perhaps as strong and disorderly as Celestina's, but are a bit more "straight," as can be seen in her resistance to Calisto's exhibitionism. The same might be said for both Elicia and Areúsa, the prostitutes who, if they follow in the footsteps of Celestina after her death, do so more timidly and crudely, not to mention heterosexually (see *autos* 15, 17, and 18).

Melibea, though, is not the only casualty of this affair; indeed, all the liai-sons end tragically, either because of greed or because of the nature and effects of love. Sempronio and Pármeno brutally murder Celestina when she refuses to share the profits of their joint venture, and are summarily executed. When his new servant confidants are harassed by low-lifes hired to avenge the deaths of Sempronio and Pármeno, Calisto fatally missteps climbing out of Melibea's garden; Melibea casts herself from her tower in order to join Calisto in death, after disjointedly telling her father their story.

Most importantly, the effects of these deaths are social as well as personal;

it is not just that Pleberio is deeply wounded by his daughter's death, nor that she feels responsible for the death of one lovesick swain. Melibea herself points to the signs of social disruption:

> Bien ves y oyes este triste y doloroso sentimiento que toda la ciudad haze. . . . De todo esto fui yo la causa. Yo cubrí de luto y jergas en este día casi la mayor parte de la ciudadana cavallería, yo dejé [hoy] muchos sirvientes descubiertos de señor, yo quité muchas raciones y limosnas a pobres y envergonzantes. (390–91)

> [I am sure you both well perceive and hear that most sad and doleful lamentation, which is made throughout all this city. . . . Of all this have I been the cause; I even this very day, have clothed the greater part of the knights and gentlemen of this city in mourning. I even this very day, have left many servants orphaned and quite destitute of a master. I have been the cause that many a poor soul hath now lost its alms and relief.]

Pleberio too, in the imprecation of fortune, love, and the world with which this section of my essay opens, tells us that Melibea's death destroys the orderly succession of goods, honors, and generations. That is, *Celestina* presents the social world as reduced to chaos, expressed in the same images typical of Mena's poem: a fearful labyrinth, wilderness filled with savage beasts, a chaotic dance impossible to follow (396–97).

In addition, though, *Celestina*'s mapping of gender and sex/uality in the *polis* contests Mena's assertion of the common folk as the locus of virtue, making them rather the locus of a violent and socially disruptive sexual diversity. It is Sempronio, Pármeno, and Celestina whose mutual avarice leads to the violent deaths set in motion by the lust omnipresent in *Celestina*'s world, a violence Pleberio is impotent to stop.[32] This contradicts Mena's assertion that the "pequeños" [small subjects] are more virtuous and natural, and that they tend not to be as given over to lust or avarice (*Laberinto* 80). In the debate about virtue and social life, *Celestina* provides no place for identity and order within its text as Mena does; the *civis* 'city' does not create a civil space. Rather, only the reader's ethical reflection on the negative examples offered in vividly concrete form — as Rojas's paratext suggests — can possibly create social order by creating individual virtue from within.

In my reading here, *Celestina* situates itself with Mena and the antifeminists in the debate by portraying the ills of society as proceeding from women and love, from *natura* as sex, shall we say, giving Sempronio's list of the gifts of *natura* to Calisto—including "grandeza de miembros" (38–39) [largeness of (members)]—a carnal twist. The semantic ambivalence of "nature" here effectively limits what can be considered "love" and not lust in the text even as it maps lust onto the female body—"qué hastío es conferir con ellas más de aquel breve tiempo que aparejadas son a deleite" (38–39) [O . . . what a loathsome thing is it for a man to have to do with them any longer than in that short prick of time that he holds them in his arms, when they are prepared for pleasure].³³ Calisto and Melibea are but one focus in *Celestina*'s portrayal of the problem of Women and Love, *eros* and the *polis,* and nowhere on its textual map, whether among the nobles or among commoners, is a positive example explicitly offered.³⁴

Carajicomedia's Cities of Brothely Love

If Mena and Rojas trace the conflicts of *eros* in the bodies that move in the *polis,* for *Carajicomedia* [Phallicomedy] *eros* is the very ground of the *polis,* offered for the reader's contemplation (148). In its mapping of prostitutes in Spain's cities, sex is the dark underbelly of a society which is itself belly-up, and the text offers absolutely no transcendental aspects to social or sexual interchange; here, the phallic remains mordantly literal rather than transcending to the symbolic or to virtue. As in *Celestina,* the city is the space of sexual action, and Spain becomes a hypocritical *pornotopia,* literally a place of prostitutes both public and *caseras* 'domestic,' some eight of which share the queen's name, Isabel.

Carajicomedia is an early sixteenth-century celestinesque parody of Hernán Núñez de Guzmán's edition of Mena's *Laberinto* (first published in 1499 and revised once in its lengthy publishing history). Published in 1519, *Carajicomedia,* concerned with the reign of Isabel (d. 1506) and Ferdinand (d. 1516), is thought to have been composed between 1506 and 1519, when it appeared in Valencia as part of the *Cancionero de obras de burlas provocantes a risa* [Songbook of Jesting Works Provoking Laughter], the latter a revised offprint of the last section of Hernán de Castillo's *Cancionero general* [General Songbook].³⁵ That is, *Carajicomedia*'s first appearance is associated with a mainstream tradition of Iberian/Castilian poetry, which, in addition to being the privileged site of the other side of the sex and gender nexus (courtly love poetry) as well as of the poetic debate on women in general, has always included bawdy poetry, often parodic, satirical, and political, its insults often couched in questions of ethnicity, gender, and sex/uality.[36]

The basic structure of *Carajicomedia* is that of Mena's poem with its prose gloss, both of which focus on the "vida y martirio" (Incipit 148) [life and martyrdom] of Diego Fajardo, or rather, of his prick, and convey a vision of this sexual world through the framework of pseudohagiography and burlesque erudition. Born under the sign of Venus, prick already erect, Fajardo is now old and impotent after years of sexual hyperactivity, and laments his penis's loss of fury (gloss to stanza 1, 150–51). In hopes of regaining his capacity to please (that is, to dominate) women who now laugh at him and doubt that he ever could, and to keep their ridicule at bay, Fajardo consults first *Luxuria* 'Lust,' and then a pair of old whores — the second more grotesque than the first — to regain his potency. In the process, Fajardo, like Mena, enarrates the whores he has known in the cities of Spain from an ekphrastic reading of their *posada* 'dwelling' (32b, 169). Throughout, the glossator maps Fajardo's verse lament onto an oral and written intertext of obscenities, all from a masculinist and pornographic point of view.

Until recently, *Carajicomedia* has been largely dismissed as simply "filthy" (*soez, procaz*) by critics and historians of Spanish literature (Varo 38–40); only recently have scholars begun taking *Carajicomedia* seriously, reading it historically and politically. It is generically a parody and thematically a satire of a fifteenth-century social vision that hypocritically places itself outside or beyond the corruption of the flesh, and punishes those not politically powerful enough to resist punishment for the same vices in which the powerful also indulge or in which they want to indulge but can't.

In *Carajicomedia*'s dissident contribution to the debate on sex and gender articulated by *Laberinto* and *Celestina*, Mena's ekphrastic world is transposed into *Celestina*'s. Rather than presenting a *mappa mundi* in the dwelling of Fortune, *Carajicomedia* traces a *mappa immunda* 'filthy map' of prostitutes in the dwelling of an Old Whore. It de-moralizes the space of *Laberinto*'s and *Celestina*'s political project, undoing the moral high ground into a morass of vice inhabited by men and women largely reduced to their orifices. In *Carajicomedia*, the instruments of phallic control are not scepters, whips, or regal swords, but plain old penises, potent and impotent, sometimes supplemented with knives (Weissberger).

Here, all of society is reduced to the level of the brothel, and Spain becomes a realm of whorehouses, including Isabel's court. The court is entangled with prostitution by the marriage of several of *Carajicomedia*'s prostitutes to royal stableboys and others associated with the court, and there are further mentions of and allusions to the queen throughout (Varo 73–90). All institutions of power and of morality — the church, the universities, the court — are implicated in this world, an aspect inscribed not only in its content but in its narrative structure. Both the supposed author of the poem (Reverend Father Bugeo Montesinos) and its continuator (Fray Juan de Hempudia) are clerics, and its anonymous glossator moves in their world and participates fully via first-person testimony of the (shall we say) "brothely" love portrayed.

Valladolid and Salamanca, both university towns, figure prominently in the text, both in the *mappa immunda* and in the first order (Salamanca and Toledo). There are also uses of the Valencian term *cadira* (*cátedra* in Castilian) 'academic chair' apropos of some of the Valencian prostitutes. Clerics — like the putative author or compiler and its anonymous glossator — cleverly pour the most sordid carnality into the church's discursive vessels: liturgy, Latin, and learning in general.[37] In addition, these university towns are sites of some of the most violent sexual encounters between prostitutes and their clients in *Carajicomedia*.

Virility as power and (im)potency turn on pleasure here, but it is sadistic pleasure alloyed with violence, with (aggressive if ineffectual) sexual power over women's privates and their insatiable desires. In this, *Carajicomedia* distorts and magnifies the world of *Celestina*, taking Mena's world a step lower than *Celestina* does; "love" is but a thing of the flesh and there is no pretense at anything else. War, a basic metaphor of courtly love, is literalized as the Realpolitik of physical war, with the genitals serving as sexual weapons. The problem with society, it seems, is that there is no place unsullied by this dirty, violent war of women and sex, and the problem with women is that they're never satisfied and never tamed.

All the women that parade through the pages of *Carajicomedia* are aggressively if not grossly sexual, an array of prostitutes of various degrees of ill repute, though these are, according to the glossator, but a drop in the bucket (87b–d, 217). One commits "el más vil crimen que Celestina nunca hizo" [a much viler crime than Celestina ever committed] by selling her virgin daughter to a local friar, but has to sell her again to someone else to get up a refund when the cleric doesn't want to deflower the girl (47 gloss, 182). Another uppity whore gets gang-banged in an admiral's house by more than twenty-five servants of the bishop of Osma, who resides there, only fleeing when they bring in two black stableboys to finish the job (58 gloss, 193–94). Yet another, tarred and feathered (honeyed and flied) protests her usefulness to the clergy in managing their sexual liaisons — speaking from the textual space of Mena's ventriloquized Macías (73–78, 206–10). Fat ones, dirty ones, one who is a howler, another who wets the bed, and so on — an entire gamut of sordidly sexual female bodies fill the pages of *Carajicomedia*, but are never filled and satisfied by the male members that engage in often violent contact with them, and are never faithful either.

Less "straight" varieties of sexual interaction are represented as well. Heterosexual sodomy — the *ley itálica* 'Italian law' — lurks beneath "normal" reproductive sex in what we now think of as the missionary position, since balls are forever neighborly with that *cagado veʒino* [shitty neighbor] even while working the proper vessel (11, 158 et passim). The *gran deporte del culo* [great sport of the asshole] ever attracts the prick, much to the irritation of the cunt (8, 156–57), to the point that Fajardo enjoins his penis to have as its rule of life to leave alone the owners of assholes ("tengan seguros los culos sus dueños") while not pardoning any cunt at all ("mas coño ninguno no le perdonar") (65, 200).

Nor is homosex/uality absent; the *nefando* 'unspeakable' sin is certainly not unspoken here. Stanza 28 is glossed with the viciously humorous story of a shepherd, Satilario, spied masturbating by a devil en route to tempt a hermit. Himself tempted with the possibility of catching Satilario at such a manifest sin, the devil unfortunately slips on the lard with which Satilario has lubricated himself, falls on the shepherd's upright member, and is thoroughly sodomized himself. There is no explicit negative judgment of Satilario who is, after all, punishing a devil. Indeed, it seems that even here it is the "great sport of the asshole" that is the motivating force in Satilario's rape of the poor "culi roto" [broke-assed] devil who never again returns (28 gloss, 166–67). One of the brothels has among its crew "Ibora Beteta" — a transvestite hired expressly for "a determined type of client" according to Varo (67–68), and toward whom the glossator expresses hostile disgust (81 gloss, 213–14). There are two potential allusions to lesbianism in the pairs of prostitutes described as "compañeras" [companions] in stanzas 49 and 51 (glosses on 187, 189), although the differential qualification of them as "companions" may not imply a sexual relationship.

As for the aged and impotent protagonist of the poem, he can't do much any more except talk, since the poem laments Fajardo's now-useless penis. The poem ends with an epic account of the latter's death in a battle between cunts and pricks that parodies the battle in which the epic hero of the circle of Mars, the Count of Niebla, meets his end in *Laberinto*. This reinscribes Mena's conflation of masculinity and *Reconquista* in that the pricks are soundly defeated by the cunts who stand in for the stormy sea and for the Muslim defenders of Gibraltar (*Laberinto* 159 ff.; *Carajicomedia* 93 ff., 220 ff.). Once dead, Fajardo's *carajo* is buried in Rome, like a relic from the body of a saint.

Clearly, *Carajicomedia* maps feminine sex/uality in two ways: first, as a function of men's sex/uality; secondly, as the lowest form of moral and physical degradation for men or for women. *Carajicomedia* is literally pornography in the etymological sense, a "writing about prostitutes"; nonetheless, it is consonant with the general *modus operandi* of the poem to map the broadest spectrum of sexual possibilities. Spain here is reduced to whores, to the acts and fluids of sexual intercourse of all varieties. Penetration is necessary to masculinity; clerics are reduced to whoremongers, many of them impotent. If there is a point to this world, it is a misogynist and not a libertarian one: that women's insatiable desires render men impotent; that all and only women should be and want to be fucked; that women are capable of astounding corruption for the sake of sex and money. And that the supposedly pious leaders of society are completely complicit in this corruption, doubly complicit if both elite and female, and impotent if male.

This pornotopic view *is* the serious political point, as Varo timidly points out and Weissberger elaborates more assertively; it is a view that must be mapped onto Isabel I, for her body is the body politic as well as that of a woman. The gender anxiety provoked by her accession to the throne was in part tamed by marriage to Fernando, but remained strong, as can be seen even in pro-Isabelline moralizing writers. For example, Juan de Lucena (d. 1506?), private counsellor and ambassador of Juan II, expresses striking ambivalence about Isabel's learning and power in his "Epístola exhortatoria a las letras" [Epistle Exhorting the Study of Letters]. Further, Fray Iñigo de Mendoza (c. 1422-c. 1492), one of Isabel's favorite preachers and a *converso* protégé of the marquis of Santillana, wrote a poem celebrating the accession of the Catholic Monarchs, "Como nuestra España es reparada" [On how our Spain is restored], in which there are only cursory references to Isabel while the poem is largely directed to Fernando. If her supporters are ambivalent about the monarch's gender, how much more virulent is this dissident response to her imposition of Mena's vision (see Weissberger and Varo).

Although Daniel Eisenberg suggests Diego Hurtado de Mendoza as a possible model for Diego Fajardo, further research has indicated as well the existence of a historical Diego Fajardo, the son of Alonso Fajardo, rewarded by the Catholic Monarchs for military services with a monopoly on the brothels in towns recovered during the final stages of the *Reconquista* (Varo 63 citing Canales). Further, the widow of the elder Fajardo made her son cede one of them to her in order to make it into a religious house for repentant prostitutes, provoking lawsuits (and documentation) in the process (Weissberger 12–13). Nonetheless, there are good reasons to see our Fajardo more as a composite figure, given the breadth of *Carajicomedia*'s political exposé, and Eisenberg's evidence remains persuasive for Hurtado de Mendoza as one element among many in Fajardo's character, including the historical Fajardo as well. At the level of *Carajicomedia*'s political critique, we should remember that Fernando the Catholic's cynical and calculating politics have been well known from Machiavelli's times to our own. In addition, he was quite sexually active outside marriage during the life of Isabel, and, after her death in 1506, spent the last ten years of his own life trying desperately to restore his sexual potency and beget another male heir, since their only son, "the prince who died of love," succumbed to sexual excess and died in his late teens (Calderón 95–100; Maura). These factors, it seems to me, make them both further targets for condensation into the character "Diego Fajardo." [38]

As for Isabel herself, the historical evidence of the granting of privileges to maintain whorehouses contrasts with the severe punishments for procurement and prostitution in Montalvo's royally sponsored edition and revision of the *Siete partidas* (a unified law code first compiled in the thirteenth century). Her refusal to discipline her son Juan's excessive sexual activity points further to a morally ambiguous dimension of the queen, rather than the moral high ground she always claimed. All this, along with the critical reading of her reign that *Carajicomedia* offers, could point to calculation if not outright hypocrisy in her dealings as well as Fernando's.

Clearly, our phallicomedian is not only up to his ears in the underworld of Spain, but views the imposition of morality by such an impotent ruling crew to be completely hypocritical. Yet whoever "he" may be, the author is no libertarian celebrator of the joy of sex, as Varo would have it. Rather, he is an exposer, not only of his own sex (in both senses of the term), but of Fernando's impotence and Isabel's hypocrisy, the latter most clearly in a stanza late in the text, where a parade of national prostitutes is read in the Order of Valencia: Francina, Estaña la Monja, la Portuguesa, la Vilara, Leonor la Aragonesa (79, 210–12; also Varo 61). Varo corrects "Estaña" to "España" in his notes to the passage and in his introductory analysis (61); the glossator reads her thus:

> Estaña la Monja es muger de buen fregado, sierva de los siervos de Dios, va por la calle, los ojos putos restrando por tierra, que parece santa. Mas yo digo: "Vade retro, Satanás." (79 gloss, 210–11)

> [Estaña the Nun is a well-scrubbed woman, servant of the servants of God, who goes through the streets with her whorish eyes dragging the ground, to appear holy. But I say, "Get thee behind me, Satan."] [39]

This is perhaps the most direct indictment of "the reestablishment of patriarchal values in Castile" whose crusade was preached by Mena and undertaken by Isabel (Weissberger 15, 16–17; Clark 9). But this contestation does not indicate that the worlds of *Laberinto*, *Celestina*, and *Carajicomedia* are that different, nor that *Carajicomedia* abandons a masculinist and racist position, since it much more explicitly maps excessive sexual prowess onto Moors (49 gloss, 186) and blacks (58 gloss, 193–94). Rather, *Carajicomedia* simply reveals that the impotent patriarchs who are supposed to impose virtue are more degenerate than the others they seek to expel — and that it is just (sexual/gender) realpolitik in the service of personal and political interests, not virtue, behind the mask of morality.

Carajicomedia seems to call the social/sexual scene in Spain as it sees it: juicy, yes, but filthy and corrupt as well. Not a moralizing imposition of anything straight, it points out how hopelessly deviant things are, as long as women are powerful and men impotent. If there aren't heroic (Castil-

ian, Catholic) men to fill their rightful place, there are always insatiable
women for whom a Moor or a Jew might be more satisfying: "[M]ás quiero
asno que me llene que caballo que me derrueque" (49 gloss, 186) [Better a
mule that fills me than a horse that throws me], as one of these "domestic
whores" says of her Morisco husband. If there is a cunt, there is always an
ass; if the brothels are full of whores, so is the court, and there is always a
queer or transvestite around as well.

As Weissberger points out, the contradictions in *Carajicomedia*'s dissidence and in its "contestatory aim" are clear (21). Its final word on this
scandalous world is a cynical and Machiavellian take on relations between
women and men, between *eros* and the *polis*, in which it textually occupies Mena's orders concerned with chastity (Luna/Diana) and sex (Venus
and Apollo) in an almost word-by-word parody through which it defines
lust and impotence. It gives the same advice to young men on how to
deal with prostitutes and to husbands on how to deal with their wives,
which I paraphrase here: First, if you're hung and hot, don't pay prostitutes but "hodedlas de balde" (67h, 201) [fuck them for nothing]—they
should learn to live more modestly (Mena's words to the great nobles in the
"Orden primera de la Luna, aplicada a Valladolid" [66–67, 200–01]). Second, marriage doesn't make sex or women virtuous no matter what Mena
says (beginning of "La última orden de Venus" [69, 202]). Finally, these are
the eroticopolitical conditions: if your wife is unfaithful, make sure you're
potent enough to keep her busy; keep it hard so she knows who's boss and
doesn't think you're submitting to her:

> CONSILIARIA DE f.
> CO. CXXXII DE JUAN DE MENA
> Y D'ESTA OBRA LXXXIX
> Por ende, vosotros, algunos maridos,
> si fuéredes tocados de amarga sospecha,
> mostrad de contino la pixa derecha,
> no piensen que'estáys del todo sumidos.
> (End of "La última orden de Venus" 89a–d, 218)

Carajicomedia, like *Laberinto*, locates the social problem not just in lascivious women but rather in insufficient virility, especially of old men. Unlike
Laberinto, though, *Carajicomedia* has a much more explicit and concrete
way of dealing with the problem, since there is no real *pudicicia* to be en-

forced by impotent rulers or fathers, and this solution can only be imposed by young and virile men (Weissberger 19). It is always penetration — even slashes across the face, in the ass, and so on (cf. especially 37, 174; and 47, 182–83) — that is the means of discipline, all within an aggressive and sadistic phallicomic mode, whether by sight, by prick, or by phallic instruments.

Conclusion

Such, then, is the world of sex, gender, and the state as mapped by *Laberinto, Celestina,* and *Carajicomedia* in their provocative readings and reinscriptions of one another and society. *Laberinto* and *Celestina* situate themselves as moral texts, and are read as such, while *Carajicomedia* sarcastically places itself in the arena of exposé cast as speculation and contemplation as well as vicious laughter, at the expense of women and old men. Its dissident intent is to critique the patriarchs' normative political and social aspirations inscribed by the former two texts, even though *Carajicomedia* is as violently misogynist and virulently masculinist as *Laberinto* and *Celestina.* It is less discreet than they are, laying out an even wider array of sex/ualities, and focusing more explicitly on impotence and vitiated masculinity in rulers and fathers, and is more openly anxious about the temptations of the queer.

Yet all three parse the sociopolitical reality of Castile through the sexual body, with all the corruption and insatiability that the sexual female body implies within this conceptual frame, centering the problems of the body politic on and projecting men's sex/uality and weakened gender identity onto the problematic bodies of women. For Mena and for Rojas, (phallic) power in the hands of women is fierce, destructive, and perverse, and all women are potentially like those "Publicias y Licinias" that without the restraint of *pudicicia* would kill their husbands without a second thought (*Laberinto* 131–32; *Celestina* 20). In *Laberinto,* Mena's epic call to Juan II to take up (phallic) arms serves as antidote and discipline to combat sexual ills and out-of-control women; in *Celestina,* the chaos that swallows up Pleberio's world proceeds from and is embodied in women, whatever their relation to men. In *Carajicomedia,* the epic battle is between the sexes (in the sense of *sexo* as genitals) in which the male sex always loses, and the terrain it maps is a violent arena of violation. Nonetheless, all these texts articulate the same economy of phallic and discursive aggression against women as quintessential other, an aggression integral to the construction of "an adequate male subjectivity" which seems to be coextensive with social order (Silverman x). Julian Weiss notes this aggression as common to Mena's lyric persona and Calisto's "rape" of Melibea, in which what is at stake is masculinity and power, that is, social order (Weiss, "Alvaro de Luna," 248–49); we may extend this to *Carajicomedia*, which locates masculinity and social order precisely in the sexual potency of younger men rather than their impotent elders. In their reforming and moralizing zeal, *Laberinto* and *Celestina* want to provoke virtue by revealing and punishing the vitiation of gender (masculine); in its exhibitionist muck-raking, *Carajicomedia* wishes to reveal the Catholic Monarchs' hypocritical show of morality, especially imputing corruption to Isabel and impotence to Fernando.

What these texts provoke in this reader, in addition to the desire to understand their workings, is a desire to question the very project of mapping social/moral order onto certain kinds of bodies as the locus of order and onto other kinds as the locus of disorder. In short, the social project of these texts suggests the necessity of analysis in its etymological sense, breaking open the tight connections of the body (gender and sex/uality) to social order, requiring the taming or expulsion of others viewed as "obscene" — dangerously and stubbornly carnal, that is, women, Jews, Moors, queers. If the "Woman Question" of the fifteenth century can be and ought to be seen as a "sex, gender, and order" question, it articulates a certain kind of social order onto certain kinds of bodies (male or female, pure [*castiʒo*] and traditional or ethnically other) and onto certain kinds of (sexual) behaviors.[40] And both sides of the question's *content* ("order" and "gender and sex/uality") as well as its *process* of collective cognition need to be interrogated.

This interrogation of the content and process of the debate in the texts of Mena, Rojas, and the unknown author of *Carajicomedia* finds a provisional answer: whether the interlocutors in the debate are "profeminists," "antifeminists," or "moralizers," they are all part of the same essentializing and therefore misogynist project (Bloch), using bodies as the primary site of culture, and the means for thinking through social dynamics and taking action on society. But the body is not a "natural" site of culture, or a natural (or unnatural) space of any simple kind (as even neurophysiology and cognitive science show), and the struggles over it that mark the fifteenth century mask other issues, "virtual" in the sense of being at the level of the imaginary and of ideology (Voestermans 245 ff.).

The reproduction of culture, while obviously connected to procreation, is not simply biological; rather, culture reproduces itself *qua* culture through ideology and the imaginary: through codes, ritual, language, and texts — precisely the terrain on which Mena, Rojas and *Carajicomedia* meet. Certainly the outcomes of the political developments of the fifteenth century were ideological and "theoretical" (in its etymological sense of "a way of seeing"), but also terribly concrete and material, at high cost in bodies and souls of a great many sexual and ethnic/religious others. If, as it seems from the scenario of contemporary U.S. and international politics, we are engaged in struggles with similar goals and strategies, perhaps this example from the past may provide a fruitful case for our own contemplation.

Notes

The title is from *Celestina*'s acrostic octaves (12–13 in the Severin/Mabbe edition). This essay is based on work for a book in progress entitled *"To Penetrate with Intellectual Eyes": Text, Vision, and Nation in Trastámara Spain;* some of the fundamental assumptions I make here about the intertextual relations of these three texts, the crucialness of ekphrasis and memory in their modalities of representation, and the moral vision of Spain that they share are much more fully substantiated and developed in that work. I wish to thank the readers for Duke University Press for their encouragement and feedback; both have made this a better essay.

1. See Cruz Tapia, which has extensive bibliography. In regard to the question of sex in Iberia's Middle Ages and early modernity, see Calderón, Cátedra, Narbona Vizcaíno, Obregón, and Sánchez Ortega.

2. These examples are necessarily strategic tokens of a much wider array of texts ranging from *cancionero* poetry to the sentimental novel, including Fray Martín de Córdoba's *Jardín de nobles doncellas,* Luis de Lucena's *Repetición de amor,* Fray Iñigo de Mendoza's *Coplas en vituperio de las malas hembras y en loor de las buenas mugeres,* etc. The debate long precedes the fifteenth century, although it has a different inflection, and continues long after.

3. On the Trastámaras in general, see Nader and Suárez Fernández.

4. See especially Rodríguez Puértolas and Scholberg. Also valuable is Márquez Villanueva ("Pan 'Pudendum Muliebris' ").

5. On reactions to Luna, see Round (8). In this volume, see Hutcheson.

6. The Mendoza clan includes such illustrious (moral) writers as Pero López de Ayala and Fernán Pérez de Guzmán, along with Iñigo López de Mendoza, marquis of Santillana. Denunciation of love and of vice is present in many of Santillana's texts; see in particular his "love trilogy," a set of texts analyzed by Deyermond.

7. For other readings of *Laberinto* as ethical, see Lapesa, Beltrán, Weiss, and Weissberger. Weissberger's readings of *Carajicomedia* and Mena's *Laberinto* are similar to mine, and my own work owes much to hers. I am grateful to Weissberger for sharing her work with me prior to its publication.

8. Dissent does not entirely disappear, but shows up in encoded forms like the sentimental novel; see, for example, Márquez Villanueva ("*Cárcel de amor*").

9. The term "sex/uality" points to persons, whether "historical" or "fictional" individuals or categories of individuals like "men" or "women," viewed in terms of sexual categories or behaviors; it does *not* indicate the kind of conflation of physical gender, erotic behavior, subjectivity, and identity which Foucault claims is forged in the nineteenth century. Hence, to talk about Celestina's "sex/uality" is not to posit "her" as a concrete individual or to subsume her "identity" within sexual attributes or positions, but rather to talk about how the text *Celestina* encodes or displays the character in sexual "action" or discourse.

10. Juan de Mena's *Laberinto* was a much copied and edited text; see the editions of De Nigris and Cummins along with Foulché-Delbosc, Street ("Hernán Núñez"), Bataillon, and Kerkhof. Although there is an early and possibly authorial commentary, it is incomplete (Weiss, *The Poet's Art* 122–23, esp. n. 22); the text was first glossed completely by Hernán Núñez, *editio princeps* 1499, revised once, and reprinted with great frequency. It was glossed again by Francisco Sánchez de las Brozas, known as El Brocense (Salamanca, 1582); I will be using the 1804 edition of this text. All quotations are from the Cummins edition and citations will indicate the stanza by number and specific verses by a lowercase letter when necessary; all translations are mine.

11. Due to this purposeful conflation on Mena's part, I will use "Mena" as well as "poet," "reader," "narrator," and "enarrator" (see note 12) to refer to any of the voices.

12. *Enarratio* is a basic element of pedagogy from classical antiquity through the Renaissance, consisting of the explanation of the text so that the reading (*lectio*) is thorough and complete, including commentary on the grammatical and figurative aspects of the text as well as its allusions and references (Quintilian 1.8.18–21). The "consummation" of this reading is *meditatio* or *contemplatio*, the ethical and spiritual application of the text to one's own life (cf. Carruthers chs. 1 and 7). I will use the term "enarrate" in part because of Núñez's use of it through-

out his *tituli* for the poem, since I take him to be a competent reader well schooled in the rhetorical and memorial traditions in which Mena himself was trained.

13. Several critics see *Laberinto* as an "interior journey," among them Post, Lida de Malkiel (*Juan de Mena*), Burke, and Nepaulsingh. However, the indications of a journey (verbs of motion, etc.) are, after the *raptus* of the poet to Fortune's house, attenuated, and, as Burke indicates, the architectonics of mnemotechnic are a structuring principle, something also signaled by Mena's use of the term *simulacra* for the objects of his *enarratio;* cf. Yates and Carruthers. In addition, the poet's attention is not at all on his own interior, but on the external world of social and political action. What *is* emphasized in the poem is precisely the visual, and the entire structure may be seen as a memorial ekphrasis not only of the throne in the circle of Mars, but also of the entire House of Fortune.

14. María of Castile, sister of Juan II and wife of Alfons el Magnanim (V) of Aragon, was also noted for her frigidity; Alfons basically abandoned their marital bed for warmer climes in Naples.

15. According to El Brocense (259), there is some confusion about who exactly the woman was (not whether she did the deed): either Doña María de Coronel, who was the daughter of Don Alonso Fernández Coronel and married to Don Juan de la Cerda in the epoch of Alfonso XI "el que ganó Algeciras" [the one who won Algeciras]; or the wife of Don Alonso de Guzmán "el bueno," who was absent at Tarifa while it was besieged by Moors, this during the reign of Sancho IV. In the latter case, it is of note that Guzmán held Algeciras until it could be aided by Castilian troops, thus holding the fort rather than giving it up to the Moors. In either case, the basic parallel structure of Reconquista and moral struggle is maintained.

16. Here, I translate *pudiçicia*, from Latin *pudicitia* "shamefastness, modesty, chastity, virtue," as "sexual shame/modesty" but there is no exact equivalent in English (Lewis 672b). Thus, after this translation, I will leave the term in Castilian. See Kaster for Roman usage of *pudicitia*.

17. There is a long tradition of two Venuses, one of whom has to do with legitimate marriage and the other with lust, a tradition much exploited by Boccaccio in his own ethical project (cf. the introduction to Cassell and Kirkham's translation of Boccaccio's *Caccia di Diana*, along with Hollander).

18. Homosex/uality is often referred to as unspeakable (*nefandum*) in discourses of the period; cf. Goodich. In *Laberinto*, it is perhaps unmentionable for any number of particular reasons, including the rumors that Luna and Juan II might be lovers (see Hutcheson in this volume).

19. *Desonesto* in Spanish is not as general as English "dishonest," but rather implies sexual impropriety.

20. Although Mena suggests that the prophecy was ambiguous (stanza 264–

65), history proved him right almost ten years after the completion of the poem, with Luna's arrest and execution in 1453 on orders issued by Juan II but master-minded by his second wife (the mother of Isabel the Catholic). Juan II died a year later, a broken man.

21. This dynamic of vitiation of male subjectivity is a salient feature of misogy-nist texts, e.g., Andreas Capellanus, *Ars amoris* III; Boccaccio's *Corbaccio;* and Alfonso Martínez de Toledo's *El Arçipreste de Talavera o Corbacho.* See, among others, DuBois; Lloyd; and Brocato ("Communicating Desire"). On Alfonso Martínez, see Brown in this volume.

22. I cite from Severin's bilingual edition of the *Tragicomedia,* which includes Mabbe's translation facing the Spanish. Mabbe's *The Spanish Bawd* (1631) is an adaptation rather than a translation of the *Tragicomedia,* if the only complete one (see Severin's introduction), and I will often make the translation more literal, in-dicating my own interventions in parentheses. Citations indicate the facing page numbers in Severin/Mabbe.

23. Cf. *Laberinto,* 12a–d: "[F]luctüosa Fortuna aborrida, / tus casos inçiertos semejan atales, / que corren por ondas de bienes y males, / haziendo no çierta ninguna corrida" [Fluctuant and abhorred Fortune, your uncertain cases seem like small unstable boats that run through waves of good and ill, making any run uncertain].

24. I have chosen to leave *Celestina's* term "auto" rather than translate it throughout because of the narrow generic reference of "act" in English. See Bro-cato 1995 regarding the difficulties of a rigid generic classification of *Celestina* in terms of twentieth-century categories.

25. Rojas claims in the Prologue to have found the first act and added fifteen more for the *Comedia,* and then to have extended the plot against his will. The textual history of *Celestina* is extremely complicated; see esp. the first volume of Marciales's edition.

26. See Gerli's essay in this volume for another analysis of the sexual dynamics of *Celestina.*

27. It might be objected that this reading strips *Celestina* of its long-admired psychological and social realism and reduces it to allegorical fable. However, classical and medieval modes of reading on different levels (the "fourfold way") depend in part on the integrity of the level of (hi)story, to progress as far as the text supports in reading at other levels. Allegorical or moral reading is often a relatively free ethical reading of a text rather than a rigidly defined one, through which the text is stored in memory to be applied to one's own circumstances. This mode of reading is as characteristic of the fifteenth and sixteenth centuries as it is of the fifth or the twelfth. See, among others, Carruthers; Yates; and Brown, *Contrary Things.* The reading offered herein is not intended to be ex-

clusive nor exhaustive of the conceptual and stylistic richness of *Celestina;* see Brocato (under submission) and the first (unnumbered) note.

28. This is demonstrated more substantively in Brocato (under submission); for reasons of concision and focus, I can only summarize its conclusions here. See the first note.

29. *Gloria* is a poetic euphemism for orgasm at this time (Whinnom 22).

30. "Más arriba lo siento, sobre el estómago," in the Mabbe translation [Lay your hand higher up toward my stomach] (190–91). On this passage see Gossy (41); and Burshatin (in this volume). Elicia points out that Celestina takes great pleasure in repairing hymens: when asked why she didn't turn to with "la de la manilla" [the girl with the bracelet], she responds, "yo le tengo a este oficio odio; tú mueres tras ello" (204–05) [but I had as lief die as go about it. . . . [Y]ou are never well, but when you are at it], translated literally, "I loathe this duty; you die for it." The phrase also foreshadows Celestina's end.

31. Gossy and Smith take up some of the same issues dealt with here, the former in terms of poststructuralist feminist theory and the latter in terms of a metadisciplinary deconstruction of *converso* identity, particularly as elaborated in the work of Américo Castro.

32. *Celestina*'s Prologue and stanza 298 of the *Laberinto* both seem to share a view of nature as violent ("tremen las ondas y luchan los vientos" [the waves shudder and the winds struggle] says line 2381 in the latter), but the final stanzas of the *Laberinto* are of later provenance and are appended to the work only from 1509 onward (cf. Foulché-Delbosc); El Brocense also discredits the attribution to Mena as early as 1570.

33. Apropos of this obscene reading of Calisto's "gifts of Nature," I offer *Celestina,* act 14, in which Melibea calls her virginity "el mayor don que la natura me á dado" [the greatest gift that Nature has given me]. Mabbe renders this "not to rob me of the greatest jewel, which nature hath enriched me with" (314–15).

34. In the closing octaves Rojas advises fleeing the bad ends he has represented and exhorts Christian devotion and fear of God, the latter of which is, after all, the beginning of Wisdom, whether *sapientia* or *prudentia* (404–05). The debate over *Celestina*'s didacticism has been heated since its publication, as the prologue indicates. Nonetheless, Rojas himself says that the text is exemplary and ethical; although he is but another reader of the text once it has been composed and revised and as such has no particular privilege, an ethical or didactic reading is still both possible and productive.

35. These dates have general consensus; cf. Eisenberg (167); and Varo (76–79). The *Cancionero de obras de burlas provocantes a risa* first appeared as the ninth section of the *Cancionero general* of 1511; as it appeared separately in 1519, it included the contents of the second and later editions of the *Cancionero general,*

restoring *Aposentamiento,* and adding *Carajicomedia* (Varo 16–20). All citations are from Varo's edition and indicate the stanza number, whether the poetry or gloss is cited, and the page number of the edition (rather than the facsimile); all translations are mine.

36. In this volume, see the essays of Blackmore and Liu.

37. The blasphemous use of religious language and Latin is clear *passim*, but see especially the glosses to stanzas 1 (150–52), 45 (180), and 59 (195). For the universities, see stanzas 34 (171), 35 (173), 48 (185), 58 (193–94), and 71 (203–05). While *Carajicomedia* has nothing to do with "love" (and everything to do with sex), like courtly love it uses the language of religion for its discursive work.

38. Cf. Calderón:

Sabemos que Fernando el Católico "estuvo dotado desde su nacimiento de admirable vigor corporal", sin embargo, la historia ha silenciado sus hazañas amatorias, dejando como único rastro visible los nombres de algunas de sus amantes: Aldonza Roig y de Yvorra, Joana Nicolau, doña Toda de Larrea, una portuguesa apellidada Pereira, etc. . . . Interesa resaltar, en cualquier caso, la actitud comprensiva de la reina católica, conocedora del 'temperamento inquieto' de su marido. (89–90)

[We know that Fernando the Catholic "was endowed from birth with a remarkable physical prowess"; history has silenced his sexual pursuits, however, leaving as the only trace the names of some of his lovers: Aldonza Roig y de Yvorra, Joana Nicolau, Doña Toda de Larrea, a Portuguese woman with the surname Pereira, etc. In any case, it is interesting to note the acquiescence of the Catholic Queen, who was fully aware of her husband's "restless spirit."]

In addition, Calderón (69) and Suárez Fernández (188) point out that, as in *Carajicomedia,* it is two prostitutes of Segovia whose first-hand testimony attests to the potency of Enrique IV "el Impotente" with other women (besides his wife), further supporting the idea that the main figures of *Carajicomedia* may be composites, condensations of several historical individuals. (Compare this to Calisto's desire for witnesses.)

39. In translating "muger de buen fregado," I have opted for "a well-scrubbed woman" to catch the suggestion both of hypocritical cleanliness and having "scrubbed" surfaces with her own back doing sexwork. This also echoes Pármeno in the first act of *Celestina:* "¡O Calisto desaventurado, abatido, ciego! ¡Y en tierra está, adorando a la más antigua [y] puta tierra, que fregaron sus espaldas en todos los burdeles" (62–63) [O unhappy Calisto, deject wretch, blind in thy folly, and kneeling on the ground to adore the oldest and the rottenest piece of whorish earth, that ever rubbed her shoulders in the stews!]. Following Severin

(116) rather than Marciales, I add "y" to separate "antigua" and "puta," although Marciales's emendation is based on the Italian translation: "In terra sta adorando alla più antica puttana vecchia ch'abbia frecate sue spalle per tuti li bordelli del mondo."

40. I have only been able to gesture toward the importance of ethnic otherness, in part because here it is subsumed in the problematics of sex. However, if we bear in mind Mena's call for a renewal of the *Reconquista*, Rojas's *converso* descent, and the scattered references to Jews and Moors as often highly sexual members of the "mundo inmundo" of *Carajicomedia*, the entanglement of issues of sex/uality and ethnicity is made plain.

Works Cited

Bataillon, Marcel. "La edición princeps del *Laberinto* de Juan de Mena." *Varia lección de clásicos españoles*. Madrid: Gredos, 1964. 9–20.

Beltrán, Luis. "The Poet, the King, and the Cardinal Virtues in Juan de Mena's Laberinto." *Speculum* 46 (1971): 318–32.

Bloch, R. Howard. *Medieval Misogyny and the Invention of Western Romantic Love*. Chicago: U of Chicago P, 1991.

Boccaccio, Giovanni. *Diana's Hunt: Caccia de Diana, Boccaccio's First Fiction*. Trans. Anthony Cassell and Victoria Kirkham. Philadelphia: U of Pennsylvania P, 1991.

Brocato, Linde M. "Communicating Desire: Self and Discourse in La Celestina." Diss. Emory U, 1991.

———. *"To Penetrate with Intellectual Eyes": Text, Vision, and Nation in Trastámara Spain*. Under submission.

El Brocense. See Sánchez de las Brozas.

Brown, Catherine. *Contrary Things: Exegesis, Dialectic, and the Poetics of Didacticism*. Berkeley: Stanford UP, 1998.

Burke, James F. "The Interior Journey and the Structure of Juan de Mena's *Laberinto de Fortuna*." *Revista de estudios hispánicos* 22 (1988): 27–45.

Calderón, Emilio. *Usos y costumbres sexuales de los reyes de España*. 2nd ed. Madrid: Editorial Cirene, 1993.

Canales, Alfonso. "Sobre la identidad del actante (léase protagonista) de la 'Carajicomedia.'" *Papeles de Son Armandans* January 1976: 74–81.

Cancionero de obras de burlas provocantes a risa. Ed. Frank Domínguez. Valencia: Albatros Ediciones Hispanófila, 1978.

Carajicomedia. Ed. Carlos Varo. Madrid: Nova Escolar, 1981.

Carruthers, Mary. *The Book of Memory: A Study of Memory in Medieval Culture.* Cambridge: Cambridge UP, 1991.

Castro Guisasola, F. *Observaciones sobre las fuentes literarias de "La Celestina".* Anejos de la Revista de Filología Española 5. Madrid: Revista de Filología Española, 1924.

Cátedra, Pedro. *Amor y pedagogía en la Edad Media.* Salamanca: Universidad de Salamanca, 1989.

Clark, Dorothy Clotelle. *Juan de Mena's Laberinto de Fortuna: Classic Epic and Mester de Clerecía.* University, Miss.: Romance Monographs, 1973.

Cruz Tapia, María Muriel. *Antifeminismo y subestimación de la mujer en la literatura medieval.* Cáceres: Ed. Guadiloba, 1991.

Deyermond, Alan D. "Santillana's Love-Allegories: Structure, Relation, and Message." *Studies in Honor of Bruce W. Wardropper.* Ed. Diane Fox, Harry Sieber, and Robert TerHorst. Newark, Del.: Juan de la Cuesta, 1989. 75–90.

Doob, Penelope Reed. *The Idea of the Labyrinth from Classical Antiquity through the Middle Ages.* Ithaca: Cornell UP, 1990.

DuBois, Page. *Amazons and Centaurs: Women and the Prehistory of the Great Chain of Being.* Ann Arbor: U of Michigan P, 1982.

————. *Sowing the Body: Psychoanalysis and Ancient Representations of the Body.* Chicago: U of Chicago P, 1988.

Eisenberg, Daniel. "Two Problems of Identification in a Parody of Juan de Mena." *Oelschläger Festschrift: Florida State University Studies presented to Victor R. B. Oelschläger in Honor of His Retirement.* Ed. Daniel Eisenberg. Estudios de Hispanófila 36. Chapel Hill: Estudios de Hispanófila, 1976. 157–70.

Foucault, Michel. *The History of Sexuality.* Vol. 1: *An Introduction.* Trans. Robert Hurley. 1978. New York: Vintage, 1980.

Foulché-Delbosc, R. "Étude sur le *Laberinto* de Juan de Mena." *Revue Hispanique* 60 (1902): 75–138.

Goodich, Michael. *The Unmentionable Vice: Homosexuality in the Later Medieval Period.* N.p.: Dorset P, 1979.

Gossy, Mary. *The Untold Story: Women and Theory in Golden Age Texts.* Ann Arbor: U of Michigan P, 1989.

Hollander, Robert. *Boccaccio's Two Venuses.* New York: Columbia UP, 1977.

Kaster, Robert A. "The Shame of the Romans." Presidential address to the American Philological Association, New York, December 1996. http://ccat.sas.upenn.edu/TAPA/kaster.html

Kerkhof, Maximilian P. A. M. "Sobre las ediciones del 'Laberinto de Fortuna' publicadas de 1481 a 1943, y la tradición manuscrita." *Forum Litterarum: miscelânea de estudos literários, linguísticos e históricos oferecida a J. J. van den*

Besselaar. Ed. Hans Bots and Maxim. Kerkhof. Amsterdam: APA–Holland UP, 1984. 269–82.

Lapesa, Rafael. "El elemento moral en el *Laberinto* de Mena: su influjo en la disposición de la obra." *De la Edad Media a nuestros días: estudios de historia literaria.* Madrid: Gredos, 1967. 112–22.

Lewis, Charlton T. *Elementary Latin Dictionary.* 1891. Oxford: Oxford UP, 1985.

Lida de Malkiel, María Rosa. *Juan de Mena, poeta del prerrenacimiento español.* Ed. Yakov Malkiel. 1950. Mexico City: Colegio de México, 1984.

———. *La originalidad artística de La Celestina.* Ed. Yakov Malkiel. 1962. Buenos Aires: Eudeba, 1970.

Lloyd, Genevieve. *The Man of Reason: "Male" and "Female" in Western Philosophy.* Minneapolis: U of Minnesota P, 1984.

López de Mendoza, Iñigo, Marqués de Santillana. *Canciones y decires.* Ed. Vicente García de Diego. 1913. Clásicos Castellanos 18. Madrid: Espasa-Calpe, 1973.

———. *Comedieta de Ponça, sonetos: letras hispánicas.* Ed. Maxim P. A. M. Kerkhof. Madrid: Cátedra, 1986.

———. *Obras completas.* Ed. Angel Gómez Moreno and Maximilian P. A. M. Kerkhoff. Barcelona: Planeta, 1988.

Márquez Villanueva, Francisco. "*Cárcel de amor:* novela política." *Revista de Occidente* 4 (1966): 185–200. Rpt. in F. Márquez Villanueva, *Relecciones de literatura medieval.* Seville: Publicaciones de la Universidad de Sevilla, 1977. 75–94.

———. "Pan 'Pudendum Muliebris' y los Españoles en Flandes." *Hispanic Studies in Honor of Joseph Silverman.* Ed. Joseph Ricapito. Newark, Del.: Juan de la Cuesta, 1988. 247–69.

Martínez de Toledo, Alfonso. *Arcipreste de Talavera o Corbacho.* Ed. Michael Gerli. Madrid: Cátedra, 1979.

Maura, Gabriel Maura Gamazo, Duque de. *El príncipe que se murió de amor: Don Juan, primogénito de los Reyes Católicos.* Madrid: Espasa-Calpe, 1944.

Mena, Juan de. *Laberinto de Fortuna.* 2nd ed. John G. Cummins. Madrid: Cátedra, 1982.

———. *Laberinto de Fortuna y otros poemas.* Ed. Carla de Nigris. Barcelona: Crítica, 1994.

Mendoza, Fray Iñigo de. *Cancionero.* Ed. Julio Rodríguez-Puértolas. Clásicos Castellanos 163. Madrid: Espasa Calpe, 1968.

Nader, Helen. *The Mendoza Family in the Spanish Renaissance.* New Brunswick: Rutgers UP, 1989.

Narbona Vizcaíno, Rafael. *Pueblo, poder, y sexo: Valencia medieval (1306–1420).* Valencia: Diputació de Valencià, 1992.

Nepaulsingh, Colbert I. *Towards a History of Literary Composition in Medieval Spain.* Toronto: U of Toronto P, 1986.

Obregón, Enrique de. *La otra historia sexual de España*. Barcelona: Martínez Roca, 1990.

Pérez de Guzmán, Fernán. *Generaciones y semblanzas*. Ed. R. B. Tate. London: Tamesis, 1965.

Post, Charles. *Medieval Spanish Allegory*. Cambridge, Mass.: Harvard UP, 1915.

Quintilian. *Institutio oratoria*. 4 vols. Trans. H. E. Butler. Loeb Classical Library 124–28. Cambridge, Mass.: Harvard UP; 1980.

Rodríguez Puértolas, Julio, ed. *Poesía crítica y satírica del siglo XV*. Madrid: Castalia, 1971.

———. *Poesía de protesta en la Edad Media*. Madrid, 1968.

Rojas, Fernando de. *Celestina*. Ed. Miguel Marciales. Illinois Medieval Monographs 1. Urbana: U of Illinois P, 1985.

———. *La Celestina*. Ed. Dorothy Sherman Severin. Madrid: Cátedra, 1987.

———. *Celestina*. Trans. James Mabbe. Ed. Dorothy Sherman Severin. Warminster, England: Aris and Philips, 1987.

Round, Nicholas. *The Greatest Man Uncrowned: A Study of the Fall of Don Alvaro de Luna*. London: Tamesis, 1986.

Sánchez de las Brozas, Francisco. *Las obras del famoso poeta Juan de Mena*. 1582. Madrid: La Imprenta de Repullés, La Librería de Castillo, 1804.

Sánchez Ortega, María Elena. *La mujer y la sexualidad en el antiguo régimen: la perspectiva inquisitorial*. Madrid: Akal, 1992.

Scholberg, Kenneth R. *Sátira e invectiva en la España medieval*. Madrid: Gredos, 1971.

Silverman, Kaja. *The Acoustic Mirror: The Female Voice in Psychoanalysis and Cinema*. Bloomington: Indiana UP, 1988.

Smith, Paul Julian. *Representing the Other: "Race," Text, and Gender in Spanish and Spanish-American Narrative*. Oxford: Clarendon, 1992.

Solomon, Michael. "Calisto's Ailment: Bitextual Diagnostics and Parody in Celestina." *Revista de estudios hispánicos* 23 (1984): 41–64.

Street, Florence. "Hernán Núñez and the Earliest Printed Editions of Mena's 'El Laberinto de Fortuna.'" *Modern Language Review* 61 (1966): 51–63.

———. "The Text of Mena's Laberinto in the Cancionero de Ixar and Its Relationship to Some Other Fifteenth-Century MSS." *Bulletin of Hispanic Studies* 35 (1958): 63–71.

Suárez Fernández, Luis. *Los Trastámara de Castilla en el siglo XV (1407–1474)*. *Historia de España*, ed. Ramón Menéndez Pidal, 15. Madrid: Gredos, 1964.

———. *Los Trastámara y los Reyes Católicos*. Historia de España 7. Madrid: Gredos, 1985.

Vanderford, Kenneth H. "Macías in Legend and Literature." *Modern Philology* 31 (1933): 35–63.

Varo, Carlos. See *Carajicomedia*.

Voestermans, Paul. "Alterity/Identity: A Deficient Image of Culture." *Alterity, Identity, Image: Selves and Others in Society and Scholarship.* Ed. Raymond Corbey and Joep Leerssen. Amsterdam: Rodopi, 1991. 219–50.

Weiss, Julian. "Alvaro de Luna, Juan de Mena, and the Power of Courtly Love." *Modern Language Notes* 106 (1991): 241–56.

———. "Juan de Mena's *Coronación:* Satire or Sátira?" *Journal of Hispanic Philology* 6 (1982): 113–38.

———. *The Poet's Art: Literary Theory in Castile c. 1400–60.* Oxford: Society for the Study of Mediaeval Languages and Literature, 1990.

Weissberger, Barbara. "Male Sexual Anxieties in *Carajicomedia:* A Response to Male Sovereignty." *Poetry at Court in Trastamaran Spain.* Ed. E. Michael Gerli and Julian Weiss. Tempe, Ariz: Arizona State UP, 1998.

Whinnom, Keith. *Spanish Literary Historiography: Three Forms of Distortion.* Exeter: U of Exeter P, 1968.

Yates, Frances A. *The Art of Memory.* Chicago: U of Chicago P, 1966.

V

THE BODY

AND

THE STATE

E. Michael Gerli

Dismembering the Body Politic

Vile Bodies and Sexual Underworlds in *Celestina*

> *Por la filosomía es conocida la virtud interior.*
> — *Calisto, in* Celestina *(Act 1)*

Celestina, the name commonly given to the *Comedia* (subsequently *tragi-comedia*) *de Calisto y Melibea*, is one of the most remarkable works produced in late-fifteenth-century Iberia. A text comprised initially of sixteen "acts" written entirely in dialogue, its earliest known edition (Burgos, 1499) was published anonymously. By the publication of the 1502 edition, however, five more acts were added, along with a prefatory "letter from the writer to a friend" and an acrostic identifying an author. Although uncertainty still clouds the identity of the individual who composed the original act 1, the remaining acts (2–21), the acrostic tells us, were written by one Fernando de Rojas (c. 1465–1541). Rojas was a lawyer educated at Salamanca and the son of converted Jews (*conversos*). Toward the end of his life Rojas served as chief magistrate of Talavera de la Reina, an important Castilian commercial center in the province of Toledo during the late Middle Ages.

The years leading up to the publication of Rojas's *Celestina* encompass a period of profound social, cultural, and political change in the kingdom of Castile. To be sure, the very decade in which Rojas published the work marks events that shook the kingdom to its foundations and held profound consequences for the rest of Europe and, indeed, the world: it signals no less than the conquest of Moorish Granada, the expulsion of the Jews, the advent of mass conversions from Judaism and Islam to Christianity, the discovery of America, the Castilian-Aragonese intervention in Italy, and, finally, the promulgation of a divinely ordained Catholic state whose purity and orthodoxy were ensured by the vigilance of the newly established

Santa Hermandad and the Holy Office of the Inquisition. As Fernando and Isabel, who are known to history as the Catholic Monarchs, sought to forge an empire through the extirpation or suppression of all signs of difference in their realms, the entire cultural spectrum of Castilian life during the last decade of the fifteenth century was distinguished by a persistent anxiety centering on questions of order and orthodoxy, power and legitimacy, truancy and heterodoxy.

In the author's prefatory letter to his friend, Rojas inscribes *Celestina* firmly within this tension of truancy and orthodoxy, order and disorder, which defines the closing years of the fifteenth century in Castilian life. In that letter, Rojas underscores sexual, class, gender, and community conflicts as his principal motivations for taking up his pen to complete the work of the anonymous creator of act 1. He explicitly conceives his *tragicomedia* as a palliative to these social ills and as a civic act of virtue intended to restore direction and reason to a confused and dissolute youth held captive by desire and exploited by "lisongeros y malos sirvientes y falsas mugeres hechizeras" (6–7) [flattering and evil servants and false witches].[1]

Translated into all the European languages and reprinted some sixty times, Rojas's *Celestina* was by all accounts one of the most popular, best read, and influential books of the sixteenth century. Celebrated by Cervantes as a "divine if human book," and imitated by, among many others, Lope de Vega, the verbal profanity and sexual license it portrays seem to have caused little distress to its readership.[2] The plot revolves around the young patrician, Calisto, and his passion for Melibea, daughter of the wealthy Pleberio. When Melibea rejects Calisto's advances, he enlists the aid of old Celestina, an unscrupulous former prostitute who now makes her living as a witch and go-between. With the help of Calisto's manservants, Sempronio and Pármeno, and some apprenticed whores named Elicia and Areúsa (who consort with Calisto's servants), Celestina persuades Melibea to relent. Just when the liaison is progressing, however, Calisto dies from a fall suffered as he scales the wall of Melibea's garden after a heated night of love. In despair, Melibea kills herself by leaping from a tower into the garden as her father watches from below. Shortly before Calisto's plunge, Celestina is stabbed to death by Pármeno and Sempronio in a dispute over spoils; the two are publicly executed by the civil authorities for the murder. Although Calisto and Melibea move in a world of ardent, idealized passion and aristocratic breeding, most of the interest in the work centers on the demonic

Celestina and her low-life confederates, who comprise a vivid picture of a sexual underworld driven by competing economic and social imperatives.

For all its achievements, *Celestina* scholarship has in the main — with the exception of the work of scholars like Castro, Gilman, and Márquez Villanueva on *converso mentalité*, and Maravall on social transformations — focused on textual technicalities, questions of authorship, characterization, and other formal, bibliographical, or artistic considerations. Conspicuous principally for its ahistoricity and its aversion to interpretation as it invokes the text's ambiguity (Russell 157), *Celestina* criticism, while it has served to resolve thorny textual issues and to illuminate the prodigious artistic achievements of the work, has declined (with the exception of the individuals mentioned) to confront the problematical connection between literature and life, text and context.

Yet a close reading of *Celestina* reveals that the church, private morals, sex, and public order were in fact in profound conflict, challenged by the existence of an increasingly visible underworld inhabited by subjects whose currency was the pleasures of the human body, lucre, personal ambition, and the proclamation of the sovereign self. It is a work that shows incontrovertibly that ideals of private freedom and their restraint were not self-sufficient, uncontested abstractions but ideas that could be construed as contradictory expressions of a single principle in late-fifteenth-century Spain — the good — whose pursuit by one and the many was capable of producing a distinctly unstable moral and cultural arrangement. *Celestina* registers and advocates definite ways of thinking about the world while it thwarts others; and it constitutes itself as a site of cultural struggle and catalyst for change whose implications are ineluctably ideological and political. The law, love, money, morality, ambition, the body, nutrition, and sexuality in particular, become in it the loci where dramatic early-modern battles of caste, rank, class, and ethics are played out.

Indeed, *Celestina,* as Maravall notes, "offers up the drama of the crisis and transformation of the social and moral values developing during the phase of economic growth, the growth of culture — of all life — in fifteenth-century society" (20). It is a work that portrays not only the blurring but the deliberate encroachment of socially consecrated boundaries of power, authority, and sexuality in order to test them and to portray new styles and mores that were daily transforming the collective imagination of fifteenth-century Castile.

Although *Celestina* quite conspicuously treats sex, love, the human body, prostitution, and morality, with the exception of Lacarra few scholars have explored how these topics, in both their orthodox and "deviant" manifestations, also affect the polity of persons depicted in the text; and how these ideas may be linked to larger cultural and ideological forces shaping the discourses of legitimacy in late-fifteenth-century Spain. The sexual underworld defined by the perimeters of Celestina's house in act 9, for example, is — more than a space for promiscuity — a precinct for heated partisan debate centered on the privileges and freedoms of the person as designated by caste, political economy, blood, and social position. It is there that, in consonance with their passionate corporality, open sexuality, and the consumption of food and other material goods, characters like Elicia, Areúsa, and Lucrecia express their radical social and civic nonconformity as they undermine their masters' authority through the exposure of what they perceive to lie behind the painted masks of their entitled lives.

The descriptions of Melibea's body in act 9 provide the iconic centerpiece for this debate and figure prominently in the scene as the concrete images around which all the apprehensions delimiting the relationship of the servants to their masters revolve. Melibea's portrait, placed there in the mouths of the two whores, Elicia and Areúsa, functions as a figural nexus that subsumes a series of symbolic connections linking sexuality, corporality, nutrition, and desire to questions of social authority, privilege, agency, money, and power. As it does this, her likeness constitutes a site for cultural negotiation, a representational structure that expresses, more than petty jealousy (Fraker 138–39; Gariano 4), deep changes affecting the social and sexual fabric of the world in which all the characters in *Celestina* live.

Pierre Bourdieu has argued persuasively that bodies harbor profound cultural significance and that they embrace a form of compressed cultural symbolism that encodes "in abbreviated and practical, i.e., mnemonic, form the fundamental principles of the arbitrary content of the culture" in which they appear (94). Bodies, according to Bourdieu, may thus be understood as domains of signification encompassing broad figurative sense and may be interpreted as illustrations of social position, cultural identity, and patterns of belief and authority.

The Middle Ages was a period profoundly preoccupied with bodily representations and both defined and constituted human bodies as crucial elements of the symbolic order. Bodies were an acknowledged medieval site for social figurations. To be sure, echoing Aristotle's *Politics,* medieval and early-modern minds viewed human bodies as microcosms (Rico), but especially as tropes capable of depicting political and social systems (Hale). Medievals read bodies explicitly as transparent cultural signs that pointed to things greater than themselves. Indeed, in the Middle Ages all manner of abstractions through the devices of allegory were given corporal form and played a prominent role in defining, mediating, and depicting society's institutions and conventions. Bodies and their representations were thus conceived as a means of knowledge of other things; they were understood as iconic devices apt to provoke thought. Looking at, reading about, talking, or writing about human bodies and their functions always implied the presence of a larger interpretive vision at work.

Personality and civic values were objectified both in the medieval physical body as well as in the marks of status and insignia used to embellish it. In the pseudo-Aristotelian *Secreta secretorum,* one of the medieval age's most widely disseminated texts, for example, Aristotle in the context of the political education of Alexander the Great invokes the science of physiognomy as key to understanding the temperament and inclinations of humankind in questions of statecraft. Similarly, the body, suitably attired and presented, came to symbolize overtly the gender, status, and nature of the person, and that individual's place in the larger sphere of the state and human polity. In the Middle Ages dignity and class came to knights from their shields and armor as well as from their genealogical person; and heraldic signs and sartorial adornment signified a means of both personal and social identification (Fox-Davies 108). The body's physical constitution and the way it was enhanced, then, were recognized forms of social textuality.

In addition to the church, which was imagined as the *corpus verum,* chief among medieval embodiments were the specifically political and civic metaphors that portrayed the state and community in concrete terms of human corpora. Ernst Kantorowicz, for example, has shown how the notion of the king's two bodies expounded the dual nature of sovereignty—both human and divine—while the depiction of the monarch as the head of society was used to account for the hierarchy of political and social differences in the order of things (Kantorowicz; Le Goff). The socialized human body often encompassed, then, the central symbolic object around which

metaphorical civic definitions, as well as the struggle for power, dominance, and spirituality, were played out (see Hale; Patterson; Dinshaw;
Brown; and Bynum, *Fragmentation, Holy Feast*).

More than for the simple transcoding of political ideals, however, bodies
—but primarily sexually disordered or infirm bodies—could be used to
portray and invoke social upheaval and threats to political and moral stability, as well as to challenge the boundaries that defined and maintained
order. Medieval imaginations, for example, failed to distinguish between
leprosy and venereal disease and specifically associated leprosy with promiscuity and sexual depravation, reading the leper's outward signs of bodily
decomposition as evidence of inner profanity, moral degeneracy, and social
undesirability. In this way, the leper incarnated an ethical, physical, and
social menace to the citizenry and was isolated in the Middle Ages by rituals, quarantines, and even legal sanctions (Brody). Corporality was thus, in
addition to being a means for representing order, a vehicle that could personify disorder and convey intangible ethical, political, and civic anxieties.
To medieval imaginations a disarranged, profane body signaled a potentially dangerous relationship to everyone in the community.

To be sure, the corporal comparison of the disordered, ailing body was
invoked with particular urgency during the wrenching debates on monarchical succession in Castile during the reign of Enrique IV, known to history as *el Impotente*. The magnate Pedro González de Mendoza explicitly
summoned it at Avila in 1465 to allude to the king, as he cautioned the supporters of Prince Alfonso's rival claim to the throne:

> Notorio es señores, que todo el regno es avido por cuerpo, del qual tenemos
> el Rey ser cabeza; la qual si por alguna inhabilidad es enferma, pareceria
> mejor consejo poner las melecinas, que la razon que cree que quitar la cabeza,
> que la nacion defiende. (*Memorias de Don Enrique IV de Castilla* 2: 489).

> [Gentlemen, it is well known that every realm may be taken for a body, of
> which the king is the head; and if that head should, through some indisposi-
> tion, suffer infirmity, the application of remedies would seem better counsel
> than following the advice of those who would remove the head, which de-
> fends the nation.]

Indeed, as the struggle for succession and political hegemony between
Enrique IV and the partisans of his half-sister, Isabel of Castile, intensified

after the death of the young Alfonso, the dynastic clash was played out upon the reigning monarch's very body. Rumored to be sexually impotent, and hence incapable of producing an heir, the right of Enrique's putative daughter, Princess Juana, to succeed to the throne of Castile was openly contested by the opposing Isabelline faction as it asserted Juana's illegitimacy. As a result, in his attempt to salvage his designated heir's claim to the crown, Enrique was compelled to submit to medical inquiries as well as cite evidence from prostitutes that refuted his alleged sexual dysfunction.[3]

It is clear, therefore, that bodily references and descriptions — but especially those linked to forms of sexuality — were something more than simply themselves, and that in fifteenth-century Iberia, as elsewhere in Europe, ordered and disordered bodies often functioned as concrete representations of social entities and ideas — conscious symbols of human polity. In effect, human bodies at all levels of society were charged with political significance as they were perceived to personify communal beliefs and contain civic significance. In this larger sense, then, bodies were envisaged as material representational spaces of community, agency, and power possessing a clear figurative economy, as their substance constituted a parable of the social condition and an image of civic stability or turmoil.

Though Melibea's body in *Celestina* has been the object of some critical interest (notably Boullosa; Fraker; Hathaway; and Hartunian), its function as a domain of social as well as sexual signification has been virtually neglected. In the impassioned discussion which her physical attributes incite at Celestina's banquet table (act 9), the description of Melibea's image is subtly transformed into something other than merely itself — it is amplified into a metonymy of the disordered civic body, as class tensions are articulated in terms of competing forms of sexuality and are suddenly projected upon and through it. Melibea's monstrous corporal representation in *Celestina* is contrived as an unequivocal image that equates corrupt social practices — privilege, plutocracy, artifice, and guile — with aristocratic sexual ideals. Norms which, according to Elicia and Areúsa (the two sluts who describe her), personify the social abuse heaped upon the humble by Melibea's empowered class. In Melibea's physical depiction as composed by the two whores, affluence and its advantages become the vehicles for the expression of not only sexual but social desire and for the portrayal of wealth's human displacements. Melibea's body thus assumes the function of a master trope for challenging and dissolving the boundaries of social and reproductive authority at the center of blood, class, caste, and legitimacy in late-fifteenth-century Castile.

Melibea's portrait as sketched by Elicia and Areúsa at the banquet stands in both stark iconographic contrast and rhetorical apposition to the one offered earlier by her aristocratic lover Calisto in act 1, whose description is also inlaid with social messages and ideological significance. Asking first that his servant Sempronio hear him out and consider "la nobleza y antigüedad de su linaje, el grandísimo patrimonio, el excelentísimo ingenio . . . e la soberana hermosura" (38–41) [the nobleness of her blood, the ancientness of her house, the great estate she is born unto, and lastly her divine beauty], Calisto launches into the following physical characterization of Melibea:

> Los ojos verdes, rasgados, las pestañas luengas, las cejas delgadas y alçadas, la nariz mediana, la boca pequeña, los dientes menudos y blancos, los labios colorados y grossezuelos, el torno del rostro poco más luengo que redondo, el pecho alto, la redondeza y forma de las pequeñas tetas, ¿quién te la podría figurar? . . . [L]a tez lisa, lustrosa, el cuero suyo escurece la nieve . . . . Las manos pequeñas en mediana manera, de dulce carne acompañadas, los dedos luengos, las uñas en ellos largas y coloradas, que parecen rubíes entre perlas. Aquella proporción que veer yo no pude, no sin dubda por el bulto de fuera juzgo incomparablemente ser mejor que la que Paris juzgó entre las tres diesas. (40–43)

[Her eyes are quick, clear and full; the hairs to those lids rather long than short; her eyebrows thinnish, not thick of hair, and so prettily arched, that by their bent they are much the more beautiful; her nose of such a middling size, as may not be mended; her mouth little; her teeth small and white; her lips red and plumb; the form of her face rather long than round; her breasts placed in a fitting height; but their rising roundness, and the pretty pleasing fashion of her little tender nipples, who is able to figure forth unto thee? . . . [H]er skin as smooth, soft and sleek as satin, and her whole body so white, that snow seems darkness unto it. Her hands little, and in measurable manner and fit proportion accompanied by her sweet flesh; her fingers long; her nails large and well coloured, seeming rubies intermixed with pearls. The proportion of those other parts which I could not eye, undoubtedly judging things unseen by the seen must of force be incomparably far better than that which Paris gave his judgment of, in the difference between the three goddesses.]

Privilege and entitlement are the concealed messages of Calisto's expression of desire for Melibea. Her measured physical attributes illustrate class power and identity and belong to a long tradition of learned descriptive conventions and "high" aristocratic discourses linked to the world of medieval romance and classical rhetoric (Colby 25–72; Curtius 180–82). Melibea's delicate, proportioned form signals the presence of caste and position embedded in a sexual ideal; she is a chosen person, an inhabitant of elevated society — the personification of cleanliness, order, and authority, as well as fertility and physical beauty. Moreover, her bodily make-up is rendered in an idiom that evokes a courtly genealogy of legible texts inscribing visions of perfection, command, and exalted passion. It commemorates the myths of heroic nobility, prerogative, and idealized desire that lie at the center of the great deeds, venerated beauties, and sentimental legends of the Trojan War, which are its literate subtext. In brief, Calisto's verbal portrait, more than a record of a particular sexual fantasy or a passionate desire, teems with emblems of cultural authority and aristocratic empowerment as it stands as an icon of lofty sensibilities, power, and courtly propriety.

On the contrary, Elicia and Areúsa's later likeness of Melibea constitutes a premeditated, dialectical deformation of those patrician principles — an attempt to cross and contest the physical boundaries that designate Melibea's lordly class, sexual desirability, and cultural command as deployed by Calisto in his earlier semblance. Artificially adorned, deformed, polluted, and spent — yet plutocratically empowered — Melibea's form, as described in act 9 by the whores, invokes an anomalous body in chaotic disarray and constitutes itself as a symbolic inversion of Calisto's sociosexual revery — it becomes a site for the expression of conflicting prerogatives and aspirations centered on the differences of wealth, lineage, and blood.

In the midst of their repast, Elicia fires the first descriptive salvo aimed at Pleberio's daughter after she hears Sempronio refer to "aquella graçiosa y gentil Melibea" (226–27) [that fair, handsome and courteous Melibea, that lovely, gentle Melibea]. Focusing on the twin themes of artifice and affluence, Elicia looses the following broadside:

¡Mal provecho te haga lo que comes, tal comida me has dado! por mi alma, revessar quiero quanto tengo en el cuerpo de asco de oýrte llamar a aquélla gentil . . . . ¡O quién stoviesse de gana para disputar contigo su hermosura y gentileza! ¿Gentil, gentil es Melibea? Entonces lo es, entonces acertarán quando andan a pares los diez mandamientos. Aquella hermosura por una moneda se compra de la tienda . . . que si algo tiene de hermosura es por buenos atavíos que trae. Ponedlos a un palo, tanbién dirés que es gentil . . . creo que soy tan hermosa como vuestra Melibea. (226–29)

[The devil choke thee with that thou hast eaten! Thou hast given me my dinner for today; now as I live, I am ready to rid my stomach, and to cast up all that I have in my body, to hear that thou shouldst call her fair and courteous, lovely and gentle. . . . [W]ho I pray had any mind to dispute with you touching her beauty and her gentleness? Gentle Melibea! Fair Melibea! Then shall both these hit right in her when two Sundays come together, or when the 10 commandments shall go hand in hand by couple. All the beauty she hath may be bought at every pedlar's, or painter's shop, and if she have any jot of handsomeness in her, she may thank her good clothes, her neat dressings, and costly jewels, which if they were hung upon a post, thou wouldst as well say by that too, that it were fair and gentle. I am every way as fair as your Melibea.]

As Elicia proclaims her own sovereignty in physical perfection and sexual allure, Melibea is reduced to an inventory of capital, a list of talismans that signify affluence over essence. Her sexual and human values are depicted only in terms of the worth of the objects she consumes and arrays in her quest to camouflage her disagreeableness. To be sure, Elicia's portrayal of Melibea's purchased charm alleges that Calisto's lover is a greater whore than she—guiltier of meretricious guile—since the acquired embellishments of her body speak of trickery, deceit, and extraneous merit rather than essential value. Melibea's sex appeal, Elicia claims, has no depth: it is a fabricated illusion—a gesture more illicit than any the low-life characters of *Celestina* could possibly contrive in their pursuit of wealth and in their efforts to make their way in the world. The fraudulence of Melibea's crafted images of desire, Elicia alleges, are the certain measures of both her moral and social worth. As a counterfeit of nature, Calisto's embodiment of aristocratic longing has been transformed into her opposite in Elicia's imagination.

The cosmetic illusion Elicia indicts Melibea of crafting conveys greater depravity than any of the wiles Celestina's whores can fashion, since Melibea fails to seduce without recourse to the ultimate deception: bodily lies.

The classic misogynistic metaphor of the courtesan—the exorbitant use of make-up, cosmetics, and other physical adornments—is ironically inverted, turned back upon Melibea by the whore in order to denounce the legitimacy of Melibea's pleasures. She, more than Celestina's sluts, Elicia suggests, is the proven woman of easy virtue, and the ultimate deceiver. The purchased ointments, salves, and unguents, plus the rich clothes she wears, constitute an artificial investment of value, as Melibea is denounced as a sexual charlatan who traffics in misbegotten sensuality. It is at this point that Elicia's indignation suddenly turns to insurgent social ideology and unites with the venerable motifs of medieval misogyny. The result is a subversion of wealth culminating in a likeness of meretricious plutocracy, as Melibea's portrait vacillates between the images of traditional medieval antifeminism and the social coordinates of Elicia's grievances. The idiom of medieval love and sexuality now unexpectedly mediates thoughts of social and political estrangement.

The attack on Melibea's sexuality is escalated when Areúsa enthusiastically amplifies Elicia's sketch, looking deeper as she magnifies the body beneath the cosmetic covering. Claiming physical nausea like her friend at the sight of Melibea, Areúsa presents Calisto's lover as a disheveled, filthy profligate:

> Pues no la has visto tú como yo, hermana mía; Dios me lo demande si en ayunas la topasses, si aquel día pudiesses comer de asco. Todo el año se está encerrada con mudas de mil suziedades. Por una vez que haya de salir donde puede ser vista, e viste su cara con hiel y miel, con unas tostadas y higos passados, y con otras cosas que por reverencia de la mesa dexo de dezir. Las riquezas las hazen a éstas hermosas y ser alabadas, que no las gracias de su cuerpo, que assí goze de mí, unas tetas tiene para ser donzella como si tres vezes oviesse parido; no parescen sino dos grandes calabazas. El vientre no se le he visto, pero juzgando por lo otro creo que le tiene tan floxo como vieja de cinquenta años. (228–29)

> [Oh sister! hadst thou seen her as I have seen her (I tell thee no lie), if thou shouldst have met her fasting, thy stomach would have taken such a loathing, that all that day thou wouldst not have been able to have eaten any meat. All the year long she is mewed up at home, where she is daubed over with a thousand sluttish slibber-slabbers; all which forsooth she must endure, for once perhaps going abroad in a twelvemonth to be seen: she annoints her

face with gall and honey, with parched grapes and figs crushed and pressed together, with many other things which, for manner's sake and reverence of the table, I omit to mention. It is their riches, that make such creatures as she to be accounted fair; it is their wealth, that causeth them to be thus commended, and not the graces and goodly features of their bodies: for she hath such breasts, being a maid, as if she had been the mother of three children; and are all for the world, like nothing more than two great pompeans or big bottled gourds. Her belly I have not seen, but judging it by the rest, I verily believe it to be as slack and as flaggy as a woman of fifty year old.]

Melibea's gross portrait, whose ugliness is now specifically contextualized in the realm of the edible, bodily regulation, and corporal exuviae (Elicia, Areúsa's, and Melibea's) — as well as sex and capital — does more than simply disavow Melibea's physical attraction: it propels her image into the contemptible sphere of lower bodies, whose iconic function is both to subvert and define structures of social authority (Bakhtin 19; Stallybrass and White 8–26). The invocation of Melibea's flaccid midriff and falling breasts, the latter doubly transformed into pendulous pumpkins (*pompeans*) by Elicia's imagination, visually denies, denounces, and converts Calisto's portrait of patrician sexuality and power into one of pollution, ingestion, and vanished desire.

Melibea's grotesque bulk is now constructed of mixed categories connoting filth, exorbitance, concealment, disproportion, protuberance, laxity, and the physical functions of the body. She comprises a multiple self composed of what Mary Douglas terms "matter out of place" (121). As such, Elicia's description reconstitutes Melibea's physical representation into a moral and social image of contamination — one that thwarts the bodily boundaries that defined the iconography of aristocratic desire symbolizing blood, class, gravity, and propriety in Calisto's portrait. The conventional metaphors of misogyny and courtly love, though present in the description, extend beyond their usual sexual, sentimental, and moral connotations as they are elusively conjoined to the metaphor of the body politic and the discourses of social legitimacy in the work, enacting a partisan drama of civic discord. The language and images of medieval sex and ethics are recast and compelled to articulate a clash of class and political economy.

Elicia's and Areúsa's insistence upon Melibea's deformity, profanity, and sexual impurity, symbolically despoils her of the insignias of prerogative and position affiliated with social elites. In fact, as Douglas has shown, physical representations like this are often crafted in order to translate questions of social authority and legitimacy into terms of bodily purity and impurity, where a despised class is generally conceived as grotesquely slovenly and unclean, just as the preferred one is imagined as free from pollution (123). In order to express the social disjunctures Melibea personifies to the marginalized women who sketch her portrait, the signifiers comprising her foul countenance are deliberately detached from their conventional semantic fields as they pose a challenge to a dominant group through displacement and disfigurement of those elements which earlier were invoked by Calisto as corporal icons of exalted status.

The vile bodily imagery employed by Elicia and Areúsa subverts Melibea's sexuality and constitutes, then, a semiological code that belongs, more than to the tradition of misogyny, which portrays women as covetous deceivers, to a counterdiscourse of bourgeois authority and political legitimacy. To be sure, Elicia's indictment of Melibea, as it incorporates familiar terms and images from medieval antifeminism, dissociates itself from the latter since her sketch separates the problem of ornament from the inherent aberrations of the female sex. Melibea is described as something degenerate, enervated and sexually spent, something that no lotion or coloring or salve can restore or purify—infertile, impotent, and incapable of plenitude—but not because she is a woman. She is a simulacrum of strangeness, disintegration, and exhausted wantonness because she belongs to a plutocratic world of license and ease denied Elicia and Areúsa. More than carnal impotency, Melibea is meant to personify a dangerous body that has lost mastery over itself and threatens others—a devitalized social standard whose meretricious essence is now revealed as she is verbally stripped of the characteristic marks of entitled beauty and exposed as a fraud by a competing class.

To Elicia and Areúsa, the ornamented, wanton, and disfigured Melibea constitutes an embodiment of the gentry's distortion of truth and nature, and her disfigurement marks the measure of their social disaffection. Their representation of Melibea's perverted and precarious female body is a proclamation of their profound civic alienation—a deformation and disfigurement of Pleberio's economic and social status as vested in his daughter, as much as it is a unique attack upon Calisto's lover.

Melibea's loathsome sexuality brutally proclaims the decomposition of authority in the civic body and signals the aristocracy's estrangement from the forces of production. More than a sign of feminine guile, the allegations of Melibea's purchased allure become figures of consumption and the power of money to transform the infamous and monstrous in nature through lies. They cast the dialogue into the realm of political economy, female commodification, and consumable goods, while linking the political, the economic, and the erotic orders (see Rubin). The revulsion provoked by Melibea's physically grotesque portrait—circumscribed by themes of barter, commerce, and exchange—registers an abhorrence not just of the person but of all she represents.

Calisto, Areúsa, and Elicia each construct verbal portraits of Melibea that offer, more than objective images of the latter's sexual charms, a likeness of the speaker's own erotic and social cravings. Each constructs Melibea as other from their positions as subject and speaks her form in the fashion they wish her to materialize. They thus implicate the portrait they draw in a clear ideological economy. The mimetic aspects of Melibea's images are mediated by two forms of yearning—carnal and social; and her body's conflicting representations may be read as explicit evidence of tension in the human polity depicted in the work. The whores' caricatures of Melibea encapsulate contradiction and irreconcilability as they give vent to a broad critique of social patterns, practices, and ideologies.

From the contrast of the two portraits, it is clear that neither Calisto's nor the servants' likeness of Melibea can be seen as gestures to picture a real-life character. The physical conventions invoked by each of the speakers constitute signs of status and moral disposition and belong to a greater web of signification pointing toward the realm of community and to a clash of sexual norms with political convictions. To Calisto, Melibea incarnates a sexuality unrelated to labor, the functions of the lower body, and other non-patrician marks. As he sees it, Melibea's body is imaginatively grounded in a learned legacy of texts and a genteel, courtly discourse rather than in nature; it constitutes for him a site of vicarious visual and sexual pleasure. Melibea personifies the notions of order, measure, and harmonic composition that lie at the heart of his and her pretensions to gentility and their claim to noble sensibilities and the rights of authority. Her sexual charms, though clearly infused with physical desire, are encoded in legendary terms that refer us to myth and to heroic times, as the most alluring parts of her body are tactfully elided, euphemized, and compared to the golden apple Paris gave to Aphrodite. Yet, simultaneously that reference to Aphrodite's apple couples Melibea's physical body to the later banquet scene at Celestina's house, where the wider links among desire, nutrition and the edible, sexuality, and the power of wealth are made explicit.[4]

At Celestina's banquet table, sex and somatic desire, as they are connected to food and prostitution, are explicitly linked to wealth and economic exchange. They are translated into a larger discourse alleging social and political guile as they point to conflict and contradiction in the social order and to the bonds between corporal regimen and regime. Norbert Elias has shown just how such seemingly trivial acts as eating and other conduct implicated in bodily regulation conceal figurative interconnections to the larger domain of ideology and subjectivity, and may be read as evidence of social class and hierarchy (150). To be sure, images and themes of material well-being, sexuality, and social power intersect at Celestina's table in a moment that underscores the servants' inner quest to be free of the regulations imposed by class, blood, and social convention. Put simply, somatic and social appetites converge there and are shown to be contingent imperatives in the servants' imaginations.

In the newly delineated space furnished by Celestina's house and table (a utopian parenthesis opened to express the servants' sense of the insufficiency of the outer world around them, as well as to proclaim their forthright sensuality) we see the confluence of the discourses of sex and bodily regimen with notions of social place. New forms of speech aimed at contesting the structures of the old civic order begin to emerge. Celestina's house thus materializes as an underground precinct for both sex and politics: a site where the questions of nutrition, procreation, and bodily control suddenly reveal their social underpinning and their connection to the struggles for power, class, privilege, and domination. Celestina's home serves as the battleground for the clash of two mutually exclusive ideologies: the economic liberalism of an emerging working class and traditional precapitalist patriarchal oligarchy.

It is not by coincidence that act 9, which exhibits Melibea's deformed countenance as the centerpiece of Celestina's table, begins by invoking hunger, poverty, and want as the forces which stir the imagination and embolden speech. Turning to Sempronio, Pármeno summons the lesson and sets the thematic preamble for the table talk and sketch to follow:

La necessidad y pobreza, la hambre, que no ay mejor maestra en el mundo, no ay mejor despertadora y abivadora de ingenios. ¿Quién mostró a las picaças y papagayos ymitar nuestra propia habla con sus harpadas lenguas, nuestro órgano y boz, sino ésta? (224–25)

[Necessity, poverty and hunger, than which there are no better tutors in the world, no better quickeners and revivers of the wit. Who taught your pies and parrots to imitate our proper language and tone with their slit tongues, save only necessity?]

Arriving late to the feast, Sempronio aphoristically excuses his delay by noting that "quien a otro sirve no es libre, assí que sojeción me relieva de culpa" (224–25) [he that serves another is not his own man. He that is bound must obey. So that my subjection frees me from blame] and pleads that they all move to the table, where they celebrate sexuality, social fellowship, and the comforts of an abundance of food underwritten by Celestina's traffic in the flesh.

Focusing on carnal pleasures, the enjoyment afforded by the surfeit of victuals, and a place to share them — as well as incessantly objecting to the misery of servitude — the dialogue at the banquet signals a ritual of social solidarity, sexual companionship, and an extended yearning for material comfort. In fact, it is as he holds forth on the pleasures of love and the camaraderie of the table, that Sempronio appeals they all seize the moment and speak about Calisto and "aquella graçiosa y gentil Melibea" (226–27) [that fair, handsome and courteous Melibea], uttering the words that kindle Elicia's and Areúsa's inflammatory ripostes and provoke their grotesque verbal portrait of her. As these two draw their loathsome sketch, the conversation becomes tangled in exchanges that persistently refer to the social issues and tensions subtending Melibea's sexuality. The interchange culminates in a dispute between Sempronio and Areúsa that shifts the focus away from Melibea's sexual body to her social one — specifically to questions of caste and lineage.

Conceding that even if Areúsa's freakish countenance of Melibea were true, Sempronio states that Calisto's passion for the patrician lady is inexorably animated by a cry of the blood, as he pinpoints the social symmetry of the lovers' desire:

> Y aunque lo que dizes concediesse, Calisto es cavallero, Melibea hijadalgo; assí que los nascidos por linaje escogidos búscanse unos a otros. Por ende nos es de maravillar que ame antes a ésta que a otra. (230–31)

> [And howbeit I should admit all you have spoken to be true, yet pardon me, if I press you with this particular. Calisto is a noble gentleman, Melibea the daughter of honourable parents; so that it is usual with those that are descended of such high lineage, to seek and inquire after each other; and therefore it is no marvel, if he rather love her than another.]

Indignant at the thought, Areúsa vehemently rejects Sempronio's views and underscores the primacy of the person in defining sexual allure and social merit, while emphasizing her own value:

> Ruyn sea quien por ruyn se tiene; las obras hazen el linaje, que al fin todos somo hijos de Adán y Eva. Procure de ser cada uno bueno por sí, y no vaya a buscar en la nobleza de sus passados la virtud. (230–31)

> [Let him be base, that holds himself base; they are the noble actions of men, that make men noble. For in conclusion, we are all of one making, flesh and blood all. For it is known that we are sons of Adam and Eve. Let every man strive to be good of himself, and not go searching for his virtue in the nobleness of his ancestors.]

From nutrition, to the repulsive denunciation of patrician power embodied in Melibea's sexual body, to a rejection of the categories of lineage, capital, and privilege, the conversation now twists back and forth until Lucrecia, Elicia's cousin and Melibea's maid servant, knocks at the door. Prefaced by Celestina's comment that Lucrecia will doubtless advance the current debate, Lucrecia's arrival stirs Areúsa's memory with the plight of domestic servitude. With this, she unleashes the full force of her social disaffection:

> [É]stas que sirven a señoras ni gozan deleyte ni conocen los dulces premios de amor. Nunca tratan con parientas, con yguales a quien pueden hablar tú por tú, con quien digan: "¿qué cenaste?; ¿estás preñada?; ¿quántas gallinas

crías?; llévame a merendar a tu casa; muéstrame tu enamorado; ¿quánto ha que no te vido? . . ." y otras cosas de ygualdad semejantes. ¡O tía, y qué duro nombre y qué grave y sobervio es "señora" contino en la boca. Por esto me bivo sobre mí, desde que me sé conoscer, que jamás me precié de llamar de otrie sino mía. Mayormente de estas señoras que agora se usan. (236–37)

[These same chamber-maids, these forsooth that wait upon ladies, enjoy not a jot of delight, nor are acquainted with the sweet rewards of love. They never converse with their kindred, nor with their equals, with whom they may say thou for thou; or so hail fellow well met, as to ask in familiar language; "Wench, what hast thou to supper? Art thou with child yet? How many hens dost thou keep at home? Shall we go make our bever at thy house? Come, let us go laugh and be merry there. Sirrah, show me thy sweetheart, which is he? Oh wonderful! How long is it since I saw thee last?" And a thousand other the like unto these. Oh aunt! how hard a name it is, how troublesome, and how proud a thing to carry the name of a lady up and down continually in one's mouth! And this makes me to live of myself ever since I came to years of understanding and discretion. For I could never endure to be called by any other name than my own, especially by these ladies we have nowadays.]

Centering first on expressions of inequality and the use of honorifics in language that mark social difference, Areúsa goes on to detail the lack of personal freedom, the humiliation, abuses, and deceptions inflicted upon all those who by social circumstance and lack of means are compelled to serve. Areúsa concludes her diatribe against the wives of the gentry by declaring that she would rather earn a living as a whore, and be her sovereign self, than serve as a domestic: "Por esto, madre, he querido más bivir en mi pequeña casa esenta y señora, que no en sus ricos palacios sojuzgada y cativa" (238–39) [And this, mother, is the reason, why I have rather desired to live free from controlment, and to be mistress in a poor little house of my own, than to live as a slave and at command in the richest palace of the proudest lady of them all].[5]

The invocation of Melibea's vile body, followed by the servants' condemnations of the privileges of class and the anathema of servitude, prevent us from seeing Elicia's and Areúsa's gruesome portrait of her sexual allure as a momentary truancy expressing feminine envy, or less, as a crude affront directed at a specific person. It is, rather, a decisive instance of what Hayden

White in his investigation of wildness calls "ostensive self-definition by negation," or a type of reflex that often appears in conflicts between social classes and political institutions seeking to authenticate their preeminence vis-à-vis one another (151–52). The traditional tropes and monstrous images of medieval misogyny are appropriated and employed here by Areúsa and her cohorts in a political way, and are hurled at Melibea in order to expound the as-yet-unpublicized anxieties of their own subjective values, fears, and aspirations. From their perspective, Melibea's sickening body incarnates their social alienation, subjugation, and exploitation — it stands as monument to their frustrated desires. Melibea's contemptible form serves to codify Elicia and Areúsa's alternative sexual and social identity through emphatic contradiction, and by means of its unnatural deformity provides a unique perspective on the ruptured civic and psychological landscape portrayed in *Celestina*.[6]

Confirmation of the iconic and socially transgressive function of Melibea's portrait follows fast, then, upon its appearance in act 9 when the conversation unexpectedly veers toward the abuses and deceptions that domestics suffer at the hands of their masters. As it unfolds, the dialogue guides us to the point where the images of Melibea's disordered sexuality intersect with grievances defined by class burdens and identity. The encounter at Celestina's table, with its denunciation of social hierarchies, prodigal wealth, abusive privilege, and ostentatious consumption, culminates symbolically in a comparison of corporalities — Elicia's, Areúsa's, and Melibea's — and, as the discourses of sex and nutrition are transformed into the discourses not simply of sexual but social craving, we are left with the impression that there is little distinction to be made between the edible, the female body, sexual allure, and social worth. To be sure, the body, sex, and other appetites, far from effecting a displacement of class conflict, become the very center of the controversy, the heart of the matter where a contest of opposing ideologies materializes in *Celestina*. The combination of diet and the images constituting other corporal necessities depicts the effective commingling of the essential forces driving the characters — desire at work, both social and somatic. Female bodies, as symbols of power, privilege, and subjective domination are assimilated to a discourse of dietary pleasure, sexual freedom, individual fulfillment, and somatic well-being as they appropriate and sublimate constitutional political ideals: social equality, agency, and personal sovereignty.

Melibea is portrayed by Elicia and Areúsa as the wanton and grotesque excluded other in a conversation ostensibly centering only on sexual desirability. Yet, as this happens, the whores blur and shift the iconographic boundaries of class and propriety. Clouding and confuting the borders that traditionally define the alluring aristocratic body, Areúsa and Elicia destabilize the notion of high-born station, blood, and agency in the world they inhabit as they betray an ideology troubled by difference and beset with anxieties about sex, caste, and identity. As they interrogate, and invert, the patrician physiognomy assigned earlier to Melibea by Calisto, Melibea's sexual body becomes the distinguishing point of tension where the integrity and position of the subject is both defined and placed into question. Elicia and Areúsa repulsively rewrite Melibea's patrician sexuality in order to dispute and encroach upon the social perimeters that customarily define her kind and exclude them from her empowered world.

Melibea's body in *Celestina* conceals, then, more than sexual covetousness and expressions of shallow envy and conceit. It constitutes an ideological crux that harbors contradictory images of contending socioeconomic convictions expressed through conflicting ideals of sexuality as it tropes class rivalries steeped in resentment. The impulses of the body emerge in *Celestina* as clear threats to the extant system of social order and control; and the desires for food, money, and sex become integral components of a larger discourse of political hegemony. The potential anarchy posed by an imperative of bodily appetites linked to social aspirations is loosed and fails to be subordinated or contained by institutional controls—by wealth and patriarchy—just as personal and group interactions crack, rupture, and finally collapse.

Celestina in this way portrays an emerging dialectical opposition between competing forms of somatic and social desire and their confrontation with civic order. The body's needs are represented first as a consumable good, and then as a threat to orderly succession and the authority of patriarchy and the family. The open expression of material, social, and sexual volition voiced by Elicia and Areúsa defiantly repudiates, as Mary Gossy states, "the legitimizing and controlling power of the church and the economic influence of the patriarchal family" (38).

In *Celestina*'s discrepant portraits of Melibea we discover nothing less than an early modern confrontation of the aristocratic and plebeian subject—a portrayal of competing forms of being and concepts of legitimacy.

Clearly, the metaphoric nature of the aristocratic body — and by extension the body politic — was undergoing profound changes and transformation. It was being subverted and displaced by new forms of sexual and social corporalities that emphasized pleasure and natural imperatives as sources of empowerment and a sense of self. However, *Celestina* superficially camouflages the discourses of subjective difference by sublimating, transcribing, and displacing them only toward the realm of sexuality. Yet, as the characters speak of passion, pleasure, and love's fulfillment we see strategies of social domination and resistance spring forth from the plot at the very point where sex is most openly commodified and defined in terms of social mobility and consumable goods. Under the guise of the traditional medieval denunciation of sexual sin, boundaries marking the frontiers of caste and class are crossed to pose stark challenges to the rights of well-born privilege.

Sex and bodies in *Celestina* thus function as a means of access for an underlying sense of civic disorder in the work; they become primary sites of ideology and serve as registers of apprehension. We see that, more than a locus of carnal pleasure or prohibition, the libidinous body is conceived as a symbolic vehicle for incarnating social conflict as well as for upending human hierarchies. Through its representation of transgressive sexualities and corporalities, *Celestina* portrays an aggregate of associated communal perils in the late-fifteenth-century Spanish imaginary and seeks to provoke, by extension, a rethinking and redefinition of the notion of political power, order, and legitimacy. Prostitution, passion, nutrition, and social stratification all intersect in the symbolic economy of sex and the body in late-medieval Castile as if they were each different facets of one subversive prism.

The representations of sexualized bodies in an author like Fernando de Rojas (not to mention others like Fernando del Pulgar, Alfonso Martínez de Toledo, and Fernán Pérez de Guzmán), capture prevailing political anxieties as they register apprehension and suggest that human corpora stand as models for social structures and behavior. As Douglas confirms, the body can never be rendered as a neutral or disinterested object — its valences are always predicated on ideological considerations — as cultures persistently turn to "the symbolism of the body's boundaries . . . to express danger to community boundaries" (122).

In brief, the discourses of the body, sexual and somatic desire, prostitution, and social trespass converge in *Celestina* to comprise a microcosm of a conflictive body politic perilously close to dismemberment. They make visible the progressive dismantling of traditional structures just as they define emerging types of subjectivity radically at odds with the governing ideology of a patriarchal culture. By the closing decades of the fifteenth century in Castile there was under way a reconfiguration of social roles just as class distinctions were being designated in and through clashing sexual and corporal representations. Figurations of alternative and competing forms of the subject like the ones depicted in *Celestina* were not contrived for idle entertainment or for insipid moralizing, but constitute testimonials of a crisis centered on the notion of the prerogatives of the individual. They were produced by fundamental shifts in ethical, cultural, and socioeconomic conditions at the close of the Middle Ages.

In *Celestina,* as in many other contemporary Iberian texts, political and civic anxieties were grounded in sex and subsumed by the body; they linked inexorably the physical constitution of the person to questions of moral worth, social legitimacy, and agency in an ongoing struggle for power, validity, and prestige. Far from innocent embodiments of nature, human bodies in late-fifteenth-century Castile could be ideologically charged vehicles for thought that directed attention beyond themselves toward community tensions — toward the body politic. As elsewhere in Europe, in early-modern Iberia crossing the boundaries of sex and the body implied crossing ideological and doctrinal frontiers.

Notes

1. Quotations in English and Spanish of *Celestina* are all taken from Dorothy Sherman Severin's modern parallel-text edition of James Mabbe's 1631 translation. Translations from all other works are my own.

2. On *Celestina*'s status as an early-modern best-seller, see Whinnom (166–68); and on the contentious opinions of its readership, see Chevalier.

3. On the full political implications of Enrique's sexuality, see Weissberger in this volume.

4. The connection between sexual desire, hunger, and the edible is made brutally explicit by Calisto when, in act 19 as he pulls her clothing off her, he responds to Melibea's protestations against his indelicacy: "Señora, el que quiere comer el ave, quita primero las plumas" (378–79) [Madame, he that will eat the bird

must first pluck the feathers]. The association of food and sex in the medieval Iberian imaginary is made explicit in the battle of *Don Carnal* 'Sir Flesh' and *Doña Cuaresma* 'Lady Lent' in the fourteenth-century *Libro de buen amor* [Book of Good Love]; see Vasvári's essay in this volume.

5. Swietlicki, centering on these remarks and looking at the episode from a feminist perspective, comments that both Areúsa and Elicia constitute "outspoken female defenders of their liberty. Areúsa . . . [embodies] a voice of class equality"; and that "Rojas' choice of two prostitutes as spokeswomen for liberty and equality was unprecedented" (5).

6. Stallybrass and White (5–6), commenting upon the representation of low others in carnivalesque discourse produced by subjects "on top," note how the images of the low other actually serve to define the writing subject in the way that Hegel describes the master-slave relationship in the *Phenomenology*. *Celestina* presents a conspicuous inversion of this dynamic: the low others (the whores Elicia and Areúsa), as they claim sexual and social parity or superiority, appropriate the rhetoric of carnivalesque corporal distortion and apply it to the subjects "on top" in their quest to define themselves subjectively. In *Celestina* the low subject thus symbolically embraces the top as an inverted eroticized component of its own desire and fantasy. The result is a psychological reliance on the excluded other who, disavowed at the level of social discourse, remains central for the definition of identity.

Works Cited

Bakhtin, M. M. *Rabelais and his World*. Trans. H. Iswolsky. Cambridge, Mass.: MIT P, 1968.

Boullosa, Virginia H. "La concepción del cuerpo en la *Celestina*." *La idea del cuerpo en la letras españolas (siglos XIII a XVII)*. Ed. Dinko Cvitanovic. Bahia Blanca: Instituto de Humanidades, Universidad Nacional del Sur, 1973. 80–117.

Bourdieu, Pierre. *Outline of a Theory of Practice*. Trans. Richard Nice. Cambridge: Cambridge UP, 1977.

Brody, Saul Nathaniel. *The Disease of the Soul: Leprosy in Medieval Literature*. Ithaca: Cornell UP, 1974.

Brown, Peter. *The Body and Society: Men, Women, and Sexual Renunciation in Early Christianity*. New York: Columbia UP, 1988.

Bynum, Carolyn. *Fragmentation on Redemption: Essay on Gender and the Human Body in Medieval Religion*. New York: Zone, 1991.

————. *Holy Feast and Holy Fast: The Religious Significance of Food to Medieval Women.* Berkeley: U of California P, 1987.

Castro, Américo. *La Celestina como contienda literaria.* Madrid: Ediciones de la Revista de Occidente, 1965.

Chevalier, Maxime. "*La Celestina* según sus lectores." *Lectura y lectores en la España del siglo XVI y XVII.* Madrid: Turner, 1976. 138–66.

Colby, Alice M. *The Portrait in Twelfth-Century French Literature.* Geneva: Librairie Droz, 1965.

Curtius, Ernst Robert. *European Literature and the Latin Middle Ages.* Trans. Willard R. Trask. New York: Harper and Row, 1963.

Dinshaw, Carolyn. *Chaucer's Sexual Poetics.* Madison: U of Wisconsin P, 1989.

Douglas, Mary. *Purity and Danger: An Analysis of the Concepts of Pollution and Taboo.* London: Routledge and Kegan Paul, 1966.

Dutton, Brian, and Joaquín González Cuenca, eds. *Cancionero de Juan Alfonso de Baena.* Madrid: Visor Libros, 1993.

Elias, Norbert. *The Civilizing Process.* Vol. 1: *The History of Manners.* Trans. E. Jephcott. New York: Pantheon, 1978.

Fox-Davies, Arthur Charles. *A Complete Guide to Heraldry.* 1909. Revised and annotated by J. P. Brooke-Little. London: Nelson, 1969.

Fraker, Charles F. "The Four Humors in *Celestina.*" *Fernando de Rojas and* Celestina *Approaching the Fifth Centenary.* Ed. Ivy A. Corfis and Joseph Snow. Madison: Hispanic Seminary of Medieval Studies, 1993. 129–54.

Gariano, Carmelo. "El erotismo grotesco en *La Celestina.*" *Vórtice* 1.3 (1975): 2–16.

Gilman, Stephen. *The Spain of Fernando de Rojas: The Intellectual and Social Landscape of* La Celestina. Princeton: Princeton UP, 1972.

Gossy, Mary S. *The Untold Story: Women and Theory in Golden Age Texts.* Ann Arbor: U of Michigan P, 1989.

Hale, D. G. *The Body Politic: A Political Metaphor in Renaissance English Literature.* The Hague: Mouton, 1971.

Hartunian, Diane. La Celestina: *A Feminist Reading of the* Carpe Diem. Potomac, Md.: Scripta Humanistica, 1992.

Hathaway, Robert L. "Concerning Melibea's Breasts." *Celestinesca* 17 (1993): 17–32.

Kantorowicz, Ernst. *The King's Two Bodies: A Study in Medieval Political Theology.* Princeton: Princeton UP, 1957.

Lacarra, María Eugenia. *Cómo leer* La Celestina. Madrid: Ediciones Júcar, 1990.

Le Goff, Jacques. "Head or Heart: The Political Use of Body Metaphors in the Middle Ages." *Fragments for a History of the Human Body.* Vol. 3. Ed. Michel Feher et al. New York: Urzone, 1989.

MacKay, Angus. "Ritual and Propaganda in Fifteenth-Century Castile." *Society, Economy and Religion in Late Medieval Castile*. London: Variorum Reprints, 1987. 14: 3–43.

Maravall, José Antonio. *El mundo social de* La Celestina. 2nd ed. Madrid: Gredos, 1968.

Márquez Villanueva, Francisco. *Orígenes y sociología del tema celestinesco*. Barcelona: Anthropos, 1993.

Memorias de don Enrique IV de Castilla: colección diplomática compuesta y ordenada por la Real Academia de la Historia. Madrid: Fortanet, 1835–1913.

Patterson, Lee. "The Wife of Bath and the Triumph of the Subject." *Chaucer and the Subject of History*. Madison: U of Wisconsin P, 1991. 280–321.

Rico, Francisco. *El pequeño mundo del hombre*. Corrected and enlarged ed. Madrid: Alianza, 1986.

Rojas, Fernando de. *Celestina*. Trans. James Mabbe (1631). Ed. Dorothy Sherman Severin. Warminster, England: Aris and Phillips, 1987.

———. *Comedia o tragicomedia de Calisto y Melibea*. Ed. Peter E. Russell. Madrid: Cátedra, 1991.

Rubin, Gayle. "The Traffic in Women: Notes on the 'Political Economy' of Sex." *Toward an Anthropology of Women*. Ed. Rayna R. Reiter. New York: Monthly Review P, 1975. 157–210.

Russell, Peter E. "The *Celestina comentada*." *Medieval Hispanic Studies Presented to Rita Hamilton*. Ed. A. D. Deyermond. London: Támesis, 1976. 175–93.

———, ed. See Rojas, *Comedia o tragicomedia de Calisto y Melibea*.

Stallybrass, Peter, and Allon White. *The Politics and Poetics of Transgression*. London: Methuen, 1986.

Swietlicki, Catherine. "Rojas' View of Women: A Reanalysis of *La Celestina*." *Hispanófila* 29 (1985): 1–13.

Whinnom, Keith. "The Problem of the 'Best Seller' in Spanish Golden Age Literature." *Medieval and Renaissance Spanish Literature: Selected Essays*. Ed. Alan Deyermond et al. Exeter: U of Exeter P, 1994. 159–75.

White, Hayden. "The Forms of Wildness: Archaeology of an Idea." *Tropics of Discourse*. Baltimore: Johns Hopkins UP, 1986. 150–82.

Mary Elizabeth Perry

From Convent to Battlefield

Cross-Dressing and Gendering the Self in

the New World of Imperial Spain

The singularly unconventional life of the person known in Spanish history as the Nun-Lieutenant (*la Monja Alférez*) began, remarkably enough, with ordinary convention. On February 10, 1592, Miguel de Erauso and María Pérez de Galarraga presented their new baby at the parish church of San Vicente Levita y Mártir in the town of San Sebastián to be baptized as Catalina.[1] Four years later, they took her to the Dominican nuns of a convent called La Antigua, where records show that they paid the nuns for boarding and training three daughters. Subsequently, their daughters Mari Juana and Isabel professed as nuns and lived the rest of their lives in this convent, but Catalina followed a different path. According to the account later published as her autobiography, she ran away from the convent, dressed as a boy, made her way to the New World, and in the conquest of Mexico and Peru made herself into a man.[2]

Catalina de Erauso's acts of self-engendering required the crossing of sexual and cultural boundaries into exciting and dangerous territory, for, as anthropologist Mary Douglas has pointed out, "all margins are dangerous," not merely external boundaries, but also "internal lines," where any disorder or passing back and forth holds the potential for both danger and power (41, 95, 122). Postulating an analogy between body and society, Douglas's analysis of boundaries and taboos provides a useful tool for examining the life of the Nun-Lieutenant. Unlike most other women known for cross-dressing, Catalina de Erauso did not assume male roles and male clothing in order to solve a momentary problem or to express a brief rebellion, after which she would return to her female identity.[3] Instead, she apparently identified herself as male early in her life, disguised herself as a male, and succeeded in gaining acceptance for her male identity even after she had to reveal herself as a woman. The life of the Nun-Lieutenant, then, raises significant questions about the relationships among sex, body, gender, self-identity, rebellion, and convention. Through an examination of Catalina de Erauso, we are able to explore the gray areas where margins meet and overlap, sometimes pushed or pulled into new alignments. Even though this atypical and anomalous person cannot be considered representative, her life acts as a prism for examining the politics of an imperialist nation as well as the politics of gender.

It seems neither fair nor accurate, however, to use exclusively feminine pronouns to refer to the Nun-Lieutenant, who worked so diligently to make herself into a man. Significantly, most historical sources referring to this person use feminine pronouns and imply that she was basically a female who dressed and lived as a man. Yet it could be argued that Catalina de Erauso should be identified as a male who did not allow his family's mistaken identity of him nor his lack of some of the physiological characteristics of males to undercut his own understanding of himself. And it should be asked if the problem is not less with the individual than with the need to conform to a dichotomized system of male and female. What the "true identity" of the Nun-Lieutenant is, like so many other questions, will not be answered by this essay. Instead, unresolved questions will be raised in hope of stimulating even better questions.

Writing about the Nun-Lieutenant raises significant questions about the limitations of gendered names and language. Should we refer to this person by her given feminine name, Catalina de Erauso, or by his masculine name, Alonso Díaz Ramírez de Guzmán, assumed in Peru, or by the last masculine name by which he was known, Alonso de Erauso? Should we use feminine pronouns throughout the story of her life or only during periods when she was known as a female? When is it appropriate to refer to this person with masculine pronouns? Realizing that there are no easy answers to these questions, I use the name Erauso as a compromise that seems less gendered without a first name; and I use both feminine and masculine pronouns throughout the essay, alternating them between sentences rather than between paragraphs in order to avoid the suggestion that certain aspects of this person's life were more masculine and others more feminine. This use of language may confuse the reader at first, but I hope that it will also serve as a reminder that our language is so gendered that we find it difficult to even conceptualize, let alone define or describe, a person who crosses gender lines without subjecting them to the tyranny of gender. In stirring up some "gender trouble," I hope to emphasize the danger, disorder, and power engendered by a boundary-crossing person.[4]

History and fiction also meet and overlap in the person of the Nun-Lieutenant, who both inspired myth and participated in his own mythmaking. If we have some historical records to verify her existence, we also note her appearance in a play, attributed to Juan Pérez de Montalván, which celebrated her life as that of a brawling, daring soldier who killed many people and, in addition, became something of a ladies' man.[5] This persona also appears in the autobiography attributed to the Nun-Lieutenant, which may or may not be authentic.[6] Catalina de Erauso wrote a much more sober version of his life in the *Memorial* that he directed to the king, which emphasized his bravery in battle and his willingness to serve, undoubtedly motivated by the hopes of a royal pension as reward. The story that she told to the cleric Pedro del Valle Peregrino attempted to establish her respectability with explanations for why she had run away from the convent and assumed the life of a man.[7] Both of these versions referred to historical "facts," but they also engaged in telling a story that would be more acceptable to those who had the power to grant him both a pension to live on and the freedom to continue dressing and living as a man. For the Nun-Lieutenant, self-engendering required not only crossing sexual and cultural boundaries but also developing a myth that explained and legitimized such boundary crossings.

To explore the process, then, by which this apparently female person made herself into a man requires us to consider far more than the question of what was myth and what was "fact" in the life of the Nun-Lieutenant. Rather than discounting myth as mere fiction, we will give serious consideration to the significance of myth so that we can better understand how this individual who began life very conventionally as a female not only changed gender identity but also won acceptance of this new identity in a period of nation building and imperialist expansion. The following pages will examine cross-dressing, redefining the body, and the making of myth, all intertwined in each of the three major stages of the life of the Nun-Lieutenant: leaving the convent and entering the New World, becoming a soldier and revealing her female identity, and winning approval to continue her life as a man.

From Convent to New World

According to the account of her life that Catalina de Erauso gave to the cleric Pedro del Valle Peregrino, she became "disgustada de aquella vida encerrada" (127) [displeased with the enclosed life] of the convent and decided to run away so that she could live as a man. About fifteen years old at the time, he pretended to be ill, took the convent key, and hid in a grove of trees near the convent. She had also taken scissors and needle and thread with her to make her habit into clothing appropriate for a young boy. Then, in a ritual similar to those that often mark the beginning of a new life phase, Erauso used the scissors to cut her hair (Douglas 97). Later Pedro de la Valle noted that the Nun-Lieutenant had no breasts and that he had told him that from an early age he used a poultice, or mixture spread on a cloth, to dry up his breasts so that they would not be noticeable.[8] She thus marked and clothed her own body, rebelling at the contours that cultural expectations imposed on her body and self as female, and scorning the long hair and developing breasts that so often symbolized the sexuality and availability of unmarried girls in this period. With these acts, Erauso began that "stylization of the body" that Judith Butler has described as so essential to gender (140).

Whether Erauso the runaway disguised herself as male because she felt more like a boy or simply wanted to survive her escape into a world in which girls seemed more vulnerable, she had to develop her own corporeal style. This required him not only to dress as a male, but also to engage in "a stylized repetition of acts"—described by Butler as "ritual social dramas"—which could legitimize and inscribe gender on the body (139–40). Erauso worked in various households as a page, using several male names including that of Francisco Loyola. She worked for an uncle, who failed to recognize her, and at another household she encountered her father, who did not recognize her. During this period Erauso undoubtedly learned by observing the body gestures, speech, and everyday movements of men who would not have been present in the convent.

Restlessly going from one household to another, the young page decided to seek passage to the New World, which seemed to promise even more freedom as a frontier land where a new identity could be established and protected. According to the account of Manuel de Mendiburu, Erauso sailed from San Lúcar as cabin boy on a galleon, captained by another uncle who did not recognize her (397–408; Erauso, *Vida* 42). Soon the new cabin boy learned the excitement of battle, for the squadron in which he sailed met a small Dutch armada and destroyed it. When his squadron finally reached land in the Western Hemisphere, Erauso jumped ship at Nombre de Dios, near the present site of the Panama Canal, taking with him five hundred pesos. She made her way to Panama aboard another ship and stayed with the captain for three months.

Erauso's education as a male continued, as he went into service for a merchant, Juan de Urquiza, who took him to Peru and put him in charge of a store and two slaves. This seemed to be an easy life until one day when she went to a theater and someone named Reyes sat down and blocked her view.

> Pedíle que lo apartase un poco, respondió desabridamente; yo a él; i díxome que me fuese de ahí, que me cortaría la cara. Yo me hallé sin armas, más que una daga, salíme de allí con sentimiento. (Erauso, *Vida* 46)

> [I asked him to move a bit, and he responded rudely; and I to him; and he told me to get out, that he was going to cut my face. Finding myself without a weapon, except a dagger, I left there with feeling.]

Erauso's antagonist from the quarrel soon learned where she worked and came to her store with a partner. When he threatened to cut his face, Erauso quickly responded,

> Esta es la cara que se corta—, i dile con el cuchillo un refilón, de que le dieron diez puntos. El acudió con las manos a su herida. Su amigo sacó la espada i vínose a mí, yo a él con la mía: tiramos los dos, i yo le entré una punta por el lado izquierdo que lo pasó y cayó. (Erauso, *Vida* 46)

> [This is the face that is cut, and from the corner of the eye I slashed him. His hands went to his wound. His friend drew his sword and came for me, and I went for him with mine: we fought, and I pierced him in the left side and he fell.]

Realizing that she now faced trouble with the law, Erauso sought refuge in a church. However, an official entered and arrested her and took her to prison, where they placed her in chains. Erauso called for his master, who argued that secular officials should not have violated the sanctity of the church. "Fui restituido a la Yglesia de donde fui sacado, después de tres meses de pleito i procedimiento del señor Obispo" (47) [I was returned to the church from which I had been arrested after three months of pleading and proceeding with the bishop]. After some discussion, Erauso and his master agreed that it would be best for him to move on to manage another store owned by the master in a different town. Like a *pícaro,* Erauso found that geographic mobility in both Spain and the New World helped her to avoid the law and also those close and continuing friendships that could threaten her new identity with awkward questions.

Avoiding intimacy could also protect Erauso from detection, but several episodes in the New World suggest that other women were attracted to her and that she may have felt some attraction, too. After he had rescued Erauso from prison, his employer, Juan de Urquiza, proposed that the best way to settle the dispute with Reyes was for Erauso to marry Doña Beatriz de Cárdenas, related to Reyes's wife. Erauso visited her several times until "una noche me encerró i se declaró en que a pesar del diablo havía de dormir con ella, i me apretó en esto tanto, que huve de alargar la mano i salirme" (47) [one night she locked me in and declared that in spite of the devil, I had to sleep with her, and I got so worried that I had to extend my hand and leave]. Erauso then told Urquiza that he would not marry this woman "por todo el mundo" [for all the world], but Urquiza urged the marriage, offering Erauso "montes de oro, representándome la hermosura i prendas de la Dama" (47) [mountains of gold, representing to me the beauty and natural gifts of the Lady]. Erauso categorically refused, perhaps to avoid the intimacy that would reveal her body as more female than male. However, it is also possible that Erauso refused marriage less from concern with his lack of male physical characteristics than with pressures to conform to social expectations of married men that threatened to curtail his freedom.

Later, after Erauso had gone to Lima to work for another merchant, Diego de Olarte, she found herself in a household with Olarte's two comely sisters-in-law. One in particular fell in love with her, and in this case Erauso seemed to have felt some erotic interest in her. When Olarte surprised the two one day, they were sharing an intimate moment in the parlor of the house, with the woman "peinándome acostado en sus faldas i andándole en las piernas" (51) [combing my hair while I reclined in her lap and stroked her thighs]. Evidently attracted by pretty faces, Erauso also delayed marriage to a mestiza, whose mother kept insisting that he become her husband. The problem, according to the autobiography, was that the daughter was very dark, "una Negra fea como unos diablos, mui contraria a mi gusto que fue siempre de buenas caras" (70) [ugly as the devil, in contrast to my pleasure, which was always for good faces]. Here Erauso may have made an allusion to racism in the ideal of female beauty held by most Spanish men at this time. However, she did not simply leave the dark-skinned mestiza, but continued to keep her company until she could no longer delay the marriage. He wrote of "dilatando el efecto con varios pretextos hasta que no pude más, i tomando una mula me partí, i no me han visto más" (70) [I delayed the marriage with various pretexts until it was no longer possible, and taking a mule I left, and they have not seen me since].

Although the autobiography suggests Erauso's erotic interests in several women during her time in the New World, it falls short as a clear description of lesbianism. It tells of no satisfying and long-lasting relationships, which may account for the tension and note of irritability that some readers sense in this section (Juárez 4). Possibly Erauso wanted to express sexual feelings, but feared the consequences of revealing not only her female identity, but also her homosexual longings. Perhaps he did not want to commit to long-term relationships, or perhaps he did not describe these relationships because he knew that they would not be acceptable in his society of "compulsory heterosexuality." [9]

No accounts of Erauso's life take on the issue of same-sex love directly, except the play written about her, when a male character, astounded at the revelation that the protagonist is a woman, blurts out, "Do I have to believe that being a woman you love another woman?" (Ferrer 246). Yet "natural order" is restored at the end of this play when Guzmán (Erauso) refuses to marry Doña Ana, but fights to defend her honor. Then, in the midst of the fight, Guzmán kneels at the feet of his antagonist, Don Diego, who replies, "Levanta, y dame los brazos" [Arise, and give me your hand], in a gesture of male bonding as well as gracious reconciliation. This play and all other historical accounts of the Nun-Lieutenant assume heterosexuality as "natural" and imply that she could not marry nor consummate a physical relationship with a woman because she lacked a penis. Providing a limited and phallic view of homoeroticism as a perversion between men only, the dominant assumption of heterosexuality completely missed the possibility of physical attraction and intimacy between women, ignoring the fact that women in this period knew about using a dildo or artificial phallus (Chaves Pt. 1).

Brawls, Battles, and Self-Revelation

In the New World in the frontier regions of Panama, Peru, and Chile, Erauso grew beyond the age of beardless preadolescent cabin boys. Here few people questioned his masculinity; mostly they assumed he was slow in growing a beard, and then later some wondered if he were a eunuch. None of the accounts of her life indicate how she disguised or stopped her menstrual periods. Apparently concentrating on the tasks of establishing "manhood" and making the body perform those acts that would inscribe on it a male identity, Erauso engaged in many brawls (Butler 140). In these rituals of insult, quick retort, and armed response, Erauso acted out the warrior ethos that had become somewhat anachronistic in post-Reconquest Spain, but appeared very appropriate in the frontier settlements of the New World. Male honor required immediate defense, and here in the regions of New Spain and Peru there were not enough peace officers to preserve the peace nor to monopolize the uses of violence.

Lacking the "civilizing effects" of marriage, Erauso and other unmarried men continued to engage in fights.[10] After she was accused of killing a man, Erauso's employer sent her to Lima, where she assumed the name of Alfonso Díaz Ramírez de Guzmán and joined a company of soldiers on its way to battle the rebel Araucanian Indians of Chile. As a soldier, Erauso won the rank of *alférez* 'lieutenant' for bravery in a battle when she rescued the flag of her company that the enemy had taken.[11] With two other soldiers, Erauso had dashed into the enemy to reclaim the flag. One was killed before reaching the flag, and the other fell from a blow of a lance just as they reached it.

Yo recibí un mal golpe en una pierna. Maté al Cacique que la llevaba i quitésela, i apreté con mi caballo, atropellando, matando i hiriendo a infinidad, pero mal herido, i pasado de tres flechas, i de una lanza en el hombro izquierdo que sentía mucho. (Erauso, *Vida* 58)

[I received a bad blow on the leg. I killed the chieftain with the flag and took it away, and held tight to my horse, trampling, killing and wounding everything, but badly wounded, struck by three arrows, and a lance in the left shoulder that hurt very much.]

Like other Spanish soldiers, Erauso fought against indigenous people such as the Araucanians of Chile who refused to accept the "civilizing mission" of Spain. Probably secure in her own purposes of legitimizing her male identity while defending Spain's imperial presence, Erauso's autobiography recalls that she fought fiercely against indigenous rebels in Peru and Chile. In one encounter, he wrote,

> me topé con un Capitán de Yndios, ya cristiano, llamado D. Francisco Guispiguarba, hombre rico que nos traía bien inquietos con varias armas que nos tocó, i batallando con él lo derribé del caballo, i se me rindió, i lo hice al punto colgar de un árbol: cosa que después sintió el Governador que deseava haverlo vivo. (60)

> [I bumped into a captain of the Indians, already a Christian, called Don Francisco Guispiguarba, a rich man who stirred us up with several arms that he shot at us, and battling with him I unhorsed him, he surrendered, and I strung him up from a tree, which afterward the governor regretted who wanted to have him alive.]

In these lands of the Western Hemisphere, Erauso encountered people of a different culture and race. Although the plight of these people evoked sympathetic responses from Spaniards such as Alonso de Ercilla y Zuñiga, a former soldier who described the Araucanians as defenders of freedom in his epic, *La Araucana*, most Spanish soldiers were engaged in defending forts and outposts against guerrilla attacks and saw indigenous rebels as barbarians they must pacify, capable of engaging in the "abominable licentiousness," human sacrifice, and cannibalism that earlier Spaniards had described.[12] In the face of such difference, Spanish soldiers scarcely noticed the fact that the young lieutenant Alfonso Díaz Ramírez de Guzmán lacked a beard. The body of this soldier became sexed only in the context of power relations, which assumed that lightness of complexion counted for more than body hair. In the New World outposts at this time the Spanish soldier had the power not only to subjugate darker-skinned peoples, but to determine the discourse used to describe this experience.[13] It is not surprising that Erauso maintained his male identity during this period, nor that his experiences as a soldier further legitimized his male identity, nor that he chose to be a soldier in the New World. As a subtext to her later explanation to Pedro del Valle Peregrino that she became a soldier because she was "inclinado naturalmente a las armas, i a ver mundo" (Erauso, *Vida* 127) [inclined naturally to arms and to seeing the world], we note that this "natural inclination" also legitimized her male identity.

Brawling continued to legitimize Erauso's maleness, as well, but it also led to the revelation of her female identity. The crisis came when he killed a man called "El Nuevo Cid" in a gambling dispute in Cuzco. Gravely injured herself, she confessed to the friar, Luis Ferrer de Valencia. "Vino el padre Luis Ferrer de Valencia, gran sugeto, i confesóme, i viéndome yo morir, declaré mi estado. El se admiró, i me absolvió, y me procuró esforzar i consolar" (102–03) [I declared my state. He was astonished and absolved me and sought to strengthen and console me]. After the friars had cared for him during four months in their Franciscan monastery, he recovered and went on his way, armed with money, mules, and slaves given to him by admirers. By moving on, she undoubtedly expected to escape any more consequences from her self-revelation.

By now, however, the noose was tightening, for both the friends of El Nuevo Cid and secular peace officers were looking for her. He hid in Guamanga from one officer who recognized him, but a big fight erupted when he then encountered some sheriffs. The bishop's secretary rescued her in this brawl and took her to the bishop's house, where the bishop questioned her the next day about who she was and what course her life had taken. Fearing death, according to the autobiography, and believing that this was a saintly man, Erauso now determined to make a second revelation of himself. She told the bishop, "Señor, todo esto que he referido a Vuestra Señoría Ilustrísima no es así; la verdad es ésta: que soi muger" (110) [Sir, all this that I have told Your Illustriousness is not so. The truth is this: that I am a woman].

The Nun-Lieutenant then told him her life story, sensing this as perhaps the best way to represent herself to this man and to save herself from hanging as a murderer. The bishop listened quietly, "i después que acabé, se quedó también sin hablar i llorando a lágrima viva" (111) [and after I had finished, he remained silent, weeping bitterly]. The autobiography does not say what moved the bishop to weep, and simply adds that he told Erauso that hers was "el caso más notable en este género que havía oído en su vida" (111) [the most notable of this kind of case that he had ever heard]. Was the bishop moved by his bravery, or by the many times Esauro had

faced death? Did he weep for all young men whose brawling subjected
them to even greater risks of early death? Did he imply that he knew other
women who had disguised themselves as soldiers, or was it Catalina's story
of femaleness that made her case the most notable?

In order to verify his story, Erauso offered to allow himself to be physically examined by matrons. "Entraron dos Matronas i me miraron i satisfi-
cieron i declararon después ante el Obispo con juramento, haverme visto i
reconocido quanto fue menester para certificarse i haverme hallado virgen
intacta, como el día en que nací" (112) [Two women examined me and swore
before the bishop that I was a female, and certified that I was a virgin intact
as the day I was born]. Hearing this, the bishop embraced him and said,

> Hija, ahora creo sin duda lo que me dixistis i creeré en adelante quanto me
> dixereis; i os venero como una de las personas notables de este mundo i os
> prometo asistiros en quanto pueda (y cuidar) de vuestra conveniencia i del
> servicio de Dios. (112)

> [Daughter, now I believe without doubt what you have told me, and I will
> believe henceforth whatever you tell me; and I venerate you as one of the
> notable persons of this world, and I promise to assist you however I can for
> your comfort and for the service of God.]

Erauso won freedom from secular justice and great notability with this
revelation, but she immediately lost the right to dress and live as a man.
When the bishop took her to the convent of Santa Clara in Guamanga,
"Salió Su Ilustrísima de casa llevándome a su lado con un concurso tan
grande, que no huvo de quedar persona alguna en la ciudad que no viniese,
de suerte que se tardó mucho en llegar allá" (112) [The bishop escorted me
with a crowd so great that not a person in the city was not there, which
delayed our arrival at the convent]. In order to demonstrate the veracity of
her story and to keep the support of the bishop, she now had to acknowledge her female identity and return to wearing the nun's habit that she had
once despised. Yet accepting the external signs of a nun did not mean acquiescence to compulsory gender identification, for the Nun-Lieutenant had
clearly demonstrated that he was not like any other nun. In fact, Erauso's
account of the response to her self-revelation suggests pride and pleasure
in the notice she had won: "Corrió la noticia de este suceso por todas las

Yndias, i los que antes me vieron, i los que antes i después supieron mis cosas, se maravillaron en todas las Yndias" (113) [The news of this event ran through all the Indies, and those who saw me before, and those that before and after knew of me marveled in all the Indies].

Crowds again came to see him in Lima, where the archbishop summoned him to visit convents and choose the one in which he would live. Erauso chose Santísima Trinidad, "gran Convento, que sustenta cien religiosas de velo negro, cincuenta de velo blanco; diez novicias; diez donadas, i diez i seiz criadas" (114) [a great convent, which sustained one-hundred professed nuns, fifty postulants, ten novices, ten lay sisters, and sixteen servants]. Here Erauso remained for two years and five months until word arrived from Spain, "razón bastante de cómo no era yo, ni havía sido Monja profesa, con lo qual se me permitió salir del Convento consentimiento común de todas las Monjas, i me puse en camino para España" (114) [that I was not, nor had I been a professed nun, which permitted me to leave the convent with agreement of all the nuns, and I took the road for Spain].

Even though the bishop in Bogotá urged her to remain there in the convent of her order, Erauso knew that she could leave the convent because she had never taken the vows that would have formally transformed her from postulant to professed nun. "Yo le dixe que no tenía yo orden ni Religión, i que trataba de bolverme a mi patria, donde haría lo que pareciese más convenirme para mi salvación" (115) [I told him that I had no order nor religious vocation, and that I was trying to return to my homeland, where I would do what appeared most suitable for my salvation]. The Nun-Lieutenant must have felt considerable tension between the male identity she had carefully established and preserved for more than twenty years and the nun's identity now expected of her. Not surprisingly, "Caí allí enferma i me pareció mala tierra para Españoles, i llegué a punto de muerte" (115) [I fell ill there and it appeared to be a bad place for Spaniards, and I arrived at the point of death], and only slowly recovered.

Approval and License

Nearly four years after confessing to the bishop in Guamanga, the Nun-Lieutenant reclaimed her male identity, but now it would be blended with public knowledge of her femaleness. When verification came from the convent in San Sebastián that Catalina de Erauso had been a postulant there, but had never professed as a nun, she left the nuns and convent in Peru to sail for Spain. What he expected to find in his homeland that would be best for his "salvation," in the words of the autobiography, is not clear, but it would seem from his subsequent actions in Spain that he considered most crucial a pension and official license to continue living as a man. Erauso no longer had to wear the nun's habit, but she had won so much fame that she could not leave behind her public identity as a nun. The nun's habit, in fact, had worked in his favor, for it brought him respect and seemed to erase any memory of the people he had killed and wounded in so many brawls (Juárez 5).

Even more important, Erauso's virginity clothed her in admiration, for her society recognized only two legitimate states for females — virgin or wife — and exalted that of virgin above all others. In fact, the intact membrane came to signify such internal virtue that nothing else that Erauso had done in his life could detract from it. If she carried out performative acts to produce her own male identity, it was what she had *not* done that guaranteed social approval once she had revealed her female identity. Maintaining the purity of his corporeal boundaries by avoiding the rupture of this most important membrane, Erauso could present himself as free from pollution. Her special position, as that of other virginal women, came not from the power to pollute and disorder, but from the power to renounce sexuality. Whether in reality he had renounced sexuality or not, Erauso knew that to get approval for the life he had made for himself, he should emphasize his virginity.

The intact hymen, in fact, protected Erauso during this trip to Spain in 1624. The autobiography tells of her gambling on board the ship and of a fight that erupted. He explains,

Allí un día en el juego se armó una rehierta, en que huve de dar a uno un arachuelo en la cara con un cuchillejo que tenía allí, i resultó mucha inquietud: i el General se vio obligado a apartarme de allí i pasarme a la Almiranta donde yo tenía paisanos. (117)

[There one day in a game a fight broke out and I had to scratch another's cheek with a small knife and much unquiet resulted so that the captain of the ship had to separate me and transfer me to the vice-admiral's ship where I had countrymen.]

Even though Erauso insulted and brawled with their men, the officers treated her very graciously. She had become a public figure whom they did not want to be accused of mistreating. Moreover, he was a virgin and was said to be a nun. If Catalina's brawling, gambling male persona most deeply impressed those whom she insulted at the gambling tables, her virginal female persona convinced the officers in authority that she should be treated as a woman deserving respect.

The Nun-Lieutenant lived in a society that had constructed a particular conceptualization of the hymen that now worked in his favor. Because a female had value in this society as an object of exchange in marriage if her hymen was intact, clerics advised parents to guard the purity of their daughters "as dragons" (Cerdá 242r). Once married, a woman also had to guard her chastity in order to verify the paternity of her children and to guarantee their "purity of blood" free from mixture with Jews or Muslims. Spanish people in this period invented meaning for the hymen by telling "stories of marriage, copulation or virginity, or both: but never neither," as Mary Gossy has written, "that is, never the story of a hymen indifferent to the phallus" (49). In addition, many clerical authorities contributed to the social construction of the hymen with their beliefs that virginity was the highest status for women and that it imparted to them a special strength (Pérez de Valdivia 167, 666).

Yet his virginity alone did not attract the crowds that flocked to see the Nun-Lieutenant when his ship sailed into Seville at the end of 1624. After all, thousands of women in Spain at this time had preserved their virginity, most in convents, but some as beatas, those women who dedicated their lives to God and took a vow of chastity but usually lived outside the discipline of the convent.[14] Nor did the crowds press around Erauso simply because she had lived and dressed as a man, for the people of Golden Age Spain also knew other cases of the "manly woman."[15] What attracted these people who wanted to see the Nun-Lieutenant was his inclusiveness as a hyphenate. Neither simply woman nor man, she was both and all, a sexual anomaly, a circus freak, a symbol of nature undone and amazed, a paradox of boundaries violated but hymen intact. In fact, the Nun-Lieutenant appeared as a living example that membranes such as the hymen could successfully negotiate the perilous transition between same and other, for he had carefully preserved his virginity even as he broke other gender constrictions on women and dressed and lived as a man (Smith 90).[16]

But Erauso determined to win acceptance for the person she had engendered. Seeking to escape the curious crowds, he went from Seville to Madrid and then to Pamplona, through France, and into Piedmont, where he was arrested and imprisoned, accused of being a Spanish spy. After she had made her way back to Madrid, the Nun-Lieutenant wrote a *Memorial* in March of 1626 in which she petitioned Felipe IV for a pension as reward for her years of service in his army. This petition differs considerably from the autobiography attributed to Erauso, and indicates a sensitivity to the need for establishing respectability. No mention is made in the *Memorial* of brawls and men he had killed. Instead, she explains that for the past nineteen years she had dressed and lived as a man in Peru, fifteen of those years in the king's army, "por particular inclinación que tubo de ejercitar las armas, en defensa de la fee católica y servicio de vuestra majestad" [because of a particlar inclination that I had for bearing arms in defense of the Catholic faith and in service for Your Majesty]. Referring to himself as "she," Erauso describes how he assumed a male name and received the title of lieutenant, as he demonstrated in many battles a "balor de hombre" [man's courage]. She acknowledges that to dress as a man is prohibited, but says that she has carried out such service for so many years and with such valor, even suffering wounds, that it would be gracious of the king to grant her a pension and some expenses so that she could return to the Indies. Felipe IV turned the petition over to the Council of the Indies, and "Su majestad me señaló 800 escudos de renta por mi vida, que fueron poco menos de lo que pedí" (119) [His Majesty granted me a pension of 800 escudos which amounted to little less than I asked].

Successfully winning the pension in Madrid, Erauso then made her way to Rome to find further legitimacy. In the autobiography he described himself as he kissed the feet of the pope and told him of his life. Significantly, she included a description of "mi sexo, i virginidad" [my sex and virginity], qualities that distinguished her from other soldiers and provided her with an ambivalent status that could have endangered the social order. Combined with the asexuality of virginity, however, this ambivalent status threatened neither the purity prescription for women nor the bravery prescription for men (122–23). "I mostró Su Santidad extrañar tal caso i con avabilidad me concedió licencia para proseguir mi vida en hábito de hombre, encargándome la prosecución honesta en adelante, i la abstinencia en ofender al próximo, temiendo la ulción de Dios sobre su mandamiento" (123) [His Holiness expressed amazement at such a case and with affability granted me license to continue to live and dress as a man, advising me to pursue an honest life henceforth, and abstinence from offending another, fearing the vengeance of God about his commandment].

During the month and a half that Erauso stayed in Rome, crowds of people tried to see her, including princes, bishops, and cardinals. His fame continued to grow as he traveled back to Spain, and a chronicle for the year 1630 records as a notable event his presence in the cathedral of Seville, dressed as a man.[17] The Nun-Lieutenant, according to this document, had run away from her convent and went to the Indies. There for twenty years he had accomplished "muchas hazañas, teniéndola todos para capón" [many exploits, everyone believing him to be a eunuch]. While waiting in Seville for permission to sail for the New World, the Nun-Lieutenant evidently sat for a portrait by Francisco Pacheco, who entitled it "El alférez doña Catalina de Erauso" [the lieutenant Miss Catalina de Erauso].

The last historical record of this individual came from a Capuchin friar who had met her in Vera Cruz about 1645. He claimed that "vio i habló diferentes vezes a la Monja Alférez Da. Catarina de Araujo (que entonces allí se llamava D. Antonio de Araujo) i que tenía una requa de mulas en que conducía con unos Negros ropa a diferentes partes" (Erauso, *Vida* 126) [he saw and spoke at different times with the Nun-Lieutenant Doña Catarina de Araujo (who was called then Don Antonio de Araujo) and that she had a pack of mules, which she and some blacks drove to take goods and clothing to different places]. "I que era sugeto allí tenido por de mucho corazón i destreza: i que andava en hábito de hombre, i que traía espada i daga con guarniciones de plata" (126) [She was believed to have much heart and skill and she dressed as a man and carried a sword and dagger with silver trimmings]. We will never know if Erauso continued the brawling that had nearly ended his life, nor if he found happiness with a partner. It seems clear, however, that she lived out the rest of her life as the masculine persona that she had so carefully engendered.

Yet the story is not so simple. In fact, Catalina's very existence raises difficult questions about sex and self-identity. Her body seemed to be female

"Catalina de Erauso," engraving from the portrait by
Francisco Pacheco. From *Historia de la monja alférez,
doña Catalina de Erauso* by J. M. de Ferrer
(Paris, 1829).

in its genitalia, but to be male in stature and structure. Although he lacked
a beard, he had small hairs above the lip as a moustache.[18] After he met her,
Pedro del Valle Peregrino wrote, "Sólo en las manos se le puede conocer que
es muger, porque las tiene abultadas i carnosas, i robustas i fuertes, bien que
las mueve algo como muger" (Erauso, *Vida* 128) [Only her hands betray her
as a woman, mostly because she moved them somewhat as a woman, even
though they were bulky and fleshy and robust and strong]. The matrons

who had examined him in Guamanga had declared his body to be that of a woman rather than a man, and they did not even suggest hermaphroditism, but could he really be seen as merely a woman? What differentiated men and women? Were there essential qualities in their bodies at birth that then determined the lives they would live, or did other factors inscribe sexual meaning on their bodies? Such questions could be especially troubling in Golden Age Spain, for most people at this time lacked any concept of a socially constructed gender, and most believed in sex as an essential quality granted at birth, integral to the "natural order," and essential to a sexually dichotomized, hierarchical, and patriarchal sociopolitical system.[19]

Yet no one raised these questions about the Nun-Lieutenant, nor did his presence stir up any gender trouble "through the mobilization, subversive confusion, and proliferation," as Judith Butler has written, "of precisely those constitutive categories that seek to keep gender in its place by posturing as the foundational illusions of identity" (33–34). As people of Golden Age Spain and its empire marveled aloud at the bravery of this person, they continued to refer to him as a female. Granted the title of lieutenant, Erauso would forever be called the Nun-Lieutenant, a feminized compound title with a feminine article, a reminder that he would never lose the nun's habit.

As a nun or virgin, Erauso could be seen as asexual as the eunuch that other soldiers had thought her to be. Such an asexual individual simply did not fit into a sexual system and thus posed no threat of proliferating categories, although we might ask why authorities did not worry that other little girls would follow Erauso's example and run away to make themselves into men, never to marry or return to feminine life. Authorities did not perceive the Nun-Lieutenant as a threat of pollution, for he kept his bodily boundaries intact and, even though he crossed sexual boundaries, he did not engage in that dangerous game of repeatedly passing back and forth across these lines. Erauso chose to be a man, dressed as a man, and lived out her days as a man.

In fact, Erauso's choosing to live as a man provided a supporting myth for the political imperatives of Golden Age Spain. She underscored the superiority and privilege of being male in this patriarchal society when she chose to live as a man, even though she defied social constrictions on her as a woman in order to make this choice.[20] Moreover, he became a unifying symbol of heroism for high- and low-born alike, and everything that he did to engender himself glorified the freedom and honor of action. Yet in no way did she threaten to overturn a sexually dichotomized and hierarchical society.

Erauso chose to go the New World, that part of the Spanish Empire that became so essential in supporting the political imperatives of a state in formation. Her desire to fight in the king's army in Peru, repeated in tens of thousands of cases, subdued the indigenous people who resisted the Spanish conquest of their lands. Soldiers such as Erauso legitimized and facilitated the transformation of this part of the earth into a major economic pillar for the Spanish state. The Spanish Crown had to grant land, its resources, and peoples, to those who could extract wealth from them; but the Crown successfully established its right to one-fifth of the gold and silver taken from the mines of Mexico and Peru. Between 1503 and 1660, the mines produced bullion imports for Spain valued at 537,385,119 ducats.[21] Although this wealth did not usually remain in Spain, it provided the collateral for loans that the Crown negotiated with banking families such as the Fuggers who financed royal efforts to retain a far-flung empire.

Moreover, the adventures of the Nun-Lieutenant publicized the attractions of the New World as a place for impoverished nobles and second sons of noble families with estates in systems of primogeniture. In her *Memorial* to the king, Erauso noted that she was the daughter of noble parents. He had served the king well, "resistiendo a las yncomodidades de la milicia, como el más fuerte varón" (132) [resisting the discomforts of the militia as the strongest of men]. Despite all the references to brawling in the autobiography, the example of Erauso could be seen as demonstrating that service to the king in the Indies did not debase nobles and might even lead to recognition and monetary rewards. For a Crown dependent on a nobility that faced major economic problems, the Indies provided opportunity to demonstrate royal largesse and support while diverting nobles' attention from serious economic hardships in Spain.

Most of all, the stories of the Nun-Lieutenant illustrated that the New World offered an arena in which to revitalize the warrior ethic of the Reconquest. This ethic had become a major part of the founding myth of the Spanish kingdom, which was said to have begun with the stubborn tenacity of Christian warriors determined to "take back" from the Muslims the lands of the Iberian Peninsula. As they fought, these Christian warriors asserted the superiority of their God and their culture, which later generations would use as a rationale for subjugating indigenous peoples in the Western Hemisphere whom they characterized as barbarians "devoted to all kinds of intemperate acts and abominable lewdness, including the eating of human flesh" (Sepúlveda 218; Castro 605, 622). They exalted the men of hard muscles and swift action, the arms they carried that supported their victories in battle, the horses that gave them impressive advantages over their adversaries. And they felt the pride of knowing that they could make a swift, sure defense of their honor. Clearly, such an ethic marked the brawling, battling stories of the Nun-Lieutenant.

Erauso succeeded in winning approval of the self he had engendered because he inscribed on his body the values of his society. She symbolized the belief that the margins and boundaries of the Spanish Empire remained intact and retained their energy to repulse attack (Douglas 114). In a very real sense, the Nun-Lieutenant became a metaphor for the Spanish kingdom. He shaped his own identity, established autonomy, and crossed into new territory. The Spanish state also sought to establish its identity in the sixteenth and seventeenth centuries, having crossed over into territory once held by Muslims, and now passing into the New World. In both cases, the preservation of traditional values seemed to nullify the dangers that could have marked such crossings. Engendering himself, Erauso had developed a myth grounded in tradition that served the political and social needs of the Spanish kingdom as it faced increasingly difficult problems in the seventeenth century.

Notes

I want to express my appreciation to the Huntington Library for permission to use their edition of Thomas Heywood's *The Fair Maid of the West, Or A Girle Worth Gold*. I am also very grateful to Josiah Blackmore, Anne J. Cruz, Gregory S. Hutcheson, and Sherry Katz for their very helpful comments on earlier versions of this essay.

1. Information about the baptism of Catalina de Erauso appears in appendix 3 of Catalina de Erauso, *Vida i sucesos de la Monja Alférez: autobiografía atribuída a doña Catalina de Erauso*, ed., introd., and notes by Rima de Vallbona (152). For documentation on her early life, see also the appendices in J. M. de Ferrer, *Historia de la Monja Alférez doña Catalina de Erauso, escrita por ella misma*, which includes the autobiography attibuted to Catalina de Erauso. The autobiography

gives 1585 as the year of birth, but Ferrer asked a local curate to check the baptismal record and he found that the date on it is 1592.

2. Her memorial directed to the king appears in Archivo General de las Indias (hereafter AGI), sec. 5, *Documentos escogidos*, legajo 1, no. 87, years 1626–30, and summarizes her brave deeds in service to the king. The New World, of course, was not at all new to those people who had been living in the Western Hemisphere for centuries; but people of Golden Age Spain usually referred to this part of the world as "the New World" or "the Indies."

3. Female transvestism is discussed in a larger context by Bullough and Bullough; Dekker and van de Pol; Garber; Gilbert; Rose; Shepherd; Wheelwright; Woodbridge; and Woodhouse. For Spain, see especially Bravo Villasante and McKendrick. Specific literary examples of women who dressed as men include Bess Bridges, who disguised herself as a sea captain in order to sail in search for her lover's body in Thomas Heywood's *The Fair Maid of the West, Or A Girle Worth Gold;* Rosaura, who cross-dressed and traveled to Poland to avenge her dishonoring by Astolfo, in Pedro Calderón de la Barca's *La vida es sueño;* and Leonora, who dressed as a man to get revenge on the man who had dishonored her in Ana Caro Mallén y Soto's *Comedia famosa de valor, agravio y mujer.*

4. The term refers to the title of a book by Judith Butler. For more on male-female dichotomization, see Rubin. For transgenderism, see Velasco.

5. Juan Pérez de Montalván, *La monja alférez, comedia famosa* (1625, reprinted in Ferrer, *Historia* 169–311). There is some question about the real author of the play, *La monja alférez.* Parker notes that the author complained about some publishers attributing to him work that was not his (69), and says that the true author may be Luis Belmonte Bermúdez. See also Dixon ("The Life and Works of Juan Pérez de Montalbán" and "Review of Profeli's *Montalbán*").

6. The most recent version of this work has been edited and published with an introduction and notes by Rima de Vallbona. All references to this work will use this edition; translations are mine. For more discussion on the authenticity of the autobiography, see Vallbona's introduction (esp. 2–22); Ferrer's prologue; Castresana; and Juárez.

7. Pedro del Valle Peregrino subsequently wrote this account in a letter dated 11 July 1626, reprinted in the Vallbona edition as appendix 1 (127–28).

8. "No tiene pechos: que desde mui muchacha me dixo haver hecho no sé qué remedio para secarlos i quedar llanos, como le quedaron: el qual fue un emplasto que le dio un Ytaliano, que quando se lo puso le causó gran dolor; pero después, sin hacerle otro mal, ni mal tratamiento, surtió el efecto" (Erauso, *Vida* 128) [She has no breasts: she told me that ever since she was a very young girl, she used some sort of remedy to dry up her breasts and keep them flat, just as they have

remained; it was a poultice an Italian had given her, and when she applied it, it caused her much pain, but afterward there were no ill side-effects and it achieved the desired effect].

9. Judith Butler discusses this phrase of Adrienne Rich and "heterosexual contract," a term of Monique Wittig, as well as her own phrase, "heterosexual matrix" (151n6). In early-modern Spain, sexual relations between men were seen as far more reprehensible than any that might develop between women, unless the latter involved penetration with an artificial phallus; for more discussion see Perry (" 'Nefarious Sin.' ")

10. The pattern was not restricted to the New World; see especially Ruggiero and also Rossiaud.

11. This account is corroborated by Luis de Céspedes, governor and captain general of Paraguay, whose signed statement is now in AGI, Indiferente, legajo 1511, no. 104. See appendix 2 of the Vallbona edition for copies of other documents that supported the truth of Catalina de Erauso's accounts.

12. See, for example, the statement of Juan Ginés de Sepúlveda in Lunenfeld (220). Note, however, that such beliefs did not prevent Spanish soldiers from taking indigenous women as concubines or wives. For a discussion of Ercilla y Zuñiga, see Korth (*Spanish Policy* 237n1).

13. Foucault often made this point; see Butler (*Gender Trouble* 96) for more discussion; and also Smith, who discusses Gayatri Chakravorty Spivak's *In Other Worlds* (17–18).

14. For more on *beatas*, see Perry (*Gender and Disorder* 97–117).

15. See, for example in Spain, Bravo Villasante; Martín; and McKendrick.

16. Erauso's apparent asexuality undoubtedly mitigated any threat posed by sexual ambiguity. Contrast this case with that of Eleno/a de Céspedes in Burshatin's essay, following, in which the subject's active sexuality provoked authorities to impose severe punishment.

17. Archivo Municipal de Sevilla, Sección Especial, Papeles del Sr. Conde de Aguila, libros en folio, "Efemérides de Sevilla," cuadro 1.

18. This is the verbal testimony of Fray Nicolás de Rentería, a Capuchin who had met Catalina de Erauso in Vera Cruz in 1645; it was given to and recorded by Fray Diego de Sevilla in Seville, 10 October 1693, reprinted in "Notas finales" in Ferrer (122).

19. For examples of writers of the period presenting this view, see Juan de la Cerda; Fray Martín de Córdoba; Juan de Espinosa; and Fray Luis de León.

20. Smith shows that Antigone acted in a similarly paradoxical fashion in both supporting and breaking the male-dominated system of ancient Greece (74–75).

21. These figures are from Hamilton (34). For a discussion of the importance

of bullion imports to the Spanish Crown, see Elliott (esp. 183–84). According to Lynch, "Spanish society and economy were built on the twin foundations of land and silver, Castilian agriculture and American mining" (1).

Works Cited

Bravo Villasante, Carmen. *La mujer vestida de hombre en el teatro español: siglos XVI–XVII*. Madrid: Sociedad General Española de Librería, 1976.

Bullough, Vern, and Bonnie Bullough. *Cross-Dressing, Sex, and Gender*. Philadelphia: U of Pennsylvania P, 1993.

Butler, Judith. *Gender Trouble: Feminism and the Subversion of Identity*. New York: Routledge, 1990.

Calderón de la Barca, Pedro. *La vida es sueño*. Ed. Enrigue Rull Fernández. Madrid: Alhambra, 1980.

Caro Mallén y Soto, Ana. *Comedia famosa de valor, agravio y mujer: apuntes para una biblioteca de escritoras españolas desde el año 1401 al 1833*. Ed. Manuel Serrano y Sanz. *Biblioteca de Autores Españoles*. Vol. 268. Madrid: Atlas, 1975. 179–212.

Castresana, Luis de. *Catalina de Erauso: la monja alférez*. Madrid: Afrodisio Aguado, 1968.

Castro, Américo. *The Structure of Spanish History*. Trans. Edmund L. King. Princeton: Princeton UP, 1954.

Cerda, Juan de la. *Vida política de todos los estados de mugeres; en el qual se dan muy provechosos y Christianos documentos y avisos, para criarse y conservarse devidamente las mugeres en sus estados*. Alcalá de Henares: Juan Gracian, 1599.

Céspedes, Luis de. *Certificación*. Archivo General de las Indias. *Indiferente*. Legajo 1511. No. 104.

Chaves, Cristóbal de. "Relación de las cosas de la cárcel de Sevilla y su trato." Vols. B–C of Papeles del Conde de Aguila, Sección Especial of the Archivo Municipal de Sevilla.

Córdoba, Fray Martín de. *Jardín de nobles donzellas*. Ed. Harriet Goldberg. University of North Carolina Studies in the Romance Languages and Literatures 137. Chapel Hill: U of North Carolina Department of Romance Languages, 1974.

Dekker, Rudolf M., and Lotte C. van de Pol. *The Tradition of Female Transvestism in Early Modern Europe*. New York: St. Martin's P, 1989.

Dixon, Victor F. "The Life and Works of Juan Pérez de Montalbán." *Hispanic Review* 32 (1964): 36–50.

————. "Review of Profeli's *Montalbán.*" *Bulletin of Hispanic Studies* 49 (1972): 1866–87.

Douglas, Mary. *Purity and Danger: An Analysis of Concepts of Pollution and Taboo.* New York: Frederick A. Praeger, 1966.

"Efemérides de Sevilla." Archivo Municipal de Sevilla. Sección Especial. Papeles del Sr. Conde de Aguila. Libros en folio. Cuadro 1.

Elliott, J. H. *Imperial Spain, 1469–1715.* London: Penguin, 1990.

Erauso, Catalina de. *Memorial.* Archivo General de las Indias. Sección 5. *Documentos escogidos.* Legajo 1. No. 87. Years 1626–30.

————. *Vida i sucesos de la Monja Alférez. Autobiografía atribuída a Doña Catalina de Erauso.* Ed. Rima de Vallbona. Tempe: Center for Latin American Studies, Arizona State U, 1992.

Ercilla y Zuñiga, Alonso de. *La Araucana.* Havana: Editorial Arte y Literatura, 1987.

Espinosa, Juan de. *Diálogo en laude de las mujeres.* 1580. Ed. Angela González Simón. Madrid: Consejo Superior de Investigaciones Científicas, 1946.

Ferrer, J. M. de, ed. *Historia de la Monja Alférez doña Catalina de Erauso, escrita por ella misma.* 1625. Paris: Julio Didot, 1829.

Foucault, Michel. *The History of Sexuality.* Vol. 1: *An Introduction.* Trans. Robert Hurley. 1978. New York: Pantheon, 1978.

Garber, Marjorie. *Vested Interests: Cross-Dressing and Cultural Anxiety.* New York: Routledge, 1992.

Gilbert, Sandra M. "Costumes of the Mind: Transvestism as Metaphor in Modern Literature." *Critical Inquiry* 7 (1980): 391–417.

Gossy, Mary. *The Untold Story: Women and Theory in Golden Age Texts.* Ann Arbor: U of Michigan P, 1989.

Hamilton, Earl. *American Treasure and the Price Revolution in Spain, 1501–1659.* Cambridge, Mass.: Harvard UP, 1934.

Heywood, Thomas. *The Fair Maid of the West, Or A Girle Worth Gold.* London: Richard Royston, 1631.

Juárez, Encarnación. "Señora Catalina, ¿dónde es el camino? La autobiografía como búsqueda y afirmación de identidad en *Vida i sucesos de la Monja Alférez.*" *La Chispa.* Ed. Claire J. Paolini. New Orleans: Tulane UP, 1995. 185–95.

Korth, Eugene, S.J. *Spanish Policy in Colonial Chile.* Stanford: Stanford UP, 1968.

León, Fray Luis de. *La perfecta casada.* 1583. Biblioteca de Autores Españoles. Madrid: M. Rivadeneyra, 1855.

Lunenfeld, Marvin, ed. *1492: Discovery, Invasion, Encounter: Sources and Interpretations.* Lexington, Mass.: D. C. Heath, 1991.

Lynch, John. *Spain under the Habsburgs*. Vol. 2: *Spain and America, 1598–1700*. New York: New York UP, 1984.

Martín, Adrienne. "Desnudo de una travestí, o la 'autobiografía' de Catalina de Erauso." *La mujer y su representación en las literaturas hispánicas*. Actas del XI Congreso de la Asociación Internacional de Hispanistas. Vol. 2. Irvine, Calif.: Asociación Internacional de Hispanistas, 1994. 34–41.

McKendrick, Melveena. *Women and Society in the Spanish Drama of the Golden Age: A Study of the Mujer Varonil*. London: Cambridge UP, 1974.

Mendiburu, Manuel de. "Doña Catalina Erauso, o la monja alférez." *Diccionario histórico biográfrico del Perú*. Lima: Enrique Palacios, 1932. 2: 397–408.

Parker, Jack H. *Juan de Montalván*. Boston: Twayne, 1975.

Pérez de Montalván, Juan. *La monja alférez, comedia famosa* (1625), reprinted in Joaquín María de Ferrer. *Historia de la monja alférez doña Catalina de Erauso, escrita por ella misma*. Paris: Julio Didot, 1829.

Pérez de Valdivia, Diego. *Aviso de gente recogida*. 1585. Madrid: Universidad Pontífica de Salamanca y Fundación Universitaria Española, 1977.

Perry, Mary Elizabeth. *Gender and Disorder in Early Modern Seville*. Princeton: Princeton UP, 1990.

———. "The 'Nefarious Sin' in Early Modern Seville." *The Pursuit of Sodomy: Male Homosexuality in Renaissance and Enlightenment Europe*. Ed. Kent Gerard and Gert Hekma. New York: Haworth P, 1989. 67–89.

Rose, Margaret B. "Women in Men's Clothing: Apparel and Social Stability in 'The Roaring Girl.'" *English Literary Renaissance* 14:3 (Autumn 1984): 367–91.

Rossiaud, Jacques. "Prostitution, Youth, and Society in the Towns of Southeastern France in the Fifteenth Century." *Deviants and the Abandoned in French Society*. Ed. Robert Forster and Orest Ranum. Trans. Elborg Forster and Patricia Ranum. Baltimore: Johns Hopkins UP, 1978. 1–46.

Rubin, Gayle. "The Traffic in Women: Notes on the 'Political Economy' of Sex." *Towards an Anthropology of Women*. Ed. Rayna R. Reiter. New York: Monthly Review P, 1975. 157–210.

Ruggiero, Guido. *The Boundaries of Eros: Sex, Crime, and Sexuality in Renaissance Venice*. New York: Oxford UP, 1985.

Sepúlveda, Juan Ginés de. "Demócrates alter de justis belli causis apud Indios." *1492: Discovery, Invasion, Encounter*. Ed. Marvin Lunenfeld. Lexington, Mass.: D. C. Heath, 1991. 218–21.

Shepherd, Simon. *Amazons and Warrior Women: Varieties of Feminism in Seventeenth-Century Drama*. Brighton, England: Harvester, 1981.

Smith, Paul Julian. *Representing the Other: 'Race,' Text, and Gender in Spanish and Spanish American Narrative*. Oxford: Clarendon P, 1992.

Velasco, Sherry. *Making a Spectacle: Transgenderism, Lesbian Desire, and the Lieutenant Nun Catalina de Erauso.* Austin: U of Texas P, forthcoming.

Wheelwright, Julie. *Amazons and Military Maids: Women Who Cross-Dressed in the Pursuit of Life, Liberty and Happiness.* London: Pandora P, 1989.

Woodbridge, Linda. *Women and the English Renaissance: Literature and the Nature of Womankind, 1540–1620.* Chicago: U of Chicago P, 1984.

Woodhouse, Annie. *Fantastic Women: Sex, Gender and Transvestism.* New Brunswick: Rutgers UP, 1989.

Israel Burshatin

Written on the Body

Slave or Hermaphrodite in Sixteenth-Century Spain

Autor: Tatuador

The life story of Eleno de Céspedes has been preserved in the archives of the Inquisition of Toledo. Eleno—known officially as the female Elena de Céspedes, according to the authorities who ruled on the question of Eleno's body and gender—was not an important personage in the reign of Felipe II. Nevertheless, she did achieve some notoriety in her lifetime, earning a place in the annals of natural history on account of her (his) claim that her body was transformed from female to hermaphrodite. Was her metamorphosis real or, as the Inquisitors of Toledo eventually concluded, a homoerotic ruse, an elaborate fabrication constructed in order to seduce other women and copulate with them as if she were a man? Eleno's case is compelling precisely because it illustrates the central problematic of early-modern Iberia through the filter of contested sexualities—the assimilation, exclusion, or negation of the "other" as indispensable elements in the construction of the hegemonic subject in the recently reconquered peninsula and the expanding overseas dominions. Framed in the context of post-Reconquest Andalusia, Eleno's dossier demands to be read as an exemplary narrative of a frontier culture whose boundaries were being displaced from the political map to the bodies of those subordinated by Castilian and "old" Christian rule—the sway of an élite buttressed by the genetic fiction of a superior ancestry supposedly free of Muslim or Jewish strains. In that increasingly racialist society, Eleno's protean subject positions bring into focus issues of race, gender, sexuality, and national identity at their points of intersection in the body of a woman born into slavery.[1]

Eleno's origins among the brown-skinned and the colonized locate her in the lowest rungs of a society that prized honor and blood "purity" above all else. Around 1545 Eleno was born female to Francisca de Medina, an African slave who was in domestic (and possibly, also, artisanal) service to the Medina-Céspedes household. This condition of servitude was inscribed on Eleno's flesh. At a very early age, her face was branded with hot coals; the resulting scars would transform her body into a tablet bearing the familiar record of slavery as written by Castilians on their human chattel. Thus branded and having joined her mother in service, Eleno's face was a text to be read as "Andalusian slave," as she would be called in a Spanish version of Pliny's *Natural History* that appeared ten years after her trial (Huerta fol. 5v). By the time of her prosecution, Inquisitors and civil authorities read the text of servitude back into Eleno's slave brand, despite the accused's brilliant career of "self-fashioning" in various artisanal, military, and medical contexts.

> Preguntado se a la dicha Elena de Çéspedes qué dos señales que tiene en los carrillos como esclava, dijo en el carrillo izquierdo quando se la quitó la señal de esclava y en cuya servidunbre a estado. Dixo que no se acuerda más de que la señal es de carbunco, que le dio siendo pequeña, e que no [h]a sido esclava de nadie. (Céspedes)[2]

> [Elena de Céspedes was asked about the two marks she has on her cheeks, like a slave, and she said that the one on the left cheek she removed, and that she was in service. She does not remember anything, except that they branded her with hot coals, when she was little, and that she has not been anybody else's slave.]

As far as Eleno's father was concerned, his reduced role in the dossier was consonant with the phallocratic rules of slavery as it was practiced in early-modern Iberia; he was but an appendage to the real and effective authority exercised by the slave-owning Medina-Céspedes family. It was up to the slave master and mistress to determine such matters as Eleno's upbringing, early training, and even her name. The name, Elena de Céspedes, was that of the mistress of the household; it was bestowed on the ten-year-old slave, along with her freedom, in "contemplation" of the deceased *señora*. The body of the young slave thereby underwent its second important transformation. In acquiring the late mistress's name, the young Elena also gained title to her own body. Her appellation and status rewritten, the sense of Elena's slave scar would also shift, from a sign that identified her as human chattel, to demeaning memento — the stigmata of dishonored origins for "old" Christians to scorn. Nevertheless, the *mulata* Elena de Céspedes gained her freedom and along with it came the notion that bodies tell stories — even conflicted ones — and that they convey history, legal status, and cultural boundaries. The trial documents reveal the surprising success that Eleno's own corporeal and sartorial transformations wrought on a stigmatized body, transforming herself from domestic slave to soldier and surgeon, from subservient female to proud transgendered subject.

During the trial, however, the formulaic recitation of family origins and autobiographical material (*discurso de su vida*) posed the gravest challenge to Eleno's career. She had to recontextualize her life according to monological and reified patterns of filiation, bloodlines, and sex. They asked whether she was of "old" or "new" Christian stock. But in the case of a woman born into slavery, questions about her nonslave father and his ancestry rang hollow. What we know of him can be reduced to this — he was called Pero Hernández and he was a farmer by trade. The father's name suggests that he was Castilian, and it has the ring of the "old" Christian caste. But should we not question Pero Hernández's paternity? He becomes a convenient legal surrogate for the master if we raise the inevitable issue regarding male slave-owners and their female possessions in sixteenth-century Castile: Might Eleno's father have been Benito, the master himself? Historians have amply documented how slave-owners took the bodies of their female slaves for sexual pleasure as well as the profits assured in slave offspring — hence the higher price fetched by female slaves from sub-Saharan Africa, who were more valuable than the males precisely because their bodies were seen as much more "productive" (Franco Silva 293).

Rather than dwell on parental filiation, Eleno's narrative articulated motifs of the body with a dazzling variety of skilled occupations. Elena's account of her performance as "Eleno" recalls the strategies of picaresque narrative. By cross-dressing and acting male, Eleno repositioned *him*self, in the words of the *pícaro* 'rogue' Lazarillo de Tormes and his mother, alongside "the good," "the powerful ones" (*arrimarse a los buenos*) of the masculine gender (*Lazarillo de Tormes* 10) — thereby crossing the boundaries erected in order to keep slaves, women, Moriscos, crypto-Jews, and other excluded groups in their subordinate positions in Habsburg Spain. But unlike any ordinary cross-dresser, Eleno's transformation was, in her own words, a classic example of the female-to-hermaphrodite metamorphosis that could be validated by appealing to natural history.

Burladora de Toledo

Esta es la justicia que manda haɀer el Santo Officio de la Inquisición de Toledo a esta muger, porque siendo casada engañó a otra muger y se casó con ella. So pena de su culpa la mandan açotar por ello y se recluya en un hospital por dieɀ años para que sirva en él. ¡Quien tal haɀe que así lo pague!
— Céspedes

[This is the justice ordered by the Holy Office of the Inquisition on this woman, because being married she fooled another woman and married her. For her guilt she is sentenced to be whipped and confined in a hospital for ten years so that she may serve there. As you sow, so shall you reap.]

The facts of the case were anything but simple, especially since one fundamental piece of evidence—Eleno's sex—was the subject of earnest and learned disputation between Inquisitors and their medical allies, on one hand, and Eleno and her/his own medical expertise on the other. Nevertheless, the facts can be summarized as follows. Having lived as a man for over twenty years, Eleno married María del Caño, the woman s/he loved. Residing as husband and wife in Ocaña, the happy couple ran into trouble when Eleno was recognized by the licentiate Ortega Velázquez, who had known Eleno in the army, from the time they had both served in the battalion commanded by the duke of Arcos in the War of the Alpujarras (1568–70). The officer denounced "her" to the authorities, alleging that it was always known that Eleno had two sexes and that he was certain that she had been married to a man. The case was heard first by the royal court in Ocaña, which on 4 July 1587, formally indicted Elena for the crime of sodomy. As in other such cases involving women, the criteria applied were "penetration" and "pollution"—that is, the signs of an unruly woman who challenged the exclusivity of the male role in bed. The specific charge against Eleno was that "con un instrumento tieso y liso . . . cometió el delito enefando de sodomya" [with a stiff and smooth instrument she committed the uspeakable crime of sodomy]. Meanwhile, the parish priest proceeded to write a letter to the tribunal of the Inquisition in Toledo, recommending that the Holy Office take over the prosecution of Eleno's case, since her chief doctrinal offense was having married another woman, thereby undermining the meaning and sanctity of the marriage vows. All the authorities soon concluded that proper jurisdiction belonged to the Holy Office, and the prisoner was escorted to Toledo, where she was brought to trial.

The charge there, however, was no longer sodomy, but *sentir mal* 'contempt' for the church and its sacraments. While sodomy was nevertheless the subject of a great deal of investigation—as well as minute and specific "fact"-finding by the Inquisitors—the tribunal opted in the end for ruling only on the least "messy" and most strictly procedural aspects of the case. Eleno was not found guilty of sodomy—a crime that in Castile was under the jurisdiction of the royal and not the Inquisition's courts anyway—but of bigamy. A few years after her manumission—and prior to her sexual transfiguration—Elena had briefly been the wife of Christóval Lombardo, a stonemason from Jaén. They cohabited for a few months, long enough to get Elena pregnant. Soon after Christóval moved away, Elena heard of his death. Eleno had withheld these facts when she sought permission to marry María. She further compromised her case in Toledo by her inability to produce to the Inquisitors' satisfaction the proper certification of her first spouse's death. Declaring that Eleno was, in fact, Elena, the Toledo tribunal convicted *her* on the technicality of having committed bigamy by marrying María without the required paperwork certifying Eleno's widowed status—an emblematic piece of bureaucratic reasoning in the reign of the "paperwork king" (*le roi paperasser*), Felipe II.

Eleno's punishment, however, merits close scrutiny, since her sexual "misdeeds" were prominently represented in the *auto de fe* and other public aspects of her sentence. While these terrible events tell us something about Eleno's own courage and self-possession, they illuminate the rising fable of early-modern sexuality, which according to Foucault originated in the double bind of secrecy and the incitement to speak (Foucault 35). The particularities of Eleno's own fable of intersex shed a special light on early-modern sexualities since they also intertwine strands of gender and race as they flourished in post-Reconquest Iberia.

On 24 December 1588, the Inquisitors of Toledo, Don Rodrigo and Don Lope de Mendoza, ordered their convicted prisoner "Elena de Céspedes"

to be taken to the town of Ciempozuelos. This was the village of Eleno's
wife, María del Caño, and the setting, two years earlier, of their betrothal,
which was celebrated only after Eleno had obtained the proper license from
Juan Bautista Neroni, vicar general of Madrid. Eleno's punishment took
the form of a humiliating return to the scene of what had been her joyful
union to María: "Mandamos que en pena de sus delitos para que a ella sea
castigo y a otros exemplo para no cometer semejantes embustes y engaños"
(Céspedes) [We sentence and punish her for her crimes as an example to
others not to commmit similar tricks and deceits]. The public sentence
transformed the church and streets of Ciempozuelos into a theatrical locale,
in which a state institution of formidable influence in society could display
its notorious "pedagogy of fear" (Benassar 94–95). Eleno's crime was publicly decried as an intolerable assault on the estate of married women. In
retaliation, Eleno's body served to stage a violent and abjecting spectacle.

While Eleno's sentence was in line with that of male bigamists, whose
typical punishment consisted of two hundred lashes and ten years of confinement and forced labor as galley slaves (Gacto 142), the actual punishment alluded to the "closeted" crime of sodomy, which was also implicit
in the charges of apostasy and heresy leveled against her by the tribunal's
promotor fiscal 'prosecuting attorney.' In the trial the chief accusation was
that Eleno was a "muger que siente mal de los sacramentos y en especial
del matrimonio" [a woman who thinks ill of the sacraments, especially that
of matrimony]. "Instigada del demonio" [instigated by the devil], "con
sus enbelecos y ynvençiones" (Céspedes) [with her machinations and in-
ventions], she pretended to be a hermaphrodite. But it was also evident
that anxiety over female sodomy structured the Inquisition's technical concern with Eleno's transgendered performance.[3] Although not empowered
to prosecute cases of sodomy in Castile, the Toledo tribunal delved into
the specifics of Elena's male impersonation, especially her "machinations
and inventions." The Inquisitors were perturbed by the parodic nature
of Eleno's sexuality, her disturbing transcontextualization of the narrative of male hegemony. After obtaining a thorough accounting of the accused's *discurso de su vida* 'discourse of her/his life' and taking depositions
from his/her wife and at least one other female sexual partner, the judges
concluded that "como hombre ha tratado y comunicado carnalmente con
muchas mugeres" [as a man she sexually dealt with many women]. The
Inquisition's interest in Eleno's sex life led them to probe into what the dis-

trict court in Ocaña had already found, that "ha cometido el dicho delicto de sodomya y contra natura finjiendo ser onbre" [she committed the said crime of sodomy and contrary to nature pretended to be a man]. Regardless of the institutional limitations on prosecuting Eleno for sodomy in their jurisdiction, the Inquisitors buttressed the case against Eleno's gender transgressions and assault on family values by documenting again and again, in prurient detail, the techniques of seduction and penetration employed by the accused, who was deemed by the tribunal's medical experts to be unambiguously female in her sex.[4]

As a female who sexually "dealt with" other females—and thereby usurped man's role in the household—Eleno was punished for mockery of the holy sacrament of matrimony.[5] But the tribunal's investigations also revealed an underlying anxiety that went beyond sodomy per se: that erotic relations between women might actually have occurred openly, in forms other than the parody of heterosex that furnished the legal definition of female sodomy. Eleno was asked on several occasions whether she thought that the church allowed a woman to marry another female:

Preguntado por qué siendo ésta muger prinçipalmente y aviendo parido se casó con otra muger como ella; si tiene ésta por líçito casarse dos mugeres, o piensa que pueden casarse dos mugeres. . . . Fuele dicho que por reverençia de Dios diga enteramente la berdad porque esto es lo que la ymporta para el descargo de su conçiençia y para que se (h)use con ella de la misericordia que en este sancto tribunal se acostumbra con los que confiesan llanamente sus culpas y espeçialmente açerca de lo que a sido preguntada del ánimo e yntençión con que se casó siendo muger y si es por tener entendido y creydo que podía líçitamente casarse una muger con otra, o que no ay sacramento de matrimonio pues en oprobrio e yrrisión dél se casó siendo muger con otra, velándose yn façie eclesie por sentir mal e haçer burla del dicho sacramento. (Céspedes)

[She was asked why was it that being principally female and having given birth to a child did she marry another woman like herself; does she think it is legal for two women to marry, or does she think that two women can marry? She was told that out of reverence for the Lord she should say the whole truth since that is most important to free her conscience, and so that she may be dealt with mercifully, as is the custom in this holy tribunal with those who plainly confess their guilt, and especially so regarding certain questions, like the spirit and intention that led her as a woman to marry, and if it was that she understood and believed that a woman could legally marry another, or that marriage is not a sacrament, since ignominiously and mockingly she, a woman, married another, and so she was wedded *in facie ecclesiae* because she is opposed to and mocks the sacrament.]

Eleno would have no part of the insinuations of same-sex desire or the accusation that his marriage to María showed his animus for the church and its sacraments. Instead, he insisted that at the time of their wedding *he* was a hermaphrodite and possessed fully working male genitalia, so there was no crime committed when *he* made love to María or his other female partners:

Dixo que ésta se casó por entender que (h)era hombre y no muger, y que podía líçitamente siendo hombre casarse con muger, que bien save que dos mugeres no pueden casarse, y ansí no lo hizo por eyrisión ni burla del sacramento, antes lo hizo por estar en serviçio de Dios. (Céspedes)

[She said that she married because she understood that she was male and not female, and could legally as a man marry a woman, that she knows very well that two women cannot marry, and so she did not do it in order to poke fun at or mock the sacrament, but to be in the service of the Lord.]

Nevertheless, the tribunal rejected Eleno's account of his sexual mutation:

Fuele dicho que ya be que todo lo que aquí tiene dicho açerca del miembro de hombre que es ficçión y enbuste, porque ésta nunca fue sino muger como naçió y es de presente, que lo que la haçe al caso para que en este tribunal se (h)use con ella de misericordia es deçir enteramente la verdad, que diga el embuste que hizo y la forma que hubo para engañar a los testigos que dixeron en favor de ésta y si les dio o prometió algo, y qué es lo que la movió, siendo muger como es, casarse con otra, y si la dicha María del Caño savía ser ésta muger quando con ella se casó. (Céspedes)

[She was told that, as she can see, everything she has said about the male member is a fiction and a lie, because she has always been female, since birth and now; that what is in her interest and to obtain the tribunal's mercy is to say the whole truth, explain how she made the lie, and the way she deceived the witnesses who testified in her favor, whether she gave or promised them anything, and what was it that moved her, being a woman, to marry another, and whether the said María del Caño knew that she was a woman when they were married.]

Eleno's only admission of wrongdoing was that she used her pharmacological and surgical skills to shrink or camouflage the opening of her vulva, a deception that enabled Eleno to pass as a man and to obtain permission from the vicar of Madrid to marry María del Caño. But the prosecutor further charged Elena with having made pacts with the devil in order to create the illusion in her sexual partners — and all those who examined her body prior to her imprisonment in Ocaña and Toledo — that Eleno was a man, pure and simple. Physicians, healers, midwives, surgeons, female lovers, male friends, and acquaintances all testified that they had been deceived, either by Eleno's extraordinary transsexual arts or her business with the devil, when they took Eleno for a man. Regardless of whether the deception was due to Eleno's artfulness or devilish connections, they agreed that at the time he possessed a penis of normal size, a pair of testicles, also well-proportioned, and that, contrary to the rumors circulating about, they never saw or touched any part of Eleno's body that resembled the female sexual organ that he was said to have as well:

> Y aviéndose alçado sus faldas el dicho Eleno de Céspedes, la dicha persona le vio su miembro genital y estuvo descubierto buen rato delante de entrambos, que tenía su proporcion y forma de miembro de hombre proporcionado a su cuerpo, nj grande nj pequeño, antes más grande que pequeño, y le parece que tenía una señal debajo de los testículos, pero no advirtió tanto a esto que pueda dezir si tenía sexo de muger. (Céspedes)

[And the said Eleno de Céspedes, having raised his skirts, the witness saw his genital member, which was uncovered a good while in front of both of them, and it was proportioned and formed like a man's, in proportion with his body, neither big nor small, rather on the large side than small, and the witness thinks that he had a small mark under the testicles, but didn't pay much attention to it to be able to say whether he had a female sex.]

As stipulated in her sentence, Elena was to receive one hundred lashes in Toledo and one hundred more in Ciempozuelos. The latter set was to follow the public reading of her conviction in the parish church. Like canny showmen, the Inquisitors even specified that the text of Elena's punishment should be made public either on a Sunday or suitable feast day, so as to draw as large an audience as possible. This concern for attendance was characteristic of the Inquisition's way with urban spectacles, which were mounted on an increasingly lavish scale, the better to capture public opinion (Maqueda Abreu 36). And so it was a "prime-time" event when the sentence was read in front of a large number of parishioners assembled on 28 December 1588, feast day of the Holy Innocents, in the presence of the parish priest, two *familiares* 'lay agents' of the Inquisition, and Elena herself, who was dressed for the occasion with the mandatory *coroza*, or conical mitre, and *sambenito,* the short, yellow tunic worn by those to be "reconciled" to the church.

While Eleno's former status of slave was not mentioned in the *Pregón,* her "queer" sexuality was injected into the event—even though, as will be recalled, Eleno was not specifically punished for sodomy or any of the other related charges. This was a sign of clemency as far as the Inquisitors were concerned:

> Fallamos por lo que del presente processo resulta contra la dicha Elena de Céspedes, que si el rigor del derecho uviéramos de seguir, la pudiéramos condenar gravemente; quiriendo pero avernos con ella con equidad y misericordia por algunas justas causas que a ello nos mueven. (Céspedes)

> [We find that if we wanted to proceed with all the rigor that the law allows against the accused for the offenses here tried, we could punish her gravely; but since we want to deal equitably and mercifully with her for some just causes which so move us.]

Regardless of the stated motivation for their restraint—which may well have been a legal formula—the Inquisitors themselves brought Eleno's sexual transgressions out of the compulsory secrecy that characterized all trials of the Inquisition, which would have shrouded this key aspect of Eleno's gender dissidence. The Inquisitors of Toledo coyly alluded to female sodomy in the *Pregón,* while at the same time they remained true to the circumlocutionary status accorded to "this utterly confused category" (Goldberg 1–26) in Castile, where it was generally referred to euphemistically as *pecado nefando* 'the unspeakable sin.' The peek a boo nature of their allusions and the accompanying cruel admonishment that Eleno's whipped flesh was compelled to embody made the spectacle of Elena's supposed return to the fold an important moment in the history of lesbian sexualities.

My purpose in using the term "lesbian" in connection with Eleno's crime and punishment is not to elide the differences and the conceptual disconti- nuities between our own (post)modern notions of lesbian, gay, and trans- gendered identities and Eleno's own "queer" self-fashioning. I believe, however, that it would be singularly unhelpful, both in terms of situat- ing my own work and in understanding early-modern Iberia, to fetishize the notion of incommensurability in the service of what I consider to be an ahistorical perception of radical alterity for things Spanish, African, or early modern (see also Traub 62–63). As the trial transcripts make clear, Eleno's brilliant career was inseparable from the "gender troubles" left in the wake of her rise from female slave to transgendered surgeon. While lesbian identities are indisputably the stuff of us (post)moderns, we may safely translate across centuries and languages the Inquisitors' anxiety over female homoeroticism with recourse to that very word.

The *Pregón* addressed a female audience with the warning that the women of Ciempozuelos should be on guard against other *burladoras* 'female trick- sters' who might, like the convict, prey upon them sexually and emotion- ally, and even walk them down the aisle in same-sex marriage ceremonies (an unexpected anticipation of John Boswell's provocative last book!). But the *Pregón* was tantalizing in its incompleteness and substituted the facile closure of the proverbial expression, "Quien tal haze que así lo pague" [As you sow, so shall you reap], for particulars of the story of Eleno—the "butch" identity assumed by Elena for the previous twenty years. In con- trast to the Inquisitors' circumspection in the public texts, the secrecy of their court allowed them to tease and cajole out of all who testified the de- tails of Eleno's anatomy, his sexual habits, and gender style. The few clues released in public, however, would have served at best as an *aide-mémoire*, since long before his arrest Eleno's "butch-femme" performance and un- usual physiology were public knowledge in Ciempozuelos and among his military comrades, "diçiendo que era pública voz y fama que ésta era macho y hembra" [for it was often said in public and with great fanfare that she was both male and female]; "y algunas personas diciendo que tenía dos sexos" [and some people would say s/he had two sexes]. It was just that sort of "gender trouble" that impressed itself on Vicar General Neroni when he first laid eyes on Eleno. Eleno's demeanor and lack of facial hair aroused Neroni's suspicions that the groom-to-be was a eunuch, a deficient male or "capon": "por su aspecto pareçía ser capón" [from his appearance he seemed to be a capon], and he therefore ordered Eleno's body to be examined by trustworthy men and medical experts before he would allow Eleno to marry his fiancée, María del Caño. Eleno was so cocky about his anatomy that he was eager to have his genitals so perused: "Y el vicario biendo a ésta sin barba y lampiña la dixo que si (h)era capón, y ésta respondió que no, que la mirasen y berían cómo no lo era" [And seeing her (*sic*) without a beard and body hair, the vicar asked if she was a capon, and she said no, that they should look at her so they could see that she was not].

The *Pregón* condemned Elena for having fooled María and other women, but there was no reference to the men whose deception made the wedding possible in the first place. Eleno's skills as a licensed tailor and surgeon served him well. With all the nimbleness he had developed in the manufacturing, cutting, sewing, and tailoring of cloth Eleno was able to style and shape his androgynous figure so that it would seem sufficiently masculine to gain him entry to occupations barred to women. His medical technique and other techniques of the self produced a body that was a site of resistance to the implied subservience in the subject positions slave, woman, and even hermaphrodite.

Y en este tienpo ésta hiço çiertos labatorios con bino y balaustras y alco[h]ol y otros muchos remedios y sahumerios para ver si podría cer[r]ar su propria natura de muger, y a que no se pudiese arrugar del todo, a lo menos que se apretase de manera que pudiese disimularse. Y con los muchos remedios que ésta hizo se le ar[r]ugó de suerte que quedó tan estrecha que no le podían meter cosa ninguna. (Céspedes)

[At this time she made certain lavations with wine, decoctions of balaustine, and alcohol and many other remedies and fumigations to see if she could close her own female sex, and in the event that it could not be wrinkled entirely, so that it would at least become tighter and concealed. And with the many remedies she made, it became wrinkled and so tight that they could not push anything into it.]

This newly transgendered subject assumed the masculine identity and the name Eleno. He was truly a worthy descendant of Fernando de Rojas's Celestina, one that also made brilliant use of the tools of his trade, the "punta de mi sotil aguja" (Rojas 157) [the point of my subtle needle]. Like Celestina, Eleno's fabrications were made of flesh and cloth, signifiers whose true meaning also depended on her/his mastery over speech.

Elena began a long apprenticeship in the garment trade, first at her mother's side, in Alhama de Granada, immediately following her freedom. She would remain in Alhama until her mother's death (c. 1565), when she relocated to Granada. There she received further training as weaver, hosemaker, and tailor. Years later, in Madrid, she would also train as a surgeon. Her progress from weaving to surgery traced a parallel rise in her position in the hierarchy of genders, from the low-paying and typically female weaver to the more lucrative male trades of tailor and surgeon (see Equip Broida). The Inquisitors read Eleno's panoply of skills with misogynistic suspicion, as further evidence of her unruliness as a female who resisted the ideology of the household. As Claire Guilhem has shown, the strategy of devaluing woman's speech was the most effective technique employed by the Inquisition in order to marginalize dissident women. Inquisition trial records are filled with the suspicious activities of women whose spirituality and perceived powers of speech merited prosecution because men — whether physicians, academics, or churchmen — could no longer control and police them. These nonconformist women — *beatas* 'holy women,' healers, and other female religious — were typically accused of deluding other women or of being duped themselves into heretical beliefs and acts. From the Inquisitors' perspective, women tended to be either fools or dangerously mischievous — either susceptible to the devil's temptations or themselves agents of artfulness and deceit.

As characterized in the trial documents, the femininity imputed to Eleno encompassed both polarities of the dominant cliché. At the hand of the Inquisitors, Eleno's moral portrait became an absurd composite of both fool and consummate swindler. Above all, the tribunal regarded *her* as an illusionist aided by the devil, capable of the most subtle deception. She was the complete (i.e., female) *burladora* 'trickster,' for by the time of her trial in Toledo, Eleno had lost her male member and testicles. But she did not allow this physical lack — which she linked to a riding accident — to stand in the way of her claims of hermaphroditism, and she reminded the court that expert medical opinion had previously supported her assertions. In earlier testimony to the vicar of Madrid, the eminent royal surgeon Dr. Francisco Díaz had certifed Eleno's apparently normal maleness. But after he examined Eleno a second time, a year and a half later, in the palace of the Toledo Inquisition, Dr. Díaz contradicted his earlier testimony and declared that what he had taken to be Eleno's male sex must have been pure feminine artistry styled by Elena herself: "algún arte tan sotil que bastó para engañar a éste así en la bista como en el tacto" (Céspedes) [an art so subtle that it sufficed to fool him by sight and by touch]. Dr. Díaz, who was Felipe II's surgeon of the chamber, thus disavowed his earlier conclusion. It is interesting to note that at the time of the first physical examination the options considered by Dr. Díaz were not male versus female, but male versus hermaphrodite, the latter being, as we have seen, Eleno's prevailing public persona since at least his army days.[6]

Dr. Díaz's first deposition, presented to the vicar of Madrid on 7 February 1586, reads like a defense of Eleno's claim to manhood, meant to correct a popular misperception of him as an intergendered subject, a hermaphrodite marvel of nature:

> Verdad que él le a visto sus mienbros genitales, y las manos puso viçinas [y] a vista de ojos, y tocadole con las manos. Y que declarávase de él así: que él tiene su mienbro genital, el qual es bastante y perfecto, con sus testículos formados, como qual quiera hombre. Y que en la parte ynferior, junto al ano, tiene una manera de arrugaçión, que a su pareçer al que tocó y vido no tiene semejança de cossa que pueda presumirse ser natura, porque procurándola tocar no pudo ni fue posible [h]allarle perforaçión alguna del que ser pudiese presumir tal cossa. Y ansí dicho e declaró que a su pareçer no tiene semejança de ermafrodita ni cossa dello. Y que ésta es la verdad para el juramento que hizo. Y firmólo de su nombre. (Céspedes)

> [It is true that he has seen Eleno's genital member, and having touched all around it with his hands and seen it with his eyes, he made the following declaration: That he has his genital member, which is sufficient and perfect, with its testicles formed like any other man, and in the lower part, next to the anus, he has something like a wrinkle, which in his opinion bears no resemblance to anything that could be presumed to be a sexual organ (*natura*), because while trying to touch it he could not, nor was it possible to find any perforation that could be presumed to be such a thing. And he thus said and declared that in his opinion Eleno does not bear any resemblance to a hermaphrodite or anything like it. And this is the truth, sworn and signed in his name.]

The Inquisitors interrogated Dr. Díaz and others who had previously declared Eleno male and, therefore, "competent" to marry María. In the end they ruled out the collusion and bribery that they had suspected and concluded, rather, that Elena alone was to blame: she had used her surgical skills and anatomical expertise to effect a transsexual illusion so convincing that it fooled not just the women she went to bed with but also surgeons and physicians of renown who had examined Eleno and certified that she was a man. The ironies did not cease with Eleno's conviction, for, as we shall see, her popular image as an androgyne—enhanced, no doubt, by racist assumptions regarding her brown skin and African origins—catapulted Eleno's fame as a medical practitioner.

Cast as a rogue female *iludente* 'deceiver' by the Inquisitors themselves, Eleno emerged as an exemplary dissident woman possessed of unregulated spiritual and healing powers. Eleno's familiarity with early-modern ideas of the transformative potential inherent in sexual difference is too complex a subject to adequately delve into here (see Burshatin, "Elena"). Suffice it to say that Eleno's command of natural history enabled him to make the most of his brown skin and gender-bending look. There is no denying that Eleno's rhetorical finesse and command of the discourses of medicine and natural history enabled him to prosper beyond the customary expectations of freed female slaves in early-modern Andalusia, many of whom would frequently exchange chattel slavery for the dubiously improved status of sex worker—prostitution being one of the most frequently recorded occupations for freed female slaves (Franco Silva 297). Eleno's corporeal and social transformations give new meaning to our own notion of the "self-made man." The physical mutations occurred in support of the male social roles he played, the various occupations he took up, and his being sexually aroused by women. In the narrative of his life, the body was the principal site of his adventures as he moved along various points in the hierarchies of sexes, occupations, and genders: woman, hermaphrodite, man, wife, husband, weaver, seamstress, tailor, shepherd, domestic servant, soldier, surgeon. But regardless of the inflection he gave to his gender performance, the trial documents show an abiding resistance to the subordination implied in the social categories, female and slave.

Eleno's account gave the specifics of how and when her sexual transformation occurred, around 1562, when she was seventeen years old. The event that caused the production of her male genitalia was the birth of her first and only child—the son fathered by her husband, Christóval. Elena's pregnant body was under great strain, and in the process of pushing out her baby, she also gave birth to a penis:

Quando ésta parió, como tiene dicho, con la fuerça que puso en el parto se le rompió un pellejo que benía sobre el caño de la orina y le salió una cabeza como medio dedo pulgar, que ansí lo señaló, que parecía en su hechura cabeça de miembro de hombre, el qual quando ésta tenía deseo y alteración natural, le salía como dicho tiene, y quando no estava con alteraçión se enmusteçía y recogía a la parte y seno donde estava antes que se le rompiese el dicho pellejo. (Céspedes)

[When she gave birth, as she has said, with the force that she applied in labor she broke the skin over the urinary canal, and a head came out (the length) of about half a big thumb, and she indicated it so; in its shape it resembled the head of a male member, which when she felt desire and natural excitement it would come out as she has said, and when she wasn't excited it contracted and receded into the place where the skin had broken.][7]

Eleno's career paths, personal style, and principal affections show that he not only rejected the subservient roles for working women in domestic service and the needle trades, but also in the bedroom and the household. Eleno's transgendered identity was usually accepted with amazing success, although with varying inflections that sometimes differed from the male image he privileged at the time of his wedding to María. And so, despite the *Pregón*'s explicit conjuring of a female audience susceptible to Elena's enticements, his charms were certainly not for women only. Many influential men were swayed by Eleno's constructions. Among those persuaded were the forementioned vicar general of Madrid and, by implication, his superior, the archbishop of Toledo and primate of Spain, as well as Dr. Díaz, and the other expert witnesses who examined Eleno's body and declared it unequivocally male in various reports to the authorities of Toledo and Madrid prior to the Inquisition's interest in the matter.

Considering Eleno's twenty-year record of living successfully across gender and other boundaries, the *Pregón*'s calculated omission of male interest in the matter emerges as a disingenuous and defensive move. If the female Elena was guilty of deceiving other women, then transgendered Eleno really hoodwinked the men. Rather than admitting to Eleno's triumph over men in authority—which would surely have constituted subversion of the phallic order of things—the *Pregón* opts for patriarchal clichés: beware the woman who behaves as a man and "fools" other women; the state shall fulfill its paternal role and punish the wife who would dare to appropriate a husband's role and sexually impersonate a man, so that all women can breathe freely and not be tricked into "lesbian" liaisons. Thus, while alluding generally to Eleno's sexual transgressions, the punishment was limited to fit that of a female bigamist who was also a very competent surgeon: two hundred lashes, public exposure and degradation of the offending body, and ten years of "community service" in a public hospital. At a time when the Inquisition increasingly hounded women out of medical practice (Perry, *Gender* 25–32), here was the Inquisition's certified female Elena, surgeoness, three months into her sentence curing indigent patients at Toledo's Hospital del Rey 'King's Hospital.' Her notoriety drew many to her care. The sick and injured were eager to be healed by a woman who had lived as a man and was reputed to have both male and female genitalia, her powers now the stuff of an *auto de fe*. The hospital director begged the Inquisitors to reassign Elena to another hospital because of the scandal she was creating. In March of 1589 the Inquisitors obliged and banished the notorious *maestra* to another hospital, in the remote town of Puente del Arzobispo. Of the many ironies found in Eleno's story, perhaps none is as transgressive of the cultural divide between masculine and feminine than the piquant spectacle of the transgendered "butch" surgeoness — in proper skirts, presumably — produced by the Inquisitors themselves.

Suspected of Being a *Monfí*

Around 1568 (the dates given are imprecise) Eleno's transgendered appearance produced two contrasting forms of cultural anxiety over his disquieting look. Some read Eleno as an effeminate male or butch female, while others took Eleno for a *monfí*, or Morisco bandit. Eleno, who was then twenty-two or twenty-three years old, had recently come out of jail in Jerez de la Frontera, where he had been arrested for stabbing a ruffian named Heredia, who had attacked Eleno for his "queer" style. While not completely costumed as a man at the time, Eleno was sporting a disguise that had aroused Heredia's hostility. The assailant's animosity was aggravated after Eleno was released from jail. With the help of other thugs, Heredia harrassed Eleno further. Eleno's testimony regarding this violent episode took the form of what Marjorie Garber has called the "progress narrative," the account that situates cross-dressing as an enabling episode in the cross-dresser's path to success (Garber 70). Eleno thus explained that having been mistreated by Heredia and friends, he then "determinó de andar en ávito de hombre" (Céspedes) [decided to go around in male habit]. The account given makes the distinction between *disfraʒarse de* 'to disguise oneself'—connoting an episodic or more permeable sort of gender construction, perhaps mixing and matching parts of masculine and feminine attire—and *tomar ávito de* 'to adopt the habit of,' which is a more formal and definitive transgendered position, expressed in a locution formed by analogy to institutionalized modes of linking dress, body, and social status, as in the "habits" worn by nuns, mendicant friars, *beatas,* and members of prestigious military orders. Eleno's personal history exhibits the desire to normalize his gender dissidence by rendering his taking up the habit of man as an armor of sorts that would enable him to make his way in the world of men outside the household, doing the work of men, but without the vulnerability that such crossing of boundaries necessarily entailed.

Eleno's butchness met with unexpected complications in the politically charged atmosphere of post-Reconquest Andalusia. His male performance was tantamount to constructing the ominous image of an empowered, brown-skinned male that the "old" Christian caste was about to face in the protracted guerrilla war of the Alpujarras (1568–70), when Morisco rebels took up arms against their Castilian masters. In Arcos de la Frontera, butch Eleno, who was then calling himself just "Céspedes," found work as a farm laborer and shepherd. But if Heredia and the other fellows in Jerez had found Eleno's previous image soft and vulnerable, the hypermanly "Céspedes" was much too threatening. His butchness, brown skin, and slave brand produced the most prevalent sort of cultural anxiety of early-modern Spain: "Céspedes" looked like a *monfí,* and he was therefore arrested as a Morisco outlaw. Covarrubias's dictionary of 1611 defines *monfí* and makes palpable the generalized concern that the ruling elite felt over the recrudescent power lurking beneath the colonized Morisco subject:

Monfíes llamaron ciertos moros o moriscos, convertidos, de los primeros que se convirtieron; y estos, por estar mezclados entre los christianos, deprendieron nuestra lengua, y assí eran señores de las dos, como oy día hay muchos, y pocos christianos viejos que sepan la suya; de do se siguen muy grandes inconvenientes, siéndonos superiores en esto y pudiendo armar las traiciones que quisieren. Dixéronse monfíes corrompido de *mofties,* que en arábigo vale tanto como si dixésemos ladinos, que saben su lengua y la nuestra. Pero Tamarid dize que *monfí* es hombre ahuyentado y retraído o vandolero (Covarrubias, s.v. *monfíes* 812).

[*Monfíes* is the name given to certain Moors or Moriscos who were among those who first converted; and these, since they mixed with Christians, learned our language, and thus were masters of both, as there are many today, and very few Old Christians know theirs; from this is a great inconvenience, as they are superior to us in this and can plot whatever treachery they wish. They say *monfíes* from a corruption of *moftíes*, which in Arabic is equivalent to saying *ladinos*, who know their language and ours. But Tamarid says that *monfí* is a man who is frightened and withdrawn, or a bandit.]

The most menacing aspect of the *monfí* was not his religion, ethnic origin, or even outlaw existence; it was, rather, his ability to move easily between the divided worlds of the Muslim and the Christian, his bilingualism and formidable "cultural literacy." They can penetrate our world, but we are strangers in theirs; this is Covarrubias's main preoccupation. In popular drama this ease of movement across cultural and political boundaries becomes the conqueror's prerogative, as in Lope de Vega's drama, *El primer Fajardo* (c. 1610–12) whose eponymous Castilian hero is the one who "passes." Fully bilingual and in Moorish garb, Fajardo brings back his trophy in the form of a Moorish bride, kidnapped in the midst of her wedding party (Burshatin, "Playing" 570–73). Eleno's own cultural literacy was also impressive. It enabled him to negotiate without much incident the boundaries of genders, sexualities, and occupations. His misidentification with the mobile *monfí*, capable of crossing the boundary and passing for "old" Christian, showed the power of impersonation, as well as the dangers of such a strategy. In Eleno's narrative, "Céspedes" as *monfí* was an unfortunate classification, since it put Eleno back in skirts. Recognized by a fellow citizen from Alhama, "Céspedes" was able to convince the authorities that he was not a *monfí*, and he was released from jail. But the memory of his old status bodied forth "Elena," and he was forced to take up both his discarded female identity and the *habitus* of menial domesticity, becoming a servant to the parish priest of the church of Santa María at Arcos. Compelled to resume the feminine habit, Eleno would nevertheless quickly return to male garb and avail himself of another opportunity at the expense of Moriscos. They had risen in protest by the thousands in the mountainous region of the Alpujarras and soldiers were needed to combat them. Eleno joined the armies of Felipe II, deployed against the brethren of his former neighbors and acquaintances in Alhama and Vélez-Málaga. (Attacks on Moriscos had been occurring for generations.)

Eleno's milieu was one in which Moriscos and their world were the object of "ethnic cleansing" at the hands of colonizers from the North who were the beneficiaries of the culture of the Christian Reconquest, with its racial-ist claims of ethnic purity and "irredentism" over the land. For a *mulata* slave like Elena, however, the horizons would normally have been even more limited than those of free Moriscos. Eleno's rise through the ranks of the needle trades in Andalusia occurred in the context of a local cul-ture in which Moriscos had formerly been associated with those particular occupations and the silk industry centered in Granada (Ladero Quesada 40–42). As a freed slave who was a licensed tailor, Eleno exemplified the social integration that many such freed slaves aspired to as they moved out of the narrow confines of domestic service into the wider economy of wage labor and small manufacturing (see Franco Silva).

In a world where Moriscos and displacement became synonymous, Eleno's strategy of "cozying up"/"assimilating oneself to the good and powerful ones," found its most logical channel. How much contact did the young Eleno have with Moriscos? By occupation and name, it is reasonable to assume that many of those who trained, employed, knew, and perhaps even "owned" Eleno were of Morisco origin, including the slave-owning Medinas, the expert weaver Castillo, who taught Elena her trade, and the licentiate Benegas, whose testimony in Arcos reassured the authorities that Eleno was not a *monfí*. The latter two were perhaps as eager as Eleno to see themselves reflected in the mirror of idealized hegemonic subjects, as was the case with many other assimilated Moriscos — Cervantes's Ricote being the most notable literary example. In the Morisco texts studied by Luce López-Baralt, ideals of physical beauty do not include dark-skinned men and women. Rather, their favorite skin color was decidedly pale or whit-ened; alas, they did not imagine themselves to have the charms of García Lorca's "moreno de verde luna" [moon-green man of color]. Instead, the preferred types tended to be "rubias fantasías godas" (López-Baralt 335; 348) [blond Gothic fantasies]. This form of double consciousness responded to the racialist turn taken by the ruling ideology of imperial expansion.

The other side of that coin, however, encouraged the production of identity positions no longer fettered to caste and race narratives canonized by the dominant culture. Eleno's career thrived on similar forms of displacement, appropriating for his own purposes and erotic pleasure the master('s) trope of the Christian Reconquest. Eleno's early training and expertise in the garment trades certainly positioned him as the beneficiary of economies and occupations associated with Muslim al-Andalus. In literary history the *Poema de mio Cid* (c. 1207) gives an early indication of the prestige of Moorish fashion. A fancy, "Moorish" fur cloak lined in red silk ("una piel vermeja morisca e ondrada") is the Andalusian souvenir requested by the Jewish moneylenders of the less-than-honest Cid as he is about to embark on his military adventures in territories to the east and south of Castile (line 178). Regardless of the actual ethnicity of those around Eleno, his artisanal training had very much been the province of Moriscos, their techniques and economies. The politics of displacement, however, were primarily the privilege of the hegemonic subject of the Christian Reconquest, and Eleno's moves retraced the strategies of the dominant classes. While Moriscos themselves had difficulty finding congenial places to live and work, Eleno easily moved into their professions.

The Alpujarras rebellion (1568–70) furnished another sort of stepping-stone. Eleno, now in an epic mode, could join with the dominant caste against the despised and feared colonial subject. Eleno served in the armies commanded by Don Luis Ponce de León, on the Crown's side of the campaigns to establish "old" Christian and Castilian sway over the patchwork of diverse religions, languages, laws, and customs that was the legacy of the frontier cultures of al-Andalus. It is ironic that Eleno's gender transgressions enabled him to espouse the interests of the ruling élite, and perhaps even bask in some of the reflected glory that fighting against Moors inevitably conferred on front-line soldiers. The site of his cultural positioning was the space vacated by Moriscos as they were "cleansed" out of the Spanish picture.

By the time of Eleno's birth, almost fifty years had passed since the storied frontier of Christian and Muslim Andalusia had ceased to exist as a political and military reality. Nevertheless, Eleno grew up and changed sexes while Spanish literary orientalism enjoyed a veritable boom in fiction, balladry, and the popular drama, as well as its curious formation in state policies aimed at staging a sort of Morisco assimilation that was as much desired as it was doomed to failure (see Cardaillac; Domínguez Ortiz; García Ballester). Eleno's transformations occurred in the context of compulsory cross-dressing. State-mandated transvestism had, indeed, become an instrument of official policy in coercing Moriscos to embrace "Spanishness" as an ostensible sign of state authority. At a time when the artifacts and signs of "oriental" splendor were cultivated by the so-called Moorish novel and other related literary and cultural forms, Moriscos themselves were forced to abandon their distinctive cultural style by a much debated royal decree, the *pragmática* promulgated in 1567, under which traditional dress, dances, songs, and Arabic surnames were to be regarded henceforth as signs of Morisco heterodoxy to be policed by the Inquisition. Thus, Castilian stage actors could dress *à l'Orientale*, but not Moriscos. The logic of this colonialist measure presupposed that clothes do, indeed, make the person. In effect, those who would most suffer by the clothing restrictions were women, according to the impassioned plea for tolerance and diversity written by a leading Morisco spokesperson, Francisco Núñez Muley (García Arenal 45–46). He even attempted to deorientalize Morisco dress by comparing it to other regional clothing styles as worn in Aragon, Navarra, or Galicia.

Despite many protests and offers of large sums to the Crown to soften some of the restrictions, the edict was implemented and armed rebellion ensued. The War of the Alpujarras, in the mountains outside Granada, gave Eleno the opportunity to enlist in the armies of Felipe II, dressed as a man and a "Spaniard" on behalf of the internal colonial agenda and its peculiar code of national cross-dressing. Eleno's own bodying forth of the male "Spaniard" mimicked the official policy of making subordinates mirror the dominant caste. Nevertheless, the effect of state-mandated cross-dressing was to bring the Morisco further under the jurisdiction of the Inquisition. In the eyes of Crown and church, the Moriscos' cross-dressed Spanish style would render them more docile to colonial policies as aspects of their private or community lives were turned into matters for state coercion and vigilance. As Deborah Root has observed, the Inquisition's role in investigating and disciplining Morisco deviance was enabled by shifting "behaviors formerly considered private" into the public sphere, under the jurisdiction of state institutions that zealously investigated whether Moriscos were properly "speaking Christian" (Root 120). The *pragmática* thus enforced the notion that identity was a publicly defined function, emblematized by one's clothing and appearance. Wear "old" Christian fashions and you, too, will act and think like one; but if you do not, you will have Inquisitors to answer to. The courts of the Inquisition thus produced "Morisco difference as heterodoxy" (Root 120). One of the finer ironies to be found in Eleno's story is that in challenging gender roles, he also adopted the state's own radical notion that the outward signs of identity were malleable and could be made to speak an enabling cultural program, one capable of overriding family bloodlines and origins. A supporter of Castilian hegemony in the Alpujarras, Eleno's own career would take off and enjoy numerous successes for the following twenty years.

The ever shrinking site of Morisco subjectivity continued to be a profitable one for Eleno as he entered the world of empiric medicine and humanist physiology. The medical field was strongly identified with Moriscos and *conversos* ("new" Christians of Jewish ancestry). Beginning around 1576, Eleno's career rise from tailor to surgeon occurred in Madrid, where he relocated after military service. There he met a surgeon from Valencia, who took him into his house and trained him in medicine and surgery. His progress was swift and he would eventually pass two certifying examinations in Madrid, one in curing and purging and another in surgery. By training under a Valencia physician he acquired an illustrious medical pedigree. With it also came the "culture wars" embedded in the practice of medicine in sixteenth-century Valencia.

This Mediterranean city was an important center of humanistic reform and innovation in Spanish medicine. But it was also the hub of the increasingly marginalized worlds of Arabic learning and Morisco culture. The Faculty of Medicine of the University of Valencia played a vital role in introducing the innovations in surgery and anatomy developed by Vesalius. Two of his disciples at Valencia, Pedro Jimeno and Luis Collado, were instrumental in establishing Valencia as the springboard of the newer, "Italian" medical humanism (García Ballester 42–43). With its large Morisco population of over a hundred thousand, Islamic medical traditions were also maintained, although the level of professional training would witness a swift and catastrophic decline under the state's aggressive policies aimed at assimilating and obliterating Islamic culture (García Ballester 44).

Morisco medicine was increasingly relegated to the nether world of "folk" healing, which combined empirical knowledge with hermetic or animistic beliefs. Their practitioners were male and female healers. These would often arouse suspicion for their alleged connections with witchcraft and would thereby run afoul of the Inquisition. As Arabic science declined with conquest and colonization, Moriscos found themselves excluded from both the old and new modes of professional accreditation. The newer path to university training would effectively exclude Moriscos for social, linguistic, and racialist reasons. Increasingly out of their reach as well was the declining medieval model of professional apprenticeship outside the university system. Given the racist conception of Moriscos as a marginal and inherently deceitful ethnic group, the "honorable" practice of medicine ("oficio honroso," "oficio que exige virtud") would not admit members of a caste that was regarded as congenitally lacking in those values (García Ballester 106). The breach opened by Morisco marginalization would prove hospitable to Eleno's social positioning. His medical training followed the "open" model, the *madrasa*, that was historically the model of choice in al-Andalus. In contrast to the "closed" university model, physicians in Islamic al-Andalus obtained both theoretical and practical training by apprenticing under a recognized master. This was followed by several years of supervised clinical practice. The training culminated with the successful completion of certifying exams administered by a municipally chartered tribunal of experts, as was still the case in sixteenth-century Valencia and Madrid. In the context of the protonationalist project of removing Moriscos from the practice of medicine, Eleno once again availed himself of the opportunities for social advancement.

Cada uno hace de su barriga un tambor

In a recent study of *Celestina* and the gendering of utterance, Mary Gossy illuminates the extraordinary conjunction of various forms of stitching — inscribing, scratching-in, untelling — and the various fabrics — society, cloth, hymens — that the go-between's technique joins together as she traverses the boundaries of sexes, genders, classes, and castes in order to "tangle with the very fabric of society and the text" (Gossy 41).[8] One such crucial moment, which occurs in Areúsa's bedroom in act 7, stitches together the discourses of sexuality and medicine on the fabric of female friendship and eroticism. In its audacity and richness of form, the scene is an exemplary moment in the culture of post-Reconquest Spain, one that furnishes congenial ground for interpreting a similar conjunction of sexualities and medicine in Eleno's body. With Pármeno waiting belowstairs, eager to lie with Areúsa, Celestina boldly initiates Areúsa's seduction. Areúsa apologizes to Celestina for being in bed — for wearing her bedclothes as if they were skirts: "Así que necesidad, más que vicio, me hizo tomar con tiempo las sábanas por faldetas" (Rojas 126). [Necessity rather than vice/pleasure made me take my time with these sheets as if they were skirts.] Menstruation is the cause of Areúsa's discomfort and Celestina happily begins to manipulate Areúsa's breasts: "Pues dame lugar, tentaré" [So make room for me, I'll touch] and in a rare moment of lesbian *jouissance*, the old bawd gives herself over to pleasure and extols Areúsa's charms, while all the time looking at and fondling Areúsa's naked body, so redolent of the special sensuality (*vicio*) of a woman alone in her room that Areúsa has already twice denied it:

> Déjame mirarte toda a mi voluntad, que me huelgo. . . . ¡Bendígate Dios y señor san Miguel ángel, y qué gorda y fresca que estás! ¡Qué pechos y qué gentileza! Por hermosa te tenía hasta agora, viendo lo que todos podían ver; pero agora te digo que no hay en la ciudad tres cuerpos tales como el tuyo, en cuanto yo conozco. No parece que hayas quince años. *¡Oh, quién fuera hombre y tanta parte alcançara de ti para goçar tal vista!*" (126, 127; emphasis mine).

> [Let me take a good look at you; what a delight. May the Lord and the archangel Michael bless you, and how big and fresh you are! Such breasts and softness! I knew you were beautiful, I could see what is plain for all to see; but let me tell you, in this whole city I know there aren't even three other bodies that stack up to yours. You don't even look fifteen. *Oh, that I were a man, so that I could hold all of you and enjoy the sight of you!*]

The demurrer—"Quién fuera hombre"—is Celestina's professional calling-card. In a world of "compulsory heterosexuality," where female go-betweens service male clients, Celestina can be trusted to observe a code of professional ethics that rests squarely on the heterosexually constituted body. According to the operative male fantasy of illicit heterosex, the procuress will observe the boundaries that male go-betweens (*alcahuetes*) will only too easily trespass — recall here the Archpriest's rebuke in the *Libro de buen amor,* in which his male emissary runs off with the lovely baker Cruz (Ruiz strophe 113). Celestina's crude penis envy is surely a timely ruse: she has her client waiting outside the door, and it is incumbent on the success of her main business venture with Pármeno's master that she produce the body that Pármeno desires. Having effectively roused Areúsa from her sickbed torpor, Celestina has completed the foreplay and tries to leave Areúsa's bed in order to usher in her randy client, only to be stopped by the needy Areúsa. She has a different idea: "Alahé agora, madre, y no me quiere ninguno. Dame algún remedio para mi mal y no estés burlando de mí" (Rojas 127) [Please wait, mother, no man loves me. Give me something to take away the pain instead of just playing with me.] Celestina's "subtle needle" locates and stitches into place the "hymen text" on which the phallic order lamely inscribes its power as the law of female chastity. But with Areúsa gender is further refigured and dislodged from phallic authority: butch Celestina is a surrogate penis, a momentary stand-in for Pármeno; motherly Celestina, in her best bedside manner, now gives voice to a tradition of female healers and rewrites the phallocratic narrative. If—and the conditional is underscored here—woman by virtue of anatomy is not competent fully to enjoy a body like her own ("Oh, that I were a man!"), then the female healer by virtue of that same body is most competent to devise strategies of caring and curing a body identical to her own: "De este tan común dolor todas somos, mal pecado, maestras" [Of this common pain, we are all, the devil take us, experts].

The contradiction is productive indeed, but it will not bear close scrutiny, since the "partner" is attired in sheets—a reversible gown suitable both to the patient and the lover. Swathed in pleasure (*vicio*) ambivalently asserted and denied, Areúsa's bedsheets/skirts are inscribed with both functions, even if, as Celestina would have it, only the medical domain is truly gynocentric. Inhabiting a common body, female physician and female patient are sisters in struggle, and the male client is an intruder who brings the marketplace—and its phallocratic order—into the intimacy of female homosociality overseen by *maestras* like Celestina herself: "Lo que he visto a muchas hacer y lo que a mí siempre aprovecha te diré" (127) [I shall tell you what I have seen many other women do and what always works for me].[9]

Women are naturally endowed to be *maestras*, to work as surgeons and healers. The female body is an enabling ground for launching a medical career. It is an irony of history—and one traceable in Eleno's dossier—that the contrary of this very notion will become a major objective of the

Inquisition in the sixteenth century, as Guilhem and Perry have shown. But in Areúsa's bedroom Celestina's notion of genders has been revealed as an elastic concept that complicates the simple assertion of the phallocratic account of woman's body as an "imperfect," interiorized and inverted image of the "telos" that the male body represents in medieval and early modern physiology (see Daston and Park; Laqueur).

The importance of Celestina's game of "let's play doctor" is that the trope of bedsheets-as-skirts emblematizes the transgressive notion that women do "naturally" desire and care for other women — friendship, passion, and healing. In a similar vein, but one with a more baroque configuration, Eleno's narrative produces an androgynous body that is the "natural" locus of transgendered desire. Against the Inquisitors' assertion of feminine artfulness and witchiness, Eleno sought to recover his own instancing of the transgendering narrative that natural history had authorized. Eleno wished to retrieve and reconstruct from the surface scars and odd wrinkles, tissues, and blemishes his lost penis and testicles. With impressive presence of mind, Eleno resisted all attempts to reduce him to the status of deceitful female patient, undeterred by the clinical gaze of male Inquisitors and their medical allies. He tried to have the authorities follow his own interpretive strategy and read the phallus inscribed on his now unremarkable female pudenda. The invisibility of Eleno's male member, ciphered in scars only Eleno could make intelligible, is rendered as a complex corporeal sign that contests the power of the always visible slave mark. That inscription was negated and partly defaced by Eleno, but its message of subordination to the phallocratic regime of slavery was reinscribed by Eleno's tormentor as he lashed and "blackened" Eleno's offending body two hundred times. Constrained, imprisoned, and inserted into natural history, Elena's slave scar would utter once again a demeaning narrative of origins and feminine wiles.

The unequal conditions of the debate over who was more competent to narrate the body, Eleno or the judicially sanctioned physicians and surgeons, can be seen in one small detail: only Eleno thought of his medical colleagues as such, as "his equals" (sus émulos). For the other medical authorities Eleno's credentials were entirely separable from his account of gender and sex changes. Elena was a sly and/or bedeviled woman. The male physicians called to testify on both sides of the case — those on Eleno's list of witnesses as well as the prosecution's — were unanimous in rejecting Eleno's assertion that if they looked attentively they would find signs of his now absent male genitalia. In arguing his own defense, it is clear that Eleno had at his fingertips Galenic and Hippocratic notions of the physiological differences between men and women. The evidence of Eleno's learning is ample and impressive. In the inventories of his possessions, which the Inquisition confiscated in order to assure itself of payment for Eleno's room and board in prison, we find the contents of his medical library. His collection of twenty-seven volumes on physiology, rhetoric, natural history, anatomy, medicine, and surgery—written in Spanish, Latin, and Italian—was acquired from a university-trained man (*licenciado*), probably a physician, judging by the book titles. Included among these volumes are works by Galen, Vesalius's anatomical treatises, studies on surgery, Cicero's epistles, and several commentaries on Galen. In his own defense Eleno cites several learned sources, including Pliny's *Natural History*, book 7, in which marvels of nature, like monstrous births and hermaphrodites, are explained and documented. His account smoothly incorporates the prevailing medical and philosophical views that rendered the female body an unstable and deficient entity, susceptible to transformations of a male sort during extremely arduous physical activities. Eleno invokes humoral theories, according to which a sudden rise in body temperature could result in the extrusion of the male sexual organs that woman was believed to harbor in her "cold" and "wet" interior.

> Porque yo con pacto expresso nj táçito del demonio nunca me fingj honbre para casarme con muger como se me pretende imputar. E lo que pasa es que como en este mundo muchas veçes se an vjsto personas que son andróginos, que por otro nonbre se llaman hermafroditos, que tienen entramos sexos, yo tanbién [h]e sido uno de éstos. Y al tienpo que me pretendí casar incaleçía e prevalesçía más en el sexo masculino, e natural mente era honbre e tenja todo lo neçessario de honbre para poderme casar. Y de que lo era hiçe información e probança ocular de médicos e zirujanos peritos en el arte, los quales me vjeron e tentaron e testificaron con juramento que era tal honbre y me podía casar con muger. Y con la dicha probança hecha judiçial mente me casé por honbre. (Céspedes)

[I never made any pact, explicit or tacit, with the devil, in order to pose as a man to marry a woman, as is attributed to me. What happens is that many times the world has seen androgynous beings or, in other words, hermaphrodites, who have both sexes. I, too, have been one of these, and at the time I arranged to be married the masculine sex was more prevalent in me; and I was naturally a man and had all that was necessary for a man to marry a woman. And I filed information and eyewitness proof by physicians and surgeons, experts in the art, who looked at me and touched me, and swore under oath that I was a man and could marry a woman, and with this judicial proof I married as a man.]

Eleno had studied the authorities and read himself into the wonders of the Book of Nature. His androgyny was not a deception, it was the work of nature, and his own account of it was properly channeled and confirmed by medical authorities, whose unanimous opinion a mere sixteen months earlier had corroborated his own observations that gender was a position along a scale of perfectability, and that he had quite naturally reached its optimum level. Along with this physiological change, he argued, came his sexual desire for women.

Who was competent to interpret Eleno's body? Were there visible signs of his having had a penis and testicles? What was that on his skin — folds of loose flesh, hemorrhoids, warts, or the scars showing where his male pudenda once were? Eleno's medical credentials notwithstanding, his authority — like his penis — vanished. Facing the tribunal, his body was but the object of male medical expertise. In the presence of the tribunal secretary, *she* was taken out to the prison patio in Toledo to be examined in the light of day by a team of physicians and surgeons, with the tribunal secretary busily taking notes. The unanimous and unequivocal conclusion they reached contradicted what some of these same men — including, as we have seen, Dr. Díaz — had sworn before. Elena was a woman, and nothing but a woman, with no signs of her ever having been what she said. While the experts shared some of Eleno's views on the transformational potential of the female body, Eleno's words were empty — a mere echo of that degraded feminine discourse that the Inquisition systematically devalued (Guilhem 137–38). The tribunal's panel of experts acknowledged that under certain circumstances the morphology of the female body could acquire male parts. But those metamorphoses were thought to be very rare. As in France at this time, the experts who testified in Eleno's trial viewed the possibility of hermaphroditism according to the Aristotelian rather than the Hippocratic-Galenic model. In the view of the former, "the sexual ambiguity of the hermaphrodite was never more than superficial, leaving the bipolar sexual order intact" (Daston and Park 422). While the experts admitted that Eleno's transformation was theoretically plausible, they rejected outright a male or transgender identity, especially one based on what *she* regarded as visible signs and evidence. The male experts did not see anything at all:

Y que aunque es verdad que todas las mugeres tienen testículos, son ynteriores en la madre, de manera que no se pueden ber ni tentar por de fuera, y que en quanto a esto diçen que es embuste deçir que los tubo fuera. Y en lo que diçe la dicha Elena de aver tenido berga de hombre, conque diçe tratava con otras mugeres, dixeron que aunque es verdad que pudo creçerle lo que llaman "nynphe opudendum" que les naçe a algunas mugeres en la matriz, pero que ésta no le tiene ni señal de averla tenido, y aunque la tubiera no pudiera salir fuera ni tener fuerza para hazer lo que la dicha Elena de Çéspedes diçe [h]açía, por donde pareçe claramente ser embuste. Y en quanto diçe que para hazerle salir el miembro de hombre que diçe tubo la rompieron un pellejo, que es falso, porque aunque tubiera la dicha "nynphe" que es a manera de berga de hombre que se afloxa e yncha con la pasión natural que les viene a las mugeres que la tienen, era ymposible salir por donde diçe la dicha Elena de Çespedes y no tiene señal de aver avido herida para haçerla que saliese ni çicatriz dello, por donde también se [v]e ser embuste. Y que si oviera de aver çicatriz donde diçe tenía el dicho miembro de hombre, avía de ser sobre el empeyne, que es la parte donde naçe el miembro viril a las mugeres hermafroditos, como todos los médicos y zurujanos diçen. (Céspedes)

[Even though it is true that all women have testicles, they are inside the womb, so that they cannot be seen or touched from the outside, and so it is a lie when she says that she had them outside. And what this Elena says about having had a man's dick, with which she says she dealt with other women, they said that although it is true that she could have developed what they call a "nynphe opudendum," which is born to some women in the womb, there is no sign that this one ever had one, and even if she had, it couldn't have come out or had enough force to do what said Elena de Céspedes says it did, which clearly shows that she lies. . . . And if she truly had a scar where she says she had the member, it would have been on the lower belly (*empeine*), which is the spot where the virile member is born to hermaphrodite women, as all physicians and surgeons say.]

The terms of the debate between female surgeon and male medical establishment were clearly political. The central question shifted to one of discursive affiliation. The issue was not whether a woman could turn into a hermaphrodite, but who could write the cultural program within which "the biology of sexual difference is embedded" (Laqueur 19). The Inquisitors and their experts asserted the privilege of patriarchy when they denied that Eleno's body contained any evidence that the internal male organs have appeared in the past. They rejected what Eleno offered as evidence. The marks around her genitalia were trivial and meaningless. More likely, they insisted, any visible irregularities would result from Eleno's own devious simulation of the scarring she claimed had occurred. Eleno's cultural program did not even register as such. Instead, Eleno's words were the untruths that women of a certain ilk in Toledo had been known to act out. True gender transitivity was out of the question as far as these male physicians and surgeons were concerned. Their moral concern, though, was that a woman would dare to question the binary gender regime of masculine versus feminine.

Spanish literary and cultural history is very familiar with the legendary sexual outlaw Don Juan, "el burlador de Sevilla" [the trickster of Seville]. One of the new lessons that Eleno's dossier teaches us is that the notion of a female *burladora* was also in circulation. The term designated a distinctly queer practice. The medical experts in Eleno's trial expressed concern for certain *burladoras* 'female tricksters' from Toledo. Eleno was one of those *burladoras* who fashioned *artificios* 'dildoes' for themselves out of the sheepskin normally used for making *baldreses* 'bellows.' The tribunal concurred with the experts that all the acts she performed as a man were one big *embuste* 'lie' and *no cosa natural* 'unnatural thing.' Elena's gender and sex were returned to their "natural" subordinate state, and all the previous evidence, once found so persuasive by the vicar of Madrid, was easily dismissed with confident misogyny as the sort of deception that women were capable of:

> Y así les pareçe que todos los actos que como hombre diçe que hizo fue con artifiçios, como otras burladoras [h]an hecho con baldreses y otras cosas como se [h]an visto, y que es embuste y no cosa natural, que el artifiçio con que hizo el dicho embuste y engaño a las mugeres, éstos no so lo saven que ella lo dirá. (Céspedes)

[And so it seems to them (to the physicians and surgeons) that all the acts she says she performed as a man were done with dildoes, as was the case with other female tricksters who have used sheepskin and other things, and that this is all a lie and not a natural thing, and how exactly she deceived and fooled other women, they don't know, let her say how it was.]

Eleno's significance to a revitalized field of Iberian cultural studies, which the articles in this volume seek to map out, consists precisely in the multiplicity of voices, bodies, genders, sexualities, and discourses that s/he devised or appropriated in the face of repeated attempts to normalize her as a subaltern. Rather than submissiveness, the Inquisition and other disciplinary mechanisms produced a countereffect that proved enormously appealing in sixteenth-century Toledo. Eleno's trial and life history became a fable of the malleability of genders, bodies, and desires. The scandal of her "marvelous" childbirth gave this *burladora* the language of natural agency with which to imbue a life at the edges of the permissible. While the authorities attempted to reduce Eleno to silence or misogynist clichés, the aura of her/his persona was greater and more variously inflected than the rigors imposed by the Inquisition's judicial-religious spectacle of bipolar gender restored. By highlighting the necessity of Eleno's dossier and placing it alongside some canonical literary texts (the *Cid, Laẓarillo, Celestina*), I have sought to challenge the notion of the uniqueness of the literary artifact that so many of us still harbor as an unexamined assumption in scholarship. At the same time, I have also endeavored to reclaim Eleno from the safely marginal and reductive readings of criminology, "strange loves" (Escamilla), or just plain tabloid history (as in Eslava Galán 114–15). Eleno's canny moves across the ideological boundaries of post-Reconquest Iberia have justly earned her/him a place of her/his own beyond the various secret closets and cabinets of wonder that have heretofore guarded this exemplary frontier actor.

Notes

An earlier version of this paper was presented at the Center for Literary and Cultural Studies, Harvard University, 6 December 1993. The title of this section, "Autor: Tatuador" [Author: Tattooer], is taken from Sarduy (51).

1. Eleno's life story can be read as an illustration of the "profound questioning of social relations" that obtained in early-modern Spain (Mariscal 14). But in explaining his exclusion of genders and sexualities from his discussion, Mariscal seems to suggest that they cannot properly be the object of study in an early-modern context because of their incommensurability with their modern counterparts (27). My working assumption is that genders and sexualities are not only constitutive of Eleno as subject, they are of central importance in the trial proceedings.

2. I cite throughout from my transcription and English translation of the dossier of the trial of Elena de Céspedes (Céspedes). The documents, numbering over three hundred pages, are written in various sixteenth-century hands. My transcriptions show some slight modifications for greater ease in reading: I resolve abbreviations (e.g., *dho = dicho*, $M^a = María$), regularize the use of *u* and *v*, and furnish accent marks and punctuation. Since the dossier lacks consistent pagination, and the order of the documents is unreliable in some cases, I provide no page or folio numbers. All English translations from the dossier, as well as from other works in Spanish cited in the text, are mine. In recent years, Eleno's case has been studied by Barbazza; Escamilla; and Folch Jou and Muñoz Fernández. Richard Kagan is also at work on the dossier (personal communication), but I have been unable to consult his study.

3. Homophobia is much in evidence in early-modern medico legal vigilance of the hermaphrodite's "grotesque" body. See Daston and Park; Epstein; Jones and Stallybrass.

4. For the legal and social status of sodomy in early modern Spain, see Benassar; Carrasco; Perry ("Nefarious"); and Tomás y Valiente.

5. The *mulier economica* of the Renaissance "is essentially a woman married, about to be married, destined for marriage, or a widow," socially meaningful only in terms of the household and marriage (MacLean 58).

6. The dossier calls Dr. Díaz, "çirujano de Su Magestad" [surgeon to His Majesty], and I believe he is the eminent physician of the same name who held the royal appointment, "cirujano de la cámara," Felipe II's "surgeon of the chamber," and was the author of two treatises, on surgery and urology, respectively. See López-Piñero; and Riera.

7. While Eleno only cites Christian and Western sources, it is reasonable to assume that having trained with a Valencian surgeon s/he also had knowledge of Arabic and Morisco medical traditions. See the parallel case of sexual transformation following childbirth mentioned in *Risālah fī l-Ubnah* [Treatise on *Ubnah* 'passive male homosexuality' (Rosenthal 45)] attributed to Abū Bakr ar-Rāzī, which records the following: "[M]any people tell of a woman who gave birth to children and then afterwards, a male organ appeared on her body" ("she revealed

a male organ") (Rosenthal 55). I gratefully acknowledge the help provided by Michael Solomon in locating this interesting resemblance to Eleno's own narrative of the "birth" of her/his penis.

8. The title of this section is taken from a statement in Montejo (39): "Yo tengo la consideración de que cada uno hace de su barriga un tambor" [I'm of the opinion that everyone makes a drum out of his or her own belly].

9. On Celestina's ability to combine language, eroticism, and the marketplace through "the verbal erotica she peddles," see Gaylord (10). See also Márquez-Villanueva for the "ethnic" subtext in the conjunction of the arts of medicine and love.

Works Cited

Barbazza, Marie-Catherine. "Un caso de subversión social: el proceso de Elena de Céspedes (1587–89)." *Criticón* 26 (1984): 17–40.

Benassar, Bartolomé. "El modelo sexual: la Inquisición de Aragón y la represión de los pecados 'abominables.' " *Inquisición española: poder político y control social.* Ed. Bartolomé Benassar. Barcelona: Editorial Crítica, 1981. 295–320.

Boswell, John. *Same-Sex Unions in Premodern Europe.* New York: Villard, 1994.

Broida, Equip. "Actividad de la mujer en la industria del vestir en la Barcelona de finales de la Edad Media." Muñoz Fernández and Segura Graiño 255–301.

Burshatin, Israel. "Elena alias Eleno: Genders, Sexualities, and Race in the Mirror of Natural History in Sixteenth-Century Spain." *Gender Reversals and Gender Cultures: Anthropological and Historical Perspectives.* Ed. Sabrina Petra Ramet. New York: Routledge, 1996. 105–22.

———. "Playing the Moor: Parody and Performance in Lope de Vega's *El primer Fajardo.*" *PMLA* 107 (1992): 566–81.

Cardaillac, Louis. *Moriscos y cristianos: un enfrentamiento polémico (1492–1640)* Mexico: Fondo de Cultura Económica, 1979.

Carrasco, Rafael. *Inquisición y represión sexual en Valencia: historia de los sodomitas (1565–1785).* Barcelona: Laertes, 1985.

Céspedes, Elena de. *Legajo 234, Expediente 24, Sección Inquisición.* Archivo Histórico Nacional, Madrid.

Covarrubias, Sebastián de. *Tesoro de la lengua castellana o española, según la impresión de 1611, con las adiciones de Benito Remigio Noydens publicadas en la de 1674.* Ed. Martín de Riquer. Barcelona: S. A. Horta, 1943.

Daston, Lorraine, and Katharine Park. "The Hermaphrodite and the Orders of Nature: Sexual Ambiguity in Early Modern France." *GLQ: A Journal of Gay and Lesbian Studies* 1 (1995): 419–38.

Domínguez Ortiz, Antonio, and Bernard Vincent. *Historia de los moriscos: vida y tragedia de una minoría*. Madrid: Revista de Occidente, 1978.

Epstein, Julia. "Either/Or — Neither/Both: Sexual Ambiguity and the Ideology of Gender." *Genders* 7 (1990): 99–142.

Escamilla, Michèle. "A propos d'un dossier inquisitorial des environs de 1590: les étranges amours d'un hermaphrodite." *Amours légitimes amours illégitimes en Espagne (XVIe–XVIIe siècles)*. Ed. Augustin Redondo. Paris: Publications de la Sorbonne, 1985. 167–82.

Eslava Galán, Juan. *Historias de la Inquisición*. 2nd ed. Barcelona: Planeta, 1993.

Folch Jou, Guillermo, and María del Sagrario Muñoz. "Un pretendido caso de hermafroditismo en el siglo XVI." *Boletín de la sociedad española de historia de la farmacia* 93 (1973): 20–33.

Foucault, Michel. *The History of Sexuality*. Vol. 1: *An Introduction*. Trans. Robert Hurley. New York: Pantheon, 1978.

Franco Silva, Alfonso. "La mujer esclava en la sociedad andaluza de fines del medioevo." Muñoz Fernández and Segura Graiño 287–301.

Gacto, Enrique. "El delito de bigamia y la Inquisición española." *Sexo barroco y otras transgresiones premodernas*. Ed. Francisco Tomás y Valiente. Madrid: Alianza Editorial, 1990. 127–52.

Garber, Marjorie. *Vested Interests: Cross-Dressing and Cultural Anxiety*. New York: Routledge, 1992.

García Arenal, Mercedes, ed. *Los moriscos*. Madrid: Editora Nacional, 1975.

García Ballester, Luis. *Los moriscos y la medicina: un capítulo de la medicina y la ciencia marginadas en la España del siglo XVI*. Barcelona: Labor Universitaria, 1984.

Gaylord, Mary Malcolm. "Fair of the World, Fair of the Word: The Commerce of Language in *La Celestina*." *Revista de Estudios Hispánicos* 25 (1991): 1–27.

Goldberg, Jonathan. *Sodometries: Renaissance Texts, Modern Sexualities*. Stanford: Stanford UP, 1992.

Gossy, Mary S. *The Untold Story: Women and Theory in Golden Age Texts*. Ann Arbor: U of Michigan P, 1989.

Guilhem, Claire. "La Inquisición y la devaluación del verbo femenino." Benassar 171–207.

Huerta, Gerónimo de. *Tradvcion de los libros de Caio Plinio Segvndo, de la historia natvral de los animales. Hecha por el licenciado Geronimo de Huerta, medico, y filosofo. Y anotada por el mesmo con anotaciones curiosas*. Alcalá: Justo Sánchez Crespo, 1602.

Jones, Ann Rosalind, and Peter Stallybrass. "Fetishizing Gender: Constructing the Hermaphrodite in Renaissance Europe." *Body Guards: The Cultural Poli-*

tics of Gender Ambiguity.* Ed. Julia Epstein and Kristina Straub. New York: Routledge, 1991. 80–111.

Ladero Quesada, Miguel Angel. *Granada: historia de un país islámico.* Madrid: Editorial Gredos, 1969.

Laqueur, Thomas. *Making Sex: Body and Gender from the Greeks to Freud.* Cambridge, Mass.: Harvard UP, 1990.

Lazarillo de Tormes. Francisco Rico, ed. Barcelona: Editorial Planeta, 1988.

López-Baralt, Luce. "La estética del cuerpo entre los moriscos del siglo XVI, o de cómo la minoría perseguida pierde su rostro." *Le Corps dans la société espagnole des XVIe et XVIIe siècles.* Ed. Augustin Redondo. Paris: Publications de la Sorbonne, 1990. 335–48.

López-Piñero, J. M. *Diccionario histórico de la ciencia moderna en España.* Vol. 1. Barcelona: Península, 1983. 278–81.

MacLean, Ian. *The Renaissance Notion of Woman: A Study in the Fortunes of Scholasticism and Medical Science in European Intellectual Life.* Cambridge: Cambridge UP, 1980.

Maqueda Abreu, Consuelo. *El auto de fe.* Madrid: Ediciones Istmo, 1992.

Mariscal, George. *Contradictory Subjects: Quevedo, Cervantes, and Seventeenth-Century Spanish Culture.* Ithaca: Cornell UP, 1991.

Márquez-Villanueva, Francisco. "*La Celestina* as Hispano-Semitic Anthropology." *Revue de Littérature Comparée* 61 (1987): 425–53.

Montejo, Esteban. *Biografía de un cimarrón.* Ed. Miguel Barnet. Mexico: Siglo Veintiuno, 1968.

Muñoz Fernández, Angela, and Cristina Segura Graiño, eds. *El trabajo de las mujeres en la Edad Media hispana.* Madrid: Asociación Cultural Al-Mudayna, 1988.

Perry, Mary Elizabeth. *Gender and Disorder in Early Modern Seville.* Princeton: Princeton UP, 1990.

———. "The 'Nefarious Sin' in Early Modern Seville." *The Pursuit of Sodomy: Male Homosexuality in Renaissance and Enlightenment Europe.* Ed. Kent Gerard and Gert Hekma. New York: Haworth P, 1989. 67–89.

Poema de mio Cid. Ed. Colin Smith. Oxford: Clarendon P, 1972.

Riera, Juan. "La obra urológica de Francisco Díaz." *Cuadernos de historia de la medicina española* 6 (1965): 13–59.

Rojas, Fernando de. *La Celestina: tragicomedia de Calisto y Melibea.* Ed. Dorothy S. Severin. Madrid: Alianza Editorial, 1976.

Root, Deborah. "Speaking Christian: Orthodoxy and Difference in Sixteenth-Century Spain." *Representations* 23 (1988): 118–34.

Rosenthal, Franz. "Ar-Rāzī on the Hidden Illness." *Bulletin of the History of Medicine* 52 (1978): 45–60.

Ruiz, Juan [Arcipreste de Hita]. *Libro de buen amor*. Ed. Raymond S. Willis. Princeton: Princeton UP, 1972.

Sarduy, Severo. "La aventura (textual) de un coleccionista de pieles (humanas)." *Escrito sobre un cuerpo*. Buenos Aires: Sudamericana, 1969. 49–52.

Tomás y Valiente, Francisco. "El crimen y pecado contra natura." *Sexo barroco y otras transgresiones premodernas*. Madrid: Alianza Editorial, 1990. 33–55.

Traub, Valerie. "The (In)Significance of 'Lesbian' Desire in Early Modern England." *Queering the Renaissance*. Ed. Jonathan Goldberg. Durham, N.C.: Duke UP, 1994. 62–83.

Index

Notes on the Contributors

JOSIAH BLACKMORE, coeditor, is Assistant Professor of Portuguese at the University of Toronto and Associate Chair for Portuguese in the university's Department of Spanish and Portuguese. He received his Ph.D. from Harvard University in 1992. His research and teaching interests center on the culture of medieval and early modern Portugal, with emphasis on the discourses of poetry, history, and sexuality, as well as representations of the forbidden. He has published articles on medieval Portuguese historiography, and is currently at work on a book-length study of Portuguese shipwreck narratives entitled *Manifest Perdition: Shipwreck Narratives and the Disruption of Historiography, 1552–1651.*

LINDE M. BROCATO is Assistant Professor of Spanish at the University of Illinois at Urbana-Champaign. She received her Ph.D. in comparative literature from Emory University's Institute of Liberal Arts in 1991. Since then she has been investigating fifteenth- and sixteenth-century Spanish literature and philosophy. Her book, *"To Penetrate with Intellectual Eyes": Text, Vision, and Nation in Trastámara Spain,* is presently under consideration for publication.

CATHERINE BROWN is Associate Professor of Romance Languages and Literatures and Comparative Literature at the University of Michigan in Ann Arbor. She is the author of *Contrary Things: Exegesis, Dialectic, and the Poetics of Didacticism* (1998) and of articles on Héloïse, Marie de France, Juan Ruiz's *Libro de buen amor,* and Hispanist Ramón Menéndez Pidal. She has also published translations of works by Federico García Lorca. She is currently at work on a book entitled *The Living Letter of the Middle Ages.*

ISRAEL BURSHATIN is William R. Kenan, Jr. Professor of Spanish and Comparative Literature at Haverford College. He has published numerous studies on the cultural role of Moriscos and Moors in medieval and golden age writing, including "Power, Discourse, and Metaphor in the *Abencerraje*," in *Modern Language Notes* (1984); "The Moor in the Text: Metaphor, Emblem, and Silence," in Henry Louis Gates, Jr., ed., *"Race," Writing, and Difference* (1986); and "Playing the Moor: Parody and Performance in Lope de Vega's *El primer Fajardo*," in *PMLA* (May 1992). He is currently working on a book-length study of the trial of Eleno de Céspedes.

DANIEL EISENBERG is Associate Dean of Liberal Arts at Regents College. He is the author of numerous studies on Cervantes, Spanish chivalric romances, and the twentieth-century poet Federico García Lorca. He is the founder of the *Journal of Hispanic Philology* and presently serves as Associate Editor of the journal *Cervantes*. He wrote the first historical survey of homosexuality in Spain, from prehistory to the present. Originally published in the *Encyclopedia of Homosexuality* (1990), an expanded version will appear as the introduction to the volume *Spanish Writers on Gay and Lesbian Themes*, to be published by Greenwood Press.

E. MICHAEL GERLI is Professor of Spanish and Medieval Studies at Georgetown University. He is the author of over one hundred publications on medieval and Renaissance literature and linguistics. His latest book, *Refiguring Authority: Reading, Writing, and Rewriting in Cervantes* (Univ. Press of Kentucky, 1995), explores the genesis of narrative in Cervantes. He also serves on the editorial board of numerous distinguished professional journals and presses both in the United States and abroad and is General Editor of the *Encyclopedia of Medieval Iberia*.

ROBERTO J. GONZÁLEZ-CASANOVAS is Senior Lecturer in Spanish, Comparative Literature, and Latin American Studies at the University of Auckland, New Zealand. He is engaged in interdisciplinary research and teaching on medieval, Renaissance, and colonial Iberian cultures. He has three books in print (two on Llull's religious utopia and missionary rhetoric and one on Iberian historiography of the Reconquest and Conquest) and two more in press (one on Spanish Golden Age discourses of self-discovery, the other on Catalan and Byzantine crosscultural representations in medieval and renaissance chronicles and romances).

GREGORY S. HUTCHESON, coeditor, is Assistant Professor of Spanish at the University of Illinois at Chicago. He received his Ph.D. from Harvard University in 1993, writing on discourses of marginality and empowerment in Juan Alfonso de Baena's *Cancionero*. He has published on both poetic art and sexuality in late-medieval Spain, and is presently at work on a book-length study of the emergence of the sodomitic Moor in Spanish historicism.

MARK D. JORDAN is Asa Griggs Candler Professor of Religion at Emory University. He is the author of numerous studies on philosophical and theological topics, including *Ordering Wisdom: The Hierarchy of Philosophical Discourses in Aquinas* (1986) and a translation of Thomas's *Summa* on faith. His writings on gay topics include *The Invention of Sodomy in Christian Theology* (1997) and *The Silence of Sodom: Homosexuality in Modern Catholicism* (forthcoming 2000).

SARA LIPTON is Assistant Professor of History at the State University of New York at Stony Brook. Working under the direction of John Boswell, she received her Ph.D. in medieval studies from Yale in 1991. She held post-doctoral fellowships at The Hebrew University and at New York University, and has taught at the College of William and Mary. Lipton is author of *Images of Intolerance: The Representation of Jews and Judaism in the* Bible moralisée (1999) and is working on a book entitled *A Question of Identity: Polemic, Policy, and Violence in the Albigensian Crusade.*

BENJAMIN LIU is Assistant Professor of Spanish at the University of Connecticut. He received his Ph.D. in comparative literature from Harvard University in 1996, writing on poetic and cultural ambiguities in the *cantigas d'escarnho e de mal di\zer.* He has published articles on laughter, obscenity, and transgression in Galician-Portuguese poetry and, with James T. Monroe, coauthored *Ten Hispano-Arabic Strophic Songs in the Modern Oral Tradition: Music and Texts* (1989). He is currently preparing a book-length study on poetry and laughter in medieval Iberia.

MARY ELIZABETH PERRY is Adjunct Professor of History at Occidental College, Research Associate with the UCLA Center for Medieval and Renaissance Studies, and author of *Gender and Disorder in Early Modern Seville* (1990) and *Crime and Society in Early Modern Seville* (1980). She is also coeditor of *Cultural Encounters: The Impact of the Inquisition in Spain and the New World* (1991) and *Culture and Control in Counter-Reformation Spain* (1992). Author of many essays and articles on marginal people in sixteenth- and seventeenth-century Spain, she is currently engaged in a study of the conflict between Christians and Moriscos.

MICHAEL SOLOMON is Associate Professor of Spanish at Emory University. Over the course of a decade he has published studies on virtually every major canonical text in medieval Spanish, although he has become increasingly interested in epidemiology as it interacts with the sociocultural climate of medieval Iberia. He has edited several medicinal tracts for the Hispanic Seminary of Medieval Studies at the University of Wisconsin-Madison, including the *Speculum al foderi* (The Mirror of Coitus) in 1990. His most recent work, *The Literature of Misogyny in Medieval Spain: The* Arcipreste de Talavera *and the* Spill (1998) explores the relation between disease and antifeminist writing in fifteenth-century Spain.

LOUISE O. VASVÁRI is Professor of Comparative Literature at SUNY-Stonybrook. She has published extensively on medieval Spanish literature and sexuality, and has edited a critical edition of Juan de Mena's *Laberinto de fortuna.* Her essay, "Festive Phallic Discourse in the *Libro del Arcipreste*", won the 1995 John K. Walsh Award for an outstanding article published in the journal *La corónica.* Her most recent book is *The Heterotextual Body* of the "Mora Morilla" (London: Queen Mary and Westfield College, 1999).

BARBARA WEISSBERGER is Associate Professor of Spanish at Old Dominion University. For over a decade she has led the vanguard of a new generation of Hispanists applying feminist literary theory and criticism to fifteenth-century Spanish literature. Much of her published research deals with the highly complex, often misunderstood genres of sentimental fiction and *cancionero* lyric. She is presently working on a book-length study of the gender ideology in the reign of Isabel the Catholic.

Library of Congress Cataloging-in-Publication Data

Queer Iberia : Sexualities, cultures, and crossings from
the Middle Ages to the Renaissance
edited by Josiah Blackmore and Gregory S. Hutcheson.
p.   cm. — (Series Q)
Includes bibliographical references and index.
ISBN 0-8223-2326-5 (cloth : alk. paper). — ISBN 0-8223-2349-4
(pbk. : alk. paper)
1. Homosexuality — Spain.   2. Homosexuality — Portugal.
3. Homosexuality and literature.   4. Sex in literature.
5. Literature and society — Spain.   6. Literature and society —
Portugal.   I. Blackmore, Josiah.   II. Hutcheson, Gregory S.
III. Series.
HQ76.3.S7Q44   1999
306.76'6'0946 — dc21   98-32016